PLATO'S ETHICS

PLATO'S ETHICS

Terence Irwin

New York Oxford
OXFORD UNIVERSITY PRESS
1995

Oxford University Press

Oxford New York
Athens Auckland Bangkok Bombay
Calcutta Cape Town Dar es Salaam Delhi
Florence Hong Kong Istanbul Karachi
Kuala Lumpur Madras Madrid Melbourne
Mexico City Nairobi Paris Singapore
Taipei Tokyo Toronto

and associated companies in
Berlin Ibadan

Published by Oxford University Press, Inc.
198 Madison Avenue, New York, New York 10016-4314

Library of Congress Cataloging-in-Publication Data
Irwin, Terence.
Plato's ethics / Terence Irwin.
p. cm.
Includes bibliographical references and indexes.
ISBN 0-19-508644-9; ISBN 0-19-508645-7 (pbk.)
1. Plato—Ethics. I. Title.
B398.E8I78 1994
184—dc20 93-40066

3 5 7 9 8 6 4 2

Printed in the United States of America
on acid-free paper

To
H.E.I
M.M.K.I

Preface

Anyone who is interested in the contribution of Aristotle, Hume, or Kant to moral philosophy can turn to at least one book in English that tries to give a fairly full and detailed account of the philosopher's main ethical views. The same cannot be said about Plato's ethics. Admittedly, the questions that face the interpreter of Plato are different from those that face us in interpreting these other philosophers; still, I believe that what has been done for their ethical views can be done for Plato's ethical views. That is what I have tried to do in this book. It is not comprehensive, since it leaves out several important aspects of Plato's ethics, but it focusses on what I take to be central questions.

I have tried to present Plato's reasons for holding his ethical views, his reasons for changing his mind about some of them, the content and implications of his views, and some reasons that might incline us towards accepting or rejecting them. With these aims in mind, I have traced the development of Plato's views in the earlier dialogues, laying special emphasis on the defence and (as I claim) re-statement of Socratic ethics in the *Gorgias*. I have devoted a large part of the book to the examination of Plato's most important contribution to moral theory, in the main argument of the *Republic*. I have added a very brief discussion of some aspects of the later dialogues, to show how they throw further light on questions raised by the *Republic*.

A proper understanding of Plato's moral philosophy requires some understanding of his views in moral psychology, epistemology, and metaphysics (the same is true, of course, of the other philosophers I mentioned), and so I have discussed these areas of his philosophy as well. Socratic method and Socratic ethics help to explain each other, and we can see the same sort of mutually explanatory connexions between Plato's metaphysics and epistemology (growing out of his reflexions on Socratic method) and his ethical theory. My discussion of some features of Plato's metaphysics and epistemology is evidently not a full treatment, but I hope it describes an aspect of the Theory of Recollection and the Theory of Forms that we may not appreciate sufficiently if we study these doctrines without reference to Plato's ethics. The different threads in my argument combine in the discussion of the Sun, Line, and Cave in the *Republic*.

These claims about Plato's development require a decision about the nature of Plato's Socratic dialogues, and, more generally, about Plato's relation to the historical Socrates. I have presented the early dialogues as embodying both the views of the historical Socrates and the views that Plato held when he wrote these dialogues. This view of the early dialogues is defended briefly in Chapter 1.

My attempt to attribute an ethical theory to Plato may suggest to some readers that I have misconceived the character of the dialogues altogether. I have ascribed a relatively systematic body of doctrines to Plato on the strength of the dialogues; but some readers strongly reject this 'doctrinal' view of the dialogues. I acknowledge an element of truth in those approaches that emphasize Plato's distance from the characters in his dialogues; still, I believe a doctrinal view is broadly correct, and that it finds strong support both in Aristotle's comments on Plato and in a fair and scrupulous examination of the dialogues. It seems to me that a doctrinal approach will be most convincing if it allows us to attribute a significant philosophical position to Plato; and so my main aim is to describe the position that he holds.

I began this book intending it to be a second edition of *Plato's Moral Theory*. The Press agreed to a moderate increase in the length of the earlier book, in the hope that a new edition would (1) offer a less one-sided presentation of some controversial issues than I gave in the earlier book; (2) expound the main issues less cryptically, with the hope of making the book more accessible to readers who are not specialized students of Plato; (3) include some discussion of the later dialogues; and (4) take account of what has been written on this topic since the publication of the earlier book. The constraints of length have meant that the first two aims have taken priority over the last two.

Recent discussion has influenced my decisions about the relative length of different parts of the book. Many critics of the earlier book focussed on the chapters that dealt with the Socratic dialogues. Moreover, these dialogues have been intensively studied in recent years (largely through the influence of Gregory Vlastos); indeed, they seem to have been discussed more intensively than the *Republic* has been. This trend has been salutary in many ways, but I have not followed it. Much of the increase in length of this book over *PMT* results from a fuller discussion of the *Republic*. It seems to me that the changes Plato introduces in the *Republic* are—as far as concerns the topics of this book—changes for the better. If *PMT* made it difficult to see my comparative evaluation of the Socratic dialogues and the *Republic*, I hope this book will make my view clearer.

In this book I have added two short chapters on the *Philebus*, *Statesman*, and *Laws*. They are by no means a full treatment of the ethical argument of these complex and rewarding dialogues. I confine myself to some suggestions about what the late dialogues add to Plato's views on some of the questions that I have explored in the early and middle dialogues.

To make room for the main text, I have (with some regret) deleted or curtailed most of the more discursive and argumentative footnotes I had written for this book. Many of the notes give bare references or the briefest indication of my reasons for taking a particular view; they do not attempt either a full report or a full discussion of the different views expressed in the secondary literature. On some points, then, the notes and bibliography are less full than those in *PMT*. In a few cases I have simply referred to one of the longer notes in *PMT*. The length of the notes has been determined, not by the importance of different issues for the understanding of Plato, but by their importance for the argument of this book.

Since the book is meant to be accessible to people who are beginning to think seriously about Plato's ethics, I have not emphasized the differences between it and *PMT*. After writing an appendix describing the main objections raised against *PMT*, and the ways I now want to accept or answer these objections, I decided not to include the appendix in this book, since it would probably be more interesting to me than to most of my readers. I do not mean, however, to seem unappreciative of the helpful suggestions and objections of the many critics—friendly, hostile, or neutral—who have taken the trouble to explain what they thought was wrong with *PMT*. I am grateful for the stimulus that these criticisms have given me to think again about Plato's ethics; even though I have probably learnt less than I ought to, I am sure that the present book has been improved by the criticisms of *PMT*, whether or not I have accepted them.

Though I began with the idea of a second edition of *PMT*, it has turned out a bit differently. None of the text of the earlier book reappears in this book, and so it seemed reasonable to present this as a new book rather than as a second edition of an old book. In one important way, however, it is more like a second edition. I have not tried to achieve the degree of distance from *PMT* that would be necessary for a fresh examination of the primary texts and the secondary literature; instead, I have re-read the primary texts, and surveyed the secondary literature, in the light of the earlier book.

In the notes I have tried to give some idea of the main contributions to discussion that have appeared since the earlier book was published. I have learnt a great deal from recent work, especially from the books of Julia Annas, Richard Kraut, and Gregory Vlastos, and from papers by Terry Penner, John Cooper, and Nicholas White. I have also indicated some new debts to older works that I have read or re-read in the course of writing this book. I had already used (for instance) Grote, Moreau, Joseph, and Murphy for the earlier book, but in re-reading them I found many suggestive remarks that had not made the proper impact on me before.

The task of working out some second thoughts on Plato's ethics has been both more complicated and more interesting than I had expected it to be, and I am very pleased to be able to thank those who have helped me in it. The Delegates and staff of Oxford University Press have always been helpful and encouraging, by publishing the earlier book, by keeping it in print, and by agreeing to an extensive revision; I have especially benefited from Angela Blackburn's advice and support at different stages. In 1990–91 I was fortunate enough to have a sabbatical leave from Cornell University and a fellowship from the National Endowment for the Humanities. My views have developed in response to questions by undergraduate and graduate students at Cornell over several years, most recently in a seminar in the autumn of 1991. I have learnt so much from colleagues in the Sage School of Philosophy that it is difficult to keep track of specific debts, but in this case I am especially conscious of having learnt from Sydney Shoemaker, David Lyons, Harold Hodes, Nicholas Sturgeon, and Allen Wood. Jennifer Whiting and Susan Sauvé Meyer made useful comments and suggestions on particular points. Daniel Devereux and David Brink gave me detailed and searching criticisms of a draft of the whole book, and I have often benefited from their suggestions. My ideas on Plato have developed on many points as a result of Gail Fine's work. She is responsible for so many changes that I cannot exclude the possibility that she has led me into new errors, but I am fairly confident that almost all the changes are improvements. Several drafts of this book have been benefited, in large and small ways, from her vigorous castigation and continual encouragement.

Finally, I must express my gratitude for the help of two colleagues and friends who have recently died. Michael Woods encouraged me in my work on Plato ever since 1974 when he read a draft of *Plato's Moral Theory* and invited me to contribute a volume on the *Gorgias* to the Clarendon Plato Series, which he edited until his death in 1993. I benefited from his perceptive advice and comments on my efforts on the *Gorgias*, and on many other topics in Greek philosophy. In 1971–72 Gregory Vlastos supervised my dissertation on Plato's ethics. Shortly before his death in 1991 he began to write a reply to my review of his book on Socrates. In the intervening years he was a constant, severe, sympathetic, and constructive critic of my views on Socrates and Plato. By precept and example, he, more than any other single person, has made the study of Socratic and Platonic ethics the flourishing activity that it is today. I would especially like to have known what he thought about my latest effort, in this book, to carry on a discussion with him that has been an important part of my intellectual life for over twenty years. I know I wouldn't have convinced him, and I know his criticisms would have thrown still further light on the questions.

Ithaca, New York T.H.I.
September 1994

Contents

Abbreviations

Works of Plato and other ancient authors are sometimes cited by abbreviated titles; full titles, with information (where necessary) about the editions used, are given in the index locorum. Plato is cited by the standard Stephanus pages and lines. I have used the Oxford Classical Text edited by Burnet [1900].

Other works are cited in the notes by author's name and date. The date is normally that of the original publication, but the pagination is taken from the second source cited. Well-known philosophical texts (e.g., Hume, Kant) are cited by author and abbreviated title, and the edition used is listed in the references. Abbreviations used in the notes and references are as follows:

AGP	*Archiv für Geschichte der Philosophie*
AJP	*American Journal of Philology*
Ap	*Apeiron*
AP	*Ancient Philosophy*
APQ	*American Philosophical Quarterly*
BACAP	*Proc. Boston Area Colloquium in Ancient Phil.*
CJP	*Canadian Journal of Philosophy*
CQ	*Classical Quarterly*
CR	*Classical Review*
DK	Diels [1952]
HPQ	*History of Philosophy Quarterly*
JHP	*Journal of the History of Philosophy*
JHS	*Journal of Hellenic Studies*
JP	*Journal of Philosophy*
OSAP	*Oxford Studies in Ancient Philosophy*
PAS	*Proceedings of the Aristotelian Society*
PASS	*Aristotelian Society Supplementary Volume*
PBA	*Proceedings of the British Academy*
Phil	*Philosophy*
Phr	*Phronesis*
PQ	*Philosophical Quarterly*
PR	*Philosophical Review*

PT	*Philosophical Topics*
RIP	*Revue Internationale de Philosophie*
RM	*Review of Metaphysics*
RP	*Revue Philosophique*
SVF	Von Arnim [1905]
YCS	*Yale Classical Studies*

PLATO'S ETHICS

1

Plato, Socrates, and the Dialogues

1. Preliminary

The aim of this book is to expound and examine Plato's moral philosophy. In speaking of Plato's moral philosophy, I refer to two things: first, to Plato's answer to the normative question, 'How ought we to live?' and, second, to his answer to the epistemological question, 'How can we know how we ought to live?' Plato's answer to the normative question relies on his views about the connexion between the virtues and happiness; and since his views about the virtues rely on his views about reason, desire, and motivation, our discussion of the normative question leads us into his moral psychology. His answer to the epistemological question rests on his account of knowledge, belief, and inquiry. Since Plato believes that knowledge is possible only if there are Forms to provide the basis of knowledge, his answer to the epistemological question requires an answer to metaphysical questions about Forms, and so we must also try to understand his views about Forms.

Every dialogue in the Platonic corpus contributes to the understanding of these different aspects of Plato's moral philosophy in this broad sense. In deciding what to discuss I have focussed on issues that seem to me to be central in answering the two main questions. This focus has determined the extent to which I have pursued different problems of interpretation. I have not, for instance, given anything like a full account of Plato's views about Forms; I have concentrated on those aspects of his views that seem to matter most for his moral philosophy. Again, many of his ethical views are closely connected with his views on pleasure, moral responsibility, politics, society, and religion; but I have not explored all these connexions, since I believe that his central views in moral philosophy can be understood independently of them, although undoubtedly a complete account of his views on morality would have to include them.

For similar reasons, this book is focussed on the dialogues of Plato's early and middle periods, giving special weight to the *Gorgias* (as the fullest statement of Socratic ethics) and to the *Republic.* I believe that in these dialogues Plato works out the most central and most important elements in his moral philosophy. In particular, I believe these central elements persist largely unchanged in the later dialogues, and that is why I have not examined the later dialogues at all fully. My discussion of the *Statesman, Philebus,* and *Laws* is extremely selective, and does not pretend to give an idea of the many ways in which these dialogues throw light on ethical topics; instead, I have traced Plato's later thoughts on some of the main ethical topics treated in the *Republic.*

Even within the dialogues that I examine in more detail, limits of space have led me to pursue some questions more fully than others. On points that matter for the main argument, I have discussed passages in some detail and given some account of the main issues about interpretation. On other points I have been rather dogmatic and simply tried to mention points of dispute, without giving details of my reasons for taking one or another view.

I have presented the main argument as an account of the development of Plato's moral philosophy from its Socratic beginnings to its most fully developed exposition in the *Republic.* I have done this partly because I believe it is historically accurate (for reasons suggested in this chapter and explained in more detail later). But I believe it would still be a good way to present Plato's theory even if it were not historically accurate; if we begin with the position I have called 'Socratic' and then we see the difficulties it raises, we can see the point and interest of Plato's own views. The 'Socratic' position defines important questions about morality and moral knowledge, and Plato's answers to these questions are successful enough to constitute a large and permanent contribution to the understanding of morality.

2. Approaches to the Dialogues

Any account of Plato must rely primarily on the Platonic dialogues.[1] If we are to use them as evidence of Plato's views, we must decide, at least in a preliminary way, how we ought to read them.

First of all, in what order should we read the dialogues? Since there is not enough external evidence to settle their absolute or relative dates, we must turn to whatever evidence we can find in language, style, and literary form.

Second, should we read them as expressions of Plato's views? Since the dialogues often present conversations between interlocutors who hold opposed positions, we ought not to assume that all these views are Plato's Have we any good reason to suppose that Plato identifies his views with those of any of the speakers in any of the dialogues?

A special question about Plato and his characters arises about the character called 'Socrates'. This is also the name of a historical figure known to us from other sources. What is the relation between the Platonic character and the historical figure? And what is the relation between either of these and Plato's own views?

We cannot set out to interpret Plato's dialogues without some preliminary answers to these questions. Our more considered answers to these questions will partly depend on our interpretation of the content of the dialogues. If, for instance, the views expressed by the character Socrates on fundamental questions fluctuate wildly from one dialogue to another, even in dialogues that appear close in date, that is a reason for denying that the dialogues are meant to express Plato's settled views. We must, therefore, begin with some account of the order and character of the dialogues that seems initially plausible, but we must keep it open to revision in the light of our interpretation of the dialogues.

A decision on these points require a discussion of complex and wide-ranging historical, literary, and philosophical questions. I will not undertake a full discussion here; I will simply offer a brief statement that is bound to be superficial and dogmatic. I simply want to clarify the point of view I take in the rest of this book. If readers disagree with my view of these questions about the dialogues, they may still find my account of their ethical doctrines worth considering; in that case they will have to modify my account in ways that I will suggest in the rest of the book.[2]

3. Aristotle and the Dialogues

Aristotle presents the first account of Socrates' and Plato's doctrines that is available to us. He includes Plato in his history and criticism of philosophical developments among his predecessors and contemporaries, and he often mentions or refers to Plato in his own discussions, both agreeing and disagreeing with him. Moreover, he was a member of Plato's Academy for the last twenty years of Plato's life. Aristotle is not infallible, and readers have often found reasons to challenge his interpretation of his predecessors.[3] But he was in a better position to know about Plato's intentions than we will ever be; and his views deserve to be taken seriously until we find some specific reason for rejecting them.

Aristotle had evidence for Plato's views that was not confined to the dialogues. He refers to Plato's 'unwritten doctrines' (*Phys.* 209b13–16), and to oral comments (*EN* 1095a32–b1).[4] He mentions Plato's early association with Cratylus (*Met.* 987a32–b1), which is not mentioned anywhere in the dialogues and could not be inferred from reading the *Cratylus* or any other dialogue.[5] Since he was in a position to compare the dialogues with other sources of information about Plato, we ought to take very seriously the fact that his approach to the dialogues is firmly doctrinal: he regularly treats the dialogues as evidence for Plato's views, and regularly attributes some of the views of the Platonic Socrates to Plato, without seeing any need to explain or defend the attribution.

In the course of criticizing Plato's Theory of Forms, Aristotle mentions the *Phaedo* (*Met.* 991b3–4) and 'Socrates in the *Phaedo*' (*GC* 335b9–17). In mentioning Plato by name he alludes to passages in the *Phaedrus* (*Met.* 1071b22–23), the *Theaetetus* (*Met.* 1010b11–14), the *Sophist* (*Met.* 1024b14–15), and the *Philebus* (*EN* 1072b28–32). He considers a question, already disputed by his contemporaries, about what Plato actually meant in his account of creation in the *Timaeus* (*DC* 279b32–280a3). In criticizing Plato he contrasts the view taken in the *Timaeus* with the view taken in the unwritten doctrines, without suggesting that either is to be taken more or less seriously as a statement of Plato's view (*Phys.* 209b11–16). Aristotle's criticism of the *Republic* and the *Laws* in *Politics* II provides a striking example of his identification of Plato with the Platonic Socrates. After speaking of the Socrates in the *Republic,* Aristotle goes on to speak of the *Laws* as another 'Socratic discourse' (1265a10–13), even though Socrates is not a speaker in the *Laws.*[6] He then goes on to treat both the *Laws* and the *Republic* as evidence of Plato's views (1266b5, 1271b1, 1274b9–10).

Aristotle's ascription of the views of the Platonic Socrates to Plato is especially impressive once we notice that in many of these passages he is engaged in criticism of Plato. If Aristotle's original audience (during Plato's lifetime or at most twenty-five years after his death) had believed that Plato did not accept the views attributed to his character Socrates, then Aristotle's approach would have been both totally unfair and absurdly self-defeating; a defender of Plato would only have had to remind Aristotle that the Platonic Socrates was not meant to represent Plato's views. If there had even been a dispute about whether the Platonic Socrates expressed Plato's views, Aristotle would have been unwise to cite the Platonic Socrates, without further comment, as the target of his criticism of Plato. The fact that Aristotle sees no need to justify his assumption, and that (as far as we know) no one thought of questioning his assumption, gives us good reason to believe that Plato's contemporaries and successors took the views of the Platonic Socrates to be Plato's views.

The doctrinal approach of Aristotle and (apparently) his contemporaries is not the only possible approach to the dialogues.[7] We might believe that the dialogues are primarily exploratory and that they expound and examine certain views that Plato thinks worth discussing, without necessarily committing himself to them. If we accept this 'aporetic' approach, we will not insist that the position of the leading speaker in different dialogues must be consistent or that it must develop along lines that would be reasonable in the thought of a single person; 'Socrates' (and so on) may simply be the mouthpiece of views that Plato chooses to discuss at different times.[8] Then again, we might think that Plato writes the dialogues in the light of some views that he does not express there. According to this 'esoteric' approach, these unexpressed views provide the background against which he assesses the views that he discusses and against which we can assess the views attributed to Socrates.[9]

These approaches conflict sharply with Aristotle's doctrinal approach that treats the main speakers in the dialogues, including the character Socrates, as expressing Plato's views. Examination of the dialogues might convince us that Aristotle is wrong; we might find that the views of the Platonic Socrates are so lacking in internal coherence or intelligible development that they are most unlikely to be Plato's own considered views. In that case we would have to try another approach to the dialogues. But until we have shown that Aristotle's view breaks down, it deserves to be our working hypothesis.

A doctrinal approach can accommodate some aspects of the other approaches. Plato may well sometimes be genuinely puzzled and want to explore a position for its own sake without having firmly made up his mind; to this extent the aporetic approach insists on an important possibility. Equally, we may find reason to suppose that in a particular dialogue Plato is influenced by views that he has not completely worked out in the dialogues; to this strictly limited extent the 'esoteric' approach might contain a grain of truth.

Still, our initial acceptance of one of these three approaches as our dominant approach will make a difference to our view of the dialogues; and since they are incompatible, we must choose between them. We are justified in following Aristotle and trying a doctrinal approach to see how far we can go with it.

4. Why Dialogues?

It is reasonable to ask, as ancient writers on Plato did (cf. Anon. *Prol.* 15), why Plato chose to write dialogues rather than to present Socrates' views and his own in continuous treatises.[10] The dialogues themselves suggest an answer, which is summed up by a later Platonist:

> Plato adopted the dialogue form because it imitates dialectic. For just as dialectic proceeds by question and answer, so the dialogue is composed of characters questioning and answering. In order, then, that, just as dialectic compels the soul to reveal the labours it undergoes (for according to Plato the soul is like a writing tablet with nothing written on it), so also <the dialogue may compel the reader> to assent to the things being said, for this reason he used this type of composition. (Anon. *Prol.* 15.40–47)[11]

In the *Apology* Socrates claims that he goes around examining people to see whether they know what they profess to know and take virtue as seriously as they should (*Ap.* 21b9–c8, 29d2–30a4), and Nicias describes this as a characteristic activity of Socrates (*La.* 187e6–188a3). In attributing this to Socrates, Plato means that Socrates practised the sort of examination that is presented in the dialogues; for the inquiry into bravery in the *Laches* is clearly meant to illustrate Nicias' point. Plato attributes to Socrates a specific method of argument and inquiry, and claims to represent this in the dialogues.

Socrates claims that the systematic form of interrogation that he practises allows him to secure his interlocutors' agreement to moral positions that they would have firmly, often indignantly, rejected before they faced Socrates' questions. The interrogation is not simply the way Socrates happens to reach his conclusion on this occasion; the fact that the conclusion is reached through this sort of interrogation is part of the reason Socrates offers us for believing his conclusion. He claims that the arguments are not simply those that strike him, but arguments that actually convince a normal interlocutor who approaches the questions in the right way.

If Plato accepts these claims about the epistemological role of the dialogue, he might reasonably find it difficult to present the essential elements of Socratic philosophy in any other form than the one he chooses. Since Plato takes Socratic philosophy seriously, he writes Socratic dialogues. To see why Socrates and Plato attach such importance to the Socratic cross-examination, we must examine the dialogues themselves. But it is worth mentioning the connexion between

Socratic method and the dialogue at this preliminary stage; for the fact that Plato wrote dialogues rather than treatises has sometimes been taken as evidence for a non-doctrinal interpretation. In fact, it provides no such evidence until we can rule out an explanation of Plato's choice of the dialogue form that is consistent with a doctrinal interpretation. Since the connexion between dialogue and Socratic method provides an easy explanation of Plato's choice that is perfectly consistent with a doctrinal interpretation, we must not suppose, without further argument, that the dialogue form itself raises a difficulty for a doctrinal interpretation.

5. Aristotle and Socrates

If, then, we agree that Aristotle's doctrinal approach is initially credible, we must also attend to his views about whose doctrines are to be found in the dialogues. We have seen that he ascribes views presented by 'the Socrates in the *Phaedo*', and so on, to Plato, and he mentions no exceptions to this rule. Sometimes, however, he ascribes specific views to Socrates, apparently referring to the historical person and not just to a speaker in a Platonic dialogue. In many of these cases he also ascribes a different position to Plato.

Aristotle seems to be quite self-conscious about his distinction between the historical and the Platonic Socrates. Indeed, he often signals it with a grammatical device. When he is discussing the character in a dialogue, he usually calls him 'the Socrates' (abbreviating, e.g., 'the Socrates in the *Phaedo*'; cf. *GC* 335b10; *Pol.* 1342a32–33), but when he speaks of the historical person he usually calls him 'Socrates' without the article.[12]

In epistemology Aristotle says that Socrates asked questions but did not answer them; 'for he confessed that he did not know' (*Top.* 183b7–8). Aristotle never attributes a similar disavowal of knowledge to Plato. The suggestion that Socrates asks questions but does not answer them fits some of the Platonic dialogues, but it clearly does not fit them all.

On Socrates' philosophical interests, Aristotle remarks that he was concerned with ethics, and especially with universal definitions, but did not concern himself with nature as a whole (*Met.* 987b1–2, *PA* 642a28–31). Aristotle's criticisms of Plato's views on metaphysics and natural philosophy show that Aristotle believes that this claim about the extent of Socrates' interests is plainly false for some of the dialogues.

Aristotle attributes metaphysical views to Socrates, but—consistently with his claims about the extent of Socrates' interests—he does not suggest that these views constituted an explicit doctrinal position parallel to Plato's and Aristotle's. He says that Socrates regarded universals as the objects of definition, but did not separate them from particulars. In Aristotle's view, the separation of Forms is a distinctively Platonic doctrine, resulting from Plato's (but not Socrates') belief that sensibles are in flux[13] (*Met.* 987a32–b10, 1078b12–1079a4, 1086a37–b11).

Aristotle's claims about Socratic ethics are especially important for our purposes. He says Socrates denied the possibility of incontinence (*EN* 1145b22–

31, 1147b13–17; *MM* 1200b25–32). He criticizes Socrates in various ways for exaggerating the importance of knowledge in virtue—for identifying courage with empirical knowledge (*EN* 1116b3–5; *EE* 1229a14–16, 1230a6–8; *MM* 1190b28–32),[14] for defining all the virtues as instances of knowledge (*EN* 1144b17–30; *EE* 1246b32–37; *MM* 1198a10–15), and for overestimating the importance of theoretical knowledge in ethics (*EE* 1216b3–10; *MM* 1183b8–11). Socrates is said to have made the false claim that it is not in our power to be virtuous or vicious (*MM* 1187a5–13). In Aristotle's view, Socrates reduced all the virtues to knowledge and did away with the non-rational part of the soul, feelings, and character, whereas Plato rightly recognized the non-rational part of the soul, but wrongly contaminated his ethical discussion with speculations about the Forms (*MM* 1182a15–30).[15]

Aristotle's remarks about incontinence clearly allude to the *Protagoras*. Those on bravery probably refer to the *Laches*. Aristotle also ascribes views to Socrates on the basis of the ethical sections of the *Euthydemus* and the early part of the *Meno* (*EE* 1247b11–15; *Pol.* 1260a22–24). These remarks about Socratic ethics are a valuable starting point for interpretation and must be examined in detail later on. For present purposes they are important because Aristotle clearly takes them to be about the historical Socrates; most of them would clearly be false if they were applied to the character Socrates in the *Republic* or *Phaedrus* or *Philebus*.

In all these contexts, then, Aristotle believes he is entitled to distinguish Socrates from Plato, even though his distinction would be baseless if he treated all the remarks by the character Socrates as evidence for the views of the historical Socrates. It follows that he does not treat all the remarks of the character Socrates as evidence for the views of the historical Socrates; in some cases he takes the character to present the historical Socrates and in some cases he takes him to present Plato's (but not Socrates') views.

The contrasts that Aristotle draws between Socrates and Plato are not casual or unimportant.[16] On metaphysical questions he largely agrees with Socrates against Plato; for he thinks Socrates was right not to separate universals, and that Plato's belief in separation was the root of the paradoxes arising for Platonic Forms. Still, Aristotle is no thoughtless partisan of Socrates against Plato. In ethics, he agrees with Plato against Socrates on most of the points that he picks out as distinctively Socratic; in fact, it would not be a gross exaggeration to describe Aristotle's ethical theory as a systematic defence of the theory that Plato develops in opposition to Socrates.

Aristotle's suggestion of a sharp contrast between Socrates' and Plato's views would be open to question if we were to find that 'Socratic' and 'Platonic' features are combined in a single dialogue, or that some purely 'Socratic' dialogues are probably later than some clearly 'Platonic' ones. If we can plausibly suggest a special point that Plato might be making through these Socratic features, then their presence in a dialogue of the 'Platonic' period need not count against Aristotle. If no plausible explanation of this sort can be found, however, then Aristotle's suggestion should not be accepted. If Aristotle is right, then we ought not to expect the characteristic ethical doctrines that he attributes to Socrates to be present throughout the Platonic corpus. We ought to be surprised, unless we can find a special explanation,[17] to find Socratic doctrines in contexts where Plato defends his beliefs in the flux of sensible things and in non-sensible Forms, or goes beyond Socrates' purely ethical concerns. If Aristotle's claims about Socrates are not confirmed by the dialogues, then either Aristotle is wrong about Socrates or else Plato's dialogues do not give an accurate account of the historical Socrates.

In fact (as we will see in detail), study of the dialogues reveals the sorts of differences that Aristotle describes; and even without his help we ought to be able to see the differences for ourselves. Without his evidence we would not know that the differences have anything to do with the historical Socrates, but we would have to take account of them somehow in our account of Plato's development.

One group of dialogues display all or most of the Socratic characteristics described by Aristotle: (1) Their concerns are entirely or predominantly ethical. (2) Socrates disavows knowledge. (3) He looks for definitions and does not find them; the conclusion is often aporetic. (4) They are characteristically exploratory rather than dogmatic or expository. (5) They express Socratic views about virtue and knowledge. (6) They do not contain the doctrines that Aristotle connects with the belief in non-sensible Forms.

These criteria pick out the *Laches, Charmides, Euthyphro, Lysis, Hippias Minor, Lysis, Euthydemus,* and *Ion;* and these count as clearly Socratic.[18] The *Apology* and *Crito* are not aporetic, but they are doctrinally similar to the other Socratic dialogues. The *Protagoras* and *Gorgias* are more elaborately constructive than the other Socratic dialogues; but they are doctrinally continuous with them. None of these dialogues contains the characteristic features of the Platonic theory of Forms.[19]

We must still, however, choose between three different explanations of these 'Socratic' features: (1) They are genuine features of the historical Socrates, as Aristotle claims, and the dialogues reflect Plato's development from agreement with Socrates to a more independent position. (2) They are not (contrary to Aristotle) genuine features of the historical Socrates, but they express Plato's views at the time when he wrote the relevant dialogues, and so it remains true that the dialogues reflect a development in Plato's thought. (3) Whether or not they are features of the historical Socrates, Plato does not introduce them into the dialogues because he believes them, but because he wants to discuss them—either because he rejects them and has his alternative views in mind[20] or because he has no definite views in mind.

The choice between the first and the second explanation depends on our estimate of Aristotle's credibility. It is difficult to believe that he reached his view simply by reading the dialogues. Although a careful reader might notice the 'Socratic' features we have mentioned, as well as the difference between these and some central Platonic positions, why should Aristotle, without external evidence, attribute them to the historical Socrates, instead of regarding them as evidence of inconsistency or development in Plato's thought? Aristotle and his audience had more information about Socrates (as well as about Plato) than we have; and Aristotle refers to stories about Socrates that he could not have known from Plato's dialogues.[21] Moreover, he regards the contrasts between Socrates and Plato as contrasts between true and false views in metaphysics (where he agrees with Socrates against Plato) and ethics (where he agrees with Plato against Socrates). It is important for Aristotle, then, that his audience should accept his historical remarks on Socrates and Plato. The fact that he sees no need to defend them (any more than he defends his use of the dialogues as evidence for Plato's views) is a further reason for believing that he and his audience took them to be obviously correct.[22]

Although a good case can be made for Aristotle's historical reliability about Socrates, this issue should not overshadow the more general importance of focussing on the features that he regards as Socratic. Whichever of the three explanations suggested here we eventually favour, it is useful to see what sort of philosophical position (if any) emerges from the dialogues with these features. Whether or not Plato ever believes this position himself, closer study of it may help us to understand the questions that he seeks to answer in his more distinctively Platonic (according to Aristotle) treatment of the same ethical issues.

6. The Order of the Dialogues

Aristotle's comments help us to identify a group of dialogues that we can in any case distinguish (without his help) on doctrinal grounds; he gives us good reason for regarding this group as Socratic. It is reasonable to infer that this group is also earlier, and that it represents the period in Plato's career when he presented Socrates' views. This inference is not completely secure, however; Plato may have been capable of presenting Socratic views even after he came to formulate his own non-Socratic views. If we are to attach chronological significance to Aristotle's testimony, we must consider any other evidence we can find for the order of the dialogues.

It would be helpful if we could find chronological indications that could be assessed independently of our interpretation of the philosophical content of the dialogues; since questions of interpretation are open to dispute, it would be useful to find a chronological scheme to serve as an undisputed starting point for philosophical interpretation. No such scheme has been found; but significant, though limited, evidence has been found.

The most useful evidence seems to come from studies of Plato's style. If we can identify stylistic features that are independent of our philosophical judgments and independent of the subject matter of the dialogues, we may be able to use these to order the dialogues. If we accept the tradition that makes the *Laws* the latest of the dialogues,[23] we can examine the other dialogues for degrees of similarity to the *Laws,* and we can look for both conscious and (presumably) unconscious features of grammar, vocabulary, syntax, and style.[24]

One chronologically significant stylistic feature appears to be conscious. At some point in his career, Plato seems to have made a definite decision to avoid hiatus (certain sequences of a word ending with a vowel followed by a word beginning with a vowel).[25] Hiatus is conspicuously avoided in the *Laws, Philebus, Timaeus, Critias, Sophist,* and *Statesman*, and to a lesser degree in the *Phaedrus*, but not in the other dialogues. This test seems to pick out a group of late dialogues (since the *Laws* is among those avoiding hiatus). Since the dialogues concerned differ widely in subject matter and form, it is fairly unlikely that Plato decided to avoid hiatus (say) only in dialogues that he intended to achieve literary polish.

The results reached by reference to Plato's avoidance of hiatus seem to be confirmed by attention to aspects of style that may be less conscious—the recurrent rhythms of the ends of sentences. Study of prose rhythms suggests the sequence *Timaeus, Critias, Sophist, Statesman, Philebus, Laws,* as the latest group of dialogues.[26]

The study of (presumably) unconscious use of particles and combinations has resulted in some conclusions about the early and middle dialogues. One fairly plausible scheme recognizes an early group containing the *Apology, Crito, Laches, Charmides, Euthyphro, Hippias Minor, Ion,* and *Protagoras;* a second group containing the *Lysis, Cratylus, Euthydemus, Gorgias, Hippias Major, Menexenus, Meno, Phaedo,* and *Symposium*, and a third group containing the *Republic, Parmenides, Theaetetus,* and *Phaedrus.*[27]

These stylistic investigations do not support firm conclusions about the order of the dialogues. For one thing, we do not know how many of the stylistic indices are influenced by the subject matter or conscious style of a dialogue;[28] if, for instance, Plato chooses to write a dialogue in a more exploratory or a more didactic or a more rhetorical manner, does this cause his choice of particles and vocabulary to change? The changes themselves need not be conscious, but they may still be influenced by his conscious decisions. This question may be satisfactorily (though not conclusively) answered for the late group, since here the stylistic evidence (prose rhythms, avoidance of hiatus) seems not to be correlated with different subject matter or choice of style. It has not been satisfactorily answered for the earlier dialogues (those in the first two groups); and so we do not know for sure what we are classifying.

Moreover, stylistic investigations do not fix a firm boundary between the first and second groups, or within each of these two groups. Although most investigators place the *Phaedo* and *Symposium* late in the second group, and place the *Meno* and *Cratylus* earlier, they do not agree on the place of the *Euthydemus* and *Lysis.* Still more important, study of the early dialogues (the first group) cannot rely on any assured results about their order, or about the relation of the *Protagoras* and *Gorgias* to each other or to the apparently earlier dialogues. Judgments about the content of these dialogues must determine our decision to trace one or another development (or none at all) in Plato's ethical thought.

Still, these chronological considerations should affect our approach to Plato's ethics. They suggest, for instance, that we ought to consider the *Phaedrus* as a revision or development of the views of the *Republic* and *Symposium,* not as an anticipation of them, and that we should take the *Statesman, Philebus,* and *Laws* to reflect three stages of Plato's later ethical thinking.[29]

Further, when we consider the earlier dialogues, we ought to compare the stylistic evidence with the conclusions we might draw from Aristotle's remarks on Socrates. All the dialogues that, following Aristotle, we counted as Socratic fall into the first two chronological groups.[30] No non-Socratic dialogue falls into the first group; and the place of the *Phaedo* and *Symposium* close to the end of the second group fits Aristotle's criteria.

To this extent, then, the Aristotelian and the stylistic criteria tend to confirm each other. This convergence should not be uncritically accepted as a decisive argument for a particular chronological order. Both sorts of criteria may just pick out dialogues that Plato chose to write, for didactic or dramatic reasons, in a 'Socratic' manner, even when he had formed his more definitely 'Platonic' views. Still, if we are willing, as we should be, to regard Aristotle's account as initially credible, we are still justified in taking it as our starting point in investigating the dialogues.

For convenience I will speak of the 'shorter Socratic dialogues' (*Apology, Crito, Laches, Charmides, Euthyphro, Hippias Minor, Ion, Lysis, Euthydemus*) in contrast to the *Protagoras* and *Gorgias*. I believe that, in fact, the shorter dialogues are earlier than the *Protagoras,* that the *Protagoras* is earlier than the *Gorgias*, and that the *Gorgias* is earlier than the other dialogues in the second group (apart from those listed among the shorter dialogues).[31] But this view needs to be defended from a closer examination of the dialogues.[32]

7. Plato's Attitude to Socrates

If Plato's earlier dialogues are 'Socratic', insofar as they present the views of the historical Socrates, to what extent do they also present Plato's philosophical views or concerns? Three views are possible: (1) In the middle dialogues Plato states his own views through the character Socrates, but in the Socratic dialogues he writes as a biographer, rather than as a philosopher, insofar as he intends simply to record, without necessarily endorsing, the views of the historical Socrates.[33] (2) In the early dialogues he is simply a reporter of Socrates, not adding anything of his own, but he writes as a philosopher, endorsing the position attributed to Socrates. (3) In the early dialogues Plato accepts the views that he attributes to the historical Socrates, but develops, extends, and defends them in his own way, to different degrees in different dialogues. In the middle dialogues he goes further in this direction and moves beyond the historical Socrates.

We can perhaps find some support for the third view against the other two, if we recognize that Plato's transition from Socratic to (non-Socratic) Platonic views is quite gradual. In the *Meno, Cratylus,*[34] and *Hippias Major,* the character Socrates explores new questions and reaches new conclusions, without reaching any of the views that Aristotle signals as characteristically Platonic. In two middle dialogues that unmistakably affirm the Platonic theory of Forms, the *Phaedo* and *Symposium,* the character Socrates is strongly, indeed ostentatiously, linked both with the historical person and with the distinctively Platonic doctrines. The *Republic* begins with a dialogue (Book I) that recalls the earlier manner of the Socratic dialogues, before the character Socrates begins an elaborate defence of the Platonic view. At the very point where Plato departs sharply from the views of the historical Socrates, he is concerned to remind the reader vividly of the historical person.

Plato, therefore, implies that the character who states Platonic views is linked to the historical Socrates. It would be odd of him to do this if (as the first view suggests) his Socratic dialogues had been meant simply to describe the views of the historical Socrates, without expressing Plato's own views. His treatment of Socrates would be less odd, but still fairly odd, if the second view were right and he had accepted Socrates' views without attempting to develop or extend them himself. His treatment of Socrates in the middle dialogues is far easier to understand if we suppose that in his Socratic dialogues he intends the character Socrates both to express the views of the historical Socrates and to express Plato's conception of how these views should be stated and defended. In the middle dialogues his biographical references to Socrates are probably meant to emphasize the continuity between the views Plato now holds and the views that he had previously both accepted as his own and attributed to the historical Socrates.

If we agree that Plato regards himself as a Socratic philosopher, not as a reporter (either detached or committed) of Socratic philosophy, we should not assume that the exposition or defence of Socrates' views is necessarily all derived directly from Socrates. If Plato is presenting his own views as well as Socrates', he may have tried to state them in the most defensible form, find his own arguments for them, or improve the arguments he had offered in other dialogues.[35]

We can perhaps appeal to Aristotle to support this account of Plato's relation to Socrates. In describing what he takes to be Plato's major departure from Socrates in metaphysics, the theory of separated Forms, Aristotle claims that it results from Plato's reflexions on the presuppositions of Socrates' search for definitions. Plato's exposure to the extreme Heracleitean doctrines of Cratylus prompted him to articulate and examine the presuppositions of Socratic inquiry, since Socrates had not tried to articulate these presuppositions for himself. This description of Plato's development is true of many other aspects of Socratic and Platonic doctrine as well; we will often find that Plato's self-consciousness about Socratic inquiry, in the light of other contemporary views, stimulates him to develop and modify the Socratic position. If this is how he sees his relation to the historical Socrates, it is intelligible that he continues to write as a Socratic philosopher, insofar as he defends the central elements (as he sees them) in Socrates' position, while he develops his distinctive and partly non-Socratic views.[36]

Some of the Socratic dialogues—and especially the *Protagoras* and *Gorgias*—become easier to understand if we suppose that they contain Plato's reflexions on the Socratic views that he thinks he has supported elsewhere with arguments that he no longer finds adequate. If we interpret the *Protagoras* and *Gorgias* in this way, we will also find it easier to understand why the middle dialogues recall the historical Socrates so strongly at the very point where Plato embarks on non-Socratic argument. As Plato probably looks at it, what he is doing in the middle dialogues is not sharply discontinuous with what he has been doing in the *Protagoras* and *Gorgias*; this in turn is not sharply discontinuous with the shorter Socratic dialogues. Throughout, Plato regards himself as trying to give the best account and defence of a basically Socratic position; as he thinks about how to do this, he comes to see that he has to reject or supplement Socrates' view on some points. If this is Plato's view of himself, then his appeal to the historical Socrates is consistent with Aristotle's testimony showing that in these very dialogues Plato develops his own position in contrast to Socrates' position.

If we want to explore these possibilities, then we must be careful in our presentation of the Socratic position. If we appeal indiscriminately to the shorter dialogues and to the *Protagoras* and *Gorgias* for evidence of Socrates' views, we may conceal significant differences between these two dialogues and the shorter dialogues.[37] Even if we do not eventually find any such differences, we must leave open the possibility of finding them.

I have argued that Plato's early dialogues present the views of the historical Socrates, that Plato defends them as his own views, and that they are distinct from the views attributed to the character Socrates in the middle dialogues. We may find that this view requires a line of interpretation that the dialogues cannot reasonably bear. If the early dialogues turn out to attribute no reasonably constant and coherent set of views to Socrates, and if the middle dialogues do not depart from Socratic views in any clear or intelligible way, then we may justifiably decide that our provisional conclusions are wrong. But at least it is fair to start with them, and to see where they lead us.

8. Socrates in the History of Greek Ethics

While giving first place to Aristotle, we must also consider further sources of information about Socrates. Some of the main features of the Aristotelian and the Platonic Socrates are recognizable in Xenophon's account. The Xenophontic Socrates is concerned with ethics, interrogates other people, and expresses some ethical views similar to those of the Platonic Socrates. But Xenophon adds a great deal of positive ethical and practical advice, as well as a conventionally pious attitude to traditional religion, and he subtracts the Platonic Socrates' frequent disavowal of knowledge. Both the additions and the subtraction match Xenophon's own religious and moral outlook and conform to his general strategy in his defence of Socrates. We have good reason to prefer the evidence of Plato and Aristotle.[38]

One other source of evidence on Socrates should not be overlooked, although it must be used with caution. Many Greek moralists after Plato claim to be inspired by Socrates. Indeed, Augustine remarks that the controversial and inconclusive character of Socrates' arguments inspired the sharply opposed schools of Cyrenaics and Cynics; both the hedonist Cyrenaics, identifying happiness with pleasure, and the ascetic Cynics, identifying happiness with virtue, claim to be genuine Socratics.[39] The Stoics also recognize Socrates as their inspiration; Cicero traces the 'paradoxes' of the Stoics back to Socrates (*Parad.* 4).

While all these moralists claim Socratic inspiration, they sharply distinguish Socratic from Platonic doctrine. Diogenes the Cynic rejects Plato's Theory of Forms, allegedly telling Plato that he can see tables but cannot see tablehood (DL VI 53). He takes to extremes the Socratic doctrine that virtue is sufficient for happiness; and this may explain why Plato describes him as 'Socrates gone mad' (DL VI 54). The hedonist Aristippus seems to have believed that Plato's dogmatic system went far beyond anything that could reasonably be ascribed to Socrates.[40] Aristippus' hedonist position is incompatible with the views defended by Socrates in the *Philebus,* and may indeed be inspired by the hedonist views that are rejected there. Similarly, the Stoic paradoxes differ sharply from the views expressed in the *Republic.* Although Stoics claim to follow Socrates, some of them criticize Plato for disagreeing with views that are both Socratic and Stoic (Plutarch, *SR* 1040d).[41] When Poseidonius criticizes the Stoic defence of the Socratic belief in the impossibility of incontinence, he defends the possibility of incontinence by appeals to the authority of Plato and Aristotle, but not of Socrates.[42]

These later moralists ascribe some definite views to Socrates that are not the ethical views of Plato's own middle and later dialogues. They may, admittedly, have misinterpreted Socrates; but their claim of Socratic support for their incompatible views is one fact to consider in trying to understand Plato's account. Plato's account of Socrates ought to seem plausible to us if we can see not only why Plato thinks that his development and modification of Socratic views are reasonable but also why his successors might believe that other views capture central Socratic claims that Plato abandons. If Plato's account of the historical Socrates can explain why later philosophers might intelligibly disagree about the significance of Socratic ethics, and might develop it in contradictory directions, that will be a further reason for us to treat Plato's account of Socrates as accurate.

2

Socrates' Method

9. Socratic Ignorance and Socratic Method

Is Socrates a constructive moral philosopher? The view that he is simply a negative critic of other people's moral views may seem a plausible conclusion from the Socratic dialogues. In these dialogues Socrates' characteristic method of argument is a systematic interrogation and cross-examination (*elenchos*) of different interlocutors who maintain some positive moral thesis.[1] This cross-examination normally leads to the refutation of the interlocutor.

The basic structure of a typical elenchos is simple.[2] Socrates asks a question, either a request to be told what some virtue is (for instance, 'What is bravery?'), or some other question about a virtue. The interlocutor affirms some proposition p in answer to Socrates' initial question; under Socrates' questioning he agrees that he also believes q and r; and he discovers, under further questioning, that not-p can be derived from q and r; hence he finds that his beliefs commit him to p and not-p.[3] Finding himself in this situation, he is 'at a loss' (*aporein*) about what to believe.[4]

It is not just the interlocutor who is at a loss. Socrates himself insists that he does not know the answers to the questions that he asks his interlocutors; and so he concludes that they are 'all alike at a loss' (*La.* 200c5). He is better off than other people not because he knows more, but because he is free of other people's false conceit of knowledge (*Ap.* 22e1–5).[5] Often in the early dialogues he disavows knowledge about the moral questions examined in an elenchos.[6] According to Aristotle, Socrates made no pretence of knowledge, but 'acknowledged that he did not know' (*Top.* 183b7–8).

In later antiquity some readers take the negative aspects of Socrates very seriously, claiming that Socrates is a negative critic because he is a sceptic; according to this view, he not only disavows knowledge but even refrains from affirming any positive convictions of his own ('ita disputat ut nihil affirmet', Cicero, *Ac.* I 16). Some believe that Plato (in all his dialogues) as well as Socrates should be interpreted as this sort of sceptic (Anon. *Prol.* 10.57–65).[7] The view of Socrates as a purely negative critic seems to be strongly supported not only by his explicit disavowal of knowledge but also by the character of his elenctic arguments; if he confines himself to elenctic argument, it is easy to see why he disavows any knowledge about morality.

Aristotle, however, does not draw this conclusion either about Plato or about Socrates; for he ascribes several definite and paradoxical views about virtue and knowledge to Socrates. The dialogues support Aristotle's view; for Socrates sometimes states some definite and unpopular moral convictions. These convictions, however, raise further questions. Do they rest on any argument? If they rest on argument, do they rest on the elenchos or on some other sort of argument? How, in any case, are we to reconcile them with Socrates' disavowal of knowledge? Can they really be Socrates' views if he admits that he does not know anything about ethics?

It is best to approach these questions by examining what Socrates does with the elenchos and what he claims or assumes about it. When we have a clearer view of the elenchos, it will be easier to understand the force of Socrates' disavowal of knowledge. For if the elenchos is purely negative, it is easier to interpret Socrates' disavowal of knowledge as a sceptic's disavowal of positive convictions. If, on the contrary, the elenchos is supposed to support positive conclusions, we ought to look for a different understanding of Socrates' disavowal of knowledge.

In this chapter and the next three, I will try to present the Socratic view without reference to the *Protagoras* or the *Gorgias*. I believe that on some important points they throw light on the claims and assumptions made in the shorter dialogues; but to see that this is so, we must begin with some account of these claims and assumptions. This point is especially relevant to the present chapter; for it is sometimes believed that the *Gorgias* advances positive claims about the elenchos that mark an essential difference from the shorter dialogues. I do not believe there is any essential difference; to show this I will examine the positive claims made in the shorter dialogues without reference to the *Gorgias*.

10. Uses of the Elenchos

At first sight it seems that an elenctic argument with a particular interlocutor who maintains some proposition p can show only that this interlocutor cannot consistently maintain p together with his other beliefs. It does not follow that p is false or that the interlocutor ought to reject p. It should be puzzling, then, that Socrates does not confine himself to this minimal conclusion from an elenctic argument.

First, he assumes that an elenchos can show that some belief of the interlocutor's is false. In the *Laches* Laches begins by asserting that bravery is standing firm in battle, but Socrates' questions show him that this assertion conflicts with his belief that one can display bravery in other ways (*La.* 190e4–191c6). Having discovered this conflict in his beliefs, Laches has to reject at least one of those beliefs that caused the conflict, but the argument itself does not show which he should reject. He could resolve the conflict created by his initial attempted definition of bravery if he retained the definition and withdrew his admission that bravery does not always require us to stand firm. He does not choose this resolution of the conflict, however; neither he nor Socrates regards it as a reasonable option. Instead, both of them assume that the initial definition has been refuted. Socrates, then, assumes that (sometimes, at least) when an elenchos reveals a conflict, there is a right way to resolve the conflict and the interlocutor will choose it.

Since Socrates assumes that the interlocutor resolves conflicts correctly, it is easier to see why he claims to be seriously trying to find a definition. In the *Charmides* he claims that he does not know what temperance is, but is inquiring (*zētein*) together with Critias for the answer (*Ch.* 165b5–c2).[8] The purpose of cross-examination and refutation is to inquire into the truth; the removal of the false conceit of knowledge is part of this inquiry (*Ch.* 166c7–e2). Socrates does not suggest that the elenchos simply exposes ignorance or that they need some other method to find out the truth; the success or failure of an attempted definition under cross-examination is taken to reveal its truth or falsity.

At the end of the *Charmides* Socrates claims that, despite the apparent tendency of the argument, he does not believe that temperance is really useless; on the contrary, he thinks (*oimai*) that he has been a bad inquirer and that, in fact, temperance is useful, indeed that it is sufficient for happiness (*Ch.* 175e5–176a1). In this case Socrates does not accept the ostensible conclusion of the elenchos, but he implies that we would have to accept it if it did not conflict with our firm convictions about temperance. He therefore assumes that this elenchos reaches prima facie credible conclusions about a virtue, and that if we do not accept them we must show that something has gone wrong in the elenctic argument.

In the *Apology* Socrates seems to assume that the conclusions of an elenchos are to be taken seriously in this way. For he suggests that engaging in the elenchos is a means to moral reform. He asks people whether they are not ashamed of devoting their efforts to accumulating possessions and neglecting the care of their souls. If they claim that they do care about their souls, he will examine them; if they claim to have virtue but they really lack it, he criticizes them for their inverted values (29d7–30a2). He does all this to persuade them to change their ways (30a7–b4).[9] Socrates advocates an 'examined life' that includes arguing daily about virtue; this life is the greatest good for human beings (38a1–6).

Socrates does not suggest that he engages in two different activities: elenctic cross-examination and exhortation to care most about virtue. He suggests that the elenchos is itself a means to persuading people to care about virtue. This is also his view in the *Crito*. He claims to reach his views about justice by 'being convinced by nothing else than the argument (*logos*) that appears best to me on each occasion when I argue it out' (*logizomenō(i)*); he still accepts the same arguments that he accepted previously (*Cri.* 46b3–c6, 48b4–6, 48d8–49a2, 49a4–b6, 49c10–e3). He believes that the elenctic argument gives him—not only the interlocutor whose beliefs are examined—good reason to accept the conclusions and to act on them.

11. Socrates' Constructive Method

If Socrates believes he can derive positive conclusions from his cross-examinations, he must assume that they show something more than the interlocutors' ability to defend their initial assertions. He must rely on some further assumptions about the character of their answers.

If a Socratic interrogation were simply meant to test someone's ability to maintain a consistent position, an astute interlocutor would not concede any of the premisses that Socrates uses to lead him into self-contradiction. Laches, for instance, would not have conceded that it is sometimes brave to run away, or that foolish confidence is bad and shameful. Do Laches' concessions show that he is simply not a very astute interlocutor? Should he demand the opportunity to reconsider (cf. *Ch.* 164c7–d3, 165a7–b4)?

This criticism overlooks the fact that Socrates is not trying to test the interlocutors' logical skills. If they altered their claims simply to maintain or to restore consistency, they would be violating a principle of the elenchos. Socrates requires them to say what they really believe about the moral question he raises. When Laches sees that the answer he is inclined to accept will raise trouble for him, he asks Socrates 'What else is one to say?' Socrates replies, 'Nothing else, if this is what one believes'; and when Laches agrees that he does believe it, he gives the answer even though it causes trouble for his initial claim (*La.* 193c6–8).[10]

This demand for sincerity is meant to distinguish Socratic argument from the 'eristic' ('contentious') form of argument displayed in the *Euthydemus*. Eristic allows the interlocutor no genuine opportunity to express his beliefs. Since the questioner demands a yes-or-no answer, the interlocutor is not allowed to add the qualifications that would express his beliefs better. In many cases the interlocutor is refuted whichever answer he gives. If we suspected that Socrates secures his points in argument by any of these tactics, we would have no reason to believe that he makes any progress in understanding the virtues.[11] Socrates rejects eristic tactics; he expects interlocutors to look at the conflicts they discover and to resolve them in the light of what they really believe. Laches, for instance, is not expected to reject his definition of bravery and to maintain that bravery is always fine unless this is what he really believes. If Socrates conducts the elenchos by these rules, it is more than a device for testing the consistency of an interlocutor's beliefs or his skill in defending a position; it also leads the interlocutor to modify his beliefs after reflexion on their consequences.

This does not yet justify Socrates in accepting the conclusions that emerge from the elenchos after this examination and reflexion. If he is to accept the conclusions himself he must also assume that (1) normal interlocutors will eventually accept the same answers to Socrates' questions and resolve conflicts in their beliefs by making the same decisions about which beliefs to retain and which to abandon, and that (2) the judgments that they rely on in answers and in resolutions deserve to be accepted. Without the first assumption, Socrates would have no reason to believe that elenctic inquiry will tend to support one moral position rather than another. Without the second, he would have no reason to believe that the interlocutors' judgments should influence our judgments about these moral questions.[12]

To see whether Socrates' assumptions are justified, we need to identify the principles that guide the interlocutors in their responses to Socrates' questions. Socrates does not list these 'guiding principles' of the elenchos; we must eventually try to uncover and examine them.[13] For the moment it is enough to notice that if the elenchos follows these guiding principles, and Socrates accepts them, he has some reason to claim that the elenchos makes moral progress and justifies definite moral claims.

12. The Demand for an Account

The normal, though not the exclusive, focus of Socrates' ethical inquiries is his demand for an account of what a given virtue is; in order to show us how Socrates examines himself by inquiring into the virtues, the shorter dialogues present his searches for definitions. Why is the search for definitions important, and why is it relevant to the practical conclusions that Socrates wants to draw from his inquiries? It will take us some time to answer these questions, and we must begin by considering the type of question that Socrates asks.

In the *Charmides* Socrates' primary question is introduced in a discussion of whether Charmides himself is temperate (157c7–158e5). Socrates suggests that if temperance is present in Charmides, he will have some awareness (*aisthēsis*) of it, which will result in a belief about 'what it is and what sort of thing it is' (*hoti estin kai hopoion ti*), which he will be able to express in words (*Ch.* 158e7–159a10). Socrates assumes that if Charmides is really temperate, he does not simply conform unintelligently to conventional rules, and does not conform to them just because other people approve of his conformity; he must also have the right view of why he is conforming to them. Socrates' request for an account is meant to identify Charmides' view of why he does the temperate actions he does, and to show whether he sees in them what the temperate person sees in them.

In the *Laches* an account of a virtue is intended to answer a different question. Socrates does not ask whether his interlocutors have a particular virtue, but whether they are in a position to give advice about how to acquire a virtue. If we are to be good advisers on this question, we must know what virtue is; if we know what it is, we can say what it is (190b3–c7). Nicias and Laches did not agree on whether the young men should have lessons in armed combat. They disagreed partly because they disagreed about whether these lessons taught anything that is relevant to virtue. Even when they agreed, their conception of what was involved in being a fine and good man was rather narrow, since they focussed on the military aspects of virtue without reference to the other qualities that make someone worthy of praise. It is appropriate for Socrates to raise the broader questions that they have ignored.

Neither the *Charmides* nor the *Laches* suggests that people disagree about the sorts of actions that are expected of a virtuous person. In the *Euthyphro,* however, such disagreements are prominent. Euthyphro recognizes that he will be thought mad for prosecuting his father for murder (*Eu.* 4a1–10), but he insists that he is entirely justified. Socrates finds this claim surprising and asks whether Euthyphro's knowledge of piety is so exact that he can defend his actions (4e4–8). Since Euthyphro's action raises doubt and dispute, he can fairly be asked for some principle supporting his interpretation of what piety requires against other interpretations. This is the sort of principle that Socrates looks for; he asks Euthyphro to tell him 'what sort of thing you say the pious and the impious is' (5c9), assuming that this is what Euthyphro has claimed to know. Socrates' request for an account of piety seems quite reasonable and appropriate to the context.

13. Accounts and Definitions

In looking for an account of a virtue, Socrates seeks to answer reasonable questions. But what counts as a good answer? The *Charmides* offers no explicit criteria.[14] When Charmides suggests that temperance is 'doing everything in an orderly and quiet way' (159b3–4), Socrates agrees that this answer reflects the common view that 'quiet people are temperate' (159b7–8). He suggests, however, that Charmides' answer does not capture what is fine about temperate actions; quietness and slowness themselves are not always fine and commendable, and we would not regard them as temperate on all occasions (159c1–160d4).[15] Socrates implies that if we simply try to describe the behaviour that initially appears to be most characteristic of temperate people, we will not really capture what is praiseworthy about these people.

Socrates speaks as though his objections justified the rejection of Charmides' proposed account. But even if quietness is not always either necessary or sufficient for fine action, might Charmides not still have found a characteristic of some range of temperate actions? Indeed, we might argue that the common beliefs about temperance are really about a number of distinguishable and separable traits of character. We might try to distinguish good sense and prudence from self-control and from moderation. If we accepted this 'piecemeal' approach to temperance, we might defend Charmides' initial reply to Socrates' demand, and say that even though it fails to cover all admirable and temperate actions, it covers some of them; the temperate actions it does not cover are temperate in a different sense of the term.[16]

In the *Laches* Laches suggests that someone who stands firm in battle is brave (190e4–6). However inadequate this suggestion may be,[17] Socrates is willing to treat it, for present purposes, as providing a sufficient condition, in order to show that it does not provide a necessary condition (191a5–8). The initial question about the nature of bravery applies to all military and non-military situations where someone acts bravely, in resisting danger in battle, on the sea, in illness, and in resisting the temptations of pleasures and appetites (191c7–e7). A single capacity—the capacity to do many things in a short time—underlies speed in running, lyre-playing, and learning; similarly, Socrates suggests, we should look for a single capacity in all cases of bravery (191e9–192b8).

Once again a piecemeal approach might seem plausible. If we accept it, we will reject Socrates' suggestion that one and the same virtue of bravery can be displayed in all sorts of situations outside danger in battle (191c7–e11); perhaps 'brave' resistance to pleasures introduces a different sense of the term.[18] If this is right, then Laches is justified in confining his attention to the cases of bravery that introduced the discussion.

The Socratic dialogues do not explain what is wrong with a piecemeal account of the virtues, but they clearly reject it.[19] In the case of bravery, Socrates suggests that the moral judgments leading us to approve of hoplite bravery also commit us to the approval of these other cases of bravery, since they all display praiseworthy determination to stick to the right course of action. Socrates raises a legitimate question about Laches' initial assumption. We ought not to rule out a single account of speed simply because speed can be displayed in many different sorts of activities; and so we should not rule out the possibility of finding a single account of bravery simply because we can recognize bravery in many different types of situations. He leads Laches through a series of examples that suggest why it is reasonable to recognize one and the same praiseworthy attitude to all these different sorts of goods and evils. Similarly, he assumes in the *Charmides* that if quietness cannot constitute what is fine about temperate actions, it cannot be what makes temperate actions temperate.

Socrates suggests that our initial conception of the virtue is too narrow; the property that we use to pick out our intuitive examples cannot be the property that makes even these cases brave or temperate. When we focus on the right property, we will see that it reveals a degree of similarity in different brave and temperate actions that we did not notice at first. If we focus too narrowly on a particular range of recognized virtuous actions, we will not really form the virtuous person's outlook. We expect a virtuous person not only to do the right actions but also to have some conception of what it is that makes them the right actions to do; we would not regard mere accidental conformity as proof of virtue. Socrates argues that if we do not see the similarity between brave and temperate actions in different circumstances, we do not really see what features of an action are relevant to its being brave, and so we do not care about the right features of brave or temperate actions. If we rejected his arguments, we would be lacking the sort of discernment that can reasonably be expected of a virtuous person.

14. Adequate Definitions

Socrates' demand for a single account is explained more clearly in the *Euthyphro*, when he insists that the pious must have some one and the same character (*idea*) in all its instances (*Eu.* 5d1–5).[20] Socrates assumes that the only satisfactory answer to the demand for an account of piety will be a definition applying to all and only pious things.

Although Euthyphro answers that 'the pious is what I am doing now' (5d8–9), he does not mean to be giving a mere example of pious action. He also gives a broader description of what he takes to be pious about his action, saying that it is pious to prosecute someone who commits injustice, no matter whether it is one's father or mother or anyone else in one's family (5d8–e2). He supports his claim by appealing to Zeus' punishment of Cronus for injustice (5e5–6a5). Socrates argues that this answer to his first demand for a definition is unsatisfactory;[21] there are many other sorts of pious things besides those that are covered by Euthyphro's description, and we need a description that covers these (6d6–e8). The question about what piety is can be answered properly only by an account that shows the one in the many.

Socrates wants an account of the single 'form' (*eidos*) or 'character' (*idea*) of piety, 'by which all pious things are pious; for, I take it, you said that it is by one character that impious things are impious and pious things pious' (6d9–e1). In saying that the form is not simply something that pious things have in common but must also be that 'by which' they are pious, Socrates takes the 'by which' to be important for deciding whether something is pious (6e4–6). The description of the one form must describe the feature of pious things that explains why they are pious.

Euthyphro identifies the pious with what the gods love (6e10–7a1). Socrates objects that since the topics of most persistent dispute are those about 'the just and the unjust, fine and shameful, and good and bad' (7c10–d5), these disputes imply dispute among the gods about what is pious (8a7–b6).[22] To prove that there is no dispute among the gods, Euthyphro would have to show that the dispute among human beings about whether his action or his father's is pious or impious can be resolved in his favour; he can tell what all the gods will agree about only by appeal to his judgment about what is clearly pious. If that is so, then his appeal to the preferences of the gods is no help to him. Socrates is willing to grant that what the gods love is coextensive with piety (since he treats it as a *pathos* of piety, 11a7), but he does not agree that this description of piety answers the question he asked.

According to Socrates, we will not find the appropriate explanatory feature of pious things until we can say why the gods love what they love. If our evaluation of piety rests not on the brute fact that the gods love it, but on the belief that the gods make true judgments about what deserves to be loved, we need to know something more about the property that the gods focus on; this property is the single form we were looking for (10d12–11b1).[23]

Socrates' questions express both an epistemological and a metaphysical demand. The epistemological demand requires us to know the pious (and so on) in the right way; the metaphysical demand requires us to identify the pious with a property that genuinely explains the relevant properties of a pious thing. We violate the epistemological demand if we introduce one of the predicates whose instances are disputed ('just', 'fine,' and 'good', 7b6–d7). In rejecting an account that can be applied only by appeal to further judgments about what is just or fine or good, Socrates suggests (without formulating the demand) that terms whose application is undisputed in some instances but disputed in other instances do not identify a property by reference to which we can say whether any action is pious.[24] We violate Socrates' metaphysical demand if we find some common feature of all pious actions, but this is in turn explained by some further feature. We meet the metaphysical demand only if we find this further feature; only the further feature will really be that 'by which' pious actions are pious.

Socrates argues that the account of piety as 'what the gods love' violates the epistemological demand. If this account were correct, we could not know which actions are pious until we knew what the gods love; but since Euthyphro has admitted that there is dispute about what the gods love, an appeal to what they love will not resolve disputes about whether something is pious. Euthyphro's account also violates the metaphysical demand, because the fact that the gods love pious actions is not the basic fact that makes the actions fine; the gods love pious actions because they are (antecedently) pious, and their loving the actions does not by itself constitute them as pious. Hence Socrates concludes that Euthyphro has not found the essence of the pious but simply described something that is true of it because it is pious (10e9–11b5). We are still looking for the description of the pious that explains why the gods love it.

Socrates insists, then, that an account saying what a virtue is must be a single definition that identifies the property that makes an action virtuous. He expects us to see that it is reasonable to ask for an account, and that it is reasonable to ask for the specific sort of account that he demands.

15. Types of Definition

Now that we have seen what sort of account Socrates is looking for, we can say more about what a Socratic definition must be like and how it differs from other types of definitions.

Aristotle believes that in searching for definitions Socrates 'was seeking the universal' (*Met.* 987b1–4):

> since he was seeking to reason deductively, and the what-is-it is the principle of deductions. . . . For there are two things that one might fairly ascribe to Socrates, inductive arguments and universal definitions—for these are both about the principle of science (*epistēmē*). (*Met.* 1078b23–30)

Aristotle claims that Socrates wanted to construct a body of scientific knowledge (*epistēmē*) about ethics, and that this was why he wanted definitions.[25]

This claim that definitions provide the first principles of scientific knowledge rests on Aristotle's distinction between nominal and real definitions. He contrasts (1) what we take the name 'F' to signify at the beginning of inquiry with (2) what the essence of F turns out to be as a result of inquiry. By finding the essence of F we ought to be able to explain the features that we initially took 'F' to signify (*APo* 93b29–94a10).[26] The essence of F is the (non-linguistic) universal that the study of F seeks to discover. In saying that Socrates sought to define the universal, Aristotle implies that Socrates was looking for real definitions; for these, in contrast to nominal definitions, are the basis of scientific knowledge.

Aristotle's claim about Socrates should warn us against an overhasty view of Socratic definitions.[27] We might suppose that Socrates is looking for definitions that capture meanings or concepts in a fairly superficial sense; these are roughly what Aristotle calls nominal definitions. One sort of definition—a summary of the usage of competent speakers—appears in a dictionary. Another sort gives an account of the concept—of the assumptions and beliefs underlying the dictionary definitions. Neither of these types of definition, however, is appropriate as a basic principle of a scientific discipline, and if Socrates regards these sorts of definitions as a basis for knowledge, he is misguided.[28]

We might argue on Socrates' behalf that nominal definitions are needed because we cannot communicate clearly or effectively if we do not grasp the meaning of our words, and we cannot grasp this if we cannot give definitions. A good objection to this argument was already presented in antiquity. Epictetus reports the criticism of Plato by Theopompus the orator, who pointed out that we can communicate without grasping forms (Epictetus, *Diss.* II 17.5–6). Socrates would be wrong if he assumed that people could not communicate unless they had an answer to his question.[29]

A real definition, by contrast, describes not the 'nominal essence' grasped by the competent speaker and hearer, but the 'real essence' they are referring to.[30] Suppose that the nominal essence we associate with the term 'gold' is described as 'shiny yellow metal'; still, we may discover that some things satisfying this description are really bits of 'fool's gold' (iron pyrites). In this case the natural kind with the inner constitution of gold does not include all the examples that satisfied the initial description.

This discovery of the difference between nominal and real essence depends on facts about the nominal essence. We must assume that we intend to use the word 'gold' to refer to a natural kind of metal. We might have had a word that was intended simply to refer to particular superficial characteristics, not to any underlying constitution; but we believe that 'gold' is not such a word, because we regard it as a name of a natural kind. When we see a discrepancy between the real essence and features of the nominal essence, we allow the real essence to determine the extension of a term that we take to name a natural kind.

If Socrates is looking for real definitions of this sort, then Aristotle is right to suppose that he is looking for the sorts of definitions that Aristotle regards as the basis of scientific knowledge. In that case Socrates can accept Epictetus' answer to Theopompus' criticism of the search for definitions. Epictetus agrees that we can speak significantly about Fs, in the light of our preconceptions (intuitive beliefs) about F, even without a scientific account; he argues, however, that we cannot 'apply our preconceptions' correctly until we articulate them through a scientific account (Epictetus, *Diss.* II 17.7–11). We need to articulate our preconceptions so that we apply them consistently and rationally to particular situations, instead of relying on the conflicting judgments that we reach if we do not articulate our preconceptions. Epictetus assumes that Socrates is trying to do for ethics what Hippocrates did for medicine, by finding an account of the reality that underlies our common-sense beliefs about the virtues. The legitimate criticisms that face Socrates if he is looking for nominal definitions do not apply to a search for real definitions.

Socrates' own remarks about definitions support the view of Aristotle and Epictetus that he is looking for real, not nominal, definitions. He asks what F is, and what all Fs have in common, not about what the word 'F' means. He wants to be told 'that very form by which all the piouses are pious' (*Eu.* 6d10), or something that 'is the same as itself in every <pious> action' (5d1). Similarly, he asks for the single power that is common to all cases of bravery (*La.* 191e9–192b8). The explanatory function that he attributes to the one F 'by which' and 'because of which' all Fs are F is fulfilled by a real essence, but not by a nominal essence.

16. Knowledge and Definition

We have seen that Socrates uses the elenchos to seek definitions, and what sort of definition he wants. If this is right, we must reject a view of Socrates' disavowal of knowledge that at first seemed plausible; he cannot consistently mean to disavow all reasonable positive convictions about morality. We must try to find an account of Socrates' ignorance that fits the rest of his outlook.[31]

To understand what Socrates means by disavowing knowledge himself, we ought to see how he exposes lack of knowledge in other people. He tested the Delphic oracle by trying to show that other people knew more than he does. He cross-examined them and discovered that after all they lacked the knowledge he thought they had; wheras the oracle's claim survives Socrates' attempts to refute it, Socrates' claim is refuted by the same elenctic testing (*Ap.* 21b9–d7).

A Socratic cross-examination, as we have seen, does not show that the interlocutors' beliefs about the virtues are all false, or that no justification could be found for any of them. Interlocutors who fail an elenchos show their inability to give a definition of the sort Socrates seeks. On this point Socrates is no better off; for he does not believe he can provide the definitions that his interlocutors fail to provide.

If failure in an elenchos is Socrates' evidence of other people's lack of knowledge, then he must take ability to give a definition to be necessary for knowledge. He assumes both (1) that knowledge of what bravery (for example) is requires a definition of bravery, and (2) that knowledge that something is brave requires knowledge of what bravery is. If he made the first assumption without the second, then the elenchos would not show that people lack knowledge about virtue, but only that they lack knowledge of what virtue is. If he made the second assumption without the first, the elenchos would not show that they lack knowledge of what virtue is.

Socrates confirms his acceptance of these two assumptions. Sometimes he implies that we cannot know the answers to certain questions about a virtue unless we know what the virtue is, and so can give a definition of it (*Eu.* 5c4–d5, 6d9–e6; *La.* 189e3–190c6; *Lys.* 211e8–212a7, 223b4–8). These demands on knowledge fall short of the explicit acceptance of the priority of definition in knowledge, but they are most easily understood and defended if they rest on the general claim about the priority of definition; the general claim is affirmed in later dialogues that present or discuss elenctic argument (*HMa.* 286c8–d2; *M.* 71a1–7, 80d1–4; *R.* 354a12–c3).[32]

Aristotle also suggests that Socrates takes definition to be necessary for knowledge. For he claims that Socrates sought definitions because he wanted scientific knowledge (*episteme*) (*Met.* 1078b23–30).[33] Aristotle, following Plato, distinguishes knowledge from mere belief; it is reasonable to attribute a similar distinction to Socrates, since he does not say that a definition is necessary for any true belief about the virtues, but does imply that it is necessary for knowledge about them.[34]

If we assume that knowledge of virtue requires a Socratic definition, we can explain both Socrates' own disavowal of knowledge and his view that his interlocutors lack knowledge. His own disavowal of knowledge is very sweeping; he insists that he is wiser than other people only insofar as he recognizes his own lack of knowledge about ethical questions (*Ap.* 21d2–7). If Socrates claimed to know ethical truths that his contemporaries do not know, he would be wiser than they are in this respect. Since he claims to be wiser only insofar as he recognizes his own lack of knowledge, he cannot consistently claim to know other ethical truths that they do not know.[35] This global disavowal of knowledge is quite reasonable in the light of Socrates' view that knowledge requires Socratic definition.

17. Difficulties about Socratic Ignorance

When he disavows knowledge, Socrates still claims 'human wisdom', the only approach to wisdom that is currently available to human beings (20d5–9, 23a5–b7); at present this wisdom consists simply in the rationally warranted recognition that his ethical convictions do not amount to knowledge (although Socrates does not claim that it is all that human beings are capable of). In speaking of human wisdom, he carefully cancels—in this context—the normal implications of a claim to wisdom, which normally implies a claim to knowledge. We are not entitled to suppose, then, that whenever he says he has some sort of wisdom or knowledge, he must intend to make the ordinary sort of claim to knowledge. If he says he has knowledge, but in a context in which he has made it plain that he claims only human wisdom, his apparent claim to knowledge may simply amount to a claim that he recognizes that his convictions do not really count as knowledge.

If we keep this point in mind, we can perhaps explain the rather surprising fact that Socrates sometimes says he knows some moral truths.[36] When he decides to face death rather than commit injustice, he says that if he withdrew from danger, he would be pretending to know that death is an evil, whereas in fact he does not know that. In contrast to his ignorance about death, he is firmly convinced about what he ought to do; 'that doing injustice and being disobedient to the better person, either god or human being, is bad and shameful, I know' (29b6–7).[37] If Socrates accepts the priority of definition in knowledge, then he cannot consistently claim to know what he says he knows. Either he does not accept the priority of definition, or he is inconsistent, or this remark does not really state a claim to knowledge.

The third of these options deserves consideration, if we take Socrates' claim to express his 'human wisdom'—a moral conviction accompanied by his further rationally warranted conviction that the moral conviction does not really count as moral knowledge. The further conviction does not undermine the original moral conviction, but simply affirms its epistemic limits. In speaking of human wisdom Socrates insists that what he has is not really wisdom at all, but simply the closest that he can come to wisdom; we may explain the claim about knowledge in the same way.

Whether or not we believe Socrates is consistent in his claims about knowledge, we ought to recognize that his disavowal of knowledge does not imply that his convictions are subjectively uncertain or practically unreliable. His convictions are superior to those of an interlocutor, since they do not collapse under an elenchos; they are stable and based on some rational defence (*Cri.* 46b4–c6). He therefore has some basis for confidence in his beliefs, even though he does not know that they are true.

18. Difficulties in Socratic Method

We have seen that Socrates believes that the elenchos is a method of moral inquiry, capable of supporting positive moral convictions; we have seen how this belief can be reconciled with his disavowal of knowledge. His belief can be supported by the appropriate assumptions about the interlocutors and about the guiding principles of the elenchos. So far we have focussed on Socrates' primary demand for an account of each virtue and on the reasons that are offered or suggested for accepting his further demand for an account expressed in a single explanatory definition. Socrates gives some reasons for believing that the demands are reasonable responses to reasonable questions, but it still remains to be seen whether he has any reasonable prospect of success. His prospects depend on whether his assumptions about his interlocutors and about the guiding principles are reasonable.

Five main questions are worth asking:

1. Does Socrates start in the right place? His interlocutors accept common-sense moral beliefs about how many virtues there are, what they are called, and which types of actions are normally virtuous. If these beliefs are largely false, the conclusions reached by the elenchos can hardly be relied on to be true; the result of adjusting false beliefs to the guiding principles may simply be a more consistent set of false beliefs.
2. Does Socrates show that normal interlocutors really accept the guiding principles? Or does he just bully, manipulate, or confuse them in the eristic

manner until they go along with his suggestions, even though they might not have accepted them if they had thought more carefully?

3. Is the degree of agreement that Socrates secures simply the result of his choice of interlocutors? Does he pick people who are initially sympathetic to his assumptions? If only such people are likely to accept his guiding principles, then his claim about their role in the elenchos is not very impressive.
4. Even if normal interlocutors (whether or not they are compliant or sympathetic) accept the guiding principles, why does that show that the principles are likely to be true?
5. If the guiding principles are true and properly applied, are they well designed to lead Socrates to a correct definition?

Socrates is most conscious of the second question. He regularly insists that interlocutors must say what they believe and tries to show that he does not use eristic tactics against them.[38] He does not take up the other questions; if we are to answer them, we must examine the dialogues in more detail. When we see what Socrates assumes about the interlocutors and what guiding principles determine his conduct of the elenchos, we will be better able to decide whether the elenchos actually gives him good reasons for believing the conclusions that, in his view, result from it. In particular, we must try to decide why Socrates does not actually reach knowledge. Does the genuine difficulty of finding an adequate definition fully explain why Socrates cannot find any? Or does Socrates make it difficult for himself by assuming the wrong conditions for an adequate definition?[39] Answers to these questions depend on our views about Socrates' specific ethical arguments.

3

Socrates' Arguments about the Virtues

19. The Character of the Dialogues

Some of the Socratic dialogues discuss the five cardinal virtues.[1] Bravery is discussed in the *Laches*, temperance in the *Charmides*, and piety in the *Euthyphro*; these three dialogues are concerned with definitions, and most obviously deserve to count as dialogues of inquiry.[2] No Socratic dialogue discusses wisdom and justice in the same way, but the *Laches* and *Charmides* say something about wisdom, and the *Apology*, *Crito*, and *Euthyphro* express some views about justice.[3]

These dialogues do not follow a standard pattern. The three dialogues concerned with definitions involve different types of interlocutors whose views raise different sorts of questions. Still, it is useful to discuss them together and to compare the common questions, themes, and approaches that emerge from the individual discussions. Socrates claims that his different arguments and inquiries support the same conclusions (*Cri.* 46b3–c6, 49a4–b6; cf. *G.* 482a5–c3, 509a4–7), and the convergences between different dialogues raising apparently different issues support his claim.

Although the *Apology* and *Crito* are not dialogues of definition and the *Apology* is not strictly a dialogue at all, they ought to be discussed in close connexion with the dialogues of definition. For they show both that Socrates holds some definite and controversial moral positions and that he claims to hold them on the strength of the sorts of arguments that are set out in his elenctic inquiries. These two dialogues warn us not to suppose that Socrates takes his inquiries to be primarily negative or exploratory; they force us to ask how these inquiries can support positive moral conclusions.

If we consider these dialogues together, we will neither dismiss their negative and inconclusive aspects as mere artifice nor be discouraged from trying to identify Socrates' and Plato's own views. To attribute a definite view to Plato is not to claim that he dismisses all the objections to it that can be raised from a particular dialogue or that he believes he has clear answers to them. Indeed, study of the objections, explicit and implicit, may help us to understand Plato's own later reflexions.

Study of the different ethical arguments in these dialogues will answer some of the questions we raised at the end of the last chapter. Once we see what Socrates assumes about his interlocutors, and what principles he relies on in his arguments, we will see how far he is entitled to claim that his elenctic inquiries are a means to moral discovery and progress.

20. Common Beliefs

Socrates does not claim, as Aristotle does, to follow the dialectical procedure that begins from common beliefs.[4] He directs his arguments towards a particular interlocutor and sometimes recognizes that this interlocutor's view may not be widely shared (*Cri.* 49c11–d5). Still, it is useful for us to begin with some idea of the moral beliefs and questions that most people would have in mind in approaching Socrates' arguments. Socrates cannot ignore common beliefs if he claims, as he does, that the results of his arguments give him good reason to regard his own moral views as correct (*Cri.* 46b3–c6). If the arguments depend on the choice of sympathetic interlocutors, and would go quite differently if Socrates began from less idiosyncratic views, then they do not make a strong case for Socrates' views.

Moreover, if Socrates believed that there are some quite widespread moral positions that he rejects but cannot refute, he would raise an objection to his description of himself. He claims that he goes around arguing with anyone he meets, 'persuading you, young and old, not to care for your bodies or possessions before or as much as your souls, to make them as good as possible' (*Ap.* 30a7–b2). If Socrates goes around arguing (as he claims) with everyone he meets, but he stops arguing with the people who reject some of his controversial premisses, then his concern is much less universal than he makes it look.

Most important, if Socrates has to admit that his most important moral claims cannot be defended against opponents who rely on common beliefs, he violates his own exhortation to an examined life (*Ap.* 38a). If, however, he can defend his controversial claims against interlocutors who are initially disposed to reject them, he shows that his claims are to be taken seriously.[5]

We ought, then, to consider not only how well Socrates deals with the views he discusses but also whether he discusses all the questions he ought to discuss. To see what questions he ought to discuss, we ought to have some idea of common beliefs on the main questions that are relevant to the dialogues.

21. Happiness

In the *Euthydemus* Socrates begins his discussion of ethics by asking whether we all want to 'do well' (*Euthd.* 278e3–6) or to 'be happy' (280b6). He assumes that this is our ultimate aim, and so the next question in ethics concerns what we must do to be happy. This question leads Socrates into discussion of virtues and other goods. Aristotle's account of common ethical views supports Socrates' assumption about the ultimate end: ‘For practically every person individually and for everyone in common there is a goal that all aim at in whatever they choose and avoid; and this, to speak in summary form, is happiness (*eudaimonia*) and its parts’ (*Rhet.* 1360b4–7).[6] This is also the view of common sense and tradition. Homer speaks of the ‘blessed’ gods who enjoy unbroken and secure prosperity. Human beings cannot expect to enjoy the same unbroken prosperity, since their successes are insecure and transitory by comparison with the gods; still, the wealth, power, and honour enjoyed by Croesus and Polycrates in Herodotus, and by Oedipus in his years as king, represent the goal of human ambition, and this success is described as ‘blessedness’, or ‘happiness’.[7]

After taking happiness as the ultimate end, Socrates asks how we are to achieve it. He takes it as obvious that we become happy by being well supplied with goods, and among goods he lists (1) wealth; (3) health, beauty, and other bodily advantages; (3) good birth and positions of power and honour in one’s own city; (4) temperance, justice, and bravery; (5) wisdom; and (6) good fortune (*Euthd.* 279a1–c8). Socrates takes all these elements in the list to be uncontroversial, except for the virtues and wisdom. Aristotle presents a similar list of goods (*Rhet.* 1360b19–23), explaining that they are generally supposed to secure the ‘self-sufficiency’ (*autarkeia*, 1360b14, 24) and ‘security’ (*asphaleia*, 1360b15, 28) that are needed for happiness. We are self-sufficient insofar as we have all the goods we could want, and we need none added; we are secure insofar as our good fortune protects us against sudden reversals and loss of happiness.

Since happiness requires security and stability, it is natural to suppose that it must require favourable external conditions that are not wholly in the agent’s control. To begin with, we seem to need the appropriate sort of ‘antecedent’ good fortune, in the provision of the right sorts of resources: wealth, health, and social position. But even if we have these and use them wisely, we also seem to need ‘subsequent’ good fortune; however talented, industrious, rich, and famous I may be, I cannot eliminate the possibility that some event over which I have no control will ruin me, as it ruined Polycrates and Oedipus.

If, however, we emphasize the importance of security and stability in happiness, we may come to doubt whether the other goods that are recognized as parts of happiness really contribute to happiness after all. The Homeric Achilles eventually chooses a short and glorious life over an obscure, inglorious, but secure and stable life (*Il.* 9.410–416; 18.95–106); but the happy lives that Solon recommends to the successful Croesus are more like the sort of life that Achilles rejects (Hdt. I 31–32). Common-sense views about happiness reflect these tensions between different apparent aspects of happiness.

22. Virtue

Among the parts of happiness, Aristotle mentions the ‘virtues’ (or ‘excellences’, *aretai*). The various virtues correspond to the different ways that agents themselves, in contrast to their resources or external circumstances, are well adapted for happiness. Hence Aristotle describes virtue as 'a capacity . . . that secures and preserves goods, and a capacity that benefits in many ways, and great ways, and in all sorts of ways on all sorts of matters' (*Rhet.* 1366a36–b1). Health and strength count as virtues according to this general description, and indeed he counts them among virtues of the body (1360b21–22).

Aristotle distinguishes, however, a narrower use of 'virtue', applying to praiseworthy traits of character. A person who has these traits is properly called *agathos*, 'good', without further specification (as opposed to a good soldier or a good carpenter). The virtues he lists are 'justice, courage, temperance, magnificence, magnanimity, generosity, gentleness, intelligence (*phronēsis*), wisdom (*sophia*)' (1366b1–3). In claiming that virtue is 'fine' (*kalon*) and praiseworthy (1366a33–36), Aristotle means that it benefits others as well as the agent (1366b36–1367a4, 1367b6–7, 1359a1–5).

This restriction of virtue to praiseworthy states of character that benefit other people is not universally accepted in Greek ethical thinking. When a Homeric hero is exhorted 'always to be best and to excel others' (*Il.* 11.784), he is not being exhorted to be more cooperative, considerate, just, or temperate than other people; he is being exhorted to be braver and more successful in battle, and this is the aspect of superiority that makes Achilles the 'best of the Achaeans' (*Il.* 1.240–4). Achilles and Ajax lack many of the virtues listed by Aristotle, but Homer never suggests that these lapses prevent them from being *agathoi* (cf. *Od.* 11.549–551, 555–558); indeed, the *Iliad* makes it clear how the single-minded pursuit of one's own honour and status may conflict, as it does for Agamemnon, Hector, and Achilles, with the welfare of one's friends or dependents. The conflict is most vividly presented in Sophocles' *Ajax*; however self-absorbed and indifferent to the welfare of others Ajax may become, he is taken to deserve the honour that is due to a hero of outstanding excellence. This Homeric conception—by no means confined to Homer—presents the *agathos* as the person who has the qualities needed for his own success in life, whether or not these qualities benefit other people, and whether or not they actually secure his success in life (they clearly do not secure it for Ajax).

Still, many of Socrates' contemporaries believe that, as Aristotle says, virtue seeks the good of others. In Thucydides' Melian Dialogue, the Athenians remark that the Spartans 'exercise the highest degree of virtue' in their conduct of their internal affairs, whereas in dealings with other states they are the most conspicuous examples of people who 'regard what pleases them as fine, and what is expedient for them as just' (Thuc. V 105.4).[8] The Athenians evidently do not mean that the Spartans display the Homeric self-assertive virtues less in their external affairs; on the contrary, they mean that the Spartans consider the common interest in their internal affairs, but in their external affairs they are aggressive, self-seeking, and unconcerned with the interests of others. Thucydides conveys this contrast by saying simply that the Spartans display 'virtue' in their internal affairs.

Thucydides describes how the dislocations resulting from war focussed people's attention on the conflicts between these two conceptions of the virtues. Some people changed their minds about which actions were praiseworthy (*epē(i)neito*, III 82.5). What would normally be called mindless daring was regarded as bravery, and what would normally be counted as temperate was regarded as cowardly hesitation (III 82.4).[9] Alcibiades expresses and exploits this dispute about the requirements of the virtues; he suggests that the patriot's love of his city (*to philopoli*; cf. *Ap.* 24b5) does not exclude conspiracy against it, but actually justifies him in trying to return to Athens by intriguing with its enemies (Thuc. VI 92.4). Plato also mentions people who dissent from ordinary views about the requirements of the virtues (*R.* 560d1–561a1).

These dissenters from conventional views deny that the virtues are to be connected with other-regarding concerns; they try to connect them with the self-assertive outlook of the Homeric ideal. They rely on a well-established tradition in Greek ethics, and so it is not surprising that Alcibiades' dissent from conventional values expresses itself in an unconventional view about what the recognized virtues require, not in an explicit rejection of the recognized virtues.

Since these controversies raise basic questions about the virtues, we might well expect Socrates to take them up. In fact, he does not take them up in the shorter Socratic dialogues. We ought to be surprised by his silence and seek some explanation. Once we have examined the questions he does take up, and the arguments he presents, it should be easier to see why he takes up some questions and neglects others.

23. Virtue and the Virtues

Socrates' interlocutors readily recognize different actions and people as displaying bravery, temperance, and piety; they seem to suppose that if we are evaluating people as good or bad, it is appropriate to ask whether they are brave, temperate, and so on. In both the *Charmides* and the *Laches* the discussion settles on one particular virtue because it seems the best way to answer a more general question about what makes a person good.

In the *Charmides* Socrates claims that the proper medicine to produce health in the soul is the sort of discourse that will produce temperance there; for temperance ensures the healthy condition of the whole soul, and health spreads from there to the whole body (*Ch.* 156d6–157c1). Temperance is not simply one among a number of recognized good qualities; it is supposed to determine whether we have or do not have a virtuous soul. This general aim of the inquiry is made clearer in the *Laches*. Although the immediate question is about whether Aristeides and Thucydides should be trained in armed combat, the broader question is about the sort of education that will make them 'fine and good' (186c4). It is because the young men's fathers want them to be good men that they want them to be trained in the specific virtues (190c8–d5).

These introductory points affect the direction of the argument. Since Socrates inquires into specific recognized virtues on the assumption that they are genuine virtues and that they make someone a good person, he seems to start with a bias against the view that temperance, for instance, is not really a virtue after all. If we must discover what temperance is by relying on our views about virtue and virtuous people, any argument purporting to show that temperance is not a virtue must apparently be rejected.

Socrates, then, examines the particular virtues to discover what a 'fine and good' person is like, assuming that everyone wants to discover this, and that the discovery will affect their views about how to live. This is why Nicias warns Lysimachus that they will find that they are examining their own past and present and arguing about how to conduct their lives (*La.* 187d6–188c3); Nicias assumes that people will want to conform to their conception of a fine and good person, and that this is why they will be interested in an inquiry into a specific virtue.

This underlying assumption is not examined, or even made explicit, but it influences the course of argument. Since it is an important assumption, we might fairly ask for an account of virtue, not simply of this or that virtue. Yet Socrates neither offers nor seeks an account of virtue in general.[10]

24. Action, Character, and Virtue

Sometimes Socrates treats 'brave' and so on as predicates of persons. In the *Charmides* he looks for the common property of being a temperate person that belongs to all temperate people. Similarly, in the *Laches* the discussion is about training that will make the young men brave people. In the *Euthyphro*, however, 'pious' seems to be treated as a predicate of actions. Socrates asks: 'Is the pious not the same as itself in every action?' (*Eu.* 5d1–2), and suggests that, if he finds what the pious is, he will find a standard to determine whether an action is pious (*Eu.* 6e3–6). The later discussion in the *Euthyphro* returns to the piety of persons.[11]

The questions about actions and about persons are distinct, but they may not be separable. We may seek to define temperate action, independently of defining a temperate person, and then define a temperate person as one who tends to do temperate actions; in this case a temperate action is prior in definition to a temperate person. Conversely, we may discover that a temperate person is prior in definition to a temperate action. Or again, we may claim that the definitions are interdependent, so that neither is prior to the other.

Socrates does not declare his view on this question about priority, but his arguments suggest that he rejects the definitional priority of actions over persons. When Charmides identifies temperance with quietness, Socrates takes him to claim that it is an external feature of a person's behaviour, parallel to slowness in walking or speaking. Socrates objects that if we take some external feature of action, without reference to motivation, to be a sufficient condition for temperance, we will find many counterexamples (159b7–160d4). Charmides' next account tries to avoid these counterexamples by turning to characteristics of persons. He suggests that temperance makes a person prone to be ashamed, and therefore is to be identified with (*hoper*) shame (160e2–5); the person who does the right thing out of temperance does it out of a feeling of shame or scrupulousness (*aidōs*).

Similarly, Socrates convinces Laches that bravery is not to be defined by reference to independently defined brave action, for the variety of actions resulting from bravery cannot be independently characterized as having some single property apart from their connexion with the virtue of persons.[12] Laches, therefore, suggests that bravery is 'some sort of endurance of the soul' (192b9–c1). He now realizes that someone cannot be trained to be brave simply by being trained to behave in certain prescribed ways in specific situations described without reference to bravery. Laches sees that we do not want brave people simply to stand firm in battle; we want them to endure in the variety of situations that demand endurance. If we are to train them to endure, we must train them to recognize the degree of danger and the importance of facing it; since this recognition is a state of the soul, not simply a behavioural tendency, bravery must consist in some state of the soul.

25. The Fine and the Good

Once it is agreed that a virtue is some state of the agent's soul, Socrates asks what state it is. In looking for a more precise answer, he assumes that a virtue must be fine and good.[13] Against Charmides' second suggestion, that temperance is shame, Socrates suggests that if temperance is fine it makes temperate people good, and therefore must itself be good; hence it cannot be the same as shame, which is sometimes bad (160e6–161b2).[14] We sometimes condemn shame as bad, if people are wrongly ashamed of doing an action that is in fact fine and virtuous (cf. *Ap.* 28b3–5; *Cri.* 45d8–46a4), so that they display shame on the wrong occasions; but (according to Socrates) we never suppose that it is bad to display temperance on this or that occasion. If this is right, then Socrates has shown that temperance cannot be, as Charmides claimed, 'precisely shame',[15] since it cannot be identical to shame.

We might still, however, identify temperance with a type of shame that excludes bad shame. This sort of account is explored further in the *Laches*. Instead of proposing that bravery is identical to endurance, Laches proposes that it is 'some sort of endurance of the soul' (192b9–c1). If some sort, but not every sort, of endurance counts as bravery, then we need a more precise description of the relevant sort of endurance, so that we can evaluate the proposal against specific cases.

Socrates develops Laches' implicit suggestion that bravery cannot be straightforwardly identified with endurance. He argues that not every case of endurance is fine and beneficial, whereas bravery is a virtue, and so must always be fine and beneficial (192c4–d5). Since foolish endurance is shameful and harmful, not all endurance can be brave.

Socrates is entitled to assume that bravery and brave action must be fine.[16] But what makes an action fine? Socrates and Laches agree that foolish endurance and daring is harmful and mischievous (192d1–2, 193d1), and that nothing of that sort could be fine. They assume that bravery is a virtue and that every virtue is fine. Fine action, we might argue, must benefit the people to whom the benefit is owed. Someone who daringly betrays his own city to a foreign enemy who will reward him has done a shameful, not a fine action; he has shown himself vicious, not virtuous, and therefore his bold and fearless action cannot be regarded as brave.[17]

The conclusion that each virtue must be both fine and good conflicts with some common views about both bravery and temperance. Many people believe that bravery makes us pursue our own aims vigorously and fearlessly, whereas temperance moderates our own aims and desires to fit our plans for our own welfare or to fit other people's demands. This general view underlies the tendency to identify bravery with standing firm and temperance with quietness. From the temperate person's point of view, the brave person is impulsive and aggressive, but from the brave person's point of view the temperate person is cold and sluggish (*St.* 306a12–308b8).[18] For similar reasons, bravery seems to conflict with justice: some people argue that the brave person pursues his own aims vigorously and that only cowardice persuades people to listen to the requirements of justice (cf. *R.* 561a1; Thuc. III 82.4).

Socrates assumes that we will reject common sense once we see the implications of our views about bravery, virtue, and the fine. Since we seek to describe a virtue, we recognize that this must be a fine and admirable state of character. If we had to admit that bravery is not always fine, we would have to admit that it is not always a virtue; since (Socrates assumes) we hold fast to the assumption that it is a virtue, we must reject any account of bravery that implies that it is not always fine.

26. Temperance and Knowledge

Once Socrates persuades Charmides that temperance cannot be identified with shame, since temperance is always fine and beneficial, Charmides suggests that temperance is 'doing one's own' (161b6). This seems to explain and correct his earlier suggestions. For we might say that the temperate person knows what is 'his own', what is appropriate for him, and that for this reason he is 'quiet', instead of being inappropriately aggressive, and would be 'ashamed' to overstep what is appropriate for him.

Socrates suggests, however, that 'one's own' or 'what is appropriate for one' is a 'riddle' (161c8–9, 162b3–6), because it is difficult to understand what is meant by 'one's own'.[19] We need some explanation of 'one's own' that allows us to say whether one or another action is an instance of it; Socrates demands this of any adequate definition (cf. *Eu.* 6e3–6).[20] Critias argues that we should interpret 'one's own' in 'doing one's own' as 'proper to oneself' and hence as 'fine and beneficial' (163c4–8).[21] The resulting account of temperance is broad and uninformative.

Critias now agrees that temperate people must know that what they are doing is good and beneficial (164b7–c6). He rushes precipitously into another account;

might suggest that in both dialogues Plato intends the perceptive reader to see that the non-cognitive component of a virtue is unjustifiably set aside. This suggestion becomes less attractive, however, once we have to admit that Plato fails even to drop a subtle hint to the perceptive reader. We should at least consider seriously the possibility that Plato believes that Socrates' move is justifiable, even though no justification of it is presented in these dialogues.

28. Temperance and the Unity of the Virtues

Once Socrates has clarified the proposal that temperance is knowledge of the extent of our knowledge and ignorance, he asks whether this proposal is correct. If we accept the suggested account of temperance, we cannot identify temperance with the knowledge of good and evil; Socrates argues that the consequences of rejecting this identification are unacceptable.[31]

Socrates suggests that if temperance is 'beneficial' (169a8–b5) it must be identified with the knowledge of good and evil. He argues:

1. Each craft is the producer only of its proper product (medicine is the science of health, shoemaking of shoes, etc.).
2. Temperance is not the science of benefit.
3. Hence temperance is not the producer of benefit.
4. Hence temperance is not beneficial to us. (174e3–175a7)[32]

This answer still seems unsatisfactory. If the product of a science is a benefit to us, surely the science is beneficial, even if is not the same as the science of what is beneficial?

Socrates might reply in either of two ways: (1) None of the products of the other sciences is good, all things considered, in all circumstances. If these products are to benefit us, they must be used by the science of good and evil. (2) None of the products of other sciences is really a good; the only science that produces a good is the science of good and evil. The first reply expresses a moderate claim about wisdom, asserting that we need the superordinate science of good and evil if ordinary goods are to be genuinely good for us (all things considered) on each occasion when we use them. The second reply expresses an extreme claim, asserting that the alleged goods produced by other sciences are not really goods at all.

Socrates seems to accept the extreme claim, since he assumes that the superordinate science of good and evil is sufficient for happiness (174b11–c3). He does not suggest that any non-cognitive condition is necessary for happiness. Equally he assumes that no unfavourable external conditions will prevent our knowledge from achieving our happiness. If Socrates is to defend his claim that knowledge of good and evil is sufficient for happiness, then he must accept the extreme view that the products of the subordinate sciences are not goods at all; for if knowledge of good and evil does not guarantee possession of the products of the subordinate sciences, and if these products are genuine goods, then knowledge of good and evil does not seem to be sufficient for happiness.[33]

And so Socrates seems to accept the extreme claim that the product of the superordinate science is the only good.

At the end of the dialogue Socrates reaffirms the extreme claim. He tells Charmides that he assumes that if we have temperance, we will be happy (175e6–176a1); although he reserves judgment about the other concessions made in the course of the argument, he emphatically insists that temperance ensures happiness (175b4–d5). If temperance is sufficient for happiness, then it must be identified with the science of good and evil, and the products of the other sciences cannot be genuine goods. Socrates' final moves in the *Charmides* are justified if and only if he is entitled to the extreme claim.

The *Charmides* ends aporetically, but we should not infer that Socrates has no firm view about the character of temperance. On the contrary, it is his firm view that creates the puzzle. He has found that the different conceptions of temperate behaviour and different criteria for temperance lead us to one virtue, not to several virtues; to that extent, he has discredited the piecemeal approach.[34] Moreover, this one virtue turns out to be identical to knowledge of the good and to be sufficient for the agent's happiness. Common sense recoils from these conclusions, and so Socrates thinks we are right to be puzzled and confused. But he believes that common sense cannot reasonably reject his arguments.

29. Bravery and the Unity of the Virtues

If Socrates' arguments in the *Charmides* are meant to show that temperance must be identical to knowledge of good and evil, then he implies that temperance is identical to each of the other virtues. For the assumptions about temperance that support Socrates' argument seem equally reasonable assumptions about each of the other virtues. This implication is not pointed out in the *Charmides*, but the parallel implication about bravery is pointed out in the *Laches*.

Socrates suggests that if Nicias is right to identify bravery with knowledge of the proper objects of fear and confidence, then it has to be identical to all the virtues (199d–e). The crucial points are these:

1. Knowledge of proper objects of fear and confidence is knowledge of future goods and evils.
2. Knowledge of future goods and evils is knowledge of goods and evils as a whole.
3. Knowledge of goods and evils as a whole is the whole of virtue.
4. Therefore bravery is the whole of virtue.

Does Socrates take this argument to be sound?[35]

We might deny that bravery requires knowledge of goods and evils as a whole. Perhaps each virtue requires its specific type of knowledge or belief about some appropriate subset of goods and evils. We might say, for instance, that bravery requires knowledge of what is good and evil in circumstances tending to arouse fear, temperance in circumstances tending to promise pleasure, and so on.

Socrates' remarks on wise endurance have undermined this answer. Foolish endurance, he says, is not beneficial, hence is not fine, and hence is not brave. Brave people do not face all dangers indiscriminately; they must know which dangers deserve to be faced. The worthwhile dangers do not include those that we face in robbing a bank or in carrying out some prank; indeed, readiness to face certain sorts of dangers (in Don Giovanni, for instance) is a mark of intemperance or injustice, not of bravery. If that is so, then the knowledge that belongs to justice and temperance is needed to find the brave action; no department of knowledge of the good is sufficient by itself for the cognitive aspect of bravery.

This conclusion may be defended by appeal to a strong version of the claim that bravery must be fine and beneficial.[36] This strong version implies that if some trait of character leads to actions that are worse and more shameful than the alternatives, that trait is not a virtue. Since each virtue without the others will sometimes lead us to actions that are worse than the actions we would do if we also had the other virtues, none of the virtues can really be separated from the other virtues. If Socrates accepts the strong claim, he has a reason to insist that the virtues are inseparable.

This defence of the inseparability of the virtues does not prove that they are identical; for it does not imply knowledge is sufficient for virtue. We might argue that knowledge of the good is a component of every virtue, but each virtue has a non-cognitive component that distinguishes it from the other virtues.[37] This reply is closed to us, however, once we accept Nicias' reduction of bravery to knowledge. If knowledge of the good is the state of the soul responsible for all virtuous action, a correct account of the virtues has no room for anything except this knowledge.[38]

Plato, then, constructs the argument of the *Laches* with some care; apparently controversial steps in the final argument are defended earlier in the dialogue, and apparently plausible objections have been answered. Not all objections have been answered, however; Socrates points out that the conclusion that the virtues are identical conflicts with the initial assumption that bravery is only a part of virtue (199e3–11). To see whether this conflict refutes the conclusion, we must consider the grounds for accepting the initial assumption.[39]

The assumption that bravery is a proper part of virtue was introduced to make the inquiry easier, because bravery seemed to be the virtue most closely connected with training in armed combat (190c8–d5). But the main question at the beginning, as we saw, was not about bravery in particular, but about how to make people 'fine and good'; bravery was introduced only as the aspect of fineness and goodness that seemed most relevant to the occasion.[40] Socrates gave no reasons in support of the initial assumption about bravery, and nothing in the argument of the dialogue depends on the assumption.

Plato never suggests, then, that the assumption that bravery is a proper part of virtue is more plausible than the premisses of the argument for the unity of virtue have turned out to be; for these premisses have been quite strongly defended. The sort of bravery that is characteristic of the 'fine and good' person will surely not be mere heedless daring or purely technical expertise; Socrates has made it seem plausible that the fine and good person acts bravely because of the sort of knowledge that turns out to be sufficient for the other virtues as well.

Plato could easily have indicated, if he had wanted to, that the main argument ought to arouse suspicions. If the crucial steps of the argument for the unity of virtue had been introduced without any previous defence, or if they clearly conflicted with something we had found good reason to believe earlier in the dialogue, these would be warning signals. Plato gives us none of these signals.[41] All the weight of the argument tends to support the view of bravery that is presented in the final argument. Moreover, doubts that might be raised by the *Laches* are partly answered in the *Charmides*, where Socrates seems to accept some of the premisses that are needed to support the argument in the *Laches*. The *Laches* in turn supports the arguments of the *Charmides*. We might object that Socrates' argument in the *Charmides* must be mistaken because it implies the unity of the virtues; the *Laches* argues that this implication does not undermine, but actually vindicates the argument of the *Charmides*.[42]

In the *Laches* as in the *Charmides*, an apparently cogent argument about bravery has challenged the common-sense belief that one virtue is distinct from all the others. Socrates regards this as a genuine puzzle, since he does not suppose that once we reach a counterintuitive conclusion from premisses he accepts we should immediately abandon all our initial beliefs. He believes that we should be willing to re-examine the question, and that once we re-examine it, we will agree that the Socratic arguments are cogent.[43]

30. Justice and the Good of the Agent

The *Charmides* and *Laches* do not show exactly what Socrates means by his crucial claims that temperance and bravery are always fine and always good and beneficial. Although we might initially suppose that 'always good' means only that a virtue is always a good (so that there is always something to be said for it), the conclusions of the dialogues rest on the strong claim that a virtue is always better than anything else (so that it is always good, all things considered). In claiming that if a virtue is fine, it must be beneficial, Socrates does not say whose benefit is being considered; is it the benefit of the agent, the benefit of those affected by the action, or both? Since the end of the *Charmides* suggests that one's temperance must be sufficient for one's own happiness, Socrates seems to accept the further strong claim that if a virtue is fine, it must also be best, all things considered, for the agent.

Socrates' position is clearer if we consider his claims in the *Apology* and *Crito* about justice; here he insists that justice is fine, and therefore best, all things considered, for the just agent. This claim seems quite implausible, since it may seem obvious that just people follow the requirements of justice even at the cost of their own interest. Socrates, however, denies this apparently obvious fact about justice.

In the *Apology* Socrates insists that his commitment to justice must not be relaxed for the sake of his own self-preservation; any man worth anything takes no account of danger or death, in comparison to the question of whether he is doing just or unjust actions, and the actions of a good or a bad man (*Ap*. 28b5–9).[44] Later, Socrates denies any conflict between being virtuous and securing one's own advantage, since he claims that no evil can happen to a good man (41c8–d2). If nothing can harm him, then his justice cannot harm him. He does not explain here why he thinks uncompromising commitment to justice promotes the agent's happiness.

He takes up this question in the *Crito*. In reply to Crito's claim that it would be both harmful and unjust, and therefore shameful, for Socrates to stay in prison (*Cri*. 46a3–4), Socrates reaffirms his rigid commitment to justice, and insists that he cannot be harmed by acting justly. He affirms that living well, rather than simply staying alive, should be our primary concern (48b3–6). Then he claims that living well, living finely, and living justly are the same (48b8–9). This claim explains why the good person cannot be harmed; he cannot be harmed if he cannot be deprived of happiness, and if he lives justly he is happy.[45]

To explain how justice is connected to happiness, Socrates claims that justice and injustice in the soul correspond to health and disease in the body (47d7–48a1). Justice, in his view, is such an important good that it is not worth living with an unjust soul; and so unjust action is to be avoided, because it produces the ruinous state of injustice in the soul. In making these claims, Socrates implies that what is fine and just must be beneficial for the agent.

This claim is by no means indisputable. In Sophocles' *Philoctetes*, Neoptolemus sharply distinguishes justice both from the public interest and from his own interest. He does not deny that Odysseus' plan is the most effective one for the benefit of the Greeks, and hence the 'wise' (*sophon*) course of action; but when he decides that the plan is shameful (*aischron*) and unjust (1234), he prefers the just course of action, and says: 'if it is just, that is better than being wise' (1245–1246).

If we consider the particular actions that Socrates counts as just, we might well expect him to agree with Neoptolemus. In the *Apology* Socrates is on trial for impiety, and for acting unjustly (19b4) by corrupting the young men and leading them to behave unjustly. In his defence he claims to have behaved in ways that the jury themselves can recognize as scrupulously just. He refused to agree to an illegal (in his view) trial of the generals after Arginusae, and he refused to cooperate in the unlawful (in his view) arrest of Leon by the Thirty (32a4–e1). Socrates does not assume that the jury will necessarily agree with what he did on both occasions; they may well suppose that in the trial of the generals he carried his concern for strict legality too far and ignored the gravity of the situation. Still, he assumes that they will recognize the same concern for justice in both incidents. This concern seems to be displayed especially in respect for what the law guarantees to individuals affected by it, irrespective of Socrates' own advantage or any plea of social expediency.

This, however, is not Socrates' view of the relation between justice and the agent's interest. On the contrary, he maintains, against Neoptolemus, that every virtue must benefit the agent; he maintains this claim most strongly in discussing the virtue that seems to falsify it.

31. Justice and the Good of Others

The *Crito* ought to throw some further light on Socrates' views about justice and interest, since it presents his defence for a particular moral position that rests on his views about justice. Having assumed that justice benefits the just person, Socrates argues that it benefits other people too. Crito agrees that since (1) we must not commit injustice, it follows that (2) we must not commit it in retaliation for injustice (49b10–11); since he also agrees that (3) treating someone badly (*kakourgein*, 49c2; *kakōs poiein*, 49c7) counts as committing injustice, he agrees that (4) we ought not to repay injustice by treating someone else badly in return (*antikakourgein*, 49c4).

What does Socrates mean by 'treat badly'? If it simply means 'harm' (*blaptein*), his step 3 is controversial and undefended.[46] Alternatively, 'treat badly' may mean 'treating other people in some way that would be morally unacceptable if they had not committed injustice'. If it is taken this way, Socrates' argument is open to at least two sorts of objections by defenders of retaliation: (a) One defence might accept (3), but deny (1), claiming that we are entitled to commit injustice in retaliation for injustice. (b) Another defence might accept (1) and (2), but deny (3), claiming that it is just for A to retaliate against B's unjust treatment of A by doing something to B that would otherwise be unacceptable.

Socrates rejects both these defences of retaliation, but he does not argue cogently against them. In order to reject the first defence, he must explain why committing retaliatory injustice damages one's soul no less than unprovoked unjust action does; he has not explained this, since he has not explained how injustice and unjust action damage one's soul at all. In order to reject the second defence, he must explain why B's previous unjust treatment of A does not make retaliation by A just.

If Socrates had argued against the second defence of retaliation, he would have had to clarify his own view on retaliation. If he claimed that the fact that A has wronged B should never affect B's treatment of A, he would imply that justice imposes absolute obligations irrespective of the effects on the agent or on other people. In that case, it would be difficult for Socrates to show that what is just and fine is also good, all things considered, for the agent and for the other people affected.

In fact, however, Socrates confines himself to the more moderate claim that A's injustice to B is not by itself a sufficient reason for B to treat A differently.[47] When 'the Laws' take over the argument, they compare the state to parents who are entitled to special consideration in return for benefits they have conferred; they argue that Socrates has made a binding agreement to keep the laws and to confine himself to persuasion if he disagrees with some law. They assert that in disobeying the laws Socrates is undertaking to destroy the laws and the city, as far as is up to him (50a8–b5); but they do not immediately assume that his action must be impermissible. They simply reject the plea that Socrates' disobedience is sufficiently justified by the mere fact that the city has committed injustice against him (50c1–2).

In rejecting this plea, the Laws rely only on the moderate claim about non-retaliation. If they rejected retaliation in all possible circumstances, they would not need to consider any further arguments for disobedience in response to injustice; but in fact they consider further arguments. They argue that Socrates will not be able to carry on his philosophical activity effectively outside Athens in present circumstances, and that he will do better for his sons if he accepts his punishment than if he tries to escape (53a8–54b1).

If Socrates needs to be persuaded on these points, then he must assume that he might be justified in disobeying if he were not persuaded that his escape would be ineffective in these ways. It is relevant for him to ask these questions if he believes the moderate claim about non-retaliation; if his disobedience could gain him these further benefits, he could claim that it is justified on non-retaliatory grounds. He therefore seems to allow that the argument from agreement established only a presumption against disobedience, and that further consideration of consequences is needed to show whether disobedience is, all things considered, just and good.

These arguments tend to confirm the view that Socrates takes just action to be both good, all things considered, and good for the just agent. They show that when he defends particular moral decisions Socrates does not violate his theoretical principles that connect the just, the fine, and the agent's good. These theoretical principles, however, are open to question at the very places where they are used to defend the most controversial aspects of Socrates' position. He does not explain how being unjust or acting unjustly harms one's soul, or what sorts of harms count as unjust treatment of another person.

Similar conclusions may be drawn from the *Lysis*, where Socrates discusses another aspect of other-regarding morality.[48] In friendship (*philia*) one person is concerned for another person's good; the dialogue explores ways in which this concern for others might be connected with a person's own good. This dialogue is a rich source of puzzles about friendship,[49] and Socrates' approach to them is quite indirect. Sometimes his objections appear to be captious and fallacious, but, as the dialogue goes on, the pattern in his questions begins to appear. The different puzzles about friendship turn out to be soluble within Socrates' general assumption that virtuous action benefits the virtuous person; initially surprising features of friendship become easier to understand if we suppose that people are to be loved for their usefulness (212c5–d4, 214e3–215c) insofar as they supply each other's needs (215b–c).[50] The object of love is something fine; by a familiar move Socrates assumes that it is also good (216d2), and so we discover that the object of love is really the good (216c4–217e2). Socrates gives no clear sign of repudiating or challenging these assumptions.[51] This should not be surprising, in the light of his claims about justice and the agent's interest.

These dialogues that discuss the relation of virtue to the interests of other people make it clear that, in Socrates' view, every virtue, precisely because it is fine and beneficial, must be both good, all things considered, and good for the agent. We saw that Socrates relies on this strong claim at the end of the *Charmides*; the dialogues we have just considered show that it is a settled part of his outlook. It is one of the most important and one of the most controversial of the principles that guide Socrates in his elenctic arguments.

32. The Guiding Principles of Socratic Inquiry

We have examined some of Socrates' inquiries into the virtues and identified some of the positive results of these inquiries. We can now identify the main guiding principles of his elenctic inquiries; they guide Socrates in asking questions and in accepting or rejecting answers, and also guide the interlocutors in answering questions and resolving conflicts. If Socrates is entitled to claim that normal interlocutors accept these principles, then he can support his view about the conclusions that will emerge from elenctic inquiry. If he has good reason for believing these principles, then he has good reason to accept the conclusions of elenctic inquiry.

The main guiding principles we have found are these:

1. The interlocutor agrees, sometimes after preliminary explanation, that it is reasonable to look for an answer to the question 'What is F?' on the assumption that there is some single informative answer that applies to all and only the genuine cases of F, and that allows us to decide whether unfamiliar cases are genuine cases of F or not (*La.* 190d7–192b8; *Eu.* 5c8–7a3).[52]
2. He agrees that he has some fairly reliable views about examples of virtuous actions and virtuous people. For when Socrates suggests that a definition that conflicts with clear and confident judgments about examples is to be rejected, the interlocutor agrees that his judgments are clear and confident and that this is a good reason for rejecting the definition.
3. He agrees that it is reasonable to identify a virtue with a state of the agent, instead of trying to define it in behavioural terms. When attempts to describe a pattern of action in purely behavioural terms run into difficulties, the interlocutor is ready to consider definitions that refer to states of the agent (knowledge, endurance, etc.) (*Ch.* 159b7–160d4; *La.* 191d3–e2).
4. He agrees that a virtuous action must always be 'fine' (*kalon*), 'good' (*agathon*), and 'beneficial' (*ōphelimon*). If an action is shameful or harmful, the interlocutor agrees that it cannot be virtuous, and that a state of an agent producing such an action cannot be a virtue (*Ch.* 160e7–11; *La.* 192b9–d9). This is part of Socrates' reason for believing that virtue must be knowledge (since he takes knowledge of the good to be necessary and sufficient for a fine and beneficial state of character).[53] When Socrates spells out the content of this principle, he makes it clear that it implies his strong claims about virtue and self-interest.
5. These previous four principles may conflict in particular cases. Indeed, the second and the fourth seem especially likely to conflict; why should we not find an apparently clear example of a virtuous action that seems clearly not to be fine and beneficial? Socrates sees the possible conflict between the two principles and uses the fourth to override the second. This is why Nicias and

Socrates reject Laches' attempted counterexamples to Nicias' account of bravery (*La.* 197a1–c9), and this is why Socrates refuses to accept the apparent result of the elenchos because it conflicts with the belief that temperance is always beneficial (*Ch.* 175e5–176a1).

These are guiding principles of the elenchos, not simply Socrates' own beliefs. For he assumes—and his assumption is proved right in the dialogues we have examined—that the interlocutor will accept these principles and be influenced by them in answering Socrates' questions. Sometimes the interlocutor needs some explanation or argument before he accepts the guiding principles or sees what they imply, but the argument proceeds only when he has assented to them.

33. The Elenchos and the Search for Definitions

The role of the guiding principles makes it easier to understand how Socrates might reasonably claim to be making progress towards finding definitions. We have seen that Socrates is looking for real, as opposed to nominal, definitions; he wants to know what actual properties we refer to in speaking of the virtues, not simply what sense we attach to different terms. If he were looking for nominal definitions, he would be foolish to suggest that the virtues may not be distinct; for it is difficult to deny that, say, 'bravery' and 'justice' have different senses. It is not so obviously foolish, however, to claim that the terms refer to the same virtue. Socrates' practice suggests that he is not looking for nominal definitions, but can he reasonably claim to be advancing towards real definitions?

We can see the problem that faces him if we compare names of moral properties with names of natural kinds. In finding the real essence underlying 'gold', for instance, we assume that (1) 'gold' is a name of a natural kind (rather than the name of a collection of observable features), and that (2) we were not far wrong about the reference of the term, so that the real essence underlying the 'gold' is the one that belongs to most of the examples, or to stereotypical examples, that we call gold.

With many names of natural kinds, these two assumptions lead to the same results. They do not always lead to the same results, however, and when they do not, we sometimes rely on the first to override the second. If some of our stereotypical samples of gold turned out to be iron pyrites, others turned out to be yellow-painted lead, and so on, we would not infer that gold is not after all the metal with this particular atomic structure; we would simply decide that these were not genuine examples.

In the case of moral properties, we must face this sort of conflict between our general assumptions and our beliefs about examples more often than we face it in the case of natural kinds. Socrates is engaged in the task that Epictetus calls the 'articulation of our preconceptions'.[54] If we are to articulate them correctly, we must reject many of our initial beliefs about which actions are virtuous. Socrates and Epictetus agree that if we are to find the real virtue underlying our use of names for virtues, we ought not to look for an answer that accepts most of our purported examples. For Socrates believes that many people are quite wrong about some examples of the virtues: (1) They count repaying evil for evil as a clear and stereotypical example of just action. (2) They count someone who achieves wealth and worldly success as a clear example of a happy (*eudaimōn*, well-off) person and someone suffering poverty and ill health as a clearly unhappy person. (3) They count someone who rushes into battle fearlessly without understanding why what he is doing is worth doing, and who gets drunk and commits rape after the battle, as an evidently brave person.

Socrates' second guiding principle implies that he cannot suppose that people are always or usually as mistaken as they are in these particular cases; evidently his inquiries could not get started unless he thought his interlocutors could recognize some examples of the virtues fairly reliably. Still, his inquiries would lead to the wrong conclusion if they had to accept all or most of the common-sense stereotypes. To avoid this error, he appeals to the other four guiding principles to justify him in overriding the second in cases of conflict. Since he cannot rely uncritically on stereotypical examples, he must rely all the more heavily on these other guiding principles. When we rely on these, we 'articulate our preconceptions' (as Epictetus puts it); for we make it clear to ourselves what is implied in being a virtue, and how these implications must modify our initial conception of this particular virtue.

34. Socrates' Treatment of Common Beliefs

Is Socrates entitled, however, to rely on these guiding principles? If they are to play the role that he intends for them in the elenchos, he must claim that they are more reliable than our judgments about particular virtuous actions, and the interlocutor must agree with this claim. But can he fairly expect a normal interlocutor to agree?

Our initial survey of common beliefs revealed disagreement about what is needed for happiness, and about the relation among virtue, the agent's good, and the good of others. Socrates strongly disagrees with the widespread view that the recognized virtues, especially justice, may conflict with the agent's own good. Since this disagreement is so important in deciding between Socrates' moral outlook and the different outlooks that stay closer to common sense, we may well be surprised that he does not openly confront interlocutors who challenge his views about virtue and happiness.

Socrates might reply that he does not need to confront such challenges directly, since anyone who accepts the guiding principles of the elenchos will see that all such challenges must be rejected. If we agree that the recognized virtues are genuine virtues, and that every virtue must be fine and beneficial (in the sense that Socrates attaches to this claim), then we can see that justice must be beneficial to the agent. He does not need to confront interlocutors who begin by claiming that justice conflicts with the agent's happiness, since the guiding principles ensure that such interlocutors will have to reject their initial claim.

This defence of Socrates, however, simply pushes the question further back. The defence succeeds only if interlocutors can be expected to accept the guiding principles. But if we begin by sharing the widespread view that the recognized virtues may not promote the agent's interest, why should we accept the guiding principle that says every virtue is fine and beneficial for the agent? If the Socratic elenchos relies on this guiding principle, it will work only with interlocutors who implicitly accept it and who agree to accept it when they see how it requires a revision in their other beliefs. But Socrates has not shown why we should accept this guiding principle if we share the widespread doubts about the connexion between virtue and happiness.

These points are enough to show not only that we ought to find Socrates' guiding principles controversial but also that his contemporaries have good reasons to challenge them. He would be wrong if he supposed that the guiding principles need no further defence. Can he offer any further defence?

4

Socrates: From Happiness to Virtue

35. The Importance of the *Euthydemus*

We have now given reasons for believing that some of the shorter Socratic dialogues express Socrates' acceptance of some controversial claims about the virtues. To test this account of these dialogues, it is useful to consider the *Euthydemus*. Here Socrates presents a 'protreptic' discourse (*Euthd.* 278c5–d5) designed to show Cleinias 'that he ought to cultivate wisdom and virtue' (278d2–3). He puts forward some very general claims about happiness and virtue. If the implications of these claims fit the views that emerge from the dialogues that inquire into the virtues, then we have a further reason for believing that we have really discovered a Socratic conception of the virtues.

The *Euthydemus* proceeds from general claims about happiness, whereas the other dialogues proceed from particular beliefs about virtues and virtuous actions. These two directions of argument complement each other; for the argument emerging from the *Euthydemus* suggests how Socrates might defend some of the guiding principles of his inquiries into the virtues, and the particular inquiries into the virtues suggest how the programme outlined very broadly in the *Euthydemus* might be defended in more detail.[1]

36. Eudaemonism

Socrates' views about happiness are important in his claims about the virtues in the *Charmides*, *Apology*, and *Crito*; but they are not explained. The *Euthydemus* offers the clearest account of the role of happiness in Socrates' argument.

Socrates takes it to be obvious that everyone wants to fare well and to be happy (*Euthd.* 278e3–6, 280b6), and once this is agreed he asks how we are to achieve happiness, and what we must do to get it (279a1–2, 282a1–4). Socrates assumes that this must be the form of every practical question; whenever we are considering what to do or how to live, the right answer will tell us what we must do in order to be happy.[2] Similarly, he assumes at the end of the *Charmides* that if Charmides has any reason for cultivating temperance, temperance must benefit him, and if it benefits him, it must promote his happiness (*Ch.* 175d5–176a5).[3]

Common beliefs, as summarized by Aristotle, agree with Socrates in taking happiness to be an end that we aim at in all our action.[4] But Socrates goes further, making happiness the overriding end that determines the rationality of any action. He commits himself to a eudaemonist position, insofar as he claims: (1) In all our rational actions we pursue our own happiness. (2) We pursue happiness only for its own sake, never for the sake of anything else. (3) Whatever else we rationally pursue, we pursue it for the sake of happiness.

These eudaemonist claims still need to be clarified, for different questions might be answered by saying that we act for the sake of happiness. We might be answering a request for an explanatory reason (answering 'Why did you pursue x?') or for a justifying reason (answering 'Why is x worth pursuing?').[5] Socrates does not distinguish these different types of reason, but it is often important to know which question he means to answer by an appeal to happiness. If he means happiness to provide the only ultimate justifying reason, then, we may say, he accepts *rational eudaemonism*; if he means it to provide the only ultimate explanatory reason, then he accepts *psychological eudaemonism*.

The remarks in the *Euthydemus* about happiness, taken by themselves, imply only that if we do not pursue our own happiness, we are not acting rationally; they do not imply that we actually pursue happiness in all our actions. So far Socrates commits himself only to rational eudaemonism. He does not draw any distinction, however, between rational and non-rational or irrational actions. If he assumes that all our actions are rational actions (in the sense that is relevant to the eudaemonist claims), then he believes that we always act for the sake of happiness and never for any other ultimate end. In that case he maintains psychological eudaemonism.

Psychological eudaemonism, in contrast to rational eudaemonism, requires the rejection of three possibilities that common sense recognizes: (1) Common sense believes that it is possible for us to benefit someone else for the other person's own sake, not for our own happiness. (2) It allows disinterested spite, malice, or resentment. (3) It believes that we often act in ways that we realize are harmful for us; for example, I may realize I would be better off without another drink, but I may still want it, and I may want it strongly enough to take it.

A psychological eudaemonist must claim that such actions cannot happen, and that common sense is misled in believing that they happen. Rational eudaemonism claims not that these actions are impossible, but that they are irrational; that claim is itself disputable, but it is less paradoxical than the psychological claim. If we can see how far Socrates' ethical claims conflict with these three possibilities recognized by common sense, we will also see what sort of eudaemonism he accepts.

37. Why Eudaemonism?

In the *Euthydemus* Socrates takes eudaemonism to be so obviously true that he does not explain why he accepts it. The *Lysis*, however, helps to explain why eudaemonism might seem reasonable. After discussing different ways of describing friendship and love (*philia*) and what it loves, Socrates finds it necessary to distinguish different sorts of things that may be loved, and the different sorts of things we may love them for. In particular, he distinguishes subordinate from primary objects of love. A subordinate object is loved for the sake of some primary object of love, whereas the primary object is loved for its own sake and not for the sake of any further object of love.

Socrates implies that only the primary object is loved for its own sake; no good that is chosen for the sake of the primary object is chosen for its own sake (219c1–d5, 220a6–b5). He concludes that 'what is truly loved (*philon*) is not loved for the sake of anything else' (220b4–5); what is truly loved is loved for its own sake, and Socrates implies that an object of love is loved for its own sake if and only if it is not loved for the sake of anything else.

Socrates believes that there must be a primary object of love because the series of objects of love must be finite. If we take one thing to be loved for the sake of a second, the second for the sake of a third, and so on, 'we must refuse, and arrive at some beginning that will not lead us on to yet another object of love, but will arrive at that first object of love, for the sake of which we say that the other things are also objects of love' (219c5–d2).[6] If we say that A chooses x for the sake of y, but we cannot see why A chooses y, then, it might be argued, we still do not understand why A chooses x; we must therefore introduce z, some further object of love that A chooses for its own sake.

These claims seem to be applied to the explanation of action, not (or not only) to justification. Socrates does not say it would be foolish to pursue one thing for the sake of another without limit; he implies (in 'we must refuse . . .') that it is impossible. He therefore maintains a psychological thesis about action and motivation, not (or not merely) a thesis about what makes action rational.

The thesis he maintains falls short of psychological eudaemonism, since he does not say how many primary objects of love there are. Perhaps the father takes his son (in Socrates' example) as a primary object of love, and the medicine administered for the sake of the son's health as a subordinate good. Socrates does not imply that happiness is the only primary object of love.[7]

In the *Euthydemus*, however, Socrates suggests that happiness is the only end that meets the conditions laid down in the *Lysis* for being a primary object of love. He does not suggest that we pursue happiness for the sake of anything else.[8] By contrast, when he considers why we pursue other recognized goods besides happiness (27914–b3), the only reason he considers is their promotion of happiness. He assumes, then, that happiness is the only end that we pursue with no further reason and hence the only one that we do not pursue for the sake of a further end.

Other dialogues confirm the suggestion made in the *Euthydemus* that we must refer to happiness to give a reason for our choice of everything that we choose besides happiness. Socrates believes that when we face a choice between virtuous and vicious action, we should not consider the costs of virtuous action as any sort of reason against it (*Ap.* 28b5–9).[9] He does not mean, however, that no reason can or should be given for the pursuit of virtue. On the contrary, he begins his argument in the *Crito* by assuming that living well is what matters most; he defends the just course of action only when he has established that living well, living finely, and living justly are the same (*Cri.* 48b4–10). To explain why he has no reason to fear the penalties threatened by his accusers, Socrates answers that the good person cannot be harmed (*Ap.* 41c8–d2); he assumes that nothing except his happiness needs to be, or should be, considered when he is deciding what to do or what to avoid. Similarly, in the *Charmides* he takes it for granted that temperance and any other craft cannot produce a good that is not subordinate to happiness.

These different remarks suggest not only that Socrates accepts eudaemonism but also why he accepts it. The passage in the *Lysis* implies that action requires reference to some primary object of love; the other passages suggest that happiness is the only primary object of love.

This argument is not conclusive, because it fails to distinguish rational from psychological eudaemonism. The *Lysis* affirms a psychological thesis that falls short of eudaemonism. The other passages clearly affirm rational eudaemonism, but it is not so clear that they also affirm psychological eudaemonism. If Socrates clearly distinguished rational from psychological eudaemonism, he might consistently maintain that there are many primary objects of love, as defined in the *Lysis* (since many ends provide sufficient explanatory reasons), but happiness is the only one of these that it is reasonable to pursue as a primary object of love (since it is the only one that provides sufficient justifying reasons). If this is right, then the passages considered so far fail to provide conclusive evidence of Socrates' acceptance of psychological eudaemonism.

38. Happiness, Wisdom, and Fortune

Socrates takes it to be generally agreed that we achieve happiness by gaining many goods (279a1–4), but he argues that the only good we need is wisdom. He argues in three stages: (1) Happiness does not require good fortune added to wisdom (279c4–280a8). (2) Wisdom is necessary and sufficient for the correct and successful use of other goods (280b1–281b4). (3) Wisdom is the only good (281b4–e5). From this Socrates concludes that if we want to secure happiness, we need not acquire many goods; we need only acquire wisdom (282a1–d3).

In the first stage, Socrates denies that happiness needs good fortune in addition to the other goods. He argues:

1. In each case the wise person has better fortune than the unwise (280a4–5).[10]
2. Genuine wisdom can never go wrong, but must always succeed (280a7–8).
3. Therefore, wisdom always makes us fortunate (280a6).

What does Socrates mean by step 1? He might be taken to mean that wisdom ensures more success, other things being equal, than we can expect if we lack wisdom; with the same materials and the same external circumstances, the wise craftsman who knows his craft will be more successful than the ignorant person. But this moderate conclusion cannot be all that Socrates means, since it does not prove his contention that we need no good fortune besides wisdom.

If we accept only the moderate conclusion, then we agree we are better off with wisdom than without it, but we must still admit that external circumstances may prevent the success that (for all Socrates has proved so far) is necessary for happiness. If happiness requires actual success in, say, making money or protecting our friends, it seems to need the good fortune that provides favourable external circumstances.

Since the moderate conclusion evidently fails to support Socrates' claim that good fortune need not be added to wisdom, he needs to assert the extreme claim that wisdom guarantees success whatever the circumstances. If we understand his step 2 to claim this, then his conclusion (in step 3) justifies him in claiming that no further good fortune is needed. But he has given us no argument for the extreme claim about wisdom and success.

39. Wisdom and the Correct Use of Assets

In the second stage of his argument, Socrates argues that it cannot be the mere possession of various goods, but only the correct use of them, that produces happiness (280b7–d7). Some of the ostensible goods that are alleged to produce happiness may be called 'assets'. If something is an asset, we are normally supposed to be better off, other things being equal, to the extent that we have it than we would be if we lacked it, but it does not actually benefit us unless we use it well. Socrates now argues that we must allow wisdom a special place among goods, distinguishing it from assets:

1. It is possible to use assets well or badly (280b7–c3, 280d7–281a1).
2. Correct use of them is necessary and sufficient for happiness (280d7–281e1).
3. Wisdom is necessary and sufficient for correct use (281a1–b2).
4. Therefore, wisdom is necessary and sufficient for happiness (281b2–4).

Once again Socrates seems to assert a more extreme conclusion than he is entitled to. His argument is valid, but the second step is open to objection. If we do not have enough assets in the first place, or if we are unlucky in the results of our correct use of them (we navigate with great skill, but an unpredictable storm wrecks the ship), then the correct use of assets does not seem to secure happiness. This objection would not work if we accepted the strong conclusion that Socrates drew from his argument against the addition of good fortune, but that argument seems to be open to objections very similar to those that arise for the present argument.

40. Wisdom as the Only Good

Socrates begins the third stage of the argument by claiming that assets do not benefit us without wisdom (281b4–6).[11] He asks: 'Would someone benefit if he had many assets and did many things <with them> without intelligence, or <would he benefit> more <if he had and did> few things with intelligence?'

(281b6–8).[12] He suggests that if we do not know how to use the assets we have, we are worse off if we have more of them, for that will make us more active and so more likely to harm ourselves. Assets include not only material resources such as wealth (281c2–3) but also strength, honour, bravery, temperance,[13] industry, speed, and acute senses (281c4–d1); indeed, they include all the recognized goods, apart from wisdom, that were initially taken to promote happiness.

Socrates now argues that wisdom is the only good:

1. Each recognized good is a greater evil than its contrary, if it is used without wisdom, and each is a greater good than its contrary, if it is used by wisdom (281d6–8).
2. Therefore, each recognized good other than wisdom is in itself (*auto kath'hauto*) neither good nor evil (281e3–4).[14]
3. Therefore, each of them is neither good nor evil (281e3–4).
4. Therefore, wisdom is the only good and folly the only evil (281e4–5).

This argument treats all recognized goods other than wisdom as assets, and asserts that wisdom has a special status that makes it different from assets.

It is difficult to be sure, however, what Socrates is saying. Two views deserve consideration: (1) A moderate view: When Socrates says that the recognized goods are not goods 'in themselves', he means that they are not goods when they are divorced from wisdom, but are goods when they are properly used by wisdom.[15] When he concludes that wisdom is the only good, he means simply that only wisdom is good all by itself, apart from any combination with other things.[16] (2) An extreme view: When Socrates says that the recognized goods are not goods 'in themselves', he means that they are not goods; any goodness belongs to the wise use of them, not to the recognized goods themselves. When Socrates concludes that wisdom is the only good, he means that nothing else is a good.

These two views correspond to the two interpretations we considered for Socrates' claims about the 'science of benefit' at the end of the *Charmides*.[17] We saw there that Socrates seems to endorse the extreme view when he asserts that temperance is sufficient for happiness. Which view does he take in the *Euthydemus*?

The moderate view makes steps 1 and 2 reasonable, but it does not explain how Socrates reaches his conclusions in steps 3 and 4. If Socrates is entitled to infer (3) from (2), then 'good in itself' must be taken to mean that health itself, say, is not good, and anything good results only from the exercise of wisdom.

Socrates' later remarks show that the conclusion he reaches in (4) is not a momentary exaggeration. The argument is meant to secure Socrates' previous claim that wisdom is necessary and sufficient for happiness, for it claims to shows that wisdom is the only good, and it has been agreed that happiness requires the presence of all the appropriate goods. Socrates makes this clear in his summary of his argument (282a1–7), and he goes on to claim that we should pursue wisdom to the exclusion of any other recognized good because 'it is the only thing that makes a human being happy and fortunate' (282c9–d1). Later (292b1–2) he reasserts his claim that wisdom is the only good; this claim is unsupported unless he has previously asserted the extreme view that assets are not goods at all.

Although Socrates maintains the extreme view, he has not defended it. To defend it he needs to convince us that we benefit simply from the use we make of whatever assets we have,[18] so that if we begin from very few assets and make good use of them, we are happy; but Socrates has not defended this view. He seems to have made the same move that he made in the first two arguments, from the claim that wisdom makes us better off, in appropriately favourable conditions, to the claim that wisdom is sufficient for happiness. If we had already been convinced that external circumstances and assets make no difference to our happiness, then we could see an argument for Socrates' conclusion that nothing else besides wisdom is a good. But Socrates has not presented the sort of argument he needs. His conviction that only wisdom matters for happiness influences his argument, but lacks defence.

Moreover, Socrates does not consider all the implications of his claim that wisdom is the only good and is sufficient for happiness. For if there is nothing good about external goods, why should a virtuous person do anything to secure health rather than sickness, in cases where health does not require any sacrifice of virtue? Socrates himself agrees that the external goods are preferable in such conditions; for he claims that if wisdom guides us in the choice of ways to use health, health will be a greater good than sickness, to the extent that health is more able to serve its leader and the leader is good (cf. 281d6–7).

This comparative claim ('greater good') need not imply that health is a good;[19] if two things fail to be large, one of them may nonetheless be larger than the other, and if two lines fail to be straight, one of them may still be straighter than the other because it is closer to being straight. In this case, then, Socrates may mean that neither health nor sickness is good, but health is a greater good because it is more of a good, closer to being a good.[20] If this is what he means, his claim is consistent with the claim that wisdom is the only good. In that case, the remarks about health and sickness do not require Socrates to take the moderate view.

41. The Sufficiency of Virtue for Happiness

If we agree that in the *Euthydemus* Socrates seems to accept the extreme view about wisdom and external goods but does not defend it very well, ought we to suppose that he seriously holds this view? We must turn to some of his remarks in other dialogues that are relevant to questions about happiness.[21]

A passage in the *Apology* might seem to support the moderate view. Socrates claims that virtue is the source of wealth and any other goods there are (*Ap.* 30b2–4). In claiming this, he seems to suggest that wealth is really a good.[22] Socrates' claim is difficult to understand, since he would destroy his whole argument in the *Apology* if he were to advocate virtue as the best policy for accumulating external goods. It would be more consistent with his general view if he meant that virtue is the source of the sort of wealth, health, and so on that is really good for a person. Perhaps he means that since desire for external goods will not distract virtuous people from being virtuous, desire for these assets will not interfere with virtuous people's happiness, and to that extent these assets will be good rather than bad for them. If this is what Socrates means, then he does not admit that virtuous people lose anything of value by being deprived of wealth and health.[23] In that case his remark does not commit him to the moderate view about external goods.

Sometimes Socrates takes virtue to be sufficient for happiness (*Ap.* 30c6–d5, 41c8–d2; *Cri.* 48b8–9; *Ch.* 173d3–5, 174b11–c3).[24] Most people think it is possible for a virtuous person to have bad luck, and therefore to lack some of the goods that contribute to happiness, but Socrates believes that common sense is confused, and that he can expose the confusion by appeal to his eudaemonism.

To expose the confusion in common sense, Socrates considers the virtuous person's attitude to virtuous action in comparison with other goods. We agree that it is fine and admirable for brave people to sacrifice their lives for the right cause, for just people to refuse to act unjustly even with the prospect of some large reward, and for friends to help each other even at some large cost to themselves. In each case we suppose that the virtuous action is actually finer when it imposes a larger sacrifice of other goods. Evidently, then (Socrates argues), we assume that virtuous people are acting reasonably when they sacrifice other goods for virtue, since we approve of what they are doing.

Socrates interprets this assumption from his eudaemonist point of view. In his view, rational action aims at the agent's own happiness, and well-informed agents have true beliefs about what contributes to their own happiness. Since virtuous people who sacrifice other goods to virtue are making the right decision and are not misled by ignorance, we must, according to Socrates, agree that they are doing what is best for themselves. It follows that virtuous people must correctly believe that their virtuous action promotes their own happiness better than any other action would.

This appeal to rational eudaemonism supports a *comparative thesis* (that virtue contributes to happiness more than anything else would). It does not, however, support the *sufficiency thesis* (that virtue is sufficient for happiness) that Socrates accepts. We could accept the comparative thesis and so defend, for instance, Socrates' decision to act virtuously rather than seek to avoid punishment, while still insisting that in the situation that faces him the virtuous action will not bring him happiness, since the harms that it brings him are large enough to prevent him from achieving happiness. Has Socrates any reason for preferring the sufficiency thesis over the comparative thesis?

Since he does not compare the two theses about virtue and happiness, we cannot be certain of his view. We can see what he might say, however, if we consider the different attitudes to virtuous action that the two theses would support. If we accept the comparative thesis, but reject the sufficiency thesis, then we will believe that the virtuous course of action is best, all things considered, but nonetheless the sacrifices involved are so large that the virtuous person has good reason to regret the cost of being virtuous. If we value external goods highly, although never so highly that they cause us to abandon virtue, we will sometimes face the virtuous action with some reluctance.

Socrates does not acknowledge that virtuous action ever involves this sort of sacrifice. He does not, for instance, tell the jury at his trial that he is justified in making the heavy sacrifice he must make to be virtuous; on the contrary, he seems to be telling them that he is making no sacrifice that he has any reason to regret. We might expect him to acknowledge to Crito that in accepting the death penalty he gives up some significant goods; but he never suggests this. To judge by Socrates' own attitude, he expects the virtuous person not only to choose a virtuous course of action but also to choose it without regret or reluctance.

Socrates would not be entitled to advocate this non-reluctant, non-regretful commitment to virtue if he could show only that the good of the virtuous course of action outweighs any cost that it may involve. He is entitled to advocate such commitment, however, if he can show that the virtuous person's choice involves no loss of genuine goods, so that there is no loss that needs to be outweighed and regretted. Socrates has a reason, then, to believe that virtue is sufficient for happiness. If he believes that, then he also has a reason to maintain that other supposed goods do not contribute to happiness at all in their own right. The extreme view that he asserts in the *Euthydemus* is not an aberration; he needs it as part of his argument for unreserved commitment to virtue.

42. Use and Misuse of Knowledge

We have argued that Socrates' belief in the sufficiency of virtue for happiness supports the extreme interpretation of his claims in the *Euthydemus*. Still, even if virtue is sufficient for happiness, it does not follow that wisdom is sufficient for happiness. If wisdom is not sufficient for virtue, then we could have all the appropriate knowledge, but still use it badly to harm ourselves; in that case wisdom also turns out to be a mere asset, not (on Socrates' criteria) a genuine good.

The later protreptic discourse (from *Euthd.* 288d5) implicitly raises this question, but does not directly answer it. Socrates points out that not every sort of knowledge guarantees happiness; a particular craft (*technē*) knows the correct use of some assets to produce a product, but this product in turn becomes a new asset that can be used well or badly, and we need a superordinate craft to use the product of the subordinate craft (289a7–b3). And so we need the sort of science (*epistēmē*) 'in which production and knowledge of how to use the product are combined' (289b4–6). Socrates calls this the 'royal science', the superordinate craft whose possession ensures happiness (289c6–8, d8–10).

What is the relevant science? We can say that it is the craft that produces happiness, but we want to know how it does that. Socrates argues that it must be beneficial and therefore must produce some good for us; since the only good we have discovered so far is knowledge, apparently the royal science must produce happiness for us by producing some sort of knowledge in us. But then the question arises: what sort of knowledge does the royal science produce in us? If we say it is the knowledge of producing the same sort of knowledge in others, we still have not said what sort of knowledge this is. Until we can answer that question, we have not said what the royal science produces (292a4–e7). The discussion ends without an answer.

Is Socrates wrong to suppose that the product of the royal science must be some sort of knowledge? He supposes this because he claims that knowledge is the only good that they have discovered; but we might want to dispute this claim. For we have found that knowledge is a good because it ensures the correct use of assets that secures happiness. If this correct use of assets were not a good, how could the knowledge of how to use assets correctly be a good? Surely, then, we have already found an answer to Socrates' question about the product of the royal science; should we not say that its product is the correct use of assets that leads to happiness?

This is not a good answer to Socrates' question. For what is the correct use of assets? To say what it is, we need a clearer conception of what promotes happiness. If, for instance, we knew that happiness requires wealth or fame, we would know that the science of happiness must secure wealth or fame for us. But Socrates has rejected these claims about happiness without replacing them with any other description of the appropriate product of the science of happiness. In raising the final puzzle, he draws our attention to this gap in his argument.[25]

Even if this objection can be answered, we might argue that Socrates makes a further assumption that makes his puzzle insoluble. For he assumes that to answer the question 'What guarantees the right use of our knowledge?' we must discover the further knowledge that guarantees the right use of the rest of our knowledge; he reduces the question about correct use to a question about a superordinate science. But we might doubt whether a superordinate science solves the real problem. Why could I not know that something promotes my happiness and still choose to act in some other way?

These difficulties are not peculiar to the *Euthydemus*. Nothing in the other dialogues we have discussed suggests that Socrates can avoid them or that he has any answer to them. The *Euthydemus*, indeed, improves on the other dialogues to the extent that it makes it easier to see how the difficulties arise.

43. Socrates' Defence of His Guiding Principles

The *Euthydemus* starts out from some general and—in Socrates' view—obviously correct claims about happiness and reaches some controversial views about the relation between wisdom and happiness. In the course of the argument, Socrates clarifies and defends some of the guiding principles that are assumed in the dialogues that start from ordinary beliefs about virtue.

The most important of these principles asserts that every virtue must be fine and beneficial. Socrates interprets this principle in a very strong sense, insisting that every virtue must be beneficial, all things considered, for the agent. The rational eudaemonism that he accepts in the *Euthydemus* explains why he believes he is entitled to this strong principle. The rational eudaemonist assumes that (1) A has good reason to choose x over y if and only if x promotes A's happiness better than y would. Socrates also assumes—and his interlocutors do not disagree—that (2) we always have good reason to choose virtue over anything else; if we discovered that a supposed virtue did not meet this condition, we would have good reason to conclude that it is not really a virtue. These two assumptions support Socrates' strong conclusions about virtue and happiness.

If we agree with this, we can see why it is reasonable for Socrates to believe that the virtues cannot be separated; for if a supposed virtue could be separated from the other virtues, there would be occasions when it would not cause us to choose what is best for us, all things considered, so that this supposed virtue would turn out not to be a virtue.[26]

The *Euthydemus* not only throws light on the principles that Socrates invites his interlocutors to accept but also helps to explain his acceptance of some of the principles that he takes for granted without asking his interlocutors. In advocating wisdom, the *Euthydemus* appears to demote the virtues to the status of assets that are not necessary for happiness (*Euthd.* 281c6–7),[27] but it demotes them only on the assumption that they are not identical to wisdom. The *Euthydemus* makes it clear that either we must regard the virtues as subordinate goods to be regulated by a superordinate science or we must identify each of them with the superordinate science itself. The *Charmides* and *Laches* suggest that Socrates chooses the second alternative; his choice is reasonable, in the light of his claims about wisdom in the *Euthydemus*.

In the *Euthydemus* Socrates assumes that if we have wisdom, we need not be concerned about the effects of external circumstances, because wisdom ensures the right use of the assets we have. If he is right about this, and he is right to identify each virtue with wisdom, then he has some support for his assumption in the *Apology*, *Crito*, and *Charmides* that virtue is sufficient for happiness.

The identification of virtue with wisdom, however, requires more than rational eudaemonism. We will insist that bravery requires endurance as well as knowledge, and that temperance requires self-control as well as knowledge, if we suppose it is possible to believe that x is better for us than y, but still to choose y over x. Rational eudaemonism does not imply that these irrational choices are impossible, and so it gives us no reason for affirming that knowledge is sufficient for virtue. Although rational eudaemonism supports the inseparability of the virtues (for the reasons given previously), it does not imply that every virtue is identical to knowledge of the good.

To show that virtue is simply knowledge, Socrates must maintain that irrational choice of the lesser apparent good is impossible; to maintain that, he must maintain psychological eudaemonism. Although psychological eudaemonism is not explicitly maintained in the *Euthydemus*, it is implied in Socrates' claim that wisdom is sufficient for happiness; this same psychological claim helps to explain why he argues in the *Laches* and *Charmides* that each virtue is identical to knowledge of the good. If psychological eudaemonism is true, then Socrates is right to ignore the non-cognitive aspects of each virtue.

44. Questions about Socrates' Defence

We have seen how the guiding principles of the elenchos conflict with the common-sense views that recognize conflicts between the virtues and between the virtues and one's own benefit.[28] If Socrates defends the guiding principles by appeal to rational and psychological eudaemonism, does he give us good reason to agree with the guiding principles?

Socrates' remarks suggest a possible answer to this question. He implies that it would be ridiculous and foolish even to ask whether we all want to fare well (278e3–6); apparently the claim that we all want to fare well is so obvious and indubitable that we do not even need to ask whether it is true. We do not know how many of the premisses in the argument of the *Euthydemus* Socrates regards as equally indubitable. But if he could convince us that his conclusion that wisdom is necessary and sufficient for happiness rests on premisses that are as indubitable as the claim about happiness, then he could reasonably claim to have defended a crucial element in the guiding principles of the elenchos.

If this is his view, then he has an answer to critics who wonder why they ought to accept the guiding principles of the elenchos even when they conflict with common-sense views about the virtues.[29] He can answer that the guiding principles rest on rational and psychological eudaemonism or on similarly indubitable premisses whose evident truth becomes clear to everyone who thinks clearly about them. If, for instance, we find ourselves compelled to agree that virtue is sufficient for happiness, we must simply dismiss the views that lead some people to believe that virtue and happiness may conflict.

This answer to critics may explain why Socrates does not actually consider common-sense views that conflict sharply with his own views about virtue and self-interest. If something strikes us as being so clear and evident that it is altogether indubitable, then we may well feel entitled to infer that any claims inconsistent with it must be given up; however plausible they may seem, the evidence for them must be misleading, since we cannot be justified in accepting anything inconsistent with what we find altogether indubitable. On some occasions this attitude may be reasonable; if we find p indubitable, but people have fabricated some misleading evidence for not-p, we need not take the trouble to unmask all their ingenious fabrications.

These would be exacting standards, however, for Socrates to meet, and he does not show that he meets them. He has not said enough about the nature of happiness or the intended connexion with virtue to justify the claims that underlie his own moral position. His premisses themselves are paradoxical, and the parts of the theory that rest on these apparently paradoxical premisses are equally controversial. His belief that knowledge is sufficient for virtue does not appear plausible if it is defended by the claim that there are no non-rational desires to threaten the supremacy of knowledge; for Socrates has given us no reason to accept this further claim if we do not begin by agreeing that knowledge is sufficient for virtue. Similarly, if Socrates wants to defend an unreserved commitment to virtue, he does not defend it very effectively by claiming that virtue is sufficient for happiness, if all he can say in support of that claim is that his defence of virtue requires it. The controversial assumptions need some independent defence.

If this is true, then Socrates' strategy of beginning with the virtues that arouse the least controversy and uncovering the indubitable assumptions that will support his more controversial claims has not succeeded. Why should we not find our confidence in Socrates' claims ebbing when we confront them with the common-sense views he rejects? Even if it does not ebb, what do we say if we find that anti-Socratic claims seem equally indubitable? And if Socrates' interlocutors find Socrates' claims indubitable, but other people would find anti-Socratic claims indubitable, how are we to decide between these inconsistent intuitions of indubitability?

This objection to Socrates assumes that he appeals to the obviousness and indubitability of his premisses, but that assumption itself rests on a speculative generalization from his remark about the desire for happiness to the other premisses of his argument. It is by no means clear that Socrates follows the strategy I have just described and criticized. I have explored it, however, to make three points: (1) It is one strategy that he might find attractive. (2) It is open to serious objection. (3) If he does not follow this strategy, he needs some other reply to the very natural and reasonable question about why we should rely so heavily on the guiding principles of the elenchos. If this is true, then the arguments of the *Euthydemus* still leave us with some serious questions about Socratic method and ethics. The *Euthydemus* gives us some reason to believe that some of the assumptions that Socrates relies on elsewhere are not bare, undefended assumptions; for it shows how Socrates might defend them. Still, the defence provided in the *Euthydemus* is quite limited; for some of the premisses Socrates relies on are themselves quite disputable.

5

Difficulties for Socrates

45. The Questions about Happiness

In the *Euthydemus* Socrates argues that wisdom is necessary and sufficient for happiness. If we are to evaluate this argument, we need to ask how he conceives happiness, and how he takes wisdom to be related to happiness. To see why we need to raise these issues, we may begin with some difficulties in understanding Socrates' apparently simple questions: 'Since we want to fare well, how might we fare well? Would we fare well if we had many goods?' (*Euthd.* 279a1–3). The most obvious answers to these questions seem to collect the various goods that Aristotle lists as 'parts' of happiness (*Rhet.* 1360b19). But what does Socrates take to be the relation of these goods (or this good, since it turns out that only wisdom is necessary and sufficient for happiness) to happiness itself?

Some of Aristotle's remarks in his ethical works, in contrast to the *Rhetoric*, show why this is a fairly complicated question. In the *Eudemian Ethics* he urges us to distinguish the question 'What does our living well consist in?' from the question 'What are the necessary conditions for our living well?', remarking that being healthy is not the same as the conditions necessary for being healthy (*EE* 1214b11–15). He remarks that a failure to distinguish these two questions is the cause of much dispute, since some people treat necessary conditions of happiness as though they were parts of it (1214b24–27). Aristotle assumes that a description of the parts of happiness answers his first question ('What does our living well consist in?') as distinct from his second.

This distinction between the two questions is not observed in the *Rhetoric*. Some of the goods listed as 'parts' of happiness seem to answer the first question; others seem to answer the second. Money and slaves seem to be simply necessary conditions. I want money for its causal properties; it offers me security and the resources I need to achieve happiness; if I could secure the causal consequences of having money without having money, that would be just as good (if, for instance, I could rely on having all the goods that I normally buy, without having to buy them). Slaves are an even clearer case; they involve enough disadvantages that I might positively prefer it if I could, say, have my land worked by some other means. By contrast, friendship does not seem merely a necessary condition. I certainly have reason to value the causal consequences of friendship, but it is not at all clear that if I could survive without friends and I did not need their services, I would be willing to do without them. I might say that I could not be happy without having friends, or that having friends is part of what it is to have a good life.[1]

In the *Nicomachean Ethics* Aristotle distinguishes different questions about happiness in order to explain why, and in what ways, people disagree about happiness. He suggests that people do not know what happiness is; they agree that it is the ultimate end, but they do not agree on the sorts of states and activities that constitute happiness (*EN* 1095a17–23). Hence their disputes are quite deep and difficult to resolve because they reflect different views about what happiness is, and these views result in different views of the parts of happiness (in the terms used in the *Eudemian Ethics*). This issue is also overlooked in the *Rhetoric*, where Aristotle does not suggest that there is any dispute about what happiness is, or that such a dispute leads to disputes about what constitutes happiness. To answer the question about what happiness is, the *Ethics* appeals to criteria for happiness (completeness and self-sufficiency) and argues that the accepted candidates for happiness—the lives of pleasure, honour, and virtue—should be rejected because they fail these criteria (*EN* I 5).

These remarks by Aristotle help us to see that the question 'How can we be happy?' (or 'What must we do for the sake of happiness?') may be used to ask two crucially different questions: (1) What is happiness; that is to say, what are its constituent parts? (2) What are the means to happiness; that is to say, given that I have a conception of what happiness is, what is needed to get it?

It is important to see that the goods picked out by the answers to these questions have different relations to happiness, even though we say they are all to be pursued 'for the sake of happiness'. In particular, the eudaemonist claim that we do, or should do, everything for the sake of happiness does not imply that everything chosen for the sake of happiness is purely instrumental to happiness (in the way that wealth or slaves are purely instrumental, as necessary conditions). The eudaemonist claim is consistent with the view that there are other goods besides happiness that are worth choosing for their own sake, and that these belong to happiness as parts rather than as instrumental means. We might say that both mending a broken violin and playing the first movement of a symphony well are actions done 'for the sake of' playing the whole symphony well, but the two actions have a different relation to playing the whole symphony well; only the second is actually a constituent of playing the whole symphony well. Similarly, if virtue or health, for instance, is a component of happiness, its role in happiness is not purely instrumental, since it is not exhausted by its purely causal contribution to a consequence distinct from itself. Both instrumental means to happiness and components of happiness are chosen 'for the sake of' happiness, but the relation indicated by 'for the sake of' is different in the two cases.[2]

Socrates does not mention these Aristotelian distinctions, and so he does not tell us which of the Aristotelian questions he means to answer when he tells us that some things promote happiness and other things do not. Is he telling us about the components of happiness or simply about instrumental means to it? We must answer this question if we are to understand Socrates' view of the relation between virtue and happiness. I will consider some arguments to show that Socrates believes virtue is instrumental to happiness; then I will consider whether there are good arguments on the other side.

46. Is Virtue Instrumental to Happiness?

In the *Lysis* Socrates argues that the primary object is not loved for the sake of anything, and that other objects of love are loved for the sake of the primary object and not for their own sakes:

> However many things we say are loved (*phila*) for the sake of something that is loved, we are evidently using an inappropriate word in saying that.[3] It seems that the thing that is really loved is that in which all these things called loves come to an end. . . . Then what is really loved is not loved for the sake of anything. (220a7–b5)

Socrates claims that whatever is loved for the sake of some further end is not really what we love, and that the only thing we really love is whatever we love without loving it for the sake of anything. He implies that if we choose x for the sake of y, we cannot also choose x for itself.[4] If this general principle is accepted, then we cannot say that virtue is a constituent of happiness; for if it were a constituent (as Aristotle conceives a constituent), it would have to be chosen both for its own sake and for the sake of happiness. Since Socrates' principle reduces anything chosen for the sake of an end to the status of a purely instrumental means, let us say that it is an *Instrumental Principle* about non-final goods.

This passage by itself does not imply that virtue is purely instrumental to happiness, since (as we have seen) it does not say that there must be only one primary object of love. But Socrates also suggests in the *Euthydemus* that we desire happiness for its own sake and desire everything else for the sake of happiness;[5] and so he commits himself to the conclusion that we desire everything other than happiness only for the sake of happiness and not for its own sake. Now Socrates believes that virtue and virtuous action are desirable, as the *Euthydemus* says, for the sake of happiness. If, then, he accepts the Instrumental Principle, he must infer that virtues are purely instrumental to happiness, and are not to be valued for their own sakes.[6]

Does Socrates actually accept the Instrumental Principle that is assumed at this stage in the *Lysis*? Many of the premisses of the arguments in the *Lysis* are certainly questionable; Socrates explicitly or implicitly questions several of them. He does not challenge the Instrumental Principle, however. To find explicit evidence of his accepting it elsewhere, we must turn to the *Gorgias*. Here Socrates claims that when we do x for the sake of y, what we want is not x but y; he states his claim more precisely when he says that in these cases we want x only for the sake of y and do not want x for itself (*G.* 468b7–c5).[7] Once again Socrates fails to mention the virtues, but he implies that since we want them for the sake of happiness, we do not want them for their own sakes.

In these two passages, then, Socrates makes claims about non-final goods that, taken together with his conviction that virtue contributes to happiness, imply that virtue is purely instrumental to happiness, cannot be chosen for its own sake, and therefore cannot be either identical to happiness or a part of happiness. He does not mention this implication of his claims; we might suggest that he is not aware of it, and that if he had recognized it, he would have reformulated the claims to avoid the Instrumental Principle. We should examine the rest of Socrates' claims to see whether they conflict with the Instrumental Principle.[8]

We can see why Socrates might incline to an instrumental conception of virtue, if we recall why he appeals to happiness in the first place. Happiness offers some standard for evaluating the claims of virtue and of other things to be reasonable objects of pursuit. If Socrates believes that the nature of happiness is agreed, whereas the instrumental means to it are disputed, an appeal to the final end helps to solve disputes about the rationality of the virtues. If, for instance, we are to choose between different techniques of carpentry, we ought to consider which of them is the best way to make a bed. This reference to the end of the craft solves disputes, provided that we have a clear enough conception of what a bed is supposed to be, and provided that the only question at issue is about how to make a bed. If the same conditions are satisfied for virtue, then an equally effective method for resolving disputes will result from attention to the final end.

If, then, Socrates appeals to eudaemonism and to an instrumental conception of the relation between virtue and happiness, he has a clear and intelligible method of arguing for the rationality of the moral virtues. If he denies that virtue is simply instrumental to happiness, an appeal to happiness may not settle disputes about the rationality of the moral virtues; for disputes about the virtues may simply reveal disagreement about the character of happiness. The Instrumental Principle and an instrumental conception of virtue might belong to an intelligible strategy for the defence of virtue.

47. Is Virtue a Craft?

Our defence of an instrumental conception of virtue used an example from a productive craft, which can explain and justify its procedures by showing how they are instrumental to the production of a product with the features that are already taken to define an appropriate end for the craft. Socrates himself assumes some degree of analogy between virtues and productive crafts. When he appears to assume that knowledge is sufficient for virtue, he illustrates his views about knowledge by giving examples of crafts (*La.* 198d1–199a5, *Ch.* 174b11–175a8). In the *Charmides* and *Laches* he never suggests that the sort of knowledge (*epistēmē*) he has in mind belongs to anything except a craft (*technē*). In the *Euthydemus* he sets out to answer the question 'What sort of knowledge secures happiness?' by trying to answer the question 'What sort of craft secures happiness?' (*Euthd.* 288d9–291d3), and he tries to answer this question by saying what sort of product this craft produces (*Euthd.* 291d7–e2). How seriously does Socrates take this analogy between virtue and craft?

To answer this question, we ought to see how Socrates treats some difficulties that we might expect to arise for anyone who identifies virtue with a craft. One serious difficulty arises once we notice that crafts can be misused for bad ends. Since Socrates takes virtue to be fine, beneficial, and sufficient for happiness, he surely does not believe that virtue can be misused for bad ends; does it not follow that virtue cannot be a craft?

Some of Socrates' arguments point to this difficulty without answering it. The *Charmides* argues that other kinds of knowledge are open to misuse unless they are regulated by the knowledge of the good (*Ch.* 173a7–d5). A similar question about misuse arises in the *Euthydemus*; it is answered by the introduction of the 'royal craft' combining knowledge of how to produce a product with knowledge of how to use the product to produce happiness (*Euthd.* 289b4–d10). These answers seem to miss the force of the difficulty. If the superordinate science is a craft (as Socrates assumes), then is it not still liable to be misused? It seems wrong to appeal to some further craft in order to remove the possibility of misuse that arises for every craft. We might conclude that either Socrates does not see this difficulty or he does not really believe that virtue can be a craft.

The *Hippias Minor*, however, suggests a further option. First Socrates states the general difficulty about misuse that seems to arise for all crafts. A craft is a capacity (*dunamis*, *HMi.* 366b7–c4), and someone who has the capacity can either use it to produce its normal product, leave it unused, or misuse it to produce a different product. The carpenter who knows how to make a bed that will hold together, for instance, will also be the most skilful at making a bed that will fall apart after a week, and the most skilful doctor will also be the most skilful poisoner. For these reasons a craft is, as Aristotle puts it, a 'capacity for contraries' (*Met.* 1048a7–11); the person who knows how to tell the truth will also be the most skilful liar, and in general it seems that the best person will be the most skilful wrongdoer (*HMi.* 375d2–e1, 376a2–4, 376b4–6).[9] If this is so, then it seems that a virtue cannot be identified with a craft.

Socrates indicates an answer to this objection when he concludes that the good person would be the one who willingly makes errors and does shameful and unjust actions, 'if there is such a person' (376b4–6).[10] He concedes that every science, including superordinate sciences, is a craft whose presence is logically compatible with its misuse. It follows that if a virtue is a craft, it is logically possible for it to be misused. But Socrates' reservation in 'if there is such a person' suggests that the mere logical possibility of misuse does not prove that virtue cannot be a craft. If the end promoted by the proper use of the supreme craft is an end that everyone wants, the logical possibility of misuse will never in fact be realized. If there is some craft whose misuse is logically possible but psychologically impossible (given actual human nature and motives), Socrates may still be willing to identify such a craft with a virtue.

Other Socratic doctrines support this solution. The supreme craft is the one whose proper use promotes the agent's happiness, and Socrates suggests in the *Euthydemus* that everyone pursues happiness as the ultimate end and pursues everything else simply for the sake of happiness. It follows that everyone who believes that the product of the proper use of a given craft is his happiness will also want to use the craft properly; every case of misuse or non-use will be the result of ignorance about the results of the proper use. Socratic psychological eudaemonism makes it easy to believe that the logical possibility raised by the *Hippias* creates no difficulty for the identification of virtue with craft.

If this is Socrates' view, then the point of the *Hippias Minor* is not to cast doubt on the identification of virtues with crafts, but to show that we must accept psychological eudaemonism if we are to identify virtues with crafts. If that is so, then the difficulties about misuse need not lead Socrates to deny that virtues are crafts.[11]

48. Aristotle on Virtue and Craft

If Socrates explicitly or implicitly identifies a virtue with a craft, what does he imply about the nature of a virtue? It is difficult to answer this question; for Socrates does not say exactly what he takes to be implied by saying that something is a craft or is similar to a craft. Nor can we assume that his hearers or Plato's readers must have been able to grasp the relevant implications without further instruction. For while Socrates' contemporaries recognize medicine, shoemaking, and carpentry as clear examples of crafts, they have no definite or explicit account of exactly what makes something a craft, as opposed to a mere knack or facility or (as we would say) technique (cf. *G.* 465a2–7).[12]

Aristotle, however, has a fairly clear and explicit view of the character of a craft, and of what would be implied by the treatment of virtue as a craft. It is useful, then, to replace the rather imprecise question 'Does Socrates treat virtue as a craft?' with the more precise question 'Does Socrates treat virtue as the sort of thing that Aristotle regards as a craft?' Admittedly, Aristotle's conception of a craft may be different from that of Socrates and of Socrates' contemporaries; still, it deserves consideration, since it cannot be dismissed as the view of an interpreter who is unacquainted with Greek views about crafts. If Socrates appears to accept the implications, as Aristotle conceives them, of treating virtue as a craft, that is a good reason for believing that Socrates treats virtue as a craft. In any case, if we show that Socrates attributes to virtue those features that Aristotle attributes to a craft, we will have discovered something important about Socratic ethics.

Aristotle rejects one crucial assumption that leads to the puzzle in the *Hippias Minor*. He suggests that the argument there is mistaken because it fails to distinguish a capacity, which can be used for either of two contrary ends, from a state (*hexis*) of character, which includes a stable disposition to use the capacity for just one sort of end (*Met.* 1025a6–13).

In this passage Aristotle does not actually attribute this mistake (as it seems to him) to Socrates or Plato. But some of his remarks elsewhere show that he believes Socrates makes the mistake. He argues that virtues of character must be identified with states because they involve the right use of capacities (*EN* 1106a6–10). Socrates, however, according to Aristotle, ignores this vital difference between crafts and virtues (*EE* 1216b2–10).

49. Aristotle on Production and Action

Aristotle partly explains his disagreement with Socrates by explaining why craft knowledge must be distinguished from moral wisdom (*phronēsis*). In his view, wisdom is concerned with action (*praxis*), whereas craft is concerned with production (*poiēsis*). Action and production differ in their relation to the ends they aim at:

> <Wisdom> is not craft-knowledge, because action and production belong to different kinds. The remaining possibility, then, is that wisdom is a state grasping the truth, involving reason, concerned with action about what is good or bad for a human being. For production has its end beyond it; but action does not, since its end is doing well itself. (*EN* 1140b3–7)

Wisdom is concerned with finding virtuous actions, and the wise person chooses these actions for their own sake (1144a11–20); Aristotle objects that we fail to capture this crucial feature of moral wisdom if we identify it with any sort of craft.[13]

Does Aristotle apply this criticism to Socrates? We have some reason to suppose he does, since we know from other passages that he takes Socrates to treat virtues as crafts. We have a more specific reason in this passage on action and production once we notice that it recalls a puzzling passage in the *Charmides*. Critias uses this same contrast to argue that 'action' (*praxis*) in the narrow sense is different from productive work (*poiēsis*) (*Ch.* 163a10–c8). But he does not use the distinction at all helpfully; he simply identifies 'action' with 'the producing of fine and beneficial things' (163c3). Socrates in turn does not try to exploit the distinction for Aristotle's purposes.[14] Indeed, on one vital point he implicitly rejects Aristotle's reason for distinguishing action from production. Just a little later in the dialogue he rejects Critias' suggestion that a science need not have any product distinct from its exercise; indeed, he insists that every science must have a product that is 'something other than the science itself' (166a3–7).[15] Socrates refuses to draw Aristotle's distinction between productive and practical knowledge, and his attitude to Critias' suggestion is a natural result of his refusal. He does not suggest that wisdom (*phronēsis*) is to be distinguished from craft, or that it is to be distinguished along Aristotle's lines.[16]

The final puzzle in the protreptic interlude of the *Euthydemus* (292d8–e7) offers Socrates a further opportunity to deny that wisdom is a craft producing some product distinct from itself. If he denied this assumption, he would be able to disarm the puzzle, but we have no reason to believe that he chooses this solution.[17]

Aristotle, then, believes, contrary to Socrates, that there is an important distinction to be drawn between production and action. He insists that this distinction expresses a vital difference between craft knowledge and moral wisdom. He therefore implicitly criticizes Socrates for failing to see the importance of the distinction.

The fact that wisdom is concerned with actions that are ends in themselves explains, in Aristotle's view, why it requires temperance: 'For the principle of what is done in action is the goal it aims at; and if pleasure or pain has corrupted someone, it follows that the principle will not appear to him. . . . For vice corrupts the principle' (1140b16–20). Aristotle remarks that not every grasp of a principle is corrupted by vice. A purely theoretical grasp of the nature of a triangle is undamaged by vice, and Aristotle implies that the grasp of a craft is equally undamaged by vice. Only principles about action (*praxis*) are affected by vice (1140b14–15).

Aristotle now explains how he deals with the paradox in the *Hippias Minor* about misuse: 'Moreover, there is virtue of craft, but not of wisdom. Further, in a craft, someone who makes errors voluntarily is more choiceworthy; but with wisdom, as with the virtues, the reverse is true. Clearly, then, wisdom is a virtue, not craft-knowledge' (1140b21–25). If virtue were a productive craft, then the person with more virtue would be the one who is better able to make mistakes voluntarily; for since voluntary error rests on a wrong conception of the end that ought to be pursued, this sort of mistake is quite consistent with full possession of a craft that is concerned only with instrumental means. Aristotle argues that we can justifiably deny that wisdom makes us more capable of voluntary error if and only if we see that it is concerned with ends and is therefore not a productive craft.

We know that Aristotle criticizes Socrates for his error in treating virtue as a craft. He does not explicitly claim that Socrates' error includes the error of treating virtue as productive. But since he alludes to passages in the *Charmides* and *Hippias* where Socrates fails to challenge assumptions that (in Aristotle's view) imply that moral wisdom is simply a productive craft, he probably means that Socrates fails to distinguish practical wisdom from productive knowledge, and that this is one of the errors included in the conception of virtue as a craft. If we are unaware of the distinction between production and action, we may not notice the difference between virtues and crafts; equally, if we are already attracted by some analogies between virtues and crafts, we may deny or overlook differences between action and production.

50. Virtues, Crafts, and Instrumental Means

We have seen some support in the dialogues for Aristotle's view that Socrates fails to distinguish production from action and therefore fails to distinguish moral wisdom from craft knowledge. Socrates does not mark the Aristotelian distinctions; on the contrary, the difficulty raised in the *Hippias Minor* is readily solved if we treat virtue as a superordinate craft and accept Socratic psychological eudaemonism.

This conclusion is important for answering our previous question about whether Socrates regards virtue as purely instrumental to happiness. Part of the point of Aristotle's distinctions is to show how virtue is not purely instrumental. If moral wisdom were simply about production, it would prescribe instrumental means to some end that is distinct from virtue and virtuous behaviour (in the way in which an effect is distinct from its efficient cause). Since, however, wisdom is about action, in which the end is not distinct from the action itself, the virtuous action is itself the end, and is therefore a part of—not simply an instrumental means to—the final good that is happiness. Aristotle sees that virtue and virtuous action cannot be purely instrumental to happiness, because virtuous and vicious people do not disagree purely about the instrumental means to happiness; they also disagree about what happiness consists in, and virtuous people's actions express their distinctive convictions about the nature of happiness, not simply about how to get it.

Socrates' failure to protest against the analogy between virtue and craft is quite intelligible if he believes that virtuous and vicious people do not disagree about the nature of happiness, but only about whether virtuous or vicious action promotes happiness. If we suppose that Socrates implicitly accepts the Aristotelian distinctions, we must find it puzzling that he treats the analogy between virtue and craft so uncritically. His uncritical attitude is quite intelligible, however, if he believes virtue is purely instrumental to happiness.

We have now considered four independent arguments to show that Socrates takes virtue to be purely instrumental to happiness: (1) He does not ask Aristotle's question about the nature and constituents of happiness, and so he does not suggest that a defence of virtue requires a revision of our conception of happiness; hence he does not consciously set out to prove that virtue is a component of happiness. (2) Passages in the *Lysis* and the *Gorgias* commit Socrates to an instrumental conception of the relation between virtue and happiness. (3) Aristotle probably attributes an instrumental conception of virtue to Socrates. (4) Socrates does not draw any of the distinctions that Aristotle draws to mark the difference between virtues and crafts.

None of these arguments would by itself vindicate an instrumental interpretation if we could find clear evidence on the other side. For if we had clear contrary evidence, we might decide that Socrates' silences are unimportant, that his explicit remarks about non-final goods misrepresent his real views, or that Aristotle misinterprets him. Still, all these arguments point in the same direction. Although any one of them may be inconclusive, their cumulative weight requires us to take an instrumental interpretation seriously.

51. Why Is Virtue Sufficient for Happiness?

We might suppose, however, that there is clear evidence to show that Socrates cannot hold a purely instrumental view of virtue. He claims emphatically that virtue is sufficient for happiness. He must mean by this, we might argue, that his commitment to virtue influences his life so deeply that it actually determines his conception of what happiness is, so that he and other people are not really trying to achieve the same constituents of happiness by different means. In particular, his attitude to choices involving virtue may seem to conflict with any purely instrumental view. For he maintains that we should consider only what the virtuous course of action is, counting nothing on the other side (*Ap.* 28b5–9).[18] If we accept an instrumental view, we must agree that instrumental considerations may in principle count against virtue; and so Socrates' commitment seems to exclude a purely instrumental view of virtue.

This argument, however, proves too much; if it shows that Socrates cannot be an instrumentalist, a parallel argument shows that he cannot be a eudaemonist. For if he is a eudaemonist, then he must recognize that prospects for happiness may in principle conflict with virtue; in that case, it may be argued, he cannot really be 'counting nothing on the other side' against virtue, and so he cannot be committed unreservedly to virtue.

An argument that concludes that Socrates cannot be a eudaemonist is clearly unsound. In reply, we may point out that if he is a eudaemonist, he can still be committed unreservedly to virtue, provided that he is convinced that the virtuous action always promotes happiness better than any other; he refuses to listen to any contrary consideration on a particular occasion only because he has already concluded that nothing contrary to virtue could promote happiness as well. But if this account shows how unreserved commitment to virtue is compatible with eudaemonism, a parallel argument shows how Socrates could be unreservedly committed to virtue but still believe that virtue is purely instrumental to happiness. Hence his unreserved commitment to virtue creates no difficulty for the view that he treats virtue as strictly instrumental to happiness.

How, then, might an instrumental view of virtue support Socrates' claim that virtue is sufficient for happiness? We all agree, according to the *Euthydemus*, that there is such a thing as happiness, that it is the ultimate end, pursued only for its own sake, and that if we get it our desires will be fully satisfied (since we have no desire for anything that lies outside happiness). Socrates may assume that this is a determinate enough description of happiness to vindicate his claims about virtue. If he can show that virtue ensures the satisfaction of the virtuous agent's desires, he will have shown (he may suppose) that virtue is sufficient for happiness.

A virtuous person clearly cannot expect to satisfy all the desires that an ordinary non-virtuous person might have. The ordinary person strongly desires not to face the sort of death that Socrates has to face, and so such a person will suppose that Socrates suffers some serious harm. Socrates can reply, however, that he is unreservedly committed to being virtuous, and so he has no desire to do anything that conflicts with his commitment to virtue. Once he discovers that in some circumstances wealth or safety, even self-preservation, conflicts with the requirements of virtue, he has no desire to pursue any of these recognized goods in these circumstances. Although non-virtuous people in Socrates' situation might suffer frustration of their desires, Socrates does not suffer the frustration of any of his desires; but it is his desires for himself, not the desires that other people would have for themselves if they were in his situation, that determine whether he is happy. He claims that since he wants to be as virtuous as he can be and has no desire for anything that conflicts with being virtuous, he suffers no loss of happiness, and hence no harm, if he loses any of the supposed 'goods' that the virtuous person has to forgo.

Socrates might also fairly claim that the virtuous person is less liable to frustrated desire than a non-virtuous person, since a non-virtuous person is liable to failures that do not affect a virtuous person. If I desire honour or wealth or political success as means to happiness, it is not up to me whether I achieve them; even if I act wisely, I may be unlucky, and so I may have my desires frustrated. Socrates claims that this frustration does not face him if he sets out to be as virtuous as he can be;[19] for this aim is in his power to achieve, and he is not liable to be disappointed by external circumstances.

In that case Socrates' belief that virtue is sufficient for happiness does not rule out his believing that virtue is purely instrumental to, and not a part of, happiness; for the conception of happiness we have described would support the claim that virtue is an infallible instrumental means to happiness. We do not have to prove that Socrates accepts this conception of happiness and this argument to show that virtue is instrumental to happiness; the possibility of such an argument is enough to show that his claims about virtue do not, by themselves, rule out his taking an instrumental view of the relation of virtue to happiness.

52. Virtue, Craft, and Non-Rational Desires

We have considered some of Aristotle's reasons, relying on his distinction between production and action, for distinguishing moral wisdom from productive crafts, and we have seen why Socrates seems not to draw Aristotle's distinctions. It is equally important to consider another aspect of Aristotle's division between virtues and crafts. In some of the passages cited earlier (*EN* 1106a6–10; *EE* 1216b2–10),[20] he insists that the virtues cannot be identified with mere capacities, because virtues require the appropriate training of feelings, which partly determine whether we will use our capacities well or badly. On this point virtues differ sharply from crafts, which, being capacities, do not require the same training of feelings.

According to Aristotle, Socrates' willingness to treat virtues as though they were productive crafts reflects his failure to recognize the importance of non-cognitive elements in virtue. In identifying virtue with knowledge, Socrates does away with the non-rational parts of the soul and therefore with feelings and states of character (*MM* 1182a15–23). This is why he rejects the possibility of incontinence.

The Socratic dialogues give us ample reason to accept Aristotle's description of Socrates' position. Non-rational desires disappear from consideration in both the *Laches* and the *Charmides*, and the *Euthydemus* does not suggest that they might be necessary for virtue. If Socrates does not believe there are any non-rational desires, then he cannot recognize non-rational desire as a source of error that prevents the correct use of knowledge. If this is Socrates' view, it explains why he does not regard the argument in the *Hippias* as a serious objection to the conception of virtue as a craft.[21]

Does Plato write these dialogues in order to raise difficulties for a strictly cognitive view of the virtues?[22] The puzzles raised in the *Hippias* do not support this suggestion, since we have seen how Socrates can answer them. Aristotle does not ascribe the argument in the *Hippias* to Socrates, but his other remarks show that he believes that Socrates fails to draw the distinction between capacity and state of character that is needed to reject the argument in the *Hippias*. Aristotle implies, therefore, that Socrates takes the analogy between virtue and craft very seriously, and that he is right to take it seriously, given his views about the nature of virtue.

Aristotle's distinction between moral wisdom and productive craft turned on the difference between action and production and explained why moral wisdom could not be misused in the way that a craft could be misused. His distinction between virtue and craft differs from that previous distinction insofar as it does not primarily concern the nature of moral knowledge and does not primarily focus on misuse; instead it focusses on non-use.

Aristotle focusses on cases where someone who has the right cognitive condition fails to act on the appropriate knowledge. Non-rational desires do not cause us to use our moral knowledge for the wrong end, but they seem to prevent us from using it correctly. Incontinent people do not use their knowledge that, say, it is better to be clear-headed tomorrow than to enjoy another drink tonight, and hence they do not misuse it; but they leave it unused if their desire for another drink is strong enough. Since perverted non-rational desires prevent the right use of knowledge, a virtuous person must have them turned in the right direction and so must have a state of character including the right cognitive and affective states.[23]

In his remarks about wisdom, Aristotle insists on distinguishing it from the productive knowledge that belongs to a craft; in his remarks about learning virtue, he accuses Socrates of being misled into treating features of crafts as features of virtue. It is clearer in the second case than in the first that Aristotle is criticizing Socrates, but the fact that in the second case he claims that Socrates relies on the analogy between virtue and craft makes it reasonable to claim that he intends the same claim about Socrates in the first case also.

53. Implications of an Instrumental View

Since nothing in the dialogues rules out an instrumental view of virtue and happiness, and since some of Socrates' claims suggest, as we have seen, that he accepts an instrumental view, we ought to conclude that this view fits the dialogues best. It is unlikely that Socrates rejects the instrumental view or sees anything misleading in this application of the analogy between virtue and craft.

Still, it would be unwise to infer that Socrates would actually accept an instrumental view if he clearly formulated it and examined its implications. We have seen why it would answer some pressing questions for him and why it might offer an apparently attractive way of explaining why we have good reason to be virtuous. However, he might well not welcome all the consequences. In particular, an instrumental view might not provide the most plausible defence of all his central convictions.

We might argue, for instance, that his attachment to justice would be more intelligible and persuasive if he presented it as a conviction about the nature of happiness, not just about the instrumental means to it. Equally, we might be impressed by Socrates' vigorous defence of the importance of inquiry into the virtues and the search for rational understanding of our moral convictions (*Ap.* 38a1–6).[24] We might doubt whether the best defence of his convictions about the value of moral inquiry and understanding ought to rely on the instrumental view. Indeed, an instrumental account of Socrates' moral convictions might seem to deprive these convictions of their power and fascination for readers of the dialogues, both ancient and modern.

These doubts about the instrumental conception of virtue should be neither stifled nor allowed to control our interpretation of Socrates. If we are trying to understand Socrates' own theoretical account of virtue and happiness, insofar as he has or presupposes one, we ought to be persuaded that he accepts an instrumental view. Even if it does not offer a very plausible defence of some of his convictions, that is not by itself a good enough reason for supposing that he does not accept the view; many philosophers have accepted theories that fail to justify some of their convictions.[25]

Still, it remains possible that Socrates does not see that he must choose between an instrumental and a non-instrumental account of the relation between virtue and happiness, and that for this reason he does not notice the controversial assumptions implied by the analogy with a craft. These controversial assumptions, we might say, are vivid to Aristotle because he is aware of questions that Socrates simply overlooks. In the dialogues Socrates never asks what happiness consists in, or what is implied by the claim that we must pursue virtue for the sake of happiness. Since he does not raise these Aristotelian questions, it is not surprising that he does not ask how an instrumental view affects his basic moral convictions.

Perhaps, then, we can go no further in saying what Socrates really believes. Still, the conclusion that Socrates does not reject an instrumental conception of virtue is most important if we want to understand Plato's reflexions on Socratic moral theory. If this conclusion is right, we must agree that if Plato explicitly endorses the non-instrumental view of virtue and happiness, he departs from Socrates. If Socrates does not straightforwardly affirm an instrumental view, Plato's acceptance of a non-instrumental view may not lead him into open conflict with Socrates; but if our account of Socrates is right, the rejection of an instrumental view requires Plato to ask some basic questions that Socrates fails to ask. Moreover, if some of Socrates' central convictions about virtue seem more plausible than the instrumental view that is supposed to justify them, that may help us to understand some of Plato's reactions to Socrates; for we will see that Plato revises Socrates' views precisely on the points that affect the defence of these central convictions.[26]

6

The *Protagoras*

54. The Aims of the Dialogue

Socrates examines Protagoras' claims about the value and usefulness of sophistic teaching. Since Protagoras claims that he teaches something useful because he teaches virtue, Socrates examines Protagoras' claim to be a teacher of virtue. First, he raises doubts about Protagoras' claim by raising doubts about whether virtue can be taught. The Athenian practice of taking political advice from everyone, recognizing no experts, leads him to suppose virtue cannot be taught, whereas Protagoras' claims lead him in the contrary direction (320b4–8). As sceptics usually do, Socrates cites the 'conflicting appearances' of different people and finds himself puzzled as a result.[1] Protagoras answers these doubts by arguing at length that virtue can be taught.

At the end of the dialogue the situation is different. Socrates remarks that the argument they have had would ridicule them if it could speak in its own voice. It would point out that Socrates has abandoned his initial doubts about whether virtue can be taught, because he has been 'undertaking to demonstrate' that all the virtues are knowledge, which would imply that virtue is teachable (361a6–b7). Protagoras, on the other hand, has been undertaking to deny that virtue is knowledge, and so he has undermined his own previous claim that virtue is teachable (361b7–c2). Socrates says he would like to take the discussion further and consider what virtue is before turning again to consider whether it is teachable (361c2–d2). Although the Socratic search for definitions is not the central focus of the dialogue, Socrates reminds us of its relevance to the questions that have been discussed.

The dialogue ends with a puzzle rather than a definite solution to the opening question. It does not follow, however, that Plato believes neither speaker has defended the true answer; the true answer may have been found even if it turns out to have puzzling consequences.[2] To see what the dialogue actually shows, we must consider both Protagoras' and Socrates' conceptions of virtue. Protagoras sets out his conception at length in his Great Speech. Socrates develops his conception only in the course of the argument.

55. Protagoras and Socrates on Virtue

Protagoras' Great Speech (320c8–328d2) presents the sophist's conception of virtue and teaching. In order to show that the Athenians and he teach virtue, he must show both that what they and he do counts as teaching, and that what they teach is really virtue. To succeed in these tasks, it is not enough to show that the Athenians and he succeed in training people to conform to the patterns of behaviour that they describe as virtuous. Protagoras also needs to say why these patterns of behaviour count as virtuous; for if he cannot say what real virtue is, he cannot communicate any articulate understanding of the virtues to other people, and so he throws doubt on his claim to be a real teacher (cf. *La*. 190b3–c7).

Protagoras claims that the Athenians and he teach certain virtues. These are 'shame and justice' (322c2, 332c4, 322c7, 322d5), 'justice and the rest of a citizen's virtue' (323a6, 323b2), 'justice' (322b6, 327c5–6), 'justice and virtue' (327b2), or 'justice and piety and the whole of a citizen's virtue' (323e3–324a1, 325a1–2; cf. 325d3–4). According to the myth that Protagoras recounts to explain his view, virtue is given to everyone because it is necessary for social life; and so the virtues that are taught should be the virtues of good citizens.

But are these the virtues that the sophist teaches to his pupils? In his opening remarks (318e-319a), Protagoras offers something that is advantageous for his pupils: ability to deliberate about their own and the city's affairs and to manage them well. Socrates suggests that this amounts to teaching the political craft and making the pupil a good citizen, and Protagoras agrees; but they seem to overlook a serious issue. For it is not clear how far the skills and abilities that promote an individual's success are connected with the virtues of justice and shame that are attributed to all the citizens alike. If my own success requires ruthlessness and deception rather than justice, will Protagoras teach me to be ruthless or to be just?[3]

Protagoras' account of his own aims raises the sorts of doubts and disputes that are widespread in Greek views about the requirements of virtue. In the shorter dialogues Socrates does not openly confront these doubts and disputes. Nor does he confront them in the *Protagoras*;[4] indeed, he accepts Protagoras' assumption that genuine virtue must be beneficial both for the agent and for other people. He argues, however, that Protagoras does not see the implications of this assumption about the virtues.

The issue about the relation between virtue, the good of the agent, and the good of other people is raised in a series of preliminary arguments for the unity of the virtues (329c2–334a6). Socrates asks Protagoras how many virtues he thinks there are: are the different names he has used really names for one and the same virtue, or are they names of distinct 'parts' of virtue (329c2–d2)? Socrates formulates the Unity Thesis (the claim that all the names of the virtues are really names of one and the same thing, so that the virtues are identical) and distinguishes it from the claim that the virtues are similar and from the

Reciprocity Thesis (the claim that they imply each other, and are therefore inseparable) (329b5–330b6, 349a8–c5).[5]

This discussion defines the issue more sharply than the shorter Socratic dialogues have defined it. We have seen two sorts of arguments in the shorter dialogues: (1) In order to show that every virtue is fine and beneficial, Socrates argues that no virtue can prescribe actions that are rejected by any of the other virtues. He infers that the virtues are inseparable, thereby supporting the Reciprocity Thesis. (2) He also argues that knowledge is sufficient for virtue and that therefore all the virtues can be identified with knowledge of the good. Only the second argument actually defends the Unity Thesis. The *Protagoras* clarifies the issue by distinguishing the Reciprocity Thesis from the Unity Thesis and arguing specifically for each in turn.

56. Preliminary Arguments for the Unity of the Virtues

When the different possibilities have been distinguished, Protagoras claims not only that the virtues are distinct and dissimilar but also that they are separable. He has accepted Socrates' suggestion that he was speaking of justice, temperance, and piety as parts of virtue (329c2–d4), and he does not at first suggest that these are separable. But then he introduces bravery and wisdom, too, and suggests that we can be brave without being just, and just without being wise (329e2–330a2).

In reply, Socrates suggests that a person cannot display one virtue while displaying any of the vices. The temperate person, he suggests, cannot also display foolishness (332a4–333b6); and Protagoras is reluctant to admit that a temperate person could act unjustly (333b7–c3). If Protagoras had not diverted the discussion, Socrates would have argued that a temperate person cannot do anything that is not beneficial, and that acting unjustly is harmful (333d4–e1).

These suggestions will seem plausible if we accept a strong form of the assumption that virtuous action must be fine and beneficial.[6] In the shorter dialogues, Socrates seems to assume that if any allegedly virtuous action is open to objection from the point of view of any of the other virtues, then it is not really a virtuous action; apparently brave action, for instance, that is not guided by temperance and wisdom is not brave after all. Although Socrates does not say so, he seems to assume that if an allegedly brave action is foolish or unjust, it cannot be fine and beneficial, and therefore cannot be brave.

The arguments in the *Protagoras* do not defend the assumptions in the shorter dialogues, but they articulate those assumptions more clearly. Still, the arguments are not adequate for their purpose. The premisses that Socrates needs might be accepted by one of the more compliant interlocutors of the shorter dialogues, but they do not convince a more resourceful and critical interlocutor such as Protagoras, who refuses assent at the crucial stage (334a3).

Although Protagoras raises difficulties for Socrates' position, his objections to Socrates also raise a question, not mentioned by Socrates, about Protagoras' own account of the virtues. Protagoras rejects the Reciprocity Thesis, but by rejecting it he raises a serious difficulty for himself. If the Reciprocity Thesis is correct, then Protagoras is right to assume that we cannot acquire the self-regarding virtues, aiming at one's own success, without also acquiring the other-regarding virtues of the good citizen. Since Protagoras rejects the Reciprocity Thesis, however, he has no defence against the suggestion that we might be well advised to cultivate the self-regarding virtues without the other-regarding virtues. The apparently counterintuitive Socratic thesis turns out to provide a better defence of Protagoras' view of teaching virtue than Protagoras can provide from his own resources. The sophist is shown not to understand the conception of virtue that underlies his own claims about teaching virtue; and so he is shown to need the sort of enlightenment that results from a Socratic inquiry.

These preliminary arguments defend the Reciprocity Thesis, but Socrates himself does not make this clear. He speaks as though he had shown that temperance and wisdom are 'one' and as though justice and piety are practically (*schedon*) the same (333b4–6); he seems to assume, then, that he has been defending the Unity Thesis.[7] Perhaps he is right about wisdom and temperance, but he is not so obviously right about justice and piety or about justice and temperance. In these latter two cases, Reciprocity, not Unity, seems to be the main issue; indeed, Socrates would have had a more convincing argument about wisdom and temperance if he had argued for Reciprocity rather than for Unity.

It is reasonable to infer that Socrates distinguishes the Reciprocity Thesis from the Unity Thesis and believes both, but has not sorted out the arguments that support each thesis. In particular, he does not remark that the guiding principles of the elenchos—and specifically the claim that virtue must be fine and beneficial—tend to favour the Reciprocity Thesis,[8] but do not vindicate the Unity Thesis. It may be significant, however, that he leaves these arguments incomplete and turns to a different sort of argument for the Unity Thesis; he may recognize that the considerations underlying the claim that virtue is fine and beneficial do not really support the Unity Thesis.

57. The Appeal to Hedonism

The discussion of the unity of the virtues resumes (349a8) with an argument about the relation of bravery to the other virtues (349d2–8), specifically about its relation to wisdom (349e1–350c5).[9] Protagoras insists that bravery cannot be identical to wisdom, because it requires 'nature and good training of the soul' (351a3–b2), for which wisdom is insufficient.[10]

Here Socrates focusses directly on the crucial question about the Unity Thesis. We could reject the Unity Thesis if we believed that knowledge is insufficient for virtue and that different virtues have different non-cognitive components. The *Laches* and *Charmides* do not explore possible reasons for believing that the virtues must have non-cognitive components,[11] but Protagoras' dissent raises this possibility very clearly.

To answer Protagoras, Socrates appeals to more general claims about choice and motivation. First, he puts forward a hedonist thesis (351b3–c6). Protagoras rejects it, as most people do (351c7–e8). Instead of replying immediately, Socrates turns to the denial of incontinence; on this, Protagoras agrees with him against the many (352a1–353b6). Socrates argues that the many wrongly accept incontinence because they wrongly reject hedonism. Socrates asserts his own belief in hedonism before he turns to argument with the many (351c4–6).[12] He defends hedonism (353c1–354e2); then he argues against incontinence (354e3–357e8); finally, he argues directly for the Unity Thesis, appealing to hedonism and to the impossibility of incontinence.

Socrates argues for hedonism (353b-354e) through a diagnosis of our apparently anti-hedonist claims about choice. Sometimes we say that x is painful and y is pleasant, but nonetheless x is better than y; such claims seem to conflict with hedonism. Socrates disagrees. When, for instance, we take an unpleasant-tasting medicine or force ourselves to face some danger we would like to escape, we expect the 'painful' course of action to yield more pleasure than pain, and the 'pleasant' course of action to yield more pain than pleasure, when their total effects are considered.[13]

Socrates suggests that this explanation of our claims about good and pleasure applies to all our actions in pursuit of pleasure. He asks the many, 'Don't you pursue pleasure as good and avoid pain as evil?' (354c3–5), and they agree. Then they also agree that in pursuing x rather than y as good they pursue x in the belief that it yields greater overall pleasure than y.[14] Socrates is entitled to conclude that whenever we pursue x rather than y for x's pleasure, we pursue it because we believe that x yields greater overall pleasure than y.[15]

The many have now accepted three claims about pleasure and good: (1) We believe x is better on the whole than y if and only if we also believe x yields more pleasure on the whole than y. (2) If we believe x is better on the whole than y, we believe this because we believe x yields more pleasure on the whole than y (354b5–d3). (3) We pursue pleasure as good and avoid pain as evil.

The first of these claims commits us to believing that what is best is also most pleasant, but it does not say how these beliefs are connected. The second claim affirms that the belief about goodness is founded on a belief about pleasantness. It is the epistemological counterpart to the belief that what is good is good because it is pleasant. Since Socrates regards 'pleasant' and 'good' as two names for the same thing, he believes that the same property can be described correctly as both pleasantness and goodness. This identification of the good with the pleasant is meant to be reductive, claiming that in some ways pleasantness is more fundamental. In Socrates' view, we regard things as good because we suppose they are pleasant, whereas we do not regard things as pleasant because we suppose they are good. Socrates brings out this difference between 'pleasant' and 'good' in persuading the many that pleasure is the end they have in view in calling things good (354b5–e2).

It remains true that we desire and pursue pleasure because we regard it as good, and to this extent good must be motivationally prior to pleasure. Whereas x's yield of pleasure makes x good, x's yield of pleasure gives us a reason to pursue x because we regard pleasure as good and we pursue the good; we do not need to be persuaded that the good is pleasant in order to believe that we have some reason to pursue the good. Socrates does not offer hedonism as an alternative to eudaemonism, but as an account of the good that eudaemonism takes to be our ultimate end.[16] Let us say, then, that he affirms *epistemological hedonism*, taking judgments about pleasure to be epistemologically prior to judgments about goodness.

Socrates asks the many to consider carefully whether they are convinced by his argument for hedonism; for he believes that if they accept it, they can no longer maintain their belief in the possibility of incontinence (354e3–355b3). Why does he believe that epistemological hedonism undermines the possibility of incontinence?

58. The Denial of Incontinence

The issue about incontinence is clearly relevant to the question about the unity of the virtues. To prove the Unity Thesis, Socrates wants to prove that knowledge is sufficient for virtue, so that virtues do not differ in having different non-cognitive components. But if bravery requires something besides knowledge, knowing what is better is insufficient for choosing what is better. The many believe that knowledge can be 'dragged about' by various non-rational desires and impulses (352a1–c7), and so they reject the view that knowledge is sufficient for virtue.

Socrates argues that belief in the possibility of incontinence leads to absurdity. His argument is this:

1. Suppose (as common sense does) that A chooses y rather than x, knowing that x is better overall than y, but overcome by the pleasure of y (355a5–b2).
2. 'Pleasant' and 'good' are two names for the same thing (355b3–c1).

Since (2) licenses the substitution of 'pleasant' for 'good' in (1), we can replace (1) with

3. A chooses y rather than x, knowing that x is better overall than y, but overcome by the goodness of y (355d1–3).

This argument does not make it obvious why (3) is ridiculous, but Socrates believes that this will be obvious once the many are reminded that they accept hedonism (354e3–355b3).[17] Socrates attributes epistemological hedonism to the many; we need to see what difference this makes when it is added to the explicit steps of the argument.

The many have agreed that they pursue pleasure as good and avoid pain as evil (354c3–5), and that if they pursue something as good they pursue it for the sake of maximum overall good.[18] Now the allegedly incontinent person clearly pursues pleasure; that is how the many explain his incontinent action. He must, therefore, pursue this pleasure as good, and so must pursue it because he believes it will result in maximum overall pleasure. Epistemological hedonism, therefore, implies

2a. When A chooses y over x, A chooses y because A believes y is pleasanter than x overall.[19]

Since (as the many agree) incontinent action is free, unforced, intentional action (355a8), it must, because of (2a), rest on the belief that the action being chosen is pleasanter than the alternative. But this belief conflicts with the belief—necessary for genuine incontinence, according to (1)—that the action being chosen is worse than the alternative.

Socrates seeks to display the relevant conflict of beliefs by substituting 'pleasant' and 'good'. Is he justified in doing this? He assumes that if 'pleasant' and 'good' are two names for the same thing, it is legitimate to substitute one term for the other in a statement of the agent's reasons ('because he believes y is better—because pleasanter—than x').[20] We might suppose Socrates relies on an illicit substitution; it would be illegitimate to argue from 'A bought the Porsche because A believed it was fast and reliable' and 'A believed the Porsche was ruinously expensive' to 'A bought the Porsche because A believed it was ruinously expensive'.[21]

The fact that this particular substitution is illegitimate does not show that Socrates' substitution is also illegitimate. For the connexion between 'pleasant' and 'good' implied by epistemological hedonism justifies us in saying both that A pursues x because A believes x to be most pleasant (since A believes that something is good on the basis of beliefs about pleasure) and that A pursues x because A believes x to be best (since A desires pleasure because A believes pleasure is the good). Socrates has made sure that the many have accepted the premisses that he uses to undermine their belief in incontinence; they believe in a connexion between pleasure and goodness that licenses the substitution justifying the move from (2) to (3). Since Socrates must appeal to epistemological hedonism to justify the exchange of 'pleasant' and 'good', we have a further reason for believing that he accepts epistemological hedonism.

Once we exchange 'pleasant' and 'good', the rest of Socrates' argument is persuasive. For we must now admit that (3) implies:

4. A chooses y over x, knowing that x is better than y overall, because A believes that y is better than x overall.

Since the many must agree that (3) implies (4), and (4) attributes contradictory beliefs to the incontinent agent, Socrates thinks it is ridiculous for the many to accept (3).[22] This is why Socrates believes that the acceptance of his version of hedonism undermines the belief in incontinence; for epistemological hedonism licenses the substitutions that reveal the absurdity concealed in the common-sense belief in incontinence.

59. The Last Argument for the Unity of the Virtues

Socrates introduces epistemological hedonism to explain why incontinence is impossible; once he has explained this, he has undermined an objection to the unity of the virtues. In the last main argument of the dialogue (from 359a2), he shows how his conclusions about hedonism and incontinence combine to support the further conclusion that all the virtues are simply knowledge of the means to maximum pleasure.

Since Socrates believes that the belief in incontinence is ridiculous, he looks for an alternative explanation of the error that the many describe in these ridiculous terms. The actual error consists in choosing smaller goods at the price of greater evils (355e2–3),[23] and Socrates explains the error; since short-term pleasures and pains seem greater than they really are, we make mistaken judgments about pleasure and pain, and so we choose the result that will actually be less pleasant because we believe it will be more pleasant (356c4–e4). This description differs from the ridiculous belief of the many, insofar as it denies that, when A chooses y over x, A knows or believes that x is better than y. If we are to avoid the error that the many describe as incontinence, we need the measuring craft that calculates the prospective quantities of pleasure and pain. Since this craft guarantees right action (359e1–360b3), it is identical to each of the virtues.

In identifying virtue with a hedonic measuring craft, Socrates relies on epistemological hedonism. For the brave person finds the brave action by considering what course of action will maximize pleasure; that is why the craft of measuring pleasure (not some different craft that coincidentally maximizes pleasure) determines right action. This claim would be false if, for instance, the brave person believed that brave actions are most pleasant only because he believed they are fine and that fine actions are most pleasant. The judgment about pleasure must be basic.

If Socrates accepts epistemological hedonism, then he faces a relatively precise task if he wants to show that he has described the virtues correctly. He must show that the measuring science of pleasures and pains, relying on no further ethical judgments, reaches the conclusions that are characteristic of each of the virtues. His treatment of bravery suggests how in general he argues for this view. He suggests that when we consider short-term and long-term pleasures and pains together, we will see that the maximization of pleasure over the longer term, in our life as a whole, requires us to face the pains that the brave person faces. We can see how this hedonist analysis might be taken to explain some brave actions; a similar analysis might be applied to temperance. Socrates does not suggest a parallel analysis for justice, but he needs one if he is to defend the unity of the virtues on a hedonist basis.

60. Questions about Socratic Hedonism

This section of the *Protagoras* argues from epistemological hedonism for the denial of incontinence and the unity of the virtues. So far, I have assumed that Socrates accepts both the conclusions and the hedonist premisses. This assumption, however, needs some defence; for some critics believe that Socrates does not accept the hedonist thesis himself, but simply uses it as a popular view that serves his purposes in this argument with the many.

This 'ad hominem' interpretation of hedonism rests on three main arguments: (1) Socrates tries to show how the many are committed to hedonism; he does not argue that it is true, but only that they cannot avoid it. And so we cannot infer that he accepts hedonism. (2) The truth of hedonism is unnecessary for Socrates' rejection of incontinence and his belief in the unity of the virtues, and Socrates and Plato must have realized this. (3) None of the other Socratic dialogues affirms hedonism; indeed, it is incompatible with the ethical doctrines of the other dialogues, and Socrates and Plato must have realized this.

The first argument rests on the fact that Socrates seeks to show that the many implicitly accept hedonism. This is a poor reason for supposing that he does not accept it himself. It is quite common for Socrates to argue that although his interlocutors initially disagree with him, they are also committed to principles that require them to agree with him. This is how he convinces Crito to abandon his initial opposition to Socrates' remaining in prison, once Crito carefully examines the implications of his own sincere beliefs (*Cri.* 49c11–d1). Socrates assumes that the conclusions reached by the interlocutor through the elenchos are true.[24] The second-person character of the elenchos and its appeal to the beliefs of the interlocutor are pervasive features of Socrates' use of the elenchos in his pursuit of truth.[25] Nothing about the argument in the *Protagoras* with the many makes it ad hominem in any sense that distinguishes it from elenctic argument in general.[26]

We would have a better argument for an ad hominem interpretation if we found that Socrates is careful to confine the hedonist claim to the many and to dissociate himself from it; but this is not at all what we find. In fact, Socrates himself proposes hedonism, against the initial opposition of Protagoras and the many, as the first step of his argument for the unity of the virtues (351b3–c6). Only when he has already asserted hedonism on his own account does he try to show that the many actually agree with him without realizing it.[27]

The second argument for an ad hominem interpretation maintains that the *Protagoras* is meant to show only that the many and the sophists must accept the Socratic doctrine of virtue since they are committed to hedonism; these hedonist arguments do not (on this view) give Socrates' reasons for accepting his doctrine.[28] This argument appeals to the fact the hedonist premisses are sufficient, but not necessary, for a valid argument in support of the Socratic doctrines; a non-hedonist argument could reach these doctrines from Socrates' eudaemonist assumptions without appeal to hedonism.

This point, however, does not support an ad hominem interpretation, since not every valid argument would also be plausible or non-question-begging in this context. We have seen that the common-sense belief in incontinence constitutes a strong objection to Socrates' psychological eudaemonism. If Socrates is to answer this objection, he cannot fairly take psychological eudaemonism for granted, but he must argue for it. The hedonist argument is all that he offers. Nothing in the *Protagoras* or in the shorter dialogues suggests any other argument that could do the same work. The hedonist argument does what Socrates needs it to do only if he believes it.

And so the first two arguments for an ad hominem interpretation fail. The counterarguments constitute a strong case for the view that Socrates accepts epistemological hedonism. This case is not conclusive, however; we may still favour the ad hominem interpretation if we are convinced by the third argument. We must ask, then, why hedonism might seem attractive or unattractive in the light of the ethical doctrine of the Socratic dialogues.

61. Eudaemonism and Hedonism

Hedonism is meant to give an account of goodness and hence of happiness. According to hedonism, we identify happiness with the predominance of pleasure over pain in our life as a whole. To see whether hedonism ought to seem plausible in the light of the Socratic dialogues, we ought to see how this account of happiness fits with Socratic eudaemonism.

Since Socrates commits himself to both rational and psychological eudaemonism, he regards happiness as the only end that brings explanation and justification to a halt, because it needs no further explanation or justification, but makes other aims intelligible and justifiable.[29] This claim about happiness, however, does not say exactly how an appeal to happiness plays the appropriate role in explanation and justification.

One common approach to knowledge and justification maintains that the only acceptable way to avoid a vicious regress of justification is to find some self-justifying foundation. If we also reject an infinite regress in the explanation and justification of action (*Lys*. 219c5–d2), then this foundationalist line of thought will lead us to believe that there must be some object of desire that is self-justifying and self-explanatory. And this is one way to describe the role of happiness in rational action.

A different approach to justification rejects any self-justifying foundation and claims to find justification in the relations of coherence and explanation between the propositions believed. We might think of happiness along similar holistic lines, not as one particular self-explanatory or self-justifying object of desire, but as a system of ends in the light of which each particular desire and each particular end can be explained and justified. We will be doubtful about the foundationalist approach if we doubt whether there is really any end that is completely self-explanatory outside any context at all, and whether any such end (supposing we could find one) would really justify the pursuit of every other reasonable end. If we accept the holistic conception of happiness, we avoid this difficulty.

Holism raises the opposite difficulty, however. For mere coherence seems to justify too many beliefs and desires, if it allows any consistent but crazy set to be justified irrespective of its content. This difficulty seems to lead back towards a foundationalist conception of justification. If we reject foundationalism, we must say that the relevant sort of coherence is more than mere consistency. We need to say which desires should be counted as initially reasonable, so that we can look for coherence among these rather than among some arbitrarily selected set of desires.

Hedonism seems to support the foundationalist version of eudaemonism. Pleasure seems to be an ultimate and self-explanatory object of desire. Socrates takes it as immediately obvious that everyone pursues happiness,[30] and it might be thought equally obvious that everyone pursues pleasure. If (as the foundationalist eudaemonist claims) there is only one completely self-explanatory and self-justifying end, and if pleasure is a completely self-explanatory and self-justifying end, it follows that happiness and pleasure must be identical.

We have found some reason to believe that a foundationalist outlook appeals to Socrates. He appears to suggest that the guiding principles of the elenchos can be supported by evident and obvious truths about happiness and virtue.[31] If this is his strategy, he has some reason to welcome hedonism. For pleasure seems to be an indubitably choiceworthy end; if it can be presented as a self-justifying starting point for the defence of Socrates' moral position, then Socrates can vindicate his indirect approach to opposing views.

62. Advantages of Hedonism

Even if Socrates has these reasons for taking hedonism seriously, its further implications might still lead him to reject it. We must, then, consider these implications.

In the *Euthydemus* Socrates appeals to happiness in order to claim that some recognized goods are worth pursuing because they are necessary for happiness and that others are not worth pursuing because they are unnecessary for happiness. How might he defend this claim? If you find the Socratic virtues worthwhile because they contribute to your happiness, as you conceive it, but I find them a waste of time because they do not contribute to my happiness, as I conceive it, then an appeal to happiness has not solved our dispute about the value of the virtues, or about which of the recognized virtues are genuine virtues. We have simply transformed the dispute about virtue into a dispute about happiness that seems to raise the very same questions.

Socrates can settle this dispute if he can find a more determinate and specific conception of happiness. The argument in the *Euthydemus* about the supreme science ends with a puzzle that would be solved if we could reach a clearer conception of happiness. Socrates looks for the science whose possession would be sufficient for happiness, but he cannot say what science this is until he can say what its content is. It is the science of happiness, but he cannot say anything more informative about what this science is the science of, until he can say more definitely what happiness is.

Hedonism seems to provide a suitably precise description of happiness. Aristotle mentions 'a pleasant life with security' (*Rhet.* 1360b15) as one of the general descriptions of happiness. His other general descriptions are 'doing well combined with virtue', and 'self-sufficiency of life', and 'prosperity of possessions and slaves combined with the power to keep them and act with them'.[32] We might argue that the first of these accounts is the most fundamental; perhaps we regard virtue, self-sufficiency, and assured possession and use of external goods as valuable only because they increase pleasure and reduce pain. If Socrates argues in this way, he can appeal to hedonism to solve the puzzle in the *Euthydemus*.[33]

This argument for taking hedonism seriously would be weakened if we knew that no reputable thinkers among Socrates' contemporaries would be disposed to take hedonism seriously. The initial resistance of Protagoras and the many suggests that Plato believes anti-hedonism is intelligible enough to his contemporaries to need no elaborate explanation. On the other hand, the view that happiness is closely connected with pleasure and enjoyment was also quite common. Indeed, the contemporary moralist who apparently shares Socrates' belief in the importance of virtue and care of the soul also seems to be a hedonist; for Democritus' goal of 'good spirits' (*euthumiē*) easily allows a hedonist interpretation. Some of his advice about pursuit and avoidance of pleasures can be understood with the help of the distinctions between short-term and long-term pleasure that are drawn in the *Protagoras* as well.[34]

We have no reason to suppose, then, that Socrates' contemporaries in general thought hedonism too disreputable to deserve discussion.[35] On the contrary, we might well be surprised that the shorter Socratic dialogues do not explicitly take account of hedonist views about the good. Once again the *Protagoras* fills a gap that might strike a moderately perceptive reader of the shorter dialogues.

63. Hedonism and Instrumentalism

If Socrates appeals to hedonism in order to clarify his claims about happiness, what must he say about the relation between virtue and happiness?

In the *Euthydemus* Socrates asks how we are to be happy and answers this question by mentioning virtues, and eventually wisdom, but he does not say whether he takes virtue to be a component of happiness or instrumental to it. Epistemological hedonism makes it more reasonable to say that virtue is purely instrumental to happiness. For if epistemological hedonism is correct, then judgments about goodness must be derived from judgments about pleasure that do not themselves rely on judgments about goodness. If, however, virtue is a component of happiness, it must constitute a special kind of pleasure that we enjoy only insofar as we regard virtue as good for its own sake; in that case judgments about goodness are prior to judgments about pleasantness, contrary to epistemological hedonism. To argue, within the constraints of epistemological hedonism, that virtue promotes happiness, we must argue that virtue can be shown to be the source of greatest pleasure, estimated without appeal to any further judgments of goodness; hence we must argue that virtue is instrumental to happiness.

Ought Socrates to find this consequence of hedonism welcome or unwelcome? The shorter dialogues have given us some reason to believe that he takes virtue to be instrumental to happiness, and no reason to believe that he takes it to be a component of happiness.[36] If this is right, then his views about happiness should incline him towards epistemological hedonism.

Some of Socrates' instrumentalist remarks about virtue are connected with the analogy between virtue and craft; epistemological hedonism is relevant to that analogy. We can settle difficulties and disputes about the right way to practise a craft if we can identify the product by some description that can be accepted and applied independently of our beliefs about the correct practice of the craft; we form our conception of the right way to make a coat by reference to our view of a good coat, not the other way around.[37] We might wish we could settle disputes about virtue in the same way, but we might also believe that our wish is empty because we cannot form a suitably independent conception of happiness.

Epistemological hedonism seems to answer this objection. For apparently we can tell, independently of our moral views, whether one or another action results in greater pleasure. Insofar as we can tell that, we can tell which action contributes more to happiness. A clear and precise sense can be attached to the claim that virtue is the craft promoting happiness.

64. Hedonism and the Virtues

We have seen how the *Protagoras* argues from epistemological hedonism in support of the Socratic doctrines that virtue is knowledge and that all the virtues are one. These are not the only Socratic doctrines about virtue that are more plausible in the light of hedonism.

Hedonism allows Socrates to claim not only that each virtue is a craft but also that all the virtues are the same craft aiming at the same end; for, according to the *Protagoras*, the only relevant difference between one pleasure and another is quantitative (356a5–c1).[38] If this is right, then Socrates' belief in the unity of the virtues becomes more plausible. The Unity Thesis is not secured if we simply agree that all the virtues aim at happiness; if happiness is just a collection of heterogeneous, even conflicting, goods, and if one virtue aims at one of these goods and another at another, we have no reason to suppose that the two virtues are really identical. If, however, pleasure is a uniform and homogeneous end, then the virtues that all aim at it have a better claim to be the same knowledge of the same good, and therefore to be the same virtue. Hedonism allows Socrates to anticipate and to answer a line of objection that was left unanswered in the shorter dialogues.

Epistemological hedonism and the unity of the virtues suggest how we might answer Socrates' demand for a definition of the virtues. In the shorter dialogues Socrates is not satisfied by any of the proposed definitions of the virtues; his epistemological constraints on acceptable definitions explain why he is not satisfied.[39] In the *Euthyphro* he suggests that moral terms ('fine', 'just', 'good', and their opposites) introduce disputes and that disputes are removed only when we can replace these with terms referring to properties that can be determined by measurement—presumably by quantitative judgments that everyone accepts no matter what position they initially take in a particular dispute (*Eu.* 7b6–c8). Socrates does not actually present this as an explicit condition for a successful definition of a virtue, but he suggests no other way to reach a definition that will resolve disputes about what the virtues require.[40]

Epistemological hedonism makes such a constraint on definitions seem both reasonable and satisfiable. Pleasure seems to offer a more determinate description of happiness because it seems easier to say whether someone is enjoying himself than to say whether someone is happy. To say whether someone is happy, we need a more determinate description of happiness; the reference to pleasure seems to provide this more determinate description. The question about whether an action or state of character promotes happiness can be reduced to a question about how the action or state affects a person's feelings; at least we know what sort of evidence to look for to answer this question. And so an account of virtue referring to pleasure seems to open the prospect of an adequate Socratic definition.

It would be wrong to claim that in the shorter dialogues Socrates implicitly accepts hedonism, or that he is committed to it by his other views; each of these claims would go unjustifiably far beyond our evidence. On the other hand, these shorter dialogues make it easy to see why Socrates might intelligibly accept hedonism. They do not show that it would be surprising if he committed himself to hedonism in the *Protagoras*. On the contrary, a defender of Socrates might naturally and reasonably turn to hedonism.

The appeal to hedonism in the *Protagoras* is intelligible if the dialogue presents Plato's reflexions on Socratic method and ethical theory. This view of the *Protagoras* would probably be more widely accepted if many readers were not convinced that Plato cannot take this version of hedonism seriously. But nothing in the shorter Socratic dialogues conflicts with the acceptance of this version of hedonism, and so we cannot appeal to these dialogues to show that Plato must reject hedonism. Since the hedonism of the *Protagoras* presents a reasonable defence of the moral theory of the shorter dialogues, it is fair to conclude that this is also Plato's intention.

We cannot, then, be certain that the innovations (as they seem to be) in the *Protagoras* represent the views of the historical Socrates. We must remain uncertain if we look at external evidence. Although Aristotle cites the *Protagoras* as evidence of Socrates' rejection of incontinence, he says nothing one way or the other about Socrates and hedonism. We perhaps learn something more definite from the fact that one group of Socrates' followers, the Cyrenaics, were hedonists. This would be surprising if Socrates had already rejected hedonism, and if most people believed that his views were clearly incompatible with hedonism. It is not at all surprising, however, if the Cyrenaics supposed they were developing the sorts of arguments that appear in the *Protagoras*.[41] The outlook of the Cyrenaics certainly does not by itself prove that Socrates must accept the hedonism of the *Protagoras*; it simply suggests that he probably does not reject hedonism.

Some of Socrates' other followers, the Cynics, were vigorous anti-hedonists who perhaps took Socrates' belief that virtue is sufficient for happiness to exclude any hedonist defence of virtue.[42] Just as it would have perhaps been difficult for Cyrenaics to present themselves as Socratics if Socrates had been widely believed to reject hedonism, it would also perhaps have been difficult for Cynics to present themselves as Socratics if Socrates had been widely believed to endorse hedonism without hesitation. It is most reasonable to regard the formulation of hedonism in the *Protagoras* as Plato's contribution, to recognize the Socratic sources of it, and to admit uncertainty about how much is Socratic and how much is Platonic.

65. Socratic Method in the *Protagoras*

We have found some reasons derived from examination of Socratic ethics for taking the hedonism in the *Protagoras* to express Plato's considered view. This conclusion is further supported by some features of Socrates' method in the *Protagoras*. In several ways he tries to give us reason for confidence in the seriousness and soundness of his arguments.

First of all, Protagoras is more evenly matched with Socrates than the interlocutors in the shorter dialogues were. He answers Socrates' doubts about whether virtue can be taught by presenting an elaborate and persuasive defence of his own conception of virtue. Socrates' questions do not unsettle him, and he defends his position quite ably. Plato uses Protagoras' independent and critical attitude to Socrates to assure us that Socrates is taking account of plausible objections and alternatives in the course of defending his own view. Moreover, Socrates is not content to answer the objections that Protagoras wants to raise; he actually presses Protagoras to put forward reasonable objections that Protagoras himself is willing to waive (331b8–d1, 333c1–9).

Socrates' aims set him apart from Protagoras. For Protagoras assumes that he and Socrates are primarily concerned to win the argument, and so he argues that each of them should be free to choose the tactics that seem most likely to win (334d6–e3, 335a4–8). Socrates, however, denies that victory is his main aim;[43] he wants to examine the actual merits of arguments and to see what someone is really committed to by holding one or another position.[44]

Socrates' aim of examining views and arguments, as opposed to the statements of particular interlocutors, is particularly important in the argument about incontinence. Socrates and Protagoras agree about the impossibility of knowing what is better and doing what is worse, but Socrates does not want the rest of the argument to rely simply on what Protagoras accepts (352d4–353b5). And so the argument about hedonism is an imagined conversation between Socrates and Protagoras, on the one side, and the many, on the other side. Socrates wants to rely not simply on Protagoras' agreement but also on the reflective agreement of the many; hence he insists that they are free to retract their agreement if they can see any alternative to hedonism (354e8–355a5). The crucial argument about incontinence is even more complicated. It is a conversation between Socrates and Protagoras, representing the view of the many, and an imaginary interlocutor who claims to refute these views. The use of an imaginary interlocutor allows us to examine the merits of the argument apart from our view of the particular person who may defend it well or badly on this particular occasion.

The end of the dialogue underlines this contrast between Socrates' and Protagoras' attitude to the argument. Protagoras is unwilling to continue to play his part as interlocutor when he sees that he has been refuted; he suggests that Socrates is being competitive in pressing him to answer so that everyone will see that Socrates has won (360b6–e5).[45] Socrates rejects this account of his aim; he insists that he just wants to make clear the implications of their argument about virtue (360e6–361a3).

Socrates personifies the conclusion of the argument, describing how it arbitrates between the initial positions taken by him and Protagoras (361a3–c2). Socrates is not claiming victory for himself; he is claiming that the actual merits of the argument require both of them to modify their original claims. The personified conclusion says that Socrates has actually undertaken to prove the unity of the virtues;[46] he has not simply been defending that thesis for the sake of argument, and he has defended it in the face of the contrary view seriously maintained by Protagoras. Socrates claims that the discussion has reached a conclusion about the merits of their opposing views. Protagoras has not taken account of the possibility of securing such a result by Socratic cross-examination.

Protagoras' misunderstanding of Socrates' methods and aims prevents him from understanding the implications of his own claims about virtue and about himself as a teacher of virtue. Socrates suggests Protagoras' failure of understanding in a rather surprising way, by presenting the argument against incontinence as a defence of sophists. The many, he claims, refrain from buying a sophistic education for their children because they do not recognize the sufficiency of knowledge for virtue; since they believe in incontinence, they do not realize that all we need is to have our ignorance cured (357e2–8). We should not dismiss Socrates' conclusion as mere irony. There is no reason to doubt the sincerity of his claim here (and in *Meno* 91b2–92c5) that most people are prejudiced against the sophists for bad reasons. But we would be missing the point of Socrates' argument if we supposed that he intends no criticism of sophistic. He does not say that Protagoras and the others can cure the ignorance that results in error; he says only that they claim to be able to cure it (357e3–4). He has given reasons for doubt about their claim.

The main reason for doubt emerges in the discussion of the Unity Thesis. On the one hand, Protagoras claims that bravery is separable from the other virtues, and so he rejects the Unity Thesis. On the other hand, he rejects the possibility of incontinence (352c8–d3), since he agrees with Socrates' view that knowledge is sufficient for right action and cannot be dragged about; indeed, he says, it would be shameful for him above all to deny that knowledge has this power (352c8–d3).

We may be surprised that Protagoras agrees with Socrates, after previously rejecting Socrates' suggestion about bravery and wisdom; for if knowledge is sufficient for right action, why should anything besides knowledge be needed for bravery? Plato is not treating Protagoras unfairly. Socrates might argue that if Protagoras really claims to teach virtue, and not simply to teach a skill that can be used well or badly, then he must agree with Socrates' view that knowledge is sufficient for virtue.[47]

Protagoras' attitude to hedonism betrays a further confusion. For though he rejects incontinence (and so undermines his reason for believing that bravery is separable from the other virtues), he initially rejects hedonism, whereas, according to Socrates, the argument against incontinence depends on hedonism. Whether he accepts or rejects incontinence, he raises difficulties for some of his other claims.

His attitude to the unity of the virtues raises a still deeper question. As we noticed, his claim that the virtues he teaches are those that both benefit the agent and benefit the community would be much easier to maintain if he also maintained the Unity Thesis or the Reciprocity Thesis. Since, however, he maintains that bravery is separable from the other virtues, he allows a critic to ask why we should not cultivate the self-regarding virtues independently of the other-regarding virtues. We cannot say for sure that Plato means us to see this apparent incoherence in Protagoras' position, but it is a further incoherence that displays the same sort of confusion that Plato points out. However proud Protagoras may be of having improved on common beliefs (328a8–b5, 352e2–3), he often relies on unexamined common sense. Because he has not examined his own position, he has not seen that his objections to common sense conflict with his own views.

The Socratic elenchos, on the contrary, seeks to discover unsuspected conflicts in common sense; in exposing the conflicts in Protagoras' position, Socrates vindicates his own more critical attitude to common sense. In his argument for the unity of virtue, Socrates has defended the most counterintuitive parts of his own view and has shown how it can pass the sort of critical examination that Protagoras fails.

In emphasizing these aspects of Socratic method, Plato seeks to reassure a critic who is dissatisfied with the use of the elenchos in the shorter dialogues. Socrates does not rely simply on the agreement of a sympathetic interlocutor; Plato wants to show that the conclusions rest on a fair examination of the merits of the case, as they appear to someone who is not initially disposed to agree with Socrates. These claims about Socratic method should encourage us to treat the premisses and conclusions of the ethical arguments in the dialogue as expressions of Plato's actual views.

7

The Argument of the *Gorgias*

66. The Main Issues

Just as the *Protagoras* illustrates the difference between the methods of argument favoured by some of the sophists and those advocated by Socrates, the *Gorgias* illustrates the difference between rhetoric and Socratic elenchos. Socrates attacks rhetoric for its irrationality and lack of understanding. Rhetoric, he argues, produces persuasion and conviction, which may be either true or false; it is contrasted with crafts that have a method for reaching true beliefs with rational understanding (454c–455a, 465a).

Socrates claims that his elenctic method deserves the rational confidence that rhetoric does not deserve. To defend this claim, he denies that his aims or tactics are those of an eristic, and he sharply distinguishes the dialectical pursuit of truth from the eristic pursuit of victory in argument (457c4–458b3).[1] To this extent, Plato seeks to defend the method of argument used in the shorter dialogues. Just as in the *Protagoras,* however, he does not simply present the method of the earlier Socratic dialogues as a fixed point for comparison with rhetoric. He also develops his method to answer correct criticisms of the earlier method and to show more clearly why the earlier method is not in fact open to some criticisms that might have seemed reasonable.

It is not surprising that a defence of Socratic method leads Socrates into a defence of his moral convictions. Plato's influential contemporary Isocrates regularly defends the moral and educational benefits of rhetoric against the claims of eristics, whose quibbling arguments result in bizarre moral claims that no one could be expected to take seriously. Several of Isocrates' charges are presented by Callicles; in the *Gorgias,* in contrast to the shorter Socratic dialogues, Plato defends Socratic philosophy and Socratic morality against Isocrates' criticisms.[2] Since Socratic method is ridiculed on the ground that it allows Socrates to defend bizarre moral claims, it is important for Socrates to show that the claims he defends are not bizarre after all.

In order to defend Socratic morality, Plato focusses on a central Socratic claim that is likely to provoke the ridicule of a critic such as Isocrates. In the shorter dialogues Socrates assumes that justice is sufficient for happiness, but he does not argue for his assumption; common sense might reasonably conclude that in his eagerness to defend justice he has trapped himself and his credulous interlocutors in an altogether incredible paradox.

In the *Gorgias* Plato sets out to defend the Socratic belief about justice. He wants to show that Socratic method can produce a cogent argument, compelling even a highly critical interlocutor to accept the Socratic belief, and that the Socratic belief is an inevitable, even if surprising, consequence of moral beliefs that we cannot reasonably abandon.[3]

67. Objections to Rhetoric

The criticism of rhetoric in the *Gorgias* develops a line of argument that is sketched and suggested in the *Protagoras*. In the *Protagoras* Socrates suggests that the people who trust sophistic are misguided, and that even the people who distrust it do not see what is really wrong with it. In the *Gorgias* he argues that people do not see what is really wrong with rhetoric, because they have not examined the false assumptions, both epistemological and moral, that underlie the standard views about rhetoric. Rhetoric is similar to sophistic, insofar as it seems plausible to us only insofar as we share some false assumptions about virtue and knowledge that Socrates wants to undermine. His main concern is not with the sophists, rhetoricians, and orators themselves, but with the people who listen to them.[4]

Socrates argues that neither the orator himself nor his audience has any reason to value rhetoric. It is not a genuine craft, because it lacks any rational method based on understanding of its subject matter (454c–455a, 462b3–c3, 465a). Rhetoric cannot give an account (*logos*) or reason (*aitia*) of why it does what it does, and it does not understand the nature of the things it uses. Something that lacks these rational aspects of a craft must be a mere empirical 'knack' (465a1–7). Orators and rhetoricians have no good reason for believing that they ought to be persuading other people to believe one thing rather than another, and so their audiences have no reason to trust their advice.[5]

In Socrates' view, the fact that fancy cooking, cosmetics, and rhetoric are not crafts is somehow connected with the fact that they aim at what will please their customers rather than at what is really good (464a3–e2). The expert in a craft refers to an objective norm that determines how the product should be, apart from what happens to please the consumer. We do not refer to the right sort of norm if we can say only that people like the results. Although there is a craft in making cars (since they are required to run without too many repairs, to be reasonably safe and durable, and so on), there is no craft, according to Socrates' criteria, in designing cars to appeal to popular taste; for then the designer's aim is fixed by whims and impulses.

Socrates must agree that our preferences about cars are relevant to explaining why a good car should not break down too often and should not be so big that it needs to be kept in a hangar; these are features of a good car because they are connected with what customers want cars for. But this does not mean that the norms for a good car are not objective; for sensible car buyers want a car to have certain objective properties apart from a tendency to please the customer. If a car tends to please me (because of its colour or appearance, say, or because it has been effectively advertised) but is not actually reliable or safe, then I have good reason to be suspicious of it.

This feature of a craft explains why the fact that rhetoric does not rely on the appropriate objective norms is a reason for suspicion of it. Sometimes we may be well aware that someone practises 'flattery' (as Socrates calls it), because he has the knack of pleasing us. If, for instance, we realize that bakers of doughnuts are adept at pleasing us, but do not know about healthy food, this will not necessarily undermine our confidence; for we do not go to them for a healthy diet in the first place. But if we discover that the doctor or the car maker has this skill in 'flattery' without achieving any further good, we have reason for suspicion; for we do not go to these experts in order to be flattered, but in order to be really healthy or in order to buy a really reliable car.

This comparison is damaging to rhetoric. From the point of view of its 'consumers'—the audience that is persuaded by the orator—the separation of rhetoric from knowledge of the good should be a ground for doubts about the value of rhetoric. Indeed, Socrates suggests that the value we tend to attach to rhetoric is inconsistent with understanding the nature of rhetoric. For the orator's political advice persuades us not because we think he knows effective techniques for persuading us, but because we believe his advice is good; if we then come to realize that we believed his advice was good only because he had effective persuasive techniques, and not because his advice was really good, we will reasonably find his advice less persuasive. Once we understand why the orator is persuasive, we will find him less trustworthy and so less persuasive.[6]

68. Rhetoric and Justice

Gorgias can answer Socrates' objection if he can show that the orator's advice to us rests on reliable convictions about what is good for us. He suggests that when rhetoric is used justly, it produces a worthwhile product, as other crafts do (456a8–457c3). The fact that some people misuse rhetoric is not a reason for general distrust of it.

Socrates argues that Gorgias' position is inconsistent. Gorgias believes both (1) that orators may misuse rhetoric in the service of unjust purposes and (2) that if his pupils do not know about justice and injustice, Gorgias himself will teach them. But he also accepts (3) that if someone has learned justice, he is just and will not want to commit injustice (460a–c); and (2) and (3) together conflict with (1).

Is Socrates' objection fair? Gorgias has no basis for complaint; for all these steps are made explicit and Gorgias accepts them all. It is more difficult, however, to see why he needs to accept both (2) and (3) if he is to defend his claim that the rhetorician is not to be blamed if his pupils misuse their rhetorical skill.[7]

Polus suggests that Gorgias should not have accepted (2), and that he accepted it only because he was ashamed to deny it. He should, according to Polus, have been frankly indifferent to the questions about justice and said that he taught people to be good speakers no matter how they might choose to use their skill (461b3–c4). This attitude is close to the position that Plato attributes to Gorgias elsewhere.[8] If Plato had begun the *Gorgias* by attributing this view to Gorgias, no contemporary reader would have accused him of being unfair. Since he conspicuously refrains from attributing this position to Gorgias, and since Polus draws attention to the position, Plato must intend to expose a difficulty that ought to make Gorgias hesitate to accept the position that Polus offers him.

If Gorgias had followed Polus' advice, he would have undermined two points in his defence: (a) His ability to persuade a patient to accept beneficial medical treatment shows how political oratory is useful. (b) We should not hold a rhetorician responsible for his pupils' misuse of rhetoric. Gorgias' first point is plausible only if we can normally count on orators to be guided by a true conception of the interests of their audience; but if orators learn rhetoric without learning justice, we cannot count on them to care about the interest of their audience, let alone to have a true conception of it. And so the first point in Gorgias' defence collapses. The second point collapses with it. For if he knew that his pupils would probably use rhetoric unjustly, but he did nothing about it, then he could reasonably be blamed even if he hoped they would not use it unjustly; in the same way (to pursue Gorgias' comparison) we would rightly blame a gun dealer who sold guns knowing that the buyers were going to use them to commit murder.

These difficulties that result from rejecting (2) might suggest that Gorgias should retain (2) and reject (3). Socrates believes (3) because he believes that knowledge is sufficient for virtue, but why should Gorgias agree? Why should he not simply say that he can teach people about justice and injustice, but cannot ensure that people become just through his teaching?

This reply to Socrates would also undermine points (a) and (b) in Gorgias' defence. For if instruction in justice does not make orators just, we have no reason to trust their advice; if Gorgias admits that although he informs people about what is commonly considered just and unjust, he is well aware that they will not act justly, then his informing them does not count as even trying to ensure the just use of the craft.[9]

It is reasonable, then, for Socrates to expect Gorgias to agree that someone who learns justice and knows justice is thereby just. If Socrates is right on this point, then Gorgias has a defence against objections to rhetoric; but in that case, as Socrates points out, Gorgias ought not to concede that people who have really learned rhetoric and justice will use rhetoric unjustly. Alternatively, if it is possible for people who have learned rhetoric and justice still to use rhetoric unjustly, then Gorgias has not shown why this unjust use is not a good reason for suspicion of rhetoric. Once again, the better we understand rhetoric, the less reason we have to trust it.

This objection to Gorgias' position would lose some of its force if, as he suggests, it could be applied to any craft that can be used unjustly. If Socrates' argument were fair, would it not equally show that a doctor or a gymnastics teacher must teach his pupils justice? If we do not blame the doctor for the unjust actions of his pupils, why should we blame the rhetorician?

Socrates might fairly point out that the aim and product of rhetoric make the question about justice more pressing. An unjust carpenter is capable of making a perfectly good bed; we might buy his bed if we make sure that he does not cheat or overcharge us. We simply need to make sure that he practises his craft competently. If an orator is unjust, however, can we still rely on his ability to give us good advice? He is skilled only in techniques of persuasion, and we have no reason to value their effect on us if he is not also just. We cannot guard against the effects of his injustice by making sure that he practises his skill competently. His injustice, then, seems to interfere with his ability to produce a worthwhile product, whereas it need not interfere with this ability in a genuine craftsman. Socrates' objections about rhetoric and justice give us a special reason for distrusting the advice that an orator gives us.

Socrates' argument against Gorgias, then, does not rely simply on a dogmatic appeal to Socrates' view that knowledge is sufficient for virtue. It shows that Gorgias has no adequate reply to the suspicions raised by the unjust use of rhetoric, and that therefore we have no reason to accept his defence of rhetoric. We noticed that Protagoras claimed rather incautiously to be able to teach virtue, without having thought carefully about what virtue must be like if it is to be teachable; when this question is raised, we can see why it is not unreasonable of Socrates to suggest that Protagoras ought to accept Socrates' position.[10] Similarly, Gorgias' position is more difficult to maintain if he rejects the Socratic view. In both cases Plato shows why the Socratic view is more difficult to reject than we might at first have thought.

69. Power and Justice

Like Protagoras, Gorgias claims that he teaches something that will be good both for his pupils and for the community as a whole.[11] Still, he recognizes a possible conflict between the orator's own interest and the requirements of justice, and does not explain why the orator has any reason to be just if he gains something from being unjust. Polus raises this question more sharply; he rejects Gorgias' claim to teach justice, suggesting that only shame led Gorgias into this mistaken claim (461b3–c4). When Socrates argues that rhetoric is not a genuine craft because the rhetorician and the orator do not know what is beneficial for the people they advise (464e2–465a7), Polus replies that Socrates is considering the wrong people's benefit. Polus focusses (as Gorgias did, 452e1–8) on the benefit of rhetoric for the orator, claiming that the orator has great power, which is clearly good for him (466a9–c2). In order to refute Socrates, Polus needs to show that the orator's great power is good for him, all things considered,[12] whether or not he is just.

First of all, Socrates points out that the mere ability to do what seems good for me does not ensure that I will always get what is actually good for me, all things considered, (since I may not know what is actually good for me); hence this ability is not always good for me, all things considered (466d5–468e5).[13] Next he focusses on the specific abilities of the orator to imprison, expropriate, and execute. He shows that it is not good for us to exercise the ability to kill or rob people if we act in ignorance of what is good for us (469c8–470b8).

Polus answers that the abilities of the orator, together with knowledge of the right time to use them in unjust action, enable him to win the power, wealth, and status of the usurper Archelaus, and anyone who achieves this condition is happy. Although Polus abandons his first claim that rhetoric by itself is always good, all things considered, he still maintains that the knowledge one needs to use rhetoric for one's benefit is the knowledge of how to imitate Archelaus, not knowledge of how to be just.

Socrates answers Polus by claiming that justice is necessary and sufficient for happiness (470c1–471a3). Unlike Crito (*Cri.* 48b8–10), Polus refuses to accept this controversial Socratic claim, and so Socrates sets out to defend it. In defending it, he introduces another assumption that is always accepted in the shorter dialogues, that since virtuous action is fine it is also beneficial.[14] Polus rejects this assumption (474c9–d2), and so Socrates has to defend it.

Socrates seeks to show that Polus' position is inconsistent. He argues as follows:

1. Committing injustice is more shameful, and therefore worse, than suffering injustice (474d3–475c9).
2. Polus would not choose (*dechesthai*) what is worse and more shameful over what is better and less shameful (475d1–e3).
3. Hence he would not choose to commit injustice rather than suffer it (475e3–6).
4. Hence it is better for him to suffer injustice than to do injustice.

Socrates concludes that he has refuted Polus' initial claim that we can be happy without being just.

Socrates gives a reasonable defence of (1), if (1) is taken to mean that committing injustice is worse for the community (or for those affected) than suffering injustice is. Socrates is also justified in inferring (3) from (1) and (2), provided that 'worse' is understood in (2), as in (1), to mean 'worse for the community'. He does not seem justified, however, in inferring (4). Why should Polus not defend (3) by arguing that I have strong moral reasons to choose fine actions, since they are better for the community? Apparently he could still reject (4) by arguing that these actions are worse for me than some shameful actions would be.[15]

Polus, however, has already deprived himself of this answer to Socrates. Earlier he denied that doing injustice is worse for the agent than suffering injustice. When Socrates suggested that Polus and everyone else 'think doing injustice is worse than suffering it and that not being punished is worse than being punished' (474b3–5), Polus denies this; 'for', he asks, 'would you choose to suffer injustice rather than do it?' (474b6–7). At this stage 'worse' must mean 'worse for the agent', since that is the issue in dispute. Polus assumes that since we do not choose suffering injustice over doing injustice, we cannot think it is better for us. He therefore implies that if we thought it better for us, we would choose it (474b9–10). Polus, then, commits himself to:

5. If A believes x is better than y for A, then A chooses x over y (474b6–10).

Once Polus has accepted (5), he cannot accept (1) through (3) without also accepting (4).[16]

Admittedly, (5) is a Socratic assumption, expressing a part of Socrates' psychological eudaemonism. But it is not thrust on Polus without warning; Socrates has previously asserted the eudaemonist position (468b1–7, d1–7),[17] and Polus has accepted it. It did not occur to Polus that in accepting both Socrates' eudaemonist assumption and the common-sense belief that just action is worth choosing because it is fine, he committed himself to the Socratic view that whatever is fine is beneficial to the agent; but Socrates points out that Polus is indeed committed to this conclusion, however surprising he may find it.

The argument with Polus answers an objection that might reasonably be raised against the argument with Gorgias. Socrates assumes, and Gorgias agrees, that anyone who knows what justice is will also be a just person; but Socrates at first gives no reason for assuming this. Polus' views about justice and power implicitly challenge Socrates' assumption, since they imply that one's unjust action is sometimes beneficial to oneself. In arguing against Polus, Socrates defends his assumption about justice: when we know what justice is, we will also know that it is fine, and if we know that whatever is fine is good for us, we will want (according to Socratic eudaemonism) to be just.

The initial dispute about rhetoric has now allowed Plato to focus attention on two connected assumptions underlying the argument of the Socratic dialogues. Socrates regularly assumes that justice is sufficient for happiness and that whatever is fine must also be beneficial to the agent. The discussion with Polus has shown that these assumptions can be defended against the doubts of an interlocutor who is initially hostile to Socrates' position. Indeed, Socrates claims to have shown that Polus cannot avoid agreeing with Socrates.

This defence of Socratic ethics is not yet complete, however. For Socrates has still taken for granted without argument not only the truth of eudaemonism but also the common-sense assumption that other-regarding justice is fine. This assumption is the next one to be challenged.

70. The Argument with Callicles

Callicles claims, as Polus did, that Socrates traps interlocutors by exploiting their embarrassment at being committed to claims that would conventionally be found shocking; even though Polus saw that this tactic was used against Gorgias, he fell into the same trap himself (482c4–e2). Both Gorgias and Polus are caught because they attach some value to other-regarding principles of justice; for if we accept Socratic eudaemonism (which Callicles does not challenge), we find that Socrates' claims about the connexion between justice and happiness are supported by common-sense assumptions about other-regarding justice. Callicles asks: if we reject these common-sense assumptions, can Socrates convince us that we have good reason to accept them, or must he admit that they cannot be defended in the light of anything more fundamental?

In the *Crito* Socrates might be taken to argue that no further defence of justice is possible. In arguing with Crito that he ought to suffer injustice rather than do injustice, he requires Crito to agree that justice promotes happiness, and he offers Crito no further reason for agreeing on this claim (*Cri.* 48b8–10). In the *Gorgias,* by contrast, he offers Polus a reason to believe that justice promotes happiness; since Callicles rejects the reason given to Polus, Socrates agrees to re-open the question. In accepting Callicles' challenge, Socrates implies that he does not regard the interlocutor's commitment to other-regarding justice as a fundamental point of agreement; he believes that the elenchos can convince an interlocutor that he is wrong to reject this commitment.

Since Socrates wants to examine and defend his moral position without relying on unexamined conventional assumptions, he is right to suggest that Callicles is an especially suitable interlocutor.[18] Callicles will not make mistaken agreements because of stupidity, embarrassment, or insincerity (487d7–e6); his 'frankness' (487a7–b5) ensures that he will stick firmly to his anti-conventional position. Still, Socrates seems to exaggerate when he claims that whatever the two of them can agree on will be the truth (486e5–6, 487e6–7). For the argument still requires Callicles to agree on some points at the beginning; why should he not withdraw his agreements and so wreck Socrates' argument? Even if he sticks to his agreements, what does that show about the truth of the conclusions? Callicles points out that if Gorgias and Polus stick to their agreements, that shows something about Gorgias and Polus, but not necessarily about the truth of their claims. Socrates needs to convince us that the agreements between him and Callicles are not open to the objection that Callicles raises against the previous agreements.

71. Callicles' Moral Position

Callicles argues that Socrates has no good reason to value other-regarding justice. He claims that it is not really justice at all, and is really shameful rather than fine;[19] it is just and fine 'by convention', but not 'by nature' (482e2–483d6). Callicles agrees that it is just to give people what they deserve, what is owed to them, and what is appropriate for them, but he argues that common-sense views about justice are formed by a mistaken consensus about what is appropriate for different sorts of people. This consensus reflects the outlook of inferior people, who want to restrain and inhibit the aims of superior people (483e1–484a2).

Callicles regards other-regarding justice as the product of convention rather than nature. In his view, natural justice requires the subordination of inferior people to superior people, so that the superior people can have what is appropriate for their superior abilities and aims. Callicles does not try to show that it is fine and beneficial for inferior people to observe the principles of natural justice, but he argues that it is fine and beneficial for superior people to observe natural rather than conventional justice, and that it is mere cowardice if such people observe the rules of conventional justice.

In appealing to justice, we normally assume that we are appealing to some impartial reason, distinct from the aims of a particular person, that supports the just course of action.[20] If we accept conventional justice, we believe—falsely, in Callicles' view—that the interests of the many inferior people should determine the appropriate treatment of each person. Callicles puts forward a rival impartial principle, claiming that the interests of the superior people should set the standard for justice. This is an impartial principle in the sense that the domination of the superior people is supposed to be not merely good for the superior people themselves but also desirable from some point of view distinct from theirs.

To examine Callicles' position, we need to examine his claims that (1) violating the rules of other-regarding justice is in some people's interest, that (2) these people are superior people, and that (3) what promotes these people's interest is naturally just. Perhaps Callicles believes that the third claim follows from the second, but whatever we decide about the second and third claims, the first is independent of them.

In Callicles' view, it is part of a worthwhile life to excel—to develop one's capacities and desires and to satisfy them. A superior person's aspirations will not remain at the level of what is currently easy or readily available for him; he will want more than he has, and he will want the virtues that enable him both to translate his aspirations into practical aims and to carry out his aims. This is why Callicles values wisdom and bravery (491a7–b4). The sort of person he admires seeks political power and achievement (491b1–2) and therefore also values philosophy (in its place) and rhetorical skill (484c4–d7, 485d3–e2); he uses these skills to help himself and his friends, and to harm his enemies (492b8–c3).[21]

In presenting Callicles' criticism of other-regarding justice, Plato draws attention to a powerful line of objection to Socratic ethics that is ignored in the shorter dialogues. If Callicles is right, then some of Socrates' assumptions are completely wrong; but the shorter dialogues never argue against Callicles' position. Plato does not intend Callicles' position to be an eccentric or extremely radical point of view on conventional justice; it is simply a forceful statement of views that appeal to many of Socrates' and Plato's contemporaries. The conception of a virtue and of a good person that is focussed on the individual's power, wealth, and status is well established in Greek ethical thinking, and it co-exists uneasily with a conception of virtue that is connected with the other-regarding obligations of justice. Protagoras suggests, but does not argue, that these two conceptions of virtue are combined in the virtue that the Athenians and he teach.[22] In Callicles' view, these two conceptions are in conflict, and a correct conception of a worthwhile life requires us to reject other-regarding justice.

Socrates begins his examination of Callicles' position by asking why it is just by nature for the superior people to violate conventional rules of justice, and why it is not just by nature for the inferior people to restrain the superior people. He argues that Callicles cannot consistently identify the superiority of superior people with their greater strength. For if greater strength implies superiority, and the many inferior people are collectively stronger than the single superior person, they must also be collectively superior. It must, therefore, be naturally just for the superior person to be subject to the inferior people, contrary to Callicles' previous claim (488b8–489b6).

Callicles is no better off if he simply says that the superior people are those who have superior wisdom, if all kinds of wisdom count; for then he cannot explain why the wiser people ought to have more (490a1–491a3).[23] Socrates suggests that it is foolish to claim that better shoemakers ought to have more shoes; although it is more reasonable to claim that better farmers ought to have more seeds, this is not what Callicles meant by 'having more'.

These objections strike Callicles as Socrates' usual eristic tactics (490e9–491a3), but they have a more serious point. If Callicles is to justify his claim that the superior people's violation of conventional justice is really just, and not simply advantageous for the superior people themselves, he has to explain why the superior people's superiority entitles them to preferential treatment. Socrates presses him to describe the type of superiority that supports this appeal to natural justice.

Callicles answers that the superior people are those who are wise in the affairs of the city and brave in carrying out their purposes (491a7–b4); it is fitting for these people to rule, and justice consists in their having more because they are rulers (491c6–d3). This answer still does not explain what is naturally just about preferential treatment for the rulers; but Socrates now drops that issue by moving on to a question about happiness.[24]

72. Callicles' Conception of Happiness

Socrates apparently changes the direction of the discussion by inviting Callicles to agree that the superior people who rule over others must also rule and control themselves; by this he means that they ought to rule their pleasures and appetites (491d10–e1). Callicles answers that this suggestion requires too much restraint of desires (491e5–6, 492c4–e2). In Callicles' view, happiness requires large and demanding appetites and their satisfaction (491e5–492c8); 'how could a human being become happy <while> being enslaved to any<thing>?' (491e5–6). The happy person is free to satisfy his desires, has the resources to satisfy them, and takes advantage of his freedom and his resources to satisfy his desires.

Callicles seeks to articulate a conception of happiness that supports the rejection of justice. He must claim that all of a person's desires, especially the most demanding desires, must be expanded and satisfied. If we had a strong desire to be just and satisfied that desire, we would be no less happy (on one conception of happiness) than a person who satisfies vigorous and demanding appetites. Callicles, however, cannot accept this conclusion. He does not merely want to say that it is possible to be happy without being just; he argues that it is impossible to be happy if we are just.[25] He must therefore argue that happiness requires the development and satisfaction of the sorts of desires whose whole-hearted pursuit is incompatible with respect for justice. Moreover, he does not want to say that the desires that a happy person satisfies are especially good desires; for then a question would arise about why the desires preferred by Callicles are better desires than those that a just person satisfies. He has to insist that the only relevant fact about the desires to be satisfied is that they are as strong and demanding as possible. Hence he must refuse to discriminate among desires on any other basis.

This conception of happiness shows how superior people are different from ordinary people and why they should be given more resources. Most people, in Callicles' view, cannot achieve the sort of happiness he describes, both because they lack the necessary material resources and because they are irresolute and cowardly (492a1–3).[26] Since they are ashamed of their weakness of character, they hide it by claiming that temperance is fine and self-indulgence is shameful (492a3–b1). In Callicles' view, the right way to use abundant material resources is to treat them as material for a self-indulgent life; he suggests it is shameful if people who have these resources are deceived into condemning a self-indulgent life (492b1–c3).

Since Callicles rejects the conventional view of justice and maintains that natural justice requires the allocation of resources to superior people, he needs to explain what sort of superiority requires us to violate conventional justice. He answers that natural justice requires allocation of resources to superior people because they are the only ones who have any reasonable prospect of happiness. To give these resources to inferior people would be a foolish waste of these resources on people who are psychologically incapable of gaining happiness from them. Plato cannot fairly be accused of foisting an extreme conception of happiness on Callicles in order to make it easier for Socrates to refute him. Callicles' conception of happiness is the one he needs to support his objections to conventional justice.[27]

In defence of his conception of happiness, Callicles introduces hedonism. He argues that a self-controlled person who has moderate desires and satisfies them cannot be happy. Such a person lives like a stone, neither enjoying pleasure nor feeling pain; living pleasantly, by contrast, requires the largest possible inflow of satisfaction and therefore requires the most demanding desires, since only these require a large inflow to satisfy them (494a6–c3). Callicles argues, then, that if we identify happiness with maximum pleasure we ought to agree with his expansive conception of happiness, because someone who satisfies strong and demanding desires maximizes pleasure. Although some of these desires may seem repulsive on other grounds, happiness consists in the pleasure we gain from satisfying them; the only question is whether the pleasure is large enough (494c4–495d5).

Plato makes it clear that Callicles' claims about happiness imply the acceptance of hedonism; for Socrates points out with some emphasis, and Callicles eventually agrees, that Callicles affirms the identity of the pleasant and the good

(495d2–5). These are the very terms in which the *Protagoras* stated the hedonist position.

73. Socrates' Conception of Happiness

In reply to Callicles' claim that happiness is incompatible with self-control (491d4–e6), Socrates puts forward a different view of happiness. Callicles rejects the view of happiness that claims that 'those who need nothing are happy' (492e3–4).[28] Socrates, by contrast, describes the bad effects of uncontrolled desire, hoping to persuade Callicles to prefer 'instead of the unfilled and unrestrained life, the life that is orderly and adequately supplied and satisfied with the things that are present on each occasion' (493c5–7).

Both Callicles' and Socrates' claims about happiness might be defended by appeal to common-sense views about happiness.[29] Callicles agrees that happiness requires external success and prosperity. Since it requires favourable external conditions, we need large resources to secure these favourable conditions; and since the recognized virtues prevent us from acquiring both the large resources and the external successes that are needed for happiness, we cannot regard them as means to happiness. Callicles, therefore, appeals to one aspect of happiness recognized by common sense and argues that it is so central to happiness that it should override any common-sense views about the value of other-regarding virtues.

Socrates also takes a critical attitude to common sense, but he comes to the opposite conclusion. He appeals to the common-sense view that the happy life is 'self-sufficient' (*autarkēs*), because it needs nothing added, and 'secure' (*asphalēs*), because it is immune to misfortune (Ar. *Rhet.* 1360b14). Socrates suggests that we satisfy these conditions if and only if we adapt our desires to the conditions available for satisfying them and so assure their satisfaction. Let us call this an 'adaptive' view of happiness.[30] If it is correct, then the common-sense demand for self-sufficiency refutes the common-sense view that happiness requires external prosperity. The demand for external prosperity supports Callicles' expansive view of happiness, but it cannot be reconciled (according to Socrates) with the overriding demand for self-sufficiency and security.

This Socratic conception of happiness shows that the Calliclean conception is not the only way to form a consistent position out of common-sense beliefs about happiness. The rest of the dialogue ought to show whether the Calliclean or the Socratic solution is to be preferred.

74. Socrates' Reply to Callicles

Socrates presents two arguments against Callicles' view that the pleasant is identical to the good. Both arguments turn on a difference between the pleasure of the moment and a person's good, regarded as extending over one's life as a whole. It is difficult, however, to decide whether Socrates exploits this difference fairly, and whether he exposes any real difficulties in hedonism.

First, Socrates points out that we can feel pleasure and pain at the same time, but we cannot be well off and badly off at the same time (495e1–497d8). This difference shows that feeling some degree of pleasure or pain at a time is not the same as being well off or badly off on the whole over one's whole life, but it does not show that being well or badly off cannot be identified with a surplus of pleasure over pain over one's life as a whole. And so the argument does not refute a hedonist conception of happiness.

Indeed, it is difficult to believe that Plato could have intended this argument to refute hedonism. Callicles has made it clear that he is thinking about people choosing their way of life (491e7–492a3, 494c2–3), and Socrates has recognized that the judgment about a person's happiness is to be made about one's life as a whole (494c6–8). The first argument is probably meant to show why the hedonist must identify the good with maximum pleasure over the whole of one's life; at any rate, this is the hedonist position that Socrates needs to refute if he is to refute Callicles.

In the second argument (497d8–499b3) Socrates seeks to show that Callicles' hedonism is inconsistent with the belief that bravery is a virtue.[31] For a hedonist, a virtue is a state or capacity that is useful for maximizing pleasure, but there is no reason, according to Socrates, to believe that bravery is especially useful for this purpose. Socrates observes that in battles the coward gets at least as much pleasure as the brave person gets; and so it seems that bravery is no more effective than cowardice in securing pleasure.

Callicles admires brave people because they 'are strong enough to achieve what they have in mind, and do not shrink back because of softness of soul' (491b2–4). These strong and resolute people have plans for themselves and want to carry them out; since fears and 'softness' deter us from carrying out our own plans, agents who care about carrying out their plans will want to restrain fear and avoid cowardice. Callicles' ideal person carries out his own plans and satisfies his own appetites (491e8–492a3) without fear of what other people will think (492a3–b1).

Socrates points out that Callicles' admiration for this well-planned and resolute way of life conflicts with the particular content he assumes it will have: the unrestrained pursuit of the satisfaction of one's appetites. For the sort of planning and resolution that Callicles values commends itself to a consistent hedonist only if it is a sensible strategy for maximizing pleasure over one's life. The example of the coward shows that planning and resolution may be no better than cowardice as a strategy for maximizing pleasure; hence hedonism does not justify Callicles in preferring bravery over cowardice.[32]

In response to Socrates' argument, Callicles chooses to give up his hedonism rather than his account of the virtues. Someone who lacked bravery altogether would never persist in any rational plan if he felt any pain or reluctance; but he might still do well for pleasure, since his sensitivity to pain might make him especially pleased at relief from pain. Indeed, Callicles' discussion of pleasure and desire implies just such a proportional increase in pain, desire, and pleasure. But such a person would have a poor chance of executing his rational plans; he would disable himself from forming them, and from applying practical reason to his future states at all. Callicles is justified in refusing to make this large sacrifice of rational agency.

75. Rhetoric and Pleasure

Earlier in the dialogue, Socrates criticized rhetoric for its exclusive concern with pleasure and its indifference to the good; he suggested that from the consumer's point of view we ought to distrust rhetoric because we cannot expect that the advice that is aimed at our immediate pleasure will secure our good. He returns to this criticism of rhetoric after the refutation of Callicles' hedonism (500e4–501b1). As he often does in this dialogue, Socrates appeals to his later argument to show that an earlier conclusion was justified, even if it seemed to be open to objection at the time. The argument with Callicles shows why the orator's audience should not trust his advice and why the orator himself is misguided in following Polus' advice to pursue his own power.

If Callicles' conception of happiness were correct, then some of our grounds for suspicion of rhetoric would collapse.[33] For if happiness consists in the pleasure resulting from the satisfaction of desires as they arise, the orator might claim to promote our happiness. Since he can present a course of action in a favourable light, he can induce in us a strong desire for that course of action, and so offers us some prospect of satisfying a strong desire, if we do the action he recommends. If we are disappointed with that action, the orator can perhaps persuade us not to care so much about it, if he can propose something else that we will care about intensely.

Socrates suggests that this is the sort of satisfaction that we can expect from rhetoric. Pericles satisfied people's appetites and then increased them so that they demanded more; he even caused people to demand so much that they turned against him because he still left them dissatisfied (515b6–516d4). If we simply think about maximizing pleasure, we have no reason to say that Pericles' policy was bad for the Athenians; it would be bad for them only if their desires outran their ability to provide resources for their satisfaction.

Similarly, Callicles' conception of happiness would support Polus' contention that orators promote their own good by having and exercising the power that their rhetorical skill gives them. Socrates and Polus agree that orators do what they decide, and Callicles ought to agree that they are in a position to satisfy their appetites. If a person's good consists in nothing more than maximum satisfaction of appetites as they occur, the orator does not seem to do so badly for himself.

If, however, Callicles' conception of happiness is wrong, then those who pursue the pleasant without the good pursue the satisfaction of particular appetites as they arise, but neglect what is good for them in their lives as a whole. Although the orator is skilled in creating and satisfying particular appetites, he has no skill in creating or satisfying desires that promote our good in our lives as a whole. Similarly, the orator has no reason to trust his own skills. If he follows Polus' advice, he will be able to satisfy his appetites as they arise, but he has no reason to believe that in doing so he promotes his good.

Socrates is quite justified, then, in emphasizing the importance of his argument with Callicles about pleasure and happiness. He wants it to be clear that Callicles is committed to the premisses of this argument, so that he can show that Callicles has no escape from the conclusion. Callicles claimed that Socrates' inquiries are trivial, and cannot establish any important result, because they rely on eristic tricks. Socrates has tried to show that these objections cannot be raised against the argument he has just given. Once Callicles has been refuted, he claims that he was not sincere in conceding the crucial premisses (499b4–8), but the previous argument has shown that he cannot maintain his original claims about justice without maintaining the premisses that led to his refutation. Socrates is right to claim that he has undermined Callicles' opposition to other-regarding justice.

76. Happiness and Rational Order

In response to Socrates' argument, Callicles chooses to abandon hedonism rather than abandon his belief that bravery is a virtue. Does he make the right choice?

Socrates defends Callicles' choice by arguing that a person's good requires some sort of rational order in one's desires. In the *Crito* Socrates appealed to an analogy between health in the body and justice in the soul (*Cri.* 47d3–48a1), but he did not try to show how the two conditions are analogous. In the *Gorgias* he tries to make the analogy more precise. He distinguishes two parts of the soul with two different types of desires.[34] The part with appetites is unruly and insatiable (493b1–3); if we simply cultivate the satisfaction of desire, we strengthen this non-rational and insatiable part and make ourselves incapable of rational planning. If desires differ in this way, any concern for ourselves as continuing agents with long-term plans requires us to recognize the value of order in the soul and to restrain the desires that should not be satisfied (503d5–504e5). To have this sort of order is to have one's appetites (*epithumiai*) controlled (505b1–5).

Callicles is right, then, to value bravery, because a rational agent needs it to execute his rational plans. The brave person sticks to his rational plans and is not diverted from them by fear. Socrates points out that we have the same reason for valuing temperance; for the temperate person sticks to his rational plans and is not diverted from them by the prospect of pleasure. If Callicles recognizes that the restraint of desire required by bravery is reasonable, he must also value the psychic order that results from temperance no less than from bravery (504d1–3, 505b1–11, 506d2–507a2).

Socrates can now answer Callicles' contention that other-regarding justice is bad for us because it interferes with the maximum expansion and satisfaction of desires. Socrates argues that this fact about conventional justice is not a reason for condemning it but a reason for advocating it; for the nature of rational and non-rational desires assures us that some restraint of desire is in our interest. Since justice interferes with the expansion of our desires by requiring us to restrain some of our non-rational desires, it is beneficial rather than harmful.

This is the end of the main ethical argument of the *Gorgias*. It argues quite convincingly for an important result, that Callicles' reason for supposing that the just person is harmed by being just is not a good enough reason; for Socrates shows that Callicles cannot press his criticism of justice without committing himself to a version of hedonism that undermines his own conception of a virtuous agent. If Socrates has shown this much, he has shown that his refusal to sacrifice justice to other apparent goods is not as obviously mistaken as it might initially appear; Polus and Callicles have tried to explain what is wrong with Socrates' position, and have failed to show anything wrong with it.

As Socrates claims, his opponents have turned out to be committed to a ridiculous position (509a4–7), and his own position has remained undamaged:

> These things that appeared true to us earlier, in the previous arguments, are held firm and bound down, so I say—even if it is a bit impolite to say so—by iron and adamantine arguments; so at least it would seem so far. (508e6–509a2)

'Appeared' refers to the conclusion of the argument with Polus, but 'are held firm and bound down' refers to the confirmation provided by the argument with Callicles.[35]

To agree with Socrates to this extent, however, is not to accept all his conclusions. For he speaks as though he had argued for something more than the conclusion that we have derived from his explicit arguments. He claims to have vindicated his own claim that justice is sufficient for happiness, but all he has actually argued is that Callicles is wrong in claiming that justice is incompatible with happiness.

Has Socrates said enough in the *Gorgias* to allow us to supply the further argument that would support his stronger claims about justice and happiness? To answer this question, we must examine some aspects of his views about happiness more carefully.

8

Implications of the *Gorgias*

77. Quantitative Hedonism

Socrates' argument for justice rests on claims about happiness. He rejects Callicles' expansive conception, which he describes as a hedonist view, and he argues against Callicles by appealing to an adaptive conception of happiness. To estimate the success of Socrates' argument, we need to examine his views about happiness.

First of all, several questions arise about the treatment of pleasure in the *Gorgias*, especially about its relation to the hedonism of the *Protagoras*.[1] Callicles affirms the identity of the pleasant and the good, and Socrates denies it. The thesis accepted in the *Protagoras* and the thesis rejected by Socrates in the *Gorgias* are expressed in the very same words (*Pr.* 354e8–355a2, 355b3–c1; *G.* 495d2–5). Does Plato mean that the hedonism of the *Protagoras* requires acceptance of Callicles' conclusions about happiness?

We have seen reasons for believing that the hedonism in the *Protagoras* expresses Plato's own view and is not simply assumed for the sake of argument. If the *Gorgias* actually rejects this same hedonist doctrine, then Plato has apparently changed his mind about hedonism, and we ought to find some reason to explain this change of mind.

Perhaps, however, we ought not to assume that the hedonist doctrine rejected in the *Gorgias* is actually the same as the one in the *Protagoras*. The *Protagoras* appears to have taken account of Socrates' objections to Callicles; for it insists that pleasure is to be assessed by considering not merely the pleasure of the moment but also maximum pleasure over one's life as a whole. In this emphasis on long-term planning, the 'measuring science' of the *Protagoras* seems to express the same commitment to rational prudence that Socrates exploits to refute Callicles' hedonism.

In identifying the pleasant with the good, Callicles claims that unrestrained indulgence in any sort of pleasure whatever constitutes a person's good. This claim might suggest that he has forgotten that pleasure is to be estimated with regard to one's life as a whole. Even if we grant that the coward has more short-term pleasure, we can still argue that the brave person has greater overall pleasure. That is why the *Protagoras* takes the life of maximum pleasure to require bravery and temperance.

This is enough to show that defenders of the ethical position taken in the *Protagoras* will disagree with Callicles. It is not enough, however, to show that they are entitled to disagree with him; for we must still ask whether they are entitled to claim, on strictly hedonist grounds, that the brave person gets more long-term pleasure than the coward gets. This is precisely the question that Socrates raises in the *Gorgias.*

Does Socrates' argument to show that cowards get at least as much pleasure as brave people (497c8–499b3) collapse as soon as the hedonist distinguishes the pleasure of the moment from pleasure over one's life as a whole? Socrates implicitly challenges this hedonist reply. He remarks that the coward feels more pain when the enemy advances and more pleasure when the enemy retreats (498b2–7); the pain that results from his fear increases the pleasure of the relief when the danger passes. Now Callicles has agreed that we gain more pleasure if, say, we eat when we are very hungry than if we eat when we are not especially hungry; and since the coward is far more afraid of danger than the brave person is, he is more pleased if the threatened evil passes him by.

Moreover, if the coward's cowardice exposes him to more danger in the future, he can look forward to greater pleasure if he is lucky enough to avoid the threatened evils. Of course, he may be unlucky, but it is not clear that he is worse off, from a purely hedonist point of view, than the brave person is. For even if the brave person secures himself (again, not certainly) against some future pains, he both exposes himself to pains that the cowardly person avoids and denies himself the intense pleasures of the coward who sighs with relief when the danger is past.

It is difficult, then, for Callicles to deny that the coward's strategy is at least as good as the brave person's as a way to maximize overall pleasure. The force of Socrates' argument does not depend on any unfair neglect of the difference between the pleasure of the moment and pleasure over one's lifetime; and so the argument challenges a hedonist view that defends bravery as the best strategy for maximizing pleasure over one's lifetime.

This argument exposes a difficulty in specifying happiness in purely quantitative hedonist terms. In the *Protagoras* Socrates suggests vaguely that we do not live well if we live a life of pain, and we do live well if we come to the end of our lives 'living pleasantly' (*Pr.* 351b3–7). This suggestion needs to be made more precise, but no more precise formulation seems entirely satisfactory. It would be unrealistic to insist that a happy life contains no pain at all. On the other hand, we presumably do not secure happiness if our life contains only a tiny surplus of pleasure over pain, whereas it seems excessive (and perhaps unintelligible) to insist that we are happy only if we achieve the maximum surplus of pleasure that anyone could achieve.

Perhaps we can say that a happy life must have a sufficiently large predominance of pleasure to count as clearly pleasant on the whole. But this also seems to imply a questionable claim about happiness. Should we be willing, for instance, to accumulate severe pains, provided that the resulting pleasures are large enough to create a large surplus of pleasure over pain? Or does the absolute quantity of pain matter more? This question is raised in a trivial case by someone who is willing to itch in order to get the pleasure of scratching, and in a more important case by the coward who is willing to suffer more pain for the sake of more intense pleasure. The argument in the *Gorgias* shows us that when we try to formulate the right quantitative conception of happiness in hedonist terms, we may come to wonder whether a quantitative conception is plausible at all.

The same argument challenges the epistemological hedonism of the *Protagoras*. Epistemological hedonism claims not only that something is pleasant if and only if it is good but also that we believe that goodness just is pleasantness, and hence we believe that something is good just because, and insofar as, it is pleasant. In the *Gorgias* Socrates suggests that if we think of nothing except maximizing pleasure, the coward can make at least as good a case for cowardice as the brave person can make for bravery.

78. Pleasure and Good

In reply to Socrates' objections, Callicles seeks to distinguish good from bad pleasures, and claims that the brave person's pleasures are better than the coward's (499b4–d3; contrast *Pr.* 351c2–e7). The *Protagoras* showed how a hedonist might try to reduce the distinction between good and bad pleasures to a distinction between more and less overall pleasure. But it is doubtful whether this reduction rests on a plausible view of the nature of pleasure.

In the *Protagoras* Socrates concentrates on examples in which it is plausible to suppose we gain more of the same thing in the long term by giving up some of it in the short term; the pain in our tooth that we suffer because of toothache is similar enough to the pain we suffer from having a filling to make it easy to say that we incur a little pain now (in having the filling) to avoid greater pain of the same kind in the future. Since we can assume some uniformity in the pleasure that is lost and the pleasure that is gained, it is easy to see how we can say that we gain or lose more of the same thing.

Not every comparison of goods and evils, however, is easy to understand in these purely quantitative terms. The coward is willing to put up with the pains of ill repute and of longer-term dangers in order to gain the pleasure of relief from danger. Callicles' intemperate person prefers extravagant physical pleasures so much that he is willing to set aside the demands of justice and temperance; does this mean that in the end he gets a smaller quantity of the very same sort of pleasure that he pursues? Perhaps just people take so much pleasure in being just that they would find it intolerable to violate justice for the pleasures that appeal to the intemperate person, but might the intemperate person not say the same about his pleasures in comparison to the just person's pleasures? It is not clear how a purely quantitative comparison can explain the disagreement between the intemperate and the temperate person, and Socrates does not explain how a hedonist copes with such cases.[2]

We may argue that the coward's pleasures are bad because one ought not to be so pleased at relief from immediate danger and so little distressed by the prospect of future danger; or we may argue that the brave person's pleasures result from the exercise of rational agency rather than from passively awaiting relief from painful sensations. Each argument gives us reasons to agree with the brave person's judgment, but both abandon epistemological hedonism. If cowardly people's values determine their pleasures, and brave people's values determine their pleasures, we cannot decide who is right by some independent calculation of pleasure. As Socrates says, we must take the good as our end and choose pleasant things for the sake of goods, not the other way around (500a2–4). In affirming that the good, not the pleasant, is the end we must aim at, Socrates rejects the epistemological priority of the pleasant over the good.

If this is the right way to understand the two dialogues, then the *Protagoras* does not defend a sophisticated version of hedonism that avoids the objections raised in the *Gorgias*. On the contrary, the anti-hedonist arguments in the *Gorgias* raise serious difficulties for precisely the epistemological hedonism that is defended in the *Protagoras*. Indeed, the strength of the objections raised in the *Gorgias* might lead us to wonder whether Plato seriously intends the hedonist doctrine in the *Protagoras;* is it not likely that these difficulties strike him and that they qualify his acceptance of hedonism? This suggestion cannot be dismissed, but the *Protagoras* itself does not seem to support it, since Plato does not indicate any of the relevant doubts or hesitations. It is best to conclude that the *Gorgias* expresses Plato's further thoughts about hedonism.

79. Psychic Order

In explaining the importance of rational prudence, Socrates claims that happiness requires rational order in the soul. In his view, the virtuous person must be 'self-controlled' (*enkratē heautou*, 491d11). This talk of self-control suggests another apparent conflict with the moral psychology of the *Protagoras*. In the *Protagoras* Socrates argues that the effects normally ascribed to lack of self-control (*akrasia*) are really the effects of ignorance of the good. If this is true, then all our desires are focussed on the good, and if we discover what is good for us, no desires will divert us from the pursuit of that good. In the *Gorgias,* however, Socrates recognizes two parts of the soul and says that one part consists of appetites that make it unruly and insatiable (493b1–2). If he is speaking strictly, then he rejects the psychological eudaemonism characteristic of the Socratic dialogues. It is useful to look back at the *Protagoras,* since it offers an argument, based on epistemological hedonism, for the eudaemonist claim that is assumed without argument in the shorter dialogues. What reasons might lead Plato to question that argument?

The belief in incontinence conflicts with Socratic psychological eudaemonism. Socrates assumes that happiness provides a self-explanatory end and that every other end must be explained by reference to happiness; but if incontinence is possible, this eudaemonist claim about explanation is false. According to common sense, we may know that it would be better for us not to run away from danger, but we run away nonetheless because we are 'overcome', as we say, by fear (*Pr.* 352b5–c2). If common sense is right, this appeal to 'overcoming' provides an adequate explanation that does not refer to happiness. Socrates ought not to appeal simply to psychological eudaemonism to answer this common-sense view; such an appeal would be question-begging, since the common-sense view challenges the truth of eudaemonism.[3]

In the *Protagoras* Socrates recognizes that he cannot merely appeal to eudaemonism; for he introduces hedonism precisely to convince someone who might reject eudaemonism in the belief that sometimes we choose what we regard as most pleasant over what we regard as best. In this case a believer in incontinence interprets 'A chooses y over x because A is overcome by the pleasure of y' as meaning 'A chooses y over x because A believes y is more pleasant than x' (*Pr.* 355a5–e4). Socrates is entitled to interpret the many in this way, since he secures their agreement to the principle that we choose y over x because we believe y is more pleasant overall than x;[4] this principle follows from the other principles of choice that the many accept. His argument, then, is not question-begging against the many, given their acceptance of his suggestion that we always choose what we believe to be most pleasant overall.

It is not clear, however, that every believer in incontinence must follow the many in accepting the interpretation of 'overcome by pleasure' that assumes we always pursue what we take to be most pleasant overall. Even if we accept hedonism as an account of the good, we need not agree that we pursue maximum overall pleasure in all our choices, since we need not agree that we always pursue overall good. Socrates persuades the many to agree that we always pursue overall pleasure, by suggesting that they pursue pleasure as good (354c4). But his suggestion should not seem plausible to a believer in incontinence. If I suppose I am overcome by anger, I need not suppose I believe that taking revenge now will yield greater pleasure overall than I would obtain if I kept my temper. I may admit that the incontinent course of action is both worse overall and less pleasant overall, but still find it attractive enough for me to pursue it.

If that is so, then Socrates has not refuted the view that incontinent people are attracted by things that they regard as both worse overall and less pleasant overall than the alternatives. Another way to express this objection would be to say that what attracts and motivates us depends on other things than our judgment of overall value (however overall value is decided).[5]

Socrates would be entitled to reject this view about incontinence if he were entitled to assume that we always choose what we value most. He would be entitled to assume this if he were entitled to assume psychological eudaemonism. But it would be question-begging to assume psychological eudaemonism, since the apparent reality of incontinence is an apparent counterexample to psychological eudaemonism. If we do not rely on psychological eudaemonism, it is not clear (from anything said in the *Protagoras*) why we should assume that we always choose what we value most.

Hedonism is important in Socrates' argument, since it allows him to reject incontinence without appealing to any question-begging eudaemonist premisses.

However, the principles about choice that he appeals to are open to many of the same sorts of doubts that might lead someone to reject eudaemonism in the fact of apparent examples of incontinence. And so the appeal to hedonism does not seem to be dialectically effective against the sorts of doubts about eudaemonism that Socrates wants to remove.

80. Socratic Eudaemonism in the *Gorgias*

If our account of the treatment of hedonism in the *Gorgias* is right, then Plato has a good reason to reconsider the argument that the *Protagoras* offers against incontinence, since he rejects its crucial hedonist premiss. It is more difficult to decide whether he sees that the argument would fail even if hedonism were accepted. At any rate, his claims about self-control and the non-rational part of the soul give us some ground for supposing that he has doubts about the eudaemonist rejection of incontinence. These same doubts may explain why the *Gorgias* does not explicitly identify virtue with knowledge.[6]

Belief in the possibility of incontinence gives further point to the argument against Callicles. Socrates seems to argue that justice and health are analogous because each requires the orderly arrangement of potentially conflicting elements, and that the variety of desires implies potentially conflicting elements in the soul (504a7–d3, 505a2–b12). The possibility of psychic conflict and the resulting need for psychic order justify Callicles' preference for bravery. To neglect the virtues that ensure the dominance of rational over non-rational elements in the soul is to neglect the conditions of rational agency.[7]

If, however, the *Gorgias* sometimes rejects psychological eudaemonism, a serious difficulty arises; it also seems to affirm the psychological eudaemonist view that all desires are focussed on the good (467–468). This claim plays a vital role in Socrates' arguments against Gorgias and Polus; it is never questioned in those parts of the dialogue, even though some of Socrates' other premisses are questioned. If later in the dialogue Socrates rejects the eudaemonist claim, the *Gorgias* is internally inconsistent on this major issue.

If we are determined to avoid finding this inconsistency in the dialogue, we may take Socrates to mean that an ignorant person has insatiable desires, and for his own good must be prevented from satisfying them; but (on this view) once he learns what is really good for him, the insatiable desires will disappear and no further restraint will be needed. According to this eudaemonist interpretation of the remarks on psychic order, the *Gorgias* differs from the shorter dialogues insofar as it recognizes that the excessive satisfaction of some desires actually causes us to be indifferent to considerations of our longer-term interest; but Socrates still believes (on this view) that once we notice this feature of these desires, we will no longer be tempted to satisfy them excessively.[8]

It is difficult to decide whether Plato does or does not mean to reject psychological eudaemonism. If he allows incontinence, and so rejects psychological eudaemonism, he gives further point and force to the claims about psychic order, and this would be the better interpretation if the question of consistency did not arise. But the eudaemonist interpretation cannot be ruled out.

Even if Plato intends to reject eudaemonism and to recognize the possibility of incontinence, he apparently has not worked out an account of desire that would justify his position. In reflecting on the nature and the importance of rational agency, he suggests that not all desires are related to rational agency in the same way, but he does not develop this suggestion very far.

81. The Adaptive Conception of Happiness

Since Plato's views on rational agency suggest to him that the hedonist conception of happiness is wrong, it is reasonable for him to say what conception of happiness fits a correct account of the nature and importance of rational prudence. Socrates presents an adaptive conception of happiness in opposition to Callicles' expansive conception. Why should we accept the adaptive conception?

Socrates suggests that Callicles' expansive view of happiness rests on a confusion. We might be tempted to agree with Callicles if we believe, as Socrates does, that happiness consists in the satisfaction of desires, and we also assume, contrary to Socrates, that some demanding level of desires must be taken for granted. On this view, if I lack the resources needed to satisfy my desires, or if ill fortune interferes with their execution, I lack happiness because I have my desires frustrated. The elements of my happiness, on this view, must include all that I need for the satisfaction of my desires; hence they must include external goods.

Socrates argues that this view mistakenly assumes that my happiness requires the satisfaction of the desires I actually have. If my desires grow greater, then I must, on this view, find more and more resources to satisfy them (494b6). Such a view of desire and happiness ignores the plasticity and adaptiveness of desire. We do not necessarily think ourselves unhappy simply because we cannot fulfill clearly unfeasible desires that we might have had or once did have. The rational person will react by giving up the desires that have become unfeasible; once he has given them up, the fact that they are not satisfied no longer causes unhappiness. Since the loss of external goods causes no loss of happiness, they are not necessary for happiness.

We might object that our desires are not always plastic. Even if we realize that a desire is unfeasible, we may retain it, and so we may continue to suffer from its frustration. Socrates can answer this objection, if we concede that the persistence of unfeasible desires is always bad for us; for such desires will disappear (according to Socratic psychological eudaemonism) once we know that they are bad for us. And so failure to achieve external goods will not be bad for people who know that persistent unsatisfied desires are bad for them.

Just as the loss of external goods does not by itself cause unhappiness, so also their presence does not by itself secure happiness. We can still misuse them; however many we have, we may have such extravagant and unfeasible desires that we are still unsatisfied. Both in favourable and in unfavourable conditions we need feasible desires; according to Socrates, once we have them, we can secure happiness through the fulfillment of our desires. A wise person will see that he is better off with feasible desires; if changing external conditions make some of his desires unfeasible, he will give them up. By adapting his desires to suit the external conditions, he will secure his happiness whatever the conditions may be.

The adaptive conception of happiness does not tell us what sorts of desires we ought to form for the sake of our happiness; it sets out from common-sense views about the sorts of things that are worth pursuing, as Socrates does in the *Euthydemus* (279a–c). It advises us on the regulation, cultivation, elimination, and satisfaction of our initial desires so that they become suitably adapted to circumstances. If self-sufficiency is to be identified with the complete fulfillment of desires, it seems reasonable to adapt our desires in ways that secure their satisfaction.

82. Wisdom and Happiness

This adaptive conception of happiness fills a gap in the argument of the shorter dialogues, since these commit Socrates to claims about ways to achieve happiness but do not present any definite conception of happiness. The adaptive conception explains and supports some of the claims in the shorter dialogues.

In the *Euthydemus* Socrates claims both (1) that external goods are not genuine goods (*Euthd.* 281e3–4), since wisdom is the only genuine good, and (2) that under the control of wisdom they are 'greater goods' (281d8) than their opposites. The first claim seems to be required by Socrates' conviction that virtue is sufficient for happiness. This conviction is supported in turn by his demand for whole-hearted and unreserved commitment to virtue.[9] This demand is easier to understand if Socrates claims virtue is sufficient for happiness, but the *Euthydemus* and the other shorter dialogues do not explain what conception of happiness would support this strong claim about virtue.

An adaptive conception of happiness supports Socrates' claim. According to this conception, the wise person knows that an adaptive strategy secures happiness; this wisdom secures his happiness. If virtue is, as Socrates believes, the knowledge of good and evil, then virtue is sufficient for happiness. A virtuous person has seen that his happiness requires him to have flexible and feasible desires; he therefore cultivates these desires and eliminates others, and so ensures the satisfaction of his desires. He therefore ensures his happiness, and any loss of external goods is no threat to it. Since the virtues cause us to abandon unfeasible desires and to adapt our desires to our circumstances, they contribute instrumentally to our happiness. On this point as on others, the *Gorgias* clarifies Socrates' view of happiness and thereby clarifies some of his claims about the virtues.

83. Happiness and External Goods

Socrates does not simply claim that wisdom is sufficient for happiness; he also claims that recognized external goods are preferable to their opposites.[10] Does the adaptive conception of happiness help to explain how these claims are consistent?

Socrates mentions external goods in a list that he offers to Polus as a list of what common sense would count as goods (467e4–6). He says he would wish neither to do nor to suffer injustice (469c1). Later he allows the reflective pilot to wonder if he has benefited or harmed people by saving them from drowning (511e6–512b2). In these passages Socrates simply asks his interlocutor about commonly recognized goods; nothing in the argument depends on his agreeing with the interlocutor that these are genuine goods. The passages therefore provide very weak evidence for the view that he really counts external goods as goods. When he says he would not wish to suffer injustice, Socrates refrains from saying he would wish not to suffer it.[11] He has no reason to wish for it, since suffering injustice is in itself no benefit to him, and he can say this even if not suffering injustice is no benefit to him either.[12]

Sometimes, however, Socrates seems to believe that the presence of some external goods is more beneficial than their absence. The person who is killed unjustly is less wretched and pitiable, according to Socrates, than the one who kills unjustly (469b3–6), and doing injustice is a greater evil than suffering it (509c6–7). These remarks might be taken to suggest, even if they do not strictly imply, that there is something pitiable about being killed unjustly and something bad about suffering injustice. At least Socrates seems to concede that there is some benefit to be gained from not suffering injustice as well as from not doing injustice (509c8–d2).

If these passages are meant to imply that external goods are genuine goods, then they agree with the apparent suggestion in the *Apology* that virtue actually makes wealth and other things goods (*Ap.* 30b2–4).[13] But this suggestion seems to contradict Socrates' claim that virtue is sufficient for happiness and that therefore the good person cannot be harmed. For if nothing is good without contributing to happiness, external goods must contribute to a virtuous person's happiness if they are really goods; but if they are goods, then the loss of them should harm the virtuous person, contrary to Socrates' claim that the good person cannot be harmed.

Some of Socrates' claims would be clearer if he decided between different criteria for being a good. He might claim either (1) that x is good for me if and only if it is necessary for my happiness; (2) that x is good for me if and only if it makes me happier than I would be without it; or (3) that x is good for me if and only if it positively promotes my plans for achieving my happiness. Since he does not say what criterion he relies on, it is not clear whether an apparent denial in one place that external goods are goods really denies what he affirms when he affirms in another place that they really are goods.

If Socrates accepts an adaptive conception of happiness, his different claims about external goods can be interpreted or clarified or modified so that they make a consistent position. The adaptive conception makes it clear that the three criteria give different answers about which things are goods. Such things as health sometimes meet the third criterion but do not meet the other two criteria, whereas illness does not usually meet the third criterion. Only wisdom meets all three criteria.

This third criterion helps to explain the claim in the *Euthydemus* that health is sometimes a greater good than illness.[14] If wise people want to act, they will often find it easier to act as they want to if they are healthy than if they are sick. If I decide to walk twenty miles and I am in robust health, I can do this easily, but if I am less healthy I will need to plan my journey more carefully. To this extent, health positively promotes my plans, whereas illness does not; although wise people 'use' both health or illness, depending on their circumstances, illness is something that they must cope with rather than something that positively helps them. Still, Socrates suggests, if I plan wisely I will get to where I want to go in either case, so that I am on the whole no better off from being healthier than I would be if I were less healthy. Health itself, on this view, is not good, because what is good about using health well is the use that is made of it, not the health itself; the use that wise people make of health and the use they make of illness are equally good and equally guarantee happiness.

If, then, Socrates holds an adaptive account of happiness, he has some reason for allowing that external goods are goods (since they satisfy the third criterion) and some reason for denying this (since they do not satisfy the first two criteria). If Socrates is not sure about which of these three criteria are correct, or if he has not adequately distinguished them, it is easy to see why he might be inclined both to affirm and to deny that external goods are really goods. His statement of his view is obscure at some points, and both the view itself and the obscurities in his statement of it are intelligible results of an adaptive conception of happiness.

84. Happiness, Virtue, and Justice

Both Polus and Callicles deny that other-regarding justice promotes the agent's happiness. As Polus sees, the whole point of justice seems to be to limit my pursuit of my own interest in the interest of other people. Hence Callicles claims that the conventional rules of justice result from a conspiracy of the weak people against the strong people who are capable of defending themselves in the pursuit of their own interest (482e–484c). He rejects other-regarding justice because he believes that it requires us to restrain our desires in ways that conflict with our happiness. Socrates argues against this opposition to justice by showing that Callicles' conception of happiness is mistaken and, in particular, that Callicles underestimates the importance of rational order.

Something more is needed, however, if Socrates is to defend the strong claim he affirms, that justice is actually sufficient for happiness (470e9–11, 507b8–c7).[15] If he holds an adaptive conception of happiness, can he defend this strong claim about justice?

I will believe that happiness requires me to be unjust or intemperate, if I want the external goods secured by these vices. If I cheat, I can get the money I think I need to satisfy my desires; if I do not cheat but forgo the money, then apparently I lose something I need for happiness. An adaptive conception of happiness, however, implies that this argument is mistaken. If I forgo an external good, I simply need to adapt my desires to the new circumstances, and I need not forgo any happiness.

Polus' and Callicles' objections to justice rest on a non-adaptive conception of happiness that exaggerates the value of external goods. If we see that virtue is not sufficient for external goods, and we believe that external goods are necessary for happiness, then we will deny that virtue is sufficient for happiness. If, however, we accept an adaptive conception of happiness, we cannot claim that external goods are necessary for happiness; hence we must agree that virtue is sufficient by itself.[16]

Socrates does not state this argument connecting the adaptive conception of happiness with the conclusion that virtue is sufficient for happiness. However, he speaks as though he had proved this conclusion, he accepts the adaptive conception of happiness, and he suggests no other argument in support of his conclusion. This is a good reason for believing that he accepts the argument we have given, and hence for believing that he takes the adaptive conception seriously.

85. The Treatment of the Interlocutor

Now that we have examined the main ethical argument of the *Gorgias,* we ought to consider what the dialogue adds to the other Socratic dialogues. Socrates sets out to show that his elenctic method supports the strong moral conclusions that he affirms. Does he show this?

In the shorter Socratic dialogues, the role of the interlocutors seems to prevent the discussion from vindicating Socrates' more controversial claims; the crucial moves are not shown to have any rational claim on anyone besides this or that particular interlocutor. Socrates and the interlocutor are allowed to take for granted controversial assumptions about the virtues. They agree on the names of the virtues (*La.* 199d4–e3) and that a virtue must be fine and beneficial for the agent (*La.* 192c4–d8, 193d4). These agreements are never questioned even when they conflict with other beliefs about the virtues.

In the *Protagoras* Socrates is less willing to rest his conclusions on the agreement of this or that interlocutor; he recognizes that he needs to take a more self-critical attitude to the basic agreements than he takes in the shorter dialogues.[17] Still, the self-criticism does not go very far. Although hedonism is challenged and defended, it receives no critical examination; and the crucial assumption that each virtue, as commonly named, is fine and beneficial is still left unchallenged.

In the *Gorgias* Socrates tries not to rely simply on the agreement of a particular interlocutor. He still insists that he wants the sincere agreement of his interlocutor; in contrast to orators who introduce witnesses to sway one's judgment irrationally, the only witness he wants is the interlocutor himself (471e–472c). As usual, the interlocutors must accept the conclusions only if they still stick to their initial agreements (479c4–6, 480a1–4, 480e1–4), but Socrates claims that they have a fair opportunity for retraction or second thoughts about the initial agreements (457e-458e, 461a4–b2; cf. *Pr.* 354e8–355a5).

To show that crucial and controversial premisses are not taken for granted without good reason, Plato uses a device that is not used in earlier dialogues and introduces successive interlocutors who challenge the concessions made by their predecessors. In the *Protagoras* Socrates considers what a third party might say and how he and Protagoras ought to reply to the third party. In the *Gorgias* Plato presents the different views through participants in the dialogue. Callicles' views are not meant to be constructed simply for Plato's convenience, so that Socrates can easily refute them; they are a statement of views that Socrates' and Plato's contemporaries take seriously and that present serious objections to Socratic ethics. In his choice of interlocutors and the views they put forward, Plato wants to show that he is not leaving reasonable objections unheard.

86. The Constructive Use of the Elenchos

Plato intends his choice of interlocutors to support his claim that the elenchos reaches positive results and gives good reasons for believing that they are true. He also makes this claim in the shorter dialogues; the *Crito* presents the clearest statement of the constructive role of the elenchos, and in doing so provides a starting point for issues and arguments in the *Gorgias*.[18] None of the shorter dialogues explains how Socrates could support these claims.

The *Gorgias,* however, tries to support them. Socrates says he has proved that his conclusions are true, not only that this particular interlocutor must accept them. In arguing with Polus he claims to have 'demonstrated' (*apodeiknunai*[19]) the truth of his claims by refuting Polus' rejection of them (*G.* 479e7, 480e3). He tells Callicles that if the two of them can agree, their agreement will reach the truth (487e6–7). In concluding the refutation of Callicles, he claims to have proved by iron and adamantine arguments that his position is true; and he supports his claim by saying that while he does not know how things are,[20] no one has ever been able to disagree with his position without becoming ridiculous (*G.* 508e6–509b1).

This last passage deserves special attention. In successive sentences Socrates claims that he has demonstrated the truth of his claim by the elenchos and that he does not know how things are. The next remark shows how Socrates thinks his two claims are consistent: by showing how anyone disagreeing with him becomes ridiculous, he has shown enough to prove his own position, but not enough to justify him in claiming to know how things are. In this deliberate juxtaposition of his confident conclusion with his disavowal of knowledge, Socrates implies that his frequent disavowal of knowledge is not a disavowal of positive convictions.[21]

Part of Plato's reason for claiming to have proved his conclusions is clear from his choice of interlocutors. This is not enough, however. It is useless for Plato to introduce the right interlocutors if he does not argue fairly against them. If Socrates is an eristic, as Callicles believes, then his success in argument is no reason to believe that the argument is rationally compelling. Socrates wins, according to Callicles, simply because the interlocutor does not see through the eristic tricks that Socrates uses to confuse him; once we see these limitations in the interlocutors, we will no longer be tempted to believe Socrates' conclusions (482c4–e2, 489b7–c1).[22]

Polus and Callicles criticize Socrates not only for his eristic tactics but also for his manipulation of the interlocutor's sense of 'shame' or 'embarrassment' (*aischunē,* 461b3–e4, 482d2–e2). If we have correctly described the method of the Socratic elenchos, it is neither surprising nor unreasonable for Socrates to appeal on some occasions to his interlocutors' sense of shame. For he appeals not simply to their sense of consistency but also to their moral judgment; since feelings of shame and repulsion often reflect our moral reactions and moral judgments, they may be a good guide to the sort of answer that is relevant to Socrates' questions. Socrates suggests that someone like Laches will of course regard bravery as fine, and Laches strongly agrees (192c5–7); he would clearly find it shocking to deny that bravery is fine, and his view that this would be shocking and shameful legitimately guides him in answering Socrates' questions. On the other hand, a sense of shame can be misleading. Laches suggests it is 'daring' or 'presumptuous' of Nicias to reject the common view that people can be brave without wisdom, since he is refusing to allow these people their due honour (*La.* 197a1–5, 197c2–4). In this case Nicias is right not to be shocked by the apparent affront that his views offer to common sense.

The unreliability of the interlocutor's shame may explain why the *Protagoras,* in contrast to the shorter dialogues, avoids appeals to shame. Protagoras claims on his own behalf that he would be ashamed to say that someone could be both temperate and unjust or to admit that knowledge can be overcome (333c1–3, 352c8–d3); but in both cases Socrates refuses to rely on Protagoras' shame and insists on discussing the views of people who lack Protagoras' scruples. He does not disagree with Protagoras' conclusion in either case, but he does not want to rely on shame as its only support.

It is reasonable, then, for the *Gorgias* to avoid appeals to shame. Socrates is not saying that it is bad to be moved by shame in considering some of the questions that he puts forward, but he does not want the appeal to shame to stand alone. If someone challenges the appropriateness of shame in a particular case, then it is useless to appeal to an admission that rests simply on a particular interlocutor's sense of shame. For this reason the discussion with Callicles elaborately sets aside any appeal to anyone's sense of shame (494c4–495c2).[23] Socrates does not allow Callicles to escape from the consequences of his position by resorting to shame, but requires Callicles to admit that he sincerely assents to the consequences of his claim that the good and the pleasant are the same.[24] As an ancient commentator says, it is Callicles' outlook, not simply his assertion, that is refuted.[25]

Socrates states his conclusions about shame and truth in an important remark to Callicles: 'And it turns out that those things you thought Polus conceded to me out of shame were true . . . ; and it turns out that anyone who is to practise rhetoric correctly must be just . . . , which Polus in turn said Gorgias had conceded out of shame' (508b7–c3). Polus alleged that Gorgias had been too ashamed to say what he really believed and so had answered Socrates insincerely (461b3–c4). Callicles alleged that Polus had done the same thing (482c4–e2) because 'he was ashamed to say what he thought' (482e2). Earlier Socrates had agreed that Gorgias and Polus were shamed by his questions (494d2–4); in our present passage he neither endorses nor rejects the allegation that they were insincere in their answers to his questions. But he firmly rejects the suggestion that only shame could explain their answers; he argues that, in fact, they had good reason for agreeing with him apart from any feelings of shame.[26] The argument with Callicles is meant to show that when appeals to shame are set aside, the interlocutors still have good reason to agree with Socrates.[27]

Callicles has to agree, then, that the conclusions that he thought Gorgias and Polus had accepted because of shame have actually been proved to be true (508a8–c3). Plato has tried to assure the reader that the conclusions of the dialogue cannot be attacked on the ground that the interlocutor is too sympathetic to Socrates' position, that Socrates uses eristic tactics, or that he exploits the interlocutor's shame. The Socratic dialogue retains its character of an encounter between two people, rather than a systematic exposition of a theory; but Plato seeks to assure us that this feature of the dialogue does not deprive us of good reason for believing the conclusions of the argument to be true. On the contrary, Plato seeks to show that the argument that can overcome Callicles' objections gives us a good reason to take its conclusion seriously.

What, then, does Plato rely on? Why should we suppose that the points accepted by Callicles have some rational appeal beyond their appeal to a particular interlocutor? Socrates disclaims any ability to find arguments that will seem immediately persuasive to many people on first hearing, but he says, 'I know how to make one person a witness to the things I am saying, the person with whom I am having the discussion' (474a5–6). In claiming that he knows how to make an interlocutor agree with him, Socrates is not claiming any particular skill in argumentative tactics; if these were responsible for the agreement, we would have no reason to believe that Socrates' view has been proved to be true. He must mean that his moral position will convince any rational interlocutor who examines it on its merits and is not put off by its initial appearance of paradox. To see whether Socrates is entitled to this claim, we must consider the character and results of his moral argument.

87. The Contribution of the *Gorgias* to Socratic Moral Theory

The *Gorgias* goes beyond asserting the supreme value of justice and gives some definite argument for Socrates' claim. It addresses the sort of opponent who never appears in the shorter dialogues: an opponent who disagrees strongly with Socrates' central moral claims and in particular rejects his views about the value of the recognized virtues. This sort of opponent is not given a voice in the earlier dialogues; the *Charmides*, for instance, does not doubt the value of temperance, as Callicles does, although the introduction of Charmides and Critias as interlocutors would have made this a highly pertinent issue. In the *Gorgias* Socrates abandons the indirect approach to radical critics that he follows in the shorter dialogues. He defends the guiding principles that underlie his use of the elenchos. In particular, he defends the claim that every virtue must be both fine and beneficial for the agent. Instead of assuming that we regard other-regarding justice as a virtue, he takes on an interlocutor who rejects other-regarding justice, and he tries to explain why such an interlocutor must also reject rational prudence.

Socrates' argument about bravery explains why he believes that the argument with Callicles supports conclusions that have a reasonable claim on any rational agent, not simply on someone with the peculiarities of Callicles. Socrates suggests that if Callicles does not repudiate the coward's way of seeking maximum pleasure, he cannot endorse rational prudence at all, but must reject the value that he clearly attaches to resoluteness and rational planning. The value to be attached to rational planning is explained by appeal to an adaptive view of happiness, from which Socrates defends the sufficiency of virtue for happiness.

In focussing on rational prudence, Plato identifies one possible basis for an argument that every rational agent has to take seriously. Here the treatment of Socratic method and the treatment of Socratic ethics in the *Gorgias* reinforce each other. We might say that Plato realizes that elenctic argument ought to reach people who disagree quite deeply with Socrates, and that once he sees this, he works out the line of argument that ought to convince such people. Alternatively, we might say that Plato sees how to defend Socratic claims about justice, and that once he sees this, he sees how he can argue successfully with critics of conventional morality. Perhaps neither of these stories is quite right; Plato may take both steps at once without regarding one as prior to the other. In any case, he presents an ethical theory that has a rational claim on people who might fairly be unmoved by the sorts of arguments that are offered in the shorter dialogues.

This argument suggests why Socrates believes he can convince any rational interlocutor who participates honestly and competently in an elenchos that Socrates is right about justice and temperance. He implies that a rational interlocutor must have the characteristics of the rational agent who benefits from the virtues. To participate competently in the elenchos, we must be able to revise our beliefs in the right way, so that we retain those beliefs that are more important and abandon the less important ones that conflict with them. To estimate relative importance, we must be able to distinguish the beliefs we have good reasons for holding from those we happen to be especially attached to here and now. We may have been extremely confident, for instance, about the truth of Laches' initial claims about bravery, but if we are guided by this unreflective confidence, we will abandon beliefs that further consideration would show to be much more broadly connected to our other beliefs. The minimal competence we need is the ability to distinguish the current strength of our conviction from the rational warrant of our conviction, and the ability to revise beliefs in accordance with their rational warrant, not in accordance with their current strength.

Socrates suggests that if we draw this distinction among beliefs, we must equally draw it among desires, and we must prefer the desires with the greater rational warrant over those with greater current strength. In advocating bravery over cowardice, Callicles implicitly accepts this distinction among desires; brave people act on their conviction about what is most worth doing and discount the current strength of their desire to escape the danger. Socrates argues that when Callicles generalizes this attitude, so that he does not confine it arbitrarily to bravery, he will see that it supports a preference for temperance and justice as well.

If this argument succeeds, it supports Socrates' conviction that he can give any rational interlocutor compelling reasons to 'witness' to the truth of the Socratic position. For the argument does not depend on moral convictions or preferences that some people share with Socrates but others reject; it depends only on preferences that must be attributed to a rational interlocutor.

This ambitious line of argument succeeds only if Socrates' claims about happiness are plausible and the conclusions he draws about virtue are justified. It is better to postpone a discussion of these questions until we come to the *Republic,* for we will see that Plato's further thoughts about the argument of the *Gorgias* help to explain some of the distinctive features of the moral outlook of the *Republic.*[28] At any rate, in seeing the possibility of such an argument, Plato moves beyond the ambitions of the shorter Socratic dialogues; the *Republic* is a further attempt to carry out the task that is first proposed in the *Gorgias.*

9

Socratic Method and Socratic Ethics: The *Meno*

88. Questions about Socratic Method

In the early dialogues Socrates relies on the elenchos, but does not normally explain why he believes he is entitled to rely on it. In the *Gorgias* Plato is more self-conscious; he tries to defend some of the guiding principles of Socratic inquiry. In the *Meno* he is still more self-conscious; he examines some of the basic assumptions that underlie both Socrates' method and his conception of virtue.

The dialogue focusses on knowledge, and especially on two claims about knowledge that Socrates makes in the early dialogues: (1) It is important to look for a definition of a virtue, and since he cannot give such a definition, he lacks knowledge about the virtue. (2) Knowledge is both necessary and sufficient for virtue. The first part of the *Meno* examines Socrates' first claim, and the second part examines his second claim.

In the first part Plato tries to explain what a Socratic definition is and why it is relevant to knowledge. In the early dialogues Socrates readily assumes that certain things are virtues and relies on quite controversial assumptions about what a virtue must be like; but he never tries to justify these assumptions by raising the general question that is raised in the *Meno*.[1] In the second part of the dialogue, Plato considers some arguments for identifying virtue with knowledge and apparently rejects them.

We might reasonably wonder whether the same sort of knowledge is relevant to each of these Socratic claims. The first claim seems to refer to the theoretical knowledge that concerns someone who wants to understand virtue; the second seems to refer to the practical knowledge that concerns someone who wants to be virtuous. Socrates, however, seems to assume that the same kind of knowledge is relevant in both claims, for he seems to regard failure in Socratic inquiry as a sign of lack of virtue (*Ap.* 29e3–30a2).[2] The *Meno* might be expected to clarify this issue; either Plato ought to reject Socrates' apparent assumption, or he ought to explain why the assumption is justified.

89. Inquiry and Knowledge

When Meno asks Socrates whether virtue is teachable, Socrates suggests that an Athenian will give a modest answer:

> Stranger, it looks as though I seem to you to be some blessed sort of person; for I seem to you to know whether virtue is something teachable or how it is produced. But in fact I am so far from knowing whether it is something teachable or not teachable that in fact I don't even know at all what on earth it is. (71a3–7)

This Athenian modesty is supposed to come as a surprise to a Thessalian such as Meno, since the Thessalians are used to hearing people like Gorgias, who answered questions like Meno's 'fearlessly and magnificently,[3] as one would expect in people who know' (70b7–8). Gorgias is confident in his ability to answer any question that people ask him; in the *Gorgias* Plato contrasts this self-confidence with Socrates' disavowal of knowledge (*G.* 447c–d). The *Meno* marks the same contrast; Socrates cannot give the sort of confident answer that would reflect a claim to knowledge. Socrates is too generous, however, in suggesting that such modesty is characteristic of Athenians; Anytus' behaviour in this dialogue shows that, as Socrates claims in the *Apology*, he is the only one who recognizes his lack of knowledge.

When Socrates disavows any knowledge about virtue, Meno is surprised (71b9–c2), and Socrates surprises him further by saying that he has never met anyone else who knows what virtue is (71c3–4). Meno asks whether Socrates did not think Gorgias knew what virtue is (71c5–7), clearly assuming that Gorgias did know. The demand for knowledge is not forced on Meno; he assumes that the demand is legitimate and easily met. Plato suggests that Socrates and Meno must have in mind some distinction between knowledge and mere belief; the gradual articulation of the distinction is a task for the dialogue.

Socrates professes inability to answer Meno's question because he is so far from knowing whether virtue is teachable that he does not even know what virtue is; he assumes that if he did know anything about virtue he would have to know what virtue is. Socrates supports this assumption by suggesting that if he did not know who Meno is, he could not know whether Meno is handsome or rich or well-born (71b1–8). Meno does not challenge Socrates' suggestion. He assures Socrates that 'it is not difficult to say' what virtue is (71e1), and that 'there is no puzzle[4] to say about virtue what it is' (72a2).

So far, then, Meno is not surprised that Socrates is looking for knowledge, or that he takes knowledge of whether virtue can be taught to require knowledge of what it is. He is surprised only by Socrates' profession of failure in these apparently rather easy cognitive tasks.

90. Accounts and Definitions

In the early dialogues the interlocutors readily agree to answer the 'What is it?' question (*La.* 190c6, 190e4; cf. *HMa.* 286c8); they agree that it is reasonable to look for some account of a virtue. It takes them longer to see that the right sort of account is a Socratic definition, giving a single description of the F by which all F things are F.[5] In the *Meno* Plato tries to justify the demand for a Socratic definition.

Sometimes Socrates objects that the interlocutors' initial accounts are not comprehensive enough; he tells Laches and Charmides that many other types of actions and people besides the ones they mentioned are brave and temperate. Similarly, Socrates criticizes Euthyphro for telling him about only 'one or two of the many piouses' (*Eu.* 6d9–10). Meno's first answer, however, shows that the demand for comprehensiveness does not justify the demand for a Socratic definition. He suggests that a complete list of the many different types of virtuous action gives a suitably comprehensive account of virtue, and so he mentions the various qualities, abilities, and accomplishments that equip different classes of people (men, women, children, slaves, etc.) for different social statuses and roles (71e–72a, 91a).

Meno treats virtue as essentially heterogeneous. He thinks first of all of what an aristocrat is expected to do and expects that virtue will equip him to do it in the ways that bring honour and success. He is not necessarily indifferent, however, to other-regarding morality; when he speaks of conducting the city's affairs finely, he may be alluding to the demands of justice. Someone who recognizes these distinct, uncoordinated, and potentially conflicting elements in the common-sense view of virtue might well conclude that the sort of account that Meno offers must be right. The potential conflict between the two aspects of virtue is not recognized in the shorter Socratic dialogues; it is easier to see in the *Protagoras* and *Gorgias*.[6] It is expressed in Meno's list of the types of virtue.

In contrast to Meno, Socrates looks for one and the same non-disjunctive characteristic of being F that is present in all instances of F. He compares the parallel question about what a bee is. Once Meno agrees that 'one bee does not differ at all from another in so far as they are bees' (72a8–9), Socrates makes the parallel claim about health, largeness, and strength, and invites Meno to agree that it holds for virtue as well:

> Even if they are many and of all sorts, still they have some one identical form because of which (*di'ho*) they are virtues, focussing on which the respondent can presumably show well to the questioner what in fact virtue is. (72c6–d1)

Meno is not sure that the parallel claim is true in this case (72d4–73a5), but Socrates persuades him that such an account of virtue must be possible. Meno has assumed that virtuous people all perform their function well (73a6–7), and he now agrees that good performance of one's function involves justice and temperance, so that the same conditions must be satisfied in each case (73a6–c5).

91. Definition, Explanation, and Knowledge

The agreement between Socrates and Meno relies on assumptions that certainly need further discussion.[7] For the moment, however, we ought to notice why this discussion of definition is relevant to the initial questions about knowledge. In suggesting that different types of virtue have 'some one identical form because of which (*di'ho*) they are virtues' (72c7–8), Socrates suggests that we can recognize some one thing that explains why we count all the items on Meno's list as genuine varieties of virtue. Once Meno concedes this, he concedes that a Socratic definition is relevant to the previous demand for knowledge. For the sort of confidence that he displayed, following Gorgias, in listing the types of virtue would be challenged if he could not say why a particular item really belongs on the list; and so the ability to answer that question is necessary for the warranted confidence that Meno connects with knowledge.

This discussion, then, looks forward to Socrates' later claim that knowledge differs from mere belief because it includes 'reasoning about an explanation'. A definition of virtue tells us the explanation of why different characteristics are virtues, and this explanation, Socrates suggests, is necessary for the sort of knowledge that Meno seeks. Meno has a reason for taking Socratic definition to be important for knowledge about virtue, and so Socrates is justified in trying to clarify the further features of an adequate definition (73c6–79e6).

Meno agrees that an adequate definition has all these further features; but once they are made clear to him, he still finds himself unable to produce a definition of virtue. It is not only Meno who fails; the interlocutors in the early dialogues also find it difficult to answer Socrates' demand, and Socrates insists that he cannot answer it himself. Why are definitions so difficult to find? We might reconsider some of the features that Socrates attributes to an adequate definition and argue that an acceptable definition may lack these features; if Socrates made less strict demands on definitions, they might be easier to find.

This criticism of Socrates certainly deserves to be explored, but Meno does not consider it.[8] He believes he has found a more basic objection to Socrates' search for a definition. If he is right about this, then it is pointless to modify Socrates' particular demands on definitions, since the search for a definition will turn out to be misguided in the first place. Meno's objection, therefore, needs to be answered.

92. The Paradox of Inquiry

In Meno's view, it is Socrates' disavowal of knowledge that makes the whole inquiry into virtue futile:

> And in what way, Socrates, will you look for that thing which you don't know at all what it is? For what sort of thing among the things you don't know will you put forward and look for? And on the other hand, however true it might be that you happen on it, how will you know that this is the thing that you didn't know? (80d5–8)

Meno suggests that if Socrates really does not know what F is, then he fails the minimum necessary conditions for inquiry into F.[9]

The difficulty raised by Meno would not seem so compelling if Socrates had not affirmed that knowledge about F requires knowledge of what F is. If we could know some facts about F without knowing what F is, then perhaps we could know enough about F to pick it out as an object for inquiry. Socrates rules out this answer. Since he also insists that knowledge of what F is requires a definition of F, Meno's difficulty seems to arise. For Socrates believes we discover the definition of F through inquiry into F; but if we cannot begin inquiry into F without already knowing what F is, we must know the definition of F before we can begin the inquiry that is supposed to lead us to the definition of F.

Meno's argument, suitably expanded, seems to be this:

1. If we do not know what F is, we do not know anything about F.
2. If we do not know anything about F, we cannot distinguish F from other things we do not know.
3. If we cannot distinguish F from other things we do not know, we cannot inquire about F.
4. Hence, if we do not know what F is, we cannot inquire about F.
5. If we cannot define F, we do not know what F is.
6. Socrates and Meno cannot define virtue.
7. Therefore, they do not know what virtue is.
8. Therefore, they cannot inquire about virtue.

This expansion shows how Meno's assumptions about knowledge and inquiry—in (2) through (4)—together with Socrates' assumptions about knowledge and definition—in (1) and (5)—result in the paradox; if either set of assumptions were rejected, the paradox would be dissolved. One conception of knowledge makes Meno's assumptions plausible; another conception makes Socrates' assumptions plausible.

Socrates has given some reason for preferring his assumptions about knowledge over Meno's present assumptions. Indeed, he has made it clear that at the beginning of the dialogue Meno agreed with Socrates' assumptions about knowledge rather than with the assumptions that generate Meno's Paradox. Socrates suggested that Gorgias' authoritative confidence in his answers to everyone's questions would be justified if he really knew what he was talking about; Meno asserted that Gorgias had the appropriate knowledge. Next Socrates showed that Meno's list gave insufficient basis for justified confidence. He invited Meno to consider why his list of virtues included only these specific items and no others; if Gorgias (and Meno on his behalf) could not answer this question, then he would have no appropriate basis for confidence in his list. Gorgias' and Meno's own implicit conception of knowledge as the basis for justified confidence shows why Socrates is right to reject Meno's minimal conditions for knowledge.[10]

If Meno's assumptions about knowledge are rejected, then his conditions for inquiry should be rejected too. The assumptions about knowledge shared by Socrates and Meno at the beginning of the dialogue suggest that we do not need knowledge to begin inquiry; if we are to distinguish one object of inquiry from others, we do not seem to need the sort of cognitive state that Meno ascribed to Gorgias. However conjectural and tentative our belief about F might be, it might still serve to identity F as an object of inquiry. To resolve Meno's Paradox, Socrates needs to say that inquiry requires initial belief, not initial knowledge, about the object of inquiry.[11]

93. A Successful Inquiry

Socrates, however, does not draw an explicit distinction between knowledge and belief. Instead, he tells a story about the immortal soul and the knowledge it possessed before its incarnation. Although he expresses some reservations about the story as a whole (86b6–7), he defends the belief in prenatal knowledge by engaging in a discussion with a slave[12] about geometry.

This discussion with the slave is meant to recall the discussion with Meno.[13] The slave begins, as Meno did, by being confident that he knows the answer to Socrates' question (82e5–6); he shares this confidence with many interlocutors (cf. 71e1; *La.* 190e4; *Eu.* 4b9–5e2), who do not see that there is anything difficult about Socrates' questions. Socrates insists, as he regularly does, that his role is simply to ask questions and not to oppose one conviction with another (82e4–6). The questions cause the slave to see a contradiction between his general claim (that if one figure has sides double the length of the sides of a second figure, the area of the first figure is also twice that of the second figure) and what he thinks most reasonable in the particular case presented to him. At this point the slave is puzzled and 'numb', as Meno was when he despaired of making progress (84a3–c6; cf. 79e7–80b4; *La.* 193d11–e6; *Eu.* 11b6–8; *R.* 334b7–9).

Socrates urges that this state of puzzlement is a precondition for making progress (84c4–9; cf. *Sph.* 230c3–d4). He does not suggest that puzzlement and awareness of one's own ignorance is simply a stimulus to modesty in the assertion of one's views, or that it should make us reluctant to assert any positive claims. At this point the discussion with the slave continues where the discussion with Meno left off; further questioning causes the slave to find the right answer. When the right answer has been found, Socrates says that questioning has aroused true beliefs without knowledge in the slave, and that further questioning of the right sort will lead to accurate knowledge about the same things (85c6–d1).[14] His present state of belief without knowledge is like a dream (85c9–10), and knowledge is what corresponds to being awake (86a6–8).

From this discussion with the slave Socrates draws three conclusions:

1. The slave brings or 'gathers up' (*analambanein*, 85d4) the answer from within himself, since Socrates does not tell him the answer but he has to discover it in answer to Socrates' questions. When he has pursued inquiry further, to the point where he has achieved knowledge, he will have gathered up knowledge from within himself (85d3–4).
2. This process of gathering the right answer from within oneself is actually recollection, the gradual recovery of knowledge that we possessed in a previous existence but have forgotten in the meantime (85d6–7).[15]

3. We ought to be confident and optimistic in inquiry (86b6–c2). In particular, we ought to regard the interlocutor's puzzlement not as a reason for despondency, but simply as a necessary preliminary to progress.

Socrates declares that he is confident about his third conclusion, but 'would not be altogether insistent in defence of the argument, as far as the other points are concerned' (86b6–7). If Socrates means to endorse only the third conclusion while hesitating about the other two, his position is strange; for why should we accept the third conclusion if the discussion with the slave has given us no grounds for it? His position is more reasonable if he means that we should commit ourselves definitely only to the parts of the argument that are needed to support the third conclusion. If this is what he means, then he probably means to endorse the first conclusion and to express hesitation about the second; for if we agree that the slave has gathered up true beliefs from within himself, we have some reason for confidence about the prospects of inquiry, even if we are not convinced that this process of gathering up is also a process of literal recollection of what he once knew.

94. A Defence of Socratic Inquiry

The discussion with the slave is meant to give us grounds for confidence in Socrates' inquiries. To see how it does this, we ought to consider (1) how it gives grounds for confidence in some Socratic inquiry and (2) whether the same grounds for confidence apply to the sort of moral inquiry that goes on in the *Meno* and in the Socratic dialogues. The two questions need to be distinguished, since the discussion with the slave is an inquiry into a mathematical question, not a moral question, and we should satisfy ourselves that the two cases do not differ in some relevant respect.[16]

The discussion with the slave answers Meno's Paradox, if we are convinced that the slave has inquired successfully despite having had no initial knowledge of the things he was inquiring into. The slave begins with the sort of confidence that Meno expressed in saying there was no difficulty in answering Socrates' questions; but it turns out, as it turned out with Meno, that he has no reasonable basis for such confidence, and so he has no knowledge. Socrates makes it clear, however, that the slave has enough true beliefs to make progress; and so Meno's lack of knowledge should not lead us to conclude that he lacks the true beliefs needed for successful inquiry. The slave has not yet acquired knowledge; but his inquiry has been successful, since he has increased his stock of true beliefs.

The slave has been inquiring, and has not simply recited the correct answers, since Socrates has not taught him, but he has gathered up the correct answers from within himself. In saying that he is not teaching the slave, Socrates does not mean that he suggests nothing to him, but that the slave never gives a particular answer simply because he has been told that it is the right one. In every case he answers only when it seems to him, on the basis of his previous beliefs, that this is the most reasonable answer; this is what Socrates means in saying that the slave gathers up the answers 'from within himself'. He does just what the interlocutors in the early dialogues are told to do; they are required to answer sincerely, not saying what they think Socrates believes or what he wants to hear, but saying what seems reasonable to them in the light of their previous convictions.[17] The discussion should give us confidence in the slave's ability to find the right answer for himself from his own resources.

We have reason to believe, then, that the inquiry makes progress, because we have reason to believe it meets these conditions:

1. The slave's initial beliefs were not too far astray. Most of his judgments about particular lengths and areas were correct.
2. He was able to make his beliefs more consistent by revising them when he detected an inconsistency.
3. He was able to revise them in a reasonable direction. He did not adjust all his other geometrical views to make them fit the principle that a figure with sides double the length of the sides of a second figure also has double the area of the second figure.
4. This revision eliminated false beliefs and replaced them with true beliefs.

Since Plato has given us reason to believe that the discussion with the slave meets these conditions, he has given us reason for confidence in some Socratic inquiry.

These reasons for confidence seem to apply to the moral inquiry in the *Meno*. Meno satisfies the second condition. He also, in Socrates' view, satisfies the first, since Socrates agrees that Meno's answers to most of his questions are reasonable; these are the answers that Socrates uses to convince Meno to reject his general claims about virtue.[18] Here as in the other dialogues, Socrates assumes that in getting the interlocutor to reject one of his initial claims by appeal to the interlocutor's other beliefs, and especially by appeal to the guiding principles of the elenchos, he helps the interlocutor to make his beliefs more reasonable; therefore, Socrates must assume that the interlocutor begins with a fairly large stock of reasonable beliefs.[19]

In Socrates' view, Meno also satisfies the third condition. He could have stubbornly denied that justice and temperance are needed for all the cases of virtue that he originally listed, and hence he could have denied that there was anything inadequate about his list. In fact, he does not do this. Socrates believes that Meno's beliefs have become both more consistent and more reasonable, insofar as he has thrown out the ones that are inconsistent with the more reasonable ones, not those that are inconsistent with the unreasonable ones. In the *Meno* as in the early dialogues, Socrates assumes that if we rely on the guiding principles of the elenchos as guides for resolving conflicts of belief, we revise our beliefs in the right direction. The fact that Socrates secures Meno's agreement by asking leading questions does not matter, any more than it mattered in the discussion with the slave, as long as Meno assents for reasons that seem good to him, not simply because Socrates tells him to.

But this defence of Meno's beliefs seems to fall short of what is needed to show that they really satisfy the first and third conditions fully enough for the purposes of the argument. For we might doubt whether Socrates' judgment that some of Meno's beliefs are reasonable and that Meno revises his beliefs in a reasonable direction is reliable enough to warrant confidence in the direction of the inquiry. In the discussion of the slave there was no doubt about the right answer, and there was no room for objection to the judgments that Socrates relied on in focussing the slave's attention on one question rather than another. But we might argue that in the moral cases there is room for objection.

Socrates himself acknowledges in the *Euthyphro* that questions about the good, the just, and the fine are those that raise disputes of the sort that do not arise in questions where we can appeal to measurement. In the discussion with the slave, Plato picks a mathematical example, since it is an uncontroversial example of progress, but the feature that makes it such a good example of progress also seems to raise a difficulty for an attempt to extend the conclusion, as Plato wants to, to the case of moral inquiry.

In the *Gorgias* Plato suggests a possible answer to these objections. Socrates professes to argue from a starting point that Callicles himself accepts, outside the mere conventions (as Callicles conceives them) of ordinary moral beliefs; he tries to show that Callicles must revise his beliefs to agree with Socrates. The *Meno* does not show that it is logically impossible for the slave to hold on to his initial conviction about the areas of different figures, but we can easily see that the revisions that would be needed would make the subsequent geometrical beliefs rationally intolerable. Socrates suggests that if Callicles resists the revisions suggested by Socrates' questions, Callicles' subsequent beliefs will also lead to rationally intolerable results.

The *Meno* does not pursue this suggestion further. Plato's initial reflexions might reasonably have convinced him that a proper development of the suggestion sketched in the *Gorgias* would have to be quite elaborate. He would need to show why Socrates' starting point is rationally acceptable and why a particular direction of revision in beliefs is rationally inescapable. The *Meno* turns instead to the more basic question about whether Socratic inquiry rests on self-defeating claims about knowledge and definition. Once this more basic question has been answered, Plato can return to the questions left open by the *Gorgias*. He takes them up in the *Republic*.

95. Aspects of Recollection

We have considered Plato's answer to Meno's Paradox without reference to Plato's claim (however hesitant) that the progress we make in Socratic inquiry is literally recollection.[20] Does that claim make the issues easier to resolve?

An appeal to recollection cannot reasonably convince us that we discover truths through Socratic inquiry. For if we were not antecedently convinced that the slave had found the true answer by a process of rational inquiry distinct from what Socrates calls teaching, we would have no reason to say he has recollected anything; there would be nothing needing to be explained by an appeal to recollection. And so the introduction of literal recollection does not answer the doubts that might be raised about the reasonableness of Socratic moral inquiry and the truth of its conclusions.

Still, an appeal to literal recollection is not idle. It answers one reasonable question about Socratic inquiry. If we are convinced that Socratic inquiry makes progress towards the truth, an appeal to literal recollection helps to explain how this progress is possible. For if we actually knew moral truths before we were born, it is reasonable to expect that we will have true moral beliefs when we begin inquiry and that we will be able to elicit more in the course of inquiry. If we do not accept the appeal to recollection, how are we to explain our apparent success in Socratic inquiry? Must we simply say it is a lucky accident that we begin with many true beliefs and have the capacity to eliminate false ones through inquiry?

If Plato wanted to answer this question without appealing to literal recollection, he would have to say more about how we acquire the common-sense beliefs that Socrates begins from. If he agrees with something like Protagoras' account of how we acquire our beliefs, he certainly does not believe that the mechanisms for forming moral beliefs guarantee the truth of the beliefs that are formed. But perhaps he can show why these mechanisms are likely to produce the sorts of beliefs that are presupposed by Socratic inquiry. If (1) the virtues aim at the good of the virtuous agent and at the common good of the community, and (2) the good of individuals and the community has been advanced in the past when people have relied on their judgments about the fine and the good to correct their views about virtue, then Socrates has some reason to claim that the sort of revision that he advocates has in the past tended to bring common moral beliefs closer to the truth. Insofar as these processes tend to form the common beliefs that we begin from, we begin from a sufficient stock of true beliefs (mixed with some false ones).

Both the Socratic dialogues and the *Meno* accept the first of these claims, but they do not argue explicitly for the crucial second claim. An argument for this claim would involve some complex historical claims of the sort that are merely suggested in Protagoras' Great Speech. But Plato could make a reasonable case for this claim; he could, therefore, have offered a reasonable alternative to the belief in literal recollection.

96. Virtue as Knowledge: For and Against

After the discussion with the slave, Socrates agrees to consider whether virtue is teachable, even though they have not yet found out what virtue is (86c4–e1). Perhaps Plato means to suggest that we can profitably inquire into questions about virtue without having answered Socrates' demand for definition. He certainly suggests this in the *Gorgias*; although the main arguments against Polus and Callicles do not rest on any definition of justice or happiness, Socrates thinks he establishes his conclusion by arguments of iron and adamant (*G.* 508e6–509a4).

Still, Socrates is reluctant to begin this inquiry before inquiring into what virtue is (86d3–6). As he says at the end of the dialogue, we will know something perspicuous (*saphes*) only if we examine what virtue is before considering how it can be acquired (100b4–6). The inquiry into whether virtue is teachable may be intended to support this verdict by warning us that inquiries into questions about virtue are deficient unless they rest on knowledge of what virtue is. The *Gorgias* offers a similar warning; after drawing his conclusions, Socrates insists that he does not know they are true (*G.* 509a4–6).

After giving this warning, Socrates presents three arguments about virtue: First, he argues that virtue is knowledge and therefore must be teachable. Second, he argues that virtue is not teachable and therefore cannot be knowledge. Third, he draws a distinction between knowledge and right belief and argues that virtue is right belief rather than knowledge. Since Plato sees that the conclusions of these arguments are inconsistent, he must believe that at least one argument is unsound. The third argument challenges the first argument by suggesting that knowledge is not the only thing that leads to success in action; and Socrates emphatically endorses the distinction between knowledge and belief that underlies the third argument.

We ought not to infer, however, that Plato means to challenge only the first argument. We are advised not to rely uncritically on our initial impression that a given argument is sound (89c5–10); moreover, all three arguments precede the final warning that a satisfactory conclusion about whether virtue is teachable requires knowledge of what virtue is. In this warning Plato invites us to reconsider points at which any of the arguments might have gone astray through a mistaken conception of what virtue is. If we follow Plato's own suggestion, can we find any reasonable objections to the arguments?

97. Virtue and Benefit

First, Socrates argues that since virtue is knowledge, it is teachable.[21] He argues that is knowledge by arguing that virtue is good (87d2–3) and only knowledge is good. Socrates claims that other conditions of the soul—confidence, self-control, and so on—are beneficial if and only if they are combined with knowledge (88c6–d1). He concludes that 'according to this argument, virtue, since it is beneficial, must be some sort of wisdom' (88d2–3).[22]

How is this conclusion to be understood? Two options need to be considered: (1) It is meant to say that virtue is simply some type of knowledge, so that it requires no non-cognitive components. (2) It is meant to say that virtue is 'some sort of wisdom' in the sense that it is wisdom combined with something else. Just as bravery may be called 'some sort of endurance' if it is endurance combined with wisdom, virtue may be called 'some sort of wisdom' if it is wisdom combined with the non-cognitive aspects of bravery, temperance, and so on.[23]

The first option is a more natural interpretation of the passage, and it states the conclusion that Socrates needs in order to establish that virtue is teachable. We have some reason to hesitate, however, since only the second option fits the argument Socrates has given. When Socrates argues that confidence and so on are beneficial only if they are combined with wisdom, ought he not to conclude that virtue is confidence (etc.) plus wisdom? The argument seems to show that knowledge is a necessary part of virtue, but not that it is the whole of virtue.[24]

The claim about the beneficial character of virtue fits one of the guiding principles of the elenchos and the considerations that Socrates appeals to support the inseparability of at least some of the virtues, and so it tends to support the Reciprocity Thesis.[25] But this claim does not imply that knowledge is sufficient for virtue, and so it does not imply that all the virtues are identical to knowledge (the Unity Thesis). In the *Protagoras* Plato suggests, although he does not clearly state, the difference between the arguments for the Reciprocity Thesis and the arguments for the Unity Thesis;[26] his main argument for the Unity Thesis depends on a proof that knowledge is sufficient for virtue.

It is important to decide which thesis Plato means to express in this argument in the *Meno*. If the conclusion of this argument really states that virtue is simply knowledge, then the argument is invalid, and we must ask whether Plato recognizes the invalidity. If the conclusion expresses only one aspect of the Reciprocity Thesis, by claiming that knowledge is necessary for virtue, then Socrates is not entitled to infer that virtue is teachable because it is simply knowledge. We must ask whether Plato recognizes that such an inference is illegitimate.

98. Psychological Eudaemonism in the *Meno*

To answer this question about the argument, we ought to go back to an argument in the first part of the dialogue. Socrates has a reason to identify virtue with knowledge as long as he maintains psychological eudaemonism, and so he rules out the possibility of incontinence; we might suppose that he tacitly relies on psychological eudaemonism to justify the identification of virtue with knowledge. In the *Gorgias* we saw some reasons for wondering whether Plato still accepted psychological eudaemonism. In *Meno* 77–78 he discusses an issue connected with psychological eudaemonism, but it is difficult to be sure about his conclusion.

Socrates argues that it is superfluous to include the clause ‘desiring good things’ in a definition of virtue, because no one desires bad things (77b6–78b2).[27] This sounds like the doctrine of the *Protagoras*, that we always and only desire what we believe to be better and therefore cannot desire what we believe to be worse.

It is not clear, however, that Socrates defends the strong psychological eudaemonism of the *Protagoras*. He might be taken to argue for either of two conclusions: (1) We never desire bad things as such; that is to say, the fact that they are bad is never a feature that makes us desire them. (2) We never desire, under any description, things that we believe to be bad; that is to say, the belief that they are bad always prevents us from desiring them. Only the second conclusion affirms psychological eudaemonism, but only the first conclusion is warranted by the argument. The argument leaves open the possibility that we might want x, knowing x to be bad but still believing that it has something else to be said for it (that, for instance, it is pleasant).

Does Plato see the difference between the two conclusions, and does he see that his argument supports only the first? In summing up the argument, Socrates says that the proposed definition of virtue, 'wishing (*boulesthai*) the good things and being able <to get them>' (78b3–4), should have the first conjunct deleted, since 'wishing belongs to everyone and in this respect one person is no better than another' (78b5–6). Socrates need not mean to be asserting psychological eudaemonism (the second conclusion); he may mean simply that the good is one object of everyone's desire, not that it is the object of all desire.[28]

A further difficulty must be faced. Although Meno agrees that the proposed definition was 'wishing (*boulesthai*) the good things . . .' (78b4), Socrates actually set out to discuss an account that said 'desiring (*epithumein*) the good things' (77b3–7). Does Plato intend any distinction between wishing and (merely) desiring? Socrates introduces 'wish' in saying that no one wishes to be miserable (78b4), and he infers that no one wishes bad things, since being miserable is simply 'desiring (*epithumein*) bad things and getting them' (78b6–8). This argument does not show that Plato treats 'wish' and 'desire' as synonyms. He may mean that since no one has a rational wish to be miserable, no one has a rational wish for things believed to be bad; this would still allow us to say that some people have a non-rational desire for things they believe to be bad.[29]

The Socratic dialogues mention a distinction between 'wish' and 'desire' that Plato might reasonably exploit in this context (*Ch.* 167e1–5; *Lys.* 221a3; *Pr.* 340a7–b2).[30] He does not exploit it in the Socratic dialogues, where it would raise a serious doubt about psychological eudaemonism. In the *Gorgias* Plato perhaps implicitly distinguishes wish, which is directed towards the good (*G.* 468e5–7), from 'desire' or 'appetite' (*epithumia*), which seems to be directed towards the pleasant (*G.* 493b1, 503c4–6), but he does not explore the implications of this division for his claim that we do whatever we do for the sake of the good.[31] In the *Meno*, however, we ought not to assume that he means to leave psychological eudaemonism unquestioned.

This earlier discussion of desire and the good is relevant to the later argument about virtue and knowledge (87d–89a). If the earlier discussion was not meant to support psychological eudaemonism, then we are not clearly justified in taking psychological eudaemonism to be tacitly presupposed in the later argument; hence it is not clear that Plato takes the later argument to be a valid argument for the identification of virtue with knowledge. He may recognize that he has given no sufficient reason to identify bravery with knowledge rather than with confidence regulated by knowledge; in that case he may recognize that he has given no reason for accepting the Unity Thesis rather than the claim that virtue is inseparable from knowledge.

We cannot be sure that Plato sees the flaw in his argument for the identification of virtue with knowledge, but the case for believing that he sees it is strengthened by the fact that his earlier argument fails to support the psychological eudaemonism that would in turn support the Unity Thesis. In presenting these two arguments Plato may mean to suggest that we ought to reopen the question about what virtue is, and especially about how far it can be identified with knowledge.

99. Knowledge and Teaching

The first argument has concluded that virtue must be teachable. The second argument (89c5–96d4) argues directly against this conclusion, as follows:

1. Virtue is knowledge if and only if it is teachable.
2. Virtue is teachable if and only if there are teachers of it (89d3-e3).
3. There are no teachers of virtue (96c4-10).
4. Hence it is not teachable.
5. Hence it is not knowledge.

The first step of the argument is taken over from the previous argument and is unchallenged. The second step, however, is neither defended nor adequately explained.

The claim that virtue is knowledge if and only if it is teachable is true, if it means that virtue is knowledge if and only if it is the sort of thing that people can teach if they find out enough about it. But if this is how we understand 'teachable' in step 1, we have no reason to accept (2), if we attach the same sense to 'teachable'. If (2) is true only if a different sense is attached to 'teachable', the argument contains a fatal equivocation.

Some of Plato's remarks suggest that he sees this flaw in the argument. He draws our attention especially to issues about teachability, when we are instructed to include recollection under 'teaching' (87b5–c3). This instruction is quite surprising; for the account of recollection denied that Socrates was teaching the slave, and since recollection results in knowledge, recollected knowledge seems to falsify the claim that all knowledge is teachable. To avoid this objection, the scope of 'teaching' is extended to include recollection.

Once Plato does this, he makes it easy to see the falsity of the claim that if virtue is teachable, there must be people who can teach it. For if we can be taught virtue only through recollection, there will be teachers of virtue only if there are people who can guide recollection until it reaches knowledge. Plato shows that if the knowledge relevant to virtue is recollected, then probably no one can teach it at present; for Socrates has not shown that he knows how to guide recollection all the way to knowledge, and no one else even believes that the relevant knowledge is recollection at all.[32] If, then, we consider the very type of knowledge that Plato himself has urged on our attention, we will see that steps (1) and (2) of the argument cannot both be true if the same sense of 'teachable' is assumed.[33]

We have a good reason, therefore, for supposing that Plato does not accept all the steps of this argument. Ostensibly the failure of different people to teach virtue is offered as a reason for denying that virtue is teachable (95a4–96b4). The earlier parts of the *Meno* itself, however, give us good reasons for doubting whether the failure of these people to teach virtue shows that it is not teachable.[34] Their views are clearly affected by their conception of what virtue is and of what teaching is; Socrates has made it clear that their views on both these questions are likely to be mistaken. He has shown that it is difficult to say what virtue is and therefore difficult to form a correct conception of what is to be taught; and he has shown that the appropriate way to learn about virtue is recollection. If people who try to teach virtue have the wrong conception of what they are trying to teach and of what would count as teaching it, their efforts are likely to be wrongly directed; their failures therefore do not show that virtue cannot be taught.[35]

100. Knowledge, Belief, and Socratic Inquiry

In the third argument (96d5–100b6) Socrates assumes the soundness of the second argument and resolves the conflict between the first and second arguments by challenging the truth of a premiss of the first argument. The first argument asserted that only knowledge is beneficial, but in the third argument Socrates suggests that correct belief is also beneficial; hence we can resolve the conflict between the conclusions of the first two arguments by identifying virtue with correct belief.

Socrates claims—uncharacteristically—that one of Prodicus' distinctions is illuminating (96d5–7).[36] Indeed, he is unusually emphatic in endorsing the distinction between knowledge and correct belief (98b1–5). His emphasis is quite justified; for the whole dialogue has shown that we need to draw this distinction and that Socrates' inquiries will seem pointless and unintelligible unless we keep the distinction in mind. Knowledge differs from correct belief because correct belief by itself is unstable, whereas knowledge makes it stable by 'reasoning about the explanation' (97e5–98a8). Meno himself remarks on the tendency of his beliefs to wander away under Socrates' questioning (79e7–80b7, 95c7–8), and the same thing happens to the slave (84a3–b1). The comparison with Daedalus' wandering statues is used in the *Meno* in the same way as in the *Euthyphro*, where it is applied to Euthyphro's reaction to Socratic inquiry (*Eu*. 11b6–e1). The condition of Socrates' interlocutors illustrates the condition of someone who has correct belief without knowledge.

The instability of correct belief need not, however, result in the confusion that affects Socrates' interlocutors. For Socrates himself disavows knowledge about virtue, and yet he seems to have quite steady convictions about what virtue requires. In explaining why he lacks knowledge, Socrates does not say that his own beliefs waver; he suggests that since he cannot give an account of virtue, he lacks knowledge of what virtue is, and so lacks knowledge of other properties of virtue. Since the explicit distinction between knowledge and belief makes explanation necessary for knowledge, we can infer that knowledge of the definition of virtue provides knowledge of truths about virtue by providing an explanation to stabilize one's belief in these truths.

This connexion between giving an explanation and giving an account is assumed in the *Gorgias*. Socrates argues that a craft, in contrast to a mere knack, can give the explanation, which is manifested by the ability to give an account (*logos*) 'by which <a craft> applies the things it applies, <saying> what sorts of things they are in their nature' (*G*. 465a3–5). Giving the explanation implies ability to give the account answering a 'What is it?' question.

How, then, does a Socratic definition provide an explanation? The first part of the *Meno* does not actually use 'explanation' in connexion with a Socratic definition, but it comes very close. To give the explanation of what one does (cf. *G*. 501a2) is to say why (*dia ti*) one does it, and to give the explanation of x's being F is to give the reason why (*di'ho*) x is F.[37] When Socrates asks Meno for a single answer to the question 'What is virtue?' he says that all virtues 'have some one identical form because of which (*di'ho*) they are virtues, focussing on which the respondent can presumably show well to the questioner what in fact virtue is' (72c6–d1).

In speaking of Socratic definition Socrates clearly affirms that it answers the relevant why-question; he implies that in doing so it gives the appropriate sort of explanation. Socrates makes the same point in the *Euthyphro*, claiming that a definition of a virtue identifies the property that we can focus on in deciding whether an action is virtuous (*Eu*. 6e3–6), because the property is that 'by which' all virtuous actions are virtuous (*Eu*. 6d11–e1). A definition gives our beliefs the sort of justification and explanatory account that both Plato and Aristotle count as a distinctive feature of knowledge.

This connexion of knowledge, explanation, and Socratic definition justifies the implicit assumption of the early dialogues that the elenchos exposes people's lack of knowledge by showing that they cannot give a correct definition. The elenchos shows that people lack knowledge because it shows that they lack the particular sort of justification that a definition would supply. Although they may be right to claim *that* bravery requires standing firm against danger on some occasions and not on others, they cannot say *why* this is so. They would have the 'why' as well as the 'that', as Aristotle puts it (*EN* 1095a31–b8), if they could produce a Socratic definition. And so, when Socrates claims that he and other people are ignorant about the virtues, he claims that they lack the 'why', the explanation that would transform their beliefs into knowledge.

Plato's remarks about knowledge and recollection confirm the suggestion that a Socratic definition meets the demand for explanation. For having introduced this demand, Socrates says: 'and this . . . is recollection, as stands agreed by us in the earlier discussion' (98a4–5). 'This' refers to reasoning about the explanation; Socrates refers back to his remark that the slave had belief that could be converted into knowledge by the appropriate further inquiries (85b8–d2). This remark about the slave, however, says nothing about finding an explanation. We see the relevance of an explanation only if we connect recollection with the Socratic inquiry conducted in the first part of the dialogue, for that aims at finding the one thing because of which all virtues are virtues. We can see why Plato thinks finding the explanation has been shown to be recollection, if, and only if, we take his allusion to recollection to be an allusion to the search for a definition.

If this is correct, then Plato's explicit distinction between knowledge and belief explains what is said and done in earlier dialogues. According to the *Meno*,

Socrates is right to disavow knowledge about virtue because he lacks the appropriate sort of explanation, and he is right to seek a definition because that will provide the sort of explanation that contributes to knowledge. Since the *Meno* presents an explicit account of knowledge that is absent from the early dialogues, it gives a clear formulation and defence of claims that are implicit and undefended in the early dialogues; it does not introduce a new epistemological demand that was absent from earlier dialogues.[38]

101. Knowledge, Belief, and Stability

Plato clearly accepts the part of the third argument that affirms the difference between knowledge and correct belief, but does he accept the further premisses that lead to the identification of virtue with correct belief? That depends on what he thinks about the combination of two claims: (1) Correct belief is as beneficial as knowledge. (2) Whatever state is always beneficial is virtue. If Plato accepts both these claims, and if they both use 'beneficial' in the same sense, they constitute an argument to show that knowledge cannot be necessary for virtue.

In defending (1) Socrates explains what he means by it. Meno suggests that correct belief might sometimes go wrong, whereas knowledge never goes wrong, (97c6–8). Socrates seems to say that this suggestion rests on a misunderstanding: 'Will not the person who has correct belief on a given occasion succeed on that occasion, as long as he believes the correct things?' (97c6–8).[39] He agrees that correct belief is all right 'as long as it believes correctly' (97c10), but it is liable to wander away, and the function of knowledge is to tie it down. In claiming that mere correct belief is all right as long as it is correct, Socrates is not merely stating a tautology. He presumably means that in some circumstances the fact that my belief is not knowledge makes no difference to its reliability.

How might this happen? True beliefs are liable to wander away in two different ways: (1) I lose the relevant sort of belief in conditions where I am puzzled and do not know what to believe; this is what happens to Euthyphro (*Eu.* 11b–e). (2) I still have the same sort of belief, but it ceases to be correct, in conditions where my tenacious belief turns out to be false. Knowledge therefore binds belief both (1) by preventing it from wandering away in unfamiliar conditions and (2) by preventing it from wandering away from the truth. In the first case, the agent's belief itself is unstable; in the second case, the truth of the belief is unstable. Since Plato is concerned with the stable correctness of beliefs, not simply with tenacity of belief, he must take both kinds of wandering away into account, and knowledge must protect us against them both.

Plato also needs to consider the different circumstances that might cause true beliefs to wander away in one of these two ways, so that he can say how many circumstances are relevant to deciding whether our beliefs have the right kind of stability. Different demands for stability might rest on different standards of reliability. If, for instance, I believe that these animals are sheep, and they are sheep, then my belief is reliable for these animals, and it does not matter if I do not know what makes them sheep. If, however, I cannot tell the difference between sheep and goats and do not know why these animals are sheep rather than goats, my ignorance would make a difference if I were confronted with goats. If we are concerned about 'empirical reliability' (the tendency to be right in empirically likely conditions), my belief that animals with a certain appearance are sheep may be perfectly reliable (if I can be expected not to meet any goats). If we are concerned about 'counterfactual reliability' (the tendency to be right in counterfactual, and not necessarily empirically likely, conditions), my inability to distinguish sheep from goats makes my belief unreliable that animals with a certain appearance are sheep. In saying that my belief about sheep is counterfactually unreliable, we point out that my reason for believing that these things are sheep is mistaken, even though the mistake makes no difference to my judgments in actual circumstances.

When Plato speaks of a given belief 'wandering', he describes a fault that we might more easily recognize if it were described differently. If I identify sheep by features that do not distinguish them from goats, then I rely on false principles to reach the true belief 'this is a sheep' in an environment without goats. If I rely on the same principles to identify sheep in an environment that includes goats, I will often reach the false belief 'this is a sheep' when I meet a goat. We may want to describe these facts by speaking of three things: (1) the true token belief 'this is a sheep' (applied to a sheep in the first environment), (2) the false token belief 'this is a sheep' (applied to a goat in the second environment), and (3) the false general principle that I use to identify sheep in both environments. Plato, however, tends to speak as though the false general principle causes one and the same belief ('this is a sheep') to change from truth to falsity in different environments.[40] Once we keep this in mind, it is easier to understand what he means by speaking of beliefs 'wandering'.

If we take account of the different ways in which beliefs may be stable or unstable, we can defend Socrates' claim that mere correct belief is less stable than knowledge. If we consider mere empirical reliability, the case for saying that correct belief must be less stable is weak. For in particular empirical circumstances, I may never face the situations that will cause either my belief or the truth of my belief to wander away; and so, if these are not alternative circumstances that need to be considered, my belief may be perfectly stable, contrary to Socrates' claim. If, however, we consider counterfactual reliability, taking an appropriate range of counterfactual circumstances to be relevant, Socrates is right to claim that without knowledge correct belief must be unstable. Even if correct belief is as good as knowledge in a given range of situations, it will not remain correct if it is exposed to certain kinds of challenges that someone with knowledge can overcome.[41]

Plato gives a clear reason, then, for preferring the rational understanding and explanation that we gain from knowledge. If we know why it is right to keep promises in all the situations we have faced, we will be better equipped to discover that it would be wrong to keep them in some situation that we have not considered (cf. *Rep*. 331c), and we will be better equipped to resist specious arguments suggesting that the rule does not apply in some situation that we had not previously confronted.

If Plato takes this counterfactual reliability to be necessary for the stability that distinguishes knowledge from true belief, then the two features that appeared to distinguish knowledge from true belief become harder to separate. We might at first suppose that knowledge differs from mere correct belief both in being stable and in including 'reasoning about the explanation'; in that case we might suppose that some correct beliefs could have one of these features without the other. If, however, the relevant sort of stability requires the counterfactual reliability that focusses on the right reason for believing that p, then we cannot have the relevant sort of stability without grasping the right reason for believing that p. If this is true, then we cannot achieve stability without meeting the demand for rational understanding.

102. Knowledge, Belief, and Virtue

If this is Plato's view about the difference between knowledge and correct belief, what does it imply about the claim that correct belief is as beneficial as knowledge? Consideration of the different types of reliability suggests that the question may be difficult to answer. If we are concerned with actual results, we may conclude that only empirical reliability matters and that therefore correct belief is as beneficial as knowledge; perhaps this is what Socrates has in mind when he says that true belief achieves the result of each action no less well than knowledge does (98a7–9) and that it is no less beneficial 'for actions' (98c1–3). If, however, the relevant sort of benefit includes counterfactual reliability, knowledge is more beneficial than correct belief.

Our view about the sort of benefit being considered will also affect our judgment on the claim that whatever state is always beneficial is to be identified with virtue. If the only relevant benefit is the 'pragmatic' benefit displayed in actual results, then the identification of virtue with the beneficial state implies that only actual results matter for virtue; in that case, correct belief will do as well as knowledge. Socrates assumes this pragmatic conception of benefit in using the distinction between knowledge and belief against the earlier argument (87d–89a) for the identification of virtue with knowledge. The pragmatic conception of benefit supports the ostensible conclusion of the third argument, that virtue comes by some divine fate, and not by nature or teaching, to those who have it.

Socrates qualifies this conclusion, however, by adding that we will know something perspicuous about this only if we ask what virtue is before asking how it is acquired (100b4–6). Each of the three main arguments (from 87d onwards) is open to some doubt that raises questions about the nature of virtue. If we have correctly understood the arguments in their context, then Plato amply justifies his suggestion that they rely on disputable assumptions that need to be clarified by an inquiry into what virtue is. In this case we need to know enough about virtue to decide whether the purely pragmatic conception of benefit is the only one that is relevant to virtue.

Socrates claims that knowledge is more valuable (*timiōteron*, 98a7) than correct belief. He implies that the greater value of knowledge does not consist in its greater empirical reliability, since it may not in fact be empirically more reliable than correct belief. Knowledge may confer some benefit that is not purely pragmatic, but is nonetheless morally relevant. If A's knowledge and B's correct belief would give different answers only in counterfactual conditions, this might still be relevant to virtue; for perhaps the actual behavioural difference between A and B is not all that matters, but we should also be concerned about their motives and attitudes. If these matter to us, then the benefit relevant to virtue is not exhausted by the pragmatic benefit.

103. The *Meno* and Socratic Ethics

This question about the value of knowledge introduces one of the features that, in Aristotle's view, distinguish virtues from crafts. He argues that whereas we assess people's possession of a craft by considering how efficiently they produce the right products, we assess someone's character by considering further features that are independent of results:

> The actions that come about in accordance with the virtues are done justly or temperately, not if they themselves are in some specific condition, but if in addition the agent is in some condition in doing them—first, if he does them knowingly, second, if he does them by deciding on them, and deciding on them for their own sakes, and third, if he also does them from a firm and immoveable state. (*EN* 1105a28–33)

If Plato in the *Meno* is concerned to identify the features of virtue that Aristotle mentions here, he has good reason to insist that knowledge, not just correct belief, is necessary for virtue. Since he insists that knowledge is more valuable than virtue, while recognizing that it is no more useful in action, he raises the possibility that the further valuable element in knowledge is also an element of virtue.

If Plato takes this view of virtue, he goes beyond the attitude of the early dialogues. For in the early dialogues Socrates is silent about the differences that Aristotle sees between virtues and crafts; indeed, he appears to assimilate the virtues to crafts.[42] He never suggests that understanding the right reason for virtuous action is itself an element in virtue, apart from its consequences for action.

However, a reader of these dialogues might fairly argue that Socrates' emphasis on the importance of articulate understanding seems to go beyond anything he could justify instrumentally. Nicias warns Lysimachus that anyone who engages in discussion with Socrates finds himself having to 'give an account about himself, how he is conducting himself and how he has conducted his whole previous life' (*La.* 187e10–188a2). Socrates confirms Nicias' impression of him;

he maintains that the unexamined life is not worth living, and that it is the greatest good for human beings to argue daily about virtue (*Ap*. 38a1–6).[43] Although some instrumental defence of Socrates' activities can be given, one may well doubt whether it would really explain the importance that Socrates attaches to them.

This question about Socratic ethics and its connexion with Socratic method cannot be raised properly without the distinctions drawn in the *Meno*; that is why it is not raised in the earlier dialogues. Once Plato distinguishes knowledge from correct belief, he can consider the character of knowledge, as distinct from the practical results that it may share with correct belief, and he can ask whether the rational and articulate understanding that is characteristic of knowledge is to be valued in its own right as an aspect of virtue. In suggesting that it has some value in its own right, Plato suggests that a purely pragmatic conception of the benefit of virtue cannot explain Socrates' own conviction that knowledge is necessary for virtue. Although a grasp of the distinction between knowledge and belief tends to support the practice of Socratic inquiry, it tends to challenge Socrates' attempts to explain the character of virtue. The Socrates of the early dialogues turns out to have correct belief, but not knowledge, about the character of virtue.

In the *Meno* and especially in the discussion of recollection, knowledge, and belief, Plato introduces epistemological questions that are not examined in the early dialogues. But his introduction of these questions shows that they matter for Socratic method and Socratic ethics. Plato suggests that the historical Socrates made it unnecessarily difficult to defend his moral convictions because he confined himself to ethical discussion. Some defence of Socratic method is needed if we are to take these ethical discussions as seriously as Socrates took them, and a defence of Socratic method soon leads us into epistemology. Moreover, Socrates' emphasis on the ethical importance of rational understanding and self-examination requires a fuller understanding of knowledge and belief than Socrates himself achieved.

Many readers of the *Meno* have recognized that it expresses Plato's critical reflexions on Socrates. Some have argued that Plato's criticisms are primarily external; according to this view, he finds Socrates wanting when he measures him against epistemological and metaphysical standards that Socrates did not accept.[44] We have discovered that, on the contrary, Plato's criticisms are internal; he insists that if we want to understand and defend Socrates in the light of questions that Socrates himself must recognize as legitimate, we cannot confine ourselves to Socrates' purely ethical inquiries. To this extent the impulse behind the epistemological and metaphysical inquiries of the middle dialogues is strictly Socratic.

10

The Theory of Forms

104. Socratic Method and Platonic Metaphysics

In the *Meno* Plato examines some of the presuppositions of Socratic inquiry. He considers the conditions for an adequate Socratic definition, and he explores the distinction between knowledge and belief. He implies that knowledge is the result of recollection. In the *Phaedo* he reasserts the Theory of Recollection, but now he claims that the truths we recollect are truths about non-sensible Forms, recollected from imperfect sensible instances (*Phd*. 74e8–75a3).[1] Since recollection is complete, according to the *Meno*, when we have a Socratic definition, Plato claims that Socratic definitions must primarily apply to non-sensible Forms. The *Republic* asserts the same epistemological and metaphysical claims; Plato argues that knowledge cannot be primarily about anything sensible, but must be about non-sensible Forms.

In Aristotle's view, this belief in the epistemological deficiency of sensible things and in the epistemological necessity of Forms that are 'separated' from these sensibles is a central difference between Socrates and Plato on questions of metaphysics and epistemology (*Met*. 987a32–b10, 1078b12–1079a4, 1086a37–b11). According to Aristotle, Plato developed his theory of non-sensible, separated Forms in response to Socrates' search for definitions in ethics, because he believed that Socratic definitions could not apply to sensible things, since sensible things are subject to change. Aristotle leads us to expect, then, that when Plato argues that sensibles are deficient or imperfect, he will refer especially to change. To see whether Aristotle is right, we must find out what he means and how far his claim can be defended from Plato's dialogues. It will be easier to approach these questions once we have examined Plato's reasons for regarding sensibles as deficient.

These issues are relevant to the understanding of Plato's moral theory. It is worth examining Plato's theoretical views about Socratic definition, because his practice in the *Republic* is strikingly different from his practice in earlier dialogues. Whereas the early dialogues fail to reach the Socratic definitions they seek, *Republic* IV presents an account of each of the cardinal virtues. Does Plato's reflexion on Socratic definitions affect his views about the prospects of finding them?

105. Definition and Unity

It is useful to take up some questions that are raised, but not pursued, in the *Meno*. When Socrates suggests to Meno that a definition of virtue is needed, Meno does not immediately agree that such a definition is possible (*M.* 73a4–5). Indeed, Plato recognizes that the demand for a single account of virtue is not as uncontroversial as it is made to appear in the Socratic dialogues. Meno's initial views about the different types of virtue reflect the rather awkward coexistence in common sense of different views about what should count as a virtue. Meno thinks immediately of the Homeric conception, connecting virtue with the agent's own worldly success; Socrates gradually persuades him, returning to the same point more than once, that justice and temperance are necessary for any genuine virtue (73a6–c5, 78c4–79a2). Socrates assumes that genuine virtues must share a tendency to benefit the agent himself and other people. He does not justify this assumption, but in making it clearer that Socrates relies on it, Plato uncovers one of the controversial claims that underlie the arguments of the Socratic dialogues about the virtues.

Meno agrees quite quickly with Socrates' demand for a single definition of virtue (73a6–c5); he does not suggest that Socrates is asking the wrong question. Nor does he challenge Socrates' other criteria for a definition, even when he has doubts about Socratic inquiry. He supposes that his failure to make progress results from Socrates' attempt to inquire without previous knowledge, not from Socrates' conception of the definitions he is looking for. But it is worthwhile to raise some questions about Socrates' conditions for definitions.

When Meno offers a list of types of virtue, Socrates suggests that Meno thinks the items on his list belong on it because of some further feature that they share (besides the mere fact that they are on the list). To recognize this further feature is to recognize the 'one' belonging to all of the many (*dia pantōn*, 74a9; cf. 75a7–8), to recognize that something can be attributed 'universally' to them (*kata holou*, 77a6). This is a familiar Socratic demand, but what does it imply?

Let us suppose that Meno had not accepted Socrates' suggestion that justice and temperance are common features of all the types of virtue that Meno originally mentioned. In that case he might have said that the different types of virtue need not have anything in common except their membership in a disjunctive list. We might say, if we like, that this membership is the single feature that makes all virtue virtue.

Has Socrates any reason to reject this as an account of the 'one' that is common to the 'many'? In demanding the one in the many, Socrates seems to be influenced by the fact that we apply the single name 'virtue' to the many different types of virtue. Does he perhaps assume that whenever we apply a single word 'F' to many cases, it has a single meaning, and that this fact by itself justifies us in demanding a Socratic definition of F that reveals some form that all Fs have in common, something because of which they are all Fs, and something that we can focus on to say whether something is F?

If this is what Socrates means when he looks for a definition, then it will be relatively easy, but also relatively uninteresting, to find the one common to the many. If, for instance, 'F' is a disjunctively defined predicate, there must (on this view) be something that all Fs have in common; if the definition corresponding to 'F' is 'being G or H', then this will tell us what all Fs have in common. If that is Socrates' view, then it is easy to adapt Meno's first answer to answer Socrates' question; instead of giving a list of types of virtue, Meno should simply say that the form that they all have in common is simply being a member of the list, so that virtue will be an essentially disjunctive characteristic.

Socrates, however, does not suggest that such an answer would satisfy him. In assuming that virtue must be a single form, he seems to assume not merely that 'virtue' is a meaningful predicate but also that it corresponds to one non-disjunctive property underlying the disjunctive list of types of virtue. This single property must explain why the different types of virtue belong to one and the same kind.[2] This assumption is neither challenged nor clarified in the rest of the *Meno*. It commits Socrates to claiming that names (or some names at least) are correlated with some sort of unified explanatory properties that do not correspond directly to linguistic predicates; if, for instance, 'virtue' corresponded only to a disjunction of characteristics, it would not correspond to a genuine explanatory property. To see what Plato takes to be implied by the belief in properties of this sort, we must look outside the *Meno*. The best place to look is the *Cratylus*.

106. Convention and Objectivity

The *Cratylus* is concerned with the 'correctness of names' (383a4–b2) and specifically considers whether their correctness is conventional or natural.[3] This question divides into two further questions: (1) Is the internal character and structure of names purely conventional? (Is 'horse' a more correct name for horses than '*hippos*'?) (2) Is it a matter of nature or convention that a particular name is the correct name for a particular sort of thing? Socrates allows that an appeal to convention may give the right answer to the first question (435a5–d3), but he rejects convention as an answer to the second question.

Socrates supposes that the conventionalist answer to the second question rests on the Protagorean view that 'what things seem to each person to be like, that is also what they are like' (386c4–5). In Socrates' view, the conventionalist means that there is nothing about, say, horses themselves that makes it correct to give a single name to all horses rather than one name to horses and dogs encountered on odd days of the week and another to horses and cats encountered on even days. On this view, there is nothing about external reality itself that makes it right to classify things in one way rather than another.

Socrates' questions in the *Meno* presuppose there is something about virtues themselves that makes it correct to give them the same name. If a conventionalist theory is universally correct, however, there is nothing in the nature of virtues themselves that makes it right for us to classify all these states and characteristics as virtues. If it is simply a matter of convention that we recognize the kinds we actually recognize, and if nothing about the things classified makes one classification right or wrong, then there is no reason to follow Socrates in assuming that the things referred to by the name must have something in common besides being the things that we have chosen to classify under that name.

Socrates attacks one motive for the conventionalist view by attacking the Protagorean position. He asks Hermogenes whether 'the being (*ousia*) of things is private to each person' (385e5) or, on the contrary, things have some stability in their own right (386a3–4), so that they do not vary in accordance with variations in our views about them (386d8–e4).[4] Socrates defends his belief in objective things and properties by arguing from the fact that we distinguish better and worse people, and in doing so distinguish wise from ignorant people (386b10–12). If Protagoras were right, we would not be entitled to draw these distinctions; for since everyone would have equally true beliefs, everyone would be equally wise, and so no one would be wiser than anyone else (386c2–d1).[5]

This argument helps us to see why Socrates believes he is asking Meno the right questions about virtue. He assumes that an interlocutor will have some views about the correct answer to Socrates' questions. Even more important, he assumes that the interlocutor agrees that correct answers exist and that we can make progress in finding them. This assumption rests on the still more basic assumption that some people are wiser than others about virtue.

Once Socrates has secured Hermogenes' agreement about different degrees of wisdom, he infers that there must be something for us to be right or wrong about, and that this must be the nature that things have in their own right independently of our beliefs about them (386d8–e5). It follows that we speak correctly or incorrectly insofar as we do or do not speak of things as they objectively are (387b11–c5). Since naming is an action that is a part of speaking, naming can be done rightly or wrongly too (387c9–d8).[6] The proper function of a name is to teach and distinguish the being of things (388b6–c1), and a correct name will carry out this function.[7] Socrates suggests that a name is correct to the extent that it conveys an 'outline' (*tupos*) of its referent. The better the outline of F, the more correct the name of F; but as long as some outline of F is conveyed, the name still names F (431c4–433a2).

The assumption that some predicates are names preserving outlines underlies the discussion with Meno. For Socrates assumes that when Meno uses the word 'virtue', he preserves the outline of a genuine nature, as Socrates conceives it. Why does Socrates assume this? Presumably it is possible that some names (or putative names) are so badly correlated with reality that they preserve the outline of no genuine nature,[8] or they combine elements of two natures so confusedly that we cannot say determinately which nature is named. Meno might argue that there is nothing that the items on his list of virtues have in common, or that all they have in common is the fact that they are conventionally recognized as virtues because they correspond to conventionally recognized roles. Alternatively, he might suggest that if some quality of a person comes to be widely admired, or admired by certain people, it is a virtue, and that this is what being a virtue consists is. This answer does not divide virtue up into many, and it does not provide a mere list. But it is not the sort of answer that satisfies Socrates. In the *Euthyphro* he considers and rejects an answer of this sort, arguing against the suggestion that piety should be defined as what the gods love.

Socrates rejects this sort of answer because he believes there is something about the virtues themselves that makes it appropriate to put them on the list of virtues. He assumes that there is some question about the objective character of the virtues that we can answer correctly or incorrectly. The *Cratylus* presents the metaphysical view of language and its underlying reality that is presupposed by Socrates' demands in the *Meno* and in the early dialogues. Socrates commits himself to the existence of real kinds and genuine objective similarities that justify our classifying things as we do. He assumes, with Meno's agreement, that there is some single standard, derived from the nature of the actions and characteristics themselves, that justifies our judgment that all the types of virtue are genuine virtues.

This is why Socrates rejects Meno's attempted definition of virtue as 'ruling with justice'. Meno's suggestion is faulty not only because there are types of virtue that do not involve ruling (73d2–5) but also because a reference to justice does not properly justify our judgment about virtue. Socrates assumes that some further fact about virtue explains the fact that justice is a virtue, and the explanation provided by this further fact is needed for a proper definition of virtue.

The demand for an objective explanatory property makes the demand for a single definition more difficult to satisfy. If Socrates were satisfied with a single description corresponding to 'F' that applies to all Fs, it would be easier for Meno to satisfy him. Since, however, he demands an objective explanatory property, he is dissatisfied with answers that do not provide the right sort of explanation.

107. Epistemological Requirements for a Definition

This demand on Socratic definitions is metaphysical, since it requires a single objective property that stands in the right explanatory relations to its instances. Once we understand this demand, we must compare it with Socrates' other demands on definitions, to see whether it is reasonable to expect that they can all be satisfied.

In the *Euthyphro* Socrates combines his metaphysical demand with an epistemological demand; the appropriate account of a form must provide a 'pattern' or 'standard' (*paradeigma*) for judging that something is or is not an instance of piety. He seems to assume that such an account must eliminate 'disputed terms' (*Eu.* 7c10–d5).[9] Socrates seems to believe that we cannot use our account of the form of piety as a standard for judgment, if we can describe it only in terms that we cannot apply to particular cases without causing dispute. Since there is dispute about which actions are just, an account of piety that mentions justice will not allow us to decide which actions are pious.

This constraint is suggested rather than stated in the *Euthyphro*; although Socrates emphasizes the difficulty that arises from the use of disputed terms in an account, he does not explicitly insist that an acceptable account must eliminate them. Still, he suggests no other way to remove the difficulty that he raises. Moreover, if he believes that disputed terms must be eliminated, it is easier to understand why he never specifically claims to give a satisfactory definition of a virtue. He offers descriptions such as 'bravery is knowledge of what is to be feared and faced with confidence' (*La.* 199d1–2; *Pr.* 360d4–5) and the descriptions in the *Gorgias* of the virtues as types of psychic order (*G.* 506e2–507b8), but he does not represent these descriptions as adequate definitions. His apparent unwillingness to accept definitions of this sort is understandable if he accepts the implicit demand in the *Euthyphro* for a method of measuring and deciding that will eliminate disagreement about moral properties. If Socrates is looking for such a method, then accounts such as 'bravery is knowledge of what is to be feared' will not seem promising.

Socrates would perhaps be able to meet the difficulty raised in the *Euthyphro* if he relied on the epistemological hedonism of the *Protagoras* and so claimed that we can know what maximizes pleasure independently of our beliefs about the good.[10] In the *Protagoras* he speaks of the 'measuring craft' that settles questions about goodness and badness by estimating present and future pleasures; this seems to solve the difficulty that was raised in the *Euthyphro*. Measurement is precisely the method that the *Euthyphro* suggests for eliminating disputes, and the *Protagoras* suggests that this method is not as alien to moral questions as it might initially have seemed.[11]

In the *Meno* Plato notices the epistemological aspect of Socratic definition and distinguishes it from the metaphysical aspect. Socrates persuades Meno that the correct answer to a search for a definition must 'not only answer true things, but also through those things that the questioner additionally agrees that he knows' (*M.* 75d6–7).[12] This condition—said to be characteristic of dialectic as opposed to eristic—is applied to Meno's next attempt at definition. He eventually agrees that 'whatever comes about with justice is virtue and whatever comes about without all such things is vice' (78e8–79a1). Socrates objects that if we do not know what virtue is, we will not know what any part of virtue is; hence we will not know what justice is, and so it is illegitimate (by the standards of the dialectical condition) to mention justice in the definition of virtue (79d1–e4).

Socrates implies that we cannot know what G is if F is mentioned in the definition of G and we do not know what F is; and so, since knowledge requires definition, we cannot know what G is unless we can define F independently of G. This is not quite the same as the demand for the elimination of disputed terms, but it might be explained by that demand. For Socrates might argue that if G is defined by reference to F, but F cannot be defined independently of G, then apparently our initial disputes about what things are G will return when we consider what things are F.

If we combine the remarks in the *Euthyphro* about disputed terms with the dialectical condition in the *Meno*, we still cannot be sure exactly what Socrates or Plato means to allow or exclude. But these different remarks suggest that Socrates imposes some epistemological demand on a definition. If he does, we ought to raise a question that the *Meno* does not raise: how does the epistemological demand affect the metaphysical demand for an explanatory property?

Although the dialectical condition may seem reasonable if we are concerned about the resolution of disputes, the restriction it imposes is open to question. How can Socrates be entitled to rule out the possibility that some definitions are interdependent? If he recognizes this possibility, how can it be fair to rule out such definitions as answers to an inquiry? Such a restriction seems especially unwelcome in the light of Socrates' metaphysical constraint on definitions. If they are supposed to identify the genuinely explanatory property, how does he know that it will always be possible to specify this property in the sorts of terms required by the dialectical condition? Socrates does not consider the possibility of divergence between the epistemological demand and the metaphysical demand, and so he does not say which demand is more important.

As long as Socrates accepts both the epistemological and metaphysical demands, without saying which is more important or how we are to decide conflicts between them, he makes the task of finding a Socratic definition significantly more difficult. Meno is as unsuccessful as both Socrates and his interlocutors have been in the early dialogues. Meno does not challenge Socrates' requirements; he believes that the difficulties he faces arise from Socrates' claims about knowledge and definition. He is mistaken in this belief; when we see that he is mistaken, we may wonder whether Socrates' other demands would make it difficult for anyone to find a satisfactory definition. In studying Plato's further reflexions on the nature of forms and our knowledge of them, we might reasonably hope to find out whether Plato accepts both the metaphysical and the explanatory demands imposed by Socrates, and how he believes they can be satisfied.

108. Compresence of Opposites

In the *Phaedo* Plato discusses both the metaphysical and the epistemological sides of Socratic definition. He considers the forms (*eidê*; *Eu.* 6d9–e1; *M.* 72c6–d1) and asks how we can know them, in the light of facts about how they are. To make it clear that he is talking about the forms that concern Socrates, Plato introduces the 'just itself' and all the other things that are properly called 'the F itself' in dialectical discussions (*Phd.* 65d4–5, 74a11, 75c10–d3, 76d7–9); these are precisely the 'beings' or 'essences' (cf. *ousias*, 65d13) that Socrates sought to define.

Once he has made it clear that he is talking about the same forms that Socrates talked about, Plato makes an epistemological claim: these Forms are inaccessible to the senses (65d4–5). In support of this claim, he makes a metaphysical claim: the Form of F has properties that no sensible F can have. This fact about Forms explains why they cannot be known by the senses (74a9–b7). These claims and their supporting arguments have no parallel in the Socratic dialogues; we must try to understand their significance for Plato's view of Forms.

To show that the Form cannot be sensible, Plato claims that whereas equal sticks and stones appear both equal and unequal, the form cannot have these contrary properties (*Phd.* 74b7–9).[13] In the post-Socratic dialogues, Plato often contrasts the Form of F with Fs that are both F and not F. He sees a Heracleitean unity of opposites in a beautiful (*kalon*) girl who is also ugly (*aischron*) in comparison with gods (*HMa.* 289a2–c6). Burying our parents and being buried by our children are fine (*kalon*) in some circumstances and shameful (*aischron*) in others (293b5–e5). The many beautifuls (justs, equals, and so on) are both beautiful and ugly (*R.* 479a5–b10). In contrast to the F things that are both F and not F, the Form of F must be free from this compresence of opposites (*Symp.* 210e5–211a5; cf. *HMa.* 291d1–3).

What is wrong with the compresence of opposites, and why is Plato entitled to assert that the Form must be free of it? It would be a mistake to argue that if something is both F and not F, it is not genuinely F after all, or that it is a self-contradictory entity; Plato never relies on this mistaken argument.[14] In *Republic* IV he insists that it is impossible 'for the same thing to do or undergo contrary things in the same respect or in relation to the same thing' (436b8–9).[15] While Plato never actually remarks that the many Fs are not self-contradictory, everything he says suggests that he believes their opposite properties are perfectly compatible. When he talks about the compresence of opposites in the many Fs, he makes it clear that this compresence involves different respects or different relations, and he never relies on any argument that requires him to neglect this fact about the relevant sort of compresence. Why, then, does the compresence of F and not-F in a given F imply that this F cannot be the Form of F?

109. Compresence and Explanation

To answer this question, Plato refers to the explanatory role of Forms. Like Socrates, he wants to find the Form of F because he wants to find 'that because of which' (*di'ho*) all F things are F (*M.* 72c6–d1, *Eu.* 6d9–e1). To clarify this explanatory requirement, he cites purported explanations that would be blatantly unsatisfactory. If, for instance, we tried to explain x's being larger than y by mentioning what makes x larger than y, and we said that x is larger than y 'by a head' (*Phd.* 96d7–e1), we would have given a bad explanation, since 'by a head' explains x's being larger than y no more than it explains y's being smaller than x. Similarly, we cannot say that the combination of two things is what make things two, since it is equally true that the division of one thing makes it two (96e5–97b3).[16]

These are strange examples of attempted explanations. No doubt Plato means them to be strange, so that they illustrate an extreme version of the error that he means to avoid. He suggests that as explanations they suffer from disabling faults; a property G cannot be the explanation of x's being F if either (1) G is present in y, but y is not F, or (2) G is not present in z, but z is F (97a5–b3, 100e8–101b2). G may well be present in x and may have some connexion with x's being F (as 'by a head' plainly does if we say that Theaetetus is taller than

Socrates by a head), but if either (1) or (2) is true, then G lacks the explanatory connexion to F that G would have to have if G were what makes x F. To put it in Aristotle's terms, we cannot say that x is F insofar as x is G (that x is F qua G) if either (1) or (2) is true (cf. *Phys.* 196b24–29; *Met.* 1026b37–1027a5).

In asserting his constraints on explanation, Plato assumes that an explanation involves a contrast.[17] If being F and being G are two possible conditions for x and we want to explain why x is F as opposed to G, we have not explained this if we refer to some further state H that no more explains x's being F than it explains x's being G. And so 'by a head' does not explain x's being taller rather than shorter than y, since it no more explains this than it explains x's being shorter than z. If, then, F and G are contrasted in our demands for explanation, so that we want to know why x is F rather than G or G rather than F, we must appeal to different explanatory properties of x.[18]

These general claims about explanation show us why Plato focusses on the compresence of opposites. If we want to know what makes something just, and the alleged explanatory property no more makes something just than it makes something unjust, then we have not found the explanatory property we wanted. Plato argues that, for instance, it cannot be the fact that the children bury their parents that makes this particular action of these children burying their parents fine; for that fact might equally be found in a shameful action (if, for instance, the children had murdered their parents first).

In articulating this demand on explanations, Plato exploits some standard Socratic objections, but he develops them in a direction that has no Socratic parallel. When Charmides suggests that temperance is shame, Socrates convinces him that this is a faulty definition because shame is good (in some situations) and bad (in other situations), or 'no more good than bad' (*Ch.* 161a2–b2). He could also have pointed out to Laches, although he does not say so in precisely these terms, that endurance is both fine and shameful (cf. *La.* 192d7–8). He does not say that shame is both temperate and not temperate or that endurance is both brave and not brave. Some of the objections raised in the *Meno* against Meno's proposed definitions could be stated in terms referring to the compresence of opposites (cf. *M.* 73d6–8), but that is not how they are stated. None of these passages states the general principle that the F cannot be both F and not F, whereas various candidates for being the F are in fact both F and not F, and therefore cannot be the F. The *Hippias Major* comes closer to stating this general principle (*HMa.* 291d1–3), but it is expressed most clearly in the dialogues that contrast the non-sensible Form of F with the many sensible Fs.[19]

110. The Form and the 'Many'

Once we see why Plato contrasts the Form of F with the many Fs, we can also see what the many Fs are supposed to be and what an acceptable description of the Form would have to be like.[20] To see what he might mean, we ought to recall what Socrates means when he implies (in the *Laches*) that endurance is both fine and shameful or asserts (in the *Charmides*) that shame is both good and bad. He does not suggest that every particular case of endurance (Leonidas' last stand, for instance) or of feeling shame (for instance, the shame felt by a Spartan who ran away when Leonidas stood firm) is both good and bad (or fine and shameful). He means that some tokens of the relevant action type are good and others are bad or, equivalently, that the property in question (being a case of endurance or shame) makes some token actions good and makes other token actions bad. Equally clearly, the remark in the *Hippias Major* about burying one's parents means not that every such action token is both fine and shameful, but that some of them are fine and others are shameful.[21]

The discussion of explanation in the *Phaedo* refers primarily to properties: having a head, being taller by a head, and so on. When he contrasts the 'safe' explanation referring to Forms with the defective explanations he has illustrated, Plato insists that we should say that beautiful things are beautiful because of the Beautiful Itself, not 'by having a bright colour or a shape or anything else of that kind' (*Phd.* 100c9–d2). He seems to mean the same by saying (1) that bright-coloured things, say, are both beautiful and ugly, (2) that bright colour is both beautiful and ugly, or (3) that bright colour makes things beautiful and ugly. The third formula conveys his main point most accurately.

It would be going too far to claim that when Plato speaks of 'the many Fs', he always and unambiguously has in mind alleged F-making properties, as opposed to F particulars. In some cases it is easy not to see the distinction. For in the case of equality, largeness, and smallness, particulars as well as properties seem to suffer the relevant sort of compresence. The comparative character of largeness and equality implies that whatever is large or equal in one comparison will also be small or unequal in another. But no sound parallel argument can be given to show that the same is true for the moral properties (goodness, bravery, justice, and so on) that are Socrates' main concern.[22] Plato never implies that every single token brave action (for instance) is also cowardly, and such claims play no role in his arguments about the many Fs and Forms.[23]

111. The Role of the Senses

Now that we have seen what Plato means by his claim that the many Fs are F and not F, whereas the Form cannot suffer from this compresence of opposites, we ought to return to his claim that the many Fs are sensible, but the Form is non-sensible. This emphasis on the senses is one aspect of the middle dialogues that has no parallel in any earlier dialogues. In the *Meno* Plato introduces knowledge gained by recollection, but he does not explicitly contrast it with sense perception, and he does not discuss the role of sense perception in the process of recollection. In the *Phaedo* and *Republic*, by contrast, the contrast between sense perception and thought is closely connected with the contrast between the many and the one. Plato believes that in order to recollect the form of F that Socrates was looking for, we must distinguish it from all the sensible Fs that suffer the compresence of opposites, and so we must grasp it by something other than the senses.

The connexion between the senses and the compresence of opposites is most strongly asserted in *Republic* VII. When Plato describes the growth of reasoning and reflexion, he especially mentions mathematical properties. These are the ones for which the senses give us unsatisfactory answers: 'In some cases the things the senses give us do not provoke thought to examination, on the assumption that they are adequately discriminated by the senses; but in other cases they urge thought in every way to examine, on the assumption that sense produces nothing sound' (*R.* 523a10–b4). The cases that do not provoke thought include our perception of fingers; those that do provoke thought include our perception of their largeness and smallness.

Plato explains what it means to say that the senses sometimes do not provoke thought. He makes it clear that he is not thinking of perceptual error or illusion (resulting, for instance, from seeing fingers at a distance; 523b5–e2). He is concerned only with cases in which the senses report that the same thing is large and small, or hard and soft (523e2–524a5).

To understand this passage, we need to answer two questions: (1) What contrast does Plato intend to draw between sense and thought? (2) What does it mean to say that 'the same thing' is large and small? Plato attributes to 'the same thing' the compresence of opposites that he normally attributes to the many Fs, and we have seen that 'the many Fs' may refer to particulars or to properties and types; which does he have in mind here?

The first question does not allow a very detailed answer, since Plato does not say much here about the contrast between sense and thought. We might be inclined to draw the contrast so that sense by itself includes no thought; in that case, the contribution of sense is the basis for a perceptual judgment but does not itself include any concepts or judgments. This is the conception of sense that Plato accepts in the *Theaetetus* in order to show that sense does not yield knowledge; knowledge requires the application of concepts and judgments, and the application of these is not a task for the senses (*Tht.* 184b4–186e12).

In the present passage, however, Plato does not seem to intend such a minimal conception of sense.[24] He says that in perceiving a finger, 'sight in no case indicated to it <sc. the soul> at the same time that the finger is the contrary of a finger' (523d5–6). The judgment that this thing is a finger and that thing is not a finger is attributed to sense; it is only when sense gives conflicting judgments of this sort that thought is provoked to ask questions. Plato does not say that perceptual judgments do not involve thought, but he suggests that in some cases sense 'discriminates adequately' (523b1–2) without provoking thought to examination. The point, then, seems to be that in some cases the degree of thought needed for the perceptual judgment that this is a finger does not lead us into further questions about what a finger is.

If sense is not meant to exclude all thought, it may be easier to answer the second question about the passage. The most important point for interpretation is Plato's claim that perceptual judgments about large and small, heavy and light, in contrast to perceptual judgments about fingers, provoke the soul to ask what heavy and light are. The soul is puzzled because sense indicates that the same thing is light and heavy, or (equivalently, according to Plato) that the heavy is light and the light is heavy (524a9–10). Sight shows light and heavy confused (524c3–4), so that the soul is provoked to ask whether light and heavy are one or two (524b3–5). This sort of question is raised by cases where we cannot adequately grasp something 'itself by itself' (524d10)[25] by sense, but can grasp it only confused with its contrary (524e2–4).

The difficulty that Plato mentions seems spurious if 'the same thing', 'the light', and so on refer to particular objects, such as this finger that we take to be both heavy and light. For the mere fact that the senses attribute contrary properties to one and the same object does not seem to create any special difficulty; we do not, for instance, accuse sight of confusing squareness and whiteness if it reports that a sugar cube is both square and white. Even mutually exclusive properties need not raise any difficulty. Nothing can be both red and green all over, but if sight reports that the Italian flag is red and green in different parts, it is not confusing red and green. Equally, then, the mere fact that sight reports that something is equal and unequal, or large and small, should not lead us to say that sight confuses these two properties; if it reports that a mouse is big next to a small mouse, but small next to an elephant, that report does not by itself seem to confuse largeness and smallness. Nor is it clear why these perceptual judgments should raise a question about whether large and small are one or two.

Plato's claim is much more plausible if we take 'the same thing' and so on to refer to properties (largeness, etc.) rather than to the particular objects (this large finger, etc.) that have the properties. This is what he means by saying that the sight does not adequately see the 'largeness and smallness' of things (523e3–7). He claims that the senses confuse opposite properties, not merely that they take the same thing to have opposite properties. In saying that, according to the senses, 'the hard' is also soft (524a1–10), Plato uses 'the hard' to refer to the property that the senses identify with hardness.

Plato suggests, then, that sight counts the same things as evidence for calling something a finger in all cases, whereas it counts the same thing as evidence for attributing contrary properties in the case of large and small. The senses are open to the objection that was raised in the discussion of explanations in the *Phaedo*. If we consider what aspect of this mouse makes it big, we may mention its length, say, six inches. But if we are asked what makes it small (in comparison to an elephant that is twelve feet long), we may mention its six-inch length again. And so we are saying that the same property is both largeness and smallness.[26]

In Plato's view, Forms such as the Large, the Equal, and the Just cannot be properties that are grasped by the senses. Whatever the senses offer us to answer our question about largeness, this property turns out to be both largeness (in some things) and smallness (in other things); and so a six-inch length is one of 'the many Fs' that turn out to be both F and not-F, and cannot be the F Itself. When we are confused by this reflexion on the reports by the senses, we begin to ask what largeness and smallness are; we come to recognize that they cannot be properties that we grasp through the senses.

112. Sensible Properties

What entitles Plato to say that the properties making something a finger are accessible to the senses, and that the senses never take different views about what these properties are, whereas the property making something equal or large is inaccessible to the senses?[27]

In order to avoid judging that the same thing is both largeness and smallness, we must avoid identifying these properties with determinate lengths (or other quantities), and we must realize that whether x is large depends both on a comparison with other things and on reference to an appropriate standard of comparison. Why is it not within the competence of sight to take account of these features of largeness in informing the soul about what largeness is? Conversely, sense is supposed to be competent to find the features that make something a finger, and it never informs us that the same property makes one thing a finger and something else not a finger. Why is this?

Plato might argue that we can remove doubts about whether something is a finger if we observe the finger more carefully, whereas we do not remove the appearance that the same thing is largeness and smallness by further observation of the thing that has these opposite properties. If we are to understand that six inches is both largeness (in a mouse) and smallness (in an elephant), we must attend not only to this length but also to the relevant standard of comparison and the relevant context, and these are not features that we can observe in a particular situation. If we are thinking of mice, the mouse is large; if we are thinking of inhabitants of the zoo, the comparison with other mice is irrelevant and the comparison with the elephant is relevant, so that the mouse is small. Nothing in our observation of the mouse and its environment tells us that one or the other standard of comparison is the right one to apply. We would be misunderstanding the source of our mistake if we were to say that we ought to have observed the large mouse more carefully in order to recognize that it is small; we were not mistaken (we might want to say) in any of our observations of the mice, and we need to get the relevant information from some source outside our observation of this situation.

The same point comes out more clearly, as Plato intends it to, in the case of arithmetical properties. We can observe that there are three copies of a book on the table, that each has three hundred pages, and that each has a binding and a dust jacket. But is there one thing, are there three things, or are there at least 906 things on the table? If we are publishers considering how many new titles we have published, booksellers considering our profits, or book manufacturers considering the materials we need, a different answer is appropriate, but we do not find which answer is appropriate simply by observing these books in their present environment. The same questions arise about deciding whether something is or is not the same book or the same page as the one we were reading before; the answer seems to depend on the question we have in mind, not on something we can settle by observing the books or the pages themselves. In the cases that interest Plato, the role of contextual facts external to the observable situation implies that observation cannot provide an account of the relevant properties. What makes one situation sufficiently similar to another is an external, contextual fact that is not a matter of observation.

The relevance of context explains why compresence of opposites should be a mark of the observable instances of some properties. Being six inches long is not itself being large; it counts as being large in one context, and as being small in another. The same length may embody both properties, but which it embodies is not determined by the length itself, but by the context in which it is placed (comparison with mice or comparison with animals). Plato suggests, then, that if contextual facts are essential to the nature of a property, that property is not an observable property, and observation confronts us with the compresence of opposites. This is why the senses cannot be sources of knowledge about the properties that are the normal focus of Socratic inquiry (*Phd.* 65d4–66a8, 75c7–d5).

113. Objections to the Senses: Types of Flux

So far the dialogues confirm Aristotle's claim that Plato connects his arguments for Forms with objections to the senses. It is not so clear, however, that they confirm his claim that Plato believes in non-sensible Forms because he believes sensibles are all subject to change and flux; for the arguments we have considered so far do not mention change but refer to compresence of opposites. Have we, then, missed some important aspect of Plato's objections to sensible things? Or is Aristotle mistaken?[28]

We have good reason to believe that Aristotle is not mistaken, once we notice that Plato himself speaks of change in sensibles and seems to regard this as a reason for denying that they can be objects of knowledge and definition. In the *Cratylus* he suggests that knowledge requires the existence of unchanging forms as objects of knowledge; even if sensibles are all in flux, forms must be exempt from flux (*Cra.* 439c6–440d2). In this passage Plato does not actually affirm that sensibles are in flux,[29] but in other dialogues he seems to affirm precisely that; after he has argued that the Forms are different from sensibles, he claims that sensibles undergo constant change, whereas Forms are completely unchanging (*Phd.* 78c10–e4; *R.* 495a10–b3, 508d4–9, 518e8–9, 525b5–6, 534a2–3). If Plato believes that flux in sensibles implies that there can no knowledge of them, why does he believe this?

According to Aristotle, Plato became familiar in his youth with Cratylus and with a Heracleitean belief that sensibles are in flux and cannot be known; he held this same belief later (*Met.* 987a32–b1). Apparently, then, Plato looked at Socrates' search for definitions in the light of Heracleitean beliefs about flux.[30] What might he have taken these beliefs to imply?

In Plato's report, 'Heracleitus says somewhere that everything passes away and nothing remains, and in likening beings to the flow of a river he says that you could not step into the same river twice' (*Cra.* 402a8–10). This claim is about the succession of properties in the same subject over time. But Plato ascribes a second view to Heracleitus, that everything 'is always being drawn together in being drawn apart' (*Sph.* 242e2–3). This claim is about the compresence of opposite properties in the same subject at the same time.

Plato takes this second Heracleitean thesis to express a belief in flux. He explains how Protagoras' belief in the truth of appearances leads to the doctrine that 'nothing is any one thing itself by itself', because, for instance, you cannot call anything large without its appearing small, or heavy without its appearing light (*Tht.* 152d2–6). These appearances of compresence are the result of motion, change, and mingling, so that everything merely comes to be (hard, soft, light, heavy, and so on) and nothing stably is what we take it to be (152d2–e1).

According to Plato, this is a doctrine of 'flux and change' (152e8). In speaking of heavy, light, and so on, Plato clearly refers to the Heracleitean doctrine of the compresence of opposites; he thinks no further explanation is needed to justify him in describing such a doctrine as a doctrine of flux. He therefore assumes that it is appropriate to speak of 'flux', 'change', and 'becoming' in describing the instability that is manifested in the compresence of opposites.[31]

The *Cratylus* speaks in similar terms of the Protagorean doctrine. Plato claims that, according to this doctrine, things would be 'relative to us, and dragged by us up and down by our appearance' (*Cra.* 386e1–2). Things are 'dragged by our appearance' if we have conflicting (as a non-Protagorean would suppose) beliefs about them, so that (according to a Protagorean) contrary properties belong to them, but conflicting beliefs (of wise and foolish people) may be held at the same time. Plato does not assume that the instability Protagoras attributes to things is simply change over time; he uses terms that are appropriate for change in order to describe the instability involved in the compresence of opposites.

We ought not to assume, then, that when Plato speaks of flux he must have succession in mind; and so we ought not to be surprised when he begins by speaking of compresence and continues by speaking of change. We need not infer that Plato really intends some argument about succession or that he illegitimately infers succession from compresence; we should simply suppose that he assumes a broad interpretation of flux. The fact that he speaks of flux does not by itself tell us whether he has in mind change over time, compresence of opposites, or both at once. If we see that his arguments appeal only to compresence, not to change over time, we are justified in concluding that the type of flux he attributes to sensibles in explaining why they are unknowable is compresence.

If Aristotle sees that this is Plato's conception of flux, he does not mean to say that Plato thinks sensible objects undergo continual change over time, or that change over time is what makes them unsuitable as objects of knowledge. He may simply recognize that, given Plato's broad interpretation of flux, compresence of opposites counts as a kind of flux. We ought not to conclude, then, that Plato's argument from flux in sensibles relies on anything more than the compresence of opposites.[32]

114. The Senses and the Compresence of Opposites

Plato's claim that sensibles do not yield knowledge of forms helps to explain why Socrates did not find definitions. Socrates in the early dialogues does not speak as though his requests for definitions are unanswerable; on the contrary, he stresses the importance of answering them and works hard to find answers. But neither he nor others are said to find answers of the sort he wants. No doubt the questions are difficult, but it may well seem surprising that Socrates tries so hard to answer them, but apparently always fails. Does he impose inappropriately stringent demands on definitions?

If we are asked to say what bravery is, we quite rightly begin with our beliefs about particular brave actions and people, and we think about how we recognize them in particular situations. We observe that in particular situations brave people stand firm, temperate people are quiet, just people pay back what they have borrowed, and so on. These observations of particular situations are quite accurate, as far as they go, but Socrates points out that these observable properties (standing firm, quietness, etc.) are not the ones we are looking for, since in other particular situations we can observe the opposite properties, even though people display the same virtues, or we can observe the same properties, even though people fail to display the same virtues.

How ought we to react to this discovery? We might suppose that we have not yet found the right observable property. Socrates' interlocutors, at any rate, suppose that an account of F should mention one and the same observable feature present in every situation where something F can be observed; when they find none, Socrates points out that they have given an inadequate account of F, but he does not tell them where they have gone wrong. Does he assume that if we look hard enough, we ought to be able to find the single observable property that the interlocutors have not found?

The Socratic dialogues and the *Meno* do not actually say that Socrates assumes that observable properties are needed for a definition. But at least Socrates does not discourage the interlocutors from looking in this direction, and we have suggested, by appealing to the *Euthyphro* on disputes and measurement and to the *Meno* on the dialectical condition, that he actually requires definitions to refer only to observable properties.[33]

Plato suggests, on the contrary, that this way of looking for a definition is sometimes misguided in principle. It is easy to see why he thinks it would be a mistake to identify largeness or smallness with observable properties; but why does he believe that moral properties are among those that cannot be identified with observable properties?

115. Difficulties about Moral Properties

Sometimes Plato suggests that moral properties are especially likely to cause disagreement and dispute. In the *Euthyphro* Socrates contrasts moral properties with those that raise disputes that can be settled by measurement. In the *Phaedrus* he distinguishes 'gold' and 'silver' from 'just' and 'good' (*Phdr.* 263a2–b2). In cases of the first type we all 'think the same' when someone uses the name, but in cases of the second type 'we disagree with one another and with ourselves', and we are 'confused' (263a6–b5). Plato does not say that we disagree about whether this or that action is just or unjust, but that we have different thoughts about justice; by this he may mean simply that we have different beliefs about justice or conceptions of justice.[34]

The division between disputed and non-disputed properties seems to be connected with that between sensible and non-sensible. The properties examined in the Socratic elenchos are clearly disputed properties; they are mentioned in the *Phaedo* as non-sensible properties, and properties that involve the compresence of opposites in their sensible embodiments include moral properties. It is reasonable to assume, then, that disputed properties are a proper subset of non-sensible properties. What is the difference between these and other non-sensible properties that explains why moral properties are disputed, whereas numerical properties, for instance, are not?

No one would argue that numerical or comparative properties should be identified with sensible properties. In fact when Plato mentions accounts such as 'by a head' as explanations of largeness, his point is to show how evidently ridiculous they are. In these cases there is no serious difficulty in finding an account that is not confined to sensible properties.

Moral properties, however, are less clear. Indeed, it is easy to draw a Heracleitean conclusion that Plato wants to reject. In the *Cratylus* the discussion turns to the 'fine names' of 'wisdom', 'understanding', 'justice', and so on. Socrates suggests that the etymology of these names shows that the inventors of the names supposed that the underlying realities were in flux; but, in his view, they thought this simply because of their own waverings and confusions about the nature of these things, and they transferred the instability in their own convictions to the things themselves (*Cra.* 411a1–c5).

This remark describes a Heracleitean reaction to the compresence of opposites. Heracleiteans may argue that, for instance, justice is returning and not returning what you have borrowed, keeping and not keeping your promises, and so on. In saying this, they suppose that the different sensible properties that are the focus of dispute about justice must themselves be the only defining properties of justice.

These arguments suggest that Socrates' search for a definition of moral properties combines incompatible demands. If we suppose that moral properties must be identified with some sort of sensible properties, then the assumption that there must be one form of justice, piety, and so on, is open to doubt; it seems more reasonable to identify each moral property with a list of sensible properties. Socrates' metaphysical demand on adequate definitions is incompatible with this Heracleitean view, but if he assumes that a definition should treat moral properties as sensible properties, he is open to the Heracleitean objection.

Against this objection, Plato argues that the Heracleitean confuses different embodiments of justice in different circumstances with the property that is embodied in these different ways, so that the Heracleitean thinks the variation in these embodying properties is a variation in justice itself. In Plato's view, this Heracleitean makes the sort of mistake that we would make if we were to identify a river with the particular quantity of water that happens to fill its banks at a particular time; on this view there cannot be any continuing river. We might answer this Heracleitean view by pointing out that while the particular quantity of water constituting the river changes, the river itself remains the same. Similarly, we might argue, the compresence of opposites is confined to the sensible properties that embody justice; since each of these is just only in its specific context, it is not surprising that in a different context it ceases to be just. Since justice itself cannot also be unjust in a different context, it cannot be identical to these sensible properties that embody it.

Plato has good reasons for believing that moral properties are essentially contextual. Numerical and comparative properties are contextual because the features that determine whether one of these properties is embodied in a particular case are features external to particular observable situations. Something similar seems to be true of moral properties as well. Socrates often insists that each of the virtues is essentially fine and beneficial, and so facts about what is fine and beneficial must affect questions about whether this or that sort of action is brave or just. Whether an action is fine and beneficial may depend on, among other things, the agent's reason for doing it, the actual or expected effects of the action, and the social institutions and practices within which the agent acts. If this is so, then observation of the action itself will not tell us whether it is fine and beneficial, and so will not tell us whether an action is brave. Bravery and justice must be essentially contextual properties.

This argument could be answered if we could show, for instance, that one moral property is sensible, so that it can be defined in sensible, non-contextual terms, and that all other moral properties can be defined by reference to this one. If we could show this, we would vindicate Socrates' suggestion that disputed terms ought to be eliminated from definitions of moral properties, and we would satisfy the dialectical condition imposed in the *Meno*. Plato's reasons for believing that moral properties are non-sensible, however, apply equally to whatever property might be chosen as the basic one: just, fine, or good. If all of these are non-sensible, we have no reason to assume that one of them must be more basic than the others. If we can define the good, the fine, and the just only by reference to each other, then we cannot hope to find an account that relies only on context-free observable properties.

If this is Plato's point, and if we have correctly understood Socrates' demands on a definition, then Plato argues that Socrates' metaphysical demand for a single explanatory property conflicts with his epistemological demand that could be satisfied only by a sensible property. According to Plato, we cannot find a single explanatory property if we insist that it must be a sensible property, and therefore the different requirements for a definition that are imposed in the *Meno* cannot all be satisfied.

This argument to show that Plato intends a direct refutation of Socrates' criteria for definitions has been rather speculative at some crucial points. It must be admitted both that Plato does not affirm the essential interconnexion of definitions of moral properties and that the Socratic dialogues do not explicitly deny it. In order to show that Plato disagrees with Socrates, we have to interpret some of Socrates' demands in more precise terms than he actually uses. It is quite possible that Plato does not believe he is rejecting anything that Socrates would have said if he had been aware of its full implications.

Still, even if we do not agree that Plato deliberately rejects Socrates' explicit or implicit views about inquiry and definition, we ought to admit that he makes definite claims that Socrates does not make and rules out some approaches to definition that Socrates does not rule out. Socrates talks in general terms about finding the one in the many, a paradigm, and an explanation. If he does not see what is wrong with attempts to find definitions of moral properties that reduce them to sensible properties, then he does not see what demands on Socratic definitions are reasonable. Even if Socrates is merely silent or indeterminate on points that Plato emphasizes, Plato's arguments ought to make some difference to the search for Socratic definitions.

116. Definitions and Hypotheses

If Plato rejects an account of moral properties that reduces them to sensible properties, has he anything to say about what an illuminating account ought to be like? He comes closest to answering this question in the *Phaedo*. After rejecting the explanations that appeal to sensible properties, he offers his own preferred type of explanation. Instead of saying that things are beautiful by the presence of bright colour, symmetrical shape, or some other sensible property, he prefers to say that whatever is beautiful is so by the presence of the non-sensible Form of the beautiful (*Phd.* 100c3–e3). This remark does not tell us what an explanation referring to the non-sensible Form will be like or how the Form is to be described. To say that x is F because the Form of F is present to it is a schema for an explanatory account, not itself a satisfactory account.[35]

Plato adds something, however, to suggest how one might approach the right sort of account. He suggests that we should put forward a 'hypothesis' or assumption (100a3–7, 101c9–102a1). This hypothesis is the account that we judge strongest (100a4), and we judge how strong it is by seeing whether the consequences are in accord or discord with it. The consequences of accepting the hypothesis are not merely the logical consequences of the hypothesis alone but also the total consequences of accepting this hypothesis together with the other beliefs that we accept, and so we test the hypothesis against the whole set of these beliefs. The hypothesis is to be accepted if it explains our other relevant beliefs—this is part of its function as an explanation—and if it does not conflict with them.[36]

Plato recognizes that this sort of hypothesis may not by itself provide an adequate explanation. We may have to give an account of the hypothesis; to do this, we must find a higher hypothesis and ask the same questions about the concord or discord of other beliefs with this hypothesis. We must continue this process until we 'come to something adequate' (101e1). Plato does not say what counts as something adequate, but he emphasizes the importance of resorting to a higher hypothesis. It would be a sign of confusion if we mixed up discussion of a principle or starting point (*archê*) with discussion of its consequences (101e1–3). Plato suggests that not every sort of objection to a hypothesis should persuade us to abandon the hypothesis. In some cases we ought to retain the hypothesis and defend it, not by examining the consequences but by deriving it from a higher hypothesis. Why does Plato think it worth insisting on this point, and how is it relevant to Socratic definition?

We can see the point of appealing to a higher hypothesis if we consider a possible consequence of believing that Forms are non-sensible. In earlier dialogues Socrates sometimes seems to protest that if we must keep mentioning moral properties in our accounts of moral properties, our accounts will be uninformative and unacceptable (*G.* 451d5–e1, 489e6–8); and we have seen how the *Euthyphro* and the *Meno* might support this protest. Thrasymachus makes the same protest especially forcefully in *Republic* I, arguing that any account of the just as the expedient, the beneficial, or the advantageous is unacceptable, and that the only acceptable definition must say what the just is 'clearly and exactly' in terms that escape from this circle of accounts of moral properties (*R.* 336c6–d4).[37] If Forms are non-sensible, however, Plato cannot guarantee that circular accounts of them can be avoided.

To show that circular accounts are sometimes acceptable, Plato needs to distinguish different types of circular accounts. Circularity is open to objection if the circle of terms and definitions is too small. But the same objections do not necessarily apply if the circle is wider; for even if we cannot eliminate a circle of definitions, we may be able to make them more intelligible by displaying the right sorts of connexions between our account of moral properties and other sorts of explanations. Plato might reasonably have this point in mind when he asks for a higher hypothesis. Circular accounts of moral properties are not necessarily to be rejected simply because each of them is uninformative by itself. We should not try to replace them with a different sort of account; instead, we should place them in a theoretical context that will make them intelligible and explanatory by reference to higher, more general hypotheses.

To describe this passage as Plato's account of 'the hypothetical method' is a bit exaggerated. His remarks are too brief and imprecise to give us a very clear impression of any specific method that he might have in mind. Still, it is useful to see how they might reasonably be connected with questions that we have seen arise in Plato's arguments for non-sensible Forms. The more we can connect Plato's remarks about Forms and explanations with our account of his arguments, the better reason we have for confidence in our account.

These claims about the *Phaedo* and about the implications of the non-sensible character of Forms more generally are bound to seem rather speculative until we connect them with Plato's actual search for Socratic definitions. Fortunately, the *Republic* offers us an extended search for definitions; in fact, it presents definitions of the virtues that Socrates in the early dialogues tries and fails to define. What explains this difference between the *Republic* and the earlier dialogues? We might say that Socrates' failure was merely a pretence, that Plato is more dogmatic than Socrates, or that Plato is wrongly satisfied with accounts that Socrates would rightly have challenged. We might, however, find that in the middle dialogues Plato has formulated his task more clearly and that in the *Republic* he carries it out with more success. Our discussion of the middle dialogues should make it worthwhile to explore this question about the *Republic*.

11

Republic I

117. The Significance of Book I

The *Republic* begins with two long introductions. Book I is an apparently self-contained dialogue about the definition of justice. Book II apparently criticizes the argument of Book I; for Glaucon claims to be dissatisfied with the case against Thrasymachus (358b1–4) and seeks to restate Thrasymachus's view in preparation for a new reply by Socrates. Glaucon's comment shows that Plato intends to provoke dissatisfaction.

To see what is unsatisfactory in Book I, we ought to notice its Socratic character. It seems to have more in common with the *Laches* and *Charmides* than with the *Protagoras*, the *Gorgias*, or the *Meno*, let alone the *Phaedo* or the rest of the *Republic*. Some readers have been convinced that it actually is an early dialogue that Plato later used to introduce the *Republic*. Even readers who believe—more plausibly—that it is not an early dialogue agree that Plato writes it in order to remind us of the Socratic dialogues.[1]

We have seen reasons for believing that in the *Gorgias*, and especially in the *Meno* and the middle dialogues, Plato seeks both to defend and to revise some of the claims and arguments presented in the early dialogues. If we are right to believe this, then we ought to ask whether the specifically Socratic features of Book I are the focus of Plato's criticism in the *Republic*.[2]

We ought not to suppose that if Plato criticizes some of Socrates' claims and arguments he means to reject the main elements (as he sees them) of Socrates' moral outlook. In the *Gorgias* and the *Meno*, Plato sometimes suggests that Socrates does not give satisfactory arguments—either because he gives no arguments or because he gives inadequate arguments—but the positions he defends are nonetheless defensible. This seems to be Plato's attitude, for instance, to Socrates' beliefs that virtue promotes happiness and that knowledge is necessary for virtue. We might suppose, then, that Book I sketches some of the conclusions that Plato means to defend; the rest of the *Republic* should show us how he means to defend them.[3]

A decision on these suggestions about Book I depends on our view about the rest of the *Republic*. The suggestions are worth considering, however, in reading Book I, so that we can see what sorts of doubts might be raised by Socrates' arguments and which of his views might seem to need further defence.

118. Cephalus

Readers disagree about whether Cephalus is an attractive or an unattractive character.[4] This disagreement is intelligible, since Plato presents him in a favourable light, but also attributes some questionable moral views to him.

Some of Cephalus' views are close to the views of Socrates in the *Gorgias*. Cephalus praises the outlook of 'orderly and calm' people (329d4).[5] He implies that, as Socrates argued against Callicles,[6] we achieve happiness by first forming desires that we can satisfy and then satisfying them; happiness does not depend on the number or the intensity of desires we satisfy. To this extent, it is up to us to be happy. Cephalus also agrees with the Socratic view that justice and temperance promote peace of mind. Temperate people are not tempted to cheat or lie, since they are not so greedy that they want the benefits that can be gained by cheating or lying.

Cephalus does not take justice to be necessary for happiness; it is simply a way to secure peace of mind in facing the afterlife. We might wonder why, in that case, we could not substitute wealth for justice. Could we not make up for injustice by being wealthy, using our wealth wisely to compensate people for our past unjust treatment of them, and conciliating the gods by splendid sacrifices? On this point, justice actually seems inferior to wealth, since Cephalus believes that a just life without wealth is hard to bear (330a3–6), whereas injustice leading to wealth and comfort can be turned to our advantage. Cephalus has not explained, then, why we should endorse the unqualified commitment to justice that Socrates advocates in earlier dialogues.

This is not a purely theoretical disagreement between Socrates and Cephalus. Cephalus assumes that he will leave his wealth to his sons (330b6–7), and in fact he did. But things did not turn out as he expected. After the dramatic date of the *Republic*, but before the actual writing of the dialogue, the Thirty expropriated Cephalus' sons, Lysias and Polemarchus, and murdered Polemarchus. In his account of these events, Lysias remarks that his family had lived as law-abiding subjects of the democracy, 'neither committing any offence against other people nor suffering injustice from them' (Lysias XII 4), but their wealth made them irresistibly tempting to the Thirty (XII 6). Cephalus mentions wealth and justice as two means of securing happiness, but neither of them seemed to benefit his sons, if benefit is to be measured by Cephalus' standards. Admittedly, the Thirty could deprive Cephalus' sons of their wealth, but not of their justice, and so their justice seems more stable than their wealth; but might they not have been better off if they had been astutely unjust?

If Plato intends his readers to recall these facts about Cephalus' family, he emphasizes a question that ought to emerge in any case from Cephalus' remarks on justice. Cephalus' attitude to justice is frankly instrumental, and, given his conception of justice and happiness, his commitment to justice seems rather unstable. If Socrates agrees with Cephalus in taking justice to be purely instrumental to happiness, he ought to explain how he can justify a more stable commitment to justice.

119. Polemarchus

Socrates introduces the argument with Polemarchus by taking up Cephalus' remarks about just and unjust behaviour. He asks: 'This very thing, justice—are we to say, just like that,[7] that it is telling the truth and returning what we have received from someone? Or is it possible to do even these very things sometimes justly and sometimes unjustly?' (331c1–5). Socrates gives a counter-example to this definition,[8] pointing out that if A and B are friends and A returns B's sword to B when B has gone mad, 'one ought not to return that sort of thing, nor would the one returning it be just', and A ought not to tell the truth about everything to B (331c7–9).

Polemarchus defends the account of justice that Socrates has challenged; he argues that it fits Simonides' view[9] about justice, that 'rendering to each person what is due to him is just' (331e3–4).[10] Socrates does not say that this is a definition of justice or of just action; he examines it simply as a purported property of just action. He suggests that Simonides' view should carry some weight, but it is difficult to know what Simonides meant (331e5–8, 332b9–c1). Socrates assumes that Simonides cannot have meant to endorse Cephalus' view because it has the fault just noticed (331e8–332a8).

Socrates seeks to clarify Polemarchus' suggestion by asking what Simonides meant by speaking of what is 'due' or 'owed' to each person.[11] First, Socrates objects that it is difficult to describe a specific subject matter and a specific benefit that are characteristic of justice, since every subject matter that we suggest already seems to be taken up by some other specialized craft (332c5–333e2).[12] This objection invites the reply that justice is not an ordinary craft, but a superordinate craft of the sort described in the *Euthydemus*.[13] Socrates does not mention this reply.

He perhaps considers this reply, however, in his second objection. He suggests that if Polemarchus is right, the just person is someone who uses a craft—concerned with keeping and breaking his word—in whatever way benefits his friends and harms his enemies (333e3–334b6).[14] This conclusion is unacceptable because it implies that the just person uses both just and unjust means to help his friends and harm his enemies.

Although he rejects the conclusion that justice involves cheating people, Polemarchus maintains nonetheless that it involves harming enemies. His view implies that if we wrongly believe that certain people are bad and they are our enemies, we will be harming good people who do no injustice; but Polemarchus recognizes that such action would be unjust (334c1–d8). His own life later confirmed this judgment. After he was murdered by the Thirty, his brother Lysias complained that the Thirty treated the brothers unjustly by setting out to rob them when they had committed no injustice but, on the contrary, had shown goodwill to Athens and deserved a better return (Lysias XII 20). Polemarchus' suggestion about justice licenses the sort of treatment that he must have recognized as flagrantly unjust when he was the victim of it.

Polemarchus modifies his view further by suggesting that the just person is right to harm the bad people who are his enemies (335b2–5). In the *Crito* Socrates claims that we ought not to retaliate against injustice by treating the offender badly. In this passage he tries to support that claim by arguing for the stronger claim that it is not proper to the just person to harm anyone (335b6–d13).[15] He assumes that to harm other people is to make them more unjust and that it is not a proper exercise of justice to make other people unjust.

These assumptions, however, are controversial. The claim that to harm people is to make them more unjust would be true if justice were necessary and sufficient for happiness; for in that case the only way to make people worse off would be to make them more unjust. Even if we agree that we cannot harm people except by making them more unjust, how do we know that the just person will not make other people more unjust? Socrates answers that the exercise of justice will always benefit others and make them more just; why should we believe that?

Although these questions can certainly be raised about Socrates' argument, it still shows something wrong with Polemarchus' suggestion. For if we add up Polemarchus' different remarks about justice, he is now committed to saying that the just person is required to harm his enemy in whatever way he can, as long as the enemy is really a bad person and as long as the just person does not resort to cheating or deception. It follows that justice requires the infliction of unprovoked harm that is entirely disproportionate to any wrongdoing or vice by the bad person. It is reasonable for Socrates to suggest that this licence to harm will make the victims more unjust[16] and that such flagrant injustice cannot be characteristic of the just person.

Socrates concludes that we misrepresent Simonides if we take him to have believed that justice allows us to harm people; indeed, he suggests that this view of justice reflects the outlook of a manifestly unjust tyrant (336a5–7), not of the sages. Socrates means that a tyrant exercising his power to help his friends and harm his enemies, as the Thirty did at the expense of Lysias and Polemarchus, might well find it convenient to make his behaviour appear just, but we acknowledge that his claim would be a fraud.

120. Simonides on Justice

Socrates seems to suggest, then, that the Simonidean view should not be explained by appeal to the rule of helping friends and harming enemies. Should it be explained by some other rules of just behaviour? In raising this question, the argument with Polemarchus leads us into some of the central questions discussed in the *Republic*.

First, what is Socrates trying to define? The question he raises is about 'justice' (*dikaiosunē*). This abstract noun might be taken to pick out a property of just actions or of just people. When Socrates remarks that A ought not to return B's weapons if B has gone mad, he is speaking of the justness (if we can coin this abstract noun) of actions; when he says that A would not be just if he did this, he is speaking of the justness of persons. Book I, like the Socratic dialogues, raises questions both about just actions and about just persons, without saying how these questions are related.[17]

We might seek first to define just actions and then to define the just person as simply one who does these just actions. That is Cephalus' implicit view of justice as telling the truth and returning what we have received. Socrates examines this view throughout the argument with Polemarchus, pointing out the difficulty of stating clear and easily applicable necessary and sufficient conditions for just action independently of any further moral assumptions.[18]

Socrates argues that if we follow the rules suggested by Cephalus, we act 'sometimes justly, sometimes unjustly'. In that case, giving back what one has received is both just and unjust; it displays the compresence of opposites that Plato takes to be characteristic of sensible properties in relation to moral properties. This appeal to compresence of opposites is part of the crucial argument in Book V to show that knowledge requires knowledge of non-sensible Forms (479a5–8).[19]

Does Plato have this later argument in mind when he presents Socrates' objection to Cephalus? Certainly the objection itself would not be out of place in the Socratic dialogues, and the reader could readily understand it without knowing anything about Plato's Theory of Forms. Still, this precise claim does not actually appear in the Socratic dialogues.[20] Plato's decision to use in *Republic* I the expression that is characteristic of his arguments for Forms is a sign, although not conclusive proof, that he has the rest of the *Republic* in mind.

The claim that justice consists both in telling the truth and in giving back what we have received raises two further questions: (1) Are these the only actions required of a just person? (2) What do they have in common that explains why both are required of a just person? These are questions that Socrates raises about Meno's initial description of bravery, and they are also relevant to the discussion of the sight-lovers in Book V.

These faults in the initial description of justice are corrected in the Simonidean view; we can specify when we ought to tell the truth and return what we have been given, if we say we ought to do these things when they are 'due' or 'owed' to another person. Does Plato mean us to accept this correction of the initial description? We have some reason to believe that he does, since he does not suggest that the rejection of Polemarchus' attempted interpretations of the Simonidean view requires rejection of the view itself; Socrates says simply that they cannot have understood Simonides correctly.

If we had only Book I, we might say that this charitable attitude to Simonides is not to be taken seriously. But we are not entitled to say this once we notice that the Simonidean view is very important later in the dialogue. In Book IV it is said to be a common view that justice consists in 'doing one's own' (433a8–b1). This is not quite the same as the Simonidean view about just action, but the two views are connected. For if we assign to each person what is due to him, then he will have 'his own' (what is due to him), and if he keeps to this assignment he will also do 'his own'; when Book IV connects 'having one's own' with 'doing one's own' (433e6–434a1), it recalls the Simonidean view still more clearly.[21]

In Book VII Plato actually suggests how the Simonidean view helps to reveal the truth in the initial description of justice as returning what one has received. Socrates argues that the philosophers in the ideal city can reasonably be expected to take their part in ruling. This city has brought them up and educated them so that they develop their natural philosophical gifts; their service to the city is a fair return for what they have received (520a6–c1). Socrates appeals to justice (520a6, 520e1). The city has given the philosophers 'their own' and what was due to them, and they are asked to return what they owe.

These passages make it clear that the whole moral basis of the organization of the ideal city vindicates the Simonidean view and displays the element of truth in Cephalus' original view connecting justice with reciprocity. These later appeals to the views of Simonides and Cephalus suggest that Plato means us to notice that the Simonidean view about just action is not rejected in Book I. Plato does not intend Book I simply to dismiss erroneous views about justice; on the contrary, he defends some of the views introduced in Book I, once he has completed the long and complex task of interpreting them properly.

What needs to be added to the Simonidean view to make a satisfactory account of justice? Thrasymachus notices that it refers to what is 'due' or 'fitting', without a precise behavioural description of the sorts of actions that are due or fitting; a precise behavioural description would tell us something 'perspicuous and accurate' (336c6–d4).[22] Thrasymachus' demand is an example of the general view that a definition of moral properties should reduce them to non-moral, sensible properties. We must see whether the accounts of the virtues that are offered in the *Republic* attempt to conform to this general demand for definitions stated in non-moral terms.

121. Thrasymachus' Account

Socrates assumed that justice benefits the just person (that is why becoming unjust implies being harmed) and other people (since a just person is good, and a good person is beneficial). Thrasymachus agrees that the just person benefits other people, but he denies that justice benefits the agent. Instead, he argues that it is the advantage of the 'stronger' (or 'superior', *kreittōn*, 338c1–2). According to Thrasymachus, the common feature of just actions is that they belong to a just order:[23] they are prescribed by the laws enacted by some superior in the interest of the superior, and they actually promote the interest of the superior.[24]

In Thrasymachus' view, a just order does not exist simply because one person or group of people happens to be physically stronger than another; domination by the stronger person or people is actually injustice if it is not prescribed by laws enacted by some recognized ruler or ruling body. Nor does Thrasymachus mean that every law is automatically just; he recognizes the possibility of unjust laws, claiming that a law is just only if it actually promotes the interest of the stronger. The 'stronger' in question is the ruler 'on the exact account' who knows what is in the interest of the regime (340d1–341a4).

The care that Plato devotes to the statement and defence of Thrasymachus' definition shows that he takes it seriously as an account of justice that needs to be carefully examined and answered.[25] He could have pointed out that it fails to state a necessary or sufficient condition for justice, but he refrains from raising such objections, in order to concentrate on the plausible features of the account.[26] It accommodates the common beliefs that justice has something to do with law, that it promotes the stability of the community whose laws prescribe the just action, and that not every law is automatically just. It explains why we have difficulty in arguing that it is always in our interest to be just.

When Thrasymachus claims that justice is the interest of the stronger, he is thinking of a stable, law-abiding society in which people generally follow the rules of non-maleficence that we normally connect with justice. He is concerned with law-abiding behaviour, not with all types of behaviour that happen to benefit a stronger party (338c4–339a4), and he is concerned with behaviour by subjects, not with behaviour by rulers (343d–e). In claiming that justice benefits the stronger, he must distinguish the immediate from the ultimate beneficiary of rules of justice. If I keep my promise to return to you what I have borrowed, you are the immediate beneficiary, and I am the immediate loser. If I am punished justly, then I am the immediate loser and perhaps no one is the immediate beneficiary. According to Thrasymachus, however, the cumulative effect of the existence and general observance of these rules of justice is the greater stability of the community with its existing regime, and so the regime is the ultimate beneficiary.

If Thrasymachus' account is explained this way, has it identified the common feature by which all just actions are just, the feature that (as Socrates puts it) we ought to 'focus on' (*apoblepein*, *Eu.* 6e4) in calling things just? It does not seem to identify the feature we have in mind in calling things just; when we commend just people for acting justly, we probably have in mind the fact that they have benefited their neighbours or avoided harm to them, rather than the (alleged) fact that they have benefited the stronger.[27]

Still, even if it fails to capture our beliefs about what makes an action just, Thrasymachus' account may capture what just actions have in common in a different and more disturbing sense.[28] Thrasymachus follows Socrates' advice to seek the one in the many; the different requirements that Cephalus and Polemarchus connect with justice are all explained in his account. His point is that the ultimate beneficiary of the rules observed by just people is the community and its existing regime, and that the different requirements of justice are systematically directed to the benefit of the regime.

This explanation of the existence, content, and observance of rules of justice supports Thrasymachus' claim to have given a 'perspicuous and accurate' account of justice. It is 'perspicuous' insofar as it contains no terms (such as 'owed' or 'due' or 'appropriate') needing further moral judgments for their application, and it makes clear the real basis of justice.[29]

122. Objections to Thrasymachus: Rulers and Crafts

Socrates concedes that justice consists in obeying the laws of rulers 'on the exact account', those who correctly exercise their proper function as rulers; but he argues that if we concede this much to Thrasymachus, we cannot agree that justice should be defined as the interest of the stronger. For crafts, in Socrates' view, are properly concerned with the benefit of the object they work on; medicine as such is concerned with the welfare of the patient rather than with the welfare of the doctor. Similarly, ruling is concerned, insofar as it is the craft it is, with the interest of the subject rather than the ruler (342c8–e11). This was what Socrates assumed in the *Gorgias* about the political craft (*G.* 504d5–505b8), and now he defends his assumption.

Socrates is right to argue that if justice is laid down by a ruler exercising the ruling craft, it does not follow that justice is laid down in the interest of the ruler. But Socrates goes too far in claiming that the ruling craft must be properly concerned with the interest of the subject. Thrasymachus points out that even if every craft is concerned, as such, with the perfection or improvement of its object, this does not show that every craft is designed primarily for the benefit of the object rather than the practitioner of the craft; shepherds fatten their sheep, not in the sheep's interest, but in the interest of the shepherds who hope to sell them. If we apply this analogy to the ruler, then we support Thrasymachus' original claim about ruling and justice, and we must reject Socrates' alternative (343b1–c1).

In defending his account of justice, Thrasymachus introduces a broader issue, arguing that an unjust person turns out to be better off than a just person. Indeed, Thrasymachus suggests that this conclusion follows from his definition of justice: 'You don't know that justice and the just are in fact the good of another, the advantage of the superior and ruler, but a harm to the subject and the subservient party himself, whereas injustice is the contrary' (343c3–6).[30] Once we understand Thrasymachus' explanation of rules of justice, we can ask ourselves: If the ultimate beneficiary of these rules is the community and the regime, what is in them for me? Thrasymachus argues that once we see the point of rules of justice, we can see that we are better off if we violate them.[31] The just person always comes off worse because he is forced to sacrifice his own interest if he obeys the laws; the unjust person, by contrast, can look out for his own interest, both on a small scale and on the large scale that leads to tyranny (343c1–344c8).

In reply, Socrates accuses Thrasymachus of violating his policy of considering the craft in itself. If we consider the shepherd's craft in itself, we can see that it is concerned solely with the improvement of the sheep; the fact that shepherds hope to make money by rearing sheep is irrelevant to the nature of the craft and to what constitutes success in practising it. Similarly, the acquisitive aims of particular rulers are irrelevant to the nature of ruling; they do not affect the claim that ruling in itself is concerned with the improvement of the subjects (345b9–347d8).

Socrates is right; Thrasymachus has not proved that it is essential to rulers that they rule subjects in the rulers' interest and not in the subjects' interest. Thrasymachus cannot rely, then, on the general claim that a craft is exercised in the interest of the craftsman, since this claim has turned out to be false.

Still, even if Socrates has answered Thrasymachus' argument, he has not vindicated his own view that crafts are not designed to satisfy selfish interests. Even if the motives of individuals are not selfish, Thrasymachus might be right to say that ruling is in the interest of the stronger. For when his account of justice refers to 'the stronger', it refers to the regime; the interests of the regime may not be the individual interests of individual rulers. While it may be in this or that ruler's interest to line his own pockets and impoverish the citizens, this may well be inexpedient for the regime, since it may make the regime less stable. Therefore, the mere fact that rulers rule disinterestedly does not show that justice is not systematically directed towards the interest of the regime.

123. Thrasymachus on Justice and Virtue

Socrates now turns to consider Thrasymachus' claim that the unjust person is better off than the just person. Thrasymachus regards justice as vicious and foolish, not a virtue at all, since it is harmful; injustice is good deliberation and virtue, since it is advantageous (348c5–e3). Socrates comments that if Thrasymachus had said justice is a virtue, Socrates would have shown him 'in accordance with common beliefs' that justice promotes happiness better than injustice does (348e6–9). Since Thrasymachus denies that justice is a virtue, Socrates cannot use this argument against him.

In describing the argument 'in accordance with common beliefs', Socrates does not necessarily mean that everyone would immediately agree that justice must promote happiness. People might agree that if justice is a virtue, we ought always (as Socrates claims in the *Apology*, 28b5–9) to choose justice over injustice; and then if Socrates convinces them of the truth of his eudaemonism, which he takes to be evident, they will have to agree that justice always promotes happiness. This is why Socrates believes that people who regard justice as a virtue cannot consistently maintain that justice does not promote happiness. This sort of argument 'in accordance with common beliefs' is precisely the sort that Socrates uses against Polus in the *Gorgias*;[32] he acknowledges that he cannot use this sort of argument against Thrasymachus.[33]

The first argument (349b1–350c11) begins from the claim that 'the person who is able to do great things overreaches' (343e7–344a1). Thrasymachus said this about the unjust person who uses his opportunities to gain advantages for himself and so to 'overreach' (*pleonektein*) or get the better of other people. This is the person who goes in for 'complete unjust action' (348d5–9, 351b4–5); he takes every opportunity to commit injustice, especially on a large scale. Thrasymachus agrees that the unjust person takes this overreaching, competitive attitude to everyone. Socrates argues that competent practitioners of a craft do not try to overreach other competent practitioners; they recognize that it is foolish to try to prescribe more medicine than the right amount prescribed by a competent doctor. The indiscriminate desire to overreach is the mark of an incompetent and foolish practitioner. Measured by this standard, the unjust person turns out to be incompetent and foolish, since he tries to overreach everyone indiscriminately (349b1–350c11).

Socrates' argument is a fair answer to Thrasymachus' praise of 'complete injustice', as it has been described so far. Socrates assumes that Thrasymachus regards the unjust person as the contrary of the just person. Whereas the just person is strongly committed to just action whenever he has a choice between just and unjust action, the unjust person, as Socrates and Thrasymachus conceive him at this stage, is committed to unjust action in the same way.[34] Socrates argues that if it is characteristic of injustice—as Thrasymachus has claimed—to try to overreach or outdo other people in the accumulation of goods, then injustice is not always the best policy. Mere competitiveness in accumulation does not always seem to be advantageous.

This argument is similar to the argument about the ruling craft, insofar as it undermines Thrasymachus' actual defence. It still remains to be shown, however, that this is the most plausible way to conceive the unjust person.

124. Psychic Order

Socrates' second argument (349e11) against Thrasymachus takes up the claim that injustice is 'stronger' than justice (344c5). Socrates replies that, far from being stronger than justice, injustice always produces division, conflict, and incapacity for cooperative action in any group in which it is practised. Once again we must assume that the unjust person is unreservedly committed to unjust action, so that he will always choose it over just action. Thrasymachus accepts this assumption, since he speaks of the 'completely' unjust person and city (351b4–5). If we accept this conception of complete injustice, it is difficult to see how it can always be preferable to justice. Socrates points out that if we always choose unjust action in preference to just action, we will be unable to cooperate to the minimum degree needed for effective joint action (351c7–10).

After considering these interpersonal effects of complete injustice, Socrates turns to the effects of injustice in the soul. He argues that the unjust person will have a divided soul that is incapable of cooperative, rational action (351c7–352a9).

In defending justice by its effects on the soul, Socrates takes up a point from the earlier dialogues. The *Crito* claims that injustice harms the soul, but has no clear account of the nature of the harm. The *Gorgias* identifies justice with the order in the soul that results from the proper restraint and discipline of the agent's desires. This seems to be the point of Socrates' present suggestion too, but he does not make it clear exactly what sort of conflict he has in mind or how it arises.[35]

Nor does Socrates explain why the intrapersonal injustice that causes psychic conflict is identical to, or follows from, the interpersonal injustice that creates conflict between different people.[36] He perhaps means that if the 'completely' unjust person practises unjust action whenever he can, he will practise it on his own soul, which offers the same opportunities for injustice that are offered by interpersonal relations (351e9–352a9). If this is what Socrates means, then he interprets Thrasymachus' advocacy of complete injustice as a rather extreme position.

125. The Human Function

Socrates' last argument replies to Thrasymachus' claim that the unjust person is happier than the just person. Socrates appeals to the connexion between the virtue of F and the function, or essential activity, of F: a good knife is good at cutting, a good eye is good at seeing, and so on. He infers that the virtue of the soul depends on the soul's essential activity, which is ruling, deliberating, and living. It follows, according to Socrates, that the virtuous soul is one that lives well; since justice is agreed to be the virtue of the soul, it follows that the just person lives well and hence is happy. Hence the just person is happy and the unjust person is unhappy (352d8–354a11).

Socrates assumes that if justice is a virtue, it must promote the agent's happiness. Thrasymachus, at any rate, is not entitled to complain, since he assumed this connexion between virtue and happiness in claiming that injustice is a virtue and justice is not. It is less clear, however, that Socrates is entitled to assume that justice is the human virtue. Although he has refuted Thrasymachus' claim that injustice is a virtue, he has not thereby proved that justice is a virtue. The argument about overreaching showed that in one respect justice is more similar than injustice is to virtue (since it does not try to overreach on all possible occasions), but it did not show that justice is actually a virtue. Similarly, the argument about psychic conflict showed that extreme injustice is ruinous, but it did not show that justice is the only other option. And so the crucial premiss of the argument from function lacks the support it needs.

Even if we agree with Socrates that the just person is better off than the unjust person, we apparently do not have to agree with the stronger conclusion he draws. He asks, 'Will the soul achieve its function well if it is deprived of its proper virtue, or is this impossible?' (353e1–2). Thrasymachus agrees that this is impossible, and so he concedes that virtue is necessary for happiness. But Socrates infers, 'It is necessary, then for a bad soul to rule and attend badly, and for a good one to do all these things well' (353e4–5); from this he infers that 'the just soul and the just man will live well, and the unjust man will live badly' (353e10–11), so that the just person will be happy and the unjust person wretched (354a1–5). Socrates has given us no reason to accept his claim that justice actually guarantees happiness. This claim goes beyond what he seeks to prove against Thrasymachus, and beyond what the argument from function and virtue seems to prove. The argument from the human function begins legitimately from what Thrasymachus has already conceded, but it reaches a much stronger conclusion than anything that can be defended from the previous argument.

126. Results of Book I

Republic I considers questions that are not raised in the early dialogues. It looks for a definition of justice, whereas the *Crito* and *Gorgias* take views about justice for granted without looking for a definition. At the end of *Republic* I Socrates stresses the importance of finding a definition of justice, remarking that his argument against Thrasymachus on behalf of justice cannot be completely convincing unless they can first discover what justice is (354a11–c3). In the discussion he has also raised the question about whether justice is a virtue; this question was not raised in earlier dialogues.

The early dialogue that has most to say about justice and happiness is the *Gorgias*, and Book I seems to take up some of its arguments. Thrasymachus differs from Callicles in denying that justice is a virtue; Callicles maintained that justice is a virtue, but he had to revise ordinary views about the extension of 'justice'. Socrates implicitly recognizes that Thrasymachus is a more difficult opponent than Polus was (348e5–349a2). In some ways he is less radical than Callicles was, since he does not reject common views about the character of genuinely just actions and does not appeal to Callicles' contrast between natural and conventional justice. But he is a more difficult opponent than Callicles, since he goes further than Callicles in denying that justice is a virtue at all.

Socrates' reply raises some reasonable objections to Thrasymachus' defence of his case. Socrates shows that the mere determination to violate principles of justice is not a reliable guide for life and that therefore Thrasymachus is wrong to advocate injustice in the way he does. Socrates argues, as he argued against Callicles, that if we take injustice as our supreme principle, we eliminate psychic order and rational prudence altogether. The most plausible parts of his defence of justice suggest that something other than unrestrained injustice is needed for rational planning of one's own life. If Socrates is right, then the analogy between virtue and craft remains fairly plausible; the unjust person's commitment to injustice seems to imply ignorance of what we need to know to achieve our own interests.

This reply to Thrasymachus, however, is hardly enough for a defence of justice. Instead of conceiving the unjust person as someone who gives priority to injustice, we might conceive him as someone who simply does not give priority to justice, so that he is willing to act unjustly in cases where the just person would refuse. We might suggest that this more moderate attitude to injustice is more attractive than Thrasymachus' attitude and that therefore it is more dangerous to Socrates' case for justice. Plato takes up this suggestion in Book II.

12

Republic II: Objections to Justice

127. The Question about Justice

The first part of Book II (up to 368c7) is a second introduction to the main question of the dialogue. Glaucon and Adeimantus ask Socrates to convince them that it is in every way better to be just than to be unjust (357a4–b2). They explain 'in every way better' by insisting that a proper defence of justice should say what justice is, explain why it is worth choosing for its own sake and for what it is in itself, and show that the life of the just person who chooses justice for its own sake, no matter what the consequences, is always happier than the life of anyone who does not take this attitude to justice.

In Book I Socrates defended the less precise claim that the just person is happier than the unjust (345a2–b3, 347e2–7). Glaucon and Adeimantus are dissatisfied with Socrates' argument (358c6–d6), claiming that it did not adequately refute Thrasymachus; they argue that an argument meeting their demands is the only adequate answer to Thrasymachus.

To explain his objection that Socrates has not proved that justice is 'in every way' better than injustice (357a6–b3), Glaucon divides goods into (1) those we value for their own sake, but not for their consequences;[1] (2) those we value both for their own sake and for their consequences; and (3) those we value for their consequences but not for their own sake (357b4–d3). Socrates believes that justice, along with wisdom, sight, and health, belongs to the second class, which he calls the finest (358a1–3). Glaucon points out that if we are to defend justice as this sort of good, we cannot be satisfied with a defence that appeals simply to consequences, since such a defence fails to show that justice is not merely a good of the third, purely instrumental type.

Socrates agrees with Glaucon's view that most people put justice in the third class: 'I know that it seems so <sc. to most people> and that it has previously been condemned by Thrasymachus for having this character, whereas injustice has been commended' (358a7–9). This is rather surprising, since Thrasymachus did not say that justice was any sort of good at all. If he recognized it as an instrumental good—parallel to exercise, undergoing medical treatment, administering medical treatment, and other sorts of transactions for profit (357c5–

d1)—then he would imply that it is sometimes worthwhile to be just, and he could hardly say that justice is simply foolishness (348c2–e4).

Glaucon explains his remark about Thrasymachus by offering to 'renew the argument [or 'position', *logos*] of Thrasymachus' (358b7–c1). He and Adeimantus argue that if Socrates praises justice only for its consequences, 'we will say that what you are praising is not the just, but seeming just, and that what you are reproaching is not being unjust, but seeming unjust, and that you are encouraging people to be unjust without being detected, and that you are agreeing with Thrasymachus' (367b7–c2). They seek to explain how Socrates really agrees with Thrasymachus.

Glaucon defends Thrasymachus in three stages (distinguished at 357b7–c6), to which Adeimantus adds a fourth:

1. Glaucon describes the origin and nature of justice as the product of a social contract. This appeals to the consequences of justice as a means to secure mutual non-aggression (358e3–359b5).
2. This contractarian view makes it reasonable to suppose that 'all practise justice as something necessary, not as something good' (358c2–4). Gyges' Ring illustrates this point.
3. It is only to be expected that people take this attitude, since the life of the unjust person—apart from the prospect of punishment—is better than the life of the just person (358c4–6).
4. Adeimantus claims to confirm the conclusion of Glaucon's argument (362e1–4) by examining the defences of justice that people actually offer.

Is this argument fair? Perhaps I have reason to exercise or take medicine only because of their good consequences for my health, but since these are consequences of exercising and taking medicine, and are not consequences of seeming to exercise and take medicine, they give me reason to exercise and to take medicine, not simply to seem to do so. These examples show that the mere fact that some people regard justice as a good of the third class does not allow us to infer that they must value the appearance of justice over the reality.[2] Can Plato answer these doubts about his argument?

128. Justice and Its Consequences

In the first stage of his argument, Glaucon offers a contractarian account to show why rationally self-interested people might reasonably accept a system that enjoins just action on the members of a community. (Let us call this for convenience a *just order*.[3]) Each rationally self-interested agent has reason to prefer a just order over unrestricted aggression, which is the other available option; for while it would be better for me if I could commit injustice at will on other people than if I had to observe a just order, it would be far worse for me if I became the victim of other people's unjust actions against me (358e3–5). While each person thinks the very best situation would be freedom to commit aggression on others with impunity, people see that this is not likely, and that the next best thing is to live under a just order. This is why they agree to set up the laws and institutions that support a just order (358e5–359a4). Glaucon neither affirms nor denies that this Hobbesian argument for a just order gives a reason for someone to observe justice reliably for its consequences.

This is supposed to be an account of 'how justice came to be and what it is' (359a5; cf. 358c2). Glaucon does not claim that just and unjust action are impossible outside a state; for he allows that people treat each other unjustly in the natural condition preceding the establishment of laws (358e3–359a2).[4] The difference is that after the state is formed, laws are laid down and people call their provisions 'lawful and just' (359a4); they do not mean that the just is to be defined as what is required by the laws, but that doing what the law requires fulfills the conditions for just action. The law can claim to require just action because it requires non-maleficent restraint on the pursuit of one's own interest at the expense of others.

Glaucon claims that the fact that the laws require just action explains how justice came into being (359c5); this is not because there was no such thing as just action before there was law, but because the existence of law promotes the growth of justice: a state of just agents involving a reliable tendency to do just actions.[5] When we have agreed on mutual non-aggression and embodied this agreement in laws prescribing just action, we have some reason to become just people, since we can expect just people to benefit each other.

At first sight, this account of just action and of justice seems to conflict with Thrasymachus' view that justice is the interest of the stronger; for Glaucon might be taken to say it is in the interest of the weaker people, who cannot expect to get away with unjust action (cf. *G.* 483a7–d2). In fact, however, Glaucon's point fits neatly into Thrasymachus' account. For Thrasymachus also remarked that just actions are prescribed by the laws that the regime draws up in its interest (338e1–339a4). A just order (of the minimal sort described) is likely to preserve a regime, and since what preserves a regime will thereby benefit the people who benefit from the just order, we might perfectly well agree that just action both preserves the regime and benefits its subjects.

Thrasymachus was too hasty, then, in arguing that since just action promotes the advantage of the regime, it is bad for the subjects to obey the rules prescribing just action. To see his mistake, we need only consider the distinction between the aims of the rulers and the effects of the craft. The shepherd's craft is beneficial for the sheep (within limits), insofar as they are protected from wolves and given food and shelter; the attention of shepherds may still be in the interest of the sheep even though it is designed for the profit of the shepherds.[6]

Glaucon defends Thrasymachus by suggesting that Thrasymachus' apparently shocking account of justice as the interest of the stronger should not be dismissed, since it can be defended by appeal to a plausible view of the point and value of justice. This view has seemed so plausible that it has appealed to theorists who have rejected the rest of Plato's argument. Epicurus believes that there is no justice in itself, apart from the agreements for mutual non-aggression (*KD* 33 = DL X 150); in his view, justice is not to be chosen for its own sake, but only for its good consequences (Cic. *Fin.* I 53). In failing to recognize the plausible aspects of Thrasymachus' view in Book I, Socrates chose to refute what Thrasymachus said, rather than examining the best statement of Thrasymachus' view that he could present. In Book II Glaucon tries to explain why Thrasymachus' view might reasonably be found attractive.

129. Gyges' Ring

In the second stage of his argument, Glaucon points out that if we value justice for its consequences, we must admit it is no longer valuable if the good consequences are removed. He introduces Gyges' Ring to show that most people would commit unjust actions if they could avoid punishment for them (359b6–360d7). Gyges avoids the normal punishments connected to injustice and so gains the advantages of injustice without the normal disadvantages. Glaucon suggests (on behalf of Thrasymachus) that Gyges' attitude is also the common attitude to justice; everyone thinks that injustice is more beneficial to him individually than justice, and so people would commit unjust actions if the usual sanctions were removed (360c5–e7).

Glaucon admits that someone who refrained from unjust action in these conditions would be commended, but he argues that this does not show that people think it is reasonable to refrain. People commend the remarkably just person only because they want to discourage unjust action for fear of being its victims; they all admit that in fact unjust action is more advantageous and that someone who refrains from advantageous unjust action that he could commit with impunity is 'most miserable and most senseless' (360c8–d7).

In focussing on the fear of punishment as the deterrent to unjust action, Glaucon may seem to have forgotten an important aspect of his original account of a just order. I have reason to prefer a just order over the alternative because I stand to lose from being the victim of other people's unjust action. If I can avoid punishment for my own unjust action, I do not necessarily protect myself against the losses resulting from other people's unjust action. If Gyges' reckless use of his ring caused the breakdown of a just order in his society, then he might still suffer from other people's injustice against him; even if he were invisible, other people might steal his possessions and kill his queen.[7] Glaucon does not point out that rational agents have this sort of interest in the preservation of a just order.

If Glaucon had recognized this, would he need to change his argument? If Gyges belongs to a small, face-to-face group, where everyone knows about acts of injustice, he might see that his use of his ring will cause the collapse of a just order; since he will gain more from living in a just order than he will gain from acting unjustly and undermining a just order, he might reasonably prefer to avoid unjust action. In any larger society, however, it would be foolish to suppose that my own unjust action will cause the collapse of the just order. The good consequences of a just order may give me a reason for supporting the system of sanctions that make it more difficult for everyone, including me, to commit injustice; but my support for the system does not give me a reason not to take advantage of opportunities for avoiding the normal sanctions. Glaucon suggests quite reasonably that my motive for doing just actions—as opposed to my motive for accepting the system of justice—has to be the prospect of rewards and punishments attached to just and unjust actions.

On this point Glaucon agrees with Hobbes's 'fool':

> he does not . . . deny that there be covenants; and that they are sometimes broken, sometimes kept; and that such breach of them may be called injustice, and the observance of them justice: but he questioneth, whether injustice, taking away the fear of God, (for the same fool hath said in his heart there is no God,) may not sometimes stand with that reason, which dictateth to every man his own good; and particularly then, when it conduceth to such a benefit, as shall put a man in a condition, to neglect not only the dispraise, and revilings, but also the power of other men.

This opponent of justice does not challenge Hobbes's reasons for agreeing to the just order of the commonwealth in the first place; he simply points out that these reasons do not justify him in doing what the just order requires of him, if he can gain some greater benefit by unjust action and can avoid punishment for it.[8]

Gyges' Ring is meant to show that people 'practise justice unwillingly, as something necessary but not as something good' (358c3–4)[9] and that they practise it 'unwillingly, because of inability to commit injustice' (359b6–7). In saying that they do not regard justice as a good, Glaucon is presumably not taking back his claim that people regard justice as a good of the third class; he could equally say that we undergo surgery 'unwillingly', as something necessary, because we are unable to preserve life and health without the surgery. In saying that we do just action unwillingly, Glaucon emphasizes the fact that we recognize that we must give up something attractive in order to do just action; to this extent it is similar to undergoing surgery and different from some other instrumentally good action (which we may simply be indifferent rather than averse to, if it has no instrumental benefit). Glaucon is right to say that such a view requires us to agree that in the counterfactual conditions he describes we would have good reason to act unjustly.

130. The Choice of Lives

Gyges' Ring suggests that we care about justice only because of rewards and punishments; it does not show that we do not, in fact, care about being just. In the third stage, Glaucon adds a further counterfactual supposition to the one made at the second stage. Instead of simply considering the unjust person who avoids paying the normal penalty, Glaucon appeals to a counterfactual reversal of fortune between a just and an unjust person (360e1–362c8). He suggests that this thought experiment will give the right basis for judging between the lives of the just and the unjust person (360e1–3) and that in fact it gives a reason for judging that the life of the unjust person is preferable (362c6–8). Since most people agree that the unjust person's life is better in these circumstances, they show that they believe 'the life of the unjust person is far better' (358c5).

This conclusion is relevant to Glaucon's initial question in Book II. He asked Socrates whether he wanted to persuade them 'that it is in every way better to be just than to be unjust' (357b1–2). Glaucon takes 'in every way' to imply 'no matter what else we take away from the just person or add to the unjust person'. But is this a fair demand?

We might wonder what the relevance of the counterfactual suppositions in the second and third stages is meant to be. Why should the fact that we would prefer injustice if conditions were radically and unrealistically different show that there is something objectionable about our commitment to justice in actual circumstances? Hume remarks that some general empirical conditions are necessary if we are to be concerned about justice; but he does not take this to be a reason for suggesting that our concern for justice in these empirical conditions is not a genuine concern for justice.[10] If we say that a concern for justice in specified empirical circumstances is not a genuine concern for justice, why might we not equally say that the supposedly unjust person is not really unjust? For if there were an adequate supply of wealth, honour, and so on available without injustice, he would have no reason to value injustice. If someone can be unjust because he is willing to commit injustice in actual circumstances, why cannot someone be just because he is willing to do just actions in actual circumstances?

Plato's use of counterfactual assumptions arouses doubts among his successors. Cicero mentions Gyges' Ring in his argument to show that we should not consider the chances of detection and punishment in deciding whether to do unjust action. He acknowledges that some philosophers (probably Epicureans[11]) reject the appeal to Gyges' Ring since the example is fictitious, indeed impossible. Cicero replies that this objection is irrelevant: 'We put them on the rack, so that, if they reply that they would do what was expedient with the prospect of impunity, they admit that they are criminals' (Cic. *Off.* III 39). Carneades defends the view that Cicero rejects, arguing that in the reversal of fortune imagined by Glaucon it would be absurd to prefer the just person's situation (Cic. *Rep.* III 27). On this view, the fact that we would choose injustice if we could have Gyges' ring, or if we faced the circumstances described in the reversal of lives, does not show that, as things actually are, we really prefer the unjust person's life.

Is this a fair objection to Glaucon? It is legitimate to object to counterfactual suppositions if the situations they describe are too remote from actual circumstances to allow us to see how our moral principles might apply to them, or if they differ from actual circumstances in exactly the respects that give our moral principles their point. If, for instance, Glaucon were to describe cases in which individuals are absolutely self-sufficient and invulnerable, needing no material goods for their own welfare, he might fairly be accused of removing the circumstances that give justice its point; the fact (if it is a fact) that we would not care about justice in these counterfactual circumstances would not at all show that we are not really just or that we care only about apparent justice.

Glaucon's counterfactual suppositions, however, simply make clearer, by abstraction and exaggeration, a consideration that is clearly relevant to our decision in actual circumstances. If the only things that matter are the consequences of justice and injustice, then we must prefer injustice when it has better consequences. Although the story of Gyges describes an unrealistic situation, the sort of opportunity that Gyges takes on a large scale is open to us on a smaller scale in realistic situations. For we all have the opportunity sometimes to commit injustice with impunity; if we agree that Gyges had good reason to do what he did when the fear of punishment was removed, we must also agree that we have good reason to commit injustice when the fear of punishment is removed.

Moreover, the circumstances of the comparison of lives are not completely fantastic. For the historical Socrates pursued what he conceived to be justice when he was accused of injustice, even when he actually suffered the penalties of injustice. Lysias and Polemarchus behaved justly, but they were accused of injustice by the Thirty, who were taking the opportunity to act unjustly with impunity. Glaucon's comparison of lives focusses on exactly the sort of situation in which the historical Socrates advocated an unreserved commitment to justice. Both Gyges' Ring and the comparison of lives describe the sort of choice that we must expect to confront.

Glaucon has therefore supported his claim that those who regard justice as a good of the third class really admit that the life of the unjust person is better (358c5–6). The unjust person in actual circumstances is not someone who takes every opportunity to commit injustice, even if he is likely to be caught; he is the one who takes the opportunities that promise him advantage with no danger of discovery. Most of us have some opportunities of this sort; insofar as we are willing to take them, we show (as Cicero says) that we really prefer to be unjust rather than just.

131. Apparent and Real Justice

The fourth stage of the defence of Thrasymachus should now also seem reasonable. We might be tempted to reply to the third stage by claiming that even if we do not really care about being just, but only about the normal consequences of appearing just, still the best strategy for appearing just is constant observance of the just order. Adeimantus counters this defence of just behaviour. Most people's defences of justice actually appeal to rewards and punishments, human and divine, but astute unjust people can readily gain the same rewards for themselves (362e1–367a4). And so these defences of justice implicitly concede that if we can get away with unjust action, that is what we should prefer (365e4–366d5).

We might argue that Adeimantus' story still does not show that injustice is a practical possibility for those who regard justice as a good of the third class. For we might argue that the effort to avoid detection and punishment is too costly and strenuous to make injustice worth our while. Adeimantus mentions this argument (365c6–7), and Epicurus takes it up vigorously. He believes that injustice in itself is not an evil, but the fear of punishment is an unavoidable evil resulting from injustice and a serious enough evil to make it worth our while to be just (*KD* 34–35 = DL X 151).[12] Cicero answers quite reasonably, following Adeimantus, that Epicurus has to assume an unrealistic degree of incompetence in the unjust person (*Fin.* II 53; cf. *R.* 365c7–d6).

This four-stage argument is carefully constructed to show that I cannot both advocate being just purely for its consequences and give a good reason for being just; if I am concerned only for the consequences of justice, I must admit that I can secure these by appearing to be just rather than by being just. Plato has argued that if justice belongs to the third class of goods, it is different from some other instrumental goods in that class because a particular just agent's just action may not have any distinctive consequences that are good for the agent herself. We have good reason to prefer a genuine hammer over an apparent hammer for the sake of the consequences; if something appeared to other people to be a hammer but did not really hammer nails, it might not secure the results we want to secure with a hammer. A rational, self-interested agent's apparent justice, however, secures for the agent all the results that the agent wants to secure with genuine justice.

The egocentric character of this conclusion is important. For it would be a mistake to claim that apparent justice achieves all the good consequences of real justice. A just order is strengthened if most people actually observe the rules of justice, and it is weakened if most people are no more than apparently just. But this fact gives me a reason for wanting other people to observe the just order, and it shows that I benefit if other people are not merely apparently just; it does not show that I benefit from being more than apparently just myself. Plato shows, then, why we cannot, within his eudaemonist assumptions, both choose justice purely for the sake of its consequences and choose real over apparent justice.

132. Glaucon, Adeimantus, and Thrasymachus

We can now see more exactly how Glaucon and Adeimantus have renewed Thrasymachus' argument and what aspects of it they have rejected or accepted.

They do not accept Thrasymachus' unqualified claim that it is foolish to observe the rules of a just order; in some circumstances—in particular, when we can easily be detected in unjust action—it is sensible to observe the rules. Nor do they accept his view that the unjust person is the contrary of the just person: someone who acts unjustly 'on principle', taking every opportunity to act unjustly. Socrates exploited these extreme aspects of Thrasymachus' view in his refutation. His arguments were reasonable if and only if they were directed at a conception of the unjust person as someone who makes it his supreme maxim in life to pursue injustice.

In contrast to Thrasymachus, Glaucon explains carefully the extent to which the astute unjust person will 'overreach' (*pleonektein*). Such a person wants the benefits of injustice and the benefits of justice; he exercises craft (360e6–361a1) in doing this and will not want to 'overreach' the skilful tactics that achieve these ends; he will not, for instance, want to commit so many unjust acts that he suffers punishment. Since the astute unjust person's desire for unjust action is strictly restrained by his view of his own interest, he is rationally controlled and prudent, free of internal conflict, contrary to Socrates' suggestion in Book I.

Although the unjust person of Book II is different in these ways from the unjust person examined by Socrates and Thrasymachus in Book I, Glaucon and Adeimantus are nonetheless justified in claiming to have defended Thrasymachus' position. For they still maintain (on the basis of the contractarian account of justice) that justice is the interest of the stronger, that it is another person's good but harmful to the just agent, and that the unjust person's overreaching gives him a better life than the just person achieves by his justice (360c8–d2, 362b2–c8, 367c2–5). These are the aspects of Thrasymachus' position that most need refutation if we are to defend justice; if they can be separated from the aspects of his position that allowed Socrates to refute him, then this modified Thrasymachean position is a much more serious threat to justice than was the position that Socrates refuted. For the disturbing aspects of Thrasymachus' view can be derived from apparently quite respectable assumptions about justice.

In renewing the argument of Thrasymachus, Plato tries to answer a serious objection to Socratic argument. Later in the *Republic*, Glaucon suggests that, however cogent Socrates' argument may appear to be, most people will suppose that it seems irrefutable only because Socrates is more skilled at this game than they are and takes advantage of their errors; even if a Socratic conclusion seems to have been proved, obvious facts seem to refute it (487b1–d5). Callicles made a similar charge more briefly in commenting on Socrates' refutation of Polus.[13] In the *Theaetetus* Socrates imagines Protagoras telling him not to confine himself to the actual defence someone has offered for his position; Socrates should look for the most plausible statement of Protagoras' case and should direct his arguments against that (*Tht.* 164c2–168c2). Plato takes this advice in his restatement of Thrasymachus' position.

The only way to remove the sceptical reaction that Glaucon reports is to find the best statement of the position in question and show that even the best statement of it, however resourcefully defended, can be refuted. This is part of Plato's reason for emphasizing the importance of repeated examination (*G.* 513c7–d1; *M.* 85c9–d1). Mere repetition of the same thesis and the same arguments would be pointless; but if the same thesis is defended by different arguments and these arguments are answered, that may convince us that the thesis itself is open to serious objection. Conversely, if Plato can defend his position even against the best statement of the case for the opposition, we have a good reason for believing his position.

133. The Division of Goods

Glaucon and Adeimantus do not simply want to restate Thrasymachus' position; they want to say more clearly what is needed to answer it. The first step towards an adequate answer is an understanding of the threefold division of goods. What is needed for a proof that justice is a good to be chosen for its own sake and not simply for its consequences?

We might take 'for its own sake' or 'because of itself' to mean 'purely in its own right, and entirely without reference to any other good'. This cannot be right, however. For, according to Socrates, a good of the second class 'is loveable both because of itself and because of its results, to anyone who is going to be blessed' (358a2–3). The clause 'to anyone who is going to be blessed' shows that the three classes of goods are meant to include all the goods that might be considered as ways of achieving happiness; they are not meant to include happiness itself. The threefold division presupposes the supremacy of happiness and the subordination of all three classes of goods to happiness, since they are all chosen for the sake of happiness.[14]

Since Plato believes that we can love justice for its own sake in aiming at our happiness, he does not believe that if we love justice for the sake of happiness, we must thereby love it for its consequences as opposed to itself. If we choose justice for the sake of happiness, it is natural to say that we are choosing it as contributing to happiness; but Plato does not take this to imply that happiness is the sort of consequence that is ruled out when we speak of choosing justice because of itself. Moreover, the speakers all assume that they are saying what justice is 'in itself' when they describe 'what it does in the soul'. In speaking of what it does, they do not intend to pick out its consequences. What relation of justice to happiness allows Plato to claim that in choosing justice for the sake of happiness we also choose it for itself?

It seems obvious that in some sense of 'consequence' happiness is a consequence of justice. If we choose justice for the sake of happiness, and we actually achieve happiness, we have gained happiness by choosing justice. It seems to follow trivially that we have gained happiness as a consequence of choosing justice. Plato, then, must be assuming some narrower notion of 'consequence'.

We might suppose that Plato takes 'justice itself' to include some of the causal consequences of justice: those that can be regarded as the inevitable consequences of justice itself, not as the consequences of a combination of justice with conditions that are causally independent of it.[15] This contrast makes it easy to see why Glaucon wants to hear justice praised, apart from the honours and rewards that people normally attach to it; for these are consequences not of justice itself, but of justice together with people's normal, but not invariable, opinion. Similarly, we might say we are not describing alcohol itself if we describe the effects of drinking alcohol after taking cocaine.

This contrast, however, does not explain why Plato divides the second from the third classes of goods in the way he does. Exercise is treated as a good of the third class: Glaucon implies that if we choose it only because it results in health, we choose it only for its consequences (357c5–d2). Even if better health is the natural and inevitable result of moderate and well-planned exercise (not simply its result in some circumstances), the fact that we choose exercise only for the sake of health shows that, as Glaucon says, 'we would not prefer to have it for its own sake' (357c8). Whether the desirable consequence of exercise is a consequence of exercise itself seems not to affect the fact that exercise belongs in the third class.[16]

If, then, Plato does not use 'justice itself' to include the causal consequences of justice itself, as opposed to the causal consequences of justice together with something else, what contrast does he intend? If praise of justice for itself is distinct from praise of any of its causal consequences, how can we claim to be praising justice for itself if we praise it for making the just person happy?

We may understand Plato better if we keep in mind that 'doing' and 'making' do not necessarily introduce an efficient-causal relation between two different events. To say that being a rational animal makes someone a human being is not to say that being a rational animal and being a human being are two distinct events and the second is an efficient-causal consequence of the first. In this case the second description picks out a logical consequence of the first, and the two descriptions pick out just the same property. If Plato says that being just makes us just, he is not referring to two different events; and so he need not be referring to different events when he says that being just makes us happy or makes us better off.[17]

Similarly, then, when Plato asks what justice 'does' or what its 'power' (*dunamis*) is, he may simply be asking what difference justice 'makes' to a soul or, in other words, in what respect a just soul is different from other souls. If Plato intends 'justice itself' and 'what justice does in the soul' to describe the essential properties of the state of the soul that is justice, he is asking a reasonable question; he is distinguishing these properties from the causal consequences of justice.[18] Since this interpretation of Plato's contrast between justice itself and the consequences of justice vindicates Plato's division between the second and third classes of goods, it is to be preferred to the first interpretation (the one that takes Plato to be concerned only to distinguish causal consequences of justice itself from causal consequences of justice together with other things), which conflicts with that division.

Plato wants to find out what justice is in itself, apart from its causal consequences, because he believes that once we have found this, we will find we have sufficient reason to chose justice without reference to its causal consequences. We will not find what justice is in itself simply by finding some true description of the state of the soul that is justice; even if we are right to believe that justice satisfies Simonides' description or that it requires us to refrain from overreaching, we have not shown why we are better off being just. Plato claims, however, that when we discover the correct Socratic account of justice, it will show why justice benefits us.

134. The Superiority of Justice

Glaucon and Adeimantus ask for a defence of the comparative thesis that the just person is happier than the unjust. They do not, however, maintain that justice is sufficient for happiness.[19] The comparative thesis is weaker than the sufficiency thesis, since it is possible for A to be happier than B even though neither A nor B is happy; when Plato argues that the just person is in all circumstances happier than the unjust person, he does not imply that the just person is happy in all circumstances. He leaves open the possibility that happiness has components that are not infallibly secured by justice. Glaucon imagines a situation where the just person has the reputation for being unjust and suffers all the penalties normally attached to such a reputation, whereas the unjust person is thought to be just and enjoys all the normal benefits of a good reputation, as well as the benefits he gains by his secret injustice. Plato gives no reason to deny that the external goods lost by the just person are genuine goods. In restricting himself to the comparative claim about justice and happiness, he implicitly acknowledges that the just person suffers a significant loss in being deprived of external goods.

The rest of the *Republic* also stops short of maintaining the sufficiency thesis.[20] Plato's political argument begins from the assumption that individuals are not self-sufficient but depend on other individuals for their welfare (369b5–c8). The ideal city is designed for the happiness of all the citizens (420b3–421c6), and although justice is the basis for this happiness, the ideal city does not simply aim at making the citizens just. It is not clear whether Plato actually wants to say that the philosopher-rulers in the ideal state are happy, as opposed to coming close to happiness (420b5, 466a8, 519c5). Even if he does want to say this, he does not imply that justice alone is sufficient for happiness; for the philosopher-rulers plainly have favourable external conditions added to justice, so that they do not face the sort of hostile environment that led to Socrates' execution. The comparative claim allows us to say that these favourable external conditions (living in a just society, being reliably supplied with basic resources, receiving honour, etc.) contribute to the happiness of the philosophers.

In Book X (612a8ff.) Plato argues that the just person can in fact expect to achieve happiness, often in this life and invariably in the afterlife. But this is not because justice by itself guarantees happiness.[21] When Plato argues that, in fact, justice will secure the external goods (either through normal social processes or through the favour of the gods), he implies that just people will secure happiness once these goods are added to justice, and that they would not have secured happiness if these goods had not been added. Plato does not suggest that he has already argued that justice is sufficient for happiness. The argument of the *Republic* as a whole is quite intelligible if Plato maintains the comparative thesis, but quite puzzling if he accepts the sufficiency thesis.

135. The Relation of Justice to Happiness

Glaucon and Adeimantus want Socrates to show that justice by itself and in its own right makes the just person happier than the unjust person, even though it does not by itself make the just person happy. If these claims are to be understood as claims about justice itself, as opposed to its causal consequences, then Plato must claim that justice is a proper part, or a partial constituent, of happiness.

In relations between part and whole, it is sometimes appropriate to say both that the part contributes to the goodness of the whole and that this contribution is a feature of what the part is like in itself, not a causal (more precisely, efficient-causal) consequence of what it is like. A healthy foot contributes to the health of a body by being healthy and being a part of a body. We do not mean only that the healthy foot causally contributes (as a healthy diet does) to the health of the body; the relation is closer than causal contribution. We mean that having a healthy body is (among other things) having a healthy foot.[22]

If this parallel applies to justice and happiness, then we need to be convinced that happiness has parts x, y, and z and that justice is identical to one of them, say, x. To show this we need some other description of x, showing that x is clearly a part of happiness, and then some argument to show that x is clearly justice. We will learn something that we did not know before: that the same condition of a person both meets the appropriate standard for being a part of happiness and meets the appropriate standard for being justice.

Since Plato commits himself to the comparative claim about justice and happiness, the part-whole relation by itself does not capture the role that he envisages for justice in happiness.[23] The health of the foot is a part of the health of a body, but a comparatively minor part; if I have a healthy foot, it clearly does not follow that I am healthier than anyone without a healthy foot, no matter what else might be true of me or of anyone else. We might, however, claim that the heart or the brain is such a vital organ that its health does outweigh the healthy or unhealthy condition of the other parts of the body. We might say in this case that the health of the vital organ is dominant in the health of the body as a whole.

This notion of dominance suggests Plato's point about justice. He wants to show that although justice is not sufficient for happiness, it is dominant in happiness; being just guarantees by itself that just people will be happier than any unjust people, even if the just people are not happy, and even if all the goods that are distinct from justice belong to unjust people (in the counterfactual circumstances described by Glaucon). If Plato's claims about the intrinsic goodness of justice are consistent with his promise to prove that justice contributes to happiness, as well as with his defence of the comparative thesis rather than the sufficiency thesis, then he ought to show that justice is a dominant component of happiness.

We can therefore sum up the claims that Plato is committed to in his defence of justice: (1) Justice is identical to a part of happiness. (2) It therefore contributes non-causally to happiness by being a part of it. (3) The nature of this non-causal contribution makes justice a dominant part of happiness. (4) It contributes causally to the other parts of happiness. These claims are consistent and not obviously false; the rest of the *Republic* should show how far Plato defends them.

136. Virtue and Reliability

Glaucon and Adeimantus want to be convinced of these claims because they assume that this is the only way to show that we have reason to be a genuinely just person rather than an unjust person who puts on the appearance of being just. What is their conception of the genuinely just person?

They cannot say that the just person is the one who in actual circumstances does just actions more often than the astutely unjust person does them. For someone might refrain from unjust action only because he is afraid of its risks or does not realize how beneficial it is. Adeimantus suggests that people who take this attitude are moved by cowardice or weakness, since they would always take the opportunity to commit injustice if they thought they could really get away with it (366d1–5; cf. 360b3–c8). He allows, however, that there may be an exceptional person who 'because of <his> divine nature rejects unjust action, or avoids it because he has acquired knowledge' (366c6–d1). This person is an exception to the psychological generalization about injustice; he is the just person whose happiness is being considered.

Adeimantus contrasts this just person with those who choose just actions only for their consequences. He claims that exclusive attention to the consequences expresses an outlook that is a mere 'facade' of virtue (365a4–c6). Why should Plato believe this? He has shown that such a person is unstable, since he would be willing to act unjustly if the conditions required it. But why should we be concerned if someone's commitment is unstable to this extent?

Plato's account of knowledge in the *Meno* suggests an answer to this question. In distinguishing knowledge from true belief, he distinguishes 'empirical reliability' (the tendency to be right in empirically likely conditions) from 'counterfactual reliability' (the tendency to be right in counterfactual, and not necessarily empirically likely, conditions).[24] In saying that a belief is counterfactually unreliable, we point out that my reason for the belief is mistaken, even if the mistake makes no difference to my judgments in actual circumstances.

The same distinction may underlie a passage in the *Phaedo* where, as in *Republic* II, Plato speaks of the difference between a 'facade' of virtue and genuine virtue. He claims that philosophers are the only people with genuine virtue and that the best approximation achieved by other people is only a 'slavish virtue', which is nothing but a facade of real virtue (*Phd.* 68c5–69c3).[25] Slavish virtue relies on mercenary calculation of the effects of virtuous action on the prospects of satisfying desires that are common to virtuous and vicious people.

For all Plato says, slavish people might have all the correct beliefs about which actions are virtuous, and they might do virtuous actions on all the actual occasions that demand them. They illustrate the distinction drawn in the *Meno* between knowledge and correct belief. Plato makes it clear that in whatever sense correct belief is 'no worse' than knowledge, this does not imply that it is no worse from the moral point of view. For since correct belief only implies correct action—in the appropriate range of actual and likely circumstances—

and since virtue requires the right reasons and motives as well as the right actions, correct belief cannot be enough for virtue.

Plato suggests that it is slavish to choose virtuous action purely for its consequences. The just person's superior degree of happiness is not a consequence of justice; for justice is a component of happiness, not simply an instrumental means that has happiness as its causal consequence. While the just person and the unjust person both pursue happiness, they have different conceptions of what happiness consists in, and so they pursue different ends.

If Glaucon and Adeimantus were concerned simply about empirical reliability, the second and third stages of their argument would be misguided. For these stages ask us to consider the degree and basis of our commitment to justice in empirically unlikely circumstances. The choice of lives does not show that we will not stick closely to justice as long as the going is good; but Glaucon and Adeimantus suggest that empirical reliability is not enough to make someone just. They suggest that the purely instrumental attitude to justice is to be rejected, whether or not it weakens someone's commitment to justice in empirically likely circumstances.

137. Admiration for Virtue

We ought to accept Plato's demand for counterfactual reliability only if we agree that justice demands the right reason and motive. Ought we to agree about this? Is Plato relying on an idiosyncratically exacting conception of justice, or can he claim the support of common beliefs?

We must admit, first of all, that the counterfactual circumstances he describes are not very different from circumstances that we may well have to face. We admire the integrity and moral commitment of the historical Socrates when he faces the choice between doing injustice and exposing himself to danger; his conviction that just people stand up for justice even at the cost of other recognized goods is certainly not an idiosyncratic or fanatical view. Similarly, we are inclined to admire Sophocles' Neoptolemus for his refusal to do anything shameful and unjust even when it offers great advantages.[26]

These examples suggest that the genuinely just person is committed to just action for reasons that are not captured by the appeal to good consequences of justice. If we are not ready to reject our conviction about Socrates and Neoptolemus, then we must agree with Plato's assumption that the just person chooses just action for some reason distinct from the consequences that have already been explored.

Does this show, however, that we ought to try to prove that justice is really worth choosing for its own sake? We might argue that justice is good instrumentally since it helps to maintain a just order, and for this reason it is good (for the just order) to train people to choose justice for its own sake.[27] We can see why it is a good thing if there are just people who have the unreserved commitment of Neoptolemus or Socrates; but this is a good thing not because it is good for the agents themselves, but because it has good consequences for other people. We might agree with Adeimantus' objections to conventional defences of justice for its consequences, since it would be better if people could be trained to care about justice apart from its consequences. Perhaps, however, they could be trained to do this without believing that justice is non-instrumentally good. Suppose that an individual just person—Aristeides, say—finds he has been trained to choose just actions without regard for their benefits or harms to him. He recognizes that this attitude supports the just order. That is certainly a reason for him to retain his attitude to justice, since he values the just order and sees that it requires some restraint of his tendency to benefit himself at the expense of others.

This sort of reason, however, does not fully support Aristeides' attitude to justice. The main support of a just order is other people's commitment to justice, not his own; he benefits from a just order insofar as other people believe that he is just, not insofar as he actually is just. His best policy, then, seems to be the cultivation of genuine justice in others and of apparent justice in himself.[28] If the benefits of justice do not give a sufficient reason for Aristeides himself to be just, a true conception of the nature and value of justice seems to undermine an individual's commitment to it.

If this is true, then apparently a just order is weakened insofar as individuals understand the purely instrumental role of justice. It would be better, then, to train an individual to value justice for something more than the instrumental benefits that in fact exhaust its value; it would be better to train him to believe that justice is good for him quite apart from its consequences. Other people will gain the appropriate benefit from Aristeides' justice only if he values it for its own sake as a non-instrumental good for him; and so this attitude will be best for the maintenance of the just order.

This conclusion does not show, however, that Aristeides' justice really is good for Aristeides; it implies that we should try to form and sustain false beliefs in Aristeides. Glaucon seems to concede this possibility when he remarks that even if we believe the just person is a fool, we will take care to praise him, so that we encourage the spread of his just attitude for the sake of the just order (360d2–7). If this is all that can be said about the value of justice, then we still do not know why it is important to prove that justice is really non-instrumentally good, and our admiration for Socrates and Neoptolemus may not support the view that it is non-instrumentally good. It is important, we may agree, to convince enough people that justice is non-instrumentally good, but why should their belief be true? Apparently the just order is supported by their belief, not by the truth of their belief.

If this is right, then Glaucon and Adeimantus have not justified their demand to be shown that justice is really non-instrumentally good for the just person. They have simply shown why a just order would be better supported by the cultivation of the belief that justice is a non-instrumental good than by the less effective moral education that they describe. We might argue that someone who has reached the level of understanding reached by Thrasymachus, Glaucon, and Adeimantus can no longer maintain a commitment to justice. If that is so, then they have a good reason to make sure that other people do not reach their level of understanding.[29]

138. Virtue, Knowledge, and Perfection

Plato does not explicitly confront this issue about Glaucon and Adeimantus' argument. It is by no means anachronistic, however; Plato himself is not at all averse to the cultivation of useful fictions for the good of society (414b8–415d2), and he certainly recognizes the social value of beliefs about the benefits of justice.[30] But he implicitly defends his emphasis on proving the truth, not simply the usefulness, of the conviction that justice is non-instrumentally good.

In Plato's view, we ought to expect genuinely virtuous people to be guided by a correct conception of what a given virtue is. If some people suppose that bravery is good simply because the action they recognize as brave often provides healthy exercise and is therefore good for their health, they have not grasped what is essential to bravery and therefore are not brave, even if their belief about bravery happens to be true in their actual circumstances. For similar reasons, a just person ought to be moved by a correct conception of what justice essentially is and therefore of what matters most about justice from the moral point of view. If justice is essentially a non-instrumental good, and indeed a dominant good, then people who pursue it simply as an instrumental good are missing what is essential to it; hence they do not act on a correct conception of what is really important about justice, and therefore they cannot be really just.

If Plato is right, then if justice is a virtue and the just person ought to choose justice for its own sake, justice must really be a non-instrumental good. In supposing that society benefits if it includes just people who have false beliefs about justice, we would be denying that justice is a genuine virtue because we would be denying that it is a genuine perfection of a human agent. Plato believes that if justice is not really a non-instrumental good, the just person's outlook cannot survive confrontation with the truth. If I am not deceived, and I recognize that I have been trained to value justice for its own sake only because it benefits the just order, I see that I have no reason to value it when I can get away with acting unjustly. If, on the other hand, I have been deceived, and my attitude to justice depends on my false belief that my justice is non-instrumentally good for me, my attitude cannot survive the discovery of the falsity of my belief. In either case, justice cannot be a virtue because it requires an imperfection rather than a perfection in a just person.

The perfection of a human agent, Plato assumes, must include the knowledge of the truth about the world, specifically about what is really good and bad; and so a state of the agent that cannot be sustained in the face of knowledge of this truth cannot really be a virtue. Although Plato introduces this assumption without explanation, it is crucial in the *Republic* as a whole; it explains why a dialogue that seeks to prove what moral agents have reason to do includes an elaborate discussion of the nature of knowledge and of the reality that is revealed to us when we acquire knowledge of what is really good.[31]

This is why Plato is justified in seeing a connexion between questions about what justice is, whether it is a good to be chosen for itself, and what sort of person we are to regard as just. Our admiration for people like Socrates and Neoptolemus suggests that we suspect it is not simply an instrumental means to happiness, but a non-instrumental good. But it is not certain that our suspicion is right. If we cannot find an account of justice that shows it to be a non-instrumental, dominant good, then we will have to admit that our admiration for Socrates' commitment to justice lacks the appropriate rational basis.

139. Socrates and the Praise of Justice

Now that we have seen what question Plato wants to answer about justice, we can compare it with the questions that are asked and answered in Book I and in the Socratic dialogues. Since Glaucon and Adeimantus believe that no one has yet praised justice in the right way, they include Socrates' defence of justice in Book I among the inadequate defences of justice that fail to praise it as a non-instrumental good.[32] Is this criticism of Book I fair?

The threefold division of goods has no Socratic precedent. Socrates' explicit remarks in the early dialogues about the structure of means and ends imply a twofold, not a threefold, division. Both the *Lysis* and the *Gorgias* distinguish the things chosen for the sake of ends from the ends for whose sake they are chosen. The *Lysis* recognizes one end that is desired for its own sake; this end is the primary object of love. But neither dialogue suggests that there are any means to a further end that are also ends in themselves. On the contrary, both dialogues imply that if we choose one thing for the sake of a second, the first thing we choose cannot be chosen for its own sake.[33] This twofold division implies that no good belongs to the second of the three classes recognized in *Republic* II. Glaucon's division would often be relevant to questions discussed in the Socratic dialogues, but these dialogues never mention it.

Similarly, Book I neither recognizes nor uses the threefold division of goods. None of the arguments defends justice as a good to be chosen for its own sake. The argument about overreaching treats the just person and the unjust person as the competent and incompetent practitioners of a craft; this analogy works only if both of them are trying to produce the same product. The argument about psychic division appeals to the bad consequences of injustice. The last argument appeals to the conclusion of the first argument that justice is a virtue; and the first argument regards a virtue as an instrumental means for securing one's happiness.

Plato's attitude to *Republic* I may usefully be compared with Aristotle's attitude to Socrates. Aristotle argues that it is wrong to treat virtue as a craft, because a craft is strictly productive knowledge, whereas wisdom and virtue are concerned with action (*praxis*), which is to be chosen for its own sake. He implies that if we see the distinctively non-instrumental character of virtuous action, we will sharply separate virtue from craft. The Socratic dialogues, however, either identify virtue with a craft or at least do not sharply separate it from crafts. If Aristotle is right, this is a sign that Socrates does not clearly recognize the non-instrumental character of virtuous action.[34]

Since Plato suggests that Book I does not argue that justice is non-instrumentally good, he supports Aristotle's implicit criticism of Socrates. Moreover, the analogy between virtue and craft is prominent in Book I but not in the rest of the *Republic*; Plato thereby suggests that the use of the analogy is connected with the error in Socratic ethics that he rejects. Aristotle's claims about craft and virtue and Plato's claims about justice as a non-instrumental good may fairly be taken to express a shared judgment on Socratic ethics. In demanding a defence of justice as a non-instrumental good, Plato appeals to the historical Socrates' unreserved commitment to justice in order to criticize Socrates' views about justice and happiness.[35]

140. Socrates and the Relation of Virtue to Happiness

In Book II Glaucon and Adeimantus confine themselves to the comparative thesis that the just person is happier than the unjust. On this point also they differ from Socrates in Book I. In Book I Socrates argues that the just person is happier than the unjust (352d2–6) by maintaining that justice is sufficient for happiness; in the last argument of Book I, appealing to the human function, he maintains that the just person is happy (353e).

In defending the sufficiency thesis, Book I agrees with the Socratic dialogues. For in the *Apology*, *Crito*, *Euthydemus*, and *Gorgias*, Socrates conspicuously maintains that virtue is sufficient for happiness. Moreover, in all of these dialogues except for the *Euthydemus*, he maintains this claim about justice in precisely the sort of situation that is envisaged by Glaucon in the choice of lives. This Socratic claim is most strongly defended in the *Gorgias*, where Socrates maintains an adaptive conception of happiness; this conception makes it plausible to maintain that virtue, suitably understood, is sufficient for happiness.[36]

Since the Socratic dialogues commit Socrates so firmly to the sufficiency thesis, Plato's failure to endorse it in the *Republic* should not be dismissed as an oversight but recognized as a deliberate disagreement with Socrates.

In later antiquity some philosophers recognized this difference between Socrates' and Plato's views about virtue and happiness. In Chrysippus' view, Plato does away with justice and any other genuine virtue because he recognizes such things as health as goods (Plutarch, *SR* 1040d). Chrysippus probably has the *Republic* in mind (cf. 1040a–b); at any rate, he does not criticize Socrates for the mistake that he attributes to Plato. Probably the Stoics recognized, as Cicero did (*Parad.* 4), the Socratic origin of their views on virtue and happiness. The Stoics are partly inspired by the Cynics, and the Cynics by Socrates.[37] Since the Cynics and the Stoics take their views to be Socratic but not Platonic, they have a good reason to distinguish Socrates' view from Plato's. Plutarch, speaking as a Platonist, accepts Chrysippus' interpretation of Plato, and so finds that Plato and Aristotle agree on this point against the Stoics.

Others, however, try to identify the Platonic view with the Stoic view and therefore with the Socratic view. According to Clement, Antipater the Stoic wrote a work in three books asserting that according to Plato only the fine is good, and that therefore virtue is self-sufficient for happiness (Clement, *Strom.* V 97.6 = *SVF* III, Antip. 56). His writing a whole treatise on this question may indicate that the Stoics disagreed about the interpretation of Plato's views.

On the Platonist side, Atticus ascribes to Plato a view close to the Stoic position and so contrasts him sharply with Aristotle (Eusebius, *PE* 794c6–d13): he assumes that Plato's acceptance of the comparative thesis commits him to acceptance of the sufficiency thesis. Alcinous, another Platonist, claims, quite reasonably, that in the *Euthydemus* Plato accepts the Stoic thesis that only the fine is good (*Did.* 27 = 180.33–37); but he infers, less reasonably, that the Stoic thesis expresses Plato's view in the *Republic* as well and that Plato relies on this thesis to prove that the virtues are choiceworthy for their own sakes (181.5–9).[38]

We have found good reasons for agreeing with Chrysippus and Plutarch, against Antipater, Atticus, and Alcinous, in their interpretation of Plato and in their implicit contrast between Socrates and Plato. The difference between *Republic* I and *Republic* II foreshadows a division between, on the one side, Socrates and the Hellenistic schools and, on the other side, Plato and Aristotle.

141. Socrates and the Definition of Justice

Glaucon remarks correctly that in Book I Socrates not only failed to praise justice as a non-instrumental good but also failed to praise justice on the strength of an account of what justice is in itself, since he did not seek a definition of justice. The same is true of the Socratic dialogues. The *Crito* and the *Gorgias* argue about why justice is better than injustice and about what justice requires, but Socrates never looks for a definition of justice; he never even acknowledges, as he does for the other virtues, that it is important to find a definition.

According to Glaucon, Socrates was wrong not to seek a definition of justice, because if he had found out what justice is, he would have found out that it is a non-instrumental good. Thrasymachus has suggested that the actions characteristically recognized as just harm the interests of the agent in conditions where unjust actions would be advantageous to him. As Glaucon and Adeimantus point out, Socrates has not adequately answered this claim about the cost of just actions. He needs to show that these actions do not fully express the nature of justice. But to show this Socrates needs to say something more about the nature of justice itself.

What sort of definition of justice is needed? In studying Plato's arguments for non-sensible Forms, and in exploring the resulting differences from Socratic epistemology, we saw why Plato's views about Forms might reasonably lead him to revise some of Socrates' explicit or implicit assumptions about the character of an adequate Socratic definition.[39] Does *Republic* II give us reason to believe that Plato's disagreements with Socrates affect his demand for a definition of justice?

If Plato is right in his claims about Forms, then an attempt to define any disputed moral properties by reference to non-disputed, sensible properties is bound to fail. To show this, Plato can appeal (as he does in the case of comparatives in *Republic* VII) to the essentially contextual character of the disputed evaluative properties. The justice, fineness, and goodness of an action essentially depend on contextual features that are not to be discovered by observing the action itself in its environment; in particular, whether a type of action is just depends on circumstances, antecedents, and results that affect the fineness and goodness of this type of action.

In *Republic* I Thrasymachus apparently demands a definition of justice that avoids this circle of moral properties. Socrates and Polemarchus fail to refute the Simonidean account of justice as rendering what is due to each person, but Thrasymachus scorns this account because it is not 'perspicuous and accurate'. Judging by the accounts he rejects, he seems to mean that a perspicuous and accurate account will eliminate moral properties that cannot be understood without reference to other moral properties. Socrates expresses no view about the appropriateness of Thrasymachus' demand for a perspicuous and accurate account of justice.

In Book II, however, Plato suggests that it will be difficult to satisfy Thrasymachus' demand about justice. Glaucon argues that a definition of justice ought to imply that it is a non-instrumental good; non-instrumental goodness should be an essential, not a merely coincidental, property of justice. Glaucon's demand makes Thrasymachus' demand much more difficult to meet. For a definition that met both demands would have to define justice without the use of other moral terms in such a way that justice turned out to be a non-instrumental good. It is not easy to think of a plausible account that would satisfy both Thrasymachus' and Glaucon's demands.

If this is right, then Plato's criteria for a definition are more generous than those that seemed to be presupposed in the Socratic dialogues. The Socratic criteria are reflected in Thrasymachus' demand for a perspicuous and accurate account; once Plato rejects this demand, it should be less difficult for him than it was for Socrates to find definitions of the virtues. Since the rest of the *Republic* both offers accounts of the virtues and develops the arguments about Forms and sensibles that are relevant to questions about definition, we should be able to see how Plato answers the questions raised for him by Books I and II.

142. Are Plato's Questions Reasonable?

Although Plato rejects several Socratic assumptions, he still follows Socrates in accepting rational eudaemonism; he assumes that we have been given a good reason for being just if and only if we have been shown how justice promotes our happiness. Some moralists regard this assumption as the expression of a basic mistake about the nature and justification of morality;[40] for they argue that moral requirements and principles ought not to be subordinate to any other principles, whether these other principles refer to the agent's good or to some other valued state of affairs. From this point of view, Plato's charge that other people are slavish and mercenary in their attitude to virtue turns out to apply to his own defence of virtue as well; for he accepts the basic error of these other people in subordinating morality to some other end.

Plato might deny that he is open to these criticisms. For his view that justice is itself a component of happiness, not merely an instrumental means to it, is meant to disarm the suggestion that he subordinates morality to other ends in any objectionable sense. In saying that justice is a part of happiness, Plato implies that we cannot fully understand the composition of happiness without recognizing the non-instrumental value of justice. Morally virtuous agents are not required to subordinate morality to some non-moral conception of an end.

But if we accept this defence against the charge of subordinating morality to other ends, we may suspect that eudaemonism is not worth defending at this price.[41] For if we argue that our conception of happiness is not fixed and determinate independently of justice, then we seem to lose one of the main reasons for accepting eudaemonism in the first place. It is natural to suppose that an account of happiness gives us some basis both for the definition and for the justification of the moral virtues; we want our definitions to show how the virtues promote happiness, as previously understood, and once we have found the right definitions we will have shown why the virtues, so defined, are worth choosing for rational agents aiming at their own happiness, as already defined. If we cannot find a true determinate conception of happiness before we find an account of justice, then we cannot use it to show we have found the right account of justice. Moreover, if we cannot say what happiness is apart from justice, we cannot appeal to concerns that are recognized as rational by just and non-just agents alike in order to show that the concerns of the just person are rational. But if we cannot use our conception of happiness for these purposes, what is the point of sticking to eudaemonism at all?

If he is to meet these objections, Plato must show that he can appeal to a conception of happiness that advances the argument about justice without implying an undesirable subordination of justice to ends that are independent of it. To see whether he has any way out of the dilemma that we have described, we need to understand the objections more precisely. In particular, we must understand the claims about 'subordination', about the 'determinacy' of conceptions of happiness, and about their 'independence' of morality. If a conception of happiness can be informative without being objectionably determinate, or if a conception of justice can be connected to a partly independent conception of happiness without being objectionably subordinate to it, then Plato's appeal to eudaemonism may be relevant to the defence of his claims about justice without being open to the objection that it mistakes the relation of morality to a rational person's other aims.

In criticizing Socrates' position and in defining the questions that need to be answered, Plato raises these basic questions about the nature and aims of ethical argument. Even if the rest of the *Republic* achieved nothing, the care and subtlety of Book II would deserve our admiration.[42] We must now consider how well he answers his questions.

13

Republic IV: The Division of the Soul

143. The Argument of Book IV

At the end of Book IV Plato claims to have presented a first sketch of his answer to Thrasymachus.[1] The argument supporting his answer proceeds in three main stages: First, Plato argues for a division of the soul into three 'parts' or 'kinds'.[2] Next, he argues from this division for an account of the four major virtues. Finally, he appeals to this account of the virtues for his answer to Thrasymachus.

It is reasonable to begin by trying to understand the division of the soul, since this is used in the account of the virtues. First, we must examine Plato's principle of division so that we can tell when, by his criteria, we must recognize one part or two parts of the soul. Then we must ask whether the right application of these criteria leads us to the sorts of parts that Plato recognizes.

We cannot fully understand this division of the soul, however, without also examining the account of the virtues. In describing the virtues, Plato takes for granted some description of the parts of the soul; but his description of the virtues also says more about the character of the different parts and so completes the description of the parts. For this reason, our description of the parts of the soul has to proceed in stages, showing how different stages of Plato's argument require some addition or change.

144. Plato's Argument for the Division of the Soul

Plato takes it to be obvious that there are different mental states and activities (learning, being angry, having appetites), but he does not take it to be obvious that these states and activities belong to different parts or aspects of the soul (436a8–b3). His argument for different parts must, therefore, be intended to show something more than that there are different types of mental activities.[3] We need to know what Plato means by speaking of different parts and how successfully he argues for their existence.

The main points in Plato's argument for a division between the appetitive and the rational parts of the soul are these:

1. The same thing cannot do or undergo contraries in respect of the same aspect of itself (436b8).
2. Acceptance and pursuit of x are contrary to rejection and avoidance of x (437b1–5).
3. Appetite (for instance, hunger or thirst), willing, and wishing for x are acceptance and pursuit of x (437b7–c7).
4. Refusal, unwillingness, and non-appetite are rejection and avoidance of x (437d8–10).
5. Sometimes we both have an appetite for drink and refuse to drink (439c).
6. Since these states are contraries—by (2) through (4)—and so cannot belong to the same aspect of the soul—by (1)—they must belong to different aspects of the soul (439d–e).

Plato defends this *Principle of Contraries*, stated in step 1, by arguing that if an archer both moves and keeps still, or if a top both spins and does not move, that must be because they are moving one part and keeping another part still (436c7–e7, 439b8–c1).[4] The Principle of Contraries assumes that contrary motions must be traced to distinct states of the subject. If we reject the Principle of Contraries, we will have to say that the archer is both moving and still, without any further explanation.

These examples suggest that the Principle of Contraries rests on a demand about explanation. When we trace contraries back to different parts, we find the property 'by which' or 'in respect of which' the subject has its contrary properties. Plato discusses these sorts of explanations in the *Phaedo*.[5] He insists that x's being taller than y should be explained by appeal to the tallness in x rather than by some answer such as 'by a head', which explains being taller no better than it explains being shorter (*Phd* 96e–97b, 100c–101c). If this constraint on explanation is applied to the argument about contraries, it implies that if we seek to explain x's being F and being G (where G is contrary to F), but all we can offer is some one property H that explains being F no more than it explains being G, then we have explained neither being F nor being G. We do not, for instance, explain Socrates' being taller (than Phaedo) and shorter (than Simmias) by saying he is taller and shorter 'by a head'; 'by a head' explains neither of these properties, since it explains neither in contrast to the other.[6] We must say instead that Socrates is taller by being tall in relation to Phaedo and shorter by being short in relation to Simmias. In giving the right sort of explanation, we find two different properties 'by which' or 'in respect of which' the subject has the contraries that were to be explained. In the terminology of *Republic* IV, these two different properties 'by which' or 'in respect of which' mark out two 'parts' or 'kinds' in the subject.

Once the Principle of Contraries is accepted, Plato applies it to desires. He assumes that accepting and aiming at something is contrary to rejecting and avoiding the same thing (437b1–6), and then argues that desiring counts as accepting and aiming at its object, whereas aversion counts as rejecting and avoiding its object (437b7–d1); hence desire and aversion count as contraries falling within the scope of the Principle of Contraries. If we want to understand why S has a desire for x as opposed to an aversion to x, we cannot appeal to some property of S that would equally explain an aversion to x. The same is true (mutatis mutandis) if we want to explain why S has an aversion to x as opposed to a desire for x; and so if S has both a desire for x and an aversion to x, we must appeal to different properties, parts, or aspects of S. Since properties of S's soul are the ones that are relevant to explaining S's desires and aversions, this appeal to the Principle of Contraries seems to show that we must recognize different parts of the soul.

These general points about explanation, however, do not tell us what different parts of the soul we must recognize, for we still do not know what we are trying to explain. Plato says we are trying to explain contrary motions, but what is the relevant sort of contrariety?

145. Conflicts between Desires

Plato tries to describe the type of contrariety between desires that he has in mind (437b–439a). He describes acceptance and rejection, and pursuit and avoidance, as contrary tendencies in relation to a given object, and among acceptances and pursuits he mentions 'thirst and hunger and, in general, the appetites, and again willing and wishing' (437b7–8); among rejections and avoidances he mentions 'not wishing and not being willing and not having an appetite' (437c–10).[7] Plato goes on to describe 'the kind consisting of appetites', of which hunger and thirst are the clearest examples (437d2–4).[8]

These passages are not completely clear, but they suggest that Plato wants to distinguish appetite (*epithumein*) from the conative states that he calls 'wishing' (*boulesthai*) and 'willing' (*ethelein*).[9] For he proceeds to make some remarks about appetites in general, but he does not seem to intend these remarks to apply to wishing and willing.[10]

How does the contrast between wish and appetite clarify Plato's claims about contrariety? To begin with, three cases need to be considered and set aside: (1) I am hungry and sleepy, and I cannot both eat and sleep at once. (2) I am hungry, and so I am inclined to eat this cabbage; but I hate cabbage, and so I am also disinclined to eat it. (3) I am a long-time fan of a football team, the Wanderers, but my newfound enthusiasm for another team, the Strollers, makes me averse to my persisting enthusiasm for the Wanderers, who are their bitter rivals. In the first case, neither desire implies an aversion to the other desire or to its object; it simply happens that we cannot satisfy both desires on this occasion. In the second case, one desire implies an aversion to the object of the other desire. In the third case, one desire implies an aversion to the other desire itself, not merely to its object.

Each of these might be treated as a case of 'contrary' desires, but none of them, not even the third case, makes it plausible to claim that the desires belong to different kinds or parts. If desires are contrary just in case they cause us to pursue objects that cannot both be achieved on this occasion (as in the first case), we will have to recognize many parts of the soul. If Glaucon is sleepy and hungry, so that he both wants to eat instead of sleeping and wants to sleep instead of eating, we must certainly refer to different desires to explain his different tendencies, but this is not enough to introduce different parts. Even if one desire is an aversion for the object of the other desire (as in the second case) or a second-order desire directed to a desire (as in the third case), we still seem to be forced to recognize too many parts of the soul; why should aversions or second-order desires not conflict, just as first-order desires do? If conflicts arise among aversions and among second-order desires, then (for all we have seen so far) it seems that both aversions and second-order desires will also belong to several different parts.[11]

Plato may have an answer to these questions, if he relies on a tenable distinction between 'wish' and 'appetite', and if he can show that this distinction defines the appropriate sort of contrariety. Aristotle suggests how Plato might try to show this, for he connects contrariety with the division between rational and non-rational desires. As he puts it, 'appetite is contrary to decision, but appetite is not contrary to appetite' (*EN* 1111b15). In speaking of 'decision' (*prohairesis*), Aristotle refers to a desire resulting from rational wish (*boulēsis*) and deliberation about the good, as opposed to appetitive desires that do not aim at the good. Does Plato intend the same sort of distinction between wish and appetite?[12]

146. Rational Desires versus Appetites

This question requires closer attention to Plato's account of appetite. Taking thirst as his example, he argues that since thirst is properly defined as the appetite for drink, it must be desire for drink qua drink, not for drink qua F (qua good, interesting, healthy, etc.); if it were desire for drink qua F, it would be desire for F, not desire for drink.[13] It follows that thirst is not desire for drink qua good and, more generally, that appetites for food, drink, and so on are not the same as desires for good. If, then, we attribute thirst to an agent, we attribute an appetite distinct from desire for the good (437d8–439b2).[14]

This passage confronts an apparently Socratic thesis. For Plato tells us that we should not be put off if someone tells us that our appetite is not just for drink, but for good drink, on the ground that all of us have appetites for goods (438a1–5), since appetites are desires and all desires are for the good.[15] This thesis that we should not be 'put off' by seems to be the thesis of Socrates in the early dialogues. Whether it really is the Socratic thesis and whether Plato really rejects it must be considered after we have seen how Plato treats it.

The argument about 'thirst insofar as it is thirst' relies on a point about definitions that Thrasymachus noticed in Book I when he spoke of 'the ruler by the exact account' (340d–e).[16] Thrasymachus pointed out that the ruler qua ruler does not make mistakes, and Socrates pointed out that a craftsman qua craftsman does not make money; the features in question are not part of the definition of a ruler or craftsman. In Book IV Plato argues that if *thirst* is defined as desire for drink, and not for drink qua satisfying some further description, then it is not, qua thirst, also a desire for the good.

This parallel with Book I exposes the weakness of the argument in Book IV. Facts about rulers qua rulers and doctors qua doctors do not show that there are any actual rulers who do not make mistakes or doctors who do not make money. Similarly, facts about thirst as such do not show that any of our actual desires is a desire for drink as opposed to drink qua good. For if the Socratic dialogues are right, appetites (desires for the satisfaction of specific bodily needs and urges) do not constitute a kind of desires distinct from desire for the good. In the Socratic view, no desire conforms to the description of 'thirst qua thirst'; what we call fear, for instance, is the expectation of evils (*Pr.* 358d5–e; *La.* 198b8–9). If fear qua fear must be simply directed to something frightening, and being evil is different from being frightening, then Socrates in the *Protagoras* is wrong to apply 'fear' without qualification to the state he is describing, but he may still be right about human motivation. He can say that the desire that we loosely call 'the appetite for F' is strictly speaking not a desire for F alone, but a desire for F qua good (cf. *G.* 468c2–7).[17] That is why our desire for F depends on the belief that F is good, and so disappears as soon as we abandon our belief that F is good.

Plato needs to show, then, that there are actual desires that satisfy his description of appetites such as 'thirst qua thirst', in being simply desires for drink (and so on) rather than desires for drink as something good. To show that there are such desires, he considers someone who is thirsty and so seeks to drink. He argues: 'If there is something that pulls the soul in the contrary direction when it is thirsty, would it not be something else in the soul besides what is thirsty and is leading it like a beast towards drinking?' (439b3–5). In his support he cites the Principle of Contraries.

What does Plato mean when he speaks of 'pulling in the contrary direction' (*anthelkein*) and connects this with the Principle of Contraries? He ought not to mean that whenever the soul has a desire contrary to appetite, the contrary desire comes from the rational part. If he said this, his appeal to contrariety would leave him no room to recognize a third part of the soul distinct from the appetitive and the rational parts. And so the explanation of contrariety must be broad enough to allow more than desires of the rational part to be contrary to appetites. What notion of contrariety will mark out distinct parts of the soul?

147. Desire and Contrariety

To answer this question, we must distinguish different kinds of opposition. Opposition 'to an appetite' may be simply an aversion to this appetite for this object; alternatively, it may be opposition to acting on appetite as such. In the second case, the opposition presupposes some grounds for objection to following appetite. Since no appetite can itself be opposed to acting on appetite, the sort of desire that opposes acting on appetite must be some non-appetitive type of desire. Plato's position is reasonable if he takes the desires that are contrary to appetite to be those that are opposed to acting on appetite as such.

Plato's account of appetite suggests what is involved in being opposed to acting on appetite as such. In claiming that appetites are independent of desire for the good, he suggests that opposition to acting on appetite is opposition to acting without regard for the good; that, in other words, is what is wrong with acting on appetite. If this is what he means, then he has some reason to claim that this specific sort of contrariety between desires requires different parts of the soul; if some desires are indifferent to the good and others are not indifferent to it, this is a strong reason for recognizing two classes of desires whose members have enough in common to constitute two distinct explanatory parts.

To see whether this is what Plato means, we must understand his question, 'Are we to say that . . . sometimes some people are thirsty but are unwilling (*ouk ethelein*) to drink?' (439c2–3). He assumes that if we answer Yes to this question, we must recognize two different parts of the soul, because anything opposing (*anthelkein*) pure appetite must belong to a different part of the soul (439a9–c1). Does 'unwilling' refer to aversion in general, or does it refer to a desire resulting from a specifically rational desire for the good? If Plato refers to aversion in general, two unwelcome results follow: (1) Since he goes on to assume that the unwillingness results from reasoning, he seems to assume without warrant that all contrariety involves the rational part. (2) Not only is this assumption unwarranted, but it conflicts with Plato's next argument, which is meant to show how the spirited part may have desires contrary to those of both the other two parts. These unwelcome results of the broader understanding of 'unwilling' favour the narrower understanding, taking 'unwilling' to refer to a rational desire for the good.

We noticed earlier that in this discussion Plato has generally used 'wish' and 'will' for desires that are not pure appetites. The following remarks suggest that this is what he intends here too. First, he takes it to be obvious that unwillingness is the result of reasoning (439c9–d2); then he says that in a conflict between reason and appetite, reason 'determines that one ought not to resist (*antiprattein*)' what it says (440b5); later still, he specifies 'ought not' by saying that the rational part reasons about the better and the worse (441c1–2). By contrast, when he comes to the conflict between the appetitive and the spirited part, he does not say that the agent is 'unwilling' to follow appetite, but that 'he is annoyed and turns himself away' (439e9–10). His argument becomes more reasonable than it otherwise would be, if we assume that he intends a restricted sense for 'wish' and 'will'.[18]

Plato's claims about contrariety can now be understood by reference to his demand for explanation. He agrees with the Socrates of the early dialogues in recognizing a desire for the good that is based on the rational belief that, for instance, abstaining from drinking is, all things considered, better than drinking the polluted water; but he argues that our capacity for these rational desires cannot explain our desire to drink rather than abstain, since reasoning about what is better inclines us to abstain rather than drink. It follows that our capacity to desire things as good cannot explain all our actual desires and choices, since we sometimes desire what our capacity for rational desire causes us to reject, and the same capacity cannot explain our rejecting and our desiring.

Plato, therefore, denies the Socratic claim that all our intentional action rests on our desire for the good and our belief that the action we choose is better than our other options. If not all our desires are responsive to our beliefs about the good, then Plato has a reason for assigning them to different parts of the soul; for desires that depend on beliefs about the good seem to have enough in common to play a distinct explanatory role. But Plato needs to say more in order to say how precisely the reference to beliefs about the good is supposed to justify a division into parts.

148. The Appetitive Part

Does Plato really argue against the Socratic position, or does he take the most controversial points for granted without proper argument? We might object that he is not entitled to assert without further argument that there really are cases where we persist in our desire to drink despite recognizing that it would be better to abstain; for does Socrates not argue that we are mistaken in believing that there are such cases?

Perhaps, however, this is not the most controversial move in Plato's argument. For Socrates agrees that there appear to be cases of the sort Plato describes; in the *Protagoras* he acknowledges that the many believe there are such cases. He argues, however, that since the explanation offered by the many is incoherent, we must conclude that the appearance of such cases is misleading. If our inability to give a coherent explanation of these cases is all that justifies us in denying their existence, someone who believes in their existence need only provide a coherent explanation of them. This is what Plato tries to do.

To see whether he succeeds, we must see whether he takes account of Socrates' reasons for believing that we cannot choose contrary to our belief about the good. Socrates believes this because of his psychological eudaemonism. He believes we explain and understand an agent's action only if we refer to some end, and ultimately to some self-explanatory end; since happiness is the only self-explanatory end, actions are explicable and intelligible only if they are referred to the agent's happiness. If Socrates is right about this, common-sense views about non-rational desires make action on these desires seem unintelligible. If we say someone knew that it would be better for him to stand firm, but he ran away because he was afraid, Socrates asks why he acted on his fear. He cannot have acted as he did for the sake of his happiness, since he is supposed to see clearly that it would be better for him to do something else. He must, apparently, have acted as he did for no reason at all—as though he were simply compelled by some external force independently of his own beliefs and aims.[19]

This suggestion about compulsion raises further questions about Socrates' argument against incontinence. The recognition of compulsive non-rational desires does not conflict with the Socratic denial of incontinence, as Socrates seems to understand it; for Socrates claims only that when it is open to us to do x or y (*Pr.* 355a8), we cannot both believe that x is better and choose y. Indeed, we might even say that recognition of compulsive desires would make it easier to defend Socrates' position. Perhaps he need not say that there are no cases of believing x is better and choosing y; he might say that there are such cases, but they are cases of psychological compulsion, not of incontinence.

Socrates would be unwise, however, to rely on this line of defence. For he wants to emphasize the role of reason and knowledge in explaining human action and in forming moral character, and this role will be significantly reduced if allegedly incontinent desires turn out to be psychologically irresistible. In the *Protagoras* Socrates mentions some apparent phenomena that 'the many' take to show the possibility of incontinence: being 'overcome' by anger, fear, love, pleasure, and pain (*Pr.* 352b3–c2). Since Socrates supposes that belief in this sort of 'overcoming' would be inconsistent with his belief in the power of knowledge, he presumably does not think that the many regard these desires as being irresistibly compulsive.

We might be tempted to argue that the weakness of knowledge in these cases is no objection to Socrates' claim about the power of knowledge; for these, we might say, are cases of compulsion, but Socrates' claim applies only to cases of non-compelled action. This defence, however, protects Socrates' position by embracing a still more implausible position. He ought not to defend his position by dismissing as cases of compulsion all cases of acting against our judgment of what is better. Such a defence expands the class of compelled, rationally unintelligible action for no better reason than that the expansion helps to protect the Socratic position.

Plato's description of appetites is meant to avoid this unattractive defence of the Socratic position while answering the reasonable Socratic demand to be shown how action on appetite is intelligible if it is independent of beliefs about the good. Hunger and thirst are offered as the most evident examples of a 'sort' or 'kind' (*eidos*) called 'appetite' (437d2–5).[20] Plato does not suggest that action on non-rational desires is intelligible without further explanation; he suggests that it is intelligible insofar as these desires belong to an appropriate 'sort' or 'kind'. If acting on desires of this kind is intelligible, then acting on the different specific desires is intelligible.[21]

The relevant kind, however, is not described very clearly. Plato refers especially to basic biological urges and drives that we share with other animals. He says that thirst leads a person as though he were a beast (439b4), and that when appetites conflict with desire for what is better they are the result of 'affections and diseases' (439d1–2); the aspect of the soul in respect of which we have sexual passion, hunger, and thirst and are 'stimulated about the other appetites' is 'non-reasoning and appetitive, a companion of certain fillings and replenishments' (439d7–8).

Plato means that these desires explain and make intelligible the actions of non-rational animals and that desires of the same sort explain some of our actions in a similar way. If, then, they explain animal action without any reference to the animal's conception of its good, they should also be capable of explaining our action in the same way. The 'bestial' model of non-rational desires constitutes an appropriate reply to Socrates' implied assumption that intentional action is unintelligible without reference to the agent's desire for his good.

These remarks should not be taken to imply that all appetites are the result of diseases, that they are all bestial, or that they rest simply on basic biological urges and drives. These urges are, as Plato says (437d2–4), the 'most obvious' examples of appetites. They make it clear that we can satisfy some of the requirements that lead Socrates to his conclusion, while still resisting his conclusion. Socrates assumes that the desire for the agent's happiness explains action because happiness is a self-explanatory end, needing no further end to explain our pursuit of it. Plato may be taken to suggest that happiness is not the only self-explanatory end; the objects of appetites are also self-explanatory, since they explain some of our actions in the same way as they explain the actions of non-rational agents. If we have such desires, it is not surprising that they create conflicts with the desire for our overall good; for since they explain our actions without reference to our good, they do not automatically yield to beliefs about our good.

Plato does not point out a further feature of appetites that helps him to answer Socrates. Socrates seems to assume that an agent's actions would be unintelligible unless they were focussed on some ultimate good. A sympathetic critic might take this assumption to be an exaggeration of the plausible claim that completely pointless and uncoordinated action could not be interpreted as intentional action at all.[22] Animal action suggests how intentional action can be coordinated without being coordinated by the agent's conception of an overall good. Action on appetite displays some degree of system and coordination in its general connexion to the agent's nature and needs, without depending on the agent's conception of an overall good. If Plato had developed this point further, he would have strengthened his claim that appetites constitute a genuine part, not a mere collection of impulses.

149. The Spirited Part

So far Plato has distinguished the part of the soul that is purely appetitive from the part that is responsive to reasoning about the good (439d1–2, 439d5). This distinction, however, is still not clear, since Plato has not said what role he has in mind for reasoning. To see more precisely what distinction he intends, we must also consider the third part, the *thumoeides* or 'spirited' part.[23]

Plato begins the treatment of the third part with the example of Leontius gazing at corpses (439e). Leontius' unfortunate recreation looks even less like the product of his views about the good than physical appetites might look. Leontius is angry because of his urge to gaze at corpses;[24] this case is meant to support the division between the angry part and the appetitive part.

Since this conflict is supposed to display contrary tendencies needing to be explained by reference to different parts of the soul, we need to see whether Plato identifies the sort of contrariety that we took to be necessary for division into parts. He makes it clear that the impulses of the spirited part, like those of the rational part, are opposed not just to an appetite but to acting on appetite, as such, on this occasion. The spirited impulse is not merely an aversion to the particular appetite; it opposes the agent's tendency to be guided by appetite to this degree.

To show that the spirited part has this attitude to appetite, Plato describes its attitude to a conflict between the appetitive and the rational parts. He focusses on cases in which 'appetites force (*biazontai*) someone against his reasoning' (440b1); and he clearly means us to take Leontius as a victim of this sort of forcing. The spirited part supports the rational part against appetite, since the spirited part relies on the agent's conception of what is good and right; it does not support appetite, as such, against reasoning (440b4–7). Plato means that when we are aware of x's being better than y, and y's being more pleasant than x, our spirited part is not attracted to y because of the belief that y is more pleasant, despite being worse.

This claim does not imply that the spirited part never conflicts with the rational part, or even that it never endorses an action that is endorsed by the appetitive part and rejected by the rational part. Plato implies only that if the spirited part endorses such an action, it does so for some reason other than that the appetitive part prefers it.[25] In this example, and in the next one, about the connexion between anger and the sense of justice (440cd), Plato shows that he does not intend simply to introduce a further appetitive aversion that conflicts with appetitive desires. The spirited part has evaluative attitudes, resting on some belief about the goodness or badness of its object, apart from the fact that it is simply an object of desire.

If we accept all this, however, we may want to challenge Plato from the opposite direction. For if the spirited part supports the rational part, can it really be distinguished from the rational part? We might argue that mere aversions to appetites belong to the appetitive part, and evaluative attitudes belong to the rational part, leaving nothing to belong to the spirited part.

To counter this objection, Plato offers the example of Odysseus (441b). Odysseus' anger (at his servant girls sleeping with the suitors) moves him to want to take revenge at once. Although he realizes that this would not be the most sensible thing to do, his anger and his desire to take revenge persist against his better judgment. If his anger had been too much for him, he would have been overcome by anger (just as Leontius was overcome by appetite) against his rational desires.

Nonetheless, the attitude of the spirited part is not a mere appetite or aversion. Odysseus' spirited part has learned that the kind of treatment he suffers is an unjust harm and that he ought to punish the offender; the awareness of the harm prompts the desire to punish. The attitude is evaluative, not a mere appetite or aversion, and to this extent it is similar to the attitudes of the rational part. The desires of the spirited part, however, persist even when rational judgment shows that they ought not to be executed this time.[26]

In these cases the spirited part does not oppose the desires of the rational part in the way in which the rational part opposes the desires of the spirited part, or in the way in which the spirited part opposes the desires of the appetitive part. The spirited part is not moved by the belief that it is bad to do what seems best on the whole. It is moved by the quite different belief that it is bad to be humiliated or to let an offence go unpunished.

Plato illustrates the attitudes of the spirited part by mentioning anger, but in suggesting that it also includes a sense of shame and justice he attributes to it a wider range of attitudes. The well-trained spirited part is marked by willingness to accept punishment for its own faults (441c1–5); the spirited part endorses the just punishment and restrains the appetitive part from revolting against the painful but just treatment we receive. In this case the spirited part expresses itself primarily in pride, shame, and a sense of justice; the connexion with anger is secondary, insofar as anger is characteristically and vividly connected with these other attitudes.

In claiming that the outlook of the spirited part is evaluative, not merely appetitive, and yet different from the outlook of rational desire, Plato clarifies the nature of some emotions. If you are angry at me for taking your sandwich off your plate and eating it, you are not simply expressing your pain at being deprived of something you wanted. You might feel pain at deprivation if there just happened to be no sandwiches left, or if a dog ate your sandwich instead. If you are angry at me, you believe I caused some harm to you that I ought not to have caused you; 'harm' and 'ought' indicate the good-dependent character of your attitude. If your desire to harm me in return is based on anger, it shows itself to be a good-dependent desire, distinct from a desire to inflict pain on me for its own sake (sadism) or to prevent me from taking your food (instrumental reasoning about the satisfaction of appetite). Still, anger may not rest on a rational desire; even if I realize that this particular action of type F is nothing to be angry or feel guilty about, the anger or guilt may nonetheless remain. While reason shows us that some actions of type F are good and others are bad, emotion tends to focus on F-type actions in general, without the discrimination that results from reasoning.

This non-discriminating aspect of emotions is one of their advantages for us. For some action descriptions (such as 'he's taking what belongs to me', or 'he's hitting a defenceless victim') elicit emotions, and the emotions form a powerful desire to act in some specific way (to prevent him from taking what belongs to me, to defend the victim) that does not require elaborate reflexion on the situation, yet does not simply register my feelings of pleasure or pain. If these spirited reactions are more or less right in a fair number of cases, then their immediacy gives them an advantage over rational reflexion in cases where explicit reflexion would be inappropriate.[27] The desirable condition is not the one in which my reactions always wait on complete rational reflexion, but the condition in which my tendencies to immediate reactions have been formed by the right sort of rational reflexion, causing them to focus on the right features of situations. In this case the rational part has a regulative role, but it ought not to be giving specific advice about what to do in this situation.

150. The Rational Part

We learn about the nature and capacities of the rational part of the soul partly by seeing how it differs from the other two parts. Plato's description of the other two parts has already ruled out some initially plausible ways of describing the desires of the rational part; once we set these aside, we must see whether any plausible description can still be found.

We might suppose that a rational desire differs from an appetite insofar as one does, and one does not, involve the operation of reason in fixing the object of the desire. This division might explain the conflict between thirst and a refusal to drink. On this view, the desire not to drink the water results from, say, realizing that it is mixed with petrol and that the mixture will be poisonous, whereas the desire to drink it results from the mere appearance—without any further reasoning—that it is water.

This division implies that any desire that results from any sort of reasoning or inference thereby belongs to the rational part; if I am hungry, wonder where to find a meal, and notice that there is a restaurant across the road, my resulting desire to go into the restaurant must, on this view, belong to the rational part. If this is all it takes for a desire to belong to the rational part, very few desires will be mere appetites.[28]

This cannot be Plato's constant view, however. In Book VIII he argues that the oligarchic person is dominated by the appetitive part of his soul because he is dominated by the desire for wealth (553c4–7). Wealth is connected with the satisfaction of appetites, but to see this connexion we must be able to reason about the instrumental relation between wealth and the objects of appetite. If the desires resulting from this instrumental reasoning still belong to the appetitive part, Plato cannot believe that every sort of practical reasoning makes the resulting desire belong to the rational part. While this remark comes from Book VIII, nothing in Book IV conflicts with it.

The remarks in Book IV about the spirited part also imply that some desires of the non-rational parts of the soul depend on practical reasoning. If someone's spirited part is angry and ashamed at his running away from a battle, he must have thought that the brave thing to do would have been to stand firm, that he has failed to face the danger he ought to have faced, and that someone who does that ought to be ashamed of himself. Even though the resulting anger and shame is the product of all this reasoning, Plato thinks it belongs to the spirited part.

If dependence on reasoning is not enough, what more is needed for a rational desire? Plato says that the rational part not only reasons but also 'has reasoned about the better and the worse', in contrast to the spirited part that is 'angry without reasoning' (441c1–2); presumably the spirited part has failed to reason about the better and the worse (since, for the reasons given here, it clearly relies on reasoning about something). This seems to be a plausible ground for dividing the rational from the appetitive part; we might say that the appetitive part includes only desires that result from reasoning about how to satisfy appetites and does not include any view about whether it is good or bad to satisfy a particular appetite. If the desires of the appetitive part are indifferent to the goodness or badness of their objects, then we can see why they are liable to conflict with the desires of the rational part; the discovery that it would be bad to satisfy an appetite does not cause the appetitive desire to go away, since appetitive desires are not based on any assumption about the goodness of their objects.

This argument faces difficulties, however, if we try to distinguish the desires of the rational part from those of the spirited part. For anger, resentment, and shame seem to rest on assumptions about the goodness and badness of what was done. When Odysseus is angry at his slave girls, he does not simply register his displeasure at what they have done; he is partly moved by the thought that they have failed to show the loyalty that could reasonably have been expected of them and that they deserve to suffer for what they have done. Apparently, then, he must have concluded that it would (from some point of view) be better to punish them than to leave them alone. If this is so, the spirited part cannot be unresponsive to reasoning about what is better and worse.[29]

To grasp Plato's conception of the rational part, we must attend to a further remark. He says not only that it reasons about better and worse but also that it is capable of knowledge about what is beneficial for each part of the soul and for the whole soul in common (442c6–8). If the rational part is guided by reasoning about what is best, all things considered, for the whole soul and for each of its parts, it is different from the spirited part. For the spirited part conceives its objects as good for the agent without conceiving them as best, all things considered, for the agent. To apply the concept of 'good for me', an agent needs a conception of different things adding up to something; to think that it would be good for me to satisfy this desire, I need some conception of myself and of the sort of thing that would be good for the self that I conceive. But I may have these views without having any conception of myself as a whole or of the combination of things that would, everything considered, be best for myself as a whole.[30]

The desires of the rational part, in contrast to those of the spirited part, rest on deliberation about what would be best, all things considered, for myself as a whole. Let us say that such desires are *optimizing* desires. In claiming that the rational part is the source of optimizing desires, Plato implies that it is guided by a conception of the agent's overall happiness or welfare (*eudaimonia*) and that the other parts are not guided by it. To this extent, the desires of the rational part satisfy Socrates' description of desire in general; Plato disagrees with Socrates in recognizing desires of the other two parts, which do not satisfy Socrates' psychological eudaemonist conditions.

If practical reason contributes to the desires of all three parts, is Plato right to claim that one of the three parts has some special connexion with reason? His claim implies that optimizing desires, those that rest on reasoning about what is best for me as a whole, are especially rational. Plato shares this view with Butler, who argues that rational self-love, in contrast to the particular passions, appeals to principles and aims relying on authority rather than mere strength of desire; in choosing the ends it will follow, it is guided by reflexion on what I have better reason to do, irrespective of what I may have a stronger desire to do.[31] Butler believes that rational self-love is especially connected with practical reason because it displays no partiality to some desires or affections, but takes account of them all on their merits. If this is what Plato has in mind, he has a reason for claiming that the optimizing attitudes of the rational part are distinctively rational; they are not determined simply by the strength of some antecedent desire that provides the end for practical reason to achieve.[32] They result from consideration of what is better, all things considered, for the whole soul, not from one's strongest occurrent desires.[33]

We must examine this claim more closely to see how it distinguishes rational desires from spirited as well as appetitive desires. The spirited part is not inclined towards a particular object simply because the object is desired—that is the outlook of the appetitive part—but values it in the belief that it has some further property that deserves to be valued. But this belief about the further valuable property itself reflects the spirited part's desires and preferences; I am angry about this injustice not because I understand that injustice is bad, all things considered, but because this is how I have been trained to react to apparent injustice. Only the rational part has desires that rest on a conviction about what is best, not on the strength of other desires.

151. Reasons for the Tripartition of the Soul

If this is the right way to distinguish the rational part from the other two parts, we can now try to decide whether Plato's tripartition of the soul is reasonable. Ought he to recognize three parts, and ought they to be the three that he recognizes?

Many critics have agreed that Plato is justified in recognizing something besides the rational and appetitive parts and have seen that the attitudes of the spirited part—connected with anger, self-esteem, honour, and shame—are significantly different from appetites. It is more difficult, however, to see how these attitudes could wholly constitute a part of the soul that, together with the rational and appetitive parts, exhausts the different types of possible motives.[34]

This difficulty may be resolved if we suppose that the attitudes Plato ascribes to the spirited part are meant to illustrate, not to exhaust, the desires that are based on evaluation and are therefore not purely appetitive, but not optimizing desires either. In recognizing that some desires are neither optimizing nor purely appetitive, but involve evaluations based on desires and aversions, Plato recognizes an important class of desires that would be missed if we insisted on a bipartition.

Once we see the desires that are characteristic of each part of the soul, we can also decide how far Plato's initial appeal to contraries adequately captures his reasons for recognizing three parts. We can see that a simple reference to contraries fails to capture some important asymmetries between the parts.

If we think of moving forwards and backwards, or being pale and dark, as examples of contraries, the relation of contrariety seems to be symmetrical insofar as forwards is no more contrary to backwards than backwards is to forwards. Plato, however, describes an asymmetrical relation that includes a symmetrical relation.[35] In a parliamentary system of government, we may say that the government and the opposition are political opponents, and to that extent are symmetrically related; nonetheless, the task of the opposition is to oppose government policy, whereas the government's task is not to oppose the opposition, and to that extent their relation is asymmetrical. Similarly, if p and q are contradictory statements, their relation is symmetrical, but if speaker A asserts p without reference to the views of speaker B, and B replies by contradicting A's assertion and asserting q, there is an asymmetrical relation between the two speakers and the two assertions.

These analogies are relevant to Plato's claims about the three parts of the soul. Both the rational part and the spirited part are opposed to the appetitive part insofar as they reject action on appetite, as such, on particular occasions; the rational part is opposed to the spirited part in the same way. The appetitive part, however, is not opposed, in the same sense, to either of the other two parts, although its desires may certainly conflict with their desires. To this extent, the relations between the three parts are asymmetrical.

If this is right, then Plato's initial examples of contrariety, intended to support the Principle of Contraries, are too simple to display the special type of contrariety (including the asymmetrical element of opposition) that he has in mind. We have seen that in dividing the soul he does not appeal simply to conflicting desires, those that in fact tend to move the agent in incompatible directions; he appeals to desires that oppose other desires by explicitly rejecting them (in the sense described). Once we keep in mind the fact that Plato has this particular kind of contrariety in mind, we can object to his failure to explain how it includes more than ordinary contrariety, but we can see why he has a good reason for claiming that contrariety of this kind needs to be explained by different parts of the soul.

152. Parts of the Soul as Agents

So far we have examined Plato's account of the desires that are characteristic of different parts of the soul. We cannot, however, understand the nature of a part of the soul simply by understanding the character of its component desires. For Plato also conceives the parts of the soul as analogous to agents; he compares the rational part to a human being, the spirited part to a lion, and the appetitive part to a many-headed and multifarious beast (588c7–d5).[36] The analogy suggests that each part can be treated as a single agent, although the desires of the appetitive part show most variety (as the different aspects, good and bad, of the beast reveal themselves).

The same conception of the parts as agents underlies Plato's remarks about how they can agree with each other. Temperance requires agreement between the parts of the soul about which part should rule. In the well-governed city, 'the same belief is present in the rulers and the ruled about who ought (*dei*) to be the rulers' (431d9–e1); in the temperate soul, then, the appetitive part is expected to believe that the rational part ought to rule. In his account of elementary education, Plato argues that before we are capable of reasoning we should be habituated to enjoy what is fine (*kalon*) and hate what is shameful, so that when reason comes we will welcome it, 'recognizing it because of its kinship' (*di' oikeiotēta*, 402a3–4). If the appetitive part recognizes some kinship in the rational part, it cannot simply notice that the rational part chooses to act in ways that the appetitive part also chooses; it must also notice that the two parts are moved by some of the same considerations. Can the non-rational and the rational parts have this sort of kinship?

The rational part, as Plato describes it, reasons about what is best for each part and for all the parts in common (442c6–8). It therefore appeals to the aims of each of the non-rational parts and assures them of some reasonable degree of satisfaction. This assurance recommends the rule of the rational part to the two non-rational parts.

If we are to attribute these attitudes of acceptance and rejection to the appetitive part, we must suppose that it has some structure that makes it more than simply a collection of appetites. Agents have some attitude to their desires as a whole, and in the light of this attitude they give priority to some desires over others. The appetitive part must be able to do this, if it is to recognize that the rational part satisfies it and shares its aims, not just that the rational part shares this particular aim here and now.

Has Plato made a mistake, however, in attributing these aspects of agency to a non-rational part of the soul? If the non-rational parts agree with the rational part, they seem to have the outlook of reasonable people, but since Plato has denied that they have optimizing desires, has he not denied that they have the outlook of reasonable people? If they lack this outlook, how can they have the attitudes that they must have to do what he expects them to do?

This difficulty might suggest that Plato has made a mistake in attributing to each part the structure that makes it capable of recognizing kinship and agreeing with other parts. He seems to have pressed his political analogy too far and to have introduced a self-defeating anthropomorphic element into his description of the parts of the soul. If he treats the two non-rational parts of the soul as though they were capable of behaving like reasonable people, he seems to be treating each part as though it were an agent with its own rational part. To understand how this 'agent' makes its choices, we must presumably divide its soul into three; if we must also make each of these three parts an agent, we seem to be forced into a vicious regress.

To avoid this objection, Plato must show that a non-rational part has enough structure and unity to agree with the rational part, but still has no rational part of its own. Can he show this?[37]

153. The Unity of a Part of the Soul

If a part of the soul is to be capable of recognizing kinship in another part, it must recognize kinship to itself, and so it must apparently have a conception of itself. What might such a conception be like?

It would be very difficult to suppose that, say, the appetitive part actually includes a conception of itself as a part of a whole (in the way that someone's conception of herself might include a conception of herself as, say, a part of a community); for it would also presumably need some conception of the whole of which it is a part, and once we attribute such a conception to the appetitive part, we run the risk of reduplicating the soul whose structure we are supposed to be analysing. We will avoid this difficulty if we suppose that our appetitive part's conception of itself is a restricted version of our own conception of ourselves. What can be ascribed to the appetitive part within the appropriate restrictions?

If we have a conception of ourselves, we refer to the past and future; we are capable of regret (in the minimal sense of displeasure at something we have done in the past, if, for instance, we have foolishly forgone some pleasure we could have had) and of fear and hope. In these attitudes we connect our present appetite with a range of other past and future appetites. To this extent we have a conception of ourselves and of what satisfies us, apart from any particular desire. It is even easier to see how attitudes of the spirited part—anger, shame, pride—characteristically involve some conception of oneself as the person whose achievement is being considered, who has done something shameful, or whose interests have been harmed. From the point of view of the rational part, each non-rational part's conception of itself is also a partial conception of the self to whom the part belongs; but the part itself does not recognize this relation to a larger self.

To be aware of oneself in these ways—and so to be liable to these various feelings—is not necessarily to be capable of criticizing or modifying a present desire in the light of some conception of one's interest as a whole. A child could lack this sort of critical faculty, while still being aware of his desires as belonging to something temporally extended and containing more than one kind of appetite. The relevant conception of oneself requires some rational capacities, but it does not require the rational optimizing desires that belong to the rational part of the soul.

If the appetitive part has desires that rest on this conception of itself, then it is capable of being moved by the awareness that x is a more efficient instrumental means than y. If my appetitive part is concerned exclusively with this occurrent appetite, it will be unmoved by considerations of efficiency. These considerations tell me that one means fits better than another with my various appetitive aims, but such information will leave my appetitive part unmoved unless it has some concern for its other aims.[38]

Can we tell whether Plato takes any desires mediated by considerations of efficiency to belong to the appetitive part? We have already seen that, in his view, the desire for x is an appetite if it results from the desire for some object of appetite y and the belief that x is a means to y. Plato shows that he believes this, since he takes the desire for wealth to be an appetitive desire. If this is his view, however, he can hardly deny that reasoning about the most efficient means may also result in an appetite. It is difficult to see how we could form the steady desire for wealth as a means to satisfaction of appetites if we were unconcerned with efficiency; only if we compare wealth with the other means of satisfying appetites over time will we prefer it as a matter of policy (since, for instance, accumulation and preservation of wealth normally requires some restraint on the satisfaction of appetites in the shorter term). Plato's recognition of an appetite for wealth suggests that he regards some desires mediated by considerations of efficiency as appetites.

The appetitive part, therefore, shares two features with the rational part: (1) It is concerned for its desires over time; considerations of efficiency involve some reference to desires that I expect to have, even though there is no immediate occasion for satisfying them. (2) Its concern for the future gives it some weighted concerns; if I am concerned with efficiency, I must sometimes care more about satisfying some of my future desires than about satisfying this desire here and now. If I did not sometimes care about these future desires, I would always be indifferent, from the point of view of the appetitive part, between more and less efficient means to the same goal.

Still, even though the appetitive part has its own hierarchical preferences, it sometimes violates them. We may sometimes realize that our future appetites or appetites we care more about will be satisfied if we do not satisfy this particular appetite now, but we may choose to satisfy it nonetheless. If this is incontinence within the appetitive part, and if incontinence involves a conflict between the rational and the appetitive parts, must we admit that a rational part in the appetitive part conflicts with an appetitive part in the appetitive part? If so, Plato faces a vicious regress.

This conflict of preferences, however, does not imply incontinence, if incontinence involves a conflict between what we desire most strongly and what we recognize the best reasons for valuing. This recognition of the best reasons requires recognition of Butler's distinction between authority and strength; we must recognize the merits of a particular course of action apart from the strength of our desires. If this is necessary for incontinence, a conflict between desires for short-term and longer-term satisfaction is neither necessary nor sufficient for incontinence. While the appetitive part is capable of recognizing conflicts between short-term and longer-term satisfactions, it lacks a system of values that takes account of something more than the comparative strength of different desires.

The appetitive part, then, recognizes considerations of efficiency, but it sees no reason, distinct from an occurrent desire for long-term satisfaction, to be moved by efficiency. If a desire for some particular satisfaction becomes stronger than my desire for longer-term satisfaction, then the appetitive part no longer recognizes any reason for preferring the longer-term satisfaction. In the appetitive part, the behaviour that looks most like incontinence is really a change of mind and preference; no persisting rational evaluation opposes my current preference, and so there is no room for incontinence.

154. Relations between Parts of the Soul

This description makes it easier to see how the appetitive part can see something akin to it in the rational part, and how it can accept rule by the rational part without itself having to turn into another rational part. Since the appetitive part has some concern—not always its dominant concern—for a temporally extended self, it is capable of seeing that this sort of concern is satisfied by the rational part. Sometimes, indeed, the appetitive part will recognize that the rational part does better than the appetitive part could do by itself; for the appetitive part's overriding desire for its long-term satisfaction lapses under the pressure of intense desires for short-term satisfaction, whereas the rational part retains its overriding desire for what is best.

Most of the time, then, the appetitive part wants to secure longer-term freedom from severe pain more than it wants a particular immediate gratification; in these moods it may recognize that its aim will be better achieved if it is guided by the rational part's steady plan of pursuing longer-term freedom from pain rather than immediate gratification. Admittedly, the appetitive part will lose this preference when it forms an especially strong desire for some immediate gratification; still, it may take steps, at times when it has the far-sighted preference, to make it more difficult to violate this preference.

When the appetitive part recognizes these points of agreement with the rational part, it may also form a second-order desire to do what the rational part tells it to do; although it initially forms this desire on the basis of purely appetitive desires and their objects, the result of forming the desire may be the formation of further desires that the agent could not have had without having a rational part. This capacity of the appetitive part gives it a place in moral education. Although I do not initially care about temperate or just action, I learn to listen to the rational part (my own or someone else's) because it satisfies my longer-term appetites. Once I begin to listen to it, I come to acquire its preference for temperate and just action. Once I form this preference, it will also increase my tendency to follow my more far-sighted preferences even when I form a strong desire for an immediate satisfaction.

In this way the appetitive part is capable of adopting some of the goals of the rational part; it adopts them not for the reasons that move the rational part, but because it sees their connexion with its own goals. Although it cannot be a completely enlightened or equal partner (since it does not recognize all the reasons that move the rational part), it can cooperate with the rational part, and the more its preferences are shaped by those of the rational part, the more reliable a partner it is.

If this is a reasonable account of the structure of the appetitive part, a similar account can be given for the spirited part, which Plato takes to be less multifarious and more unified than the appetitive part. In both cases we can explain why Plato is entitled to treat the non-rational parts as though they had some of the properties of agents. Since he does not treat them as rational agents, he avoids any vicious regress in the composition of the parts.

In attributing structure to a part of the soul, Plato agrees with Socrates on a point that did not emerge clearly from the particular examples of conflict between the parts.[39] Socrates sees that a single desire by itself does not explain an action; a particular desire makes an action intelligible because the desire itself is intelligible, fitting into some longer-term pattern of choices and actions.

Socrates, however, infers that desires make action intelligible because they ultimately aim at the agent's happiness, whereas Plato sees that happiness need not be the only long-term aim that allows us to explain particular actions. In Plato's view, the non-rational parts of the soul have some of the structure that Socrates attributes to the desires of the rational agent, but only the rational part has the structure that focusses on the agent's happiness.

Since the structure of each part of the soul is essential to its explanatory role, we must suppose that Plato takes it seriously. We have found that he is right to take it seriously. His remarks about agreement and harmony between the parts are no mere metaphor or unfortunate anthropomorphism; they rest on a defensible view of the nature of the three parts. This result is important for our estimate of his account of the virtues; for this account of the virtues relies on further claims about agreement and kinship between the parts of the soul. We must see whether these further claims are defensible.

14

Republic IV: The Virtues

155. The Division of the Soul and the Account of the Virtues

Book IV presents a sharp and radical criticism of the moral psychology that is assumed and defended by Socrates in the early dialogues. Socrates' identification of virtue with knowledge depends on his belief that knowledge of what is better is sufficient for choice of what is better; it therefore depends on his rejection of incontinence. The *Protagoras* shows that Socrates recognizes this connexion between his views on incontinence and his conception of virtue. The *Gorgias* sometimes expresses the same Socratic assumptions about knowledge and action, but sometimes recognizes a distinction between rational and non-rational desires; it is difficult to decide how far it agrees with the shorter Socratic dialogues and how far Plato is conscious of disagreeing with the Socratic position. Since the *Republic* rejects the Socratic account of motivation, it is reasonable to expect that it will also reject the Socratic account of the virtues.

The *Laches*, *Charmides*, and *Protagoras* eliminate all non-cognitive components of the virtues. We might suppose, from a common-sense point of view, that someone could believe it is better to stand and face a danger, but could still be afraid to face it, so that he runs away; what he lacks is apparently 'endurance' (*karteria*), which was eliminated from the discussion of courage in the *Laches*. Similarly, it seems quite possible for someone to believe that it would be better to avoid this pleasure, but still to have disorderly appetites that make him pursue it. He lacks 'orderly' or 'quiet' appetites, which were eliminated from the discussion of temperance in the *Charmides*.

In *Republic* IV Plato restores these non-rational elements to bravery and temperance. Elementary moral education of the sort described in Books II and III is intended to fix the right non-cognitive responses in people so that they do not suffer the sort of conflict that Plato, unlike Socrates, takes to be both psychologically possible and morally dangerous. The pleasures and pains of young people are to be formed so that they go in the direction that reason will approve when it comes along; and so, once young people acquire correct rational judgment, they will welcome and accept what it says (401e–402a).

The description of the four cardinal virtues seems to reflect Plato's emphasis on the non-rational sources of right action. Bravery is no longer identified with knowledge of good and evil; instead, it is identified with a condition of the spirited part, which holds tenaciously, even in the face of danger, to the right beliefs about what should be done (429b8–c3). Temperance is taken to be a condition of the appetitive part, which accepts the rule of the two higher parts of the soul (432c6–9). Only wisdom is described as a virtue of the rational part. Justice is identified with each part's performance of its proper function in the whole soul.

These apparent differences from Socratic ethics are not surprising, in the light of Plato's tripartition of the soul. It is more difficult, however, to decide how far Plato rejects the Socratic position. In arguing that the virtues have non-cognitive aspects, Plato agrees with one aspect of common sense against Socrates. Common sense, however, also tends to believe that the virtues are separable, even opposed, and that knowledge is neither necessary nor sufficient for virtue. Socrates' views about motivation give him a reason for rejecting these common-sense views; once Plato rejects Socrates' views about motivation, does he return to common sense on these issues?

156. Connexions between the Virtues: Bravery

In the early dialogues, Socrates argues against the separability of the virtues, and hence for the Reciprocity Thesis, by arguing that every virtue must result in fine and beneficial action and that all the virtues are needed for fine and beneficial action. He does not sharply distinguish the Reciprocity Thesis from the Unity Thesis, the claim that all the virtues are identical to knowledge of the good. The Unity Thesis relies on the claim that knowledge is necessary and sufficient for virtue. In the *Meno* Plato may express some doubts about the Unity Thesis.[1] Since *Republic* IV rejects the Socratic denial of incontinence, we might expect Plato to infer that knowledge is not sufficient for virtue, and therefore to deny the Unity Thesis; if he denies it, however, he is still free to maintain some elements of the Reciprocity Thesis. What does he actually claim?

If we focus on his initial description, bravery seems obviously separable from the other virtues and therefore seems to refute the Reciprocity Thesis. Plato suggests that a brave person has stable and enduring correct belief about what is to be feared and not to be feared (429b8–c3). Education should make belief stable by non-cognitive training; the spirited part is to be trained so that the brave person retains his belief about what is better and worse despite the temptations of pleasures, pains, and fears (429b–430b). If the preservation of right belief is sufficient for bravery, then the only sources of cowardice are those temptations that change our belief about good and bad. On this view, pleasures and pains prevent us from being brave only because they make us believe that it is not so bad to avoid danger and that cowardly courses of action offer compensating benefits.

If this is Plato's view, then bravery seems to be separable from temperance;

for he identifies temperance with the control by desires and wisdom in the rational part over the desires in the appetitive part (430e–431d). Later he identifies temperance with the agreement among the parts of the soul that the rational part should rule (442c10–d1). This account connects temperance with order (*kosmos*, 430e6; cf. *Ch.* 159b3; *G.* 504d1) in the soul. If Plato assumes (1) that preservation of correct belief by the spirited part is sufficient for bravery and (2) that this preservation of true belief does not imply the agreement of the appetitive part, then he cannot consistently believe that bravery requires temperance. Does he accept either assumption?

He recognizes that an appetitive desire may conflict with a desire of the spirited part that is based on correct belief, for he suggests that a person with excessively strong and misguided appetites could still, as Leontius does, retain his belief about good and bad but fail to act on it. Plato seems, therefore, to accept the second assumption. If he also accepts the first, then someone like Leontius could be brave, but still fail to do the brave action, because his appetites move him despite his tenacious true belief about the good.

Does Plato accept this conclusion, however? If he does, then he must agree that some brave people may behave like cowards because they are both brave and intemperate. If he must say this, then his account of bravery fails to describe a reliable tendency to do the sorts of actions that are normally expected of a brave person; such an account fails a simple condition of adequacy for an account of the virtue.

Since Plato cannot accept this result, he must reject at least one of the two assumptions that lead to it. In fact, the same considerations tend to undermine both assumptions. Plato might argue that mere tenacious true belief is not really sufficient for bravery; while a certain kind of tenacious true belief is sufficient for bravery, this kind is not possible without temperance. We might argue that while someone like Leontius manages to preserve a true belief on a particular occasion, he cannot have appropriately stable true belief; the pleasure that he finds on this occasion will gradually undermine his belief that what he is doing is bad. Even though Leontius' condition may be a temporary condition of a person with an imperfectly trained soul, we need not agree that it is a stable condition; the habit of incontinent action gradually undermines correct belief. Aristotle refers to this effect of disorderly appetite when he remarks that pleasure destroys an agent's 'principle' (*EN* 1140b16–20).

We have reason to suppose that Plato agrees with Aristotle on this point. For when he describes the stable conviction that is characteristic of bravery, he mentions the 'solvents' that threaten to wash out the beliefs in the spirited part (430a6–b2). The first of these solvents is pleasure. If Plato believes that pleasure undermines true belief, but Leontius has true belief with the wrong pleasures, he must be supposing, as Aristotle does, that the solvent effects of pleasure take time. He must distinguish the 'short-term' tenacity of someone like Leontius from the 'long-term' tenacity characteristic of the brave person. Since short-term tenacity is possible without bravery, it allows incontinent action; since long-term tenacity requires freedom from the solvent effects of misguided pleasures and pains, it does not allow incontinent or cowardly action.

If, then, we are to understand Plato's view of bravery, we must not be misled into supposing that only conditions of the spirited part affect a person's bravery. He must believe that conditions of the appetitive part affect it too; and since he believes this, he must also believe that bravery is not possible without temperance. Plato's account of bravery, therefore, does not imply that the virtues are separable.

157. Connexions between the Virtues: Temperance

Plato's description of temperance as agreement between the parts of the soul implies that temperate people's appetites are not strong or wayward enough to cause them to act contrary to their true beliefs about what is good and bad. This orderly condition of the appetites seems to be separable from the tenacious belief that is needed for bravery, and so temperance seems to be separable from bravery.

It is difficult, however, to see how orderly appetites without a well-trained spirited part are sufficient to secure the normal sorts of temperate action. For even if someone's appetites are orderly, he will sometimes be tempted to some degree to pursue some pleasure contrary to what he initially thinks best. If his spirited part is not well trained, his true belief about what is best will not be stable; his mind will be easily changed by the prospect of pleasure. Plato can hardly intend this sort of fickle and self-indulgent person to count as temperate.

For this reason, genuine temperance seems to require bravery, just as genuine bravery seems to require temperance. If Plato intended the virtues to be separable, he would be forced to accept consequences that would cast serious doubt on his account. If he is not to be forced into these consequences, he ought to explain why his account of temperance does not imply that the person with orderly but wavering desires is temperate. Perhaps he can say that someone who is easily persuaded to pursue the pleasures that attract the appetitive part really lacks the right sort of psychic order. If the rational part is willing to change its mind to satisfy the appetitive part, then, Plato might argue, it is really accepting domination by the appetitive part and so cannot belong to a temperate soul. Genuine control by the rational part requires the tenacious correct belief that is secured by bravery.

Plato does not believe, then, that tenacity without orderliness is sufficient for bravery, or that orderliness without tenacity is sufficient for temperance. In starting from tenacity in the case of bravery and from orderliness in the case of temperance, Plato is starting from common sense, but he is not agreeing that these traits are the whole content of the virtues. The Socratic dialogues show that most people would readily divide bravery from temperance along these lines, and Socrates does not adequately explain why common sense is wrong. In *Republic* IV Plato confronts the common-sense view more directly and tries to show that common-sense expectations about the brave and the temperate person undermine the common-sense conviction that these virtues are separable. Common beliefs about each virtue identify some important, even distinctive, features of the virtue, but they do not justify us in separating the virtue from the other virtues. Even when we recognize different parts of the soul and allow that non-cognitive elements are necessary for each virtue, we must still insist on the inseparability of the virtues.

158. Justice and the Other Virtues

Justice raises an especially sharp question about the separability of the virtues. Plato seems to treat wisdom as the virtue of the rational part, bravery as the virtue of the spirited part, and temperance as the virtue of the appetitive part. Justice, however, has no proprietary part of the soul; on the contrary, it is the state in which each part of the soul 'does its own work' or 'performs its own function' (441e2). Does Plato believe that someone could have the other three virtues, or some of them, without meeting this condition for psychic justice? If he does, then he rejects the reciprocity of the virtues, but what would these virtues be like? If, on the other hand, he thinks each of the other virtues involves psychic justice, why does he treat it as a distinct virtue rather than as an aspect of each virtue?

First, what is required for each part of the soul to perform its own function? A connexion between justice and performing one's function has been anticipated several times in the *Republic*. It is suggested in Book I, both in the discussion of the Simonidean conception of justice and in the argument about the human function.[2] Early in Book IV, in the discussion of justice in the city, Plato remarks that it is common to see a connexion between justice and performing one's function. He exploits this connexion in arguing that the city is just when each individual does his own work by sticking to the task assigned to him by the city. A further connexion between justice and performing one's function is asserted in the discussion of justice in the individual, when Plato claims that an individual will be just and will perform his own function if the parts of his soul perform their own functions; this will make individual justice parallel to justice in the city (441d12–e2).

In this last claim, 'perform his own function' has not yet been explained. Plato is not asserting that an individual is just insofar as he does what is prescribed by the city, and so contributes to the justice of the city; if he did mean that, the content of 'perform his own function' would already have been explained, whereas Plato claims that it still needs to be explained.[3] The content is explained by appeal to the tripartition of the soul; once he has referred to the tripartition, Plato argues that the performance of one's own function that is relevant to justice in the individual consists in the right states and relations in the parts of the soul; it does not consist in outward action (443c4–d3). In speaking of function, Plato has in mind some conception of the psychic condition proper for a human being with human capacities. He argues that this condition requires the rational part to rule by its wisdom, the spirited part to support the rational part because of its affective training, and the appetitive part to remain in willing subordination to the other two parts (441d12–442b4, 443c9–444a3).

What would the other virtues have to be like if they did not require psychic justice? We would have an easy answer to this question if we thought bravery and temperance were separable; for we could conceive a brave person with a disorderly appetitive part and a temperate person with an unsteady spirited part. But since Plato does not take bravery and temperate to be separable in these ways, he cannot give this argument for separating them from justice. For the reasons we have given, each of these virtues requires cooperation between the parts of the soul.

Could this type of cooperation exist in a soul whose parts did not perform their proper functions? It is easiest to consider an alleged case of temperance in which someone's appetitive part reluctantly agrees to be controlled by the rational part. Does this constitute good order in the soul? No part of the soul departs from its proper place; the political analogue would be reluctant or grudging acquiescence by the lower classes in the rule of the guardians. In that case the temperate person would always be facing a struggle of the sort faced by Leontius; even though he would win it, his appetites would often be reluctant and recalcitrant. Does Plato count this as a case of temperance?

This is the sort of person whom Aristotle describes as 'continent' (as opposed to incontinent), but not properly virtuous (*EN* 1102b25–28). In the continent person, the non-rational part conforms to the demands of the rational part, but conforms reluctantly. In the virtuous person, however, the non-rational part is in harmony with the rational part insofar as it does not have the sorts of desires that cause the continent person's reluctance (1102b25–28). Whereas the continent person regrets having to give up these particular appetitive satisfactions, and so has to struggle to do the right thing, the temperate person has well-trained appetites that do not cause regret or reluctance.[4] Although Plato does not draw an explicit distinction corresponding to Aristotle's, it is useful nonetheless to ask whether he takes conformity to be sufficient for virtue or whether he agrees with Aristotle and demands harmony as well.

Some of his remarks might suggest that conformity is sufficient for virtue. He describes temperance as 'self-mastery' and 'control over pleasures and appetites' (430e6–431a2). This description anticipates Aristotle's description of continence. A similar view of bravery might be defended. These remarks suggest that control by the rational part and conformity by the non-rational part are together sufficient for virtue. If this is what Plato means, then his conditions for some virtues are similar to Aristotle's conditions for continence and so are less demanding than Aristotle's conditions for virtue.

This sort of conformity cannot constitute psychic justice. Even if the parts of a continent person's soul remain in their proper place, they do not perform their proper function for the good of the whole soul; for it is not the proper function of the lower parts to be resisting or complaining about the rule of the rational part. If, then, Plato believes that Aristotelian continence is sufficient for Platonic temperance and bravery, but insufficient for Platonic justice, he must agree that justice is not necessary for temperance and bravery. Whereas temperance and bravery seem to demand only conformity by the parts of the soul to the rules prescribed for them, justice also seems to require the right attitude of one part to another.

It is doubtful, however, whether this contrast between justice and the other virtues can be maintained. Plato's rejection of it is clear in a political context. Reluctant conformity by the lower classes in a city would not be the ideal condition, but we are supposed to look at the ideal city to understand the character of the virtuous person. When Plato applies this analogy, he makes it clear that he does not in fact take conformity to be sufficient for temperance. Although he first describes temperance as conformity and control, he also describes it as concord (431d8, 432a6–9) and even friendship (442c10–d3) between the three parts under the wise control of the rational part. These later descriptions anticipate Aristotle's description of virtue in contrast to continence (*EN* 1102b25–28).

This distinction between conformity and friendship is justified by Plato's view that a part of the soul has some of the characteristics of an agent.[5] Since each non-rational part has some concern for itself as something more than a mere collection of desires, it can see that the rational part is concerned for the ends of the other two parts. Friendship results from the recognition of these shared concerns and interests; friendship between the parts of the soul under the correct guidance of the rational part is Aristotelian virtue, not simply Aristotelian continence.

Temperance and bravery, therefore, are not separable from justice, for the concord and friendship required by temperance and bravery are possible only if the different parts of the soul perform their proper functions as they do in a just soul. Plato wants to distinguish justice from the other conditions for virtue, not because he believes it is separable from the other virtues, but because he wants to mark the Aristotelian distinction between continence and virtue. In distinguishing justice as psychic harmony from mere conformity and control, he makes it clear that genuine virtue requires more than mere conformity and control.[6]

159. Is Knowledge Necessary for Virtue? The Political Analogy

If Plato believes that three of the virtues are inseparable, does he also believe that each of the three requires wisdom? Does he, in other words, accept the Socratic view that knowledge is necessary for virtue? In the *Meno* some questions are raised about the Socratic view.[7] Some aspects of *Republic* IV might suggest that Plato actually rejects the Socratic view, but we have already seen that some of Plato's descriptions of the virtues may mislead us if we do not interpret them in the light of the whole argument.

If Plato attributes the virtues of bravery and temperance to members of the non-ruling classes in the ideal city, then he must reject the Socratic view; for these people have stable right belief, ensured by their non-cognitive training, but they do not have knowledge.[8] Does he suppose, then, that their stable right belief (with the appropriate states of the non-rational parts of the soul) ensures virtue?

It would be clear that he supposes this, if a particular interpretation of his analogy between soul and city were right. Plato claims that the same 'kinds and characters' are in the city and in the individual soul, and that they are present in the city because they are present in individual souls (435e1–436a7; cf. 544d6–e2).[9] If this general claim means that any virtue in the city must be present in the city because it is present in the individuals who are distinctively responsible for its presence in the city, then Plato implies that the individuals in the military class are brave, since this class seems to be distinctively responsible for the bravery of the city (431e10–432a2). Correspondingly, since temperance and justice in the city must come, on this view, from temperate and just individuals, and no one class is distinctively responsible for these virtues in the city, it seems that everyone must have the virtues.

This interpretation of the 'political analogy' has very little support. When Plato agrees that 'kinds and characters' in the city must be derived from those in individuals, he refers to the different motives and tendencies belonging to the parts of the soul; he gives us no reason to extend the same point to virtues. When he claims that the structure of the virtuous soul corresponds to that of the ideal city, he implies only that it must have the same parts in the same relations; he does not imply that individuals in a city that has a given virtue must also have that virtue. No cogent argument from the political analogy supports the claim that Plato thinks knowledge is unnecessary for virtue.

Indeed, when Plato applies the political analogy to the individual soul, he seems to maintain the Socratic view. For he speaks of wisdom (*sophia*) and knowledge (*epistēmē*, 442c6) as the virtue of the rational part and assumes that this is the virtue that produces the right instructions for the other parts of the soul.[10] He does not definitely say that someone who has any of the other virtues must have wisdom also; although he easily could have mentioned correct belief as well as knowledge in the relevant places, he does not mention it. His silence on this point would be quite puzzling if he had meant to claim that individual auxiliaries are brave because of their tenacious right belief. If he did not mean that, however, his silence is quite intelligible.

If the political analogy, correctly interpreted, suggests that knowledge is necessary for virtue, we must look at Plato's remarks on the particular virtues to see whether they support the conclusion of this argument from the political analogy.

160. Virtue without Wisdom?

The interpretation of the political analogy that we have rejected gains some support from some of Plato's remarks about bravery and temperance in the non-ruling classes in the ideal city. He describes bravery in the city as the preservation of right belief about what is and is not to be feared (430b2–5), and he suggests that the auxiliary class has a special role in the preservation of the relevant right belief. If Plato means that each individual in the auxiliary class is brave, then he implies that an individual can be brave without having knowledge. He also claims that temperance is 'spread throughout' the city (432a2–6). He might be taken to claim that, whereas only the auxiliaries need to be brave in order to secure the bravery of the city and only the rulers need to be wise in order to secure the wisdom of the city, everyone (or most people) must be temperate in order to secure the temperance of the city. The same argument also suggests that all (or most) of the members of the three classes in the ideal city need to be just if the city is to be just.

Despite initial appearances, however, it is not clear that Plato attributes bravery to each individual auxiliary. When he speaks of tenacious true belief (429b–430c), he may mean not that this is sufficient to make an individual brave, but that it is the aspect of the city that is distinctively responsible for making the city brave.[11] This particular causal role does not require individual auxiliaries to be brave.

To see what Plato means, we must examine his claim that the city's bravery is 'in' a particular part (431e10). He cannot mean that some condition of this part is both necessary and sufficient for the city to be brave; for if the rulers did not give the right orders, the well-trained souls of the auxiliaries would not suffice for bravery in the city. The claim that different virtues of the city are 'in' different parts may refer to the distinctive characteristic of each virtue; although wisdom in the ruling class is necessary for bravery, it is not distinctive of bravery in contrast to the other virtues.

If this is what Plato means by saying that bravery is 'in' the auxiliary class, then he need not mean that individual auxiliaries are brave. On the contrary, if the distinctive aspect of the city's bravery is the fact that the military class follows the instructions of rulers who have wisdom, then, as Plato himself suggests, the appropriate parallel is the brave person with the right contribution from wisdom in the rational part and tenacity in the spirited part (442b5–c4).

A similar explanation allows us to understand Plato's remarks about temperance without assuming that everyone in the temperate city is temperate. The well-trained appetitive parts of the citizens are distinctively responsible for the temperance, rather than the bravery or wisdom, of the temperate city; but this does not imply that the citizens who have these well-trained appetitive parts are themselves individually temperate. And so Plato's remarks about the particular virtues do not imply that people who lack moral knowledge can have these virtues.

It is reasonable to infer that in *Republic* IV Plato maintains the Socratic view that knowledge is necessary for virtue. We might still resist this inference, however, if we could see no good reason for him to insist that knowledge, rather than right belief, is an appropriate condition for virtue. To see why he might agree or disagree with Socrates on this point, we must examine Plato's conception of knowledge to see how it might be connected to his demands on virtue.

161. Knowledge and Stability

It is difficult to compare Plato's and Socrates' views on the necessity of knowledge for virtue, for in the early dialogues Socrates neither defines knowledge, as distinct from belief, nor explains why it is necessary for virtue. Plato faces these issues in the *Meno*, where he introduces an explicit distinction between knowledge and true belief and then suggests that knowledge differs from true belief because of the stability that results from rational understanding (*M.* 97e2–98b9). As long as true belief remains true, it is just as useful in action as knowledge would be; but we need stable true beliefs if we are to prevent true beliefs from wandering away in difficult conditions.

We might argue that from the moral point of view stability is the only feature of knowledge that makes it preferable to true belief, so that if we could find stable true belief without the rational understanding that constitutes knowledge, that would do just as well as knowledge from the moral point of view. The *Meno* does not consider this argument. In *Republic* IV, however, Plato might well appear to accept it; for the auxiliaries are said to have stable true belief dyed into them because of their early 'musical' education (429c–430b). If stability is the only morally relevant feature of knowledge, then Plato's claim that the auxiliaries have stable belief seems to imply that they have all that is needed for virtue; knowledge will be irrelevant.

In the *Meno*, however, the sort of stability Plato has in mind cannot be separated from rational understanding; it is not the sort that the auxiliaries achieve through their moral education. In the *Meno* Plato argues that correct belief is less stable than knowledge; his claim is defensible if the sort of stability he has in mind is counterfactual reliability.[12] The auxiliaries achieve only empirical reliability; for they are trained to have a firm belief about what to do in a certain range of circumstances, and, we may concede, these are all the circumstances that they are likely to face. Both their beliefs and the truth of their beliefs seem to be unreliable in a wider range of relevant circumstances. If, for instance, the rulers change for the worse and try to inculcate favourable attitudes to actions that were previously rejected as unjust, people who have had elementary moral education will still do what their rulers tell them, but their moral beliefs will no longer be true.

Plato himself illustrates just this point. In Book VIII he describes the difference between a timocracy and the ideal city. The rulers in a timocracy enrich themselves in secret, even though they profess to care most about bravery and the martial virtues; they do this because they have neglected 'reason and philosophy' (548b–c). Since they have had the wrong sort of moral education, they lack 'reason mixed with musical training, which is the only thing that can be implanted in a person to dwell as a preserver of virtue throughout one's life' (549b6). If rational understanding is necessary for the sort of moral education that preserves genuine virtue, an elementary moral education without this rational understanding does not ensure that people will stick to virtue when the rulers of their society have the wrong outlook. Since the auxiliaries in the ideal city have only elementary moral education, Plato implies that their beliefs are not counterfactually reliable and therefore are not stable in the sense intended in the *Meno*.

Is Plato right to insist that a virtuous person's moral beliefs must be counterfactually reliable? Perhaps every reasonable belief is counterfactually unreliable if the counterfactual supposition is extravagant enough; it seems unreasonable to insist that a virtuous person's true belief must be reliable in all logically possible conditions. Still, some appeal to counterfactual reliability seems reasonable insofar as it reveals an agent's motives and reasons. Suppose, for instance, that q is a good reason for believing p, and r is a bad reason; and suppose that I believe p, q, and r. I believe p for the right reason q if I would still believe p if I continued to believe q and ceased to believe r, but I would cease to believe p if I ceased to believe q and continued to believe r. Similarly, if I believe x is F and G, and we ask whether I choose x because it is F (the right reason) or because it is G (the wrong reason), it is reasonable to ask whether I would still choose x if I believed x is G but ceased to believe that x is F; if I would choose x in these circumstances, I do not actually choose x for the right reason.

If, then, Plato requires the virtuous person's beliefs and choices to rest on the right reasons, he is justified in demanding counterfactual reliability, and justified in claiming that knowledge is necessary for virtue. We must consider, then, whether his conception of the virtues includes a demand for the right reasons.

162. Knowledge, Reasons, and Virtue

Plato has already shown in Book II that he is concerned about the counterfactual reliability of beliefs and motives. Glaucon and Adeimantus consider unrealistic or unlikely situations: first, Gyges' Ring, and then the just person who suffers all the consequences that usually follow injustice. They want to see whether someone would be reliably committed to justice even in these circumstances, because this sort of reliable commitment reflects the fact that the agent chooses justice for its own sake as a dominant component of happiness. Since Glaucon and Adeimantus assume that a just person must choose justice for its own sake as a dominant component of happiness, they expect a just person to display the right sort of counterfactual reliability.

The just person is required to stick to the just course of action, as Socrates did, irrespective of 'honours and rewards' (361b8–c3); he must stick to it in conditions where acting justly actually brings dishonour rather than honour. If, then, Plato's conception of the virtues captures Glaucon and Adeimantus' demands, he must assume that the virtuous person's commitment to virtue is unaffected by dishonour. Can he claim this about the auxiliaries in the ideal city?

The elementary moral education of the auxiliaries makes them reliable across some changes in circumstances. Since true belief can be lost because of pain or pleasure or fear, the auxiliaries must be trained to resist these influences that might distract them from the right course of action (413b–414a). They are therefore immune to some of the temptations to vicious action that were considered in Book II, and to this extent they meet the demand for reliability.

On one crucial point, however, they fail Plato's demand. In Books III and IV he does not mention the effect of dishonour on one's desire to act bravely or justly; this need not be considered in the ideal city, where the right things are honoured. Plato never claims, however, that elementary moral education causes people to stick to the brave course of action irrespective of honour and dishonour. Indeed, it is hard to see how he could claim this, since the auxiliaries are guided primarily by the spirited part of the soul, which is also the honour-loving part.

This question about dishonour is raised in Book VIII in the comparison between the ideal city and the timocracy. As we saw, the rulers in a timocracy lack 'reason mixed with musical training' (549b6), and so lack virtue. Plato makes the same point in his picture of the growth of the timocratic individual. This young man's father takes the appropriate attitude to justice and so is not anxious to defend his reputation by taking part in the political activities that have now become debased; his virtue is reliable in the face of honour and dishonour. His wife scolds him for this lack of concern with his honour. And so when the son hears that just people are called fools in this city and are not respected, his honour-loving aspects are encouraged, and his spirited part takes over from his rational part (550a–b).[13]

Plato implies, then, that people who are guided by the spirited part cannot be relied on to value justice for its own sake irrespective of honour or dishonour. Elementary moral education causes people to regard brave and just action as a source of honour, but they would not remain committed to bravery if dishonour and humiliation were the penalties of being brave. Since these penalties for virtue are included among those that Glaucon considers in Book II, someone whose commitment to virtue is not stable enough to hold out against these penalties cannot have the sort of virtue that Plato was looking for in Book II.

163. Degrees of Virtue

These are good reasons for concluding that the auxiliaries who have the right sort of elementary moral education, but lack knowledge, also lack the sort of reliability that Plato takes to be necessary for a genuine virtue. Since they do not know what justice, for instance, is, they do not know that it is a part of happiness in its own right even when it is not a source of honour; and so they do not know why they are better off being just. They do not choose justice for its own sake, irrespective of honour or dishonour, and so they lack the right sort of commitment to the virtues.

Glaucon and Adeimantus suggest that someone who does not pursue justice for the right reasons has simply a facade of justice, not the real virtue. In saying this, they recall the attack on slavish virtue in the *Phaedo*, where Plato denounces those who choose virtue for its consequences and not from an understanding of what it is in itself.[14] If we have found that the well-trained auxiliaries do not really choose the virtues for their own sake, must we conclude that they have only slavish virtue? This does not seem to be Plato's view, since he contrasts the 'law-abiding' belief of the auxiliaries with the sort of fearlessness that arises without training. He says that this untrained fearlessness is 'bestial and slavish' (430b6–c1), but he does not suggest that the auxiliaries are slavish.

To see Plato's point, we must see why being slavish is not the only alternative to being genuinely virtuous. The well-trained people in Book IV cannot fairly be identified with slavish people who maintain a facade of justice only for its causal consequences. For well-educated people without knowledge, the belief that an action is just will be sufficient for them to want to do it, given the rest of their outlook; if they believe that an action is just, that is one of the features that their spirited part responds to immediately, without any further inducement. To this extent the well-educated person without knowledge differs from the calculating person who merely wants to seem just because of the anticipated rewards that might equally attract a non-virtuous person. Well-educated people take pleasure in their action because they believe it is just, not simply because they believe it has other desirable causal consequences.

But it does not follow that the well-educated person without knowledge really chooses justice for itself. To choose it for itself, we must choose it under the description that makes it what it is—for the property that makes it justice. When Plato speaks in Book II of choosing justice 'for itself', he does not mean simply that we must choose it for non-instrumental reasons; we must also choose it for what it really is. In his view, virtuous people must choose justice as a certain kind of non-instrumental good because they know that it is essentially that kind of non-instrumental good.

People who value what they regard as justice in the belief that it is a non-instrumental good, but who value it for a feature it does not have or for a non-essential feature it has, are not just people. If, for instance, someone valued justice non-instrumentally in the false belief that just action is always immediately pleasant and never painful, this person would not have the virtuous person's attitude to justice. Someone who valued just action without further reward because he found it shameful and humiliating not to do just action would have a correct belief about justice; for in a well-ordered society failure to be just (as it is understood in that society) is a source of shame and dishonour. But this is not the primary motive that Plato expects of the virtuous person.

On this view, the well-trained person who lacks knowledge does not care about doing virtuous action simply because it is a source of honour. If that were all he cared about, he would not care what he is honoured for, whereas a well-educated person cares about being honoured for being virtuous. Still, his belief that he will be honoured, and not simply his belief that he is acting virtuously, is needed to sustain his attachment to virtue; it matters to him that he is honoured for his readiness to do the brave action without further incentive.[15] His uncalculating readiness to do the brave action must be sustained by honour from other people, and Plato makes it clear that an attachment to justice that depends on honour is not sufficient for genuine virtue.[16]

164. Virtue, Knowledge, and Autonomy

Republic IV, therefore, does not give up the Socratic view that knowledge is necessary for virtue. If Plato holds this view, however, he holds it for a reason that Socrates did not make clear, since Socrates did not explain why knowledge was preferable to tenacious right belief. If we must choose the virtues for their own sake, then, according to Plato, we must choose them for what they essentially are, and so we must know what they essentially are. Plato believes that it is reasonable to expect the virtuous person to have some autonomous understanding of the virtues and their value. It is autonomous insofar as it rests on reasons that he has discovered and worked out for himself; it is not simply a set of beliefs derived from habitual obedience to other people.

On this point Plato follows a Socratic demand. In the early dialogues Socrates asks people to 'give an account' of themselves and their lives (*La.* 187e6–188a3), and he assumes that their response to his cross-examinations indicates whether they are really virtuous or not (*Ap.* 29e3–30a2).[17] Socrates does not explain why he takes this rational understanding to be a necessary condition for virtue. In the *Meno* and *Republic* II, Plato gives a reason for the Socratic demand. He suggests that virtuous agents ought to be able to show that they appreciate virtue as something to be chosen for its own sake; they ought not to rely uncritically on what other people tell them. In demanding this, Plato focusses on an important feature of a virtuous character. He connects his demand with the further demand that the virtuous person should choose virtue for its own sake. Since Socrates never states this further demand, his demand for knowledge is unexplained. Plato seeks to provide an explanation and a defence.[18]

It may seem paradoxical that Plato emphasizes this Socratic demand for autonomous understanding, since the *Republic* describes an ideal city in which most of the citizens lack this sort of understanding and are guided by unreflective obedience to others. In fact, there is nothing surprising about this. When Plato formulates the Socratic demand more sharply, he also comes to believe that it is difficult for most people to meet it. He therefore maintains that knowledge is necessary for virtue, and that most people are incapable of virtue. We may well criticize Plato for interpreting the demand for autonomous understanding so strictly that only a few people can meet it, but we should not infer that the demand itself is unreasonable or un-Socratic.

165. Is Knowledge Sufficient for Virtue?

So far we have found that Plato takes bravery, temperance, and justice to imply wisdom. But if he believes the Reciprocity Thesis without qualification, he must also believe that wisdom implies the other virtues (cf. Ar. *EN* 1144b32–1145a2). Does he believe this?

He surely cannot accept Socrates' reason for believing that wisdom implies the other virtues. Socrates believes this on the strength of a purely cognitive account of the virtues. To defend this purely cognitive account, Socrates defends psychological eudaemonism and argues against the possibility of incontinence. Plato's division of the soul rejects psychological eudaemonism, since it implies that not all desires are responsive to true beliefs about what is better and worse; the cases of Leontius and Odysseus make this clear. Plato insists that bravery and temperance require the training of the non-rational parts of the soul as well as the acquisition of true beliefs in the rational part. He cannot, therefore, agree with the Socratic view that cognitive states are the only ones that make a difference to whether one is virtuous.

This disagreement, however, does not require Plato to reject the Socratic claim that knowledge is sufficient for virtue. For Plato may believe that we cannot achieve knowledge, as distinct from right belief, unless we have acquired the appropriate non-cognitive states as well. If we have knowledge, we must have a fixed and self-conscious awareness of the grounds for our correct beliefs, and we must be able to reject specious but misleading counterarguments. Plato suggests that to reject these, we must have the right affective training.

Uncontrolled fears are a source of unstable beliefs, and the proper training of the spirited part is needed to guard against these fears (413a4–e5, 429c5–d2). Danger and fear are sometimes the source of misleading counterarguments, encouraging some people to change their minds about which dangers are worth facing and which causes deserve their loyalty. If we are to have a firm and steady grasp of the right grounds for our belief, we must be free of these disturbing fears. Immoderate pleasures may have the same effect in persuading us to desert our conviction about which course of action is worth pursuing. Aristotle recognizes this influence of non-rational motives on rational convictions; that is why he argues that temperance is necessary to preserve wisdom (*EN* 1140b11–20).

These reflexions require Plato to take a complicated attitude to the Socratic claim that knowledge is sufficient for virtue. In the *Protagoras* Socrates accepts this claim on the ground that knowledge is belief about the good and belief about the good is not 'dragged about' (*Pr.* 352c2) by non-rational desires. Plato rejects part of Socrates' position, since he believes that correct belief is sometimes dragged about (as it is in Leontius) and sometimes lost (as it is in the coward who is 'scared out of his wits' and abandons his belief); but he still apparently agrees that knowledge cannot be dragged about, since it cannot be present in someone who has erratic non-rational desires.[19] Plato believes, contrary to Socrates, that purely cognitive training is insufficient for knowledge, but he may nonetheless believe that once we have knowledge, supported by the right non-cognitive training, we thereby also have the rest of virtue. If that is so, then Plato may agree with Socrates in taking knowledge to be sufficient for virtue.[20]

166. The Reciprocity and Unity of the Virtues

Plato, therefore, seems to accept the Reciprocity Thesis. We have strong reasons for believing that he takes bravery, temperance, and justice to be inseparable, and that he takes all of them to be inseparable from wisdom. We have less strong, but still plausible, reasons for believing that he takes wisdom to be sufficient for the other virtues.

It is more difficult to say whether he also agrees with Socrates about the Unity Thesis, the claim that all the virtues are identical. Once again, he cannot accept the Unity Thesis for Socratic reasons, since Socrates accepts it because he thinks all the virtues are reducible to knowledge and no non-cognitive conditions are needed. But this is not the only possible reason for accepting the Unity Thesis. In order to defend the Reciprocity Thesis and reject the Unity Thesis, Plato would need to show that the virtues are distinct, but necessarily connected, states of character. Whether he can show this depends on how he distinguishes states of character.

The last part of *Republic* IV might suggest that Plato identifies all the virtues with psychic justice. For, he might argue, justice in the soul, requiring the proper performance of functions by each of the parts, is the single state that underlies and explains all virtue and virtuous action. If a brave person acts bravely, we will explain her action by referring to her state of mind and character, and the different features of the (supposedly) different virtues will all be relevant to explaining why she acts as she does. She displays bravery (in the condition of the spirited part), temperance (in the condition of the appetitive part), and wisdom (since the action expresses her autonomous understanding). Her success in doing all this must be explained by reference to her justice, for she does what she does willingly, without severe internal conflict or reluctance or resentment, and every part cooperates harmoniously with the others in doing its proper work. We might say that we explain her action by reference to one virtuous state of character that has these different features. If Plato agrees, he must accept the Unity Thesis.[21]

Plato does not, however, always speak as we would expect him to if he accepted the Unity Thesis. His characteristic way of distinguishing the virtues is to say that we are brave 'by F', and temperate 'by G'.[22] In these phrases 'F' and 'G' cannot be substituted for each other, for each virtue is connected with a different fact about the tripartite soul. This probably marks a contrast with Socrates. For Socrates also claims that people are brave by bravery, temperate by temperance, and so on (cf. *Pr.* 332a6–c2); but his arguments require substitutions in the 'by . . .' phrases, so that, for instance, we can argue: (1) We are temperate by temperance. (2) Temperance is identical to knowledge of the good. (3) Hence we are temperate by knowledge of the good. Plato, by contrast, does not seem to intend these substitutions.[23]

This point about explanation suggests how justice may differ from the other virtues, even though the virtues require each other. Temperance, for instance, involves control by the rational part and agreement by the non-rational parts that the rational part should rule; this agreement implies that each part does its own work, so that temperance requires justice.[24] Still, Plato can argue that the agreement of the parts is the state that explains the orderly behaviour characteristic of the temperate person, in contrast to the tenacious behaviour of the brave person; the psychic state that causes the different parts to do their own work underlies the agreement of the parts but does not explain exactly what agreement explains, and so it is not the same state.

It is plausible to believe that different virtues explain different virtuous actions, if we recognize that there are different psychic tendencies that need to be corrected by the virtues, and that each virtue corresponds to a distinct type of correction. We need bravery because we tend to be fearful and unsteady, and bravery is the virtue that corrects these tendencies; temperance, not bravery, is the virtue that corrects our tendency to overindulgence in pleasure on occasions when there is nothing to be feared.[25] Justice is not concerned primarily with the tendencies that are corrected by bravery and temperance; it is needed to ensure that the correction does not simply result in the right action, but produces the correct relation between the parts of the soul. This distinction between the virtues is defensible even if we also recognize that each of these virtues requires the others.

In claiming that different virtues are distinguished by the fact that they correct different errors, Plato expresses his disagreement with Socratic moral psychology. For Socrates, correction of our beliefs about the good and the ways to achieve it also corrects the different errors involved in each vice. For Plato, different vices reflect different defects in the non-rational parts of the soul, and different types of training are needed to correct these defects. He stresses this point in Books II and III and returns to it in Book IV (441e). This difference supports the view that different types of training result in different virtues, even though each will be a complete virtue only in a soul that has the other virtues too. The tripartition of the soul shows Plato that common beliefs about the distinctness of the virtues are closer to the truth than Socrates supposed they were.

It is difficult to say, however, whether these reasons for disagreeing with Socrates also justify the rejection of the Unity Thesis, and whether Plato actually rejects the Unity Thesis. The role of (supposedly) different virtues in explanations of different actions might be taken to show, not that bravery, for instance, is a different state from the other virtues, but that in speaking of bravery and of temperance we are speaking of different aspects of the same state. Commonsense distinctions may be defended by saying that the names for the virtues have different senses, so that 'bravery' means (roughly) 'the state that corrects tendencies to fear', not 'the state that corrects tendencies to indulgence in pleasure'. But this distinction between senses does not show that the underlying states are really different; on the contrary, we might argue that *Republic* IV shows that the state correcting these two tendencies is really one and the same state, entitled to the name of both virtues.

It must remain uncertain, then, whether Plato takes the accounts of the virtues to show that they are distinct, although inseparable, or that they are really one and the same virtue. But even if he maintains the Unity Thesis, he disagrees sharply with Socrates' reasons for maintaining it. Since Socrates believes that there is nothing to virtue besides the right sort of knowledge, he lacks the basis for distinctions among the virtues that rests on the tripartition of the soul. The tripartition allows Plato to display the complexity of each of the virtues in ways that are not available to Socrates.

167. The *Republic* and the Socratic Dialogues

Reflexion on Plato's discussion of the virtues should warn us against exaggerating the extent of his rejection of Socratic doctrines. Sometimes he appears to disagree with Socrates (on the necessity and sufficiency of knowledge for virtue, and the unity of the virtues), but further reflexion suggests that he might well still accept the Socratic doctrine, suitably interpreted. Still, if he accepts the Socratic doctrine, he does so for different reasons; for his deeper disagreements with Socrates (on moral psychology and on the role of knowledge in virtue) prevent him from relying on Socrates' reasons.

Plato might argue, then, that he is really defending Socrates, insofar as he defends Socratic doctrines from more plausible premisses than those that Socrates used. He accepts the Socratic demands for flexible response and rational understanding in the virtuous person. These demands are summarized in the claims made on behalf of knowledge in the *Meno*; *Republic* IV shows, despite first appearances, that Plato still imposes these demanding intellectual conditions on virtue.[26]

These contrasts between Socrates' views and the views of *Republic* IV rest on the assumption that when the Socratic dialogues appear to identify virtue with knowledge, they state the views of the historical Socrates and of the early Plato. We have taken the Socratic dialogues to present a relatively systematic Socratic ethical doctrine. It is most improbable that they are independent essays discussing particular puzzles in isolation. The same moves are made in different dialogues in treating different problems, and some dialogues contain arguments and claims that help to remove difficulties raised in other dialogues. In exploring difficulties, Plato is guided by a coherent doctrine that emerges from the dialogues of inquiry and is stated consecutively in the *Euthydemus*.

Some critics point out, however, that Plato is careful to suggest some objections to the 'solutions' that are presented in these early dialogues and that he exploits these objections in later dialogues, especially in the *Republic*. These critics infer that Plato cannot really have believed the solutions that are presented in the early dialogues. If we accept this argument, we may conclude either that the dialogues of inquiry are strictly aporetic, or we may accept the 'unitarian' view that Plato already has in mind the solution offered in the *Republic*.[27]

We must admit that the solution in *Republic* IV corresponds closely to the problems set in the early dialogues. If, for instance, we had insisted that some sort of endurance is a part of bravery, we would not have found ourselves tempted (at least not for the reasons that convince Socrates and Nicias) to identify bravery with the whole of virtue, and we would not have run into conflict with the initial assumption in the *Laches* that bravery is only a part of virtue. Equally, if we had insisted that some sort of orderliness or quietness is a part of temperance, we would not face the difficulty raised in the *Charmides* about the difference between temperance and the knowledge of good and evil as a whole. The *Laches* and *Charmides* are explicitly aporetic dialogues; we might suggest that in Plato's view the purely cognitive conception of the virtues needs to be rejected in order to solve the final puzzle. Why should we not suppose, then, that Plato means us to draw these morals and that he therefore sees the importance of the non-cognitive aspects of the virtues?

This suggestion appears less plausible once we notice that the purely cognitive view seems to be assumed in other contexts where it does not seem to be regarded as the source of difficulties. In the *Euthydemus* it is assumed without argument that knowledge makes the decisive difference between being happy and being unhappy.[28] In the *Gorgias* Socrates assumes psychological eudaemonism in order to show that orators do not get what they want and therefore have no power; psychological eudaemonism is essential to his argument, and he raises no doubts about it.[29] It is unlikely that in the Socratic dialogues Plato accepts the position of the *Republic* and then temporarily abandons it in the *Gorgias*.

For these reasons we ought not to suppose that the Socratic dialogues are intended to suggest that the identification of virtue with knowledge is the crucial error in the argument. Admittedly, Plato notices some of the difficulties raised by the Socratic position, and he does not offer tidy solutions to all the puzzles he presents. But we have found no reason to suppose that Plato intends to point us towards the solutions suggested by the *Republic*. Socrates could answer some of the puzzles by explaining how virtue is instrumental to happiness and how knowledge of what is better is sufficient for right action. These solutions are quite opposed to the position of the *Republic*, but the early dialogues give us no reason to deny—and some reason to believe—that when Plato writes these dialogues he accepts the 'Socratic' rather than the later 'Platonic' solution.

A decision between these different views about the Socratic dialogues and the *Republic* depends partly on the interpretation of the *Protagoras* and the *Gorgias*. If in the shorter dialogues Socrates means to maintain a purely cognitive account of the virtues, then the arguments of the *Protagoras* against incontinence and in favour of hedonism are entirely appropriate; they explain how someone might reasonably maintain a purely cognitive view. If, however, this is not the view Plato intends in the shorter dialogues, then either the argument in the *Protagoras* is not meant seriously or it marks a change of course by Plato (and Socrates?). This dialogue provides a strong presumptive argument for attributing the cognitivist view to Socrates. We ought to overturn this presumption only if the early dialogues, taken by themselves, make it incredible that Socrates should affirm this view in the *Protagoras*. We have found, however, that the early dialogues taken by themselves should incline us to believe that Socrates accepts a cognitive conception of virtue. The most plausible presumption about the early dialogues, combined with the most plausible presumption about the *Protagoras*, results in an entirely credible account of Socrates' position; the *Protagoras* turns out to be a defence and elaboration of the cognitive view of the virtues that is accepted in the early dialogues.

The 'unitarian' view would be more attractive if we could agree that any attempt to develop a purely cognitivist theory is clearly absurd, or at least that the attempt in the *Protagoras* to develop such a theory is clearly absurd. In that case, we ought to conclude that the argument in the *Protagoras* is probably not meant seriously. But in fact there is no reason to suppose that Socrates or Plato thinks that a purely cognitive view is absurd.

We have seen that a similar conclusion should be drawn from the *Gorgias*. This is different from the *Protagoras*, insofar as it shows some doubts about the Socratic cognitive view. To that extent, it is closer to *Republic* IV, but it does not seem completely consistent in its attitude to Socratic moral psychology. Its position is far easier to understand if we suppose that Plato has not yet worked out the position of *Republic* IV than if we suppose Plato writes it with *Republic* IV in the back of his mind.[30]

168. Socratic and Platonic Doctrines in Greek Ethics

The judgment that the Socratic cognitive theory deserves consideration as a position that a philosopher might actually hold is not just our judgment of what is philosophically reasonable. At this point the later history of Greek ethics helps us. Aristotle has no doubt that Socrates held a cognitive view and that the early Platonic dialogues provide evidence for it; in fact, the doctrine we have found in the early dialogues corresponds very closely with the views that Aristotle ascribes to the historical Socrates. Aristotle criticizes Socrates specifically for identifying bravery with knowledge[31] and more generally for identifying the virtues with knowledge (*EN* 1144b17–21). The most controversial positive doctrine put forward in the *Laches* as Socratic (as Nicias claims, *La.* 194c7–d3) seems to Aristotle to be authentically Socratic. This external evidence supports the view that both the historical Socrates (the person depicted in the dialogue) and Plato (the writer of the dialogue) endorse the claims about bravery and about virtue in general that are developed in the course of the discussion.

Aristotle's comments on Plato, founded on the middle dialogues, never accuse Plato of any of the mistakes about virtue that Aristotle takes to be involved in the Socratic position. His references to Plato's ethical (as distinct from metaphysical or political) doctrines sometimes express agreement with Plato (e.g., *EN* 1104b11–13, 1172b28–30); in his explicit remarks about Plato, he never seems to refer to the ethical doctrines of the Socratic dialogues. Once, in fact, he claims that Plato avoids Socratic errors about virtue and knowledge by recognizing the division of the soul (*MM* 1183a23–26).[32] Although Aristotle certainly rejects Socrates' view of the virtues, he does not suggest that it is so absurd that it need not be taken seriously. On the contrary, he thinks Socrates sees part of the truth about virtue, and that his position is mistaken mainly because it is one-sided (*EN* 1144b17–30).

Greek ethics after Aristotle confirms this view of Socrates and in particular of the *Protagoras*. For hedonism, cognitivism about virtue, and the denial of incontinence are all defended quite seriously by later Greek moralists. Epicurus seems to defend all three views; the Cyrenaic followers of Socrates defend hedonism; the Stoic defence of the last two views is recognized as a revival of the Socratic position.[33] If these later philosophers could mean such views seriously, there is no reason to assume that Socrates could not mean them seriously; on the contrary, we have reason to suppose that Socrates was widely believed to maintain these views. Critics of the Stoics never suggest that the Stoics derived their Socratic paradoxes from Plato; when Poseidonius criticizes Chrysippus for failing to see the importance of Plato's tripartition of the soul, he never criticizes Chrysippus for disagreeing with Socrates.[34]

These later philosophers, then, all seem to take the view of the Socratic dialogues and *Republic* IV that we have seen to be most plausible on internal grounds. We might well be puzzled by Plato's reintroduction of endurance, psychic order, and other non-rational components of virtue, if he had not rejected Socrates' views about reason and motivation. In fact, however, we have seen that he rejects these views very firmly, in affirming the tripartition of the soul. In the light of this tripartition, it would be most surprising if he did not reject the Socratic account of the virtues. Both internal and external arguments, therefore, suggest that *Republic* IV marks a genuine difference from the Socratic dialogues. We have noticed that Plato still maintains the characteristically Socratic claim: that knowledge is necessary for virtue. Moreover, we have noticed that he does not explicitly reject other Socratic claims: that knowledge is sufficient for virtue, and that all the virtues are really one virtue. We have seen, however, that Plato's defence of these Socratic claims relies on quite non-Socratic and anti-Socratic premisses. For these reasons, we ought to conclude that *Republic* IV marks a partial rejection and thorough revision of the Socratic theory of the virtues.

15

Republic IV: Justice and Happiness

169. The Questions about Justice

The division of the soul and the account of the cardinal virtues lead up to Plato's main purpose in Book IV. He sets out to answer the original question raised by Glaucon and Adeimantus, by saying what justice is. It was agreed in Book II that an answer to this question ought to show whether it is a non-instrumental good and whether the just person is always happier than the unjust. In Book IV Plato claims to have given a preliminary (although still incomplete) answer to the problem raised in Book II (444e7–445b8).

An answer clearly requires an account of what justice is, and Plato claims to have given this in Book IV. He does not point out that we also need some account of what happiness is. If, for instance, we shared Callicles' view of happiness, we would not agree that the just person is always happier than anyone else. Plato needs to show why Callicles is wrong. In Book IV he claims to have shown both that justice is an intrinsic good and that it is dominant in happiness. What conception of happiness should we attribute to him as the basis for these claims? Once we have answered that question, we ought to be able to say what feature of justice makes it a non-instrumental good.

If we understand Plato's explicit account of justice and his implicit views on happiness, then we can ask whether and how justice, as he conceives it, promotes happiness, as he conceives it. If we accept his answer to this question, we must still ask whether he has the right views about the nature of justice and the nature of happiness. We cannot reasonably expect him to believe everything that Thrasymachus, Glaucon, and Adeimantus maintained about the characteristics of the just person and just action; part of the point of defining justice is to correct some of their misconceptions. But we must be satisfied that the virtue Plato defines is the same as the one that Thrasymachus and Glaucon were talking about, so that we can be sure that he is actually answering the question that they asked.

First, then, we must consider Plato's view of the nature of justice, then his views about happiness, then his argument to show that justice promotes happiness (as he conceives them), and finally his success in answering the question he was asked.

170. The Function of the Rational Part

In discussing the parts of the soul and the cardinal virtues we have introduced some aspects of justice; but to see how it is appropriately related to happiness, we must examine it further.

We have found (1) that the desires of the rational part do not rest on purely instrumental reasoning about the satisfaction of this or that desire of a non-rational part, but they are rational optimizing desires; and (2) that justice requires not only conformity to the judgments of the rational part but also willing cooperation between the parts. This, however, may not be a sufficient description of justice. In a just soul, the rational part, like the other parts, must perform its proper function; do all optimizing desires result from the proper functioning of the rational part?

In some people the rational part forms its rational optimizing desires by choosing to follow the desires of a non-rational part. The rational part might choose to do what the appetitive part, for instance, wants to do at any moment. Alternatively, it might endorse the far-sighted preferences of the appetitive part, and endorse my preference for not feeling ill tomorrow against my preference for overeating today. In these cases we might say that the rational part is guided by the preferences of the appetitive part; the appetitive part does not challenge the decisions of the rational part, since it exercises the predominant influence on these decisions.

According to Plato, however, the function of the rational part is to form desires resting on wise deliberation about what is good for the whole soul. The mere fact that someone's non-rational parts accept the decisions of the rational part does not ensure that the agent also acts on wise deliberation about what is good for the whole soul. If someone thought that the most important thing in life is making money, made rational plans for doing so, and attached his feelings of anger, shame, and pride to these rational plans, he might claim to be controlled by reason. But Plato might reasonably deny that such a person acts on a view about what is good for the whole soul; if the rational and the spirited part serve appetite, they do not perform their own functions.

We can see why Plato believes this if we consider a political analogy. If the ruling class in the ideal city simply followed the preferences, even the more settled preferences, of the lower classes, and decided that it would always be best to follow these preferences, it would not be doing what Plato expects of it. The lower classes do not, according to Plato, form a conception of the city as a whole and of its good; they simply have the preferences that reflect their own character and outlook. If the ruling class simply followed these preferences, it would not form the preferences of the lower classes in the light of its own independent judgment of what is best for the whole city and its parts. In this case the rational element in the city would be dominated by the non-rational elements, although the type of domination would be different from the sort that would result if the lower classes were actually the rulers. If the ruling class simply endorsed the preferences of the lower classes, it would not be performing its proper function.

Plato has equally good reason to argue that in an individual soul a rational part that simply endorses the preferences of the non-rational parts is not performing its proper function, and that therefore a soul with this structure lacks psychic justice. The rational and spirited parts are ill equipped to pursue the good of the whole soul because they have no conception of this good. Each non-rational part has some of the characteristics of an agent, and in particular each has a conception of itself and its aims; but this conception does not include a conception of the whole self to which the non-rational part belongs. A non-rational part has no conception of the value of the aims of the other parts, or of the nature of the whole soul that is composed of these parts. Only the rational part has a view of the whole. A rational part that simply takes its cues from the preferences of the non-rational parts is not exercising its distinctive capacities and functions, and therefore the soul that is guided by such a rational part is not just.

If Plato believes that a rational part performing its function should exercise independent and critical judgment on the preferences of the other two parts and should not simply endorse them, what sorts of considerations should the rational part rely on in forming its judgments? Plato describes these only in very general terms. He says that the rational part relies on deliberation about the better and the worse, and about what is best for the whole soul and for each of the parts.

When Plato requires the rational part to consider the good of each part of the soul, it is reasonable to infer that the preferences of the non-rational parts of the soul will not be accidentally related to their good; for it is difficult to see what could be good for the appetitive part that did not include a reasonable degree of appetitive satisfaction. Indeed, if we look at the rational part's judgments from the appetitive part's point of view, we must reach the same conclusion; for it is not clear why the appetitive part should agree with the judgment of the rational part unless it sees some reasonable appetitive satisfaction in following that course of action. The rational part does not simply endorse the longer-term preferences of the appetitive part; it must modify them in the light of its view about the good of each part and of the whole. Still, the appetitive part, looking at the rational part's decisions, can see that they promote the satisfaction of its own longer-term preferences.

Plato suggests, then, that the outlook of the rational part will be wider than that of the other two parts, insofar as it has some conception of their good and has some conception of them as forming parts of a whole. Its view is more objective, insofar as it can incorporate and explain the outlooks of the two non-rational parts. If we can see all four sides of a building, we can understand the points of view of four observers each of whom can observe only one side; although there is something misleading about each of their points of view, and although we will still be misled if we simply try to add up the four points of view, we can see that they are reliable to some extent, if we also look at the whole of which they observe parts.[1]

The rational part takes this wider point of view on the desires and interests of the non-rational parts, so that it can satisfy their interests better than it would if it simply chose to be guided by their desires. If a leg could understand what is in its interest, it would realize that it is better off connected to a whole living animal than it would be by itself, even if the demands of the whole animal tire it out more than it would prefer on its own account; the fact that the whole animal is aware of considerations that the leg itself is not aware of actually benefits the leg, even though the leg itself cannot take account of these considerations.

171. The Role of Practical Reason

Plato insists that the rational part's proper function requires it to deliberate about the good of the soul as a whole. He therefore forms a more complex conception of the character of practical reason than the conception he derives from Socrates. As we might expect, a sharper distinction between the rational and the non-rational parts also results in a more precise description of the distinctive features of the rational part. In the Socratic dialogues, practical reason has no role beyond reasoning about instrumental means.[2] Although Socrates does not explicitly deny that practical reason has any other functions, he recognizes none. Plato implies that the Socratic dialogues offer an inadequate and partial description of rational agency. If practical reason is limited to instrumental calculation, it is limited to only one of the functions of which it is capable, and the agent who is guided by only this aspect of practical reason is incompletely guided by the rational part.

This fact about the rational part is especially important for the argument of the *Republic*; for Plato's whole way of framing the question about justice and happiness requires a role for the rational part that goes beyond instrumental reason. According to the position that Glaucon and Adeimantus want Socrates to defend, justice is a non-instrumental good and a part of happiness, but many people, including Thrasymachus, do not realize this. If we are to discover this fact about justice and act on it, we must be capable of forming rational desires for non-instrumental goods that we can rationally discover; someone who is not guided by the results of this rational discovery is not fully guided by the rational part of the soul.

If Plato had raised the question he raises in Book II but had said nothing to modify the Socratic instrumental conception of rational desire, he would have failed to explain how the intended conclusion of the *Republic* could make any practical difference to our choices. In Book IV Plato clarifies the non-instrumental character of rational desire insofar as he distinguishes independent and critical rational judgments from those that simply endorse the preferences of the non-rational parts. The rational part discovers what is good for us by considering our nature as a whole, and not simply the aspects of our nature that are evident to the non-rational parts.

If the rational part performs these functions, then the just person is the one who is most completely guided by practical reason. In the just person, practical reason discovers the ends that are worth pursuing; it does not simply seek ways to satisfy the desires of one or another part, but discovers the good of the whole soul by rational reflexion on the nature of the soul. Since the just soul is guided by this rational reflexion and other souls are not, the just soul realizes a capacity for rational activity that is not realized by other souls.

If the just person is happier than any others, Plato ought to be able to show how realizing a capacity for rational activity is connected with being happy; for consideration of the nature of justice shows that the realizing of this capacity is distinctive of the just soul in contrast to souls that are less completely guided by the rational part. If Glaucon and Adeimantus were right to claim that, once we see what justice is, we ought to be able to see how it promotes happiness, our account of justice ought to have told us enough to convince us, in the light of a plausible conception of happiness, that the just person is happiest.

172. Socrates on Happiness: Some Objections

We must, therefore, consider what Plato regards as a plausible conception of happiness. At the beginning of the *Ethics*, Aristotle sees that it is important to form some conception of happiness before trying to decide whether different claims about how to acquire happiness are justified. We noticed that the Socratic dialogues do not take up Aristotle's question. In the *Republic* Plato does not take it up either, but we must try to identify the assumptions about happiness that convince him that the just person is happier than the unjust.

The *Gorgias* offers an answer to critics who deny that justice contributes to happiness. We ought to ask whether the conception of happiness that is presupposed in the *Gorgias* ought to satisfy Plato in the light of what he has said in the *Republic*. If we can answer this question, we can decide whether Plato ought to try to strengthen the main line of argument in the *Gorgias* or ought to try a different sort of argument altogether.

In the *Gorgias* Socrates' adaptive conception of happiness explains why virtue is instrumental to, and sufficient for, happiness.[3] This conception of happiness is open to objection, however, if the mere fulfillment of desire does not seem to be sufficient for happiness. We can imagine someone whose desires have such trivial or absurd objects that we do not want to have his desires, even if we could expect them all to be fulfilled; we might reasonably prefer to have desires with less trivial and absurd objects, even if we suffered more frustration. An adaptive conception counts as happy some lives that we recognize as inadequate for rational agents; and therefore it cannot give us a true account of happiness.

Callicles perhaps suggests this objection. He complains that Socratic happiness is fit for a rock or a corpse rather than a human being (*G*. 492e5–6), since rocks and corpses need nothing, have no unsatisfied desires, and so seem to be good candidates for Socratic happiness. Socrates does not do justice to this objection. He thinks it rests on the mistaken belief that happiness consists in a large quantity of pleasure and therefore requires extravagant desires. Callicles' protest, however, might also suggest the more plausible objection that mere satisfaction is consistent with a low level of rational agency.

One of Socrates' own arguments actually suggests the same objection. In challenging Callicles' hedonism, Socrates claims that the coward's life maximizes his pleasure, but should not appeal to a rational agent such as Callicles who cares about himself as someone who plans for his own future. Socrates infers that the life maximizing pleasure cannot be a happy life, because it damages rational agency. His objection is reasonable; it suggests that we are not indifferent to the objects that we take pleasure in, so that we are not concerned simply about the quantity of our pleasure. As Aristotle puts it, 'No one would choose to live with the mind of a child throughout his life, taking as much pleasure as possible in what pleases children, or to enjoy himself while doing some utterly shameful action, even if he would never suffer pain for it' (*EN* 1174a1–4; cf. *EE* 1215b22–25). This is a good objection against Callicles, but the same objection seems to work against Socrates' own adaptive conception of happiness.

Republic II gives us some reason to believe that Plato has doubts about the adaptive conception of happiness that he assumes in the *Gorgias*. If such a conception were correct, then virtue would be sufficient for happiness; but we have seen that in Book II Plato sets out only to prove the comparative thesis, not the sufficiency thesis.[4] He never suggests in the *Republic* that the just person is happy despite all the possible misfortunes that Glaucon and Adeimantus describe. Nor does he suggest that, as the adaptive conception implies, a virtuous individual is self-sufficient.[5] Probably, then, Plato sees that he cannot appeal to an adaptive conception of happiness in order to reply to Thrasymachus.

Moreover, an adaptive conception does not offer a very good defence of justice. It seems to make justice at most instrumental to happiness; the psychic order that Socrates identifies with justice is a means to a distinct result, the elimination of unfeasible desires. Since Glaucon and Adeimantus insist that justice must be defended as a non-instrumental good, Plato ought not to be satisfied with the sort of defence allowed by the adaptive conception of happiness.

This objection suggests an even more serious difficulty in the argument offered by the *Gorgias*: it does not seem to offer a defence that applies specifically to justice. For apparently I could have well-adjusted and easily satisfied desires that would involve no particular concern for the interests of others. Socrates may convince me that my happiness does not require me to profit at my neighbour's expense; but if my desires are flexible and feasible, I can secure happiness for myself even if I refuse to do any of the actions of the just and brave person. If I feel greedy or malevolent or cruel or extravagant, an adaptive account of happiness does not prohibit the satisfaction of these inclinations if I have the opportunity to satisfy them.

Republic II exposes this flaw in the *Gorgias* by insisting that justice is above all the virtue that is concerned with the interests of others, and that a defence of justice must be shown to defend a virtue that involves this concern. If Glaucon and Adeimantus are right, then Socrates' choice of Callicles as his opponent does not fully take the measure of the case against justice. Callicles opposes justice because he accepts a conception of happiness that opposes restraint of desire, and so he is refuted once his conception of happiness is refuted. We need not, however, agree with Callicles' conception of happiness in order to have doubts about the value of justice. We might argue that the real objection to justice is not the mere fact that it requires some restraint of our desires, but that it requires us to subordinate our interests to other people's interests. Surely we could have the ordered desires advocated by Socrates while still rejecting the other-regarding aspects of justice? This objection suggests that Plato needs to be more careful to show that he has an argument for justice and not merely for some prudential psychic order that is compatible with injustice. *Republic* II suggests that Plato is more aware of this issue than he is in writing the *Gorgias*.

This point becomes clearer if we compare Book I with Book II. In Book I Socrates appeals, as he appeals in the *Gorgias*, to the analogy between justice and health, suggesting that justice can be defended by appeal to efficiency (352a). If psychic justice is simply a matter of efficiency, then someone who is guided by instrumental reasoning directed to the satisfaction of his appetites seems to have a 'healthy' soul. If this is what Plato means, then he is not necessarily disagreeing with Thrasymachus about the nature of happiness; if justice is to be defended on grounds of efficiency, the just person is better off simply because he is better at getting the sorts of things that both just and unjust people take to constitute their happiness. If injustice involves unrestrained overreaching and psychic conflict, it does not seem to promote what most people count as happiness.

Book II shows why this reply to Thrasymachus is inadequate. Glaucon and Adeimantus argue that an ordinary view about happiness supports a more moderate attitude to injustice than the one Thrasymachus takes, but still fails to support justice. If happiness consists in the secure possession of honours, material wealth, and power, and in the pleasure resulting from the satisfaction of desires formed by these possessions, then the central part of Thrasymachus' position is left standing, and it is not clear how the specifically other-regarding virtue of justice promotes the agent's happiness.

If, then, Plato were still satisfied with the conception of happiness that is assumed in the *Gorgias*, it would be difficult to see why he states the problems about justice and happiness as he states them in the first two books of the *Republic*. The solution to the problems he has raised cannot rest on a purely adaptive conception of happiness.

173. Socrates on Happiness: Some Ambiguities

To see how Plato might modify Socrates' conception of happiness, we ought to notice a strand in the argument of the *Gorgias* that is separable from an adaptive conception of happiness. Socrates appeals to an analogy between psychic justice and bodily health; once we see what sort of good health is for the body, we are supposed to see that justice is the same sort of good for the soul (*G.* 504e).[6] But this comparison with health is not straightforward; different views about the goodness of health may lead to different claims about the goodness of justice, and may presuppose different views about the nature of the good.

We might suppose that the comparison with health is meant to suggest how psychic justice promotes efficiency in planning and action. If we are too unhealthy, we cannot carry out many of our plans effectively. Similarly, someone whose soul is completely chaotic will be unable to act effectively in his own interest, because he will always be liable to conflict and self-frustration. Such an argument fits an adaptive conception of happiness.

Sometimes, however, Socrates uses the comparison with health differently. He argues that it does not benefit a person to live with his body in bad condition, since he is bound to live badly (*G.* 505a2–4). This claim seems to conflict with Socrates' adaptive conception of happiness. If bodily illness is bad for us because it frustrates desires that we cannot help having, then he must admit the failure of an adaptive strategy for securing happiness, since we cannot completely proportion our desires to the resources available for satisfying them.

Alternatively, Socrates might argue that even if we cease to desire the health we cannot have, we still lack happiness because of how we are, not because of how we feel about it. If he takes the analogy this way, Socrates may identify happiness with the fulfillment of our nature and capacities, not simply with the fulfillment of desire. But then virtue does not seem to be sufficient for happiness. For a virtuous person may be in bad health; if bad health deprives him of happiness, some evil can happen to him, and his wisdom cannot make good fortune unnecessary for his happiness. An appeal to human nature and capacities relies on a normative conception of happiness, since it appeals to some view about the proper or appropriate way for a human being to live; hence it demands more than the satisfied desires required by an adaptive conception of happiness. And so the normative conception seems to conflict with some of the assumptions that allow Socrates to defend the sufficiency of virtue for happiness.

These questions about happiness cast some doubt on Socrates' use of the analogy between justice and health (*G.* 506c–507c). If we argue that the unjust person is mistaken simply because he has a non-adaptive conception of happiness, then the defence of justice is subject to the limitations inherent in the adaptive conception. If, on the other hand, we appeal to the normative conception of happiness, then it seems difficult to prove that justice is necessary (as health seems to be) for happiness, or that (unlike health) it is sufficient for happiness.

Obscurities in Socrates' conception of happiness raise further questions about the contribution of psychic order to happiness. If an adaptive view of happiness is right, then psychic order contributes to happiness by making sure that we are guided by our feasible desires and not by the demanding desires that cannot be satisfied. If, however, Socrates sometimes accepts a more normative conception of happiness, he must take a different view of psychic order; for, according to the normative conception, a disorderly soul is undesirable because it allows only a low level of rational agency and so is not suitable for a rational agent. Socrates' comparison of psychic justice with health suggests this conception of the value of psychic justice, but such a conception implies that virtue is insufficient for happiness.

174. Happiness and the Human Function

The suggestion in the *Gorgias* that happiness is connected with the fulfillment of one's nature and capacities may be taken up at the end of *Republic* I, where Socrates offers the 'function argument' (352d8–354a11). He suggests that something will not perform its function well if it lacks its proper virtue: a knife does not cut if it lacks the appropriate sharp edge, and so on. We can see in outline how this form of argument might connect something's virtue with some function, if 'function' is construed as some task that it is designed for or expected to do. We might say that a pilot's virtues are those she needs to perform a pilot's functions well: aeronautical skill, quick reactions, ability to stay awake, and so on.

But this sort of function is difficult to connect with the good or happiness of the agent. For it may not be good for the person who is a pilot to have the virtues of a pilot. (Perhaps they cause stress, anxiety, and mental breakdown; compare the virtues of a boxer.) If the virtues of a human being (as opposed to a pilot, a boxer, etc.) are those that are expected of all human beings irrespective of their particular social roles, why are these virtues good for the agents themselves? Perhaps we want people to be just and cooperative because these traits are good for other people; that does not make them good for the agents themselves.

Plato needs, and sometimes suggests, an interpretation of 'function' that does not refer to the role that something is designed for or expected to fulfill. The function of the soul, he says, is 'supervising, ruling, and deliberating' (353d5) and, in general, living (353d9). These are functions that are natural and necessary for a soul and for the human being (the sort of ensouled creature being considered here) who has a soul. These claims about natural and necessary functions are relevant to the questions about happiness that are raised by the *Gorgias*; for Socrates' argument against Callicles suggests that the good life must involve some exercise of reason, and Callicles' argument suggests that it must involve activity, not just a state of satisfaction.

In Book IV Plato appeals once again to health. In explaining the analogy, he does not appeal to efficiency; instead, he argues that both health and justice involve a natural order (444d3–6). The healthy condition is natural because the predominant forces controlling the body are the naturally suitable ones; similarly, in a just soul the naturally suitable forces predominate.[7]

This claim about natural suitability must rely on assumptions about the activities proper to a human being as a whole. These are not the same as assumptions about efficiency. Someone might be more efficient as a miner if he could get his eyes used to seeing in the dark and could get his limbs used to being bent or contorted for a long time, but nonetheless these conditions are bad for his health, because they are bad for the characteristic functions of a human body (which might still be true even if they did not happen to shorten his life). A fairly simple and plausible claim about the nature and characteristic activities of a human being supports the claim that the physical constitution of a miner, however efficient it may be for mining, is bad for his health.

Plato suggests that we have a similar conception of what is naturally suitable for a soul with the structure and constitution of the human soul; the just state of the soul is the one in which it advances its good by doing what is naturally suitable for it. He expresses this claim in his description of justice as performing one's own function.[8] Psychic justice is doing what is most fully and completely 'one's own' (443c–d), insofar as it concerns, not merely external actions, but the attitudes and relations of the parts of one's soul, which is truly oneself.

It is easy to see why claims about natural suitability arouse doubts and suspicions; for we may well wonder whether we can reach any precise views about what is naturally suitable for us without already taking a stand in the ethical controversy that we hope to solve by appeal to natural suitability. Plato believes, however, that psychic justice can be shown to be natural and appropriate for human beings. We can see how he might try to show this if we consider his conception of health as a natural order. If extreme development of one limb or organ interfered with the normal functions of the whole animal, it would be unhealthy and naturally unsuitable for the animal; to see this we would need to take the point of view of the whole animal rather than the point of view of a part.

It must be admitted that Plato does not explicitly connect his claims about function with his conception of happiness; he uses function primarily to explain virtue rather than happiness. If our suggestion is right, however, he implicitly connects function with happiness as well. When Aristotle wants to present an account of happiness 'in outline' (*EN* 1098a20–22) before discussing the virtues, he argues that happiness should be identified with the fulfillment of the human function, and therefore with the life of the rational part of the soul, and more specifically with an activity of the rational soul in accordance with complete virtue in a complete life (1096a16–18). We have suggested that Plato implicitly accepts the same sort of connexion between happiness, function, and rational activity. To see whether this suggestion is right, we ought to examine Plato's account of psychic justice to see whether it supports the claim that justice partly constitutes happiness, if happiness is conceived in the way we have suggested.

175. Justice and the Human Function

To say that the good of a human being must involve rational activity is still quite vague, but it is the closest Plato comes to describing the sort of function that might suit his argument. If he shows that an essential component of a life including the appropriate sort of rational activity is the state of character that turns out to be identical to justice, then he answers Thrasymachus.

The comparison between justice and health suggests that Plato relies on this argument in order to connect justice with happiness. Justice is analogous with health insofar as it maintains the order and structure of desires that is suitable for our nature as a whole. For the rational part rules in the interest of the whole soul, not simply of a part. If we identify ourselves with something more than a restricted range of desires, we can agree that rule by the rational part realizes our capacities as whole selves, rather than simply satisfying desires that constitute only a part of ourselves.

If the rational part is guided by this concern for the good of the whole soul, it differs from the other parts in appreciating its own distinctive conception to the good of the whole. For part of the human function is rational activity; and the rational activity of the rational part is not simply a means to secure the good of the whole but also a part of the good it secures. The rational part is not an external adviser that deliberates wholly about the interests of the other two parts without considering its own. Its own characteristics are important characteristics of the agent whose interests it is considering.

From this point of view also, it is better to be controlled by the rational part, for the human good essentially requires rational activity, and the virtues are the states of soul that embody the rational activity that is required for the human good. The practical reasoning of the rational part is an aspect of our nature that is incompletely realized if either of the other two parts of the soul is dominant. If it is part of our good to realize our capacities as a whole as rational agents, then psychic justice is part of our good because it is the realization of rational agency.

Plato implies that I do not achieve my good equally fully if rational planning is taken out of my hands. Suppose that someone else offers to do all the planning that I normally do for myself, and I am confident that the answers he finds will be at least as satisfactory as those I find for myself. Plato assumes that if I accept this offer, I am worse off in one respect, whatever the consequences; he attaches intrinsic value to the very fact that I determine what is good for my whole soul by the exercise of my practical reason. He must say this if he believes that justice is good in itself and that the just soul is the one that is actually directed by practical reason.

These claims take more defence than Plato gives them in Book IV; we ought to see whether he defends them further in the rest of the *Republic*. So far, however, we have at least seen that he takes happiness to involve the exercise of essential human capacities, and in particular of rational activity.[9] He accepts the view of the human good that is defended by Aristotle, supporting claims about the human good from claims about human nature and the human essence. These claims about happiness fit the assumptions that we have found in Book II. Plato needs some conception of happiness that would make it plausible to claim that justice is a component of happiness, and in Book IV we can see in outline what conception he has in mind.

176. The Dominance of Justice

Plato believes that the analogy between justice and health helps to explain not only why justice is an intrinsic good but also why it dominates other goods (444e7–445a4). If justice were simply a minor non-instrumental good, it might not always be preferable to injustice; some of the pleasures that were mentioned as intrinsic goods (357b) are appropriately sacrificed for more important goods. Plato believes, however, that once we see the place of justice in happiness, we should also see that nothing could compensate for its loss. Glaucon thinks it is obvious that life is not worth living with one's physical health shattered, and he infers that it should be equally clear that life is not worth living with an unjust soul (445a–b). He assumes that the argument so far has supported a suitably strong version of the analogy between justice and health.

A rather strong version of the analogy must be true if Glaucon's inference is legitimate. For the collapse of health that makes life not worth living must be quite severe. Glaucon presumably does not mean that we could never reasonably sacrifice any degree of health for any other good, or that every decline in health should convince us that life is not worth living. If we could choose between, in one case, having complete justice in the soul at the expense of other goods and, in the other case, sacrificing a little justice for the sake of other goods, the analogy with health does not show us why we ought not to prefer the second option.

The absence of health makes life no longer worth living only if I cannot perform any significant human activities to a worthwhile degree (if, for instance, I have to be kept alive in a state of very elementary consciousness by extreme measures, or I suffer such continuous and severe pain that I cannot think about anything else or take an interest in anything). In such a case I am justified in choosing health (more exactly, a sufficient degree of health to avoid this intolerable condition) over any combination of other bodily or external goods; for if my health is wrecked, no other goods are of any use to me, since they cannot contribute to any worthwhile activities for me in my present condition. Health, therefore, is dominant over other bodily or external goods.

Perhaps Plato could argue that justice dominates other goods in this way, if he could show that psychic injustice involves the complete collapse of practical reason, so that the agent is incapable of guiding his actions by deliberation at all. This is not Plato's view of injustice, however; someone who deliberates about ways to satisfy his appetites may have a well-organized life, in no danger of psychic chaos or ineffectiveness, but Plato regards such a person as unjust. If we take the analogy with health to imply that psychic justice is necessary for minimal agency, then Plato cannot defend the analogy.

He need not take the analogy this way, however. When Glaucon asks, rhetorically, whether it is worth living with an unjust soul, he asks whether it is worth living 'when the nature of that very thing by which we live is disturbed and corrupted' (445a9–b1). He has been convinced that injustice implies the disturbance of the naturally suitable order of elements in the soul. If this order is disturbed, we no longer fully realize our rational agency. If we value other goods above psychic justice, we are overlooking the connexion between essential human activities and the human good.

This conception of psychic justice will show that it dominates other goods if Plato can show that without psychic justice other goods cannot have the value for us that we expect them to have. The just person has the right conception of his own good, and so he is able to pursue the other goods to the extent that they benefit him as a rational agent; the unjust person may have other goods, but without justice he cannot use them for his benefit, because his use of them is not fully guided by practical reason.

Plato's argument for this conclusion will be more convincing if his description of the difference between psychic justice and psychic injustice makes it clear what the unjust person is missing. In Book IV Plato maintains that psychic justice is the proper order of the parts of the soul in which each part does its own work, but he does not say much about what the just soul will be like; we have seen that his conception of psychic justice is more demanding than it may at first appear, but it is yet not clear enough to show what sorts of attitudes and aims we can expect of the just person.

It is reasonable, then, that Socrates both agrees with Glaucon's answer about the dominance of justice, and yet does not think it is time to drop the question. While he believes that his account of the tripartite soul and the virtues suggests an answer, he believes also that a convincing answer requires a clearer conception of what psychic justice and injustice actually involve. In Books VIII and IX, where the discussion resumes after the digression in V–VII, he defends the answer in Book IV by describing the nature and effects of psychic injustice more fully.

177. An Objection to Plato's Account of Justice

We have now seen how Plato argues, or might argue, that justice, as he conceives it, is a component of happiness, as he conceives it. Moreover, his conception of happiness as the realization of our capacity for rational agency is quite defensible. Many doubts, however, have been raised about his conception of justice; indeed, this is often taken to be a crucial flaw in the argument of *Republic* IV.

The main objection arises from the apparent difference between (1) the justice that is introduced as one of the virtues of the soul in Book IV—this is *psychic justice* (p-justice); and (2) justice as commonly understood, the virtue that is discussed in the argument with Thrasymachus—let us call this *common justice* (c-justice). C-justice is the virtue that Thrasymachus described as 'another's good'; he described it in these terms because it requires me to avoid grabbing more from other people than is due to me, and so prevents me from pursuing my own good at their expense. Glaucon and Adeimantus also assumed that justice involves some sort of respect for others; that is why it needs some special justification for an agent concerned primarily with her own interest. P-justice, by contrast, is the psychic virtue corresponding to justice in the city. It is defined by reference to the relation of the parts of the soul to each other, not by reference to the agent's relation to other people. It seems to be a purely self-regarding virtue, concerned with the good of the agent's soul.[10]

Why, then, should we suppose that this virtue of p-justice is the c-justice that concerned Thrasymachus? While p-justice might be worth having, a defence of it does not seem to show why we should respect the interests of others in the ways required by c-justice. If someone has p-justice, why should she not promote her own good at the expense of others and therefore display c-injustice? If that is possible, then Plato has not proved that the virtue involving respect for the interests of others is really part of an agent's happiness; but this is what he needs to prove if he is to answer Thrasymachus.

178. Common Views about Justice

Before we examine Plato's answer to the question about c-justice and p-justice, we ought to frame the question more carefully, with the help of some further terminology. In speaking of c-justice, we might mean (1) justice, according to the *common description* of it; or (2) the virtue of justice that is recognized by *common intuition*. The common description of justice is what people say about justice if they are asked about it and before they reflect under elenctic examination. The common intuition is what they will acknowledge they believe when the elenchos shows them the difficulties that arise in their first answers. Clearly, it is not easy to say which claims about justice reflect mere descriptions and which actually express intuitions; people's intuitions may not even be among the claims they initially make about justice. One task of the elenchos is to sort out people's intuitions from their descriptions of a virtue and to make them see that their intuitions are beliefs they have held all along without seeing their implications. This is the task that Epictetus calls the articulation of our preconceptions.[11]

We must distinguish common descriptions from common intuitions, since they may give us crucially different views of c-justice. The first of the two suggested conceptions of c-justice assumes that the common description of justice accurately describes the condition that common sense has in mind; if, then, the common description describes justice as simply a tendency to abstain from unjust actions, that tendency is the c-justice that Plato ought to be discussing.[12] The second account, however, leaves open the possibility that the common description of justice to some extent misrepresents the condition that common intuition has in mind; we may discover that common intuition regards justice as admirable in ways that are not explained by the common description of it as a habit of abstaining from unjust action. If we accept the second account of c-justice, then we may still argue that Plato is arguing about c-justice even though he does not entirely accept the common description of justice.

We can see what Plato might be trying to do if we consider his treatment of common beliefs in his discussion of the other three virtues. In each case Plato believes that common sense is right in recognizing a virtue with this sphere of concerns, but that common sense is misled by a false description of the motives and actions to be expected from the virtuous person. Most people believe, for instance, that bravery requires steadfastness in the face of danger; they are right about this. Many also believe that it is separable from temperance and justice; they are wrong about this. When Plato rejects common descriptions, he argues from common intuitions; he suggests how difficult it would be to regard bravery or temperance as a genuine virtue if we took it to be entirely separable from the other virtues. Can he argue similarly on behalf of his claims about justice?

A superficial conception of c-justice seems to underlie much of Thrasymachus' argument. In explaining how just people come off worse than unjust people, he remarks that they must give up certain benefits because they do not profit at other people's expense. Glaucon and Adeimantus also describe the good results of unjust actions and the losses that a just person may suffer as a result of doing just actions; they reassert Thrasymachus's claim that justice is another person's good (367c2–5), and in saying this they are referring specifically to the effects of just actions. All these objections would raise serious difficulties for c-justice if c-justice consisted in nothing more than a tendency to avoid unjust action, and if an agent's reasons and motives made no difference to whether she is c-just.

If, on the contrary, 'c-justice' refers to the genuine virtue of justice recognized by common intuition, it may include much more than unreflective common sense includes in the common description of justice; in particular, it may include a characteristic motive of the just person. We ought to remember that Glaucon and Adeimantus take Thrasymachus's question to refer to the virtue of justice, not simply to just behaviour; for they insist that people who do just actions with the wrong motive have a mere facade of virtue.[13]

Glaucon and Adeimantus, then, are not interested in those allegedly just people who are willing to abandon just action when unjust action offers more external goods; they are interested in people whose commitment to justice extends to cases where only someone who cared about justice for its own sake would still prefer just action over unjust. In their view, this outlook is properly identified with c-justice; hence they ask to be shown what justice is like in the soul, expecting that the answer to this question will show whether the just person is really better off than the unjust.

If c-justice is taken to be the genuine virtue of justice, Plato can argue that this is the virtue recognized by common intuition; although it is not the only possible source of some c-just actions, it is the genuine virtue underlying recognized just actions. Common intuition recognizes Plato's distinction between a genuinely just person and someone who simply does just actions for some reason that the just person would reject. In focussing attention on virtues and motives, Plato is not abandoning common intuitions about justice; but he rejects the common view about which aspects of justice are most important for deciding whether justice is beneficial.

Plato wants to prove that people who have the virtue of justice are thereby happier than anyone else. Not everyone who performs c-just actions (actions that a c-just person would do; cf. Ar. *EN* 1105b5–9) is thereby c-just, and Plato is not committed to showing that every c-just person will perform all the actions that are commonly recognized as just. His aim makes his task harder in one way but easier in another way: His task is harder than the task of showing that it sometimes pays to do just actions; as Glaucon and Adeimantus argue, a limited defence of just actions is relatively easily found, but it is more difficult to show that we benefit from being just and from being willing to act justly in conditions where we suffer for it. By contrast, Plato's defence of p-justice focusses on the benefits of a specific state of the soul; this argument has some prospect of being relevant to c-justice if c-justice is properly identified with a state of the soul rather than a type of behaviour.

If Plato has a good argument for focussing on states of the soul rather than simply on behaviour, he still needs to show that he has focussed on a state of the soul that can plausibly be identified with c-justice. We might object that he has focussed on the wrong state of soul, since what he calls p-justice is really an aspect of virtue as a whole. Plato seems to have described a necessary component of every genuine virtue, rather than a virtue with its own range of actions; and so, we might argue, p-justice cannot be the same as c-justice.

He can answer this objection, however, by pointing out that it is difficult to isolate a distinctive and separate range of actions for bravery and temperance; why should it be any easier for justice? Plato can actually appeal to common sense for some support; for some remarks on justice tend to identify it with virtue as a whole, rather than with one virtue in contrast to the others. Aristotle actually distinguishes two types of justice. One of these, 'particular justice', is concerned with violations of equality and fairness in the allocation of external goods (*EN* 1129a32–b11, 1100a32–b5); but another type of justice is properly identified with complete virtue as a whole. This second type, 'general justice', is the type that is said to be 'another's good' (*EN* 1130a3–5). Here Aristotle picks up Thrasymachus' comment on justice; he must suppose that this is the type of justice that Thrasymachus and Socrates discuss.[14]

Still, Aristotle recognizes that general justice completes virtue by directing it to the good of others (*EN* 1129b25–1130a1). If Plato is recognizably talking about justice, he must also show that p-justice has this other-regarding aspect. For the feature of justice that arouses Thrasymachus' doubts is its tendency to benefit others, to respect their interests, and to refrain from satisfying one's own desires at other people's expense. If Plato believed that no genuine virtue includes any tendency to benefit other people, he would have to show that we are mistaken in believing that in training people to be concerned for the interests of others we are training them to be virtuous. But the development of his argument in the *Republic* gives us no reason to believe that this belief is mistaken; on the contrary, the account of justice in the ideal city claims that each part of the city does its proper work for the benefit of the whole city, and Plato clearly supposes that the rulers of the ideal city can be relied on to seek the good of the city. He makes this still clearer in Book V, when he insists that the rulers will be deeply concerned for the interests of other citizens (462a2–463c7). He gives us every reason to suppose, then, that common sense is right in supposing that some virtue is other-regarding; justice seems to be the most plausible candidate.

It is fair, then, by Plato's own standards as well as the standards of common sense, to expect him to vindicate an other-regarding virtue of justice. If p-justice does not imply regard for the interests of others, we have good reason to infer that it is not justice and that therefore a proof that the p-just person is happier than anyone else does not prove that the just person is happier than anyone else. If Plato's argument about p-justice is to prove that justice promotes happiness, he must prove that p-justice is other-regarding.

179. An Answer to Thrasymachus?

Plato recognizes that it is fair to raise the question about the connexion between p-justice and c-justice. For he offers some 'commonplace' indications of the c-justice of the p-just person, suggesting that such a person will avoid flagrantly c-unjust actions (442d–443b).[15] He suggests that the p-just person refrains from these c-unjust actions because of p-justice. Unfortunately, he does not tell us in any detail why we can expect the self-regarding concern of the p-just person to result in c-just actions.[16]

Is he entitled to his confidence about the p-just person's behaviour? He might reasonably claim (1) that many c-unjust actions are the product of spirited impulses or of appetites and (2) that the p-just person has moderate and controlled spirited and appetitive parts, so that (3) the p-just person will see no reason to commit these c-unjust actions. Excessive appetites may result in greed; the wrong development of the spirited part may result in vindictiveness and violent outbursts. Plato argues, quite reasonably, that the p-just person lacks some motives that make c-unjust actions attractive to many people and therefore avoids some c-unjust actions.

But do c-unjust actions appeal only to someone with a disordered soul? It might seem obvious that even someone with a well-ordered soul can see good reason to act c-unjustly. Suppose that someone has a prudent, rational, long-term plan for maximizing his wealth or improving his social status. Both of these plans seem to suggest that c-unjust actions might be quite useful for him. Does this refute Plato's claim about justice?[17]

This objection fails to reckon with Plato's emphasis on the importance of finding out what justice is, and with the answer he gives to this question in his description of the proper function of the rational part. He does not concede that someone who is instrumentally rational in making and executing plans for acquiring wealth and so on is thereby p-just; for he does not concede that if the rational part carries out purely instrumental tasks, it thereby performs its proper function.

This reply, however, invites a further question. Even if we admit that p-just people will not be tempted to act c-unjustly for the specific reasons that would tempt people who are dominated by a non-rational part of the soul, how can we be sure that c-unjust action will never tempt them? Plato has not answered this question in Book IV because he has not said much about what the rational part does or about how the different parts do their own work. Since he has not said much about the outlook of a p-just soul, it is not clear why one sort of action rather than another should result from having a p-just soul. That is one of the questions that need to be answered by a fuller account of the virtues of the soul.

Even if Plato answers this question convincingly, he must face further questions. Even if a p-just person lacks any motive for doing c-unjust actions, and so avoids them, does this show that she is really a c-just person? Does c-justice simply require negative conditions—avoiding c-unjust actions against other people, whatever our motive may be—or does it require something more positive? I might refrain from robbery or cheating simply because I do not want the results of these c-unjust actions, even though I do not care at all about the interests of other people. If a c-just person must avoid c-unjust actions out of a specific motive—say, out of concern or respect for the interests of others—then Plato has not shown that the p-just person is c-just simply by showing that she lacks any motive for c-unjust actions.

In understanding this issue, it is useful to return to the difference between Thrasymachus' question about c-justice and Glaucon's and Adeimantus' question. Thrasymachus' objection to c-justice seemed to be its tendency to avoid c-unjust actions; to meet this objection it is enough to show that I am better off with a condition of soul that includes this tendency to avoid c-unjust actions. Glaucon and Adeimantus, however, focus more clearly on just agents, not simply on just actions. Since Plato himself agrees that the just person must act on the right sort of motive, an argument to show that p-justice is justice must show that p-just people act on the motives characteristic of just people.

If an adequate answer to the question about justice must meet this condition, we now have a clearer idea of how Plato ought to fill some of the gaps in the argument in *Republic* IV. He needs to explain more clearly what control by the rational part implies, and what sorts of attitudes and choices we can reasonably expect from the person who has genuine psychic harmony. An answer to this question should also help us to answer the question about justice. For once we see what the p-just person really prefers and chooses, we should be able to see whether the p-just person also has the just person's characteristic concern for the good of others. The rest of the *Republic* does not completely answer these questions, but it shows how Plato might reasonably try to answer them.

16

Republic V–VII

180. Socratic Definition in the *Republic*

In Books V through VII Plato interrupts the argument about justice to emphasize and defend some apparently paradoxical features of the ideal city that has been described. He spends the most time on the defence of his claim that the virtue of wisdom ascribed to the rulers of the ideal city must include philosophical knowledge and that therefore the rulers must be philosophers. The argument in Book V seeks to show that knowledge requires the knowledge of the one nonsensible Form of F, in contrast to the many sensible Fs. In Books VI and VII he says more about what this knowledge is like and how it is acquired.

This contrast between the one Form and the many sensibles is relevant to the Socratic search for definitions and hence relevant to the main argument of the *Republic*. In the Socratic dialogues, Socrates looks for definitions of the virtues but does not claim to have found them; in fact, the dialogues normally end with a confession that he is still puzzled. Socrates regularly insists that he does not know the answers to his questions about the nature of the virtues. *Republic* IV, by contrast, presents accounts of the virtues, and they are not accompanied by any of the usual Socratic disavowals or expressions of puzzlement.

To explain this difference, we need to resolve some questions about Socratic definition. At the beginning of Book I the Simonidean view of justice is not refuted, but Socrates and Polemarchus cannot explain it in observational terms that are easily applied to particular situations. If what is 'due' to people is simply what one has taken from them, we can replace 'due' with a term that is easier to apply to particular situations, since it takes less moral judgment to recognize that we have taken something from someone than it takes to recognize what is due to someone. But this attempted replacement of 'due' is unsatisfactory, and Socrates and Polemarchus find no satisfactory replacement.

Thrasymachus deplores this failure; he demands a 'perspicuous and accurate' account that would eliminate terms such as 'due', 'appropriate', or 'beneficial' in favour of terms that allow easy application to particular situations. Thrasymachus' demand corresponds quite closely to criteria that Socrates seems to accept implicitly in the early dialogues.[1] If Socrates does indeed accept them, it is easy to see why the early dialogues do not find definitions of the virtues that satisfy him; for the demand for elimination of references to moral properties makes it difficult to find acceptable accounts of the virtues. In *Republic* I, however, Socrates does not explicitly accept Thrasymachus' demand for a perspicuous and accurate account; moreover, Glaucon and Adeimantus' demands in Book II would be very difficult to satisfy if Thrasymachus' demand were also accepted.

The middle dialogues give reasons for rejecting Thrasymachus' demand, since they argue that sensible properties provide inadequate answers to the Socratic demand for a definition.[2] These dialogues suggest that something is wrong with the implicit claim of the Socratic dialogues (agreeing with Thrasymachus) that knowledge of the single form of justice, for instance, requires a single account that mentions only sensible properties.

These questions about definition should affect our view of the accounts of the virtues presented in Book IV. For these accounts do not satisfy Thrasymachus' demands, and so they do not seem to satisfy the demands of the Socratic dialogues either. Bravery is described as preservation of right belief under the control of the wisdom in the rational part; temperance is concord between the parts under the control of the wisdom in the rational part. Each of these accounts mentions the rational part and its wisdom, which is its knowledge of the good. Similarly, justice consists in each part doing its own work under the control of the wisdom in the rational part. These accounts would eliminate moral terms only if we could specify knowledge of the good in non-moral terms; to do this, we would need an account of the good in non-moral terms. Plato says nothing to suggest that he can provide such an account, nor does he suggest that he needs such an account in order to give an adequate account of the virtues.

Plato does not claim, then, that he can do exactly what Socrates was trying to do in the early dialogues. For Socrates was trying to meet criteria for definition that Plato takes to be misconceived, or at least Socrates did not realize that he ought not to try to meet these criteria. According to Plato, Socrates found it difficult to answer his questions because he had the wrong criteria for an adequate answer. *Republic* IV implicitly draws the conclusion we would expect Plato to draw from his arguments in the middle dialogues about the non-sensible character of Forms.

Perhaps, however, Plato ought not to conclude so readily that the Socratic dialogues went wrong in focussing on sensible properties, and perhaps we ought not to be so easily satisfied with the accounts that he offers in *Republic* IV. We might say that Plato's arguments show that since justice, for instance, is not a single sensible property, it cannot be a single property at all. In that case Plato is wrong to follow Socrates in looking for the single F by which all F things are F (*M.* 72c6–d1).

Plato believes that this would be the wrong conclusion to draw from his arguments about sensible properties; in his view, Socrates' assumption that knowledge of F consists in knowledge of a single form of F is correct, and so we ought to deny that the F can be identified with any sensible property. In the middle dialogues, however, he does not defend this view of the Socratic project against the more radical view that would reject the single form altogether. It is reasonable, then, that he returns to these questions in *Republic* V.

181. The Philosophers and the Sight-Lovers

In Book V Socrates describes the philosophers as lovers of the truth, in contrast to the 'lovers of sights' who are interested only in sensible things and properties (475d1–e4). The just and the unjust, for instance, are two, and each is one, but each is combined with different bodies and actions. To the extent that the same sensible things are both just and unjust, justice and injustice are combined in these sensible things (475e6–476a8).[3] These facts about the F in contrast to the many Fs explain the difference between the philosophers and the sight-lovers; for, according to Plato, the sight-lovers cannot grasp these facts about Forms.

The error of the sight-lovers is described in four ways:

1. The relations of forms to sensibles causes each of the forms to appear many (476a7). The sight-lovers accept beautiful shapes, colours, and so on, but 'their thought is unable to see and accept the nature of the beautiful itself' (476b6–8), whereas the philosophers are able to see the beautiful itself 'in its own right' (*kath'hauto*, 476b10–11).
2. The sight-lover 'recognizes beautiful things, but neither recognizes beauty itself nor is able to follow if someone leads him towards the knowledge of it' (476c2–4).
3. The philosopher 'thinks there is some beautiful itself, and is able to discern it and the things participating in it, and neither thinks that participants are it nor that it is the participants' (476c9–d3). The philosopher sees the difference between two sorts of things that resemble each other, one of which is a copy and the other the original (the many Fs and the F itself). Since the sight-lover does not see this difference, he is dreaming.[4]
4. The sight-lover 'thinks there is no beautiful itself and no one character (*idea*) of the same beauty that is always in the same condition, but takes the beautifuls to be many'. Hence he 'in no way puts up with it if anyone says the beautiful is one, and the just, and the others in the same way' (478e7–479a5).

The second of these passages, taken by itself, might suggest that the contrast is this: (1) The sight-lovers deny that there is anything properly called 'the beautiful' in contrast to beautiful sights, sounds, and so on. The first passage, however, suggests a different contrast: (2) Both the philosophers and the sight-lovers recognize something properly called 'the beautiful', but the sight-lovers think there are many of these things, and the philosophers think there is just one. This second contrast is also suggested by the third passage.

The fourth passage makes it clear that Plato intends the second contrast rather than the first. He takes the claim that the beautifuls are many to be opposed to the claim that the beautiful is one; the latter claim is clearly his own view that there is one form of beauty. If the former claim is simply that there are many things (horses, temples, institutions, and so on) properly called 'beautiful' (or 'fine', *kalon*), Plato does not disagree; indeed, he takes the existence of 'many beautifuls' (in this sense) to be obvious. Since he plainly disagrees with the sight-lover's belief that there are many beautifuls, Plato must take the sight-lover to believe that there are many things properly called 'the beautiful', not simply that there are many things properly said to be beautiful.

When the sight-lover affirms that the beautifuls are many, he means that there are many different properties that give equally good answers to the 'What is it?' question, and there is no one property that gives an adequate answer for all cases.[5] The point of saying 'the beautifuls are many', rather than just 'there are many beautifuls' might be clarified by interpreting it as 'the beauties are many'. The sight-lover believes that the right answer to the Socratic question refers to the many different properties that make different things beautiful.[6]

182. The Importance of the Sight-Lovers

The sight-lovers' position is worth discussing because it rejects Socrates' standard view, in the early and middle dialogues, about an adequate account of a virtue. The sight-lovers suppose that we have a satisfactory answer to the Socratic question if we say that, for instance, justice in these actions is giving back what you have borrowed, in those actions not giving back what you have borrowed (cf. 331c), or that beauty in this case is bright colour, in that case symmetrical shape, and so on.

On this point the sight-lovers agree with Meno, whose first answer to Socrates' request for an account of virtue is a list of different types of virtue in different sorts of people. They are more persistent than Meno, however, since they firmly reject a Socratic presupposition. Once Socrates explains to Meno the sort of thing he is looking for, Meno agrees (although hesitantly, *M.* 73a1–5) to look for a single form of virtue. The sight-lovers insist that failure to look for a single form may reflect not a misunderstanding of Socrates' method, but a reasonable doubt about the existence of any single form. Plato sees that he has to answer this doubt.

In this passage, but not in the *Meno*, Plato suggests that if we are to turn away from the many Fs to the F itself, we must turn from the senses to reason and reject any accounts mentioning only sensible properties. This difference from the *Meno* is important; for Socrates never suggests (in the *Meno* or in earlier dialogues) that it is wrong to look for sensible properties like those that Meno mentions in his account appealing to the many virtues. On the contrary, Socrates seems to insist that an acceptable definition must satisfy the 'dialectical condition', requiring it to mention only properties that the questioner agrees he knows.[7] This condition implies that no definition can mention any property that is not yet known; although this condition does not actually say that only observable properties can be mentioned, they seem to be the only plausible candidates for being already known.

In *Republic* V Plato suggests that we cannot consistently maintain two

Socratic demands: (1) the demand for the one rather than the many and (2) the dialectical condition requiring previous knowledge of properties mentioned in a definition. Plato suggests that if we insist on the second condition, we will restrict ourselves to sensible properties, and none of these will ever give us an account of the one form. If this is right, then Socrates' failure to find satisfactory definitions is readily explained; it is the result of his combining two incompatible demands. If the sight-lovers were right to suppose that Socrates' question can be answered only by mentioning sensible properties, they would also be right to suppose that each of the relevant predicates ('just', 'beautiful', and so on) corresponds to many properties.

Some remarks in the *Phaedrus* suggest that the sight-lovers have not made much progress in recollection. In this dialogue Plato treats the Theory of Recollection as an account of how we find the 'one' by beginning from the 'many': 'For a human being must understand what is spoken of in accordance with a form, by going[8] from many perceptions to a one that is gathered together by reasoning; and this is recollection of the things that our soul once saw' (*Phdr.* 249b6–c2). This ability to go from the many to the one is not explicitly connected with recollection in either the *Meno* or the *Phaedo*. The *Phaedrus* adds a significant point to Plato's previous remarks in connecting recollection explicitly with the Socratic search for the one F explaining the many Fs. We take the first step in this recollection when we see why the sight-lovers are wrong, and why we have to look for the single property F that is not reducible to the many properties that embody it in different situations.

183. Knowledge and Belief

In order to show that the sight-lovers are wrong, Plato begins by distinguishing knowledge from belief. Once he has done this, he argues that if we focus on the many sensible Fs, we cannot meet the appropriate conditions for knowledge of the F. The main steps in the argument are these:

1. Knowledge is set over what is true, ignorance over what is not true, belief over what is and is not true.
2. The many Fs (beautifuls, justs, and so on) are both F and not F.
3. The views of the sight-lovers about the beautiful, just, and so on are between being true and not being true: neither wholly true nor wholly false.
4. Hence their views are not knowledge, but belief.

While the argument raises many difficulties of interpretation, we ought to focus on the issues that bear most directly on the questions about knowledge and Socratic definition.

First, we may be surprised that Plato omits one characteristic of knowledge that he emphasizes in the *Meno* and *Gorgias*; he does not say that knowledge differs from belief in its ability to give an account.[9] The *Republic* does not give up this claim about knowledge; Book VII maintains that ability to give an account is characteristic of dialecticians (531e4–5). Why could Plato not have said in Book V that the philosophers who have knowledge differ from non-philosophers with mere belief because they can give an account of their beliefs? The search for accounts and justifications is an important part of the search for knowledge, and it may well seem strange that Plato is silent about it in Book V.

We can see the point of Plato's silence if we understand the place of this argument in the dialogue. If Book V is meant to take up questions about Socratic definition that have been raised by the dialogue so far, Plato assumes that we already agree that knowledge requires an account. The sight-lovers do not deny that knowledge of beauty requires an account of it; on the contrary, they believe they are giving the correct account when they mention the many sensible properties that, in their view, constitute beauty. If Plato is to refute them, he has to show that not every account gives us knowledge. He assumes that knowledge requires an account, in order to distinguish acceptable from unacceptable accounts. This task occupies him explicitly in the *Theaetetus*; in *Republic* V he implicitly recognizes its importance.[10]

Since Plato cannot argue that the sight-lovers provide no account, he focusses instead on the other difference between knowledge and belief, the necessary connexion between knowledge and truth. He expresses this connexion by saying that knowledge is 'set over what is'. By this he means that knowledge of a proposition p implies that p is true, whereas belief that p does not imply the truth of p; whereas it is possible for what is believed to be true or false, it is necessary for what is known to be true.[11]

The point of this description of knowledge and belief is easier to see if we notice that Plato introduces it at the start of an argument that is meant to persuade the sight-lovers of their mistake (476e7–477a5). Plato has already taken it to be obvious—to us, but not to the sight-lovers—that since the sight-lovers believe that the many Fs are all there is to the F itself, they must have belief rather than knowledge about the F. The many Fs resemble the F itself, but the sight-lovers make the mistake of supposing that there is no F itself apart from them; that is why the sight-lovers are similar to dreamers who do not recognize that real trees are different from the apparent trees they are aware of in their dreams (476c2–7). Plato argues that since some of their beliefs about the F are false, they cannot have knowledge of the F. If, then, he wants to persuade them of the soundness of his argument, it is reasonable for him to begin with the uncontroversial assumption that knowledge implies truth.

This explanation of 'is', 'is and is not', and so on, should guide us when 'is and is not' is applied to the contents of belief. The claim that the contents of belief 'are and are not' is readily intelligible if it means that they are and are not true, so that beliefs include both true and false beliefs. The claim that belief is true and false whereas knowledge is always true is equivalent to Plato's claim that knowledge is infallible and belief is fallible (477e6–7). We must suppose that 'is and is not' is applied to the whole set of propositions that are believed; we could also say that what is believed is sometimes (or in some cases) true and sometimes false, whereas what is known is always true. To say that ignorance is about 'what is not' is not to say that all false belief counts as ignorance rather than belief; it is to say that whereas belief includes both true and false beliefs, ignorance does not include true beliefs.

Once we have distinguished knowing and believing a proposition, we can also say what it takes to have knowledge and belief about some object—about beauty or justice, for instance. If some of what we say about the nature of beauty is true and some is false, then we can have only belief about beauty; if what we say is completely false, then we are ignorant about beauty. If we know about beauty, then our account of the nature of beauty must be true, with no elements of falsity. We are now in a position to see whether the sight-lovers have knowledge, belief, or ignorance about the forms.

184. Plato's Objection to the Sight-Lovers

Plato now argues that the sight-lovers cannot give the right account of the beautiful if they confine themselves to the many beautifuls. He points out, as he does in the *Phaedo* and the *Symposium*, that the many beautifuls suffer compresence of opposites, since each of them will also appear ugly (479a5–b10). Compresence of opposites disqualifies a property as an explanation, for reasons that Plato gives in the *Phaedo*: if bright colour, say, is both beautiful and ugly, it explains why something is beautiful no better than it explains why something is ugly, and so it cannot be the right explanation of why something is beautiful.[12]

The next steps in Plato's argument raise serious questions. (1) After mentioning that the many sensible Fs cannot be thought of firmly either as F or as not F (479b11–c5), he says they should be placed between 'being and not being' (479c6–d1); here it is reasonable to take him to mean 'between being F and not being F'. (2) Then he infers: 'We have found, then, that the many conventional views (*nomima*) of the many about the beautiful and the other things oscillate somewhere between what is not and what fully is' (479d3–5).[13] (3) He remarks that it had been previously agreed that anything of this sort belongs to belief rather than knowledge (479d7–10).

If our previous account of the difference between knowledge and belief was right, then the third step interprets the second step as having said that the views of the many about the beautiful and so on 'oscillate' because they are both true and false; hence 'what is not' and 'what fully is' in the second remark must be taken in the veridical sense. The first remark, however, uses 'to be' in the predicative sense (as in 'is beautiful', and so on). The sense of 'to be' shifts between (1) and (2). Does this introduce a fatal equivocation into the argument?

We must consider what Plato is entitled to say on the basis of the previous argument. In believing that beauty is bright colour, symmetrical shape, and so on, the sight-lovers are right to some degree. This bright-coloured temple, for example, is indeed beautiful, and its bright colour contributes to its beauty. The sight-lovers are right, then, insofar as the many beautifuls all contribute to making things beautiful in the right conditions; but they are wrong in believing that these many beautifuls are what beauty is.

If Plato is trying to say this about the sight-lovers in the last part of his argument, then we should not take (2)—the remark that the views of the many are between being completely true and being completely false—to ascribe partial truth to each belief of the sight-lovers. Plato invites us to look at the body of their views about, say, the beautiful, and to ask whether these views constitute belief or knowledge about the beautiful. When we find that their views about the beautiful include both true and false views, we are entitled to infer that, as a whole, their views constitute a body of belief rather than a body of knowledge about the beautiful. Their views are not so far off the mark that they count as complete ignorance about the beautiful, but they cannot count as a body of knowledge either. If this is right, then the earlier description of the content of belief as both true and false can be applied without any equivocation to the views of the sight-lovers about the beautiful, the just, and so on.

We might well suppose that if Plato had been completely clear about his different uses of 'is and is not', he would not have said exactly what he says. We might fairly conclude that he is not completely clear about what he is saying and about the conclusion he needs and intends to draw. Nonetheless, we need not find any damaging equivocation in his argument; his conclusion can be fairly drawn from his account of the sight-lovers and their attitude towards the properties that they try to define.

185. Are the Sight-Lovers Refuted?

The argument might still appear to be unfair to the sight-lovers. Admittedly, they must agree that since bright colour makes some things beautiful and others ugly, 'bright colour' cannot be the right account of beauty in all cases. This agreement would embarrass the sight-lovers if they claimed that bright colour is the property that makes all beautiful things beautiful. But this is precisely what they deny; in their view, bright colour makes some things beautiful, symmetrical shape makes other things beautiful, and so on. The fact that each of the many beautifuls suffers from compresence of opposites is precisely the sight-lovers' reason for supposing that there are many properties of which each is the beauty in a given kind of thing, and that there is no one property that is the beauty in all beautiful things. Plato might seem to have missed this point; his objection, we might suppose, would be fair only if the sight-lovers were trying to give a single account of beauty.

This defence of the sight-lovers suggests that we must distinguish two claims about the compresence of opposites. Suppose that the sight-lovers claim that bright colour is beauty in statues. In reply, Plato might say: (1) Bright colour is beautiful in statues but not in, say, Leonardo's cartoons. (2) Bright colour is beautiful in some statues but not in others. The first claim is harmless to the sight-lovers. The second claim, however, damages their case, for it suggests that within the restricted range of cases in which they believe bright colour can be identified with beauty, it is sometimes not beautiful, and so it cannot be the beauty in statues.

Which of these two claims does Plato intend when he says that each of the many beautifuls will also appear ugly?[14] The many beautifuls are the many properties that the sight-lovers identify with beauty; these properties are not bright colour, symmetrical shape, and so on, without qualification, but bright colour, and so on, in specific circumstances. Unless Plato is confused, he is claiming that such things as bright colour in statues (not simply bright colour without qualification) are beautiful and ugly. In that case he makes the second claim about compresence of opposites; if this claim is true, it damages the sight-lovers' case.

Is Plato entitled to the second claim in all the relevant cases? *Republic* I shows how he might defend it. 'Returning what one has borrowed' (as opposed to what one has been given as a gift) is a description of one of the many justs, but Socrates shows Polemarchus that it is not specific enough to avoid the compresence of opposites; for sometimes it would not be just to return what one has borrowed. If this is so, then justice, even in this restricted area, cannot be identified with returning what one has borrowed.

This objection leads Plato to a crucial question: how do we judge that bright colour makes this statue beautiful and that one ugly, or that returning what you have borrowed is just in this case and not in that case? Two answers seem to be possible: (1) Our judgment rests on nothing further; we simply remember a list of properties that make certain objects beautiful or just and a list of cases in which these properties do not make something beautiful or just. It is a brute fact that these items and no others are on the list. (2) There is some further reason underlying our judgment about the many Fs in these different cases, and this further reason leads us back to the one Form, the single property that really explains our judgments about rules and exceptions to rules.

The sight-lovers are committed to the first answer, but it does not seem plausible for the cases that display, or might display, the compresence of opposites. For we can surely explain why we think it would not be just to return a gun we have borrowed from our neighbour, if he has gone mad and threatens his own and other people's lives. We normally expect just actions to benefit rather than to harm the people primarily affected by them; this general expectation underlies both our conviction that normally it is just to return what we have borrowed and our conviction that sometimes doing so is not just. Our reasoning in such a case would be difficult to understand if the sight-lovers were right and our conception of justice rested on nothing more basic than our recognition of the many types of just actions.[15]

This line of objection to the sight-lovers explains why Plato believes they display another frequent characteristic of people who have belief without knowledge: they lack a rational basis for criticism of conventional views. Although they try to give an account of, for instance, justice they simply identify justice with the commonly recognized features of just actions (people, laws). Plato tries to show that this is a superficial reaction to the defects of conventional rules of justice; and so he suggests that failure to recognize non-sensible Forms imprisons us in conventional rules, preventing us from understanding their inadequacies and, equally important, the extent to which they are defensible (493e2–494a4). This aspect of the sight-lovers' attitude is discussed further in the image of the Cave.[16]

186. The Sun

The argument of Book V says something about what knowledge is by saying what Socratic definitions are not; since Socratic definitions cannot be confined to sensible properties, knowledge must be knowledge of non-sensible Forms. It is reasonable to ask Plato to say more about what this knowledge is like. In Books VI and VII he turns to this task by offering the three connected images of the Sun, the Line, and the Cave.[17]

The Sun tells us something more about the connexion between knowledge of the Forms and awareness of the Good. It describes two conditions of sight that illustrate two cognitive conditions of the soul:[18]

s1. Sight in the dark without sunlight looks at visible things.
s2. Sight in sunlight looks at visible things (508c4–d2).
S1. The soul looks at the many Fs without reference to the Form of the Good, and has only belief (508d6–9).
S2. The soul looks at the Forms, referring to the Form of the Good, and has knowledge (508d4–6, 508e1–509a5).

The contrast between S1 and S2 is meant to be the contrast that was drawn in Book V, between the sight-lovers who appeal to the many Fs and the philosophers who appeal to the Forms (507a7–b11). The Sun begins to explain that contrast, by insisting that an appeal to the Forms requires reference to the Good.

Socrates reminds Glaucon and Adeimantus that they accepted an account of the tripartite soul and the cardinal virtues that fell short of completeness and accuracy (504a4–b8). A complete and accurate account requires arguments and proofs that can be reached only by the 'longer way', which requires knowledge of the Form of the Good (504e7–505a4).[19] Since justice and the other virtues are essentially good and beneficial (505a2–4), knowledge of these virtues requires knowledge of the Good.[20]

The Sun makes it clear, however, that appeals to the Form of the Good are not confined to those who have mastered the longer way and have achieved knowledge of the Good. Plato insists that some appeal to the Good guides everyone who succeeds in turning from the many sensible Fs towards the Form of F; for it is the Good in S2 that makes us recognize the Forms, just as the sunlight in s2 illuminates visible objects for us. Although he may insist that complete knowledge of any Form requires knowledge of the Good, he must allow Forms to be grasped by some cognitive state, superior to mere belief, that does not require knowledge of the Good. Indeed, he must claim that the moral theory of the *Republic* rests on some such cognitive state. For since he claims to have given definitions of the virtues, he must claim to have discerned some of the features of the relevant Forms; but he denies that he has knowledge of the Good.

187. The Form of the Good

Why should it be easier to give accounts of the virtues than to give an account embodying knowledge of the Good? Plato answers this question when he considers different attempts to say what the good is.[21] The 'many' identify the good with pleasure, but they have to admit that there are bad pleasures, so that they are compelled to admit that 'the same things are good and bad' (505b1–2, 505c6–11). As usual, the claim about compresence of opposites must be applied to types rather than tokens; Plato objects that since pleasures are sometimes good, sometimes bad, simply achieving pleasure cannot be identified with achieving the good.

The difficulty in identifying the good with wisdom is presented differently. Plato suggests that people who say that the good is wisdom or knowledge 'cannot show what sort of wisdom it is, but in the end are compelled to say that it is wisdom about the good' (505b8–10). The difficulty is not that their account applies to the wrong cases, but that it appeals all over again to the good, instead of explaining what it is.

The two rejected accounts present a dilemma. We might try to defend the account of the good as wisdom by identifying it with knowledge in general, not with knowledge specifically about the good; but then we would have to allow that some kinds of knowledge without knowledge of the good are bad for us. In that case we would have introduced something that is both good and bad, so that the objection urged against the hedonists would also apply to us. Alternatively, we might defend the hedonist account by identifying the good only with good pleasure; but then we would have appealed to the good instead of explaining it, and the objection urged against the account of the good as wisdom would apply to us. The two rejected accounts offer us the unwelcome choice between an account that is too broad and an account that presupposes what is to be explained.[22]

Plato chooses the second horn of this dilemma. In Book IV he has shown that accounts of the virtues can be useful even if they appeal to evaluative properties that are not wholly reduced to non-evaluative properties. The claim in Book V that knowledge requires reference to non-sensible Forms in contrast to sensible properties defends the type of account offered in Book IV. In Book VI Plato claims that an ideal definition of the virtues cannot be expected to rely on a definition of the good that avoids appeal to the evaluative properties that are to be explained. When he says the Good is 'beyond being', not itself one of the beings whose reality and knowability come from it (509b6–10),[23] he implies that it is not identical to any of the other Forms; but in denying that it is itself a being, he suggests that it is not a Form that is independent of the totality of the Forms whose goodness it explains. We insist on pursuing other things only insofar as they are good and beneficial (505d5–10), but this does not mean that we pursue them for the sake of some good that is independent of them.

To defend his claim, Plato can turn to his views about the value of justice; we do not value justice because of its contribution to a good that is independent of it, but because it partly constitutes the achieving of the good. The good, then, may be understood not as something independent of the virtues and other specific goods, but as the appropriate combination and arrangement of them. This is why Plato believes the Good is not a 'being' in its own right, but beyond being; while the good is superior to the different specific goods that constitute it, it cannot be understood, defined, or achieved without reference to them.

Plato has already argued that justice is not purely instrumental to happiness, but a dominant component of it, so that the good cannot exist without justice. Even if this is so, it does not follow that the good cannot be understood independently of justice (even if, for instance, the healthy condition of the body is a certain balance of the four elements, I could understand what health is even if I had never heard of the four elements); in fact, however, Plato also denies the independent intelligibility of the good. Our understanding of the human good is not completely prior to our understanding of the nature of the different virtues; it consists in our understanding of the connexions between the virtues, not in our understanding of some good that could be understood without seeing the value of the virtues.

If this is what Plato means by his claim that the Good is beyond being and is not a being in its own right, then this claim fits his practice in the *Republic*. His accounts of the virtues have not tried to meet the conditions that were apparently imposed on adequate definitions in the Socratic dialogues. His claims about the goodness of justice did not try to show how justice contributes to some good that can be understood independently of it. His remarks about the Form of the Good show why it was reasonable for him to present his ethical argument in this way. Plato warns us that if we look for a 'perspicuous and accurate' account (as Thrasymachus puts it) of the Good, we will find a false account.

Plato makes Socrates insist that he cannot appeal to knowledge of the Good in support of his argument about the virtues (506b2–e5). When Glaucon and Adeimantus ask for an account of the Good parallel to the accounts that Socrates gave of the virtues, he professes inability to give such an account (506d2–8). His inability is intelligible if we take account of the connexion between the good and order and system. We will begin to form an adequate conception of the good once we understand the virtues and other goods well enough to see how they fit together and how they should be combined with each other. The accounts in Book IV, Plato suggests, do not give us this degree of insight into the virtues and other goods; they are simply the starting points for such insight. The political analogy allows us to form a conception of the rational part of the soul and its ends and so allows us to form conceptions of the virtues, but these conceptions are imperfect. If we understand the rational part and its aims better, then we will also understand the virtues better, and we will see how they combine with each other and with other goods to constitute the good.

In these remarks Plato suggests that we can have something more than mere belief about Forms even if we lack the sort of knowledge that requires knowledge of the Good. This suggestion is explained in the image of the Divided Line.

188. The Divided Line

The Line presents four cognitive states:

L1. Imagination (*eikasia*): awareness of images of sensible things.
L2. Confidence (*pistis*): recognition of the sensible things of which the items in L1 are images.
L3. Thought (*dianoia*): reliance on assumptions and on the use of sensible things as images.
L4. Intelligence (*noēsis*): dispensing with assumptions and images by finding the first principles underlying assumptions.

Plato devotes the most space to explaining the top two stages of the Line, but some difficulties about these are easier to solve if we consider the point of the image as a whole.[24]

The four segments of the line result from subdivision of the two cognitive states (S1 and S2) mentioned in the Sun (509d1–8). In that case both L1 and L2 (which divide S1) are correlated with sensibles, while both L3 and L4 (which divide S2) are correlated with Forms; indeed, Plato makes it clear that the objects about which we lack intelligence when we are at L3 are the very objects that are objects of intelligence at L4 when we find the appropriate principle (511d1–2).[25]

In assigning to L3 the arguments that rely on assumptions, Plato relies on his discussion of assumptions or 'hypotheses' in the *Phaedo*. The description of hypothetical method in the *Phaedo* follows the argument to show that sensible properties give an inadequate account of Forms.[26] Similarly, the *Republic* introduces L3 after Plato has argued—more fully than in the *Phaedo*—that sensible properties cannot give an account of the Forms and, in particular, cannot give an account of the Form of the Good. In both dialogues Plato appeals to the hypothetical method to show why his rejection of definitions by sensible properties does not make the search for definitions futile.

The *Republic* marks more sharply two approaches to a hypothesis that are distinguished in the *Phaedo*: (1) We defend a hypothesis against one sort of objection by showing that its consequences are acceptable in the light of our other beliefs. (2) We defend it by appealing to a higher hypothesis until we 'come to something adequate' (*Phd.* 101d5–e1). In the Line the first approach is characteristic of people at L3; they examine the consequences of their assumptions, but do not give any further defence of the assumptions themselves. They appeal to images and analogies to make the assumptions seem plausible, but such appeals do not count as a defence from a higher principle. A defence from a higher principle is characteristic of L4. Plato amplifies the remark in the *Phaedo* about 'something adequate', by arguing that the adequate basis will be a principle that is not itself an assumption (511b3–c2). The discovery of this non-hypothetical principle and the tracing of its consequences are tasks for dialectic.

This description of L3 and L4 tells us rather schematically how the account of the virtues offered in Book IV takes us beyond mere belief, but not as far as the complete knowledge that is achieved at L4. But how are we to advance from one of these stages to the other? Plato cannot tell us precisely, since a precise account would require the knowledge of the Good that he disavows. Since he cannot reach L4, he uses one of the devices characteristic of L3, relying on images to convey his point. To describe progress towards the Good he introduces the image of the Cave.

189. The Cave on Belief

Just as the Line divides each of the two states illustrated in the Sun (S1, divided into L1 and L2, and S2, divided into L3 and L4), the Cave divides the two illustrative states in the Sun (s1, divided into c1 and c2, and s2, divided into c3 and c4). The Cave, therefore, differs from the Line in that the four conditions it describes are purely illustrative, not necessarily examples of the states that they illustrate. The four stages of the Cave are these:

c1. Illustration of imagination: the prisoners in the cave look at shadows, reflexions, and so on.
c2. Illustration of confidence: the prisoner is released and recognizes the dummies as the source of the shadows.
c3. Illustration of thought: the released prisoner is outside the cave and discovers the visible objects that are the source of the dummies, first by looking at images of them, and then by looking at the objects themselves, eventually by sunlight.
c4. Illustration of intelligence: he looks at the sun and recognizes it as the source allowing him to see the visible objects he has seen.

The Cave also differs from the Line in being explicitly progressive; it sets out to show how someone can progress through the different stages it distinguishes, and so it ought to illustrate how someone can progress through the different stages of the Line.[27]

The Cave tells us more than the Sun and the Line tell us about the two lower cognitive conditions (L1 and L2). Socrates explains that the Cave illustrates 'our nature, as far as education and the lack of it are concerned' (514a2, 515a5). Most people remain in the condition illustrated by the inhabitants of the cave, and at least some people remain in the condition illustrated by the prisoners (516e8– 517a7); for someone who appears in a court of justice has to deal with 'the shadows, or the figures (*agalmata*) behind the shadows, of the just' (517d8–9). Even in the ideal city, most people are in the condition of the inhabitants of the cave; for when the philosophers rule, they have to 'descend into the cave' (520c1–6, 539e2–3).

From these points about the Cave, some conclusions about imagination can be inferred: (1) Imagination cannot be defined as a state in which we are literally confronted with nothing but shadows and images of sensible objects, for everyone is literally confronted with actual sensible objects, and not just with their shadows and images, and yet many people fail to progress beyond imagination in the area Plato is concerned with. (2) The area he is concerned with is morality, both in actual cities and in the ideal city.

These features of imagination are intelligible if imagination about Fs is the condition of someone who lacks standards for distinguishing real Fs from mere likenesses of Fs. Someone who has only imagination about horses draws no distinction between horses, pictures of horses, shadows of horses, and images of horses appearing in dreams. The prisoners in the cave suppose that (what are in fact) the images appearing to them are actual horses, because they cannot distinguish what looks like a horse from what really is a horse; that is why they suppose that 'horse' is the name for a certain sort of appearance (which, unknown to them, is just a shadow).[28] We would be in this condition if we were looking at a real horse, but had no idea of how to distinguish it from other things that look like horses.

This is a plausible account of imagination because it fits the moral case well, as Plato clearly intends. Even though everyone passes beyond the condition of imagination in their relation to horses, tables, and chairs, not everyone passes beyond it in relation to morality. If we simply accept, without question or criticism, the views we have been brought up with or have absorbed from our social environment, we cannot distinguish appearance from reality in this area. Plato takes this to be the condition of the sight-lovers in Book V; it is also the condition of the sophists who simply repeat and elaborate popular views without any criticism (493a6–c8). In this condition, people will not listen to any talk of the just itself in contrast to the many justs (493e2–494a3), because they have not recognized that the many justs yield no understanding of justice.

This account of imagination shows why the beliefs of people at this stage need not be largely false; indeed, they may be largely true. Plato shows that this is his view, since he implies that in the ideal city those who have had no philosophical training are still in the condition illustrated by prisoners in the cave (519d5, *desmōtas*). Since they have been brought up to have true beliefs, as far as they are capable of grasping them, it must be their lack of critical understanding that places them at the lowest stage of the Line.

Once we have seen the nature of imagination, the Cave gives us a clearer understanding of confident belief. It tells us (as the Line does not) that we make progress from the first stage to the second stage by undergoing Socratic elenchos (515d1–8). We are not to suppose that at c2 elenctic inquiry has completely reached its goals, for since the released prisoner cannot see the real horses outside the cave, he cannot say correctly what the dummies are; still, he can see enough to recognize that what he had previously called horses are in fact distorted and imperfect likenesses of the originals he now sees.

Plato implies that a Socratic elenchos can improve an interlocutor's beliefs even if it does not lead to an answer to the Socratic question; for when we compare, say, our initial attempts to say what bravery is, or our initial beliefs about the sorts of actions that are brave, with our firm intuition that bravery must be fine and beneficial, we have some basis for assessing and criticizing our initial beliefs. We could not do this if our initial beliefs did not have the right sort of implicit rational structure, and if we were not capable of following Socrates' suggestions about the right direction for the revision of our initial beliefs.[29]

These remarks about the beneficial effects of Socratic elenchos must be compared with Plato's objections to its harmful effects (537e1–539d2). Plato argues that in some young people the effect of elenchos is scepticism about the moral principles they have learned, and this scepticism undermines any moral beliefs that restrain them from following their tastes and appetites. This is the effect of practice in being refuted and in refuting other people; after this, some people form a taste for destructive argument and use it to undermine conventional moral beliefs.

People who react to the elenchos in this way have evidently failed to learn that Socratic elenchos is a method for improving as well as rejecting beliefs. Plato does not imply that Socrates did anything wrong in practising the elenchos on young Athenians, some of whom would fail to listen to everything he had to say.[30] Nor does Plato imply that he himself will not engage young people in the elenchos. If Socrates or Plato had confined the elenchos to Athenians over the age of thirty, their interlocutors would have been so set in their erroneous conventional beliefs and practices that there would have been little hope of freeing them from their errors. In the ideal city the elenchos is not needed to free people from grossly false beliefs (since they have been educated correctly), and therefore people need not be taught to practise it at a dangerous age.

Does this imply that in the ideal city people do not move to the stage of confident belief until they reach the age of thirty? Plato need not go quite so far. Elenchos may point out to us the inadequacy of our initial beliefs and stimulate us to improve them, without teaching us to practise elenchos ourselves. This is the condition of Nicias, for instance, who reflects constructively on his beliefs without going in for Socratic inquiry or cross-examination himself (*La.* 187e6–188c3). We may learn, for instance, to distinguish the various behavioural rules we may have been trained to follow from the deeper intuitions that underlie them; we learn that our belief that a virtue is fine and beneficial is more important than our belief that, say, bravery requires us to stand firm in battle. Since we can learn this from the elenchos without ourselves being equipped to refute others, a prohibition on young people practising refutation does not imply a prohibition on the use of the elenchos. And so we need not infer from the later passage on the elenchos that Plato advocates the postponement of all use of the elenctic method until the age of thirty.

Since the historical Socrates used the elenchos constructively without finding definitions of the virtues, does Plato intend us to put Socrates at L2? This is unlikely. For the released prisoner who has reached c2 does not suspect that there is anything outside the cave; Socrates, however, looks for the accounts that will explain his moral beliefs, and so he recognizes the existence of forms beyond the 'many Fs'. On this important point he is beyond the second stage.

190. The Cave on Knowledge

In contrast to the Line, the Cave describes the first two stages in some detail, allowing us to see what states Plato has in mind and how we progress from one to the other. He uses the description of the first two stages to clarify the upper two stages as well. At the upper two stages, we continue the search for explanation that we began at the second stage. When we see the dummies clearly, we understand better why the shadows are as they are; when we reach the world outside the cave, we gradually come to understand why the dummies are as they are, because we recognize the originals of the dummies. Eventually, this process of seeking explanations is complete, once we look at the sun and come to see why the living creatures in the outside world have the sort of life they have (516b4–c6).

This part of the Cave makes it easier to see the difference between L3 and L4. Plato wants us to see that at L3 accounts of the virtues resting on assumptions explain the beliefs about the virtues that have survived critical scrutiny at L2, even though we do not yet understand why these accounts are the right ones. We understand why they are the right accounts only when we reach L4 and see how they combine systematically to give us knowledge of the good.

In the Line, Plato told us that to pass from L3 to L4 we must go beyond assumptions by looking for their principle. Here he tells us again that this task belongs to dialectic, and specifically that it requires the practice of the elenctic method, carrying out an elenchos 'not in accordance with belief but in accordance with reality' (534c2). This dialectical cross-examination is systematic, seeing what things have in common with each other (531c9–d4) and seeking a synoptic view of things (537c6–7). The result of this is that dialecticians 'give an account' of what they study, and so meet a necessary condition for knowledge (531e4–5, 534b3–6).

These remarks about dialectical method suggest how dialectic is supposed to 'remove' assumptions and, at the same time, to 'confirm' them (533c7–d1). Plato assumes that we have found accounts of the virtues that fit the well-founded beliefs elicited at L2. We now try to see the systematic connexion between these different accounts, so that we can eventually give an account of the good that modifies these previous accounts and confirms the revised accounts. Each account of a virtue rests on some assumptions about the good, since we assume that each virtue promotes the good; to see if our accounts are satisfactory, we need to see whether they all agree about the nature of the good. When we have examined the implications of our accounts of the virtues for our views about the good, we may find that the implications conflict; if so, we must modify our accounts. When we have an adequate account of the good that is the goal of the different virtues, we will also have adequate accounts of the virtues. In doing this we will have 'confirmed' our assumptions, insofar as we have confirmed the claims we previously put forward as assumptions. Having confirmed them in this way, we will no longer need to treat them as assumptions, and so we will have 'removed' the assumptions.

Plato does not say much about this sort of dialectical inquiry, but consideration of Book IV suggests what he intends. We might be persuaded that both bravery and temperance promote the good, but unable to give a unified account of the good that they both promote; for we might say that temperance promotes placidity, and bravery promotes aggressiveness, and that these two tendencies often clash.[31] If we reach this result, Plato suggests, we must reconsider the accounts we have given of the virtues to see whether we can modify them to yield a more coherent account of the good. Similarly, if we suppose that wisdom requires selfishness and justice requires unselfishness, we introduce a conflict into our account of the good, and we ought to reconsider our account of these virtues to see whether we can remove the conflict. If we have absorbed the argument of *Republic* V and the discussion of the Good in Book VI, we will not seek an account of the good that is independent of our accounts of the virtues; nor will we simply accept our initial accounts of the virtues uncritically.

Since Plato does not claim to have completed this critical examination of the accounts of the virtues, he does not claim to have reached an account of the Good, and so he does not claim to have reached L4, the state that is properly called 'intelligence' or complete knowledge. He seems closer to L3, where we rely on assumptions. And yet, just as Socrates (as presented in the early dialogues) could not be placed at L2, Plato, as the writer of the *Republic*, does not belong at L3.

As examples of people at L3, Plato mentions mathematicians; they rely on assumptions that need further justification, but they do not recognize they are doing this, because they take their assumptions to need no further justification, and they reason from them as if they were genuine principles (510c1–d3). As mathematicians, they do not need to look beyond their starting points; it is left for the dialectician to see that the mathematicians make assumptions that need (for philosophical, not mathematical, reasons) further justification.

Although Plato also uses assumptions, he sees that they are assumptions and that they need further justification; since he understands the character and limitations of L3, he cannot himself be at L3. Similarly, he uses images derived from visible things, as people at L3 do. The Sun, Line, and Cave are themselves examples of Plato's resort to images; the analogy between the city and the soul is the image on which he rests his account of the virtues. But since Plato not only recognizes that he uses images but also points out their limitations, he cannot himself be at the uncritical cognitive state that he describes.[32]

191. Epistemology and Moral Theory

The Sun, Line, and Cave complete the explanation of the division between knowledge and belief that is marked at the end of Book V. Plato has a good reason for inserting this discussion of epistemology and metaphysics immediately after his first answer to Thrasymachus. For that answer rests on the definitions of the virtues, especially of justice; Plato recognizes that someone who examines these definitions in the light of the Socratic dialogues might well be dissatisfied with them. The point of Books V–VII is to remove this dissatisfaction.

In arguing that the Forms are non-sensible and that they cannot be known by people who confine their accounts to sensible properties, Plato discourages us from seeking accounts that would satisfy Thrasymachus' demand for something 'perspicuous and accurate'. In rejecting accounts of the Good that attempt to break out of the circle of evaluative properties, he rejects attempts to support accounts of the virtues by an appeal to some conception of the good that can be accepted independently of our beliefs about the virtues. We saw why it was reasonable to believe that Socrates aimed at some such independent conception of the good. Since the *Republic* rejects any such conception, it rejects the restrictions that prevented Socrates from offering accounts of the virtues.

Still, Plato does not want his claims about the Forms to be primarily negative. He insists that rejection of an independent account of the Good still allows the appeal to the Good to play an important role in defending an account of the virtues. We can reasonably expect our views about the virtues to reveal some systematic goal of the virtues, and we ought to modify our accounts of the virtues until they reveal a suitable goal. Does this advice help to strengthen the main ethical argument of the *Republic*?

17

Republic VIII–IX on Justice

192. The Place of Books VIII–IX

After the discussion of epistemological and metaphysical questions in Books V through VII, Socrates returns at the beginning of Book VIII to the promise he made at the end of Book IV to consider whether it is in our interest to be just or unjust (444e7–445b8). He describes the deviant constitutions—timocracy, oligarchy, democracy, and tyranny—that embody successive deviations from the best constitution that is embodied in the ideal city.[1] The point of this description is to distinguish the four types of deviant people who have souls analogous in structure to the deviant constitutions. Plato seeks to show that the deviant constitutions are worse than the ideal, aristocratic constitution, and that therefore all the people with deviant souls are less well off than the person with a just soul. If the deviant people exhaust the possibilities for having unjust souls, then the p-just person is happier than any p-unjust person.

What does this elaborate comparison add to the argument of Book IV? Plato suggests at the end of Book IVthat he has answered Thrasymachus (445a5–b5). But he equally insists that the argument in Book IV rests only on a outline account of the division of the soul, and that more needs to be said to support that division and (by implication) to amplify the description of the three parts. Plato recognizes that argument in Book IV is incomplete, even while he insists that it is correct; as Aristotle says in such cases, what has been said is 'true, but not perspicuous (*saphes*)' (*EN* 1138b25–26), and Plato wants to make it as perspicuous as possible (*hoion te saphestata*, 445b6).[2] We should not assume, then, that the later books are simply illustrative. Since Plato now tells us what is involved in having one's soul controlled by a non-rational part, he suggests what is required for control by the rational part and for psychic justice.[3]

The later books cannot completely fill the gap left by Book IV. For Plato believes that to fill the gap we would need to follow the 'longer way' and give an account of the Good, but he denies that he can give an account of the Good.[4] The rational part of the soul is guided by reasoning about the good, and the other parts do their proper work when they are appropriately influenced by this reasoning about the good; and so we cannot fully understand the characteristic desires of the rational part until we have given an account of the good. Plato renounces the aim of giving a full account of the parts of the soul in the *Republic.*

Still, the later books may clarify Plato's conception of the rational part and therefore his conception of psychic justice. Even if we cannot give an account of what the rational part does when it performs its proper function, we may still be able to grasp more of what it does by seeing what it must avoid. If we can see more of the outlook of unjust souls, we can see what errors a just soul must avoid; 'if being in this condition is extremely wretched, we must earnestly flee from vice and try to be virtuous' (Ar. *EN* 1166b26–28). Each of the deviant souls, according to Plato, is unjust because the parts, especially the rational part, do not perform their proper functions.

193. Sources of Psychic Injustice

If we are to decide whether the deviant people have unjust souls, we must recall Plato's conditions for having a just soul. We have seen in Book IV that not every sort of control by the rational part is the sort of control that Plato takes to be characteristic of psychic justice.

Even if my desire is irrational and incontinent, it may lead to purely technical practical reasoning (about ways to satisfy my incontinent appetite, for instance); if I follow the conclusion of this reasoning, I rely to some degree on the rational part. We have seen that Plato does not believe that desires resulting from this technical reasoning belong to the rational part; and so he does not believe that someone who acts on such desires is thereby controlled by the rational part.[5]

If we avoid incontinence and act on rational plans directed to the fulfillment of our long-term aims, the operation of practical reasoning is not restricted to instrumental deliberation on particular occasions; it must also consider the relation between different aims in my life as a whole (questions of jam tomorrow versus jam today). Concern to find the most efficient means to a given end requires me to attend to my concern for my other ends; for I must refer to these in order to decide which of several equally effective means is the most efficient and economical. Still, these functions of the rational part are strictly instrumental. The prudential deliberation of reason takes for granted the sorts of ends that I will pursue, and confines its attention to ordering them.

This concern for efficiency may be found in a non-rational part. Plato attributes some features of an agent, including this one, to a non-rational part of the soul; it has a conception of itself and its aims and uses practical reason to achieve them.[6] And so the mere fact that someone avoids incontinence and acts steadily on the conclusions of reasoning about the most efficient course of action does not by itself show that he is controlled by the rational part; for this pattern of action is equally characteristic of a non-rational part.

It is less easy to decide, on the basis of Book IV alone, what Plato wants to say if I consider the sorts of ends I ought, in my own interest, to pursue in life and decide to follow the aims of the spirited or the appetitive part. In this case, I am taking a step beyond merely instrumental deliberation; my choice of which ends to follow is a choice made by the rational part. It is important for Plato to take a definite view on this sort of agent; for if he believes that this pattern of deliberation and action is really control by the rational part, he must agree that such an agent is psychically just. If he agrees about this, then it is difficult to see how psychic justice necessarily involves any concern for the good of others, and correspondingly difficult to see any connexion with common justice. For many c-unjust people seem to be guided by a rational choice in favour of the aims of the spirited or appetitive part.

We found that Plato's conception of psychic justice gives him a reason for denying that a rational choice to pursue the aims of a non-rational part is the choice of a p-just soul. He insists that the rational part that dominates the p-just soul is concerned with reasoning about the good of the whole soul and of each part.[7] Measured by this standard, a choice to prefer the aims of a non-rational part seems to ignore the interests of the whole soul and the interests of the parts whose aims are not chosen.

Although Plato could have made this point in Book IV, he certainly does not make it clearly; for he does not consider the sort of case just described, or directly deny that it is a case of p-justice. This is why it is important to consider Books VIII and IX; since these books present different kinds of unjust souls, they allow us to see the implications of Plato's standards for p-justice. The deviant souls are clearly c-unjust, and so it is important for Plato to show that they are clearly p-unjust as well. He must therefore show how they are dominated by the non-rational parts in a way that prevents them from being p-just. Since we have just seen that there are different ways of being dominated by a non-rational part, and different roles that practical reason can play in determining our choices, we must not oversimplify the questions about the deviant people. We must consider the different types of rational control to see which ones they have and which they lack.

194. The Decline of the Soul

Plato describes a process of decline from a just constitution, in which the rulers know what the common good is and are concerned to realize it in the city, through the different types of unjust constitutions, in which different ruling groups are responsible for different types of injustice that harm the city. In the city we can see the sources of injustice in the different classes, and we can see the effects in political change. A parallel narrative describes the decline from a just soul through different types of unjust souls, so that we can understand the effects of injustice in the soul by examining the effects of injustice in a city. In the individual we can see similar effects, in changes of individual characters. Each p-unjust condition of the soul can be traced to the domination of one of the non-rational parts of the soul. The timocratic person is dominated by the spirited part; the oligarchic, democratic, and tyrannical people are dominated in different ways by different aspects of the appetitive part.

What is the nature of this domination? It would be easy to see how the deviant people are p-unjust if they were incontinent. This is the sort of domination that Plato describes on a particular occasion in Leontius; someone who is regularly guided by non-rational impulses contrary to any rational aims he may form might reasonably be said to be dominated by the non-rational parts. This is the sort of person whom Callicles praises, or finds himself forced to praise.[8] Someone who trains himself to act on his immediate impulse and to reject any desires resulting from reflexion on his longer-term good might, for the reasons that Socrates urges on Callicles, maximize his pleasure; by making this a habit, he might become a creature of impulse altogether, rejecting any significant role for rational planning in his life.

The closest parallel to this sort of person in the *Republic* is the tyrannical person, with his dominating and demanding desires and aims.[9] If Plato meant that this sort of person habitually acts against his rational plans, or fails to form rational plans altogether, then we could understand his view of domination by the non-rational parts.

This explanation of 'domination' does not work, however, for the other deviant people.[10] The timocratic, oligarchic, and democratic people have rational plans for their lives and execute them steadily, without especially frequent lapses into incontinence. The timocratic person need not be especially prone to imprudent bursts of anger; indeed, his plans encourage him to control his appetites and emotions in order to pursue his long-term aim of honour and reputation more efficiently. The single-minded and systematic planning of the oligarchic person is strongly emphasized (553b–d). The democratic person acts on a variety of desires with no clear hierarchical structure, but this is not because he cannot control his desires. On the contrary, his rational plan is precisely to leave his different desires a certain degree of freedom, and in acting on them he does just what he rationally plans to do.

It is not even clear that the tyrannical person is habitually dominated by appetite in opposition to his practical reason and deliberation. He is dominated by a particular demanding urge or 'lust' (*erōs*) (573d), but this lust does not cause him to reject or violate his rational plans and desires. On the contrary, his obsessive lust controls his rational plans too; and so he follows these plans in his actions. Like the other deviant people, he is guided by his rational plans and need not be prone to incontinence.

For these reasons, Plato could not plausibly argue that the deviant people are p-unjust in the most obvious way, by acting incontinently or without any rational order in their choices.

195. Choices in Unjust Souls

Since Plato treats the non-rational parts of the soul as having some of the features of agents, he might explain the orderly and prudent aspects of the deviant people by saying that they are dominated by the aims—especially the longer-term aims—of one or another of the non-rational parts, and that the rational part is confined to instrumental reasoning on behalf of these aims.

Plato's description of the transition from one psychic constitution to another certainly treats the different parts of the soul as having some characteristics of agents. Someone becomes an honour-lover by 'handing over' (*paradidonai*) rule in his soul to the spirited part (550b6); someone becomes oligarchic by setting his appetitive part on the throne (553b–c). In describing how someone acquires a democratic soul, Plato speaks first of a struggle between different appetites (559e4–561a5) in a young man, but then he suggests that when someone grows up he may himself take an active role in allowing some of the previously ejected desires to return and may not abandon himself entirely to unnecessary appetites (561a6–b6). A tyrannical soul develops when demanding and lawless appetites grow (572d5–573c10) and clamour for attention (573e3–574a11); it seems to be the person himself who pays attention to them and acts on them.

The parts of the soul are treated as agents to the extent that each has a relatively steady and coherent set of goals that it pursues. Since different p-unjust people are dominated by one or another of these sets of goals, perhaps Plato means that this domination is also the domination of a non-rational part. In that case, the deviant people are p-unjust because the rational part does not set the goals that they pursue in their lives.

This view of the deviant people fits some of Plato's description, but it does not fit his claim that someone 'hands over' rule in his soul to one or another part. The agent (or partial agent) who hands over rule to the appetitive part, for instance, cannot actually be the appetitive part; if it were, then no handing over would be necessary. But why would one of the other two parts hand over rule to a different part? If Plato does not mean that the agent handing over power is a part of the soul, perhaps he means that it is the person or soul composed of these three parts. But where does this agent fit into Plato's tripartite analysis of the soul? The tripartition is meant to explain the choices that we attribute to a person; if the explanation reintroduces the choices of the person without further explanation, the tripartition seems to fail in its explanatory task.

These difficulties about the role of the person in relation to the parts of his soul might be resolved in one of three ways: (1) The reference to the person is not to be taken seriously. Plato means only that the domination of one part is replaced by the domination of another. (2) The reference to the person is to be taken seriously because Plato has a conception of the person as something beyond the three parts of the soul. (3) The reference to the person is to be taken seriously, but it refers to a special role of one (or more) of the three parts of the soul.

Admittedly, Plato may well fail to distinguish these answers, or he may shift confusedly from one to the other. Nevertheless, it is worth asking which one fits his remarks best.

196. Rational Choices in the Decline of the Soul

If the first of these answers is right, then we ought not to take the remarks about 'handing over' very seriously. They suggest that there is some agent who has a choice about what to do, but we might suppose that this suggestion is misleading; perhaps Plato really means to describe a purely psychological, rather than a rational, process. On this view, when circumstances strengthen someone's spirited or appetitive part, it comes to dominate his plans and to set the ends pursued by practical reason. If the choices that a person makes simply result from the comparative strength of the desires of different parts of the soul, there is no distinct stage in which the person 'hands over' control to the strongest part of the soul; once a given part of the soul is strong enough, it dominates the person's choices without any handing over. On this view, handing over is simply a feature of the political process that Plato transfers to the decline of the individual soul; he does not mean it to describe a distinct phase in the history of the individual.

This solution, however, does not account for Plato's actual claims about handing over; for he describes the process in enough detail to show that he believes it has some distinct psychological reality. Indeed, he says enough to make it clear that the process is not purely psychological, but also rational. The deviant person reflects on his life and comes to see more point than he previously saw in taking the desires of a different part of the soul (or a different arrangement of the desires of the same part) as the basis for setting his ultimate ends. Plato suggests reasons that someone might give for abandoning one way of life in favour of another. The fact that these reasons are given suggests that the rational part is involved in each of the stages of psychic decay, and that at each stage it approves of the change in the balance of power among the parts.

The appeal to the rational part is clear at the first stage of psychic decline. When a formerly good city starts producing badly educated people, the virtuous person finds himself dishonoured by other people. Although he realizes that he ought to put up with this, his son is not so easily persuaded; the son could make a reasonable case to show that his father's way of life does not really do justice to all the parts of his soul.[11] The son's reasoning reflects a general principle that Plato applies at each of the later stages as well: people turn from Life 1 to Life 2 when it seems to them that Life 1 fails to achieve its own ends and that Life 2 offers a better prospect of setting reasonable ends that they can hope to achieve.

The same pattern of rational choice and deliberation is repeated in the other deviant people. The instability of the honour-loving life leads to the gain-loving life, but someone who lives this life has to use force against his many unnecessary desires. The failure of this use of force suggests the egalitarian democratic attitude to appetites. The democratic person assumes that any discrimination between desires involves arbitrary and unjustifiable force; for he sees that this is true of the oligarchic person's attitude, and sees no better basis for discrimination. He therefore rejects any suggestion that some desires and their resulting pleasures deserve to be cultivated and others do not (561b7–c5). Even though some of his desires do him harm that has to be repaired by deprivations that he could have avoided (561c6–d2), this does not deter him; he esteems and cultivates all desires equally, just as they strike him, and allows them all satisfaction (561b2–6).

This democratic policy is self-defeating. Since the democratic person accepts and cultivates all desires without discrimination, he has to accept and cultivate an obsessive and demanding desire (*erōs*) that is not content with equal shares. This desire uses the toleration granted to it by democratic attitudes to undermine the democratic way of life itself. For since the democratic person pursues any desire that strikes him, he has to pursue the sort of desire that completely absorbs him. Since the obsessive desire becomes stronger and stronger, the democratic policy itself requires him to pursue this desire until it dominates him completely.

These remarks suggest that Plato is not being careless in suggesting that the transition from one stage to another is a rational process involving the person who hands over control. If this is correct, then one aspect of the political analogy has to be modified when it is applied to the individual soul. In the sequence of political changes, one government is turned out and another is installed, and there is no single source of authority that consents to all the changes of government. In the individual, however, Plato seems to intend the person to remain the permanent source of authority; every change of domination in the soul is accepted by the soul itself.

197. The Rational Part of an Unjust Soul

If Plato's remarks about 'handing over' are to be taken seriously, then we cannot suppose that psychic decline is treated as a purely psychological process. If it is a rational process, must we suppose that it belongs to the person, as opposed to a part of the soul, or can we attribute it to the rational part of the soul?

The reasons that persuade the agent to cede control to a different part or a different desire seem to be reasons that the rational part of the soul accepts. The process is intelligible, then, if the rational part is persuaded by the different reasons that are offered to justify the rule of different sorts of desires. Plato does not suggest that the agent makes choices that do not express the desires of any of the three parts; he probably means that when the agent decides which desires will control him, this decision consists in a choice by the rational part.

We ought not to suppose that if the interests of the whole soul are being considered, it must be the person, as opposed to the rational part, who is moved by them. For we have seen that it is distinctive of the rational part that it considers the interests of the whole soul; although it is one of the parties whose interests are considered, it is capable of considering itself and the other two parts as constituting a whole.

The impartial outlook of the rational part explains why it need not always demand control for itself. The oligarchic person, for instance, chooses to confine the rational and spirited parts to subordinate roles that support the guiding aim of his acquisitive appetites (553d1–7). If we are right to say that these choices are made by the rational part, then the rational part chooses to assign itself a subordinate position in the government of the soul, even though it retains the capacity to change this government and replace it with another.

Although the rational part does not disappear or lapse into inactivity, it is affected by the different governments that it sets up; the mistakes that the rational part makes at an earlier stage warp its outlook when it considers what to do next. If someone who decided to be an honour-lover sees that he has been disappointed, he does not reinstate the rational part in control; since his preferences have been affected by his honour-loving life, he cannot see any alternative to acceptance of the preferences of one or another non-rational desire, and so he decides to cede control to his acquisitive appetites.

In ceding control, the rational part deliberately chooses to reduce its influence in the soul. A rational choice to follow the aims of a non-rational part involves inaction or abstention by practical reason. If I decide to follow the ends of the spirited or the appetitive part, I decide to stop exercising in the choice of ends to be pursued on particular occasions the sort of practical reason that I am exercising in the choice of ends as a whole. In Hobbes's terms, the rational part gives up its right and authorizes the non-rational parts to choose the ends to be pursued.[12]

This self-restraint by practical reason is intelligible if the rational part believes it cannot actually carry out the deliberative task that might appear to be open to it. If I simply acquiesce in the preferences of one or another non-rational part, I imply that practical reason has no basis for assessing the aims of non-rational desires, but must simply choose among them. In that case I recognize my incompetence to make any independent rational decision about ends that goes beyond the preferences of the non-rational parts.

If this is the outlook of the rational part in deviant souls, what is wrong with it? It looks as though deviant people can argue that they are p-just after all, for their souls are controlled by the preferences of the rational part deliberating about what is best for the soul as a whole. They answer this deliberative question by deciding to follow the aims of one or another non-rational part; but since that is a decision by the rational part, the fact that they follow the aims of a non-rational part does not show that they are not controlled by the rational part. Indeed, if they are right to say that the rational part cannot guide our particular choices unless it follows the preferences of a non-rational part, we cannot expect to be any more p-just than the deviant people are.

198. The Functions of the Rational Part

If Plato is to show that the deviant people are not p-just, he must show that they are not controlled by the rational part performing its proper function. The proper function of the rational part is to deliberate about the good of the whole soul and of each part. Plato must claim that to carry out this function we must deliberate about how far to accept the ends of the non-rational parts. If we take deliberation this far, we do not accept the policy of inaction or abstention that is favoured by the deviant people. Rather, we assume that practical reason is capable of deciding on its own account about the merits of the preferences of the non-rational parts. If we take this attitude to the non-rational parts, we will decide to adopt our ends on particular occasions (or on types of occasions) by the exercise of practical reason, not simply because we have decided to acquiesce in the goals of the spirited part or the appetitive part.[13]

The deviant people might concede that the questions that Plato takes to be open to deliberation are perfectly intelligible questions; it looks as though we can ask how far we ought to acquiesce in the ends of non-rational parts. The deviant people deny, however, that there are any rationally defensible answers. Can Plato answer this sceptical attitude to the claims he makes for the competence of practical reason?

The deviant people are not represented as extreme sceptics about the competence of practical reason. It is useful to see how large a role they allow to practical reason, so that we can focus on the grounds for their scepticism.

If we allow only instrumental reasoning to the rational part, we confine it to Kant's imperatives of skill ('technical imperatives') and of prudence ('pragmatic imperatives').[14] The deviant people have practical reason performing each of these roles, and on some views of practical reason these are the only roles for practical reason. We might believe, for Socratic or Humean reasons, that reason has no non-instrumental role—that questions about the sorts of ends to be pursued cannot be answered by appeal to practical reason, but must simply be answered by desires that are independent of reason.

Someone who sees only this instrumental role for practical reason implicitly denies that Butler's distinction between strength and authority applies to the choice of ends. In Butler's view, reasonable self-love is distinguished from the particular passions insofar as it acts on reasons for doing x that are recognized as distinct from the strength of my desire for doing x.[15] In deciding whether to do x or y, rational self-love does not simply try to register the comparative strength of my desire for x and for y, but considers the comparative merits of the actions themselves. If a strictly instrumental view of practical reason were right, then there would be no basis apart from comparative strength of desires for deciding between one end and another.

It is difficult to believe the strictly instrumental view, if we are persuaded, contrary to Hume, that it is rational to plan for the efficient satisfaction of our desires.[16] If we allow that this is rational, then we seem to accept, contrary to the previous suggestion, a non-instrumental role for practical reason. The efficient planner agrees that if I have desires of equal strength for A, B, and C, and if x will get me A and B, whereas y will get me only C at the cost of A and B, then I have reason to chose x over y. But the same sort of reasoning also seems to justify some discrimination among ends. If at the moment I care equally about A, B, and C, but I realize that any pursuit of C will prevent my getting A and B, whereas pursuit either of A or of B does not interfere with the pursuit of the other, why is it not rational for me to abandon C in favour of A and B? If comparative considerations can induce me to adjust my choice of means, why can they not also induce me to adjust my choice of ends?

Concern with efficiency is characteristic of each of the non-rational parts; for Plato attributes to each part a conception of itself and of its interests as a whole, distinct from the satisfaction of each non-rational desire as it arises.[17]

The rational part in turn has a conception of the interest of the whole soul that is distinct from the satisfaction of the desires of each part. The rational part cares about efficiency and coordination in the choice of means and ends because it cares about the satisfaction of the future self that will have different desires with different degrees of strength. Insofar as it has a conception of a self that is independent of current desires and their strength, it has a point of view that allows it to criticize the aims of current desires.

The deviant people accept all this; but if they accept it, can they still make a convincing case for their view that all the rational part can do to promote the interests of the whole soul is to adopt the ends of one of the non-rational parts? In deviant souls the rational part deliberates to some extent about ends; for the deviant people discard a way of life because it frustrates their own main aims. Beyond this general test of consistency for a whole way of life, can we say that some aims are, and others are not, appropriate for the rational part? We might think that ends themselves must come from the non-rational parts and that the rational part can only decide to turn over the function of setting goals to one or both of the non-rational parts.

199. The Rational Part and the Choice of Ends

From Plato's point of view, the sceptical attitude of the deviant people underestimates the importance of the rational part's concern for the whole soul, and the difference between this concern and the more partial concerns of the non-rational parts. The rational part sees that each non-rational part relies on considerations that are independent of the considerations appealing to the other part, and that both sorts of considerations deserve some independent weight. The fact that something satisfies our appetites is a point in its favour, whether or not it appeals to our sense of honour and shame; the fact that something appeals to our sense of honour is a point in its favour whether or not this fact is reflected in any of our appetites.

The non-rational parts cannot see these facts about the desires of other parts of the soul. Although each non-rational part has some features of an agent, it has no conception of itself as a part of a whole. Each non-rational part is moved by considerations appealing to the other part only insofar as they coincide with considerations appealing to itself. The appetitive part does not decide to assign a certain appetitive weight to certain actions because they appeal to the spirited part's sense of honour; it simply sometimes feels like doing what the spirited part in fact wants, but not because the spirited part wants it.

In contrast to the non-rational parts, the rational part decides by considering the merits of different desires and their objects, from the point of view of the whole soul rather than a part. Once we recognize the one-sided outlook of the non-rational parts, we will see that we cannot adopt such an outlook if we are concerned with the good of the whole soul; even if we do not know what the good of the whole soul consists in, we can see that the non-rational parts are too one-sided to give us any reason for confidence in them. We must see, then, that we are unjustified in acquiescing in their goals as the deviant people do.

Plato's account of the decline of deviant souls shows why we ought not to have confidence in their policy of simply adopting the ends of one part of the soul without criticism; the one-sided outlook of each non-rational part of the soul changes the desires of the rational part so that they become more and more one-sided and so have less and less claim to express any conception of what is good for the whole soul. The timocratic person pursues the aims of the rational person insofar as they satisfy his sense of honour, but his exaggerated focus on honour makes him too easily disappointed, and his disappointment induces him to adopt the narrower goal of the oligarchic person. Since the oligarchic person's policy encourages the growth of further appetites that are more and more difficult to restrain, he gives up his unsuccessful efforts to discriminate between desires and adopts the democratic policy of trying to satisfy each desire as it comes. Once the democratic person settles into his way of life, he finds that he has no argument against the clamorous demands of lawless and destructive desires, and so he finds no argument against the tyrannical outlook. Acquiescence in the one-sided outlook of a non-rational part condemns us to more and more one-sided outlooks.

These objections to the non-rational parts suggest that we are better off if we are guided by the rational part, since the outlook of the rational part is impartial between the aims of the non-rational parts and comprehensive in its concern for the whole soul. Plato has some reason, then, for taking his description of unjust souls to vindicate the life of a just soul guided by the rational part. When Socrates asks Glaucon to order the deviant souls by their degrees of happiness, Glaucon takes it to be obvious that the person with the 'kingly' soul controlled by the rational part is also the most just and the happiest (580a9–c8). Socrates describes this as the first 'demonstration' (*apodeixis*, 580c9) of the truth of his answer to Glaucon's original question about justice and happiness. The faults of the non-rational parts should have persuaded us that we are better off if we are guided by the rational part, even though we have not learned much about its outlook.

200. The Pleasures of the Rational Part

Plato does not leave his argument there, however. To his first demonstration he adds three more. The second argues that the psychically just person's judgment is the most reliable guide to the degrees of pleasure to be found in different lives, so that his judgment that his own life is the most pleasant should be accepted (580c9–583b2). The third demonstration argues that the psychically just person has the truest pleasures and therefore has the most pleasant life (583b2–588a11). The fourth demonstration introduces yet another image to suggest the nature and relations of the three parts of the soul. Plato compares the three parts to a human being, a lion, and a many-headed beast, all enclosed within the shape of a human being; and he defends the rational part by arguing that it protects the interests of the human being (588b1–592b6).

The arguments on pleasure raise several difficult questions, but some points in them are especially relevant to the issues about the deviant souls and the nature of control by the rational part.[18] Socrates agrees that since the proponents of each way of life are dominated by just one part of the soul, they will prefer their way of life to the others (581c–582e); he argues, however, that only the person dominated by the rational part develops and uses the capacities needed for judging one way of life over another; these capacities are experience, wisdom, and reason (582e7–9). The one-sided outlook of each non-rational part disqualifies it from finding the right aims for a person's life.

It is often objected that the person dominated by his rational part is really not as well qualified as Plato claims he is, since he cannot really have the right sort of knowledge and experience.[19] Although he has had experience of appetites, he has been (we suppose) educated properly, and so he has not had the experience of being a mature adult dominated by the appetitive or the spirited part. Does he not need that sort of experience, however, if he is to compare the situation of an appetitive or spirited person with his own experience?

The objection fails, once we recognize that the attitude of the rational part to the other parts is not the same as their attitude to it. They have no capacity to represent the interests of the rational part within their conception of their own ends. Hence the rational person ought not to be confined to their conception of his ends; for once we are confined to that outlook, we have no easy way out of it, as Plato has shown in his description of the decline of deviant souls. Insofar as we are dominated by the non-rational parts, we suffer from a distorted view of the value of satisfying these parts, because we have no basis for attributing value to the desires and pleasures of other parts of the soul.

Since the rational part has grounds for valuing the satisfactions of spirited desires and of appetites, it evaluates its experience of the pleasures of the other parts from the appropriately comprehensive point of view. Those who are guided by the rational part have no reason to believe that they miss any relevant experience simply because they lack the experience of being dominated by either of the other two parts.

201. The Special Concerns of the Rational Part

This defence does not say how the rational part considers its own interests in relation to those of the other two parts. In the argument to show that the psychically just person is a better judge of pleasure, Plato suggests an answer to this question. He describes the rational part as 'philosophical', devoted to the exercise of reason (581d10–e4). In the argument about true pleasures, he suggests that the pleasure resulting from rational thought is truer because it is concerned with what is true and unchanging rather than with what is changing (585b11–c5).

We might take these remarks to mean that the rational part has the sort of one-sided attachment to its activities and pleasures that make it indifferent to the aims of the non-rational parts. On this view, control by the rational part would imply that the aims of the other parts are regulated simply with a view to maximizing theoretical activity.

For reasons we have seen, this cannot be the whole truth about the rational part. For Plato insists that it has a 'holistic' outlook, concerned with the good of the whole soul and of each part, not simply with the good of the rational part or with the satisfaction of the rational part's special desires. This fact about the rational part, however, does not solve the problem about its special concerns. For if the rational part has both a purely rational, theoretical concern and a holistic concern, the two concerns seem liable to conflict, and the rational part does not seem to count as a single part of the soul after all.[20]

Plato's view is more plausible if he takes the holistic outlook of the rational part to satisfy the distinctively rational concerns of the rational part, because deliberation from the holistic point of view is itself an exercise of rational thought aiming at the truth. We want to pursue the good of the whole soul because we want to be guided by the real merits of different activities, not simply by our degree of inclination towards them. To this extent we regard ourselves as essentially rational agents who want to form and to act on true judgments about our good. Forming and acting on these judgments is not simply a useful instrumental means towards securing our good; it is also part of the rational activity that is itself part of our good.

This fact about the role of practical reason does not show that the pursuit of theoretical activity can never conflict with the holistic concerns of the rational part. But it shows that we cannot consistently value theoretical activity for Plato's reasons, treating it as a way to knowledge of the truth, without also valuing the holistic outlook of the rational part. For these two aspects of the rational part reflect the same value that the rational part properly attaches to its own activity.

It should now be easier to see why Plato believes that the rational part is a better judge of true pleasures. From the point of view of the non-rational parts, ends are to be chosen simply by reference to the strength of our inclinations for them, since a non-rational part cannot conceive itself as anything beyond a subject of inclinations. Inclinations are unreliable, however; the strength of an inclination depends on the conditions forming the inclination, and these conditions may distort our expectations about our future satisfaction. Drinking, for instance, is pleasant against the appropriate background of thirst, but if the background changes, drinking may no longer be pleasant (583c10–584a11). Since the non-rational parts are moved by present inclination when they form their aims, they are easily misled by misleading features of the background that forms their present inclination.[21]

The rational part, by contrast, is concerned to find what is really better and worse on the whole. This concern with truth leads it to pursue the true good of the whole soul. If it takes this point of view, it does not form its aims simply on the basis of the strength of its inclinations, and so it will not make its choices in the distorting conditions that influence the non-rational parts (585b12–c5, 585d11–586b4).

Although the details of these arguments about pleasure are open to question, their general point makes an appropriate conclusion to the arguments about psychic justice.[22] Plato suggests why the aims and preferences of the rational part make its choices best for the whole soul. This is why the non-rational parts of the soul do best for themselves if they follow the guidance of the rational part (586d–587a). They will simply harm themselves if they consistently pursue the satisfaction of their own desires 'without reasoning and intelligence' (586d1–2). Plato appeals to the superiority of the rational part in resolving intrapart conflicts for each of the non-rational parts. Both from the external point of view of the rational part and from the internal point of view of each non-rational part itself, Plato can argue that the rational part does best for each of the non-rational parts.

202. The Good of the Whole Soul

The rational part's concern for the good of the whole soul supports Plato's fourth demonstration, relying on the comparison of the rational part to a human being within a human being (588b10–e1). The fact that the 'inner man'—the rational part—itself has the shape of a man suggests that the outer appearance of a man is not completely misleading about the real nature of a man. Since the human being consists of three parts, the inner human being would be a perfect image of the outer if it also contained three parts; but this conception of the inner human being would lead to an infinite regress. The rational part cannot, therefore, include an appetitive part and a spirited part in the way the outer man does. Still, the image implies that the rational part must 'contain' the non-rational parts in some way.

The previous discussion suggests how the demand for the non-rational parts to be 'contained' within the rational can be satisfied without absurd consequences. The point of the image is clear if we remember that the interests of the other two parts are represented fairly within the concerns of the rational part, whereas the non-rational parts have no capacity for fairly representing the interests of the rational part. The rational part can therefore claim to be concerned with the interests of the whole man, not just with the aims resulting from concern for rational activity. Plato insists that the agent whose interests are to be considered is the man who is composed of the three subagents (588e3–589b6).[23]

If our previous account of the difference between the deviant souls and the p-just soul was correct, it supports the claims Plato makes here. To be dominated by a non-rational part of the soul is to reject the claim of practical reason to make rational choices of ends instead of acquiescing in the preferences of the other parts. If we do not try to make rational choices in such areas, we cannot evaluate the ends we have or acquire through our non-rational desires. Since the person guided by the rational part attaches value to the aims of the whole soul, he will have the experience of appetitive and spirited desires and satisfactions that he needs to be an experienced judge of their relative value.

When the rational part considers the good of the whole soul and each part, it will not just try to strike a balance between different appetites or between appetitive and spirited desires. It also has itself to consider. It achieves its own aims in two ways: by planning for the exercise of reason as well as the fulfillment of other desires, and by exercising reason in this very planning. Plato attaches great importance to the theoretical reasoning that is, in his view, the concern of the first task of practical reasoning; that is why the rational part finds it important to satisfy its own desires for philosophical activity. But it is important not to neglect the fact that it also satisfies some of its own desires in the very action of rational planning itself.

We can see how the rational part is a better ruler than either of the non-rational parts if we consider the different attitudes of the three parts to both intrapart and interpart conflicts. The appetitive part (and the spirited part, although perhaps not to the same degree) is bad at ensuring its own future interest.[24] In its calmer moments it prefers to ensure the satisfaction of its future desires, and so does not want to damage its prospects for the future. Still, its conviction that this long-term policy is preferable is rather unstable, since it varies with the comparative strength of its occurrent desires. Moreover, the arguments about pleasure show that even when a non-rational part forms its longer-term preferences, it forms them in distorting conditions, since the apparent pleasantness of a future condition is affected by the deprivations we are currently suffering.

A well-informed non-rational part must therefore realize in its calmer moments that it cannot even ensure that it follows the sort of policy that it prefers (in these calmer moments). It may realize that it can follow such a policy more effectively if it forms a desire to do what the rational part tells it; this further desire provides some counterweight to the strength of other occurrent appetites.

In interpart conflicts it is still more obvious that the non-rational parts are not to be relied on. For neither of them is guided by principles that appeal to authority; each of them must simply register the comparative strength of different desires. There is no reason to suppose that guidance by strength of desires results in a policy that benefits the soul as a whole, or that it resolves conflicts between the parts in any mutually satisfactory way. Since the attitude of the rational part to the claims of both non-rational parts is more sympathetic than the attitude of either non-rational part towards the other, each non-rational part will recognize that it is better off if it follows the rational part than if it must always be clashing with the other non-rational part.

203. A Fuller Conception of Psychic Justice

Plato is entitled to claim that the argument of Books VIII and IX has developed and strengthened the argument of Book IV. For we can now see why someone controlled by the rational part of the soul has the sorts of aims that exclude the lives of the deviant people. In Book IV Plato insists that p-justice requires each part of the soul to perform its own function; but he does not say much about the function of each part of the soul and, in particular, says little about the functions of the rational part. Until we know about the functions of the rational part, we cannot say when someone is or is not dominated by one of the non-rational parts. Books VIII and IX answer some of these questions; for when we see more clearly the functions of the rational part, we see why the rational part in the deviant people does not perform its proper function.

A full understanding of the proper function of the rational part would require a full understanding of the human good, and Plato warns us not to expect this full understanding, since he disavows any knowledge of the Form of the Good. But we can still be guided by well-founded beliefs about the good.[25] Plato relies on such beliefs when he indicates what the deviant people lack. He implies that they lack an essential element of the good, insofar as they lack the appropriate sort of rational activity: practical reason determining the rational choice of ends. We can see why it is better not to be excluded from this rational activity once we see what happens to the deviant people when they exclude themselves from it. They cannot properly consider the interests of the whole soul, and the p-just person must consider these.

Since Plato has explained his conception of p-justice mostly by describing the types of p-injustice that it excludes, he has not said much about the sorts of actions that p-justice requires. He tells us in general terms that they will not result from mere acquiescence in the preferences of one of the non-rational parts, and that they will result from a larger exercise of practical reason, reaching a comprehensive outlook that the deviant people lack. But we still do not know exactly what actions will result from this outlook. It is still difficult, in particular, to answer the question raised at the end of Book IV, about the relation between p-justice and c-justice.

The negative argument used in Book IV still applies here, and has a wider scope. Plato is justified in claiming that many unjust actions seem attractive because we have our souls in the condition of the deviant people, and that if we have our souls controlled by the rational part, these actions will seem less attractive to us. This analysis of the sources of injustice becomes more plausible in the light of Books VIII and IX than it might have seemed in Book IV. For Plato has now shown that many c-unjust actions that might have seemed to appeal to a p-just soul actually appeal only to the p-unjust souls of the deviant people. If we thought that the conditions for p-justice allowed the deviant people to be p-just, we would suppose we had a series of counterexamples to refute Plato's claim that p-justice implies c-justice. But once we see that the deviant people are not p-just, this line of objection to Plato's view collapses.

This does not mean that all reasonable objections have been answered. Plato's form of argument ought not to convince us that all c-unjust actions will be unattractive to the p-just person. In any case, we have already seen the difficulty in ascribing any necessary positive concern for the benefit of others to the p-just person; if he lacks that, we may doubt whether he is genuinely c-just.

Plato might still, therefore, be asked for some further account of what the rational part will decide when it deliberates about the good of the whole soul; and so he must face a further question that calls for some more definite conception of the good. He has an answer to the question, although the answer is not direct or completely explicit. To understand it, we must consider his account of love.

18

Platonic Love

204. The Questions about Justice and Interest

In Plato's view, the rational part performs its own function only if it is not subordinated to ends that are set by one of the non-rational parts; it must reach its conception of ends by consideration of the good of the whole soul and of each part, not by acquiescence in the goals of one of the non-rational parts. But can we say anything more about the outlook that results from following Plato's requirements? In particular, can we defend Plato's conviction that someone with a p-just soul will have the other-regarding concerns that are appropriate for justice?

To find any positive description of the p-just person's outlook in the *Republic*, we must turn to Plato's remarks about the philosopher. He begins with the just person, but eventually describes the philosopher, in order to answer the earlier questions about the just person (581b5–10, 586e4–587b10, 588a7–10, 590c8–d7). He does not believe he is changing the subject; for he supposes that the philosopher's outlook reveals the sort of outlook that can reasonably be expected of the p-just and c-just person.

The description of the philosophers raises further puzzles. Once they have contemplated the Forms, they will suppose they are living in the Isles of the Blessed and will not willingly undertake the task of ruling in the ideal city (519c). It would be bad for the city if they were allowed to contemplate the Forms without interruption; for they are the best qualified to rule, since their knowledge of the Forms allows them to understand the shadows and likenesses in the cave (520c–d). If it is necessary, they will embody their conception of the Forms in the institutions of the city and the characters of its citizens (500d), and since the interest of the city demands it, it becomes necessary for them to take their part in ruling.

Glaucon is surprised by all this and asks whether it is not unjust to demand this of the philosophers, since they are required to have a worse life when it is possible for them to have a better life (519d8–9). Socrates replies that the ideal city is designed for the happiness of all the citizens, not for the exclusive happiness of a single group (519e9–520a4); it is best for the whole city if it is ruled by people who do not regard ruling as a prize to be fought over, and so it is just to expect the philosophers to rule the city as a repayment for their upbringing (520a6–d8).

205. Philosophers as Rulers

Does this explanation adequately answer Glaucon's question? Socrates does not deny that the philosophers are asked to give up a better life, since they are required to give up a purely contemplative life. Indeed, he seems to insist that the philosophers are reluctant to rule precisely because they could lead a happier life.

If this is Plato's view, then he believes that the philosophers prefer, all things considered, to remain contemplating the Forms, and only literal compulsion by the authorities in the city makes them take part in ruling.[1] If they were free to follow their own decisions, they would not, according to this view, undertake the obligations imposed by justice. In that case Plato must accept Thrasymachus' main objection to justice. If the philosopher, who is supposed to have a just soul, has to be forced to do c-just actions, then Plato has not met Glaucon's demands; the p-just person seems to have nothing more than a facade of genuine justice, and so no one has been shown to have a good reason to be just.

Plato probably believes, then, that the philosophers prefer, all things considered, to take part in ruling. Some of his other remarks also suggest this view. They are just people and therefore will recognize that justice requires them to take part in ruling the city (520e1), even though they will regard ruling as 'necessary' rather than 'fine' (540b4–5). They accept the 'necessity' (500d) that requires them to express their conception of the Forms in the city. The relevant sort of necessity is not legal or physical compulsion imposed by the coercive power of the rulers; for since the philosophers are just people, they want to do what justice requires and do not need to be coerced into doing it. They recognize that ruling is necessary if they are to fulfill the requirements of justice; this sort of necessity need not involve coercion.

In contrasting the necessary with the fine, Plato does not intend to suggest that the philosophers do not prefer to rule. The contrast is relevant, however, because it recognizes an element of truth in Thrasymachus' case against justice. Thrasymachus argued that justice requires us to make unwelcome sacrifices; if the just person is a ruler, he has to forgo the advantages that an unjust person would gain from holding office, and so he must take on the burdens of office without any compensating gain (343e1–7). The sacrifices imposed on a just person lead Glaucon to suggest that justice is necessary, but not good (358c3). In Book I Socrates suggests that the just person finds the advantages to be gained from ruling so unappealing that in a city of just people the rulers will rule unwillingly (347b5–d8). In Book VII Plato agrees that the obligations imposed by justice are disagreeable; they result from circumstances that we would prefer to be absent.

But in agreeing with Thrasymachus thus far, Plato does not agree with his view about which aspect of justice is unwelcome. Thrasymachus supposed that the unwelcome fact is that we are required to attend to other people's interests, rather than to our own exclusive interest, but Plato has not agreed that this fact is unwelcome to the just person. More needs to be said to explain what Plato takes to be the unwelcome aspect of ruling for the philosophers.

Let us suppose, then, that the philosophers prefer to accept the requirements of justice and therefore prefer to rule. Why do they prefer to do this? If the purely contemplative life would be a better life, we might conclude that they are sacrificing their own interest to the requirements of justice.[2] By ruling they achieve some good, but apparently this is not the greatest good for themselves; their overriding concern, we might suppose, is with the Good, not with their own good.[3]

If this is Plato's view, he seems not to have answered Glaucon's demand to be shown how the just person is happier than everyone else; for if this view of the philosophers is right, he must admit that just people have to sacrifice their own interests for the sake of justice. Glaucon asked to be shown that justice is by itself the greatest good in the soul for the person who has it (366e5–9, 367c5–e5); Plato cannot show this if justice requires a sacrifice of one's own interest. If it requires such a sacrifice, then the happiest person would apparently be the one who could contemplate the Forms while evading the obligations of justice. Even if Plato designs the ideal city to prevent this evasion of the duties of justice, he has not shown that justice itself is the greatest good for the soul, but only that it is a necessary, but regrettable, concomitant of the greatest good in the circumstances of the ideal city.

The character of Glaucon's question also shows us why it would not be enough to argue that in the actual circumstances of human life a purely contemplative life is not a practical possibility. Let us grant that the philosophers could not contemplate as well as they do if they did not live in the ideal city, and that the ideal city will collapse unless all the philosophers are willing to take part in ruling. Even so, if that is their only reason for caring about the requirements of justice, they do not choose justice for its own sake, and justice itself is not a non-instrumental good for them.[4]

To see what options are open to Plato, we need to distinguish two aspects of ruling as it presents itself to the philosopher. It is certainly a daily round of administrative tasks concerned with the multifarious needs of the city and the three classes in it. This aspect of ruling reveals nothing more than its instrumental value; no one who could engage in philosophy would reasonably prefer to, say, plan the conduct of a war for its own sake. The actions involved in ruling are, as Aristotle puts it, laborious (*ascholoi*) and burdensome and not to be chosen for themselves (*EN* 1177b6–18). But Plato maintains that ruling has a second aspect: it is just action required by principles of justice that demand action for the common good and proper return for the benefits one has received. If the ruler's tasks are just actions, then a just person will choose them for their own sakes, insofar as they are just. This second aspect of ruling, not the first, makes it choiceworthy (in the right conditions) for its own sake to the just person.

If Plato is to answer Glaucon, he need not argue that the philosophers have reason to prefer ruling, as such, over uninterrupted contemplation, for the sake of their own happiness. He needs to argue that the philosophers have reason to prefer ruling insofar as it is just action, over pure contemplation that is indifferent to justice, for the sake of their own happiness. If justice requires each philosopher to take her turn in the disagreeable tasks of ruling, it still does not represent ruling as a good in its own right; and so Plato is still entitled to say that the philosophers will not be eager to cling to office.

Plato ought, then, to argue that the philosophers choose to rule because they regard it as just and they regard the just action as part of their happiness, so that they recognize no conflict between duty and interest. If he cannot defend this view, he leaves a serious gap in the main argument of the *Republic*. We ought to see, then, whether Plato can show that it is in the philosophers' interest to fulfill this specific other-regarding requirement of justice.

206. The Aims of the Rational Part

When Plato raises this question about the philosophers' attitude to ruling, he has claimed that they are especially well qualified to rule because they have a single goal in their life, and one ought to aim at such a goal in doing everything that one does in private or in public life (519c2–4). The philosophers have acquired the appropriate goal by the education that is represented in the Cave image and that culminates in the grasp of the Form of the Good.

Plato uses the Cave to insist on a vital difference between the training of the rational part of the soul and the training of the other two parts. In his view, the education of the rational part is not primarily the acquisition of information that we previously lacked. Such acquisition would be like putting sight into blind eyes (518b6–c2). The proper education of the rational part is a process of turning the soul towards what it needs to see, so that it can use its own capacity to see it (518c4–d1). This feature of education is illustrated in the Cave insofar as learners draw their own conclusions about the different objects they are confronted with. If prisoners are released, they are not told what they are looking at, but have to work it out for themselves. The same is true, Plato implies, at the later stages of their progress.

This turning of the soul is necessary, in Plato's view, if the rational part is to pursue the right ends. Whereas virtues, so called, of the non-rational parts are the products of habituation, the virtues of the rational part are different. If the soul is not turned in the right direction, the rational part will choose to devote itself to instrumental reasoning for the sake of the ends, good or bad, of the other parts of the soul (518d9–519b5). This mistaken choice of the rational part is illustrated at length in the different deviant people.

In order to avoid this mistake about the proper function of the rational part, Plato prescribes the study of mathematics. He advocates it not simply because it involves turning away from sense perception but also because it is constructive reasoning pursued without reference to immediate instrumental usefulness (525b11–c6, 526d7–527b11, 527d5–e6, 530b6–c1). This aspect of mathematics is relevant to practical reasoning as well, since the rational part has to become accustomed to reflecting on the merits of different courses of action, not simply on their instrumental usefulness in satisfying one of the non-rational parts.

Plato claims, then, that the rational part will acquire the right 'single goal' for private and public life if we are asked the right questions and encouraged to work out the answers by reasoning that does not focus exclusively on the satisfaction of non-rational desires. He claims that this process eventually leads to a grasp of the Form of the Good, and thereby to the appropriate goal for private and public life.[5] This emphasis on working out the answer for ourselves is the same emphasis that underlies Plato's contrast between recollection and ordinary teaching; just as he appealed to recollection to explain how Socratic inquiry could succeed, he suggests that the process of turning the soul proceeds by Socratic inquiry (515d4–5, 534b8–c1).

207. The Puzzles about Love in the *Republic*

If the turning of the soul is to have these results, it must affect the philosophers' desires as well as their beliefs. Plato suggests how this might happen. He claims that philosophers must be lovers of truth and reality (501d1–2); in the *Phaedo* (68a–b), similarly, he attributes love (*erōs*[6]) for wisdom (*phronēsis*) to them. He insists that they must be trained to cultivate this sort of love (485a10–d5). The genuine lover of truth and knowledge will not have fulfilled his eros and desire until he has completed his pregnancy, had intercourse with true reality, and begotten intelligence and truth (490a–b).[7] His desire will be fulfilled only when he comes to know the Forms. The proper government of cities requires philosophers to take control, or the rulers or their sons to acquire an eros for philosophy by divine inspiration (499c1–2). This eros explains why the philosopher who is aware of the Forms will imitate them; imitation is the natural result of 'admiring intercourse' (501c6).[8]

These passages go beyond metaphor.[9] They rely on an appeal to eros to describe and explain the philosophers' mental development. This appeal is rather surprising, since the other remarks in the *Republic* about eros do not treat it as a desire of the rational part. In Book IV eros is connected with sexual desire and is firmly attributed along with hunger and thirst, to the appetitive part (439d6–8). This is an ordinary conception of eros.

In Book IX the tyrannical soul is said to be dominated by eros, to which all the soul's other desires are subordinated; this is what is supposed to be fundamentally wrong with the state of the tyrannical soul. This is a non-literal or extended use of 'eros', insofar as it is not applied, as it is in Book IV, exclusively to sexual desire.[10] But 'eros' is still a clearly appropriate name insofar as the desire shares some salient features with some types of sexual desire. As Plato describes the tyrannical person's eros, it is irrational and obsessive, tending to dominate the soul even when it is destructive to one's other interests and concerns.

The *Republic* throws no more light on Plato's views on rational eros. But if we cannot understand it better, we cannot understand an essential element in Plato's account of the turning of the soul towards the truth. Since this turning of the soul is necessary for the grasping of the right end that makes philosophers good rulers, we will not understand why philosophers are good rulers unless we understand the eros that leads them to the right end.[11] Plato suggests, then, that an essential element in the argument of the *Republic* cannot be fully understood from the *Republic* itself. In alluding to eros, he authorizes us to look for further statements of his views; for his rather elaborate development of the metaphor of sexual intercourse, pregnancy, and birth is not readily intelligible by itself. Since his views on eros are developed more fully in the *Symposium* and *Phaedrus*, it is worth turning to them to see whether the views presented in the *Republic* are defensible.

208. Aspects of Eros

In the *Symposium* and the *Phaedrus*, no less than in the *Republic*, Plato recognizes the normal scope and associations of eros, but he modifies them until they support an account of the philosopher's eros.

Plato recognizes that common sense regards eros as the type of sexual desire that expresses attraction to a particular person, arising from awareness of beauty in the object of eros. Because eros is connected with sexual desire, Plato takes it to be connected with the desire for reproduction. Since eros is normally taken to be a form of passionate and intense, rather than calm and mild, desire, it is often supposed to be demanding, irrational, even obsessive; the *Protagoras* mentions it as one of the impulses that can, in the view of most people, overcome one's knowledge of the good (*Pr.* 352b8).

The conversation between Socrates and Diotima in the *Symposium* begins with the sexual aspect of eros, as desire for the beautiful (204d). But this description is soon supplemented or replaced by two others: eros as desire for the good and for happiness (204e), and eros as the desire to 'give birth in beauty' (206b7). Plato uses 'eros' not in its usual restricted sense, but to refer to the generalized desire for the good from which more specific desires are to be derived (205a–d). In doing this, Plato implies that he can explain a more specific love of persons, and in particular a more specific love of beauty, by appeal to this more general desire.[12]

From the point of view of the *Republic*, however, Plato's silence in the *Symposium* about the tripartition of the soul obscures one important aspect of the philosopher's eros. Nothing in the *Symposium* explains why someone might be tempted to describe the dominant desire of the tyrannical soul as a form of eros. From the point of view of the *Symposium*, it is no more true that the tyrannical soul is dominated by eros than that any other soul is; and so the *Symposium* does not suggest that if we attribute a kind of eros to philosophers, we are attributing something with the intensity and apparent irrationality that is commonly attributed to eros. To this extent, the *Symposium* eliminates the common conception of eros in favour of the Socratic conception of desire.

It is reasonable, then, for the *Phaedrus* to distinguish different types of eros. Socrates argues that the common way of dividing eros from other things is mistaken, and that when we find the right account of eros, we will also find the right distinction between types of eros. Indeed, these are not two separate inquiries; for we understand the nature of eros only if we see that it is more various than some people have supposed, and in particular that it is present in the rational part of the soul as well as in the non-rational parts.

The *Republic* already suggests the importance of correct division; while we might be inclined to oppose desire (*epithumia*) and pleasure to reason, Plato insists that a specific type of desire and pleasure belongs to the rational part of the soul, and that the other two parts have different types of desires and pleasures (*R*. 580d7–8). He adds that the different desires of different parts make people lovers (*philo-*) of different things (581c3–4); he does not claim that different people have different sorts of eros, but that claim would be a natural way to connect the division in the *Republic* with the account of eros in the *Symposium*. This connexion is made clear in the *Phaedrus*.

In the first speech of Socrates, eros is assigned to the non-rational part, because it is an expression of madness, and madness seems to belong to the non-rational part (238b7–c4). Desire or appetite (*epithumia*)[13] belongs to the non-rational part; it is opposed to 'acquired belief aiming at the best' (237d8–9). In suggesting that belief or rational belief aims at what is best (cf. 237e2–3), Socrates suggests that it can move or restrain us in ways that conflict with the urgings of some particular non-rational appetite, but he does not suggest that it has any further function than to arrange for the orderly satisfaction of non-rational desires as a whole. Eros is dismissed as irrational because it sometimes interferes with the demands of instrumental prudence. This speech entirely overlooks the view of the *Republic* that the rational part has its own desires (affirmed in Books IV and IX) and pleasures (affirmed in Book IX) that are not focussed simply on the satisfaction of the desires of the other two parts.[14]

Socrates' second speech, however, treats eros as a type of madness that belongs to the rational part (249c8–e4). He claims that the rational part includes some forms of madness, because he rejects the conception of the rational part that confines it to instrumental prudence. From the point of view of people who regard only instrumental prudence in the service of the non-rational parts as rational, the outlook of the just person is mad because it conflicts with this purely instrumental prudence.

This conflict might explain why Socrates in the *Apology* imagines someone asking him whether he is not ashamed of himself for exposing himself to the danger of death (*Ap*. 28b3–5). The same thought might underlie Callicles' repeated suggestion in the *Gorgias* that Socrates is foolishly neglecting his own interests by exposing himself to the sort of danger that he actually faces in the *Apology* (*G*. 486a4–c3, 521b2–d4).[15] In the *Republic* and *Phaedrus*, Plato reaffirms that there is no basis for 'common deliberation' (*Cri*. 49d2–5) between the just person and other people. The Socratic dialogues do not explain why there is no basis for common deliberation. The *Republic* and *Phaedrus* suggest an explanation: common deliberation requires an agreed specification of the end to be achieved, and the just person and his opponents do not agree on such a specification. The just person's opponents are right, insofar as the commitment to justice that Socrates affirms in the *Apology* threatens the just person with the sorts of sufferings that Glaucon describes in *Republic* II

The purely instrumental task of the rational part is the only task that the deviant people in *Republic* VIII and IX assign to it. We will suppose they are right about the character of the rational part, if we do not see what is involved in the rational part's performing its own function. Plato rejects the purely instrumental attitude, describing it as merely 'mortal' temperance (*Phdr.* 256e3–257a1); it displays the error that *Republic* denounces as a mere 'facade' of virtue.[16]

The *Phaedrus* explains the lover's madness as an aspect of recollection.[17] When the rational part of the soul is reminded of the Form of Beauty (249e4–250b1), its reaction is mad, since it is moved to neglect the normal requirements of instrumental prudence. In appealing to recollection here, Plato expresses the point that he expresses in the *Republic* through the account of mental development conveyed by the Cave. In both dialogues he insists that the rational part, if it is turned in the right direction, forms its conception of the good from its own resources, not dominated by the aims of the other parts.

In the *Republic* Plato does not say, as he says in the *Phaedrus*, that in working out their own conception of the good, philosophical souls display a kind of madness. Still, he recognizes the feature that the *Phaedrus* describes as madness; he insists several times in Books VI and VII—often recalling the conflict between Socrates and his fellow citizens—that the philosopher will not impress other people as someone who displays intelligence in the conduct of his own life or in his advice to other people. Most people think the philosopher is eccentric and useless, indeed harmful (487c4–d5); this is because they cannot grasp the Forms in contrast to the many sensibles, and so cannot carry out the task that the *Phaedrus* assigns to recollection (493e2–494a3; *Phdr.* 249b6–d3).[18]

The argument of the *Republic* explains why the apparently cognitive task of grasping the unity of the Form, in contrast to the plurality of the properties offered by the sight-lovers, also affects our motives and attitudes. If we do not think much about our ordinary beliefs about justice, we may be inclined to suppose there is nothing more to justice than the common descriptions that mention the observance of certain rules, such as those suggested by Cephalus and Polemarchus; we may in turn be tempted to agree with Thrasymachus' view that these rules are so many devices for securing the interests of others against our interests. In that case it is easy to infer that the right attitude to the requirements of justice is the 'slavish' attitude recommended by Socrates' first speech in the *Phaedrus* and by the oligarchic person in *Republic* VIII. When we understand what justice really is, however, we will also understand that it is a non-instrumental good; once we believe that, we will adopt attitudes to justice that seem absurd to people who are content with the views of the sight-lovers.

It is only to be expected that when the philosopher has to deal with the people who have the outlook of the cave, he will seem ridiculous and incompetent, and that they will want to do to him what they did to Socrates (*R.* 516e8–517a6). Since he does not aim at the goals pursued by other people, his behaviour will seem senseless. This is the very aspect of the philosopher that the *Phaedrus* identifies as madness, resulting from the recollection of the Form and the recognition of the difference between the Form and the many sensibles.

When Plato contrasts the philosopher with 'most people' and emphasizes the gulf between his outlook and theirs, we must qualify this contrast by reminding ourselves that what most people say about the philosopher and about the virtues does not adequately express their own implicit intuitions. When we engage in an elenchos, we begin by assenting to the views of the sight-lovers, since they seem to match common descriptions of justice; but if their views adequately represented our most tenacious intuitions, we would be unable to see the force of Socrates' objections to their views.[19]

Sometimes Plato claims that the sight-lovers and the sophists simply serve up the views of the masses, but this is only part of the truth about the masses. Since ordinary people are susceptible to Socratic elenchos, their beliefs must go beyond the relatively superficial account of them that is offered by the sophists. Plato recognizes that fact when he claims that the hostility of the many to the philosophers is not unalterable; since they are susceptible to Socratic elenchos, they must also be capable, with the proper training, of sharing some of the just person's conception of justice as a non-instrumental good.

In the *Phaedrus* Plato combines his different claims about eros in the *Republic* and the *Symposium*. He insists that, as the *Symposium* claims, one sort of eros belongs to the rational part. But he also argues that this eros shares some of the intensity and apparent irrationality of non-rational appetites; that is why 'eros' is the right name for it. If we take a narrowly instrumental attitude to practical reason, even rational eros seems irrational, but Plato rejects this narrowly instrumental attitude. The three dialogues develop different aspects of Plato's theory, starting from different elements in the ordinary conception of eros. They focus on the non-instrumental aspect of rational desire and practical reason that is assumed, but not developed at length, in the *Republic*. We need to see whether Plato's discussion of this feature of the rational part supports his claim that the p-just person chooses other-regarding justice as a part of happiness.

209. Concern for the Future

In the *Symposium* Diotima claims that an enlightened desire for one's own good results in a desire to give birth in the beautiful. She argues that since we want the good to be present to us always (206a), we must want to be immortal in possession of the good (207a); but we can be immortal, to the extent that is possible for us, only by giving birth in beauty.[20] She appeals to the desire for immortality to explain the desire for propagation, in the literal sense; we may call this *interpersonal propagation*, bringing a different person into existence.[21]

Diotima believes, however, that the desire for propagation also explains *intrapersonal propagation*, expressed in my concern for my own future. Within a single lifetime, as we ordinarily conceive it, in which an animal 'is said to be alive and to be the same' (208d4–5), we change in body and soul, so that our characters, personalities, memories, aims, and so on, all change. We keep ourselves in existence insofar as the 'old' self successfully plans for a 'new' self with the right kind of connexion between the old features and the new: 'In this way every mortal creature is preserved, not by being always the same in every way, as a divine being is, but by what goes away and gets old leaving behind in its place some other new[22] thing that is of the same sort as it was' (208a7–b2). Execution of the desire for our own persistence involves the propagation of new selves by old.

What does Plato mean? Both ancient and modern readers have supposed that he believes so-called intrapersonal propagation is really just interpersonal propagation.[23] We might infer this from Diotima's remarks about the new self succeeding the old; if she means that every change involves the destruction of the self that underwent the change, then she implies that an ordinary lifetime is really a succession of lives of short-lived people.

There is no good reason, however, for supposing that Plato must mean this. Nothing in Diotima's argument implies that the person with the new traits is not identical to the person with the old traits. When she says that the old gives way to the new, she may mean that the same person's old traits give way to the new traits, not that one person is replaced by a second person. The remarks about propagation are quite intelligible if Plato simply means that the persistence of the same self is more like interpersonal propagation than we might think it is, since it transmits my character and personality to someone who in some ways is different from myself. Persistence of a single person does not require any one component of the person to stay qualitatively the same through a person's lifetime, but only requires the appropriate causal and qualitative connexions between different stages.[24]

What are the appropriate connexions? Since we are not gods, and hence not wholly free from change (cf. 208b), it would be futile for us to want our future selves to be exactly the same in every respect as our present selves. Which features of me, then, should I want to survive? Suppose my future self has nothing in common with me except such trivial tastes and preferences as liking sugar in tea. It is not clear why I should be concerned for my survival if this is all I could expect to survive, and if everything else were totally discontinuous and unconnected.

Nor can the mere quantity of traits that survive in a later self be decisive. I would have less concern about a later self that preserved many trivial traits and no important ones than I would have about a later self that preserved a smaller number of my past traits but preserved the most important ones. The future self that I have reason to be concerned about must carry on some of the traits that I value. This is the aspect of propagation that concerns Plato when he says that our desire for propagation is a desire for propagation in the 'beautiful' or 'fine' (*kalon*).

Plato's tripartition of the soul separates desires that rest on some estimate of the overall value of the object from those that do not rest on such an estimate. When Plato claims that our concern for intrapersonal propagation relies on an estimate of what is fine, he refers to desires of the rational part, since he refers to concerns based on our values and not simply on the strength of our desires. In the *Symposium* Plato does not mention the tripartition of desires, but when we take account of it, the point of his demand for propagation in the fine becomes clearer. He rejects the attitude that the deviant people in *Republic* VIII and IX take towards the desires of the rational part.

Further reflexion on the significance of propagation in the fine requires us to modify the claim that we want the same traits to persist in our future selves. Even if I distinguish traits that I value from traits that simply reflect my tastes and inclinations, I may not want the traits I value now to persist in my future self. For I may learn more in the future about what is fine. In *Republic* IX Plato describes the rational part as a lover of the truth (*R.* 581d10–e2), in contrast to appearances; he exploits that characteristic in claiming that we want the persistence of what is fine, not simply of what appears to us to be fine.[25] If I care about the fine, not simply about what I now regard as fine, I will want my future self to have the traits that result from learning more about the fine. The fact that my future self has an outlook that is a rational development of my present values should matter to me; this rational development concerns Plato in his discussion of the 'ascent' of desire (*Symp.* 210–11).

What matters, then, in self-concern, as Plato understands it, is the preservation of what I value in myself (understood with the modification just mentioned) and the fact that this preservation results from my action. The presence of these connexions makes it true that the later person is the same person as me, despite the various differences between my present self and my later self. If these connexions were not present, then the future person would not be me. Still, it is not the bare fact that the later person is the same person as me that gives me a reason for self-concern, any more than the bare fact that a person is my 'other half' gives me reason for concern (cf. *Symp.* 205d10–206a2). If it happened—impossibly, in Plato's view—that someone could be my later self without having these connexions with me, we could not understand why I should be concerned about him. When the later person is identical to me, my concern about him is understandable insofar as he preserves (or improves) valuable features of the earlier person.

210. Concern for Others

Plato began by using interpersonal propagation (in ordinary reproduction) to explain the character of intrapersonal propagation (in self-preservation). Now he returns from intrapersonal to interpersonal propagation. But the type of interpersonal propagation that is explained by intrapersonal propagation is not the type of interpersonal propagation that was initially described. The initial form of interpersonal propagation was the literal propagation of children by their biological parents: bringing new people into existence. But the propagation that Plato describes later is the alteration of already existent people, when we propagate ourselves in them. It involves making people new, not making new people. Diotima appeals to this sort of motive to explain the actions of legislators, poets, and others who achieve their desire for immortality by impressing the effects of their own actions on the minds and characters of others (208d–209a).

Plato suggests that his analysis of intrapersonal propagation makes this new type of interpersonal propagation easier to understand. He has argued that what I value about intrapersonal propagation is the propagation of the valuable aspects of myself in a person who will exist in the future. Now he points out that the person in whom I propagate these aspects of myself need not be me in the future; it may be another person who already exists now. I can therefore achieve what I value about intrapersonal propagation if I propagate these aspects of myself in another person; if I value intrapersonal propagation, I ought to value interpersonal propagation. Indeed, I sometimes ought to prefer interpersonal propagation, since I cannot always ensure my own continued existence, and this limitation may prevent me from fully realizing in myself everything that I might want to realize in myself. In these cases the reasons that lead me to care about intrapersonal propagation should lead me to prefer propagation of these valuable traits in another person.[26]

In this passage of the *Symposium*, Plato suggests that interpersonal propagation is the next best thing to personal immortality.[27] We might infer that we would have no reason to be interested in interpersonal propagation if the relevant aspects of our characters were immortal. Plato's views about the gods, however, suggest that the mortality of a given trait need not be a necessary condition for the desire for propagation of that trait. In the *Republic* Plato insists that a god cannot be the source of evils, and that a god who is good must also be beneficial (*R*. 379b1–c7). In the *Timaeus* Plato describes the creation of the ordered world as the work of a good god who is free from spite,[28] and so would not make anything worse than he could make it; since he wants everything to be as good as possible, he makes an ordered world out of the precosmic disorder (*Tim*. 29d7–30c1).[29]

Plato wants to explain why the god created a better world rather than a worse world, given that he had to create something. But he also assumes that the god wanted to create something good, rather than simply leaving things as they were. Why does the god care about this? Since he is not mortal, he does not turn to self-propagation as a second best to immortality. Plato seems to assume that the god will want to express his goodness, even when his self-preservation does not require it. The god wants to express his goodness by exercising his capacity to create the sort of goodness that he has, and this desire for self-expression does not depend on any limitation in his capacity to preserve himself.

If, then, we want a full picture of the motives that Plato takes to support interpersonal propagation, we must include the desire to express and extend the traits one values about oneself and to embody them in other things. In mortal agents this desire for extension results in a desire for temporal extension through interpersonal propagation. The *Republic* and *Timaeus* suggest that the desire for self-expression is a source of interpersonal propagation that is prior to the desire for self-preservation.

The remarks about propagation throw some light on the role of happiness in rational desire and on the connexion between happiness and other goods. Plato accepts the rational eudaemonist assumption that every rational agent's ultimate end is her own happiness (*Symp.* 204e3–205a4).[30] He agrees that the rational part of the soul must have a holistic outlook; it transcends the limited and one-sided views that are characteristic of the non-rational parts. He now points out that if my rational part has a holistic and comprehensive outlook, it must also be temporally comprehensive and so must look forward to my future interests. He argues that an appropriately comprehensive concern for my present and my future cannot allow my concerns to be confined to myself; for since I cannot always preserve myself, I must seek to propagate the valuable aspects of myself in other people.

211. Propagation and Love of Other Persons

If Plato has shown that our valuing intrapersonal propagation gives us good reason to value interpersonal propagation, what has he shown about love of particular persons? Diotima suggests that genuine love for other persons can be understood as a case of interpersonal propagation (209a–c). A is attracted to B because B already seems beautiful and fine: a suitable person for receiving the sort of character and personality in which A seeks to propagate himself. The proper process of education causes A to change his mind about the sorts of features that he wants to propagate him in B, and as A corrects his views about what is fine, he also (Diotima assumes) improves his love for B, forming a truer conception of B's good.

When a lover examines different sorts of fine and beautiful things, he eventually comes to see the Form of Beauty itself and so comes to understand the features that all these genuinely admirable things have in common (210a–211c). Still, this ascent of desire from bodies, through souls, characters, knowledge, and so on, to the Form of Beauty does not lead away from concern for persons. Diotima insists that we all seek our own happiness as our ultimate end, and that when we are properly enlightened, we will express our self-concern through interpersonal propagation. Since we want to propagate what is valuable about ourselves, our view about what we want to propagate reflects our view about what is valuable; and the ascent of desire to the Form changes our view about which traits we want to propagate. But a change of view on this question gives us no reason to abandon our concern for persons; for since we are persons, nothing that we can affect can embody the traits that we value in ourselves as well as a person can.[31]

Does this attitude to other persons really have the sort of ethical significance that we normally attach to love of persons? One type of love for persons is a non-exploitative, not purely instrumental concern for the good of others. Is this the sort of love that Plato describes? Why does the fact that another person is suitable for propagating us require us to be concerned about the other person's good?

Plato speaks of the effects of love as 'educating' or 'moulding' (*Phdr.* 252d5–e1) the beloved into the shape that the lover thinks appropriate. What has this to do with the interests of the beloved? If B is moulded into the shape in which he best satisfies A's desire for self-propagation, it seems to be A's interests rather than B's that guide the changes A tries to produce in B. If I make a statue out of a piece of wood, I might be said to 'love' the statue, insofar as I might admire the work I have done (cf. Ar. *EN* 1168a5–9); but this falls short of concern for the interests of the wood (since it has no interests; cf. *EN* 1155b29–31). Why should attitudes to persons be any different, from Plato's point of view?

Plato's eudaemonism helps to explain why Platonic love includes concern for the interests of the other person. Since A is concerned for B as a way of propagating A, and since A cares about A's own interest for A's own sake, A will also care about B for B's own sake, not instrumentally to some further end. For insofar as B propagates A, B deserves the sort of concern that A applies to A. Although A certainly does it all for A's own sake, doing it for B's sake is doing it for A's sake, if B is A's way of propagating A. Just as A cares about the future stages of A as the results of intrapersonal propagation, A has the same reason to care about B as the result of interpersonal propagation. For if B really carries on what A regards as valuable about A, then A has good reason to care about B in the same way as A cares about A.

212. Platonic Love and Platonic Justice

If we accept these claims about Platonic love, do they show why someone whose eros has been appropriately enlightened will also be a just person? In the *Phaedrus* Plato acknowledges that the desire for self-propagation is not confined to people whose souls are completely controlled by the rational part. For he recognizes that different types of lovers mould other people into different types of characters with different outlooks (*Phdr.* 252e–253c). Even if we agree with Plato's theory of love far enough to agree that he has found some basis for a desirable type of concern for the interests of others, we need not agree that this concern gives us the right reason for being just. If Platonic love is conceived as a relation between individual persons, it seems surprising that my concern for another should be based on my success in making him like myself. This may seem an objectionably domineering attitude. How does it constitute a just person's concern for the good of others?

According to Plato, people make mistakes in interpersonal propagation because they take a narrow and one-sided view of themselves, attaching the wrong sort of priority to the outlook of one or another of the non-rational parts. In order to care about self-preservation and propagation, they must be taking the point of view of the rational part, but they do not take this point of view steadily enough to form the right conception of the self to be propagated; as the *Symposium* puts it, they have not ascended far enough through different conceptions of the fine. This is why they take a competitive attitude towards their good and other people's good, believing that the more someone else gets, the less they will get themselves; the goods that they recognize are the 'contested' goods (*Rep.* 586a1–d2). In accumulating these goods for themselves, they form the wrong conception of the self for whom they are accumulating these goods.

Plato's views about self-propagation may be explained by reference to the different degrees of rational control that are described in *Republic* VIII and IX. The deviant people are guided by the decision of the rational part about the ends worth pursuing.[32] But they are still guided by the non-rational parts, insofar as the rational part reaches its decision by simply acquiescing in the ends that appeal to the non-rational parts. The *Symposium* suggests more clearly what would be different if the rational part made decisions on its own initiative without simply acquiescing in the preferences of the non-rational parts.

In describing self-propagation, Plato denies that my conception of my happiness can be fixed independently of my moral beliefs. My conception of my happiness depends on my conception of the kind of future I want for myself; my conception of this future depends on my conception of my future self; and my conception of my future self depends on what I want to 'propagate in the fine', and so on my view of which traits are valuable enough to be propagated. Since I care about my future existence insofar as I regard it as a worthwhile existence, I must have some conception of worthwhile existence that is not simply conceived as a means to continued existence; this conception will tell me whether the satisfaction of my future desires is propagation in the fine. This normative aspect of propagation makes it reasonable to suppose that we discover the composition of happiness by reflexion on justice and the other virtues; we cannot expect to derive our view of the virtues from some prior assumptions about happiness.

In particular, Plato suggests that once we think about what we value and care about in our own future, we will see that our concern for self-preservation should lead us to revise our conception of our good. We will want our pursuits to promote the preservation of ourselves and the states and activities that we value, not simply the satisfaction of the desires that we have now. Once we discover the primacy of rational activity in our good, we discover that p-justice is a component of our good that dominates the external goods on which other people concentrate their efforts.

For this reason, Plato believes that someone who is really guided by the rational part of the soul differs from the deviant people in his attitude to the good of others. The p-just person wants to maintain the control of the rational part in his own soul and therefore will want other people's souls to be guided by the rational part also. But guidance by the rational part, as far as this is possible, is, in Plato's view, more in a person's interest than anything else is.[33] Someone who has the Platonic concern to propagate, and also has a correct conception of his own interest, will be reliably concerned with the good of others.

If this argument succeeds, then Plato's conception of love helps to fill a gap in the argument of the *Republic*. For, according to Plato's view of self-interest and intrapersonal propagation, a rational person has reason to be concerned about other people in whom he propagates himself, just as he has reason to be concerned about future states of himself. We can therefore expect a p-just person to be concerned about the interests of the other people in whom he propagates his p-justice. Since he has this non-instrumental concern for others, he has a reasonable claim to have c-justice. Hence Plato is in a position to claim that his defence of p-justice is also a defence of the c-justice that Thrasymachus originally challenged.

Will this be concern for the good of others for their own sake? Plato cannot justify completely unconditional concern, since the p-just person has no reason to be concerned with another person's interest simply because it is the interest of another person. On the other hand, he can claim to justify non-instrumental concern for another, for the other's sake. In his view, the relevant sort of concern does not imply that we are concerned for the good of others simply because of some further benefit to ourselves. For if we actually propagate ourselves in other people, then we have the same sort of reason to care about the other people as we have to care about ourselves. Plato forces us to ask whether it is reasonable to require a just person to be unconditionally concerned for others. If this is not a reasonable demand, then Plato's defence of concern for others should not be dismissed.

A further doubt may be raised about the extent of concern for others that is justified by Plato's argument. If we grant that concern for propagating myself justifies intrinsic, non-instrumental concern for some others, this does not seem to require concern for many others. Could I not propagate myself, then, without being concerned for many others? We might understand how Plato's theory of love could explain concern of one individual for another in a friendship between individuals—this is how it seems to be used in the *Phaedrus*. But this does not seem to justify the more generalized sort of concern that we demand from morality.

213. The Justice of the Philosopher-Rulers

Plato partly answers this question in the *Republic* by arguing that the philosopher-rulers will be concerned about their community. Plato's remarks about love suggest that the philosophers ought to believe that ruling is in their interest. Their desire for self-propagation leads them to discover and value the qualities that are fully embodied in the Forms, and their desire for interpersonal propagation moves them to want to embody these same qualities in other people. The *Symposium* mentions legislation as a way of expressing one's desire for self-propagation by interpersonal propagation (209a); and such a motive explains the assumptions that Plato makes in the *Republic*.

The philosophers' concern for particular other people is mediated through concern for a larger community. Plato suggests that the desire for propagation is satisfied best by the larger community, and that concern for particular others rests on their relation to the community. Once again he does not imply that the concern for particular people is purely instrumental. If concern for the larger community is justified, then concern for others will not be restricted to a very few people. To this extent Plato can claim to satisfy the moral demands of justice, as they were described at the beginning of the *Republic*.

To show that he has done what he set out to do, Plato introduces three aspects of justice, as it affects the philosopher-rulers, and he argues that the philosophers take proper account of them all: (1) The philosophers' eros has led them to knowledge of the Form of the Good, and this knowledge has given them a single goal for all their actions (519c2–4). (2) They are ready to do their part in a city that is focussed on the common good, not on their own good (519e1–520a5). (3) They are ready to make an appropriate return for the benefits they have received from the city (520d6–e1).

These three aspects of justice have appeared in reverse order in the formulation of the problems about justice in Books I and II. The third aspect recalls Socrates' first statement of Cephalus' claim about justice, that it consists in giving back what one has received (331c1–3). The second recalls Thrasymachus' objection that justice is the good of another, but a harm to the agent (343c1–5). The first expresses the point of view from which Thrasymachus' objection seems powerful; if we are concerned with our happiness, then the other-regarding demands of justice seem indefensible. The argument has followed an 'upward' path from Cephalus' first thoughts about justice to the Form of the Good, and now it follows a 'downward' path (511b3–c2; cf. Ar., *EN* 1095a30–b4) back to the initial beliefs about justice. Although Plato's argument is not at the fourth stage of the Line (since he insists that he lacks knowledge of the Good), he suggests how such an argument ought to go.

His account of eros is meant to show how the self-concerned outlook of an agent seeking his own happiness leads to acceptance of the outlook of a community that is focussed on the common good. The arguments about propagation explain why concern with one's own happiness requires enlightened agents not to focus on their own happiness, to the exclusion of other people's happiness, in all their actions. Propagation requires concern for others in a community, and a community precludes an exclusive focus on the happiness of some members as opposed to others (420b3–421c7); for if the philosopher-ruler were not concerned for the happiness of others—and therefore for their psychic justice—for their own sake, she would not be taking to them the attitude that she takes to her future self, and therefore she would not be propagating herself in them.

From this point of view it is reasonable to demand a fair return for benefits received. This demand for reciprocity and the more general demand to render to others what is due to them (expressed in the Simonidean view of justice, 332a7–8)[34] raise difficulties if we consider the interest of the agent alone (as the calculating unjust people do in *Republic* II); but it is intelligible in the light of concern for a community that rests on reciprocal benefit (secured, in Plato's ideal city, especially by the division of function between the different classes).

In connecting these three aspects of justice, Plato shows how he believes one central area of morality is to be understood. His defence of Cephalus and Simonides also explains why we should accept other claims about justice that Socrates stated without much defence in Book I: the just person is a source of benefit rather than harm (335b–e), and the best rulers are those who are least eager to rule (347b5–e2). Plato recognizes the features of justice that lead us to believe that it expresses an impartial point of view, not focussed on the good of a particular agent. This impartial character of justice, as justice is normally conceived, leads Callicles and Thrasymachus to conclude that a just person must forgo happiness. Plato wants to reject their conclusion without denying the impartial character of justice. The philosopher's concern for the community in which she propagates what she values most about herself gives her reasons to follow the principles that aim at the good of the community rather than her own good.

Plato argues that the philosopher, and therefore the just person, does not have exactly the same obligation to a city that lacks a just constitution and does not train philosopher-rulers to embody their psychic justice in the city as a whole (520a9–c1). In an unjust city, Plato suggests, philosophers should try to keep out of trouble, as though they were sheltering by a wall in a storm (496c5–e2). Even here, however, their conception of their own good is not so independent of the community that they recognize no obligations to it; they remain 'quiet' and 'do their own' (496d6), and avoid injustice and unholy actions (496d9–e1). Socrates in the *Crito* recognizes that he has some obligations to the city in return for what it has given him (*Cri.* 50c7–e1); he does not explain how all the grounds for obligation that he recognizes there can be explained within his general eudaemonist outlook. Plato certainly does not completely fill the gap that Socrates leaves in his account of the ordinary obligations, as he sees them, of justice; but his theory of love and self-propagation suggests how some of these obligations might be understood.

In expressing his view about the character of justice, Plato also expresses his view about the proper character of moral inquiry. He makes his view clearest in recalling so many claims from Book I at this stage of his argument. Although he has spoken harshly of the moral outlook of 'the many', he has not altogether rejected it. While the uninstructed and unreflective assertions of most people are misguided and harmful, these assertions express relatively superficial features of their moral outlook. The outlook of common sense is the one that Plato starts from and, more important, the one he returns to in defending the second and third aspects of justice.

The *Republic* gives us some glimpse of the goal it describes, even though it cannot lead us there. The philosophers enlightened by the Good are expected to see things better in the cave, once they have some practice in applying their knowledge of the Forms (520c1–d1), and the argument of the *Republic* is meant to make this claim plausible. Moral inquiry leads us beyond the 'many justs' that most people, in their unreflective state, do not explicitly distinguish from justice itself, but once we understand justice itself, we see what is reasonable in the intuitions underlying people's moral assertions. We see not only why people are right to suppose that justice requires us to render what is due to other people but also the cause of their mistaken claim (cf. Ar. *EN* 1154a22–25) that justice is not in the agent's interest. They are right to suppose that justice precludes exclusive focus on the agent's interest, since it requires concern for the common good of a community, and they are right to suppose that justice actually conflicts with the agent's interest, if we understand our interest as Thrasymachus understands it. A true conception of one's interest and its relation to the demands of justice allows us to see the truths that are reflected—admittedly distorted, but not beyond recognition—in ordinary beliefs.

In his account of why the philosophers will rule, Plato explains in outline why agents enlightened about their own good have reason to be just. In explaining this, he also reaffirms his view that ordinary moral beliefs are the proper starting point (*archē*) for the 'turning of the soul' through recollection towards an eventual understanding of their rational basis (*archē*).[35] On this point the *Republic*, no less than the *Meno*, reaffirms Plato's confidence in the constructive role of the Socratic elenchos. Although the moral theory, metaphysics, and epistemology of the *Republic* go far beyond Socratic theories, Plato has good reason to regard them as a defence of Socrates' beliefs and commitments about morality and about moral inquiry.

If Plato can justify other-regarding justice to this extent, it does not follow that he can justify all the legitimate demands of morality. For we might insist that the moral claims of other people on us do not depend on their being our friends or on their belonging to some community that we care about. The mere fact that they are other people seems to imply that they are entitled to have their interests taken into account. If we take this view of morality, then we might draw either of two conclusions from Plato: First, we might decide that what can be justified by his sort of argument is only a part of morality, the part that is concerned with fellow members of some community; the rest of morality, on this view, has to be justified by some other sort of argument. Alternatively, we might argue that Plato's form of justification is capable of justifying morality as a whole; on this view, we ought to extend his conception of a community so that it allows concern for other people who do not antecedently, apart from their moral claims on us, belong to the same community, but can properly be regarded as fellow members of a community with us. Although Plato's argument does not answer this question for us, its defence of some other-regarding moral concern is reasonable enough to raise these questions about its connexion to morality as a whole.

214. Conclusions from the *Republic*

Has Plato shown that psychic justice, as he eventually conceives it, is a good in itself, not to be chosen simply for its consequences? We might agree with such a claim about some minimal form of control by the rational part. But the type of control that Plato turns out to have in mind is the type that requires rational choice of ends.[36] Do the reasons that might persuade us that some minimal degree of continence is a good in itself also persuade us that this strong form of rational control is also a good in itself?

We have seen that as the argument of the *Republic* develops we must take more seriously the demand that the rational part of the soul should perform its proper function. If we accept Plato's demand, we can see why the demand for rational control seems reasonable; but we ought to pause for longer than Plato pauses on the claims about the good of performing one's own function as a rational agent.

A further question leads us to the same issue. Does Plato show that p-justice, as he eventually conceives it in the *Republic*, is a dominant part of happiness, important enough to ensure that the p-just person is always happier than the p-unjust person, no matter what else is true of them? We might agree that life is not worthwhile if it involves complete psychic chaos; but why might it not be worth sacrificing some p-justice for a larger supply of other goods? To answer this question, we need to know more about why p-justice is a good in itself and about the ways in which other goods are good; we also need to reexamine the character of the human good and its relation to rational activity.

When we see that this question arises, we come to the most important unfinished element in the argument of the *Republic*. Plato insists, often and appropriately, that we need to examine the nature of justice carefully and that misconceptions about it encourage the belief that justice does not promote happiness. Plato does not insist with equal emphasis on a re-examination of the other apparent source of misconceptions: common descriptions of happiness. But he must plainly have some implicit views on this question; for he cannot expect that the condition of the p-just person will immediately strike everyone as preferable to that of the p-unjust person with abundant external goods and opportunities to use them.

Some of these questions are answered by the theory of love, insofar as Plato suggests that the proper object of self-concern is the propagation of our rational agency. If we can formulate the conception of a person's good that underlies these claims about love, we can see what Plato assumes in arguing for the connexion he sees between justice and happiness. The dialogues themselves say enough for us to sketch the relevant conception. Some of the later dialogues, in particular the *Philebus*, develop the conception more fully. But proper explanation and defence of Plato's conception of the good are left to later Greek moralists, especially Aristotle and the Stoics. The *Republic* is as important for the lines of argument that it suggests as for the conclusions it reaches. Plato correctly suggests that some arguments about the good are worth taking seriously, even though he does not fully defend them himself.

19

Pleasure, Intelligence, and the Good

215. The Scope of the *Philebus*

The *Philebus* begins with a dispute between Socrates and Philebus about whether pleasure or intelligence (or wisdom; *phronēsis*) is the good; Philebus takes the hedonist side, and Socrates defends the claims of intelligence. In *Republic* VI Plato rejects both these accounts of the good (*R.* 505b–d) and, indeed, expresses doubt about the prospects of any attempt to define the good reductively, by reference to properties that can be understood independently of the good.[1] In the *Philebus* Plato examines both pleasure and intelligence more thoroughly.

The first issue concerns the classification and evaluation of different types of pleasures. In the *Republic* Plato claims that the good cannot be identified with pleasure, because there are both good and bad pleasures; nonetheless, he claims that insofar as just people have the best life, they also have the most pleasant life.[2] The presuppositions of these claims are examined in the *Philebus*. In arguing against the claim of pleasure to be the good, Socrates insists on the diversity of pleasures (12c–d) and claims that the initial questions about the value of 'pleasure' (in the singular) ought to be reconsidered once we have a clearer idea of the different pleasures and their different values. In fact, the bulk of the dialogue is taken up with the classification and discussion of types of pleasure. This discussion ought to explain how we can legitimately compare the pleasure in different lives, and whether such comparison supports the conclusions drawn in the *Republic*.

In the *Republic* Plato opposes the identification of knowledge with the good by arguing that the relevant sort of knowledge would have to be knowledge of the good, so that a reduction of the good to knowledge would fail. The *Philebus* examines the claims of knowledge in its broader examination of intelligence; it examines the different types of knowledge and their different places in the good life.

Plato's claims in the *Republic* about pleasure and knowledge presuppose some claims about the good. He presupposes further claims about the good in his defence of justice; for in claiming that the just person is always happier than the unjust person, but not that justice is sufficient for happiness, he appeals to some conception of the good and its composition, but he does not try to defend this conception. In the *Philebus* he argues for a conception of the good that explains the failure of pleasure and intelligence; it may also clarify the claims made in the *Republic* on behalf of justice.

These questions about pleasure and the good are explored in the context of a metaphysical discussion that is inserted into the discussion of pleasure. First, Socrates raises the problem of the one and the many. Later he introduces the limit and the unlimited. These discussions are meant to help us to answer the Socratic 'What is it?' question about pleasure, intelligence, and the good. Although this question is Socratic, Socrates in the early dialogues does not ask it about these things. In the *Republic* Plato presents his views more explicitly than Socrates did, but only the *Philebus* focusses directly on the nature of intelligence, pleasure, and the good.

The *Philebus* is interesting partly because its argument is complex and detailed. It is also obscure and difficult in many places. Any attempt at a brief account of its contribution to Plato's developing views on ethics will oversimplify. But an oversimplified account may nonetheless be useful if it suggests a plausible sketch of the argument and of the significance of the dialogue for the understanding of Plato's moral views.[3] There is good reason to suppose that Aristotle is influenced by the *Philebus*;[4] the dialogue is therefore especially important for understanding the connexion between Platonic and Aristotelian moral theory.

216. The Diversity of Pleasures

In the opening discussion, Socrates warns against any general pronouncements about the value of pleasure. He mentions the great variety of pleasures and the variety of people who enjoy them:

> We say that someone acting intemperately takes pleasure, but we also say that someone acting temperately takes pleasure in acting temperately itself. Again, we say that someone who is being foolish and is full of foolish beliefs and hopes takes pleasure, but we also say that someone who is being intelligent takes pleasure in being intelligent itself. (12c8–d4)

Socrates remarks that the temperate person takes pleasure precisely in being temperate, whereas he does not suggest that the intemperate person takes pleasure in being intemperate or in acting intemperately. Such a suggestion about the intemperate person would be false; for an intemperate person is one who enjoys, say, some particular physical pleasure and is indifferent to the question of whether this is an intemperate enjoyment. The temperate person, by contrast, is not indifferent to the fact that this is a temperate action.

In marking this difference, Plato draws attention to the distinction between the cause and the intentional object of a pleasure. It is true to say both that the cause of an intemperate person's pleasure is an intemperate action and that it is a physical pleasure; but only the second description picks out the intentional object of the pleasure by saying what he enjoys about the action. The cause and the object of pleasure may be the very same event, but only some properties of the event constitute the object of the pleasure.[5]

The distinction between cause and object is relevant to Protarchus' claim about the variety and uniformity of pleasure. In reply to Socrates' remarks about the variety of pleasures, he says: 'Yes, Socrates, these pleasures are from contrary things, but they are not themselves contrary to each other. For how could one pleasure not be most similar of all things to another pleasure, since it is the similarity of a thing to itself?' (12d7–e2). Protarchus points out correctly that a mere difference in the cause of two pleasures does not show that there is any relevant difference between the pleasures themselves. Oil from different wells or milk from different cows might not differ in anything except its origin; if this is the only difference between pleasures, the fact that both good and bad people enjoy pleasures does not show that some pleasures are good and others are bad.

In Plato's view, this answer fails to meet Socrates' claims about the variety of pleasure. Socrates claims more than that different pleasures have different causes; he also claims that they have different objects and that this difference justifies the claim that the pleasures themselves are contrary to each other. Plato believes that the fact that a cruel person, say, enjoys inflicting pain on someone else is not bad simply because someone else will suffer or because it is bad to be cruel. A hedonist might say that the cruel person's pleasure is one good feature of the situation, however much the goodness may be outweighed by bad features of the situation. According to Plato, however, the cruel person's enjoyment is a further bad feature. Even if we set aside the other bad aspects of cruelty, and even if we can avoid the bad effects on other people, the fact that someone takes pleasure in this sort of thing is bad in itself.

Protarchus objects that Socrates' own belief in the one thing called 'the F' common to the many Fs actually conflicts with Socrates' claim that pleasures themselves are contrary to each other because of their objects.[6] Since all pleasures must have in common the property of being pleasures, they cannot be different 'in respect of being pleasures' or 'qua pleasures' (*kath'hoson ge hēdonai*; 13c5); hence, Protarchus infers, they cannot be contrary to each other, and we cannot say that some are good and some are bad in respect of being pleasures.

Socrates explains why Protarchus' argument misuses the Socratic claim about the one and the many. The argument exploits an ambiguity in 'qua pleasures', which might mean (1) 'qua some pleasure or other' or (2) 'qua the sorts of pleasures they are'. Even if G and H are essentially species of F, and so share the properties essential to being F, it may nonetheless be essential to G and H to be contrary to each other, qua the species of F that they are.

This point is made clear in Socrates' examples of colours and shapes (12e3–13a5; cf. *M.* 74b2–75a9). Red does not differ from green in respect of being some colour or other; for (we suppose for this purpose) the same definition of colour applies to both. But nothing can be simply colour without being some specific sort of colour, and the features that make one colour red are different from those that make another colour green. Red and green do not differ simply in properties external to what is necessary and essential for being colour; they do not, for instance, differ only insofar as red happens to be found on berries and green on leaves. In offering Protarchus this illustration, Socrates seeks to show that the contrariety between pleasures cannot be dismissed as mere contrariety in their causes; it is also contrariety in the specific sorts of pleasures themselves.

Socrates has shown, then, that Protarchus has no good reason for rejecting his suggestion that the character of the object of a pleasure infects the character of the pleasure itself. While further argument is needed to vindicate his suggestion, his remarks so far suggest why the suggestion is plausible. If there were nothing to choose between different pleasures themselves, then I ought not to mind whether I get the pleasure resulting from being a cruel person or the pleasure resulting from being a kind person, if I consider the pleasure itself; my objection ought to rest simply on the cruel person's choice of means. But the cruel person's pleasure essentially involves the thought that someone else is suffering as a result of his action; a pleasure that did not involve looking favourably on the content of such a thought would be a different sort of pleasure. The kind person will reject the pleasure that involves such a belief. It is not simply that the cruel person must have acted cruelly; if that were all, then the evil would be over and done with by the time the cruel person takes pleasure in what he has done, and the fact that he enjoys having done it would be no more objectionable than the fact that he has done it.[7]

If this is the right way to understand Socrates' examples and arguments, then we ought to expect him to argue more fully for the connexion that he assumes between pleasure and belief. Examination of his remarks about temperate and intemperate people's pleasures suggests that his objection to Protarchus rests on his view that the relation between pleasure and belief cannot be the purely external relation that would have to hold if Protarchus' view about the goodness of all pleasure were right.

217. One and Many

Before he examines pleasure, Socrates takes up more general issues about the one and the many. He suggests that Protarchus' claims about pleasure rest on a misunderstanding of the relation of one and many (13e2–14c10).

Two problems about one and many are taken to deserve attention: (1) Man is one in the many particular men. (2) Sound is one in the many different types of sound. The first of these problems is about universals and particulars; the second is about relations between more and less determinate universals.[8]

Plato seems to refer to the first problem in his remarks about positing 'man as one, and ox as one, and the fine as one and the good as one' (15d4–6). These 'units' (*henades*, *monades*) are contrasted with things that come to be and perish (15a1–2); this contrast recalls the description of Forms in the middle dialogues.[9] The discussion of sounds in connexion with grammar and music suggests the second problem rather than the first (16c5–17a5); the task seems to be to distinguish different types of sounds, not to distinguish different token sounds from the universal sound that they instantiate.

It is not surprising, however, that Plato takes these two problems to be connected. In the middle dialogues, references to 'the many Fs' often mark the contrast between various types of F and the F itself. When Plato considers how concentration on the many Fs can prevent us from finding and defining the F itself, he might be taken to warn against confusion of the universal with its many particular instances; normally, however, he criticizes the error of those who appeal to sensible properties in the belief that a list of them provides an adequate definition of the F itself.

The *Philebus* helps us to see why Plato speaks in such similar terms of two different errors.[10] If we understand the first error, it is easier to understand the less obvious second error. We will not find a Socratic definition if we simply give a list of particular examples, for there is no limit in principle to the number of particular Fs, and their number is irrelevant to the nature of F. The definition of F is supposed to explain what makes a member of the list an appropriate member of it, and we do not answer this question simply by giving the list. If this is the objection to particulars, an equally strong objection may be raised against an appeal to a list of specific types. Such a list also includes irrelevant features, and it does not explain why the different types making up the list properly belong on it. This is Meno's error, repeated by the sight-lovers in *Republic* V. It is not surprising or unreasonable, then, if Plato thinks that the two relations between the one and the many raise similar questions when definitions are considered.

The *Philebus* adds an important point to this contrast between the one F and the many Fs. Plato insists that we have not understood the nature of F if we simply offer a description of the F and contrast this with the many Fs. For even if our description is right, it does not help us as it should towards understanding the F-ness displayed in the many Fs. A proper understanding of the F and a proper understanding of the species of F go together.

In the *Meno* Socrates does not deny that Meno has correctly identified the species of virtue. In fact, his illustration, referring to the nature of shape, assumes that we can correctly identify square, triangle, and so on as species of shape; he does not challenge this classification of shapes. In *Republic* V, however, Plato seems to challenge the classification offered by the sight-lovers. At any rate, his argument is effective only if it claims that each of the many Fs is also not-F in the precise area in which the sight-lovers identify it with the F (so that justice, for instance, cannot be simply returning what you have borrowed, even in transactions between individuals).[11] If this is right, the properties favoured by the sight-lovers cannot divide justice into the appropriate species.

In the *Phaedrus* Plato makes this objection clearer by emphasizing the importance of dividing reality at the naturally appropriate joints (*Phdr.* 265e1–266b1). It would be a mistake to take our classification of types of F uncritically from common sense and to confine ourselves to looking for one F in those many Fs.

Instead, we ought to expect that the discovery of the nature of the one F will lead us to change our minds about the important respects in which the various Fs are similar or different.

Similarly, the *Philebus* raises a question about the proper division of pleasures: should we include the objects of different pleasures among the differentiating features that divide pleasures at the natural joints? If we agree with Protarchus, we will suppose that the different objects reflect superficial and irrelevant differences between pleasures; if we agree with Socrates, we will suppose that different objects reflect essential differences among pleasures, corresponding to the differences marked in the *Phaedrus* among types of eros.[12] Plato argues that an answer to this question is inseparable from an answer to the Socratic question about what pleasure is.

218. Limit and Unlimited

Plato introduces a distinction between the limit (or 'determinant') and the unlimited (or 'indeterminate') into his discussion of the One and the Many. He speaks of the many as 'the things that come to be and are unlimited' (15b5), suggesting that the many Fs are to be identified with the unlimited. To recognize the one F and the many Fs is only the first step (16c9–d2); when we recognize the many, we should not at once regard them as unlimited. Between the one and the unlimited, we should recognize a definite number, and only when we have found the appropriate number should we dismiss the one into the unlimited (16d3–e2). In Plato's example of sound, the finding of the definite number seems to be the identification of specific vowels and consonants (17b3–9). He refers, then, to the discovery of the right species of the original genus, and contrasts this with the recognition of indeterminacy.

Once again the argument of *Republic* V may help to clarify Plato's concerns. He describes the sight-lovers as identifying beauty with different sorts of colour, shape, and so on. A correct account of beauty itself will not necessarily accept these as the appropriate species of beauty, and so they will not be included among the 'limited number' that we discover in our inquiry into the genuine species of beauty. For this reason we will not be satisfied by the simple dichotomy between the one and the unlimited many. It is nonetheless true that beauty shows itself in the different properties recognized by the sight-lovers and in the many different particulars that instantiate these properties; and so we must recognize this fact also. Plato describes our recognition of this fact as our dismissal of the original one into the unlimited.

Plato argues, then, that if we understand the Socratic demand for a definition of the one F in the many Fs, then we must seek an account of the variety of Fs. In this case, understanding the right principles for classifying pleasures is the same as understanding what pleasure is. For this reason the *Philebus* continues Socratic inquiry, even though the form of its questions may seem different from the questions in the Socratic dialogues.

219. Limit and Norm

When Socrates returns (23c1–d1) to the division among the unlimited, the limit, and the limited that results from the imposition of a limit on the unlimited, he adds a fourth item, 'the cause of the mixture' (23d7–8), which imposes a limit on the unlimited. Does he mean to draw the same distinctions that he drew in the earlier introduction of this division?[13]

The examples that are introduced at this stage seem to suggest a different distinction. Earlier the imposition of a limit on the unlimited seemed to be the recognition of the principles of division of the genus into species. Now, however, Plato is concerned with things, properties, and states of affairs that are capable of conforming to, or embodying, some norm, but do not contain any normative principle within themselves. If we consider things as hot and cold, we are not thereby thinking of them as approaching any completion (*telos*; 24b1) or norm; to be hot is not to approximate any standard of complete or perfect hotness beyond which nothing hotter is possible. By contrast, lines are straight or circular, colours match, and shoes fit to some degree that approximates to some complete or perfect limit beyond which no increase is possible.

This distinction between unlimited and limited does not necessarily divide things into two disjoint classes. On the contrary, as Plato suggests, a given pan of water may be described as hot, and as hotter than the water in the refrigerator; to this extent it has an indefinite or 'unlimited' property. But if it has been heated to the right heat for making tea, it also has an appropriately definite or 'limited' degree of heat; as Plato says, 'it has got a <definite> quantity' (24d3). Other examples of the 'imposition of limit'—health and seasonable temperature (25e–26b)—also belong to things that have the 'unlimited' properties, but do not merely have these, since they have reached the appropriate norm.[14] Being 'limited' does not involve simply having some determinate temperature (one hundred degrees Celsius, say), but having the right temperature in relation to some norm.

Socrates wants to use this contrast between limit and unlimited to support a further claim about the source of the appropriate limit. This source is the 'cause of the mixture'. The principle he extracts from the discussion is this: (1) If (a) W is some whole of which F and G are constituents, (b) W is H, (c) H is a 'limited' property, similar to straightness, etc., and (d) F and G are 'unlimited' properties, similar to hotness, etc.; then (e) the cause of the H in W is something external to F and G (27a–b). If this principle is correct, then it follows that if we want to explain why W is H—if we want to identify the feature of W that explains W's being H—then the relevant feature cannot be F or G; for F and G do not explain the normative and limit-imposing element that is essential to H and hence to explaining why W is H. To explain why someone's body is healthy, for instance, it is not enough to say that heat and cold are present in it. A complete explanation must say that heat and cold are present to the right degree, and in the right balance, to reach the norm implied by the nature of health. We therefore need to show that a healthy body contains something that combines hot and cold appropriately, not simply that it contains heat and cold.

Socrates applies his principle (1) to the question about the good life (27c–d). He reaches (without explicitly formulating it) this principle: (2) If (a) happiness (= the best life) is a whole of which pleasure and pain are constituents, (b) happiness is good, (c) goodness is a limited property, and (d) pleasantness and painfulness are unlimited properties; then (e) the cause of the goodness in happiness is something external to pleasure and pain. This principle implies that an account of happiness must describe it as something more than a quantity of pleasure and pain. There must be some other normative component in happiness that determines the appropriate level of pleasure and pain to ensure that they constitute something good.

220. Questions about Limit and Unlimited

The connexion between Plato's different remarks about limited and unlimited is difficult to see. His earlier remarks seemed to apply to all generic properties and their species; now, however, Plato seems to suggest that some properties (e.g., hotness) are inherently unlimited, whereas others (e.g., the right heat for making bread rise or the boiling point of water) are inherently limited. Moreover, the present discussion does not seem to be connected specifically, as the previous discussion was, with taxonomy; the right heat for bread to rise, the right heat for the crops to grow, and so on, are not species of heat. In one case the relevant 'limits' seem to be taxonomic; in the other they seem to be normative.[15]

We must conclude that Plato does not mean to make the same point here that he made earlier in contrasting limit and unlimited. Why, then, does he use the same terms? Are his points closely enough connected to justify him in speaking of them in the same terms?

He has some reason for using the same terms if he wants to show that in some cases the taxonomic and the normative divisions are connected. The connexion is clear in the examples of spelling and music: these disciplines not only classify different sounds or letters but also describe their permissible combinations in correctly spelled words and correctly played chords. While it is not clear that knowledge of permissible combinations underlies the taxonomy of sounds, considered in themselves, it is reasonable to claim that it is part of the understanding of types of musical notes, spoken sounds, or written letters. We understand, for instance, the different shapes that can be used to form a letter A, by knowing about writing and spelling; mere inspection of the physical shape of a letter will not tell us what letter it is unless we also know that it can appropriately be used in spelling this or that word. In these cases the proper taxonomy results from normative constraints.

Normative classification is examined further in the *Statesman*, in a discussion of measurement (beginning at *St.* 283c3).[16] Plato distinguishes two types of crafts. Some crafts involve the measurement of quantities in purely quantitative terms to determine which is greater than another; other crafts involve comparison with a norm. In the second case we do not compare larger and smaller against each other; we compare both with a third thing, the 'norm' or 'measure' that fixes the degree of each that is appropriate for the purpose (283e8–284b2). In choosing an amount of something, we can say we are aiming at a 'mean' or 'intermediate' quantity, but this quantity is not itself determined by purely quantitative means; we find the right 'measure' by finding the appropriate quantity to reach some standard that is itself defined in non-quantitative terms (284e2–8). This measure is the sort of 'limit' that Plato is looking for in the *Philebus*.

The connexion between the taxonomic and the normative 'limits' elucidates Plato's discussion of pleasure. We might suppose that the appropriate division between pleasures would depend on features of pleasures that could be defined and recognized from an ethically neutral point of view, without reference to any views about their goodness. Plato rejects this view about pleasure; he argues that a correct understanding of pleasure presupposes a normative 'limit' that depends on a true conception of the good life and of the relations of different types of pleasure to the good life.

The demand for a normative limit explains and generalizes Plato's objections in *Republic* V to the procedure of the sight-lovers. If they were right, then we could understand justice by referring to types of just action (people, and so on) classified by rules stated in non-evaluative terms (giving back what you have borrowed, and so on).[17] Plato argues that the relevant rules have to be stated in evaluative terms; giving back what you have borrowed is just only in some circumstances, if it is done, as Aristotle says, 'when one ought, as one ought', and so on (*EN* 1106b18–23). The discussion of measure in the *Statesman* indicates this connexion among the objections to the sight-lovers, the demand for a normative limit, and Aristotle's doctrine of the mean.

In the middle dialogues Plato uses this feature of moral properties to explain why they cannot be sensible properties. The *Statesman* refers to this objection to sensible properties when Plato remarks that 'the most important and most valuable things' cannot be explained by appeal to sensible likenesses (*St.* 285d9–286b7). This remark immediately follows the division between two types of measurement; the whole passage in the *Statesman* helps to show the connexion between the concerns of *Republic* V and those of the *Philebus*.[18]

It is reasonable, then, for the *Philebus* to discuss both (1) the classification of different types of pleasure (31b), and (2) the imposition of limit on pleasures in order to achieve the good.[19] The completion of the second task presupposes completion of the first; for how will we know which types of pleasure belong in the good life if we do not know what types of pleasure there are? It is less obvious that the completion of the first task requires completion of the second; but if Plato is right to claim that in some cases classification rests on normative principles, he may be able to show that this is true in the case of pleasures. If the right classification of pleasures depends partly on our view about their relation to the good, we cannot expect to postpone our inquiry into pleasure and the good until we have found an ethically neutral classification of pleasures. Why should we suppose, however, that the right classification of pleasures depends on the right conception of their relation to the good?

221. The Choice of Pleasures

Plato argues that the general principles about limit and unlimited apply to pleasure and good because pleasure is unlimited, and the good requires the imposition of limit. In this case limit must be imposed by intelligence. To indicate the role of intelligence in the good life, Socrates (28c) describes the role of intelligence in the universe as a whole. The cosmic function of intelligence in the cosmos as a whole is to produce fine, admirable, and beneficial results from elements that, left to themselves, would produce only disorder (30b). Similarly, in the individual person's life, intelligence is needed to find the combination of pleasures whose pursuit achieves one's good.

The claim that pleasure is unlimited is simply the claim that being pleasant does not imply any approach to complete pleasantness, beyond which no further degree of pleasantness is possible. A life is good, by contrast, insofar as it approaches complete goodness, which requires just the right amount of pleasure. Insofar as the good is the end we are aiming at in pursuing pleasure, 'good' and 'pleasant' are not the same concepts.

Philebus believes he can make this concession without abandoning hedonism (27e7–9). Indeed, he actually assumes that the unlimited character of pleasure follows from its being uniformly good: 'for pleasure would not all be good if it were not in fact naturally unlimited in quantity and in degree <of more or less>' (27e7–9).[20] We can agree that pleasantness is unlimited, and therefore distinct from goodness, while still advocating the maximization of pleasure. The rational person planning her life can follow simple rules prescribed by intelligence, with the aim of maximizing the balance of pleasure over pain. This might be said to impose some formal 'limit', since the goodness of the good life is imposed by something outside the pleasure and pain themselves. But it is a rather minimal limit that imposes no restriction on the maximization of pleasure. Philebus suggests that a minimal interpretation of Socrates' claims about goodness and limit really involves no substantial restriction on the pursuit of pleasure.[21]

Socrates, however, maintains that the way in which goodness requires limit and order implies that the pursuit of pleasure has to be restricted by intelligence. He still needs to argue at length for this claim, but he has already given some reason for taking it seriously. In the opening discussion he claims that, at least in some cases, different objects of enjoyment imply different pleasures. The policy of maximizing pleasure would be intelligible if we could set out to maximize a single quantity, but if pleasures differ according to their objects, it cannot be reasonable simply to accumulate pleasures without regard to their objects.

Socrates suggests that pleasure taken in good states and activities is good pleasure and that pleasure resulting from bad states and activities is bad pleasure. To distinguish the different types of pleasure, we must distinguish good and bad activities; hence we must refer to the good in distinguishing types of pleasure. The task of intelligence, therefore, cannot simply be the task of picking some definite quantity (defined in purely qualitative terms); it is primarily the task of picking the right sorts of activities and the pleasures attached to them.

We have now said enough about Plato's views on pleasure to understand the point of his remarks about the one and the many and about the limited and the unlimited; the initial claims about pleasures and their objects show that he is developing a single line of argument: (1) He has emphasized the importance of inquiring into species. The pursuit of an answer to the Socratic 'What is F?' question ought not to divert us from an examination of the species and varieties of F; for sometimes that is the only way to understand the nature of F itself. Socrates' remarks on the variety of pleasures illustrate this point. If we did not understand the variety and contrariety of pleasures, we would not understand the internal connexion between a pleasure and its object; if we did not understand that, we would not understand the nature of pleasure itself. (2) He has spoken of the limit and the unlimited both in connexion with classification and in connexion with normative design. Both aspects are relevant to those cases of classification that involve normative discrimination. Socrates has suggested that the classification of pleasures is one of those cases; for the right division of pleasures depends on the goodness or badness of their objects, and so depends on the place of different pleasures in a good life.

222. False Pleasures

Plato has already suggested that someone who takes pleasure in the wrong things makes himself worse off precisely insofar as he enjoys such things, because they are the things he enjoys, not because of some further effects. On this view, judgments of value enter not simply in considering the consequences of the pleasures but also in the estimate of the value of the pleasures themselves. This point is developed in the discussion of false pleasures. At first sight, the prominence of these rather unusual pleasures in an ethical discussion is surprising, but it is easy to understand once we see that Plato focusses on the connexion between pleasure and belief, and argues that the beliefs and judgments connected with a pleasure are not extrinsic to its value but determine whether the pleasure itself should be accepted as a part of a person's good.

The discussion of falsity in pleasures concerns four varieties:

1. False anticipatory pleasures: I take pleasure in something by anticipation, when in fact it will not happen (32b–40e).
2. False pleasures based on false anticipation of the degree of pleasure: my comparison of a future state with a present pain leads me to expect that the future state will be more pleasant than it will, in fact, turn out to be (41a–42c).
3. Falsity arising from misconception of the middle state: I suppose there is nothing more to pleasure than relief from pain, and so I suppose I have

achieved pleasure in cases where in fact I have really achieved something different. In these cases I confuse the intermediate life with the life of pleasure (42c–44a).

4. Falsity arising from misunderstanding of a mixed condition: I think I am simply enjoying pleasure, but in fact I am in a mixed condition of pleasure and pain (44a–50e).

These are different ways that falsity can arise in pleasures; they are not all varieties of 'false pleasures' in the same sense of the phrase. In the first two cases the false pleasures are still genuinely pleasures, not some other state. Plato insists that he does not mean that they are not pleasures, any more than he thinks false beliefs are not beliefs; indeed, he strongly insists on the analogy between pleasure and belief (40b2–c2).[22] In the third and fourth cases, however, the falsity is rather different. In the third case we do not have a genuine pleasure, but confuse pleasure with a different state, whereas in the fourth case we confuse a state of pleasure with a mixed state of pleasure and pain. In the third and fourth cases, as opposed to the first two, our state is not an unqualified state of pleasure.

Plato believes that all these aspects of falsity in a life aiming at pleasure help to explain why maximization of pleasure cannot be a reasonable policy for the best life. He need not show that a convinced hedonist can be persuaded by hedonist arguments to admit that a life devoted to these sorts of pleasures is bad. On the contrary, if hedonist arguments could explain what is bad about the pursuit of these sorts of pleasures, objections to a life devoted to such pleasures would not constitute an objection to hedonism. Plato's task is more complicated. He has to show that there is something clearly bad about each of these lives and that a hedonist cannot identify what is bad about them.

Plato need not, however, assume the falsity of hedonism from the start. A detailed account of pleasures helps to show what beliefs about the good affect our judgments about pleasure. Plato does not simply assert without argument that our intuitive views about the good rule out pleasure as the good. He also shows how plausible judgments about different types of pleasures rely on these intuitive views about the good, and so he shows how difficult it is to reject these intuitive views.

False anticipatory pleasures illustrate Plato's general point. On hedonist grounds, these pleasures seem no less desirable than any other pleasure, since the false belief is (according to Protarchus' original view) simply the cause of the pleasure and so does not affect the character of the pleasure itself. If false pleasures are unwelcome to a hedonist, this is only because discovery of the falsity of the anticipation produces the pain of disappointment.[23]

This hedonist response does not seem to explain what is really wrong with false anticipatory pleasures. We object to them because we do not want our pleasures to rest on deception. The hedonic disadvantages of false pleasures might be outweighed or mitigated if we could get used to forming less intense feelings of disappointment in the frustration of our expectations, or if we could avoid finding out the truth in cases where the instrumental disadvantages of deception would not be too serious.[24] But Plato might reasonably point out that these strategies for removing the disadvantages (from the hedonist point of view) of false pleasures do not really persuade us that they are desirable; indeed, the view that these strategies would make false pleasures desirable or unobjectionable betrays failure to see what is wrong with false pleasures in the first place. If our reason for avoiding false pleasures does not fall under hedonist instrumental strategies, then hedonism cannot give an account of what we take to be valuable about these aspects of a person's life.

The account of false anticipatory pleasures suggests the general form of Plato's objection to the different sorts of false pleasures. In order to have false anticipatory pleasures, we must suffer from some recognizable defect, in this case the cognitive defect that gives us the false anticipations. We are justified in preferring to be free of this defect, and so the sort of life that cannot exist without the defect cannot be the best life. We can perhaps go further. If we could have a life that contained pleasure without the cognitive defect involved in false anticipatory pleasure, then we would have reason to prefer that life over the one containing false anticipatory pleasure; but the hedonist requires us to say that the two lives are equally good. This is the basis of a legitimate objection to hedonism.

In other cases misconceptions about the nature of pleasure and its relations to pain and to the intermediate state actually cause us to believe that we are having pleasure when in fact we are in some different state. This possible misconception about pleasure and pain is especially relevant to the sorts of pleasures that Callicles advocates in the *Gorgias*; Plato alludes to these in discussing the especially intense pleasures that seem to grow more intense according to the size of the gap they fill (44b–c). These pleasures require greater pains and deprivations in order to produce greater pleasures, and so seem to require us to make ourselves worse off in order to enjoy the maximum pleasure.

This is the point that Socrates makes against Callicles in describing the coward's special susceptibility to pleasure. The intense pleasures that require a background of pain absorb more and more attention; they therefore reduce the range of other activities that we might otherwise prefer. This is why Plato suggests that they depend on some bad condition of body and soul, and not on a virtue (45e5–7).[25] This is the sort of life that an advocate of such pleasures has to regard as the happy life (47b4–7). If this is so, then the hedonist who advocates such pleasures cannot explain our view that some particular conditions of body and soul are better than others.

223. Better and Worse Pleasures

Plato's objection to the intense Calliclean pleasures helps to explain how he picks out better pleasures. Calliclean pleasures, like other false pleasures, require us to harm ourselves in order to enjoy them, insofar as they require some defect of knowledge, physical condition, or character. The pure pleasures, by contrast, do not require us to harm ourselves in order to enjoy them; and so to that extent they do not conflict with our other judgments about suitable parts of a good life. The virtuous person's pleasure in acting virtuously depends only on the true belief that one is acting virtuously. It therefore does not rely on some background of pain or ignorance that evidently makes a life worse. Plato's objections to some forms of pleasure help to explain his reasons for accepting other forms of pleasure.

Pure pleasures are clear examples of the sorts of pleasures that do not require the cultivation of a defective state as their background. Plato does not mean, however, that virtuous people allow only pure pleasures in their lives (62e3–64a6). When he includes some pleasures and excludes others, he does not consider primarily whether they involve the satisfaction of bodily needs and deficiencies; he considers whether they 'go with health, temperance, and the whole of virtue' (63e3). A virtuous person and a vicious person may both enjoy eating a meal, but they do not enjoy the same aspect of it. The virtuous person enjoys it as a healthy and appropriate physical pleasure, while the vicious person enjoys it simply as a physical pleasure. Once again, the object of their enjoyment determines the value of their pleasure.[26]

Plato's reasons for accepting some forms of pleasure into a good life do not imply acceptance of hedonism. For the judgments that explain why the virtuous person's pleasures are better than the intense but unhealthy physical pleasure of the vicious person are not available to a hedonist. The hedonist cannot recognize a difference between the two ways of life except as strategies for maximizing pleasure; Plato argues that the hedonist cannot give grounds for preferring the virtuous person's life on this basis.

It is not necessarily unfair if Plato picks some rather gross physical pleasures. It is no reply to him if we say that more refined hedonists prefer more appealing pleasures; for the question is whether the refined hedonists can justify their choice on hedonistic grounds.[27] Plato might concede that two different people, applying hedonist principles, could choose different types of pleasures. But if there is nothing to choose between their two lives on hedonist grounds, that is itself an objection to the hedonist conception of value. Plato need not argue, then, that a hedonist must advocate the pursuit of the grossest pleasures; he need only show that a hedonist cannot explain why we should avoid such pleasures.

This objection to quantitative hedonism is first presented in the *Gorgias*, when Plato suggests that if purely quantitative considerations are all that matter, the coward's pleasures may be equal to, or greater than, those of the brave person.[28] To support this objection, Plato needs to show that the disadvantages of cowardice cannot be adequately represented in purely hedonist terms; but he does not try to show this in the *Gorgias*. *Republic* IX does not directly confront hedonism, although it provides one important element of the line of argument in the *Philebus*, insofar as it suggests that the object of a pleasure makes some important difference to the character of the pleasure itself.

The *Philebus*, then, marks a significant advance in Plato's reflexions on pleasure. He sees that pleasure deserves to be studied in its own right and that a proper understanding of the connexion between pleasure and its object strengthens his objections to hedonism as an account of the good. The point of his argument is not to show that a consistent hedonist position is impossible. He wants to show that the unrestricted pursuit of pleasure rests on judgments of value that turn out to be unacceptable as soon as they are clearly formulated.

224. The Character of the Good

We may still find it unsatisfactory, however, if Plato relies simply on intuitive judgments about the goodness and badness of different states that underlie different types of pleasure. These judgments deserve more confidence if Plato can show that they reflect a reasonable conception of the good. We have seen that in earlier dialogues, and especially in the *Republic*, he relies heavily on judgments about the goodness of justice and the contribution of justice to happiness, without trying to show that he has the right conception of the good. In the *Philebus* he tries to fill this gap in his argument. Aristotle argues that a discussion of virtue and happiness must begin from an account of the nature of happiness and, in particular, must recognize that happiness is complete and self-sufficient (*EN* I 7). In the *Philebus* Plato sees the importance of Aristotle's question about the nature of happiness and answers it in ways that closely anticipate Aristotle's answers.

Socrates says he has had a dream (or perhaps he was awake) and heard that the good is neither pleasure nor intelligence but some third thing, different from both and superior to each (20b6–9). He secures agreement on four features of the good:

1. It is complete (*teleon*; 20d1).
2. It is adequate (*hikanon*; 20d4).
3. It is universally attractive; every agent who knows it pursues it, wants to get it, and cares nothing about anything else unless the agent can achieve this other thing together with goods (20d7–10; cf. *Rep.* 505de).
4. It lacks nothing, needs nothing added (20e5–21a2).[29]

Probably the fourth condition is intended to express, or to follow from, the previous ones; Socrates introduces it not as a new condition for the good but as the appropriate question to ask once we consider the choice between two lives that both represent themselves as realizing the good. It therefore seems to be what he means by the first two conditions.

The third condition is puzzling. The point of it seems to be that a reference to the good should be omnipresent in explaining the desires and concerns of an agent who knows it. Perhaps Plato means this as a test for an accurate description of the good; it must be one that makes the good universally attractive to an agent who knows that it meets this description. If we say that the good is F, then we must be able to show that any agent will want to get F and care nothing about anything besides F unless the agent can get this other thing together with something F.

Plato probably means that if we describe the good as F, then it should be clear that an agent who knows this about the good will regard getting something F, or something contributing to F, as a necessary condition for the desirability of other things. If this is what Plato means, he is repeating the demand for completeness and adequacy. Suppose our description of the good as F did not describe something complete. In that case we might desire x as G, even though G contributed nothing to being F; G would be a desirable property that fell outside being F. If, however, F is complete, then anything desirable as G must also be desirable for its contribution to F.

If the third condition refers to the demand for completeness, this demand still needs some explanation. Plato explains it by adding a fifth condition: (5) Life L is complete if and only if we would choose L all by itself with nothing further added to L (20e). This appeal to choice, however, is rather hazardous, as Plato himself notices in *Republic* IX (582d–e). We might take completeness to depend on a choice within a life: (6) Life L is complete if and only if someone living L would, from the point of view of someone living L, choose L all by itself with nothing further added. But this condition seems to make the good relative to different people's desires and limitations. For some lives may actually make people lose the desires or knowledge that would make them want more than they have in their present lives.[30]

Plato shows that he sees this difficulty in (6) as an interpretation of (5). Although Socrates asks Protarchus if he would choose the life of pleasure all by itself, he shows that he does not intend (6) to specify the right conditions of choice. For Protarchus claims that he 'would have everything' (21b2) if he had enjoyment. He might be right, if he means that he would satisfy (6); for within the life he would be leading, he might not miss anything and might not want any of the things outside it. Socrates, however, points out that in a life of pleasure without intelligence we would be living the life of some elementary form of animal, not of a human being (21c6–8). He does not mean that within the life of pleasure we would still want something else. On the contrary, the fact that we would not want anything else is part of what is wrong with the life of pleasure.

In rejecting the life of pleasure without intelligence, Plato relies on his original statement of the question about pleasure and the good. Socrates and his interlocutors agree to look for the state of soul that makes the life of human beings happy (11d4–6); hence they seek the best form of life (11e11–12a1). It is fair, then, for Socrates to ask Protarchus what sort of life he would choose for himself (21c8–9) and to consider whether the life of pleasure without intelligence is a good life (21d3; cf. 22b6). Socrates is asking how Protarchus would want his whole life to be. If we simply think of ourselves at a moment, we may overlook some desirable features of our state of mind that become clear only when we think of our whole life, and so think of ourselves over time.

Socrates points out, therefore, that the life of pleasure without intelligence lacks the different forms of rational consciousness that involve the agent's thinking of himself as a rational agent persisting through his different experiences and pleasures. Since we lack memory, we do not remember that we had pleasure; in lacking belief, we lack the awareness that we are having the enjoyment we are having; in lacking rational calculation, we lack the ability to calculate that we will enjoy ourselves in the future (21c).

Socrates would be dealing unfairly with the hedonist position if he meant to recommend these forms of rational consciousness simply as means to greater pleasures.[31] For he has already conceded that the unmixed life of pleasure includes the greatest pleasures (21b3–4). If the various forms of rational consciousness are necessary as means to these pleasures, then they are already included in the life of pleasure, but since they are purely instrumental to pleasure (according to a purely hedonist view), they presumably do not themselves constitute any of the goodness in the life of pleasure. Plato is therefore justified in considering the life of pleasure without these aspects of rational consciousness and asking whether it contains all the elements of intrinsic value that we think should be included. The hedonist does not concede that rational consciousness is one of the elements constituting the intrinsic value of the life.

This may still seem to be too brusque a reply to hedonism. For a hedonist might reply that the best life consists of pleasures taken in forms of rational consciousness. On this view, not all pleasure is part of the good, but nonetheless the good is altogether constituted by some specific pleasures. Would this not be a defence of hedonism against the mixed good? In speaking of a life, Plato seems to impose a more generous criterion than he would if he simply spoke of the good; for we might say that the good life includes other things besides those that are, strictly speaking, the good in it.

If Plato can convince us that pleasure taken in rational consciousness presupposes the intrinsic goodness of rational consciousness itself, then he can show that an argument proving that the good consists in this specific sort of pleasure is not really a defence of hedonism. For if the pleasures are essentially tied to their objects, and if they involve the belief that the object is intrinsically good, then we cannot ourselves be hedonists if we believe that the good life consists in these sorts of pleasures. And so a closer examination of an apparently hedonist doctrine shows how a proper account of the relevant sorts of pleasures in rational consciousness gives us a reason not to be hedonists. Plato's analysis of types of pleasure seeks to show that purely hedonist arguments cannot explain the badness of bad pleasures (taking false pleasures as the examples) or the goodness of good pleasures.

The rational consciousness that concerns Plato is the sort involved in being aware of myself over time; memory, self-consciousness, and rational calculation are different ways I am aware of myself as the same agent in all these experiences. Plato does not speak simply of memory of pleasure in the past; he speaks specifically of my remembering that I was previously pleased (21c1). Part of what is good about a life—and part of what is missing in the unmixed life of pleasure—is the awareness of myself as a rational agent in my different experiences.

Plato points out, then, that we will not admit pleasure as the good unless we think of it as constituting a pleasant life whose stages are connected by the different forms of rational consciousness. Next, he asks us to consider why we care about this connexion in rational consciousness and activity. Since we do not value it simply instrumentally, we must value the exercise of rational agency as a part of our good in its own right, not simply as a means to pleasure.

This objection to the life of mere pleasure suggests how Plato must interpret completeness. His condition 5 describes a life as complete if 'we would choose it' with nothing further added. We can see why condition 6, claiming that a given form of life is complete if a person living that life would not want anything further added, gives the wrong result. Plato's objection to pleasure suggests this interpretation of completeness: (7) Life L is complete if and only if a rational agent taking proper account of his nature as a rational agent would choose L all by itself without anything added to L. If (7) is what Plato means, then the appeal to choice is less useful than it may initially have seemed. For he turns out to be imposing quite strict conditions on the sort of choice that counts. Even informed choice is not adequate for his purposes; for he plainly does not mean to accept the choice of someone who has been told that he is a rational agent but is unconcerned about it. To determine the right choice, it is necessary to know what is involved in taking proper account of one's nature as a rational agent. Since the pursuit of Calliclean pleasures conflicts with prudence and self-concern, it fails to take account of one's rational agency.

In the end, therefore, the appeal to choice leads us back to the questions that are raised in the *Republic* by appeals to the human function. Socrates assumes, in his argument against Protarchus, that a rational agent's life is not worthwhile for him unless it includes, as an aspect of its intrinsic value, the sorts of rational activity that are involved in the agent's conception of himself as a rational agent, lasting from one time to another and making plans for his future. He insists that this aspect of a rational agent cannot reasonably be treated as a subordinate and merely instrumental aspect of such an agent's life.

225. Completeness and External Goods

Plato uses the demand for completeness to show that the life of mere pleasure cannot be the best life, because the best life must include rational activity as a constituent of, not a mere means to, its goodness. On the other hand, Protarchus insists, and Socrates does not deny, that a life of intelligence alone, without pleasure, would also be unacceptable for a human being or for any other animal capable of both intelligence and pleasure (21d–e; for the scope of the claim see 22b). Plato does not expect the agent making the choice between lives to regard herself as a purely rational agent, with none of the desires and feelings resulting from the non-rational aspects of human nature. The complete life for a human being cannot make her 'unaffected' (*apathēs*) by the normal feelings and passions of human beings (21e1–2). 'Freedom from affection' (*apatheia*) appeals to Plato no more than it appeals to Aristotle (*EN* 1104b24–6).

The question about the unmixed life of pleasure is a purely counterfactual question, if it turns out that some pleasures essentially involve recognition of the intrinsic value of something other than pleasure. The same point applies to the examination of the unmixed life of intelligence. For if some forms of rational activity necessarily involve pleasure, then the life that includes them involves pleasure. Socrates wants us to set this possibility aside, however, and focus on the question of whether the pleasure is itself a part of what is good about a good life. If it is part of what is good, then intelligence alone cannot be the good.

Plato has now clarified the question about whether pleasure or intelligence is the good. He does not simply want to know whether either of them is the best state of consciousness, since he asks the question about a life as a whole, not simply about episodes of consciousness within it. Nor, however, does he simply want us to identify the life that embodies the best form of existence, for it might turn out that either the life that includes the best pleasure or the life that includes the best form of intelligence embodies the right mixture of pleasure and intelligence, but neither 'life of the best pleasure' nor 'life of the best intelligence' is the right answer to Plato's question.[32] The right answer must identify the property of the best life that makes it best by capturing the element of intrinsic value in it. To identify this feature of the best life, we must describe it as the mixed life.

If we attend to this aspect of the complete good, it is clearer why the *Republic* is right not to affirm that virtue is sufficient for happiness. Lack of pleasure, even if the virtuous person is willing to put up with it for the sake of being virtuous, reveals an aspect of his life that could be better and, indeed, must be better if his life is to achieve a complete good. If we apply the test of 'universal attractiveness' (condition 3) and claim that rational consciousness and activity are the whole of the good, then someone who found reason to pursue pleasure would have found something valuable that made no contribution to the good; and that shows we have not found the complete good. Even if we believe that the just life in fact maximizes pleasure, this does not show that justice is properly identified with happiness; we must recognize that pleasure is another part of happiness in its own right. Plato implicitly recognizes this in *Republic* IX; his argument to show that justice produces the greatest pleasure aims to show that, by being the sort of intrinsic good that it is, justice secures a component of happiness that is distinct from justice.

If this is Plato's argument to show that happiness must include pleasure as well as virtue, does it also tend to show that happiness must include the 'external' goods mentioned in the *Republic*? The answer to this question may depend on how we apply the requirement that the good lacks nothing. If S has virtue and pleasure and is indifferent to worldly success, does this show that worldly success is no part of S's happiness? If Plato applies his test for a complete and self-sufficient life, then he will not agree that external goods are irrelevant to S's good if S does not care about them. He might reasonably argue that if we care about rational planning, we also have reason to care about its success—that is why we plan to do one thing rather than another. If we apply the test of completeness to the just but unlucky person described in *Republic* II, we must say that something could reasonably be added to a just but unlucky life; Plato recognizes this himself in *Republic* X, when he restores to the just person the external goods that were taken away for the purpose of the main argument.[33]

On these questions, then, the *Philebus* goes some way towards filling a gap in the *Republic*. While the *Republic* makes a number of claims about the relation of justice to happiness, it does not connect them to any definite view about the nature of happiness. The *Philebus* explores some general questions about the human good; answers to these questions provide essential support for a claim that this or that state or activity is part of the good.

226. The Special Role of Intelligence

Once Socrates and Protarchus have agreed that the mixed life is preferable to the unmixed lives of pleasure and intelligence, Socrates makes a further claim on behalf of intelligence. Now that neither pleasure nor intelligence gets the first prize, there is still a further question, he says, about which of them is the 'cause of the mixture' (23c–d), and he defends the claims of intelligence on this score. This, he says, amounts to awarding intelligence the second prize.

What is required for intelligence to be the cause of the mixture in a sense that would qualify it for the second prize, as the second highest good? In the *Philebus*, as in the *Republic*, 'intelligence' does not refer simply to practical reasoning but also includes the sort of intellectual activity that Plato admires so much in the *Republic*: philosophical study and reflexion, and other theoretical activity undertaken for its own sake. Understood this way, intelligence is an important component of the good and might turn out to be a more important component than pleasure.

At several points in the *Philebus*, it is difficult to decide what Plato has in mind in speaking of intelligence; but at this stage an appeal to purely theoretical intelligence would not support his argument in the right way. Purely theoretical intelligence might be regarded as a primary formal cause (in Aristotle's terms) of the goodness in the best life, since it is a constituent that makes the best life good by being present in the best life. It does not seem to be a cause of the mixture, however; Plato has not shown how it interacts with other constituents to produce the best combination. To find a cause of the mixture, we must turn to the practical function of intelligence.[34]

This practical function also seems inadequate for Plato's purposes if its value is taken to be purely instrumental. Practical intelligence is important in planning for the right sorts of enjoyments on different occasions and for the right resources to supply the enjoyments. This instrumental function of intelligence distinguishes it from pleasure; but it does not help Socrates' case since it does not show that the intelligence used in planning is itself any part of the good.[35]

Plato needs to say, then, that the very fact that the best life is the product of practical intelligence is part of what is intrinsically valuable about it. He must be attaching intrinsic value to the practical, instrumental activities of intelligence. On this view, the mixed life is valuable not only because it contains the right things but also because it has come into being in the right way; the facts about its causation contribute to its intrinsic value.

To defend this claim about intelligence, Plato must show that other elements of a person's good are elements of it only if intelligence chooses them and they are part of a life guided by intelligence, whereas the same is not true of intelligence in relation to the other goods. Plato might reasonably appeal to his argument against the unmixed life of pleasure. Socrates argues against Protarchus that such a life lacks the essential element of rational consciousness and planning that connects the different episodes of pleasure into a life for a rational agent. If they are left unconnected, the different pleasures are still goods, and they are raw material for a good life; but they do not constitute parts of a good life until they are connected and arranged by the right sort of rational consciousness.

The life of intelligence alone is not open to a similar objection. Even if we are deprived of pleasure, we do the best that can be done for a human being in our circumstances, and we have a crucial part of our good, even though we lack some of its necessary elements. Plato claims this in the *Republic* about justice in relation to other goods, and a similar argument will show how he might defend his claim that intelligence, in contrast to other goods, is the cause of the good mixture in the mixed life.

When Plato claims that intelligence is the cause of the good mixture, he refers partly to efficient causation; the practical reasoning and planning of intelligence produces the proper order and arrangement of other elements in the good. But he also refers to formal causation. The goodness in the mixed life partly consists in, and does not simply result from, the practical role of intelligence; that role is a necessary part of a life that is organized and connected in ways that make it good for a rational agent.

20

Reason and Virtue

227. Questions Raised in the Late Dialogues

The *Philebus* marks an important development in Plato's thought on some moral questions discussed in the *Republic* about the relation between pleasure and goodness and about the nature of the good itself. Plato does not reject the doctrines of the *Republic* but he expands and strengthens its argument at some crucial places.

The other main ethical topic in the *Republic* is the nature of the virtues and their connexion to the nature of the soul. The later dialogues show that Plato's thought develops in these areas, too, but their treatment of the questions is less elaborate than the treatment of pleasure in the *Philebus*. Hence it is difficult to say exactly what the significance of the developments is and how far it involves a drastic change in the positions taken in the *Republic*. The dialogues that are especially relevant here are the *Statesman* and the *Laws*, but the treatment of the relevant questions is often rather brief and therefore leaves many questions unresolved.

We cannot, then, always expect to reach a definite conclusion about the theoretical significance of Plato's remarks, but they are important enough to deserve discussion. On most points they agree, or at any rate do not clearly disagree, with the *Republic*; but on one important issue, about the connexion between virtue and knowledge, Plato seems to reject (and probably intends to reject) the position he takes in the *Republic*.

228. The Disunity of the Virtues

In the *Statesman* the Stranger remarks that the view that the parts of virtue are in conflict is unpopular, an easy target for disputatious people who rely on popular views (*St.* 306a8–10). This is a surprising claim; the view that the Stranger represents as unpopular seems quite similar to the one that Protagoras defends as the popular view in the *Protagoras*. In the early dialogues, the unpopular view seems to be the Socratic view that the virtues cannot conflict. In the present context, the Stranger does not even raise the question of whether the virtues are really one or many; he takes it for granted that they are many and takes himself to be defending an unusual view in claiming that they are antagonistic to each other (306a12–c1).

The Stranger supports his claim about the mutual antagonism of the parts of virtue by examining bravery and temperance. He identifies bravery with vigour, self-assertiveness, and intensity, and identifies temperance with restraint and orderliness (306e9–307b3). When these tendencies are inappropriate for the occasion, we criticize them in opposite ways (307b5–c7). People who are dominated by temperance tend to be cowardly since they are too slow to face dangers that ought to be faced; people who are dominated by bravery tend to be intemperate since they are so impetuous in pursuing their desires that they do not stop to think about reasons for not pursuing them.

This is a bad argument for the claim that bravery and temperance are distinct and opposed parts of virtue. For a start, it is not clear that the Stranger has even been talking about bravery and temperance. If we appeal either to the early dialogues or to the *Republic*, we can apparently argue that he has been talking about the natural tendencies underlying the virtues, not about the virtues themselves. Both the Socratic and the Platonic conceptions of the virtues suggest that a genuine virtue requires both the cultivation of a natural psychological tendency and its control and modification by beliefs about the good. In the *Republic*, indeed, Plato notices the natural tendencies underlying the different virtues, but does not claim that they actually are virtues (*R*. 410e). Aristotle marks the relevant distinction by separating 'natural virtue', which is a natural tendency facilitating the acquisition of a given virtue, from 'full virtue', which results when a well-trained natural tendency is combined with wisdom (*EN* 1144b4–9). Does the argument in the *Statesman* simply ignore this vital distinction?

The Stranger seems to give some answer to this question, since he says what needs to be added to an impetuous or a calm natural disposition if one is to be trained to be a virtuous person. Moral education results in stable true belief about fine, just, and good things and their contraries (309c5–8); this conviction belongs to the divine part of the soul (309c1–2). When a brave soul acquires the appropriate conviction, it becomes gentle and just, rather than wild (309d10–e3); when a temperate soul acquires this conviction, it acquires the wisdom to do what is required by justice.[1] We might suppose, then, that moral training eliminates the initial opposition between the temperate and the brave person. Each of them will have acquired wisdom and justice, and in doing so will have eliminated the natural tendencies that made temperance and bravery seem opposed to each other and to the requirements of virtue.

This does not seem to be the Stranger's view, however. For he assumes that the opposition between brave and temperate people still remains, even after they have been properly educated; this is why the statesman will try to combine brave and temperate characters by arranging marriages between them (310a7–e3). Marriages need to be watched carefully, since brave people and temperate people will tend to be attracted to those who are similar to them, and their psychological tendency will appear in an exaggerated form in the next generation.

What conclusion should be drawn from these remarks on the virtues? The Stranger has not made a good case for his claim that different virtues are opposed to each other. Bravery and temperance should apparently be regarded as the outcome of moral education, not as the natural tendencies that have to be educated. If this is right, then it is arbitrary to focus on the natural tendencies in seeking to argue for an opposition between the virtues. On this issue Aristotle seems to express the position that Plato implicitly accepts in *Republic* IV; it is puzzling that the *Statesman* seems to neglect the *Republic*'s view about the necessary conditions for a virtue.

Nonetheless, the *Statesman* may help us to understand something about the differences between the parts of virtue. In *Republic* IV Plato identified them by connecting three of the virtues with the different parts of the soul; then he had to explain how justice could involve all three parts of the soul. The *Statesman* does not connect the virtues so clearly with the parts of the soul; bravery might apparently be shown in the pursuit of objects of appetite no less than in any other activity. Instead, Plato insists that some aspects of virtue involve the modification of natural tendencies, and others involve the redirection of those tendencies towards the ends prescribed by reason. Both wisdom and justice are the result of the beliefs of the 'divine' part of the soul; and virtue might be conceived simply as the justice that results from the proper harmony between one's well-trained natural tendencies and one's rational convictions. Bravery and temperance, on the one hand, and justice, on the other hand, turn out not to be virtues of character on the same level; bravery and temperance seem to be treated as the raw material for justice.[2]

One effect of this view is that Plato firmly repudiates any suggestion that we can have well-trained non-rational parts of the soul without a well-trained rational part. We argued that, in fact, he does not accept this suggestion in *Republic* IV either, and that he insists that every genuine virtue requires knowledge in the rational part of the soul; but many readers of *Republic* IV have supposed that he takes a less stringent view of the virtues. The *Statesman* leaves no room for such a view. It clearly insists that the well-trained moral agent must be controlled by the rational part. On the other hand, Plato no longer requires knowledge in the rational part; stable true belief seems to be sufficient (following appropriate training of one's natural tendencies) for the relevant sort of wisdom (*phronēsis*; 309e6) and justice.

It would be unwise to insist that the *Statesman* must be intended to repudiate the account of the virtues that Plato offers in *Republic* IV. It would be equally unwise to claim that Plato's views change for the better; for it seems easy to defend the account in *Republic* IV against the objections apparently raised in the *Statesman*. Still, the remarks in the *Statesman* ought not to be neglected either; for they suggest lines of argument that either clarify some claims in the *Republic* or suggest options that deserve to be explored.

229. Pleasure and Desire

Some of the difficulties raised by the *Laws* are similar to those raised by the *Statesman*; it is often uncertain whether apparent differences from the *Republic* should be attributed to a different emphasis, to a less exact formulation resulting from the specific purpose of the *Laws*, or to a genuine change of doctrine. Still, the apparent differences from the *Republic* add up to a general picture that differs from it in interesting ways. Moreover, even when the different claims in the *Laws* do not mark a contrast with the *Republic*, they sometimes throw further light on topics treated in the *Republic*.

The discussion of pleasure in the *Laws* helps to explain why Plato believes this is an important topic in ethical argument. In other dialogues he assumes it is important, but does not explain so fully why he thinks so. In both the *Protagoras* and *Republic* IX Plato sets out to show that the virtuous person's life is more pleasant than anyone else's. In the *Protagoras* he wants to show this because he believes that pleasure is the ultimate end of desire and that judgments about goodness must ultimately be justified by appeal to judgments about pleasure. In the *Republic* he affirms neither the psychological nor the epistemological claim about pleasure; the *Philebus* gives reasons for rejecting these claims, in the light of the internal connexion between pleasures and their objects. Nonetheless, Plato refuses to concede that the virtuous person's life may be less pleasant than someone else's.

In the *Laws* Plato affirms that the three appetites for food, drink, and sex are basic in human nature, so that for human beings everything is 'dependent' (*ērtēmena*) on them; virtue results when these appetites are led rightly, and vice results when they are led wrongly (782d10–e1). Under the influence of these appetites, people pursue pleasure and reject pain (782e4–6). It is important to train these appetites by 'turning them towards the best as opposed to what is called pleasantest' (783a4–5). Plato suggests that under the influence of these basic appetites we judge different courses of action by their prospects for pleasure; when we train these appetites properly, we judge actions by considerations of better and worse rather than pleasure and pain. It is not clear what he means by this, however. When we have educated our basic appetites, do we simply change our mind about what is most pleasant, and identify the best with the most pleasant? Or do we form some conception of what is best that is independent of our conception of what is most pleasant?

Plato suggests that pleasure and pain are 'sources' or 'springs' that have to be turned in the right direction in order to ensure happiness. They are the 'most natural' for human beings (732d4–5), and everything depends on them. They are unintelligent (*aphrone*) advisers (644c6–7), however; that is why the virtuous person has to control his tendencies to pleasure and pain (632e1–6, 635c3–d8). Their promptings need to be regulated by a rational principle discriminating better from worse; this rational principle is the 'golden cord' that must be in control if we are to live well (644d7–645b8).

These claims about the fundamental character of pleasure and pain as human motives, and about the importance of training them, neither imply nor exclude a hedonist view of motivation. Plato might consistently accept hedonism and insist on the importance of controlling pleasure; in that case, his remarks about control mean that we must learn to regulate our appetites for immediate pleasure and our aversions to immediate pain by our views on what maximizes pleasure and minimizes pain in the long run. But while the contrast between the pleasant and the good might be explained in these hedonist terms, Plato does not choose to explain it this way. If we cannot find him offering a hedonist explanation, the remarks we have found so far do not justify us in attributing a hedonist position to him.[3]

230. Pleasure and Happiness

We might suppose we have found more positive evidence of hedonism, however, when we see how closely Plato wants to connect claims about pleasure with claims about happiness. He urges that when we commend the virtuous life, we must commend it as more pleasant than its rivals, and that we must not allow any separation between happiness and pleasure. He wants to show that the just person is happy[4] whether he is rich or poor, strong or weak (660d11–e5), and that the unjust person is miserable, no matter how healthy, strong, and powerful he may be (661d6–e4). But he is not content to claim that the just person is happier than the unjust; he also believes it is important to insist that the just person has more pleasure.

Plato defends his claim by considering what would follow if it were false; he argues that since the consequences of its falsity are unacceptable, the claim must be true. If we separate the most just life from the most pleasant, we must decide which of them is happier. Plato assumes it would be intolerable in these circumstances to have to say that the most pleasant life is happier than the just life (662c5–d7). He imagines a father telling his son that the most pleasant life is happier; the son will ask in turn why his father kept telling him to be just, since he surely wanted the son to be as happy as possible (662d7–e8).

Plato assumes here that there is no good reason for recommending a way of life to us if it is admitted that it will not promote our happiness better than any alternative will. Plato does not actually say that the son's reaction to his father's advice is correct, but he seems to suggest that it is. He refuses even to consider the counterfactual possibility of the gods saying what the human father says; in his view, we should not even contemplate the thought of the gods telling us to be just while agreeing that the just life is not the happiest.

It might seem more reasonable to suggest that the just life is happiest, while admitting that it is not the most pleasant; on this view, maximum happiness diverges from maximum pleasantness. Plato, however, rejects this suggestion too. He says that anyone who hears this suggestion will wonder what fine and good thing greater than pleasure we could be praising in the happy life. He explains this by adding: 'For what could turn out to be good for a good person if it is separated from pleasure? Tell me, are we to say that fame and praise from human beings and gods is good and fine, but without pleasure, and that ill-fame is the opposite?' (663a1–4). It would be difficult to persuade anyone of the truth of such a claim: 'for no one would be prepared to be persuaded to do willingly something that is not followed by more pleasure than pain' (663b4–6). Even if it were not true that the happiest life is also the most pleasant, we ought to persuade people it is true, so that they will be ready to be just when they are persuaded that the just life is happiest (663d6–e4). At the same time, however, Plato is convinced that it is true, and not merely a useful fiction, that the just life is the most pleasant (663d2–5).

To decide whether Plato is right, we must decide whose point of view we are to adopt. From the unjust and vicious person's point of view, the life of justice seems less pleasant, but from the just person's point of view, it seems more pleasant, and in this case we should follow the just person's point of view (663d7–8). Plato is not offering to prove, then, that the just life will appear more pleasant to anyone at all who contemplates it. Nor does he imply that there is some neutral point of view, committed neither to justice nor to injustice, from which we can see that the just person has more pleasure than the unjust. In order to be persuaded that the just person has more pleasure, we must first agree that the unjust person's point of view is distorted and that there is no neutral point of view.

Plato returns to the question about the relation between pleasure and happiness in another passage, where he emphasizes that the desire for pleasure is fundamental. In our life as a whole, we want a surplus of pleasure over pain; 'if we say that we want something contrary to this (or 'beyond this'; *para touto*[5]), we are saying this because of some ignorance and inexperience of the ways of life that there actually are' (733d4–6). Our account of Plato's view here depends on how we take '*para touto*'. If he means that we have no desires or motives apart from the desire to maximize pleasure and minimize pain, then he asserts a strong form of psychological hedonism. This, however, does not seem to be his usual view in the *Laws*. We ought to attribute it to him here only if his other remarks in the context seem to require it.

When he explains why the virtuous life contains more pleasure than the vicious life contains, Plato says that this view will be accepted by anyone who 'knows' this way of life (733e6–734a8). What does 'knows' imply here? We might suppose (1) that Plato has in mind some neutral observer who has observed virtuous and vicious people and who reaches this conclusion after a comparison made from his neutral point of view. Alternatively, we might suppose (2) that Plato refers to someone who knows what it is like to lead a virtuous life as a result of leading it himself. If Plato takes the first view, he goes beyond what he said in the previous passage, where he restricted himself to hedonic claims made from the virtuous person's point of view. If he takes the second view, he repeats what he said in the previous passage.

A remark at the beginning of our present passage suggests that Plato might be taking the second view. He claims that we ought to praise the finest life on the ground that 'if one is willing to taste it and does not become a fugitive from it when one is young, it is superior in what we all seek, greater enjoyment and less pain over one's whole life' (733a1–4). Here Plato recognizes that one's acceptance of virtue makes a difference to the pleasantness of one's life. Unfortunately, the remark is still ambiguous. It might mean (1) that we can see from a neutral point of view that someone who accepts the virtuous point of view has a pleasanter life, or (2) that someone who accepts the virtuous point of view will judge that the virtuous person's life is more pleasant.[6] The first interpretation commits Plato to the recognition of a neutral point of view for comparisons of pleasure and pain. The second interpretation allows him to insist that comparisons have to be made from the virtuous or the vicious point of view.

We cannot reach a confident conclusion about Plato's attitude to the pleasure of the virtuous life. We have no reason, however, to conclude that he says anything inconsistent with his most detailed discussion in the *Laws*. In this discussion, he rejects any neutral point of view. Instead, he argues that in order to see the greater overall pleasure in the just person's life, we must first agree that the just person's estimate of comparative pleasure is correct.

If this is what Plato means, then his claims in the *Laws* rest on the sort of argument that is developed in the *Philebus*. If the value of a pleasure is not to be assessed apart from the value of its object, then we cannot correctly assess the value of different pleasures without relying on judgments about the value of the states and activities that are the objects of the pleasures. In that case we must rely on the correct point of view for evaluating the objects of different pleasures.[7]

If Plato takes this view, we will be less surprised that he appears to make large concessions to hedonism, in rejecting the apparently reasonable position that praises the just life as the best life but not necessarily as the most pleasant life. This position seems reasonable as long as we assume that we can judge what is more and less pleasant by some purely quantitative criterion independent of our judgment of value about the objects of pleasure. If that assumption is right, then the claim that the virtuous life is the most pleasant appears to be a rather hazardous empirical hypothesis. Plato does not take it to be an empirical hypothesis, however; he takes it to be a consequence of recognizing that the virtuous life is best and understanding the relation of pleasure to non-hedonic value. If we supposed that the virtuous life could fail to be the most pleasant, we would, in Plato's view, be taking for granted a conception of hedonic value that he attacks in the *Philebus*.

231. Virtue and Happiness

Just as Plato's claims about pleasure sometimes appear to make a stronger claim than he can justify about the connexion between the virtuous life and the pleasant life, some of his remarks about virtue and happiness appear to say more than we have found him saying elsewhere. In the case of pleasure and happiness, we have found that the appearance is deceptive; is the same true of virtue and happiness?

Special difficulties arise from remarks that seem to go beyond Plato's comparative thesis that the just person in all circumstances is happier than anyone else. In the *Republic* Plato maintains this thesis in contrast to the Socratic sufficiency thesis, according to which the just person is happy. The *Laws*, however, sometimes appears to assert the sufficiency thesis. In Magnesia everyone will be taught to believe that the virtuous person 'is happy and blessed, whether he is tall and strong or short and weak, and whether or not he is rich' (660e3–5). In the context, it is understandable that Plato does not explain, as Glaucon and Adeimantus do in *Republic* II, how bad circumstances may be for the unlucky just person; but does he mean us to generalize from his remarks here and infer that, no matter how bad external circumstances may be, the just person is happy?

This is not the only way to generalize from Magnesian defences of the virtuous life. In our present passage Plato is pointing out that we do not need to excel in non-moral goods if we are to be happy; we can be happy without being as rich as Croesus (cf. Aristotle, *EN* 1179a1–16). This falls short of claiming that we can be happy no matter what non-moral goods we lack and no matter what non-moral evils we suffer. Since Plato does not affirm this stronger claim, he does not revert to the Socratic view that virtue is sufficient for happiness.

These claims about virtue and happiness ought to be connected with Plato's view of the relation of non-moral goods to virtue and vice. In the *Euthydemus* Socrates tries to reconcile the view that non-moral goods have some positive value with his belief that virtue is sufficient for happiness; he argues that for the virtuous person they are 'greater goods' than their opposites. In the *Laws* Plato affirms more unambiguously that wealth, health, and other recognized assets are bad for the vicious person, since they allow him to act in more thoroughly vicious ways, but good for the good person, since he uses them correctly in virtuous action (661b4–d4; cf. *M.* 88b–d).[8] This is why we will not want people's prayers to be answered unless their prayers are guided by wisdom, leading them to ask for the external goods that will really be good for them (687d1–e9). As Aristotle explains, we ought not to pray for external goods unless we have the wisdom that makes us use them correctly, so that they are really good for us (*EN* 1129b1–6).

These claims about the relation of external goods to virtue suggest that Plato takes them to contribute to the virtuous person's happiness; for since they are good for a virtuous person, they must contribute to happiness, if happiness includes all intrinsic goods. We cannot infer with complete confidence that Plato takes external goods to be necessary for happiness, since we cannot say for certain that in the *Laws* Plato holds this comprehensive conception of happiness. Still, it is rather difficult to believe he does not hold it. For he repudiates the view that the virtuous life is not the most pleasant life; he insists that if it is the happiest, it must be the most pleasant. It is easy to see why he maintains such a view if he holds a comprehensive conception of happiness; it is less easy, however, if he believes there are significant goods not included in happiness.

The political aims of the *Laws* strengthen the case for attributing a comprehensive conception of happiness to Plato. While he often emphasizes the superiority of goods of the soul, specifically the virtues, over bodily and external goods (e.g., 631b6–d1, 697a10–c4, 728c9–729b2, 743c5–744a7), he also advocates the pursuit of non-psychic goods, in their proper place. He does not speak as though he advocates them for the sake of some good other than happiness. On the contrary, he assumes that the proper aim of legislation is the happiness of the city and its citizens (683b1–6, 697a10–b2, 743c5–6). The laws of Magnesia aim at the happiness of the citizens, not simply because they make virtue prior to non-moral goods (we could do this while neglecting the pursuit of non-moral goods) but also because they provide for the effective pursuit of non-moral goods in proper subordination to virtue.

For these reasons, we ought not to suppose that the *Laws* departs from the comparative thesis about justice and happiness. On the contrary, the comparative thesis makes good sense of Plato's repeated comments on the hierarchy of goods. The hierarchy would be difficult to understand if we attributed the sufficiency thesis to Plato; we have no good reason to place this difficulty in the way of understanding the *Laws*. Since the comparative thesis fits the *Laws* best, we also have a further reason (though certainly not sufficient by itself) for attributing it to Plato in the *Republic*. For Plato's claims in the *Laws* about the hierarchy of goods fit naturally with the *Republic*; in both dialogues Plato is emphatic about the supreme contribution of justice to happiness, without excluding non-moral goods from happiness altogether.

232. The Cardinal Virtues

In the *Statesman* Plato affirms an opposition between bravery and temperance that seems to mark a sharp disagreement with the *Republic*; but it is difficult to say how far he really disagrees with the substance of the account of virtue in the *Republic*. The *Laws* raises similar difficulties, both internally and in comparison with the *Republic*.[9]

In some places Plato seems to have no doubts about the separability of the virtues; he criticizes the Spartans for their concern with bravery to the exclusion of the other virtues. Among the parts of virtue, bravery is the fourth in importance (630c6–d1, 631a2–8). This view of bravery treats it as a natural tendency, present in children and animals (963e1–8) and clearly separable from temperance and the other virtues. Mere bravery is treated the same way as it is treated in the *Statesman*, as natural fearlessness; it leads people to be confident, even impetuous, in pursuing their ends despite any dangers or obstacles they may face. This tendency is not good without qualification, since it may encourage us to persist in bad as well as good purposes; if it is not combined with temperance, it makes someone even more unrestrained and intemperate (696b6–10).

In the *Statesman* Plato treats temperance as a natural tendency parallel to bravery, with contrasting good and bad points. In the *Laws* it is less prominent in this role, and Plato seems doubtful about whether it is really parallel to bravery. When the Athenian asks whether temperance without the other virtues is honourable, Megillus is unsure what to reply, and the Athenian says he is right to be unsure; for while temperance is a component of something that deserves honour, it is not so clear that it deserves honour by itself (696d4–e6). This natural tendency is later called 'popular temperance' (710a3–b2), as opposed to the state we refer to when we 'compel temperance to be wisdom as well' (710a5–6).[10]

In recognizing that one type of temperance requires wisdom, Plato suggests that we might also recognize a type of bravery that requires wisdom, in contrast to the primitive form of bravery that the Spartans cultivated. He seems to commit himself to this view about bravery insofar as he recognizes that bravery and temperance are products of moral education; people are trained from early youth to be brave by overcoming their fears, and they are trained to be temperate by moderating their pleasures (791b10–c2, 815e4–816a3). What people acquire from education is not simply a stronger tendency leading them to do what naturally brave and temperate people do; they are educated to resist fears and pleasures in the appropriate circumstances. This is why the right moral education is needed if people are to be 'brave without qualification, and free' (635d5–6). In speaking of 'bravery without qualification', Plato recognizes grounds for saying that the 'bravery' of naturally fearless people is not the genuine virtue of bravery ('unqualified' bravery), but simply its natural basis. In saying that justice results from the mixture of wisdom, temperance, and bravery, Plato seems to be speaking of the bravery found in the virtuous person, not that found in the merely fearless person.

If this is the right account of bravery and temperance, it remains puzzling that Plato speaks of them in these different ways. Would it not have been clearer if he had simply accused the Spartans of cultivating a tendency that is the starting point for bravery and of failing to cultivate the virtue itself, which also requires the other cardinal virtues? Perhaps Plato shrinks from the paradoxical claim that the Spartans—universally recognized as brave soldiers—did not succeed in cultivating bravery. He ought not to have shrunk from this paradox, however, for once we see what he means by recognizing bravery as a virtue, we can see that in denying that the Spartans cultivated bravery he would not be denying any obvious facts about them.

Even if Plato must agree with Aristotle's distinction between the 'natural virtue' and the 'full virtue' of bravery or temperance, he still seems to stop short of saying that all the virtues are really one virtue, and so he seems to reject the Socratic Unity Thesis. The members of the Nocturnal Council are supposed to learn what the virtues have in common, so that they understand the 'one' as well as the 'many' (965c9–e2), but Plato's statement of this point does not compromise the plurality of the virtues. The 'one' that the Councillors recognize is the common feature of the different virtues, the feature that makes them all virtues; but recognition of this common feature does not imply that they are not distinct virtues. Plato seems to be sufficiently impressed by the difference between the natural sources of the different virtues to insist that, even when they are combined in a character that is regulated by justice and wisdom, they remain different virtues. On this point he may be expressing more distinctly the view accepted in the *Republic*.[11]

233. Wisdom and Virtue

Among the virtues Plato accords some sort of primacy to wisdom (*phronēsis*). He says that instead of praying to get whatever we want, we should prefer our wants to be guided by wisdom (687e5–9), and that the 'leader of all virtue' is 'wisdom, understanding, and belief, with passion (*erōs*) and appetite (*epithumia*) following them' (688b1–4). Wisdom belongs to the rational part of the soul, to the 'golden cord' that regulates our pursuit of pleasure and our aversion to pain by reference to consideration of better and worse (644c9–645b8). We need wisdom to make sure that we use non-moral goods correctly (631c4–5), and wisdom itself is the leader among the goods of the soul (631c5–d1).

What is required for this wisdom? It is contrasted with 'foolishness' (*amathia*). The foolish person recognizes that something is fine and good, but he hates it, or else he recognizes that something is base (*ponēros*) and unjust, but loves and welcomes it nonetheless (689a5–7). Foolishness is discord between rational belief, on the one side, and pleasure and pain on the other (689a7–9). This account of foolishness suggests that wisdom involves concord between rational judgment and pleasure. Plato simply says that concord is necessary for wisdom: 'For how . . . could even the least sort of wisdom come about without concord? It could not. Rather, the finest and greatest of concords would most rightly be called the greatest wisdom (*sophia*)' (689d4–7).

This remark suggests that wisdom is to be identified not with any specific cognitive condition, but with psychic harmony. Indeed, it becomes quite difficult to distinguish wisdom from temperance; moreover, the sort of temperance that is something more than a natural tendency seems to include wisdom (710a5–6). If wisdom and temperance are to be identified, however, it becomes difficult to see why Plato regards wisdom as the leader among the virtues, and temperance—the developed virtue, not the natural tendency—as one of the virtues following wisdom (631c5–7). Wisdom is supposed to differ from the other virtues insofar as it involves rational judgment (963e5–8); and so it can hardly be mere psychic harmony.

It is difficult, then, despite what Plato says about discord and concord, to suppose that the foolish person and the wise person could agree in all their rational judgments of value. If they could agree this far, they would differ simply insofar as the wise person's feelings of pleasure and pain would follow his judgments of value, whereas the foolish person's pleasures and pains would conflict with his judgments of value. If this were Plato's point, then the wise person would differ from the foolish person simply because the non-rational part of his soul differs. This is surely not the conclusion that Plato intends.

How, then, are we to understand the connexion between concord and wisdom? Plato's position becomes intelligible if we distinguish the foolish person's judgment that x is fine and good from his judgment that x is good, all things considered, for him. His feelings of pleasure may diverge from his rational judgments because he is not convinced that x will contribute to his own happiness.

If this is right, then the wise person differs from the foolish person insofar as he recognizes that what is fine and good is also good for him; that is to say, he has been convinced by the arguments that Plato wants to be universally accepted in Magnesia.

If we suppose that pleasure and pain follow one's judgments about one's happiness, then we can see why the divergence between the rational judgments of the wise person and of the foolish person will lead to a divergence in their hedonic judgments too. This connexion between judgments about happiness and judgments about pleasure is not surprising if we agree with Plato's claim in the *Philebus* that some pleasures are internally related to their objects.

In this way people's judgments about good and evil affect their tendencies to feel pleasure and pain. It would also be reasonable for Plato to emphasize the influence of pleasure and pain on judgments of value. In *Republic* IV he suggests that misguided pleasure and pain tend to cause wavering in beliefs.[12] This is the sort of wavering that Aristotle refers to when he says that temperance is needed to preserve wisdom, because misguided pleasure 'corrupts the principle' (*EN* 1140b11–20). If Plato means to emphasize this role of pleasure and pain in forming and sustaining true judgments of value, he need not be reducing wisdom to agreement among the parts of the soul, and he need not be suggesting that wise people differ from foolish people only in having their non-rational parts in a good condition.

Plato's different remarks in the *Laws* about wisdom seem quite unsystematic. He talks about different aspects of wisdom without explaining how they fit together. Still, the unsystematic appearance of the remarks may be a bit misleading; for when we ask how they might reasonably be fitted together, we can see their affinities both with *Republic* IV and with Aristotle's conception of wisdom. While we cannot be sure that this is the systematic view that Plato relies on, it gives a reasonable explanation of what he says.

234. Conditions for Wisdom

While Plato's remarks in the *Laws* about wisdom and temperance may not reflect any serious disagreement with the *Republic*, he seems to depart more sharply from his earlier view when he considers who has wisdom. In the *Republic* Plato consistently intends, despite some appearances to the contrary, to require wisdom in any virtuous person.[13] This requirement implies that only the rulers in the ideal city—and therefore ultimately only the philosophers—can have genuine virtue, and that the lower classes in the ideal city are guided by their non-rational parts. Although their souls have rational parts and these rational parts absorb the correct values, members of the lower classes are guided by the strength of different desires, not by their authority.

In the *Laws* the distinction between knowledge and true belief remains important, and wisdom is sometimes identified with knowledge (*epistēmē*); it is what the members of the Nocturnal Council have (632c4–6). From the moral point of view at any rate, the members of Nocturnal Council have the sort of knowledge that is expected of the philosophers in the *Republic*. They are expected to recognize the one F present in the many Fs (962d1–964b6, 965b7–966b8) and to have a conception of the goal that guides and regulates all the city's laws and institutions (962a5–c3; cf. *R*. 519b7–c7). These demands are parallel to those imposed on the philosophers in *Republic* V–VII.

These demands, however, do not apply to everything that Plato calls wisdom in the *Laws*. He expects all the citizens to have the sort of education that results in their being guided by the rational part of the soul, the 'golden cord' controlling their feelings of pleasure and pain (644c4–645c6), and he believes that when citizens have reached this condition, they have all the cardinal virtues, including wisdom (631c1–d1, 688a1–b3). In that case wisdom must require less than the level of knowledge that is demanded of the Nocturnal Council. Indeed, we have seen that in some places Plato warns against exaggerating the purely cognitive character of wisdom; he tells us to prefer the person with the well-ordered soul to the person with much greater intellectual ability in a disorderly soul (689c6–e2).

These claims might lead us to suspect that the apparent difference between the *Republic* and the *Laws* does not reflect a genuine theoretical difference. For (we might suggest) what Plato says about wisdom in the *Laws* is really no different from what he says about right belief in the *Republic*. When the *Laws* allows wisdom to all the citizens and not just to the highest class, Plato need not be saying that they have achieved something that the lower classes in the *Republic* did not achieve; he may simply be saying that what the lower classes in the *Republic* did achieve deserves to be counted as wisdom (in the reduced sense that he introduces in the *Laws*).[14]

We ought to reject this attempt to reconcile the *Republic* and the *Laws*. In the *Laws* Plato makes demands on ordinary citizens that are not made in the *Republic*, and in doing so he shows that he is not simply restating the view of the *Republic* in different words. Nothing in the *Republic* corresponds to the demand that moral education should aim at achieving control by the rational part. Indeed, when the *Republic* discusses this question, the difference from the *Laws* is significant. Plato argues that the next-best thing is to be ruled by one's own reason and wisdom, but if this is not possible, the best thing is to be ruled by someone else's reason and wisdom; this second condition is the one Plato intends for the lower classes in the ideal city (*R*. 590c2–d6). He neither says nor implies that the wisdom and reason of the ruler guides the subject through the subject's own reason and wisdom; this is not surprising, since he never suggests that the members of the lower classes are ruled by their own rational parts.[15] The *Laws*, by contrast, is quite explicit on the very points that the *Republic* passes over in silence. Plato agrees that the wisdom of ordinary citizens depends on the wisdom of other people; nonetheless, he insists that wisdom and control by reason is the condition that ordinary citizens achieve.

Does Plato expect anything more from people with wisdom than he would expect from them if they simply had correct belief? In some striking and important passages of the *Laws*, Plato makes it clear that he expects them to display one distinguishing feature of knowledge in contrast to belief. They must understand why the things they are told are right and good really are right and good; they must not simply take other people's word for it. To explain this demand, Plato introduces a comparison with doctors. On the one hand, the slave doctor, who also gives treatment to slaves, just gives instructions without giving any reason for them. The free doctor, on the other hand, who treats free people, explains why the treatment prescribed is the best one for the patients. Instead of simply giving orders, the free doctor discusses the patients' conditions with them and tells them enough to persuade them that the treatment being prescribed is the best one for them (719e7–720e5). This discussion involves communicating some theoretical understanding to the patient; as Plato remarks, a bystander listening to the free doctors might protest that they are treating the patient as a medical student, not as a patient (857c6–e6).[16]

In Magnesia the city is supposed to follow the practice of the free doctor. It persuades and educates the citizens by explaining to them why a particular law is reasonable, so that they can see the point of the law and recognize the legislator's purpose (822e4–823a6). The prefaces to the laws are intended to have this explanatory role, so that the law does not just give orders like an arbitrary tyrant (720c6–7, 821a2–5, 859a1–6).

Evidently the kind of understanding and justification that the citizen acquires from being persuaded by the Magnesian authorities is different from what the members of the Nocturnal Council are supposed to acquire; but it is not altogether different in kind. In both cases Plato agrees that genuinely virtuous people should be able to 'give an account' of what they do and believe, and that this account should explain why the actions that they take to be right really are right. It is difficult to see how they could do this without recognizing some common features of, say, justice and temperance that make them good for the just and temperate person.

In the *Republic* Plato recognizes that the demand for an explanation and justification can be satisfied to different degrees. The third stage of the Line refers to a type of knowledge and therefore must refer to someone who has to some degree answered the demand for an account; but Plato sees that we can give an account supporting our initial moral beliefs without necessarily being able to show why that account is the right one. This division between two grades of knowledge is not used in the *Republic* to justify the attribution of any knowledge to the lower classes in the ideal city (since they are all at the bottom stage of the Line), but it may suggest the general point that Plato exploits in the *Laws*.

The demand for wisdom and understanding shows that the *Laws* differs in substance, not merely verbally, from the *Republic*. Plato believes that ordinary citizens ought to have some level of wisdom because he believes it is reasonable to expect a level of understanding that goes beyond mere acceptance of what one is told. Plato retains the Socratic conviction that virtue requires understanding and reason as well as right conduct and right belief. Socrates in the early dialogues does not face the implications of his conviction; in particular, he does not say how many people can be expected to meet his demand for a rational account. In the *Republic* Plato relies on the Socratic conviction to justify his claim that only a few people can be virtuous. In the *Laws* Plato implies that the position in the *Republic* is too restrictive; he wants to maintain the Socratic conviction while insisting that it leaves virtue within the range of ordinary people. On this point the *Laws* is truer than the *Republic* to the spirit of Socratic moral inquiry.

Notes

Chapter 1

1. For discussions of Plato's moral theory, the most important question about authenticity arises about *I Alc.*, which I believe is spurious. Some serious objections to its genuineness are raised by Vlastos [1975], 155–61; contrast Annas [1985].

2. On Plato and Socrates see esp. §§7, 53, 64, 87, 139, and 167.

3. Aristotle's interpretation and criticism of Plato are sharply attacked by Cherniss [1944]; they are more favourably assessed by Fine [1993], 28f. Even Cherniss, however, accepts Aristotle's claims about Cratylus and about the difference between Socratic and Platonic metaphysics (206–19).

4. The imperfect tense used here suggests that Aristotle refers to something Plato used to say, not something written in the dialogues (for which Aristotle normally uses the present). See Stewart [1892] and Gauthier and Jolif [1970].

5. On the importance of the reference to Cratylus, see Ross [1924], I, xlvii. On the other side, see Kahn [1981a], 49, note 13.

6. Aristotle's remark about the *Laws* is discussed by Morrow [1960], 146.

7. Different approaches to the interpretation of the dialogues are briefly discussed by Kraut [1992b], 20–30; and Irwin [1992b], 73–78.

8. Grote [1888], I, chap. 8, esp. 407f., comes close to this aporetic view (although sometimes he suggests a more 'gymnastic' view, that Plato thought it worthwhile to examine the puzzles for their own sake).

9. Defenders of an esoteric approach appeal to some passages in dialogues and letters; see Krämer [1990], 42–46.

10. The philosophical functions of the dialogue form are discussed by M. Frede [1992], 215f. (who seems to me to underestimate the doctrinal element in the dialogues).

11. On dialectic see Proclus, *in Alc.* 169.12–171.6. On the connexion between dialogue and dialectic, see DL III 48.

12. This rule about the use of the article ('Fitzgerald's canon') is stated briefly by Fitzgerald [1853], 163. It is defended by Ross [1924], I, xxxix–xli. Difficulties are discussed by Deman [1942], 35, 61f., 95; and by Nehamas [1992], 169–71. The exceptions to the general rule do not undermine its general reliability. In any case, our decision on this point does not affect the main evidence demonstrating Aristotle's desire to distinguish the historical Socrates from Plato.

13. See note 3 on Cratylus.

14. Whereas the *EN* uses *ho Sōkratēs*, the *EE* and *MM* use plain *Sōkratēs*, referring (see note 12) to the historical person.

15. I believe the *MM* is substantially authentic; see Cooper [1973], criticized by Rowe [1975]. If the order of Aristotle's ethical works is *MM*, *EE*, *EN*, he displays decreasing degrees of asperity in his criticism of Socratic ethics.

16. See Deman [1942], 125f.

17. *R.* I requires a special explanation. See §117.

18. On the date of the *Lys.* see chap. 3, note 48. On the *Euthd.* see chap. 4, note 1.

19. Some of these features belong to dialogues that are not usually counted as Socratic: the *HMa.* and *Meno* need further discussion. The character of the Socratic dialogues is discussed by Vlastos [1991], chaps. 2 and 3; Penner [1992b].

20. The view that Plato presents Socrates' views with his own views in mind is defended by Shorey [1903], 10, 12. See §167.

21. See Plutarch, *Col.* 1118c (Ross [1955], p. 73); DL II 45–6 (part in Ross, p. 71); Ar. *Rhet.* 1398a24–26. Two passages correspond to passages in Xenophon: *Rhet.* 1393b3–8 (cf. Xen. *M.* I 2.9), *EE* 1235a35–b2 (cf. Xen. *M.* I 2.54).

22. See Vlastos [1991], 97f., opposed by Kahn [1992], 235–40.

23. See DL III 37; Anon. *Prol.* 24.13–19. This does not imply that the whole of the *Laws* must have been written after all the other dialogues.

24. The best survey of stylistic studies is Brandwood [1990], summarized in Brandwood [1992]. A recent statistical study is Ledger [1989] (on which see Brandwood [1992], 112f.).

25. Brandwood [1990], 9, 153–62.

26. See Brandwood [1990], 206.

27. This list is taken from Brandwood [1976], xvii. Other lists are given by Ross [1951], 2; Ledger [1989], 224f.; Vlastos [1991], 46f.; Penner [1992b], 124.

28. This issue is raised, but dismissed rather brusquely, by Ledger [1989], 88.

29. For our purposes it is not as necessary as it would be if we were studying Plato's metaphysics to form a definite view about the relation of the *Parm.* and *Tim.* to the late dialogues. I do not believe that Plato regards (or should have regarded) the arguments of the *Parm.* as fatal to the conception of Forms maintained in the middle dialogues, and so I do not accept the main reason offered in Owen [1953] for placing the *Tim.* before the *Parm.* See Fine [1988]. On the *Phil.*, see chap. 19, note 9.

30. On *R.* I, see chap. 11, note 1.

31. This is not intended to apply to the *Mnx.*, on which I offer no opinion.

32. See §64 and chap. 7, note 3.

33. This biographical view is defended by Graham [1992]. His argument rests on the dubious claim (158) that the version of Heracleiteanism accepted by Plato (see §113) conflicts with the claims about crafts that are made in the Socratic dialogues.

34. On the *Cra.* see §106.

35. My conclusion agrees with Vlastos [1991], 50f., but my argument about the Socratic character of the middle dialogues is unacceptable to him (see 131).

36. See §§103, 115.

37. Vlastos [1983b] remarks on his reliance on the *G.* (71–74). See also Nehamas [1992], 165; Kahn [1992], 251f.

38. On Xenophon see Lacey [1971]; Morrison [1987]; Vlastos [1991], 99–105. The accounts of Socrates by Zeller [1885] (see chap. 5, note 25) Boutroux [1912] (see chap. 2, note 25), and Brochard [1912] (see chap. 5, note 25) rely heavily on Xenophon.

39. See Augustine, *CD* VIII 3, XVIII 41.

40. See Ar. *Rhet.* 1398b30–33; DL II 60, III 36. See further chap. 6, note 41.
41. On the Stoics, see further §140. On attitudes to Socrates, see Long [1988].
42. On Poseidonius, see §168.

Chapter 2

1. On the use of the term '*elenchos*' see Vlastos [1983 a], 28. It is one of Socrates' legal terms (for other legal terms cf. *Ap.* 29e4–5; *La.* 188a3; *G.* 486d4, 487a1). See *G.* 473e6–474b5, 475e7–476a2; *Rep.* 534c1–3; *Phdr.* 267a1, 273c3, 278d5. In later dialogues (*Phil.* 52d10; *Sph.* 230d7, 231b5–6, 239b1–3, 242a7–b5, 259d5) it has a more specialized use. Sometimes (e.g., *G.* 458a, 473b10), but not always (see *Ap.* 39c6–d3; cf. *La.* 187d10), *elenchein* implies actual refutation.

2. On types of elenchos see Robinson [1953], chaps. 2 and 3.

3. On self-contradiction see especially *Sph.* 230b5–8.

4. See *Ch.* 162b9–11, 169a3–6; *La.* 194a6–b4, 196a7–b2, 200e1–5; *Eu.* 11b6–8; *M.* 79e7–80b4; *R.* 334b7.

5. On the false conceit of knowledge cf. *M.* 84a3–c9; *Tht.* 168a2–7, 210b11–c4; *Sph.* 230b4–e4; *I Alc.* 118a15–c2.

6. See *Ap.* 21b1–d7; *Eu.* 5a3–c8, 15c11–16a4; *Ch.* 165b5–c1, 166c7–d6; *La.* 186b8–187a8, 200e2–5; *Lys.* 212a4–7, 223b4–8; *G.* 509c4–7. For similar remarks in later dialogues see *M.* 71a1–7, 80d1–4; *HMa.* 286c8–e2, 304d4–e5; *Symp.* 216d1–4.

7. On the treatment of Socrates and Plato as sceptics, see Annas [1992]; Glucker [1978], 35–50; Woodruff [1986]; Barnes [1988], 233–36.

8. This use of *zētein* leads ancient critics to classify all the Socratic dialogues except the *Ap.* and *Cri.* as dialogues of inquiry (*zētētikoi*) in contrast to the dialogues of exposition. See DL III 49; Grote [1888], I 291–95.

9. On this passage see §20.

10. On sincerity see also *Cri.* 49d1; *Pr.* 331b8–d1 (see §65); *G.* 495a5–b6, 500b; *R.* 346a; *Tht.* 154c7–e6; Vlastos [1983a], 35.

11. On eristic see further Irwin [1986], 61–63; Benson [1989].

12. Socrates' assumptions are discussed by Vlastos [1983a], 52–56; Kraut [1983], 65–68; Brickhouse and Smith [1984], 188–92.

13. On the guiding principles see §32.

14. See Santas [1973], 110.

15. Difficulties in the argument are examined by Santas [1973], 112–17; Kosman [1983], 203–8.

16. Santas [1973], 108–10, argues that the *Charmides* is meant to show Plato's sympathy with the piecemeal approach. For different views about Plato's attitude to apparent homonymy, see Shorey [1903], 19f.; Stokes [1986], 92.

17. On Laches' suggestion, see Stokes [1986], 73.

18. On this passage see Vlastos [1956], xlvii–xlix; Santas [1969], 187; Stokes [1986], 74–76.

19. On piecemeal approaches see §§28, 105.

20. I translate 5d1–5: 'Is the pious not the same as itself in every action, and is the impious in turn not contrary to all of the pious, and similar to itself, and all of it having some one character corresponding to piety <in the case of the pious>, whatever is to be impious?' I read *kata tēn hosiotēta* in 5d4, and *pan, hotiper* in 5d4 (following

Heidel). For different views see Robinson [1953], 57f.; Guthrie [1975], 120 and notes; Vlastos [1991], 57 and notes.

21. On the misunderstanding of Socrates' questions by his interlocutors see §110; Nehamas [1975b]; Benson [1990b].

22. In 8b7–9b3 Socrates defends his claims about disputes among the gods.

23. The best discussions of *Eu.* 10–11 are Cohen [1971] and Sharvy [1972] (who especially emphasizes the explanatory aspects of Socrates' conception of definition).

24. On disputed terms, see §§64, 107. On the metaphysical and epistemological demands, see esp. §115. In describing the demand for an explanatory property as metaphysical rather than epistemological, I do not mean that the concept of explanation is wholly non-epistemological, but only that it is not purely epistemological.

25. Socrates' search for a moral science is emphasized by Boutroux [1912], 36, who relies exclusively on Xenophon.

26. See further Irwin [1982a].

27. My views about the nature of Socratic definitions are close to those of Penner [1973a] (reconsidered in 1992b); Fine [1993], 46–49. Such views are opposed by Vlastos [1981b].

28. It is unwise, however, to try to draw a sharp line between conceptual inquiries and the Socratic search for a definition. 'Concept', 'meaning', 'understanding', 'sense', and so on can themselves be understood in different ways in different theories.

29. See Grote [1888], I 450–52. He also appositely cites Origen, *Cels.* V 47.

30. On nominal and real essence see Locke, *Essay*, III 3.13–17.

31. On the disavowal of knowledge, see further §86.

32. The significance of these passages is discussed by Geach [1966]; Irwin [1977a], 40f.; Burnyeat [1977]; Santas [1972], [1979], 116f.; Kraut [1984], 267–79; Beversluis [1987]; Benson [1990a]; Vlastos [1990]; Fine [1992], 200–204. Although I believe there is good reason to hold that Socrates believes a definition of moral properties such as justice is necessary for knowledge about justice and about what things are just, it is another question whether everything he says is consistent with this belief; see §17.

33. For Aristotle's view, see §15.

34. On knowledge and belief, see §100.

35. This point about the scope of Socrates' disavowal of knowledge is emphasized by Vlastos [1991], 238, against the solutions offered by Lesher [1987] and Woodruff [1990]. It also raises difficulties for the view defended by Reeve [1989], 32–53.

36. Vlastos [1985] suggests that Socrates uses *know* in two senses. Against this suggestion, see Irwin [1992a].

37. This passage is discussed by Vlastos [1985], 7–10; Beversluis [1987], 117f.; Mackenzie [1988], 338; Reeve [1989], 53–62.

38. On eristic see §11.

39. On Socrates' conditions for definition, see §107.

Chapter 3

1. The cardinal virtues are listed at *Pr.* 329c6–d1, 329e6–330a2.

2. On 'dialogues of inquiry' see chap., note 8.

3. On *R.* I see §117.

4. See Ar. *EN* 1005a22–30, 1145b2–7; Polansky [1985], 249–53; Vlastos [1991], 94, 111.

5. On Socrates' defences see §§44, 85, 94.

6. *Eudaimonia* is often taken to include more than a mental state; many Greeks supposed that being rich, prosperous, and successful were ways of being *eudaimōn*, not simply means to a feeling of happiness. For this reason, 'prosperity', 'well-being', or 'welfare' suggest aspects of *eudaimonia* that might be concealed by the rendering 'happiness'. On *eudaimonia* and happiness, see Sidgwick [1907], 92f.; Ackrill [1974], 23f.; Kraut [1979]; Dybikowski [1981].

7. See Homer, *Od.* 6.39–46; Herodotus, I 32; III 39–43; Sophocles, *OT* 1186–1204. On different views of happiness, see Dover [1974], 174. His emphasis on material prosperity may be corrected by reference to De Heer [1969], chap. 3, esp. 80f., 99f.; McDonald [1978], chap. 1.

8. The passage is explained well by Andrewes ad loc. in Gomme et al. [1945]. For further discussion, see Creed [1973]; Adkins [1975].

9. On the sense of the passage, see Wilson [1982]; Hornblower [1991], ad loc.

10. On virtue in general, see §§91, 105.

11. 12e5ff. might refer either to actions or to persons, but the introduction of a craft at 14e6 implies a reference to the piety of persons. See further Vlastos [1981a], 435f; McPherran [1985], 237, note 34. On properties of actions and of persons, see 11, note 17.

12. On actions and persons, see §120; Joseph [1935] 6f.; Burnyeat [1971], 230f.; Dent [1984], 28–30.

13. Socrates' refutation of Charmides' first account of temperance also rests on the assumption that temperance must be fine.

14. The argument is this: (1) Temperance is fine (160e6–7). (2) Temperate men are good men (160e9). (3) If anything makes people good, it must itself be good. (4) So temperance is good (160e13). (5) But shame is both good and bad (161a6). (6) Therefore, shame is not temperance (161a11–b2). Socrates does not say that he is arguing from (1) to (2), but if he is not, (1) plays no role at all in the argument, and (2) is left without support that it needs.

15. See 160e4–5, *hoper aidōs*. Contrast 'some sort of quietness', *hēsuchiotēs tis*, 159b5. For this use of *tis*, cf. §97; *La.* 192b9–c1; *M.* 73e1; Graeser [1975], 174f. (answering Detel [1973], 8 and note); Stokes [1986], 76–80.

16. See 179c3; the 'fine actions' of the elder Aristeides and Thucydides certainly included brave actions. Aristotle's comments about the virtues and the fine support Socrates' assumption; see §22.

17. Contrast Stokes's explanation of 'harmful' [1986], 85.

18. On conflicts between temperance and bravery, see §228.

19. Socrates begins with a simple interpretation of 'one's own' (the cobbler mends only his own shoes, the teacher of writing writes only his own name, etc.; 161d–162a) and shows that this is unacceptable. He does not assume that he has refuted the account of temperance.

20. He sees the same sort of 'riddling' in an account of justice that mentions what is 'owed' without explaining what this is (*R.* 332b9–c3). See §§14, 107.

21. On Aristotle's use of this passage, see §49.

22. See *apergazetai*, 165c11. On crafts and products, see chap. 5, note 13.

23. On the transition from self-knowledge to knowledge of knowledge, see Dyson [1974], 103–5; Irwin [1977a], 298, note 45.

24. In contrast to Socrates, Critias has no idea of how to defend his suggestions or of the difficulties they raise, and so he lacks the degree of self-understanding that Socrates has achieved.

25. In *Cri.* 47d3–48a4 Socrates compares justice with psychic health, which the

G. connects with psychic harmony and conflict; see §§79–80. In the *Cri.*, however, this comparison simply implies that justice is highly beneficial to the soul and injustice is extremely damaging to it; Socrates suggests nothing about conflict or harmony, and so he does not allude to the doctrines of the *G.* or the *R.*

26. O'Brien [1967], 125f., suggests that Plato has *R.* IV in mind.

27. The point is relevant to the earlier question about training in armed combat, 181d8–184c8. For it now turns out that if such training did what it was supposed to and gave someone expertise in hoplite tactics, it would make bravery less necessary; it would provide a substitute for bravery rather than bravery itself.

28. On the relation between the *La.* and the *Pr.* on bravery and knowledge, see chap. 6, note 9.

29. Some readers argue that Plato intends us to conclude that a correct account must include some reference to endurance as a distinct element, independent of knowledge, in bravery. See O'Brien [1963], 139; Devereux [1977], 135–36. Stokes [1986], 88, and Kahn [1986], 18, are less confident. Devereux refers especially to 193e8–194a5. But all that Socrates commits himself to is the view that they ought to endure; he can still claim this even if endurance is not a distinct element of a definition of bravery (this would be true if, for instance, knowledge automatically produced the right sort of enduring behaviour). In *ei ara pollakis*, 194a4, Socrates does not endorse the truth of the suggestion that endurance is bravery.

30. Socrates suggests as a possible objection to Nicias' account the 'bravery' of lions and boars (196e). Laches embraces these 'agreed' (197a3) examples as counterexamples to Nicias, but Nicias disallows them, arguing that fearlessness is not the same as bravery (197a–b). Nicias is right, given that Laches is not willing to abandon his previous admission that bravery is always fine; for surely the sort of mindless fearlessness that Laches has in mind here would not always be fine, but would sometimes be foolish and regrettable.

31. Socrates suggests that knowledge of what I do or do not know about (170d1–3) might be morally and politically useful (171d1–172a5). He implicitly challenges an assumption made by those who advocate oligarchy as a temperate form of government; he argues that the temperate person will want to be assured that rulers have the right sort of knowledge to qualify them as rulers.

32. On this argument see Santas [1973], 130f.; Ferejohn [1984], 113–15.

33. This argument assumes that happiness includes all goods. Socrates appears to assume this, as Vlastos's account of Socrates on happiness makes clear. See §41; Vlastos [1991], chap. 8; Irwin [1992a], 252f.

34. On the piecemeal approach, see §13.

35. Vlastos [1972], 266–69, argues that Socrates accepts the account of bravery in (1), but rejects (2), so that he does not believe that (1) conflicts with the view that bravery is a proper part of virtue. Vlastos later rejects this account, however, at [1981a], 443–45; his later view agrees with Devereux [1977], 137–41; [1992], 771–73, that since Socrates both takes the argument to be valid and takes bravery to be a proper part of virtue, the argument is directed against (1). Vlastos considers the issue again in [1993], chap. 5.

36. On the inseparability of the virtues, see §56.

37. On the reciprocity in contrast to the identity of the virtues, see §§43, 56, 97, 166.

38. Contrast Gould [1987], 277.

39. On the claim that bravery is a proper part of virtue, see Vlastos [1981c], 421f.; [1991], 132, note 8; Ferejohn [1984], 108f.; Devereux [1977]; Stokes [1986], 67–69;

Penner [1992a]. In *M.* 78d–79c, Socrates allows (1) that there are distinct parts of virtue and (2) that there are many other virtues besides the cardinal virtues (79a3–5). Since he probably does not endorse (2), we should not assume (as Vlastos and Ferejohn do) that he endorses (1); he merely concedes (1) to Meno for the sake of the present argument. See Irwin [1992a], 244; contrast Taylor [1991] 221f.

40. On fineness and goodness, see §23.

41. On warning signals in the *M.*, see §99.

42. Some of these conclusions about the unity of the virtues are supported by the *Eu.* Socrates examines the claim that the pious is a part of the just (11e7–12d10). Euthyphro's last suggestion runs into difficulty because he suggests that in being pious we do what is agreeable (*kecharismenon*; 15b1) to the gods, and therefore loved by them; this brings us back to the suggestion that the pious is that part of justice that the gods love, and 'what the gods love' was previously rejected as a definition of piety (15b1–c9). (This aspect of the argument is discussed by Weiss [1986], esp. 450f.) Euthyphro would avoid this difficulty if he maintained (as his earlier remarks implied, 4b7–c3, 7b7–9) that all just actions are pleasing to the gods, precisely insofar as they are just. But to say this is to deny that piety is a proper part of justice. A further argument is needed to show that justice cannot be distinguished from the other virtues; the last argument in the *Ch.* fills this gap. The relation between the *Eu.* and the doctrine of the unity of the virtues is discussed by Taylor [1982], 114–17; McPherran [1985], 221f.

43. Schulz [1960], 267f., argues that (1) the argument of the *La.* suggests that Plato believes bravery is the knowledge of good and evil, so that (2) the aporia is not genuine. I do not believe (2) follows from (1).

44. On Socrates' attitude to virtue, see §§41, 51; Vlastos [1991], 209.

45. On virtue and happiness, see §41.

46. On the sense of *kakourgein*, see Kraut [1984], 26f.; Vlastos [1991], 196. On treating badly and harming, cf. §119.

47. The extreme principle of non-retaliation is this: (R1) If (1) A has done injustice to B, and (2) B's doing x to A would be unjust if A had not done injustice to B, then (3) B is not justified in doing x to A. The moderate principle is: (R2) If (1) A has done injustice to B, and (2) B's doing x to A would be unjust if A had not done injustice to B, then (3) the fact that A has done injustice to B does not justify B in doing x to A. Kraut [1984], 35–38, implicitly denies that Socrates accepts R1. Vlastos [1991], 190, also seems to attribute only R2 to Socrates; his view is less clear at 194–97.

R1 is much stronger than R2, since R1 implies that it is never permissible for B to treat A in ways that would have been unjust if A had not treated B unjustly. R1 excludes, whereas R2 permits, retributive elements in punishment. We may believe that retaliation is not by itself a sufficient reason for punishment, but still believe that the harm involved in punishment ought to be inflicted only on those who have committed injustice, and that it would actually be unjust to inflict it on people who commit no injustice; this belief would violate R1, since it implies that A's previous unjust action affects the legitimacy of B's treatment of A. This place for retributive considerations is defended by Hart [1968], 11–13.

48. I treat the *Lys.* as a Socratic dialogue. The attempts to see references to the Platonic Theory of Forms (see Levin [1971]) are answered by Vlastos [1973], 35–37.

49. Many of the puzzles in the *Lys.* are taken up in Aristotle's discussions of friendship. See Dirlmeier [1963], 435f.; Annas [1977], esp. 532–38; Price [1989], 9–14. Adams [1992] points out the systematic character of the puzzles.

50. On means and ends in the *Lys.*, see §§37, 46.

51. The self-interested character of the assumptions about friendship in the *Lys.* is emphasized by Vlastos [1973], 6–11, who is challenged by Price [1989], 10f.

52. Allen [1970], 69f., mentions this principle as an example of the 'regulative' role of the forms in dialectic.

53. On the claim that knowledge is sufficient for virtue, see §§97, 98, 165.

54. On Epictetus, see §15.

Chapter 4

1. The date of the *Euthd.* is disputed. I agree with Aristotle in regarding it as Socratic; see *EE* 1247b15, referring to 'Socrates' (not 'the Socrates'; see §5). It probably precedes the self-critical reflexions of the *G.* and *M.* See Dodds [1959], 22f., and contrast Hawtrey [1981], 4–10. Sometimes it is dated late because its claims about dialectic (290b–c) are taken to presuppose *R.* VI and VII (see Gifford [1901], ad loc.; Hawtrey is more hesitant); but they do not seem to imply anything more about dialectic than is suggested at *Cra.* 390c (which is intelligible without reference to the *R.*).

2. At *G.* 472c7–d1; *R.* 344e1–3, the question, 'How am I to live?' (see *R.* 352d5–7, *La.* 187e10–188a2, *G.* 492d3–5, 500c1–8) is identified with the question 'How am I to be happy?'

3. On temperance and benefit, see §28.

4. On common beliefs about happiness, see §21.

5. On the difference between explanatory and justifying reasons, see Hutcheson in Raphael [1969] I, §361 (distinguishing exciting from justifying reasons); Raz [1975], 15–19 (distinguishing explanatory from guiding reasons); Smith [1987], 37–41 (distinguishing motivating from normative reasons).

6. In 219c6 I read *iontas kai* with the mss (Schanz [1874–1879] and others read *iontas ē*). For the relevant sense of *apeipein* (for giving up doing x and doing y instead), Stallbaum [1877] cites *Phdr.* 228b3; cf. also *Cra.* 421e3.

7. The relation between the *prōton philon* and happiness is discussed by Versenyi [1975], 193; Vlastos [1991], 210f.

8. This claim about the good and happiness is implied still more clearly by *G.* 468a5–b8, 499e8–500a1; *Symp.* 205a1–3.

9. On Socrates' attitude to virtuous action, cf. §51.

10. Socrates' argument requires us to understand *eutuchia* so that it implies success, but not necessarily success resulting from sheer luck. His use of '*eutuchia*' does not introduce any fallacy into 279c–280a. For discussion see Stewart [1977], 23; Sprague [1977], 60; Hawtrey [1981], 81.

11. 281b8, *hōde de skopei*, signals a new argument (cf. *Phd.* 74b7).

12. In 281b8 I read *ē mallon oliga noun echōn* with the mss; see Long [1988], 166, note 59. Iamblichus' paraphrase has only *mallon ē oliga* (*Protr.* 5, p. 57.12 [Des Places]), but he may have altered the text simply for the sake of brevity.

13. In 281c6 some editors (e.g., Gifford [1901] and Hawtrey[1981]) wrongly delete *kai sōphrōn.*

14. My translation of 281d3–4 agrees with Hawtrey [1981] and Sprague [1965], against Gifford [1901] and Waterfield [1987].

15. This view is well explained by Vlastos [1991], 228f., 305f., who effectively criticizes the view (for which see, e.g., Klosko [1981], 98f.) that 'good in itself' is being contrasted with instrumental goodness. See also Zeyl [1982], 231; Kraut [1984], 212;

Ferejohn [1984], 111; Brickhouse and Smith [1987] 6; Reeve [1989], 128 and note. The sort of view that Vlastos accepts is well criticized by Long [1988], 166f.

16. See Grote [1888] II, 204; Shorey [1933], 162, 519f.; Taylor [1937], 94; Moreau [1939] 176; Festugière [1973], 46; Guthrie [1975], 270.

17. On the end of the *Ch.*, see §28.

18. He has suggested this point, if we retain *noun echōn* in 281b8; see chap. 4, note 12.

19. At *Lys.* 218e5–219a1 Socrates lists external goods among goods; he is simply setting out from the common-sense view, without challenging it himself at the moment. He does the same at *Euthd.* 279a4–b3. In both dialogues, however, he goes on to challenge the claim of external goods to count as genuine goods (*Lys.* 219e5–220b5; *Euthd.* 281e2–5).

20. *M.* 88c6–d1 concedes that external goods are in some circumstances actually beneficial. The claim here, therefore, seems to be different from the one in the *Euthd.* See §96.

21. Socrates' views on the relation of virtue to happiness are discussed by Vlastos [1991], chap. 8 (on which see Irwin [1992a], 251–64); Zeyl [1982]; Brickhouse and Smith [1987]; Klosko [1987].

22. Burnet [1924], ad loc.; and Vlastos [1991], 219 and note, translate *Ap.* 30b2–4: 'from virtue wealth and the other things become goods' (taking *agatha* as predicate). I prefer the usual translation ('wealth and the other goods come from virtue'), which provides a better balance with the previous clause ('virtue does not come to be from wealth'). The translation of *chrēmata* by 'wealth' is contested by Burnyeat [1971], 210.

23. On health and justice, see §§30, 76, 173.

24. On virtue and happiness, see §30.

25. On misuse of knowledge, see §§47, 62.

26. More precisely, this argument supports the claim that wisdom is necessary for the other virtues. In order to show that wisdom is also sufficient (which must be shown, if the virtues are to be inseparable), the nature of wisdom must be more carefully examined. See §165.

27. Ferejohn [1984], 117f., believes that this is Socrates' considered view.

28. On Socrates' attitude to alleged conflicts between virtue and happiness, see §30.

29. On the treatment of common beliefs, see §34.

Chapter 5

1. Aristotle, *EN* 1169b3–10, rejects a purely instrumental conception of friendship, repudiating the view expressed in Euripides, *HF* 1336–39; *Or.* 665–68. Greek views of friendship are discussed by Adkins [1963]; O'Brien [1967], 31–37; Blundell [1989], 32–36.

2. Aristotle recognizes this distinction between purely instrumental means and components, *EN* 1095b1–5 (cf. *EE* 1214b11–27; *MM* 1184a25–29), 1140b6–7, 1144a3–6. It has been used by many writers on Aristotle, following Greenwood [1909], 46–48; see, e.g., Ackrill [1974], 19f. On Socrates, see Zeyl [1982], 231 and note; Vlastos [1991], 205–7. The distinction is explored by Lewis [1946], 486f. (on 'instrumental' v. 'contributory' value).

3. At 220a7–b1 I follow Stallbaum [1877] and the mss in reading *heneka philou tinos, heterō(i) rhēmati*. Schleiermacher[1977] and Wright [1910] translate this text.

It counts against the suggestions of Kraut [1984], 212 and note; and Lesses [1985], 171f. (See also Bolotin [1979], 60, note 72.)

4. On this passage see Versenyi [1975], 193f.; Glidden [1981], 57; Klosko [1981], 99f.; Zeyl [1982]; Lesses [1985]; Vlastos [1991], 306. Contrary to Lesses, 171f., and Glidden, 56–58, Socrates implies that regarding x as *philon* is equivalent to regarding x as good (218e6, 219a4, 219b2, 220b7) and to choosing or being concerned for x (219d5–220a6).

5. On the desire for happiness, see §37.

6. Lesses [1985], 169, assumes that if we apply the schema in the *Lys.* to the *Euthd.* we ought to discover that wisdom is the *prōton philon*. Vlastos [1991], 230f., suggests that happiness is the *prōton philon*.

7. This passage is discussed by Vlastos [1991], 303f. In 468c2–5 Socrates argues that we do want tokens of intermediate actions (i.e., action types that, as such, are neither good nor bad) when they promote the good; 467d6–e1 should therefore be modified as follows: 'whatever things we do for the sake of something, we want them only for the sake of that for which we do them'. This still implies that we do not want these things for their own sake.

8. It would be illegitimate to appeal (as Versenyi does, [1975], 193) to *R.* 357b–d in order to interpret the *Lys.* See §139.

9. Socrates need not show that, for instance, just people will often use their knowledge of justice to commit injustice (cf. *R.* 333e3–334b6); it is enough for his purposes if people are no less just whether they use their knowledge to keep their agreements (e.g.) or to break them. The argument about misuse is discussed by Weiss [1981]; Vlastos [1991], 275–80.

10. The importance of this qualification is often remarked. See, e.g., Taylor [1937], 37f.

11. On the relevance of psychological eudaemonism, see Penner [1973b], 142.

12. Conditions for *technē* are suggested at Hippocrates, *VM* 1.11–16 (Loeb); *De Arte* 4–5; Democritus, DK 68 B 197. Greek conceptions of *technē* are discussed by Schaerer [1930], part 1; Festugière [1948], xv–xvii, 32; O'Brien [1967], chap. 2; Kube [1969], part 1; Nehamas [1986], 298–300; Nussbaum [1986], 94–99; Cambiano [1991]. The significance of Socrates' and Plato's use of analogies between virtue and craft is discussed by Gibbs [1974] and Tiles [1984].

13. In *MM* 1197a3–20 (cf. 1211b26–33), Aristotle mentions lyre-playing as an example of an action that is not done purely for the sake of an external end. He assumes that it is not a *poiēsis* and is not the concern of a *technē*. It is striking that Socrates never offers this sort of action as an example of what a *technē* does. (Contrast the arguments of Gosling [1978], 100f., and Taylor [1979], 599.)

14. Moreau [1939], 116, admits that Critias does not explicitly draw the Aristotelian distinction, but still claims that this distinction is the one 'à laquelle acheminait toutes les analyese précédentes, celle qui se dégagera avec une extrème clarté de ce dialogue et qui deviendra classique avec Aristote'. I believe it will emerge from the dialogue only if we read the dialogue from an Aristotelian, not a Socratic, point of view. I agree with Gauthier and Jolif [1970] on *EN* 1140a2–3, against Hirschberger [1932], 18, 55–57. Although Socrates does not actually credit the distinction between *poiēsis* and *praxis* to Prodicus, he suggests it is similar to Prodicus' distinctions (*Ch.* 163d3–4), which he often takes—in the light of his own ethical views—to be theoretically unimportant. Contrast chap. 9, note 29.

15. On this passage see Klosko [1981], 102; Zeyl [1982], 229 and note; Roochnik [1986], 187. While it is true that Socrates does not require a *technē* to produce a physi-

cal object distinct from the exercise of the craft itself, this fact does not show that he does not regard *technē* as—in Aristotle's terms—productive; for a physical artifact is not necessary for production, as Aristotle conceives it.

16. On the use of '*phronēsis*' before Plato see Schaefer [1981], chap. 1. Socrates uses it appropriately for the practical wisdom needed for bravery. (For other practical contexts see Democritus, DK 68 B 2, 119; *Cri.* 44a9, 47a10; *Lys.* 209c5, 209d3, 209e2, 210a4, 210b1; *Euthd.* 281e8, 285b6. Contrast *Pr.* 337c3.) But he also uses it for crafts, *La.* 192e, and he speaks of a virtue as *phronēsis*, as *epistēmē*, and as *technē*; see *La.* 193b5, 195a1, 195c11. He need not take the three terms to be synonymous; but he assumes that the sort of *epistēmē* appropriate for practical *phronēsis* will be a *technē* (contrast Stokes [1986], 80, 93). See further Schaefer [1981], chap. 3.

17. Contrast Moreau [1939], 188, who believes that the argument is meant to draw our attention to a basic disanalogy between virtue and craft: 'car l'art du bonheur, s'il consistait comme les autres techniques à réaliser un objet de possession quelconque, cesserait par là mēme, en vertu du principe, d'assurer le bonheur; en sort qu'il n'a avec les techniques qu'une ressemblance formelle; il se caractérise par la pure forme de l'activité réfléchie'. This Aristotelian line of interpretation lacks support in the Socratic dialogues. In assuming that wisdom could not ensure happiness if it produced some product distinct from itself, Moreau fails to take account of Socratic psychology. (Taylor [1937], 99; Sprague [1976], 51–53; and Hawtrey [1981], 137f., accept a view similar to Moreau's.) On this puzzle, cf. §62.

18. See Vlastos [1991], 205, note 24.

19. If Socrates believes that virtue requires knowledge and that he lacks knowledge, then he cannot believe that he is virtuous. Hence the aim that he is capable of achieving is being as virtuous as he can. Cf. chap. 8, note 21.

20. For Aristotle's comments on Socrates on craft, cf. §48.

21. According to Vlastos [1991], 280, Socrates 'failing to discern that moral virtue would be underdescribed as a power or a craft, since if it were only this it could be used for either good or evil ends, he finds himself betrayed into concluding, however hesitantly, that he who uses such power voluntarily for evil ends must be the better man.' Vlastos does not agree (279 and note) that Socrates accepts other aspects of the craft analogy.

22. Gomperz [1905], 296, argues that the *HMi.* is meant to undermine the conception of virtue as a craft.

23. This is part of Aristotle's reason for believing that wisdom itself requires virtue of character; cf. §165.

24. On the value of knowledge see §103.

25. Zeller [1885], 148–53, argues strongly that Socrates accepts an instrumental account of the relation of virtue to happiness, claiming that Socrates determines the good 'eudaemonistically'. (By 'eudaemonism' Zeller means roughly what I mean by 'instrumentalism'; he uses the term with its Hegelian sense.) He concludes (153–62) that this instrumental account of the goodness of virtue conflicts with Socrates' belief in the supreme value of care for one's soul. This conclusion is effectively contested by Brochard [1912], 42f.

26. For Plato's revisions of Socrates see esp. §§102, 103, 139, 164.

Chapter 6

1. Similarly, the *Dissoi Logoi* (DK 90 §6) argues on both sides of the question of whether virtue can be taught.

2. On puzzling conclusions, see §§28, 29.

3. Protagoras' claims about what he teaches are discussed by Adkins [1973]; Taylor [1991], 72, 81–83.

4. On disputes about the virtues, cf. §§22, 23, 68.

5. Issues about the unity of the virtues are discussed by Vlastos [1972; 1981c]; Penner [1973a]; Woodruff [1976]; Ferejohn [1982]; Taylor [1982; 1991], 103–8, 221–24; Devereux [1992]. The most important unresolved issues are these: (1) What thesis does Socrates set out to defend against Protagoras? (2) What thesis is compatible with Socrates' other claims about the virtues? The section 349a8–e5 strongly suggests a definite answer to (1), that Socrates seeks to prove that the five virtues are identical. Doubts about this answer arise primarily from the view that this belief in the identity of the virtues would conflict with Socrates' other views. The alleged conflicts are these: (a) The Unity Thesis would conflict with Socrates' belief that virtue has parts. (b) It would conflict with Socrates' belief that the virtues have different definitions. On (a) see chap. 3, note 39. On (b) see §15. Once we understand the nature of a Socratic definition, we ought not to assume that the (allegedly) different virtues must have different definitions; we could assume this only if we assumed falsely that a Socratic definition of F must consist in some expression synonymous with 'F'.

6. On virtue as fine and beneficial, cf. §29. On the assumptions underlying this argument, see Taylor [1991], 132; McKirahan [1984], 22.

7. On Socrates' formulation of his conclusions, see Taylor [1991], 115f., 121 (on 332a2–4).

8. For the reservation in 'tend to favour', see chap. 4, note 26.

9. The view that *La.* 192e1–193d10 (cf. §27) is meant to correct this passage in the *Pr.* is unwarranted. The two passages make different points. The *Pr.* argues that mere fearlessness without understanding of the risks does not count as bravery, but as madness (350b1–6), and the *La.* does not disagree. The *La.* passage insists that not every sort of knowledge constitutes bravery; the *Pr.* does not raise this question, since it is not relevant to the issue that Socrates wants to raise for Protagoras. For different views see Taylor [1991], 154; Devereux [1977], 136f.; Gould [1987], 270–72; Vlastos [1991], 50, note 20; [1993], chap. 5.

10. Protagoras' objection may result from a misunderstanding of Socrates' argument, which is itself difficult to interpret; see Taylor [1991], 160. But the objection itself is quite fair.

11. On non-cognitive components of the virtues, see §§26, 27.

12. On 351b–e, see Taylor [1991], 162–70; Gosling and Taylor [1982], 47–58. I translate 351c4–5: 'For I say: to the extent that things are pleasant, are they not to that extent good, not if (*mē ei*) anything else results from them?' (following Schleiermacher [1977], against most editors and translators). The *mē ei* . . . clause (see Adam and Adam [1893], ad loc.) explains the previous clause by saying that no result other than pleasure is relevant to something's being good. This gives Protagoras a good reason for attributing hedonism to Socrates at 351e5.

13. On Socrates' use of 'pleasant', see Taylor [1991], 179; Gosling and Taylor [1982], 56. On this rather rough formulation of hedonism, see §77.

14. I treat 'overall' and 'all things considered' as equivalent. Cf. chap. 7, note 12.

15. Richardson's suggestion [1990], 15–18, that Socrates allows incommensurable pleasures conflicts with 354c4–6, 355a1–5, 356a5–9.

16. On this issue Socrates' eudaemonist hedonism is apparently different from the version of hedonism defended by Aristippus and (perhaps) by Epicurus, who take the pursuit of pleasure to be motivationally prior to the pursuit of good. See Irwin [1991].

17. I believe the ridiculous character of the view of the many is meant to be indicated by 355d1–e2; cf. chap. 6, note 23. For different accounts see Taylor [1991], 181–86; Gallop [1964]; Vlastos [1969a], 81–83; Santas [1979], 202–9; Klosko [1980], 314–16.

18. On pleasure and good, see §57.

19. In claiming that Socrates has argued for (2a) I disagree with Taylor's claim [1991], p. 80, that the argument is invalid. His claim suggests, however, a good objection to the soundness of the argument; see chap. 8, note 5.

20. A related question about substitution arises at *Eu.* 10e9–11a4; cf. §14.

21. For this objection, see Taylor [1991], p. 180f.

22. Admittedly, some contradictory beliefs are psychologically intelligible; often, for instance, we hold beliefs with contradictory implications because we have not seen these implications. But this defence will not help the many; for they believe that incontinence is possible when all the relevant evaluative beliefs are explicit; the explicitly contradictory beliefs in (4) have not been shown to be psychologically intelligible.

23. On the force of '*anti*' see Taylor [1991], 185–87. Santas [1979], 204–7; and Vlastos [1969a], 82f., believe that 355a2–3 is meant to display the 'ridiculous' aspect of the view of the many (cf. chap. 6, note 17). I believe (with Taylor) that it is meant to describe accurately the phenomenon that the many describe as 'being overcome by pleasure'.

24. *G.* 472b6–c2, 474b6–8, and 479c8 are even more explicit on these points.

25. See Vlastos [1983a], 46–48.

26. Socrates' argument is taken to be ad hominem by Sullivan [1961]; Zeyl [1980], 250–57; Stokes [1986], 358–70. Hackforth [1928], 41f., replies effectively to such views.

27. Later on, Socrates assumes that Protagoras and the other sophists will agree with the hedonist account of the good (360a2–8); this account is defended in the discussion with the many, but nowhere else. If the defence of hedonism had been addressed only to the many, Protagoras would have been given no reason to accept hedonism.

28. The view that hedonism is the view only of the many and the sophists is briefly and convincingly answered by Vlastos [1956], p. xl, note (although Vlastos changes his mind in [1969a], 76, 86f.). It is held by Moreau [1939], 65f.; Sullivan [1961]; Weingartner [1973], 121 and note, 129f.; Dyson [1976], 42f.; Klosko [1979]; Zeyl [1980].

29. On rational and psychological eudaemonism, see §§36, 37.

30. On the pursuit of happiness, see §36.

31. On Socrates' attitude to the guiding principles, see §44.

32. On common beliefs about happiness, see §21.

33. Grote [1888], II 208, suggests that the hedonism of the *Pr.* solves the puzzle in the *Euthd.*: 'Good is the object of the Regal or political intelligence; but what is Good? . . . There is only one dialogue in which the question is answered affirmatively, in clear and unmistakable language, and with considerable development—and that is, the Protagoras: where Socrates asserts and proves at length that Good is at bottom identical with pleasure, and Evil with pain. . . .' For other views of this argument, see §49.

34. On Democritus on *euthumiē* see DK 68 A 167, B 3, 4, 188, 191. On pursuit and avoidance of pleasure see B 74, 207, 232, 235; Taylor [1967], 16–19; Gosling and Taylor [1982], 27–37.

35. In Xenophon's report, Prodicus' story of Heracles' choice between virtue and vice is a defence of long-term over short-term pleasure (Xen. *M.* II 1.21–34; pleasure is often appealed to in 29–33). Xenophon does not suggest either that Socrates' and Prodicus' views are vulgar and unenlightened, or that they are radically unconventional. See further Gosling and Taylor [1982], 14f.; Stokes [1986], 366.

36. On Socrates and the instrumental conception of virtue, see §§46–50.

37. This claim that we have some independent conception of a good product of the craft need not be true of absolutely everything that might be called a *technē*. See chap. 5, note 13.

38. On objections to quantitative hedonism, see §§77, 78, 200, 216.

39. On epistemological constraints on definitions, see §§14, 42.

40. Hedonism might also be taken to satisfy the demand for explanation involved in Socrates' conception of definition. See Sharvy [1972], 136 (who does not mention hedonism).

41. On the Cyrenaics see Irwin [1991], 57–62. Their relevance to Socrates is noticed by Zeller [1885] (discussed in chap. 5, note 25); Grote [1888], I 178, 199–201; Vlastos [1991], 301.

42. Some ancient sources attribute the remark 'I would rather go mad than experience pleasure' to Antisthenes; see DL VI 3 (= Giannantoni [1983] V A 122). Aspasius, *in EN* 142.8–10 (= Giannantoni [1983] V A 120), claims that Antisthenes regarded pleasure neither as an intrinsic good nor as a coincindental good.

43. Prodicus' distinction at 337a6–b3 alludes (although not very exactly) to this contrast.

44. The contrast between the constructive aim of Socratic argument and the agonistic character of Protagorean argument is made especially clear in the passage devoted to discussion of Simonides; at 348c5–7 Socrates emphasizes his main concern. Just as the *Euthd.* presents examples of eristic argument, the *Pr.* presents an example of agonistic argument. See Vlastos [1991], 135–39. It is a mistake to use this passage, as Klosko [1979] does, as evidence supporting the view that the dialogue as a whole is eristic.

45. On the accusation of competitiveness, see §86.

46. See 361c1, *epicheirōn apodeixai.*

47. Plato does not emphasize this consequence of Protagoras' views, and there is no reason to suppose that the historical Protagoras noticed it. The same is true of Gorgias on rhetoric; see §68.

Chapter 7

1. On eristic and dialectic, see §11.

2. For Isocrates' views, see *Antid.* 50, 84–85, 270, 285; *Helen* 1, 5; *c. Soph.* 7.

3. The relative date of the *G.* and the *Pr.* is discussed briefly and well by Rudberg [1953]; Dodds [1959], 16–21. For recent discussion, see Kahn [1988]; Taylor [1991], pp. xviii–xx. My main reasons for taking the *G.* to be later than both the *Pr.* and the shorter dialogues will emerge from the discussion of hedonism (§§77, 78) and of Socratic method (§§85, 86).

4. I use 'rhetorician' for a professional teacher such as Gorgias, who teaches the skills of public speaking, and 'orator' for the public speaker who uses these skills.

5. Socrates' argument against rhetoric is discussed by Penner [1987a] and Vickers [1985], 83–120.

6. *Phdr.* 271a–272b suggests how rhetoric might have a legitimate use in the light of understanding of the good and of the psychology of persuasion.

7. The argument against Gorgias is discussed by Penner [1987a], 323–25.

8. At *M.* 95c1–4 Gorgias ridicules the sophists who claim to teach virtue; he claims only that he makes people clever speakers. At *Ap.* 19e Gorgias is one of those who profess to educate people, but he is not said to claim that he teaches them virtue. Neither passage implies that Gorgias is a sophist.

9. Kahn [1983], 80–84, notices these reasons for Gorgias to agree with Socrates, but he infers without warrant that Gorgias makes 'a concession . . . which is not only false but known to be false by Gorgias as soon as he makes it' (84). Cf. §86 on 508b–c.

10. On Protagoras and Socrates' position, see §65.

11. On Protagoras' teaching, see §55.

12. By 'x is good for A all things considered' and 'x is good for A overall' I mean that x promotes A's happiness more than any alternative to x would promote it. I have supplied 'all things considered' or 'overall' where Plato simply says 'good' or 'better' or 'beneficial', at 467e4, 468b2, 468b7, 468c3, 468d3. (At 468b6, 468d3 it is clear that he has in mind what is good for the agent.) It is reasonable to understand Polus' and Socrates' claims this way; if Polus simply maintained the weaker claim that the ability conferred by rhetoric is a good that can sometimes be bad, all things considered, for the agent, he would not have refuted the Socratic claim that the orator needs to be just in order to secure his overall good.

13. I have stated the conclusion of the argument in 466d5–468e5 in terms that ignore some of the controversial moves that Socrates makes. See Irwin [1979], ad loc.; McTighe [1984]; Weiss [1985]; Vlastos [1991], 148–54; Penner [1991]. I see no reasonable basis for the claim that Socrates is being deliberately deceptive.

14. On *Pr.* 333d and the relation between the fine and the beneficial, see §56.

15. Polus is rather unfairly accused of hypocrisy by Canto [1987], 71.

16. Socrates' argument against Polus is examined by Santas [1979], 233–40; Irwin [1979], ad loc.; Mackenzie [1982]; Kahn [1983], 84–97; McKim [1988], 44–48; Vlastos [1991], 139–48.

17. These two passages make it clear that the good that an agent pursues is the good for the agent himself.

18. Cf. *Pr.* 348d5–349a6; Socrates suggests that Protagoras' profession makes him a suitable interlocutor.

19. This is a difference between Callicles' and Thrasymachus' objections to other-regarding justice. See §123.

20. On the impartiality of justice, see §213.

21. On the use of power to help one's friends and harm one's enemies, cf. *R.* 343e5–7; Blundell [1989], 50f. Failure to use this power is a sign of cowardice, *anandria*; cf. *Cri.* 45d8–46a4 (on the *Cri.* and the *G.*, see chap. 8, note 18).

22. On Protagoras' conception of virtue, see §55.

23. Cf. Thrasymachus on overreaching, §123.

24. The question about the relation between the interest of the rulers and the common interest is pursued in the *R.* See §213.

25. Contrast Callicles' position with that of Thrasymachus and of Glaucon and Adeimantus; §§123, 132.

26. Olympiodorus, 152.1–3, mentions only most people's lack of material resources.

27. Callicles' conception of happiness is discussed by Kahn [1983], 104f.; Rudebusch [1992].

28. 'Need', *deisthai*, might be replaced by 'lack' or 'want'.

29. On common-sense views of happiness, see §21.

30. This conception is closely related to some of the adaptive strategies discussed by Elster [1983], esp. chap. 3.

31. The argument is discussed by Santas [1979], 270–76; Irwin [1979], 202–4.

32. This aspect of the argument with Callicles is discussed briefly by Lafrance [1969], 25f., and more fully by White [1985]. White's suggestion that Callicles' ver-

sion of hedonism reflects the view that only the present matters in assessment of one's well-being (149f.) is attractive, but I am not convinced by it. (It seems to me more appropriate for a Cyrenaic view; see Irwin [1991].) I believe the expansive aspects of Callicles' conception answer the questions about 498b–c that White wants to answer by appeal to his view of Callicles (p. 152).

33. On the connexion between the refutation of Callicles and the verdict on rhetoric, see also White [1985], 149f. His account differs from mine for reasons suggested in chap. 7, note 32.

34. Socrates does not actually use any word for 'part'; he just uses the neuter article and adjective (493b1–2). See chap. 13, note 2.

35. The crucial distinction between 'appeared' (the aorist *phanenta*) and 'are held firm and bound down' (the present *katechetai* and the perfect *dedetai*) is clearly marked by Cope [1883]; Woodhead [1953]; Schleiermacher [1977]; Canto [1987]. It is blurred by Croiset and Bodin [1923]; Robin [1950]; Kahn [1983], 87.

Chapter 8

1. The hedonist doctrines in the *Gorgias* and *Protagoras* are compared by Gosling and Taylor [1982], 70–75; Kahn [1988] 72f., 93–95; Rudebusch [1989], 37f.

2. The suggestion that pleasures taken in different kinds of actions differ qualitatively may underlie Prodicus' distinction, mentioned at *Pr.* 337c1–4, 358a6–b2 (see Taylor [1991], 137f.). As usual (in the Socratic dialogues; contrast chap. 9, note 29, §100), Socrates suggests that Prodicus' distinction is unilluminating.

3. On Socratic eudaemonism and incontinence, see Vlastos [1969a], 83–88; Santas [1979], 209 (appealing to *G.* 468c and *M.* 77b–78b); Zeyl [1980], 262. On *M.* 77b–78b, see §98.

4. This is step (2a) in Socrates' argument; see §58.

5. This line of objection is suggested by Santas [1979], 209–14; Taylor [1991], 180, 188f. Taylor, however, tends to speak as though incontinence can be displayed only in an irrational preference for the present and the immediate. Davidson [1969], 30, shows why that is too narrow a conception. Socrates' move from superior value to superior attractiveness is defended by Nussbaum [1984], 112f.; [1986], 115f.; and by Rudebusch [1989], 29f. Wiggins [1978], 257, describes an argument from superior value to superior attractiveness, but does not endorse it.

6. See Kahn [1988], 89f.

7. Olympiodorus 174.23–25 perhaps suggests this interpretation.

8. This interpretation is defended by Cooper [1982], 580–85.

9. On virtue, see §41.

10. On the status of external goods, see §40.

11. Kraut [1984], 38 and note, and Vlastos [1991], 229, explain the passage differently.

12. This account also explains *Ap.* 30c6–d5.

13. On *Ap.* 30b2–4, see §41.

14. On health and illness, see §40.

15. Olympiodorus' paraphrase of the argument (178.21–179.3; 184.11–19) suggests that Socrates is claiming only that the happy person has the virtues, not the converse. He attributes the converse claim, however, to Socrates earlier in the dialogue (102.12–17).

16. This is the argument that Olympiodorus presents (153.1–5).

17. On the elenchos, in the *Pr.*, see §65.

18. On parallels between the *Cri.* and *G.*, see §§70, 76; chap. 7, note 21; Irwin [1979], 5; Kahn [1988], 74f.

19. 'Demonstrate', *apodeiknunai*, appears only rarely in the shorter Socratic dialogues. At *Ap.* 20d2 it appears in a legal context, when Socrates offers to 'show' that the charges against him are unfounded. Hippias uses it in this sense at *HMi* 367c3 (cf. *Euthd.* 285e3, 285e5). In the *Pr.* Socrates uses the word for what he is doing in the elenchos, at 354e6 ('show'), 357b8–c1, and 361b1 (where 'prove' is appropriate). In the *G.* the term is used to refer both to 'showing' or 'proving' in general (454a2, 470d3) and to the elenchos in particular (479e8). Socrates presents the elenchos as providing an *apodeixis* where his opponents cannot provide one (466e13, 527a8–c2). Socrates' willingness to speak of an *apodeixis* suggests Plato's confidence about what the elenchos can achieve.

20. In saying *tauta ouk oida hopōs echei*, Socrates means that he does not know whether the propositions he claims to have proved are true. Instead of claiming to know *hopōs echei*, he says that he takes it that things are a certain way; *tithēmi tauta houtōs echein*, 509a7–b1 (cf. *ei de houtōs echei* immediately following). In picking up *hopōs echei* with *houtōs echein*, Socrates makes it clear that the propositions he takes (*tithēmi*) to be true are the very ones he does not know to be true. Contrast Reeve [1989], 52.

21. On the disavowal of knowledge, see §16. Does 521b4–7 imply that Socrates regards himself as good, and therefore (since virtue requires knowledge) claims to have knowledge after all? (Cf. chap. 5, note 19.) Socrates does not claim that he is virtuous. In this context he is asking whether Callicles is urging him 'toward' (*epi*) the practice of flattery or towards the genuine political craft (521a2–7). Socrates claims that if he practices the political craft, someone who prosecutes him will be a bad man prosecuting a good man (521b4–7). If he possesses the political craft, he will have the knowledge needed for virtue, but he does not claim that he actually possesses the political craft. He claims only that he 'undertakes' (*epicheirein*) it (521b5–7), and undertaking does not imply possession. Hence he does not claim that he is actually virtuous either. Socrates recognizes that his position will be in some ways analogous to that of a doctor being accused by a cook (521e2–522a7), but he does not say that he actually has knowledge corresponding to medical knowledge. Contrast Vlastos [1991], 240, note 21.

22. On eristic, see §11.

23. At 494e7–8 it is actually Callicles who tries to evade the implications of his position by an irrelevant appeal to Socrates' sense of shame.

24. Olympiodorus, 156.29–157.8, argues that Socrates does not allow Callicles to escape by appealing to shame, since that would prevent him from seeing the consequences of his position (*ouk anechetai aischunthēnai hōs eidōs hoti estin hote blaptei*, 156.30–31). Contrast Kahn [1983], 106 (discussed by Irwin [1986] 72 and note); McKim [1988], 41.

25. See Olympiodorus, 158.21–22: *hē gar prohairesis elenchetai, ou to legomenon.*

26. See Olympiodorus, 179.21–26; 183.25–29. Contrast Kahn [1983], 79.

27. Different aspects of shame in the *Gorgias* are discussed by Race [1979]; McKim [1988], 40–43.

28. For Plato's further thoughts on the *G.*, see esp. §§172, 173.

Chapter 9

1. On virtue in general, see §23.
2. On Socratic inquiry and virtue, see §10.

3. 'Magnificently' in 70b6 perhaps refers to the impressive character of Gorgias' answers; he did not simply answer the question, but made a fine speech too. See Bluck [1961], ad loc.; *Symp.* 199c6–7; *St.* 277b1–6.

4. 'No puzzle' in 72a2 is picked up in 80c8.

5. On Socratic definition, see §13.

6. On different aspects of virtue, see §§55, 68.

7. On assumptions about definition, see §105.

8. On Socrates' conditions for a definition, see §107.

9. Meno's conception of knowledge is discussed by Ebert [1973], 173–75; Fine [1992], 220, and note 24.

10. The fact that Socrates and Meno share these implicit assumptions about knowledge counts against the view that their disagreement about inquiry turns on different senses of 'know'. Plato is careful to avoid suggesting that Socrates relies on any such eristic move.

11. A different answer to the paradox is suggested by White [1974]; [1976], 47–50.

12. '*Pais*' (like the English 'boy' in some periods) can be used for a slave of any age, and so does not imply that the slave is young.

13. The relation between the conversation with the slave and the Socratic elenchos is discussed by Irwin [1977a], 315f; Nehamas [1985], 305–10; Benson [1990c]; Brown [1991]; Vlastos [1991], 118–20.

14. Plato does not imply that at the end of this conversation the slave has knowledge. In 85d9 *nun* probably refers to the time mentioned in 85d1, when the slave will have completed his recollection. In *Phd.* 73a9–10 Cebes says people could not give the right answers to questions about diagrams unless knowledge and the correct account 'were in them'; but he may refer simply to the prenatal presence of knowledge. Contrast Brown [1991], 608–14.

15. In 85d4 *analabōn* need not actually mean 'recollect' or 'recover' (implying that we previously had it); it may just mean 'take up' (cf. *Ap.* 22b2; *Symp.* 185e1; *R.* 606e4; *Tht.* 203a1; *Sph.* 255e9; *St.* 261c5). The crucial claim about recollection is not the claim that the slave *analambanei*, but the further claim that this *analambanein* must be recollection, 85d6–7 (i.e., what the slave does can be explained only on the assumption that he recollects). The extent of recollection is discussed by Scott [1987]; Fine [1993], 137f.

16. On the discussion with the slave and the reliability of the elenchos, see Fine [1992], 207–13.

17. On sincerity, see §11.

18. Not all of Meno's beliefs are endorsed as reasonable. On his belief in parts of virtue, see chap. 3, note 29.

19. On the guiding principles, see §32.

20. Since Plato identifies knowledge with recollection, we can say that our recollection about F is complete, or that we have recollected F, only when we have reached the appropriate true beliefs about F and bound them with the appropriate *logos*. But this does not imply that recollection, understood as the process of recollecting rather than the result that consists in having recollected, goes on only when we acquire knowledge. Although Laches, say, cannot be said to have recollected bravery, he may still have recollected some truths about bravery in the course of incompletely recollecting bravery. On the relation between inquiry and recollection, see chap. 9, note 15; Nehamas [1985], 309f.

21. This identification of virtue with knowledge does not count as a satisfactory definition; for it does not say what sort of knowledge virtue is, and, as the *Euthd.* shows, that is not an easy question to answer.

22. On the *Euthd.*, see §§38 through 40. The arguments in the *M.* and the *Euthd.* are compared by Devereux [1977], 130–32; Ferejohn [1984].

23. On 'some sort of' (*tis*), cf. chap. 3, note 15.

24. This feature of the argument might support Thompson's translation of 89a4 as (1) 'wisdom is either virtue or a part of virtue', rather than Bluck's and Sharples' (2) 'virtue is either wisdom or a part of wisdom'. While (2) is needed to show that virtue is knowledge, only (1) has been defended. This point might also support the reading *ti autou* ('some part of virtue') in 87d7 (favoured by Bluck and by O'Brien [1967], 95).

25. For a qualification of this claim about the Reciprocity Thesis, see chap. 4, note 26.

26. On the Reciprocity Thesis in the *Pr.*, see §56.

27. The move from *kala* to *agatha*, 77b6, is also open to question.

28. Santas [1979], 194, seems to attribute the rejection of incontinence to our passage (see also Nakhnikian [1973]). His account of the argument (185–89), however, does not defend this attribution.

29. On *boulesthai* and *epithumein*, see Bluck [1961] ad 78a5, who rightly rejects Croiset and Bodin's [1923] suggestion that *boulesthai* and *dokein* in *G.* 466b–468a (also cited by O'Brien [1967], 87) mark the distinction that may be marked by *boulesthai* and *epithumein* in the *M.* Cf. §145. The distinction is reminiscent of Prodicus, who is treated differently in the *M.* from the way he is treated in the early dialogues. See chap. 5, note 14; chap. 6, note 43; chap. 8, note 2. Contrast §100.

30. Kahn [1987], 91f., takes the passage in the *Ch.* to show that when he wrote it Plato did not believe that all desire is for the good. The passage shows this, however, only if we are justified in assuming that Plato does not take desire for the fine and the pleasant to be reducible to desire for the good. This assumption about Plato's view in the early dialogues is unjustified.

31. On desire in the *G.*, see §80.

32. The relevance of the claim about recollection to the claim about teachability is noticed by Wilkes [1979]. The importance of recollection is also urged by Cornford [1952], 60 and note; and Devereux [1978], who draw different conclusions from mine.

33. The argument on teachability is discussed by Bluck [1961], 21–24; Sharples [1985], 162, 168; Kraut [1984], 288–304 (the best defence of the argument); Barnes [1991]; Brunschwig [1991].

34. On Plato's attitude to Athenian politicians, see Penner [1987a], 316–20; [1992b], 165. Contrast Vlastos [1991], 125; Snider [1992].

35. This point weakens the force of the analogy offered by Kraut [1984], 289f., and the similar suggestion offered by Brunschwig [1991], 595f.

36. On Prodicus, see chap. 9, note 29.

37. On explanations, see §109.

38. On knowledge in the early dialogues, see §16. Socrates' conditions for knowledge are discussed by Kraut [1984], 280–85; Penner [1992b], 140–43.

39. The repeated *aiei* in 97c6–8 emphasizes Socrates' point.

40. Aristotle recognizes beliefs with changing truth-values at *Catg.* 4a21–b13. For Plato's views on beliefs, cf. §§183, 184.

41. The bearing of counterfactual variations and relevant alternatives on questions about reliability and justification is discussed by Dretske [1970]; [1981], 129–34; Goldman [1976], 44–50; [1986], 103–13.

42. On virtue and craft, see §§49, 50.

43. On the relevance of Socrates' claims about the examined life, see Vlastos [1991], 125.

44. An 'external' account of Plato's criticisms of Socrates is presented by Vlastos

[1991], chap. 4. He claims that Plato's interest in mathematics swept him 'away from his Socratic moorings' towards 'the "Socrates" of his middle period, pursuing unSocratic projects to antiSocratic conclusions' (131). A similar view about the relevance of mathematics is expressed by Cornford [1952], chap. 4, esp. pp. 48, 55. Vlastos' view is criticized well by Gentzler [1991a], chap. 4.

Chapter 10

1. I use an initial capital in 'Form' and in the names of Forms ('Just', etc.) to refer to the non-sensible entity that, in Plato's view, is the only thing that meets Socrates' conditions for being a form (i.e., what is defined in a Socratic definition).

2. On Socrates' demand for a single property, see §§13, 14.

3. The *Cra.* is a dialogue of uncertain date; see Luce [1964]; Mackenzie [1986]. The fact that it takes up some questions that are treated at greater length in the *Tht.* might be thought to suggest that, like the *Tht.*, it was written after the *R*. This is not a good reason, however, for thinking it must be a late dialogue; it is equally possible that in the later dialogues Plato returns to some questions that he had discussed earlier and examines them again because he thinks they need a more thorough treatment. If we take the *Euthd.* to be an early dialogue (see chap. 4, note 1), we will make the same point about its relation to the *Sph.* and the *St.*

4. On the reference to change and stability here, see §113.

5. This issue is also discussed in *Pr.* 327e–328c; *Tht.* 178a5–179b5.

6. Plato needs the assumption that naming is an action, if he is to avoid committing a fallacy of division (which Robinson [1956], 123, alleges). The correctness of names is discussed by Kretzmann [1971].

7. The next part of the dialogue considers one way in which a name might be correct; for it considers whether the etymology of names conveys the truth about the objects they name. In the end Socrates recognizes that etymology is not the right place to look for correctness (435a5–d3). Even a name whose etymology conveys false information about the object named can serve as a name for that object in the right context, just as 'Hermogenes' can be used to name Hermogenes even though he is not a descendant of Hermes (429b11–c5). In place of the etymological theory of correctness, Socrates appeals to the preservation of 'outlines' (on which see Fine [1977]).

8. '*Barbaros*', discussed in *St.* 262c10–263a1, is an example of an apparent name that fails to preserve the outline of a genuine kind. Plato does not discuss such cases in the *Cra.*

9. On disputed terms, see §§14, 26; Kraut [1984], 281 and note.

10. On epistemological hedonism, see §57.

11. On measurement, see §64.

12. I follow Thompson in reading *ho erōtōn*. In 79c2 *gnōsomenou emou* suggests that the questioner's agreement is the relevant one. The emendation *prohomologē(i)* (defended by Thompson and Bluck) is attractive, but unnecessary.

13. At *Phd.* 74b6–9 I take *tō(i) men . . . tō(i) d'ou* to be masculine (as in *HMa.* 291d1–3, *Symp.* 211a2–5) and *phainetai* to have its veridical sense (as in *HMa.* 289b5–7; *R.* 479b6–7). On this view, one person correctly judges that two sticks are equal and another that they are unequal; presumably they focus on different features of the sticks (perhaps their equal length versus their unequal width, or their being equal to each other versus their being unequal to something else with a different length). For discussion see Murphy [1951], 111 and note 1; Owen [1957], 175 and note 35 (agreeing

with Murphy, but with an important reservation based on 74c1); Mills [1957]; Kirwan [1974], 116f.; Gallop [1975], 121f.; Bostock [1986], 73–77; Penner [1987b], 20–22, 33–40, 48–52, 352; White [1987]; [1992], 280–83; Fine [1993], 331f.

14. Contrast Ross [1951], 38; Mills [1958].

15. It is relevant to appeal to this passage in *R*. IV even though it does not specifically state the Principle of Non-Contradiction. See chap. 13, note 4.

16. Different views about the fault in the rejected explanations are presented by Vlastos [1969b], 95–102; Gallop [1975], 172–74; Bostock [1986], 136–42.

17. Explanations are connected with contrasts by Dretske [1988], 42f., relying on Dretske [1972]; Van Fraassen [1980], 127f.

18. I have spoken generally of 'explanation' in order to avoid the suggestion that Plato is concerned exclusively with causal explanation, and the suggestion that he has only non-causal explanation in mind. This issue is discussed by Taylor [1969]; Vlastos [1969b]; Annas [1982]; Fine [1987].

19. On the compresence of opposites, in *R*. I, see §120.

20. On the nature of the 'many Fs' see Murphy [1951], 110; Owen [1957], 174 and note 32; Crombie [1962], II 79, 293–95; Gosling [1960] (criticized by White [1977]; White [1979], with a reply by Gosling [1977]); Nehamas [1975a], 116 (treating the many Fs as particulars; contrast his view in [1975b]). If we believe that the many Fs are types or properties, we will not suppose that Plato is arguing primarily against nominalism (as suggested by Penner [1987b], 22, 53–55, 236f.). On Socrates, see §14.

21. Plato does not argue, then, that because (for instance) standing firm is 'no more' (*ou mallon*) fine than shameful, no particular instance of standing firm is definitely fine. On *ou mallon* see Woodruff [1988], 146–50; Annas [1992], 66–68.

22. Owen [1957], Strang [1963], and Bostock [1986], 77, 79f., maintain that Plato's belief in Forms is a response to some sort of relativity in certain predicates. This view is criticized by White [1989a], 45–57; Fine [1993], 161–68.

23. Contrast Ross [1951], 38.

24. This point is made clearly by Adam [1902], ad loc.

25. In this passage '*auto kath'hauto*' clearly does not refer to existential independence (which is irrelevant to the contrast). Cf. chap. 10, note 32.

26. This view of the passage is defended by Irwin [1977a], 318; Penner [1987b], 114f., 142. A different view is taken by Adam [1902], ad loc.; Kirwan [1974], 121–23; White [1992], 286f.

27. The inadequacy of the senses is discussed by Gosling [1973], 165–68; Penner [1987b], 114–16.

28. Plato's views on flux are discussed by Weerts [1931], 6–29 (discussed by Cherniss [1944], 218f.); Cornford [1935], 99; Ross [1951], 20; Bolton [1975]; Irwin [1977b]; Penner [1987b], 216–21; White [1989a], 58; Vlastos [1991], 69–71; Fine [1993], 54–57.

29. In 439d3–4, *kai dokei tauta panta rhein* is part of the clause beginning *mē ei*. Socrates, then, does not assert *kai dokei*. . . . This passage is discussed by Weerts [1931], 24; Calvert [1970], 36.

30. The relation of Plato's views on flux to the early dialogues is discussed by Graham [1992].

31. Plato's view of Heracleitus is discussed further in Irwin [1992b], 55f.

32. None of the passages we have discussed offers any explicit basis for Aristotle's claim that Plato 'separated' Forms from sensibles. (Vlastos [1991], 259 and note, 261, claims that Plato's use of *auto kath' hauto* for Forms implies separation, but see chap. 10, note 25, and Fine [1993], 165f., 274f.) It is not clear, however, that Aristotle takes

the belief in separation to be explicit. At *Met.* 1086b7–10 he suggests that Plato took it for granted that if he had proved the existence of Forms 'apart from' (*para*) sensibles (cf. *Phd.* 74a11, 74b6–7), that would be enough to prove that the Forms must be separated. For fuller discussion, see Fine [1993], 60.

33. On the *Eu.* and the *M.*, see §§14, 107.

34. *I Alc.* 111a11–112a9 draws a similar distinction. The importance of these passages on disputed properties is rightly emphasized by Strang [1963], 195–98 (who, however, connects them too closely with Owen's views on relatives; see chapter 10, note 22). Cf. Irwin [1977a], 320f.

35. Vlastos [1969b], 91f., argues that Plato's formula in *Phd.* 100c–e is meant to allude to the demand for definitions. Strang [1963], 196; and Bostock [1986], 150f., deny this, but they take insufficient account of 78c10–d7, which makes it clear that the Forms are the objects of Socratic definitions. The same Forms are introduced again at 100c–e; it is reasonable to suppose that Plato still intends them to be definable. The 'clever' accounts of various causes (105b6–c7) offer different suggestions about how a more informative account could be given; see Taylor [1969], 48–54.

36. The sense of 'accord' and 'discord' is discussed by Robinson [1953], 126–36; Bostock [1986], 166–70; Gentzler [1991b].

37. Perhaps Plato suggests that someone who raises Thrasymachus' sort of objection is a 'contradicter', *antilogoikos* (101e2), who urges against a hypothesis an objection that really needs to be evaluated by reference to some higher principle.

Chapter 11

1. For the view that Book I is really an early dialogue, see Friedländer [1964], chap. 3; Vlastos [1991], 248–51. On the other side see Giannantoni [1957] (esp. 131, 143f., on the deliberately Socratic character of the book); Annas [1981], 17f., 47; Tarán [1985]. The 'early' stylistic features may simply indicate Plato's success in writing in his earlier style, if he intended Book I to resemble a Socratic dialogue,

2. This interpretation of Book I is presented by Reeve [1988], 22–24.

3. For this view, see Joseph [1935], chaps. 1 and 2.

4. Sharply contrasting views of Cephalus are presented by Annas [1981], 18–23; and Reeve [1988], 5–7.

5. As Adam [1902] notes, ad loc., 'calm', *eukoloi*, fits the reference to Sophocles, to whom Aristophanes applies the term at *Ran.* 82.

6. The attitude expressed in 329a4–8 fits Callicles' emphasis on the number and intensity of desires and pleasures. See §72.

7. For 'just like that', *haplōs houtōs*, cf. *Pr.* 351c7; *G.* 468c3; *M.* 73e5; *R.* 377b5, 378a2, 386b9; *Laws* 633c9, 658a6.

8. Or 'mark', *horos*, 331d2.

9. There is no further evidence of what Simonides actually said.

10. *Apodidonai* refers to giving something that is owed; see, e.g., *Phd.* 118a7–8; Gospel according to Luke 20:25. Hence it may be translated either 'give back' (Latin *reddere*, in case we are bound to return something) or, more generally, 'duly give' (Latin *tribuere*, in case we are bound to give something that we may not have previously received). Shorey [1930] uses 'return' at 331c and 332a1, but 'render' at 331e3, 332a8, 332c2; Grube [1992] switches between 'give back' and 'give' on no clear principle. See Young [1980], 404 and note.

11. On the relation between the views of Simonides and Polemarchus, see Young [1980], 407f.; Tarán [1985], 93; Lycos [1987], 35f.

12. For this sort of objection, cf. *Amat.* 136c3–e4.

13. On the *Euthd.*, see §42.

14. This objection is raised at *HMi.* 375d7–376b6. Plato recalls that dialogue at *R.* 334b1, by citing Odysseus as an example of someone who turns out to be just, on Polemarchus' account, because of his skill in cheating.

15. On the *Cri.*, see §31. A different view on its relation to *R.* I is taken by Vlastos [1991], 197 and note 58.

16. Joseph [1935], 14, makes this point in defence of Socrates' argument.

17. *Dikaiosunē* and *to dikaion* are combined at 336a9, 343c3, 367c. The neuter adjective *to dikaion* is used for the virtue at 354c1, and for just action at 364a5. The abstract noun *dikaiosunē* is used for the person at 357d4, 358c1, 358d5, 360d1, 361b1, 363a1, 366b3, 366c4, 367a6. *Dikaiosunē* is not used as the abstract noun for the justness of actions. Cf. chap. 3, note 11 and chap. 12, note 5.

18. This view of Plato's target in the argument with Polemarchus is defended most effectively by Joseph [1935], chap. 1. With this first attempt to define justice, he compares Xen. *M.* IV 2.1–20; see esp. 13, 17.

19. This anticipation of *R.* V is noticed by Grote [1888] IV, 3.

20. On compresence of opposites and the early dialogues, see §109.

21. On this account of justice, see Vlastos [1971c], 114–23.

22. On the connexion between Thrasymachus' demand and Polemarchus' assumptions, see Murphy [1951], 6.

23. 'Just order' is further explained in §128.

24. We might initially object that 'superior' or 'stronger' is still not clear: stronger in what respect? Socrates raises this very question, asking whether Thrasymachus thinks it is just for weaker people to eat the food that is advantageous for the athlete Poulydamas (338c4–d2). Thrasymachus replies by explaining that the 'superior' he has in mind is a regime that lays down laws, and so a just action is the action of a subject in obeying laws that promote the advantage of the superior (338e1–339a4).

25. Plato's treatment of Thrasymachus' argument is to be distinguished from his presentation of Thrasymachus' character, on which see Quincey [1981].

26. Two objections might be raised against Thrasymachus' account: (1) It does not state a necessary condition for justice and injustice. He agrees that it is possible for one city to treat others unjustly by attempting to enslave them (351b1–c3). It is difficult to see how it is violating the interest of the stronger in doing this. The same is true of robbers who rob an innocent traveller (351c7–10). Whether they treat him justly or unjustly seems to have nothing to do with whether they are acting in the interest of some stronger party. (2) Nor does the account seem to state a sufficient condition for justice. A supporter of the regime might decide to form a gang of assassins to murder all the opponents of the regime. Thrasymachus does not suggest that if such behaviour benefited the regime, it would be just.

27. This objection is suggested by Joseph [1935], 19.

28. On the difference between Thrasymachus' account and an ordinary definition, see Lycos [1987], 46–48.

29. We might object that 'interest' or 'benefit' is still not sufficiently perspicuous. This objection does not affect Thrasymachus, since he understands the interest of the regime to be whatever strengthens it. A broader understanding of 'benefit' brings Thrasymachus' account closer to the truth, as the later books of the *R.* show (since the

justice of the ideal city can be seen to benefit the regime, once we understand what benefit really consists in).

30. Different views of Thrasymachus' position are summarized and discussed by Nicholson [1974] and Reeve [1985]. It is sometimes suggested (see Annas [1981], 45, agreeing with Kerferd [1947]) that Thrasymachus' claim that justice is another's good conflicts with his previous claim that justice is the advantage of the stronger, since (according to the previous definition) just action by the stronger is advantageous for the stronger. This conflict disappears once we realize that in both his claims Thrasymachus means to say that justice consists in the weaker party's obeying rules that benefit the regime. He never predicates either justice or injustice of the actions of the regime. (He predicates it of the actions of individual officeholders, but each of these individuals does act in the interest of the regime—since it is not in his own interest to refrain from taking bribes—and so for the good of another.) If this is right, we ought not to follow Kerferd [1947] and Nicholson [1974] in denying that 'the advantage of the stronger' is really Thrasymachus' account (in the appropriate sense, distinct from a Socratic definition) of justice.

31. For further discussion of this part of Thrasymachus' argument, see §132; Lycos [1987], 50–53.

32. Whether or not Plato means to allude specifically to the argument with Polus in the *G.* (see Adam [1902] on 348e5), this argument is a good example of the sort of approach that is ruled out by Thrasymachus' attitude; see Murphy [1951], 4 and note.

33. In denying that justice is a virtue, Thrasymachus rejects Callicles' view that people who have the power to overreach, and who use this power, conform to 'natural justice'. See §71.

34. This aspect of the argument is noticed by Joseph [1935], 32f. Once we notice it, we can answer the objections raised by Annas [1981], 51f.; Reeve [1988], 20.

35. In particular, Book I does not try to explain psychic conflict by appeal to a conflict between rational and non-rational parts of the soul. On psychic justice in the *G.*, see §§79, 80.

36. The unsatisfactoriness of Socrates' argument is criticized by Harrison [1962].

Chapter 12

1. 'For its own sake' translates *auto hautou heneka*, 357b6. Plato uses 'itself because of itself' (*autē di'hautēn*, 367b4, 367d3) and 'itself by itself' (*auto kath'hauto*, 358b5) as equivalent to 'for its own sake'.

2. Grote [1888], IV 117f., states this objection clearly.

3. I take all 'just orders' to prescribe just behaviour. I do not assume that they are all just, or that anyone who follows their prescriptions is a just person.

4. This aspect of Glaucon's account is noticed and criticized by Gauthier [1982], 146f.; [1986], 309f.

5. On the difference between the justness of persons (*dikaiosunē*) and the justness of actions, see chap. 11, note 17. Glaucon's emphasis on the justness of persons is noticed by Reeve [1988], 35.

6. Aristotle makes this point about slaves, *Pol.* 1278b32–37.

7. Hobbes makes this point in *Leviathan*, c.15: 'Secondly, that in a condition of war, wherein every man to every man, for want of a common power to keep them all in awe, is an enemy, there is no man can hope, by his own strength, or wit, to defend himself from destruction, without the help of confederates.' Given these facts about

Gyges, Gauthier [1982], 147f., rather exaggerates Gyges' godlike character and underestimates his interest in belonging to a just order.

8. Hobbes, *Leviathan*, c.15. The fool's argument is discussed by Gauthier [1982], 136f., 144–46.

9. On the good and the necessary (cf. 347c7, 540b4), see §205; Kirwan [1965], 167.

10. See Hume, *Inquiry*, III, p. 188.

11. See Holden [1886], ad loc.

12. Cf. Seneca, *Epp*. 97.13–16.

13. On Callicles' objections, see §§70, 86.

14. Plato's treatment of happiness is intelligible if he does not believe that happiness is just one good; the threefold division may be taken to classify single goods and so not to include a compound good such as happiness.

15. Different versions of this sort of interpretation are defended by Foster [1937; 1938]; Sachs [1963], 39–42; White [1979], 75, 78f. The most thorough defence is by White [1984]. I agree with Kirwan [1965], who develops and improves the argument of Mabbott [1937]. Reeve's position [1988], 24–33, is similar. Annas' view [1981], 66–68, is difficult to classify; see Irwin [1982b], 50f.

16. This objection seems to me to damage the account of the difference between the second and third classes of goods that is offered by White [1984], 420.

17. The relation that Plato has in mind is closely connected to Aristotle's conception of the formal cause and to his own account in the *Phd.* (see §109) of the safe and the clever causes, which are not confined to efficient-causal relations. See Mabbott [1937], 60: 'What does justice "do to a soul"? What does beauty do to a poem? By its presence it renders the poem beautiful. So justice has the power to render the soul harmonious. But its harmony *is* justice and not a consequence of justice.' See also Kirwan [1965], 172f. White [1984], 410–13, rightly emphasizes the relevance of the *Phd.*'s account of causation to the division in *R*. II; but I do not believe the *Phd.* supports the view that in *R*. II Plato refers to efficient-causal consequences of justice.

18. Some causal consequences will no doubt be necessary, in virtue of the essential properties. If we find the essential properties, we will discover why some causal consequences are necessary in the way they are.

19. Justice is said to be the greatest good and injustice the greatest evil among 'the things the soul has in it', 366e8–9. Happiness is the greatest good, but if it includes external goods, it is not confined to the soul; hence this phrase does not imply that justice is identical to happiness. Grote [1888], IV 102, takes Plato to defend the sufficiency thesis.

20. Comparative claims are made at 387d (esp. 387d11, *malista . . . autarkēs*), 392cd, 580b, 588d. The analogy of health and illness, 445a, does not imply the sufficiency thesis.

21. The role of Book X is examined by White [1989b], discussed by Kraut [1992c], 337 and note 21.

22. This view of justice and happiness is discussed by White [1979], 78f.; [1984].

23. This point is raised by Reeve [1988], 30f.

24. On types of reliability, see §101.

25. This passage is discussed by Gooch [1974]; Irwin [1977a], 322; Gosling and Taylor [1982], 87–95; Weiss [1987].

26. On Neoptolemus, see §30.

27. Grote [1888], IV 107, mentions this possibility.

28. This sort of difficulty seems to arise for the answer to Glaucon's challenge that is suggested by Gauthier [1982], 144f.; [1986], 326–28, 337f.

29. A parallel conclusion is suggested by Sidgwick's argument [1907], 490, to show that utilitarians may not want the utilitarian basis of morality to be generally recognized: 'and thus a Utilitarian may reasonably desire, on Utilitarian principles, that some of his conclusions should be rejected by mankind generally; or even that the vulgar should keep aloof from his system as a whole'.

30. In *Laws* 663d6–664a8 (cited by Grote [1888], IV 107) Plato actually suggests that it would be desirable to propagate belief in the benefits of justice even if the belief were false.

31. The citizens of the ideal city who have true belief without knowledge are not open to this objection, for their true beliefs would be maintained in the face of knowledge. See §§162, 163.

32. That Socrates' argument so far has failed to meet Glaucon's criteria is made clear by 357a4–b4, 358b1–7, and 358c6–d3.

33. On means and ends, see §46.

34. On Aristotle and Socrates, see §49.

35. At 367d5–e1 Adeimantus says he expects a defence of justice, apart from its rewards, from Socrates in particular, 'because you have passed your whole life examining precisely this'. It is not clear what 'this' refers to; it might be either 'justice' (cf. 506b8–c1, a similar remark on Socrates' long study of the good) or 'the benefit of justice apart from its rewards'.

36. On Socrates, see §41. On the *G.*, see §81.

37. Chrysippus' care in distinguishing Socrates from Plato contrasts sharply with Cicero's argument for finding the Socratic position in Plato; Cicero appeals to the *G.* and *Mnx.*, raising no question about whether these present Plato's views (*Tusc.* V 35–36), even though he elsewhere recognizes a distinction between the Platonic and the historical Socrates (*Rep.* I 16). On the Stoics' concern to distinguish Socratic from Platonic views, see Long [1988], 161. On Poseidonius, see §168.

38. On the Platonists, see Dillon [1977], 251, 299. On Alcinous, see Whittaker [1990], 137 and note 443. Lilla [1971], 68–72, discusses Clement, *Str.* IV 52.1–2 (ed. Stählin [1906]), which appeals to *R.* 361e (cf. V 108.2).

39. On Plato's views on Socrates' search for definitions, see §115.

40. This objection is forcefully stated by Prichard [1968], 103–9, 118–19. Schopenhauer, *Will and Representation*, II 524, praises Plato for having avoided the eudaemonist attitude to morality, but his praise is based on misunderstanding. White [1979], 43–45, 80, denies that Plato accepts eudaemonism. See §205.

41. Eudaemonism is reduced to a rather uncontroversial position by McDowell [1980], 366–71.

42. Grote [1851], VIII 539, describes Book II well: 'Hardly anything in Plato's compositions is more powerful than these discourses. They present in a perspicuous and forcible manner, some of the most serious difficulties with which ethical theory is required to grapple'.

Chapter 13

1. Some relevant issues in Books II and III are discussed in Irwin [1977a], 330f.

2. Plato speaks of different kinds (*eidē* or *genē*, 435c1, 444a1) or parts (*merē*, 442b11) or things (neuter adjectives and pronouns, 436b9). See Joseph [1935], 47. On the correspondence between the structure of the soul and the structure of the city, see §159.

3. See Woods [1987], 26–30.

4. This example shows that the Principle of Contraries is not the same as the Principle of Non-Contradiction. See Robinson [1971], 29. From (a) x has tendency F, and (b) x has a tendency G that is contrary to F, we cannot infer that (c) x has tendency F and not (x has tendency F). If Plato thinks he is entitled to (c), he is seriously confused. There is no need to suppose, however, that he is influenced by this confusion.

5. On the *Phd.* see §§109, 133; Houston [1986], chap. 4; Woods [1987], 40.

6. On the relevance of contrasts, see §109.

7. If Plato is speaking of genuine contraries, we must understand these negative expressions as indicating positive unwillingness as opposed to mere lack of willingness; they are similar to the English 'I don't want to', which normally means 'I want not to' rather than simply 'It is not the case that I want to'.

8. Following Adam [1902], I take the genitive in *epithumiōn . . . genos*, 437d2–3 to be a defining genitive.

9. See Adam [1902], ad loc.; Krohn [1876], 56f.

10. This point is not completely certain, because of Plato's use of *boulesthai* at 439b1, commented on by Joseph [1935], 49 and note 1. On *boulesthai* and *epithumein* in *M.* 77–78, see chap. 9, note 29.

11. The issues about types of conflict and grounds for recognizing distinct parts are discussed by Joseph [1935], 53–55; Williams [1965], 167–69 (who seems, like Joseph, 53 and note, to assume that Plato does not allow conflicts of the second and third type within the appetitive part); Woods [1987], 38f.; Penner [1990], 53f. (who explicitly makes the assumption I attributed to Williams).

12. This passage in Aristotle is used to clarify Plato by Joseph [1935], 54 and note; Murphy [1951], 28 and note; Penner [1971], 96, 118, but they all take it to imply that Plato rejects the second and third types of conflict mentioned here.

13. Although the thesis that is rejected speaks of a desire for drink as opposed to desire for good drink, Murphy [1951], 45–47, points out that Plato probably means to refer to desire for drink qua something good. The two are not the same, since a drink that is a good drink (i.e., good as drinks go) may not in all circumstances (e.g., when I have already had too much to drink) be a good (i.e., a good thing).

14. In this argument about thirst qua thirst it is difficult to decide whether *epithumiai* are restricted to appetites or are meant to include all desires; unfortunately, Plato uses the term both as a generic term for all desires (cf. 431b9–d6) and as a specific term for one type of desire (Plato explains this specific use at 580d10–581a1, appealing to the intensity of the desires that characterize the appetitive part). In paraphrasing Plato's position, I have used 'desire' to indicate the generic notion (corresponding to Aristotle's use of '*orexis*') and 'appetite' for the specific use of '*epithumia*'. See Joseph [1935], 51 and note; contrast Kahn [1987], 79.

15. On *ara* in 438a3 see Jowett and Campbell [1894], II 207f; Des Places [1929], 268f., 281. See also 358c5 (and Adam [1902]), 362a4, 364b3, 364e6; Joseph [1935], 56 and note; Murphy [1951], 45 and note.

16. The expression used to specify Thrasymachus' thesis, *kath'hoson* ('insofar as', 340d7), is repeated in 437c4.

17. On Socrates on desire, cf. §80.

18. This suggestion is challenged by Plato's remark that in some cases spirit 'is unwilling to be aroused', 440c5; even here, though, he does not actually say that the person himself is unwilling insofar as his spirited part is unwilling, whereas he does say this in the case of the rational part. Once again (see chap. 13, note 10) we have to admit that Plato's terminology for desire is rather loose.

19. Psychological compulsion is discussed with reference to Socrates and Plato by Santas [1979], 214–17; Penner [1990], 51f.

20. Cooper [1984], 9f.; and Woods [1987], 41f., 45f., give different accounts of Plato's reasons for picking the specific examples of appetites that he picks in this argument.

21. On the role of parts, see §154.

22. This claim about interpretation has been developed by Davidson [1970], 221–23; [1982], 294–96, and exploited by Penner [1990], 43f.

23. The third part of the soul is rejected by Cornford [1912], 262–64; Hardie [1936], 142f.; Penner [1971], 111–13; [1990], 44. Hardie, however, rightly rejects the view, accepted by Penner, that Plato introduces the *thumos* here simply to make the structure of the soul parallel to that of the city. Plato's argument is defended by Joseph [1935], 63–69; Cooper [1984], 12–17.

24. Perhaps Plato takes Leontius' impulse to be sexual. Adam cites Kock [1880], I 739, where, however, the reference to Leontius depends on an emendation.

25. On 440b4–7 see Krohn [1876], 52; Adam [1902], ad loc. and 271f.; Murphy [1951], 34; White [1979], 126; Cooper [1984], 21 and note 19. Since this passage does not deny the existence of any conflict between the rational and the spirited part in which the spirited part prefers the action preferred by the appetitive part, it is not inconsistent with 441a or 553c.

26. The example of children who are full of 'spirit' (or 'anger', 441a8) as soon as they are born and acquire reasoning much later (if they acquire it at all) seems unsuitable for Plato's purposes. He cannot reasonably claim that a young child or a nonhuman animal reacts as Leontius reacts to his appetites; and so it is not clear that the reactions of these agents belong to anything other than an appetitive part.

27. When sudden dangers are liable to arise, brave people are better off if they are not always reflecting about the best thing to do; cf. Ar. *EN* 1117a17–22.

28. On this restricted conception see Penner [1971; 1990]; Annas [1981], 129f., 139–41; Cooper [1984], 9.

29. The fact that beliefs about good and bad are present in the non-rational parts is emphasized by Lesses [1987].

30. On the rational part's concern for the whole self, see Joseph [1935], 58–63, esp. 59: '[Reason] makes him conceive a good that is to satisfy *him*, and not merely quench this or that particular desire; and it makes him also desire this good.' Murphy [1951], 32–34, takes a more qualified view.

31. See Butler, *Sermons*, II 13–17.

32. The attitudes of the rational part may be guided by non-rational aims. See §197.

33. If this account of Plato's division is right, he does not believe that the division between rational and non-rational parts is a division between reason and desire. As Aristotle supposes, he attributes a different kind of desire to each part (*DA* 432b4–7).

34. Murphy [1951], 29f., suggests, relying on 443d7, that the tripartite division is not meant to be exhaustive.

35. This is not the only case where Plato lacks clear terminology for the different relations. When he describes sensibles as 'likenesses', *homoiōmata*, of Forms (*Parm.* 132d3), we might take him to mean simply that they are similar, *homoia*, to Forms. In fact, however, he assumes that if x is a *homoiōma* of y, then x is a copy of y; 'being a copy of' is an asymmetrical relation that includes the symmetrical relation of similarity.

36. On this analogy, see §202.

37. The anthropomorphic aspects of Plato's division are discussed by Murphy [1951], 69; White [1979], 129; Annas [1981], 142–46; Moline [1978], 10–14, 22–26; Reeve [1988], 139.

38. On efficiency see §198.
39. On incontinence and intelligibility, see §148.

Chapter 14

1. On the Unity Thesis, see §§28, 29, 59, 97.
2. On the human function, see §125.
3. The view that I am opposing here is maintained by Vlastos [1971c], 130, discussed in Irwin [1977a], 332. Murphy [1951], 12–14, warns against the sort of view that Vlastos accepts. The importance of the claim about function is rightly emphasized by Gosling [1973], 55–57.
4. Joseph [1935], chap. 6, argues for connexions between *R*. IV and Aristotle's doctrine of the mean, without mentioning the connexion I have suggested. Murphy [1951], 19 (see also Reeve [1988], 316 and note 3), suggests a connexion with Aristotle's contrast between natural virtue and full virtue of character (*EN* 1144b1–14).
5. On parts of the soul as agents, see §152.
6. This connexion between Plato and Aristotle tends to support a general observation by Brochard, [1912], 169, who comments: 'La morale est peut-ētre la partie du système de Platon qui, du moins en France, a été le moins étudiée par les historiens et les critiques'. He suggests that this may be because Plato comes between the two major contributions to moral philosophy by Socrates and by Aristotle. Against this trend he argues: 'la morale d'Aristote se trouve plus qu'en germe dans celle de son maître. Les principales doctrines auxquelles le disciple a attaché son nom ont déjà été, sinon formulées d'une manière aussi heureuse, du moins très nettement aperçues et fortement exposées par le maître. Ici, comme en bien d'autres questions, les deux philosophies, en dépit de différences notables, se continuent l'une l'autre beaucoup plus qu'elles ne sont opposées et se complètent bien loin de se contredire' (170). A full proof of this claim would require a study of Plato's later dialogues, but a good case in its favour can be made out (as Brochard sees) from the *Republic* alone.
7. On the *M*. on knowledge, see §102.
8. The view that individual members of the lower classes in the ideal city have one or more of the virtues is defended by Vlastos [1971c], 136–38 (cf. additions in [1981a], 425–27, replying to Cooper [1977a], 151–57), and in Vlastos [1991], 88–90. His view is criticized by Irwin [1977a], 322, 329; Reeve [1988], 310. Some related questions about moral education are explored by Gill [1985].
9. Plato's analogy between city and soul is discussed by Murphy [1951], chap. 4; Vlastos [1971c], 123f.; Neu [1971]; Williams [1973a], 196–200; Irwin [1977a], 331; Cooper [1977a], 153; Lear [1992]. Wilson [1976a] explains the argument especially clearly, showing why it does not need the assumption that a virtue in the city requires the same virtue in individuals; nonetheless he attributes this assumption to Plato (121f.).
10. See 442c5–10, where the rational part deliberates; b11–c3, where it issues instructions (*parangellein*); c5–8, where wisdom is present in the part of the soul that issues instructions.
11. On 430e2, *politikēn ge*, see Adam [1902], ad loc., and Irwin [1977a] 329f., taking it to refer to the bravery of the city rather than of individuals. Alternatively, the term might be explained as a reference to 'citizen bravery', a quality of individuals to be distinguished from genuine bravery. See chap. 14, note 16. The idea of distinctive responsibility (on which see Wilson [1976a], 117f.) is expressed by saying that the non-military classes in the city are not *kurioi* of the city's being brave or cowardly, 429b5–6. To say that one class or another is *kurios* of the city's bravery is not to say that no

other class contributes to it. (When Plato says that the non-military classes are not *kurioi* by being brave themselves, we might infer that the members of the military class are *kurioi* by being brave themselves; Plato, however, does not say this.)

12. On reliability, see §101.

13. On the timocracy, see §196.

14. On slavish virtue, see §136.

15. The point is made quite well by Aristotle in his description of citizen bravery, *EN* 1116a17. He contrasts the citizen's bravery, which rests on shame and honour, with the outlook of those who do the brave action for fear of punishment.

16. Both the well-educated person and the slavish person seek pleasure and honour, but the well-educated person takes pleasure in acting (as he believes) virtuously and seeks to be honoured for acting virtuously. It is not clear how far *Phd.* 82a10–e8 marks this distinction. It seems that 68c8–13 suggests that all except philosophers are brave because of fear and that therefore they are slavish; this implies that the popular and citizen virtue of 82a10ff. is a type (although presumably a superior type) of slavish virtue. The *R.*, however, never suggests that the character of well-educated members of the lower classes in the ideal city is slavish. Archer-Hind's discussion [1894], Appendix 1, uses 'utilitarian' confusingly, to describe the motives of all non-philosophers. Vlastos [1971c], 137f. [1991], 89, insufficiently distinguishes the questions: (1) Can someone be non-slavish without knowledge? (2) Can someone be virtuous without knowledge? I believe Plato can answer Yes to (1) and No to (2).

17. On giving an account, see §§10, 53, 103.

18. See §234.

19. Plato's attitude to the Socratic belief that knowledge is sufficient for virtue is discussed by Gosling [1978], 101f.; Penner [1992b], 127–30.

20. Joseph [1935], 112, argues on these grounds that Plato takes knowledge to be necessary for virtue.

21. Murphy [1951], 18, discusses the Unity Thesis. He suggests: 'Perhaps his own view might be stated more reasonably by saying that there is either one virtue (justice) or three (temperance, courage, and wisdom, each animated by justice). It is only by adding alternatives that he gets four'. This suggestion brings out clearly an important difference between the role of justice and that of the other virtues. On connexions between the virtues, see also Reeve [1988], 238–43.

22. See 442b11, *tō(i) merei*; c5, *tō(i) smikrō(i) merei*; c10, *tē(i) philia(i)*.

23. Socrates is committed to these substitutions (if he identifies temperance with knowledge of the good) by the assumptions underlying the argument in *Eu.* 10e–11b, where he claims that if the G is what the F is, then if x is F by (or because of) the F, it follows that x is F by the G. This claim is discussed, with reference to the Unity Thesis, by Vlastos [1981a], 433.

24. On justice and temperance, see Zeller [1876], 452f.; Adam [1902], 232; Larson [1951] (who exaggerates their similarity).

25. This may be part of the point of Joseph's remark at [1935], 80 and note, that 'temperance is excellence of the soul in respect of its desiderative or orectic nature' (although I do not agree with all his other remarks about the appetitive part).

26. On intellectual conditions for virtue, see §234.

27. Shorey [1903], 14, states a strongly unitarian view: 'The *Republic*, in which Plato explicitly states his solution of these problems, is a marvellous achievement of mature constructive thought. But the ideas and distinctions required for the solution itself are obvious enough, and it is absurd to affirm that they were beyond the reach of a thinker who was capable of composing the *Protagoras*, the subtle *Lysis* and *Charmides*,

or the eloquent and ingenious *Gorgias*'. A similar view is accepted by O'Brien [1967], 122–27, 144–48; a more qualified position is held by Kahn [1986], 19–21. Devereux [1977; 1992] accepts Aristotle's testimony about the views of the historical Socrates, but argues that the *Laches* is intended as a criticism of these views.

28. On the *Euthd.*, see §42.

29. On psychological eudaemonism in the *G.*, see §80.

30. Kahn [1988] agrees with this point and so dates the *G.* very early. See chap. 7, note 3.

31. *EN* 1116b3–5 speaks of 'the Socrates' but *EE* 1229a15 and *MM* 1190b28 speak of 'Socrates'. See §5. Aristotle does not say that Socrates actually identified bravery with *empeiria*, but that the tendency to identify *empeiria* with bravery in a given area underlies Socrates' identification of bravery with knowledge.

32. On Aristotle's view of Socratic ethics, see §§48, 49, 52.

33. On Cicero's view, see chap. 12, note 37.

34. For the most relevant passages on Plato in Poseidonius, see Edelstein and Kidd [1972], T 95–97, F 142–44, 146, 152. See Kidd [1988] II 1, 82f. Galen, *HPP* 588.27–33 (De Lacy [1980]), distinguishes the historical and the Platonic Socrates, but he never ascribes Plato's tripartition of the soul to Socrates.

Chapter 15

1. Bosanquet [1906], 365 (cf. Murphy [1951], 32), remarks: 'The rank of the intelligence comes primarily from its power to represent the whole.' In this way the outlook of the rational part might also claim to be more objective, if 'objectivity is advanced when we step back, detach from our earlier point of view toward something, and arrive at a new view of the whole that is formed by including ourselves and our earlier view point in what is to be understood' (Nagel [1980], 97).

2. On Socrates' view of practical reason, see §§49, 50.

3. On virtue and happiness, see §82.

4. On the comparative thesis, see §134.

5. On self-sufficiency, see chap. 12, note 20.

6. He has used this analogy in *Cri.* 47d. See §§30, 41, 76.

7. This appeal to natural suitability does not exclude an appeal to efficiency also, but it is not the same as an appeal to efficiency.

8. On the interpretation of 'doing one's own work', see §158. Mohr [1987] connects doing one's own work (understood as Vlastos [1971c] understands it) with Plato's conception of happiness.

9. On happiness and rational activity, see §224.

10. This objection is presented at length by Grote [1888], IV 102–20. He contrasts other-regarding justice with self-regarding Platonic justice, claiming that the other-regarding sense 'is that which is in more common use; and it is that which Plato assumes provisionally when he puts forward the case of opponents in the speeches of Glaukon and Adeimantus' (103). According to Grote, Plato proves (at most) that self-regarding psychic justice promotes happiness. In commenting on the argument of Book IX, Grote objects: 'But when this point is granted, nothing is proved abut the just and the unjust man, except in a sense of these terms peculiar to Plato himself' (120). Some of the many further discussions are Prichard [1968], 106; Sachs [1963]; Vlastos [1971c]; Kraut [1973a]; White [1979], 131–33; Annas [1978; 1981], chap. 6

11. On Epictetus, see §15.

12. This first conception of c-justice is assumed by Grote [1888], IV 1–3f.; Annas [1981], 162f. The importance of distinguishing the two accounts is suggested (although not with this point in mind) by Vlastos' remarks at [1971c], 138f.

13. On the question in Book II, see §136.

14. Grote [1888] IV, 102f., argues that Plato sets out from Aristotelian particular justice in Books I and II, but turns to general justice in Book IV. Vlastos [1977], 3–11, and Annas [1981], 12, argue that Plato is concerned with particular justice, since this is the virtue that avoids *pleonexia*. These arguments do not take proper account of *EN* 1130a3–5 (general justice as an *allotrion agathon*).

15. 'Commonplace' 442e1 might also be rendered 'vulgar'. Cf. Ar. *EN* 1178b16; it is 'vulgar' to praise the gods for not being temperate, because such praise falls so far below what is appropriate that it is vulgar even to mention it.

16. At 444c10–e6 Socrates remarks that just actions tend to promote p-justice. He introduces this fact as a reason for believing that we are better off doing just action; this is how Glaucon takes it at 444e7–445b4. It is not meant as the just person's reason for doing just action; 443b1–3 refers to the opposite direction of causation.

17. This line of objection is stated by Sachs [1963], 48: 'Intelligence, courage, and self-control are . . . prima facie compatible with a variety of vulgar injustices and evil-doing. . . . In this regard it is tempting to assert that the most that can be said on behalf of Plato's argument is that crimes and evils could not be done by a Platonically just man in a foolish, unintelligent, cowardly, or uncontrolled way.'

Chapter 16

1. On Thrasymachus' demand, see §§120, 141.

2. On sensible properties, see §112.

3. On the 'combination' referred to in this passage, I agree with Owen [1957], 174 and note, against Adam [1902], ad loc.

4. This feature of the sight-lover is discussed by Austin [1979], 205.

5. Aristotle describes the sight-lovers' view by saying that it involves predicating the F itself homonymously. See Alexander, *in Met.* 83.7–11; Fine [1993], 150–55.

6. Adam [1902] explains the point well: '*ta kala* is here [sc. 479a3] the plural, not of *kalon ti*, but of *to kalon*; and Plato means that the *philotheamōn* has many *standards* of beauty'.

7. On the dialectical condition, see §107.

8. I read <*to*> *kat'eidos legomenon*, and *iont'*, with Hackforth [1952]. He cites *R.* 476b10, a telling parallel (but not in favour of Hackforth's general interpretation, as Scott [1987], 361f., points out).

9. On giving an account, see §100.

10. Questions about the nature of the 'account' required for knowledge are raised in the last part of the *Tht.*, from 201c8.

11. This line of interpretation is presented in detail by Fine [1978; 1990]. Some aspects of it are defended by Kahn [1981b], 112–15. Doubts about it are raised by Annas [1981], chap. 8.

12. On explanations, see §109.

13. The many *nomima* about F are the many standards of F-ness; the *nomima* refer to the many Fs, but are not themselves the many Fs. Contrast Penner [1987b], 236.

14. I take 'appear' to be veridical. See chap. 10, note 13.

15. On the many types of just action, see §217.

16. The conventional and uncritical character of the sight-lovers' outlook is emphasized by Nettleship [1901], 196f.; Bosanquet [1906], 215.

17. I use initial capitals for the names of the images, and lowercase letters for the items (the sun, etc.) mentioned in the description of the images.

18. I use lowercase letters ('s1', etc.) for the states mentioned in the illustration, and capitals ('S1', etc.) for the states illustrated by the states with the corresponding number.

19. On the longer way, see §192.

20. On the Form of the Good, see especially Shorey [1895]; Joseph [1948]; Gosling [1973], 62–71; Santas [1980; 1985]. The connexion of the Form of the Good with questions raised in the Socratic dialogues about the good is especially emphasized by Shorey [1895], 39–41.

21. I use an initial capital for the Form of the Good, but a lowercase initial letter for the good that is an object of pursuit. The virtues promote the good (= happiness), not the Form of the Good, which, as Aristotle remarks (*EN* 1096b31–35; see Kraut [1992c], 335 and note 29) is not an object of pursuit. But the good that they do promote has the goodness it has because it participates in the Form of the Good.

22. Pleasure and wisdom as candidates for being the good are discussed further in the *Phil.*; see §§215, 226.

23. On *epekeina tēs ousias*, see Joseph [1948], 23f.

24. An idea of some difficulties in the interpretation of the Line and the Cave may be gathered from Joseph [1948], chap. 4; Ross [1951], chap. 4; Cross and Woozley [1964], chap. 9; Irwin [1977a], 334–36; White [1979], 184–86; Strang [1986]; Fine [1990].

25. Questions about the objects assumed at L3 are succinctly discussed by Ross [1951], 58–65. Among later contributions see Annas [1975], 160–64; Burnyeat [1987].

26. On hypotheses, cf. §116.

27. Issues about the Cave and *eikasia* are discussed by Ross [1951], 68, 77f.; Malcolm [1981]; Karasmanis [1988], 159–62.

28. In 515b4–5 perhaps *tauta hēgē(i) an ta parionta onta nomizein onomazein* should be read and translated: 'Don't you think they would suppose they were naming the passing things [sc. the shadows] as beings [sc. being a horse etc.]?'

29. The relation of c2 to Socratic elenchos is discussed by Wilson [1976b], 119–22; Malcolm [1981], 65f.; Fine [1990], 103.

30. The view that this passage expresses Plato's criticism of Socrates' use of the elenchos is maintained by Ryle [1966], 11, 18, 155f.; Nussbaum [1980], 87f. (esp. note 87); Vlastos [1991], 110.

31. On conflicts between bravery and temperance, see §228.

32. The relation of the *R.* itself to the Line is discussed by Gallop [1965], 121–24; [1971], 195–98; Cooper [1966]; Austin [1979].

Chapter 17

1. I will not discuss the political and historical implications of the cycle of constitutions (criticized by Aristotle, *Pol.* 1316a1–b27).

2. This passage is interpreted differently by White [1986], 34–41.

3. The best discussions of *R.* VIII and IX are by Kraut [1973a]; and Annas [1981], 294–305.

4. On the longer way, see Murphy [1951], 9–11, 152f.

5. On instrumental reasoning, see §150.

6. On parts as agents, see §153.

7. On the rational part in the p-just soul, see §175.

8. On Callicles, see §76.

9. The tyrannical person is discussed (and his degree of rational control underestimated) by Annas [1981], 303–5; Kraut [1992c], 325f.

10. The rational aspect of deviant people is emphasized by Morris [1933], 135f.; Kraut [1973a]; Cooper [1984], 20 and note 13.

11. The main blame for putting this idea into his head is actually laid on the just man's wife, whose excessive desire for her own honour (549c8–d1) is presumably a result of the 'privatization' (*idiōsasthai*, 547c1) of families.

12. See Hobbes, *Leviathan* c.17: 'I authorize and give my right of governing myself, to this man . . . and acknowledge all his actions in like manner'.

13. Plato's view of the different roles of practical reason partly corresponds to Taylor's distinction ([1977], 19) between 'second-order desires on the basis of weak evaluations' and desires based on 'strong evaluations'. He refers to Plato at [1989], 122. Plato's division perhaps suggests some answers to the criticisms of Taylor by Flanagan [1990].

14. See Kant, *Grundlegung*, Ak. p. 414f.

15. On Butler, see §§150, 153.

16. See Hume, *Treatise*, II 3.3, p. 416: ''Tis as little contrary to reason to prefer even my own acknowledged lesser good to my greater, and have a more evident affection for the former than the latter.'

17. On a part's conception of itself, see §153.

18. The best discussion of the relation between these arguments and the main argument of the *Republic* is by Murphy [1951], chap. 10. Joseph [1935], chap. 5, is less favourable to Plato. See also Kraut [1992c], 312–14. Difficulties are fully discussed by Gosling and Taylor [1982], chap. 6.

19. A similar objection is often raised against Mill's use in *Utilitarianism* (chap. 2) of a similar appeal to experience as a test for judging the relative value of pleasures. See Joseph [1935], 137–41.

20. Different aspects of the rational part are discussed by Bosanquet [1906], 350f.; Murphy [1951], 94–96, 211. See §226.

21. See Bosanquet [1906], 363.

22. Some of these issues about pleasure are discussed further in §222.

23. In 588e3–4 *toutō(i) . . . tō(i) anthrōpō(i)* makes it clear that Plato is considering the interest of the man who is the compound (also referred to in *autō(i)*, e5) rather than the 'inner man' (589a7).

24. On the appetitive part and its interests, see §154.

25. On beliefs about the good, see §191.

Chapter 18

1. This seems to be the implication of the view of Adkins [1960], 290–92, that Plato cannot solve the difficulty he has created.

2. The view that philosophers sacrifice their interest to justice is maintained by Foster [1936], 301f., and defended in detail by White [1986]. It is contested by Kraut [1992d]; Mahoney [1992].

3. As Morris [1933], 138, puts it, 'the philosopher is moved by the knowledge of the Idea of the Good, not by desire for his own good'. See also Cooper [1977a], 55f.;

Annas [1981], 267–69; White [1986], 41–46. Waterlow [1972] makes the rather different suggestion that from the philosopher's point of view, his own good is not distinguished from the good of others.

4. Reeve's argument, [1988], 202f., is open to this objection.

5. Plato does not say that the Form of the Good is itself the goal that the philosopher-rulers pursue; it is more plausible to suppose that he means they form their goal by reference to the Form of the Good. See chap. 16, note 21.

6. For convenience I will use the word without italics or accent.

7. This combination and arrangement of different aspects of male and female sexual activity is characteristic of Plato on eros. See Price [1989], 15f.

8. Like the English 'intercourse', *homilein* can be used in sexual and non-sexual contexts (it is less precise than *migeis*, 490b5), and so it is especially useful to Plato in remarks about eros. Cf. *Symp*. 209c2; *Phdr*. 252d5, 255b1. For 'admiration', *agasthai*, in such contexts, cf. *Euthd*. 276d2.

9. For metaphorical uses of 'eros', see *Euthd*. 276d2; *Pr*. 317c7; *G*. 481d1–482b2; *M*. 70b3; Dover [1978], 156f.; Price [1989], 15. In these passages, the term indicates enthusiasm (being 'crazy about' something), but does not imply any theoretical claim about the nature or source of the enthusiasm.

10. Although 573b6 introduces *erōs* in a sexual context (this is what *legetai* refers to), 573d4–5, *diakuberna(i) ta tēs psuchēs hapanta*, shows that Plato now intends *erōs* to have a much wider scope.

11. The relevance of Plato's theory of eros to questions about justice in the *R*. is urged especially by Demos [1964] (criticized by Wilson [1977], 594–96) and by Kraut [1973b].

12. Plato need not be claiming that he can explain every sort of erotic attraction to another person by reference to this desire for the good. If he accepts the division of the soul defended in the *R*. and the *Phdr*., his account of eros in the *Symp*. will not apply to spirited and appetitive desires. In the *Symp*. he neither endorses nor rejects this division of the soul, since he neither affirms nor denies psychological eudaemonism. See Moravcsik [1971], 290–93. Contrast O'Brien [1967], 224f.; Markus [1955], 137f.

13. On the difficulties in Plato's use of '*epithumia*', see §145.

14. Hackforth [1952], 40–42, and Ferrari [1987], 101, 253, argue that the conception of the soul and virtue that underlies Socrates' first speech is crucially different from the conception Plato holds in the *R*. Contrast Rowe [1986], 184; Nussbaum [1986], 204–10.

15. I say 'might explain' and 'might underlie' to indicate that these are not the terms that the historical Socrates uses.

16. On facades of virtue, see §136.

17. The connexion between madness and recollection is discussed by Griswold [1986], 111–14.

18. On the function of recollection described here, see Scott [1987], 359–63. *R*. 493e–494a (together with 476a, which he cites, 362) tends to support his general view of recollection. See chap. 16, note 8.

19. On 'descriptions' and 'intuitions', see §178.

20. The claim about immortality might be challenged (as involving a misreading of 'always' in the claim that we want the good to be present to us always), but Plato is entitled to the weaker claim that we want to remain in existence in possession of the good. This weaker claim is enough to explain the desire for giving birth in beauty.

21. Further questions arise about what sorts of desires are being attributed to nonhuman animals in 207a–c.

22. Or 'young' (*neon*).

23. See Seneca, *Ep.* 58.22–24; Plutarch, *De E* 392c–e; Anon. *in Tht.* 70.5–26 (see Long and Sedley [1987], #28 B); Price [1989], 21–25 (who believes this is Plato's view of the body, not of the soul).

24. 'Leaving behind' indicates the causal connexion. 'Of the same sort as it [sc. the person at the previous stage] was' indicates the qualitative connexion. The role of these relations in survival and identity is discussed by Parfit [1984], chap. 12. Their implications for concern for oneself and others are discussed by Warner [1979]; Wolf [1986]; Whiting [1986].

25. On the rational part and truth, see §201.

26. This issue is discussed by Price [1989], 33–35.

27. On questions about immortality, see Price [1989], 30f.

28. On spite (*phthonos*) Taylor [1928], 78, cites *Phd.* 61d9; *Phdr.* 247a7; Aeschylus, *Ag.* 263. Plato rejects the view of the gods expressed in, e.g., Herodotus I 32, III 40.

29. Taylor [1928], 78, suggests that in Plato's view, 'it is of the nature of goodness and love to "overflow"'. Cornford [1937], 34f., criticizes Taylor for speaking of overflowing love; he neglects the similarity between this description of the god and Plato's views about eros.

30. On rational eudaemonism, see §36.

31. For different views about the significance of the 'ascent' passage in 210–11, see Moravcsik [1971]; Vlastos [1973], 30–34; Warner [1979]; Price [1989], 43–45. The *Phdr.* focusses specifically on the effects of recollection of the Form of Beauty in love between individuals. It does not explain the basis of such love in the desire for one's own happiness. By contrast, the *Symp.* does not examine, as the *Phdr.* does, the relations between individuals. But there is no reason to believe that Plato takes his conception of love, or its ethical implications, to be different in the two dialogues. (Rowe [1986], 190, partly agrees with this claim.)

32. On the deviant people, see §198.

33. 'So far as this is possible' allows for the limited extent to which members of the non-ruling classes in the ideal city can be guided by reason. See 590c2–591a4; §234.

34. On the Simonidean view, see §120.

35. The two uses of '*archē*' are derived from Ar. *EN* 1095b2–8, which immediately follows the remark about Plato. In *R.* VI and VII Plato confines his use of '*archē*' to the theoretical principle.

36. On psychic justice and rational control, see §199.

Chapter 19

1. For the rejected accounts of the good, see §187.

2. On the just person's pleasures, see §200.

3. On the usefulness of a synoptic view of the dialogue, see D. Frede [1992], 425f.

4. On Aristotle, see esp. §§45, 174, 224.

5. In the case of false pleasures, discussed in §222, the cause and the object of pleasure are different events.

6. Protarchus' view is endorsed by Gosling [1975], 73f., 162; Gosling and Taylor [1982], 134.

7. On the relevance of Socrates' argument to the main aims of the dialogue, see Gosling [1975], 142.

8. On the two problems, see Gosling [1975], on 17b4.

9. The relation between the Forms in the *Phil.* and in the middle dialogues is a matter

of controversy. See D. Frede [1992], 462 and note 40. I believe that a correct account of the theory of Forms in the middle dialogues undermines many arguments for the view that Plato later abandons that theory. A unitarian view of the *Phil.* is defended by Hampton [1990], who relies on an account of the middle dialogues that I would not accept. See further chap. 1, note 29.

10. On the many Fs, cf. §§110, 181. On the connexion between the two errors, see Fine [1993], 71–76, on Aristotle's arguments about indeterminacy.

11. On the sight-lovers, see §185.

12. On the *Phdr.* on eros, see §208.

13. On Plato's different claims about the limit and the unlimited, see Gosling [1975], 155–81; Waterfield [1980], 280–82.

14. On the relation between limited and unlimited, see Crombie [1962], II 426–36; Striker [1970], 47–58; Gosling [1975], 194; Cooper [1977b], 715.

15. On taxonomic and normative limits, see Gosling [1975], 187f.; Cooper [1977b], 715.

16. The connexion between the *Philebus* and the *Statesman* is discussed by Bury [1897], 196f.; Skemp [1952], 78–80; Cooper [1968]; Striker [1970], 69; Gosling [1975], 189; Waterfield [1980], 276–80.

17. On rules about just action, see §§120, 185.

18. Strang [1986], 23, connects *St.* 285d9–286b7 with the search for definitions. Owen [1973] takes this passage to make a narrower point.

19. On Plato's strategy, see Gosling [1975], 208–10.

20. The ms. text *pan agathon* in 27e8 might be defended as meaning 'good, all of it'. Bury [1897], Hackforth [1945], Gosling [1975], and Waterfield [1982] emend to *panagathon*, meaning (less appropriately) 'completely good'.

21. On Philebus' interpretation of Socrates' claim, see Gosling [1975], 185.

22. Among the many discussions of pleasure and falsity see Williams [1959]; Penner [1970]; Gosling and Taylor [1982], 429–53; Frede [1985].

23. There will also be instrumental disadvantages in the opportunities forgone because of my false belief that, say, I am going to be able to go to a film, when a different belief would have resulted in a different plan for the evening.

24. The examples offered by Nozick [1974], 42–45, and Kraut [1979], 177–79, illustrate this sort of strategy.

25. Contrast the suggestion by D. Frede [1992], 450, that Plato relies on purely 'scientific-medical' criteria.

26. On the virtuous person's pleasures, see Cooper [1977b], 728f.

27. Mill, for instance, claims to be a hedonist, and also distinguishes higher from lower pleasures (*Utilitarianism*, chap. 2). It has been disputed whether he can rely on purely hedonist principles to draw the distinction he wants.

28. On the pleasures of the coward, see §74. This argument is briefly restated at *Phil.* 55b1–5.

29. On these terms, see Bury [1897], 211–14.

30. This difficulty about appealing to choice is noticed by Gosling [1975], 182. On *R.* IX, see §200.

31. Gosling [1975], 183, takes Plato to be making a hedonist point.

32. On the interpretation of Plato's question, see Gosling [1975], 140.

33. On external goods, see §134.

34. The importance of the practical role of intelligence is emphasized by Murphy [1938], 118f.

35. On the place of craft knowledge in the good, see Cooper [1977b], 725f.

Chapter 20

1. This is the sense attached to *hōs ge en tē(i) politeia(i)*, 309e6–7, by Skemp [1952] ('prudent, or at any rate prudent enough, to meet its public duties').

2. Murphy's comment about the role of justice (see chap. 14, note 21) is even more applicable to the *St.* than to *R.* IV.

3. The role of pleasure in the *Laws* is explored by Stalley [1983], chap. 6.

4. On the relation of this claim to the comparative thesis about virtue and happiness, see §231.

5. Translators render *para touto*, 733d4 by 'outside this range' (Saunders [1970]); 'any other consideration than that of preponderance of pleasure' (England [1921]); 'any object other than those aforesaid' (Taylor [1934]); 'si par hasard nous prétendons avoir quelque désir en dehors de ces limites' (Des Places and Diès [1951]). The passage is discussed by Stalley [1983], 67–69.

6. This ambiguity is noticed by Crombie [1962], I 271.

7. Stalley [1983], 63, criticizes Plato's claim that the virtuous life is the most pleasant.

8. On the *Euthd.*, see §40. On the *M.*, see §97.

9. The consistency of the *Laws* on the virtues is discussed by Görgenmanns [1960], 113–55; Stalley [1983], chap. 5.

10. Saunders's [1978] rendering, 'an exaggerated and twisted use of language', seems to go beyond the Greek in suggesting that there is something actually incorrect or strained in using 'temperance' for the condition that includes wisdom. Taylor's [1934] 'high and forced sense' (following England [1921]) conveys the same unwarranted suggestion. (Des Places and Diès [1951] render similarly.) The rendering by Robin [1960] is better: 'à laquelle on donnerait une certaine noblesse, en attribuant de force à la modération dans les actes le nom de sagesse dans la pensée'. Görgenmanns [1960], 133, discusses the passage.

11. On the attitude of the *R.* to the unity of the virtues, see §166.

12. On the role of pleasure, see §165; Stalley [1983], 52–54.

13. On virtue and wisdom, see §§162 through 164.

14. On the lower classes in the *R.*, see §§159 through 163.

15. See chap. 18, note 33. Contrast Kraut [1973a], 216–22.

16. The nature and point of persuasion are discussed by Bobonich [1991], esp. 386.

References

Ackrill, J. L. [1974]. 'Aristotle on eudaimonia', *PBA* 60, 339–59. Reprinted in Rorty [1980], chap. 2.
Adam, J., ed. [1902]. *The Republic of Plato*. 2 vols., Cambridge.
Adam, J., and Adam, A. M., eds. [1893]. *Plato: Protagoras*. Cambridge.
Adams, D. [1992]. 'The *Lysis* puzzles', *HPQ* 9, 3–17.
Adkins, A. W. H. [1960]. *Merit and Responsibility*. Oxford.
———. [1963]. '"Friendship" and "self-sufficiency" in Homer and Aristotle', *CQ* 13, 30–45.
———. [1973]. '*Aretê, Technê*, democracy, and sophists', *JHS* 93, 3–12.
———. [1975]. 'Merit, responsibility, and Thucydides', *CQ* 25, 209–20.
Allen, R. E. [1970]. *Plato's Euthyphro and the Earlier Theory of Forms*. London.
Annas, J. [1975]. 'On the "intermediates"', *AGP* 57, 146–66.
———. [1977]. 'Plato and Aristotle on friendship and altruism', *Mind* 86, 532–54.
———. [1978]. 'Plato and common morality', *CQ* 28, 437–51.
———. [1981]. *An Introduction to Plato's Republic*. Oxford.
———. [1982]. 'Aristotle on inefficient causes', *PQ* 32, 311–26.
———. [1985]. 'Self-knowledge in early Plato', in O'Meara [1985], chap. 5.
———. [1992]. 'Plato the sceptic', *OSAP* supp., 43–72.
Anton, J., and Kustas, G., eds. [1971]. *Essays on Ancient Greek Philosophy*. Albany.
Anton, J., and Preus, A., eds. [1983]. *Essays on Ancient Greek Philosophy, II*. Albany.
———. [1989]. *Essays on Ancient Greek Philosophy, III*. Albany.
Archer-Hind, R.D., ed. [1894]. *Plato's Phaedo*. 2d ed. London.
Austin, J. L. [1979]. 'The Line and the Cave in Plato's *Republic*', in Urmson and Warnock [1979], chap. 13.
Barnes, J. [H. Maconi] [1988]. 'Nova non philosophandi philosophia', *OSAP* 6, 231–53.
———. [1991]. 'Enseigner la vertu?' *RP* 181, 571–89.
Benson, H. H. [1989]. 'A note on eristic and the Socratic elenchus', *JHP* 27, 591–99.
———. [1990a]. 'The priority of definition and the Socratic elenchus', *OSAP* 8, 19–65.
———. [1990b]. 'Misunderstanding the "What is F-ness?" question', *AGP* 72 (1990), 125–42. Reprinted in Benson [1992], chap. 8.
———. [1990c]. 'Meno, the slave-boy, and the elenchos', *Phr* 35, 128–58.
———, ed. [1992]. *Essays on the Philosophy of Socrates*. Oxford.
Beversluis, J. [1987]. 'Does Socrates commit the Socratic Fallacy?' *APQ* 24 (1987), 211–23. Reprinted in Benson [1992], chap. 7.

Bluck, R. S., ed. [1961]. *Plato's Meno*. Cambridge.
Blundell, M. W. [1989]. *Helping Friends and Harming Enemies*. Cambridge.
Bobonich, C. [1991]. 'Persuasion, compulsion, and freedom in Plato's *Laws*', *CQ* 41, 365–88.
Bolotin, D. [1979]. *Plato's Dialogue on Friendship*. Ithaca.
Bolton, R. H. [1975]. 'Plato's distinction between being and becoming', *RM* 29, 66–95.
Bosanquet, B. [1906]. *A Companion to Plato's Republic*. 2d ed. London.
Bostock, D. [1986]. *Plato's Phaedo*. Oxford.
Boutroux, E. [1912]. *Historical Studies in Philosophy*. E.T., London.
Brandwood, L. [1976]. *A Word Index to Plato*. Leeds.
———. [1990]. *The Chronology of Plato's Dialogues*. Cambridge.
———. [1992]. 'Stylometry and chronology', in Kraut [1992a], chap. 3.
Brickhouse, T. C., and Smith, N. D. [1984]. 'Vlastos on the elenchus', *OSAP* 2, 185–95.
———. [1987]. 'Socrates on goods, virtue and happiness', *OSAP* 5, 1–27.
Brochard, V. [1912]. *Études de philosophie ancienne et de philosophie moderne*. Paris.
Brown, L. [1991]. 'Connaissance et réminiscence dans le "Ménon"', *RP* 181, 603–19.
Brunschwig, J. [1991]. 'Pouvoir enseigner la vertu?' *RP* 181, 591–602.
Burnet, J., ed. [1900–1907]. *Platonis Opera*. 5 vols., Oxford.
———. [1924]. *Plato's Euthyphro, Apology, and Crito*. Oxford.
Burnyeat, M. F. [1971]. 'Virtues in action', in Vlastos [1971b], chap. 10.
———. [1977]. 'Examples in epistemology: Socrates, Theaetetus, and G.E. Moore', *Phil* 52, 381–98.
———. [1987], 'Platonism and mathematics: A prelude to discussion', in Graeser [1987], 213–40.
Bury, R. G., ed. [1897]. *Plato's Philebus*. Cambridge.
Butler, J. [1970]. *Fifteen Sermons*, ed. T.A. Roberts. London.
Calvert, B. [1970]. 'Forms and flux in Plato's *Cratylus*', *Phr* 15, 26–47.
Cambiano, G. [1991]. 'Remarques sur Platon et la "technè"', *RP* 181, 407–16.
Canto, M., tr. [1987]. *Platon: Gorgias*. Paris.
Cherniss, H. F. [1944]. *Aristotle's Criticism of Plato and the Academy*, vol. 1. Baltimore.
Classen, C. J., ed. [1976]. *Die Sophistik*. Darmstadt.
Cohen, S. M. [1971]. 'Socrates on the definition of piety', *JHP* 9, 1–13. Reprinted in Vlastos [1971b], chap. 8.
Cooper, J. M. [1973]. 'The *Magna Moralia* and Aristotle's moral philosophy', *AJP* 94, 327–49.
———. [1977a]. 'The psychology of justice in Plato', *APQ* 14, 151–57.
———. [1977b]. 'Plato's theory of the human good in the *Philebus*', *JP* 74, 714–30.
———. [1982]. 'The *Gorgias* and Irwin's Socrates', *RM* 35, 577–87.
———. [1984]. 'Plato's theory of human motivation', *HPQ* 1, 3–21.
Cooper, N. [1966]. 'The importance of *dianoia* in Plato's theory of forms', *CQ* 16, 65–69.
———. [1968]. 'Pleasure and good in Plato's *Philebus*', *PQ* 18, 12–15.
Cope, E. M., tr. [1883]. *Plato: Gorgias*. London.
Cornford, F. M. [1912]. 'Psychology and social structure in the *Republic*', *CQ* 6, 246–65.
———. [1935]. *Plato's Theory of Knowledge*. London.
———. [1937]. *Plato's Cosmology*. London.
———. [1952]. *Principium Sapientiae*. Cambridge.
Creed, J. L. [1973]. 'Moral values in the age of Thucydides', *CQ* 23, 213–31.

Croiset, M., and Bodin, L., tr. [1923]. *Platon: Oeuvres Complètes*, vol. 3. Paris.
Crombie, I. M. [1962–1963]. *An Examination of Plato's Doctrines*. 2 vols., London.
Cross, R. C., and Woozley, A. D. [1964]. *Plato's Republic*. London.
Dancy, J., ed. [1988]. *Perceptual Knowledge*. Oxford.
Davidson, D. [1969]. 'How is weakness of will possible?' in Feinberg [1969], chap. 8. Reprinted in Davidson [1980], chap. 2.
———. [1970]. 'Mental events', in Foster and Swanson [1970], 79–101. Reprinted in Davidson [1980], chap. 11.
———. [1980]. *Essays on Actions and Events*. Oxford.
———. [1982]. 'Paradoxes of irrationality', in Wollheim and Hopkins [1982], chap. 17.
De Heer, C. [1969]. *Makar, Eudaimôn, Olbios, Eutuchês*. Amsterdam.
De Lacy, P. H., tr. [1980]. *Galen: On the Doctrines of Hippocrates and Plato*. 3 vols, Berlin.
Deman, T. [1942]. *Le témoignage d'Aristote sur Socrate*. Paris.
Demos, R. [1964]. 'A fallacy in Plato's *Republic*?' *PR* 73, 395–98. Reprinted in Vlastos [1971a], chap. 3.
Dent, N. J. H. [1984]. *The Moral Psychology of the Virtues*. Cambridge.
Des Places, E. [1929]. *Études sur quelques particules de liaison chez Platon*. Paris.
———, tr. [1989]. *Jamblique: Protreptique*. Paris.
Des Places, E., and Diès, A., trs. [1951–1956]. *Platon: les Lois*. 4 vols., Paris.
Detel, W. [1973]. 'Zur Argumentationsstruktur im ersten Hauptteil von Platons Aretedialogen', *AGP* 55, 1–29.
Devereux, D.T. [1977]. 'Courage and wisdom in Plato's *Laches*', *JHP* 15, 129–41.
———. [1978]. 'Nature and teaching in Plato's *Meno*', *Phr* 23, 118–26.
———. [1992]. 'The unity of the virtues in Plato's *Protagoras* and *Laches*', *PR* 101, 765–89.
Diels, H., and Kranz, W., eds. [1952]. *Die Fragmente der Vorsokratiker*. 10th ed., 3 vols., Berlin.
Dillon, J. M. [1977]. *The Middle Platonists*. Ithaca.
Dirlmeier, F., tr. [1963]. *Aristoteles: Magna Moralia*. Berlin.
Dodds, E. R., ed. [1959]. *Plato: Gorgias*. Oxford.
Dover, K. J. [1974]. *Greek Popular Morality in the Time of Plato and Aristotle*. Oxford.
———. [1978]. *Greek Homosexuality*. Cambridge, Mass.
Dretske, F. I. [1970]. 'Epistemic operators', *JP* 67, 1007–23.
———. [1972]. 'Contrastive statements', *PR* 81, 411–37.
———. [1981]. *Knowledge and the Flow of Information*. Cambridge, Mass.
———. [1988]. *Explaining Behavior*. Cambridge, Mass.
Düring, I., and Owen, G. E. L., eds. [1965]. *Aristotle and Plato in the Mid-Fourth Century*. Gothenburg.
Dybikowski, J. C. [1981]. 'Is Aristotelian *eudaimonia* happiness?', *Dialogue* 20, 185–200.
Dyson, M. [1974]. 'Some problems concerning knowledge in Plato's *Charmides*', *Phr* 19, 102–11.
———. [1976]. 'Knowledge and hedonism in Plato's *Protagoras*', *JHS* 96, 32–45.
Ebert, T. [1973]. 'Plato's theory of recollection reconsidered', *Man and World* 6, 163–83.
Edelstein, L., and Kidd, I. G., eds. [1972]. *Poseidonius: Vol. 1, the Fragments*. Cambridge.

Elster, J. [1983]. *Sour Grapes*. Cambridge.

England, E. B., ed. [1921]. *The Laws of Plato*. 2 vols., London.

Everson, S., ed. [1990]. *Companions to Ancient Thought 1: Epistemology*. Cambridge.

Feinberg, J., ed. [1969]. *Moral Concepts*. Oxford.

Ferejohn, M. T. [1982]. 'The unity of virtue and the objects of Socratic inquiry', *JHP* 20, 1–21.

———. [1984]. 'Socratic thought-experiments and the unity of virtue paradox', *Phr* 29, 105–22.

Ferrari, G. R. F. [1987]. *Listening to the Cicadas*. Cambridge.

Festugière, A. J., ed. [1948]. *Hippocrate: l'Ancienne Médecine*. Paris.

———. [1973]. *Les trois Protreptiques de Platon*. Paris.

Fine, G. [1977]. 'Plato on Naming', *PQ* 27, 289–301.

———. [1978]. 'Knowledge and Belief in *Republic* V', *AGP* 60, 121–39.

———. [1987]. 'Forms as causes: Plato and Aristotle', in Graeser [1987], 69–112.

———. [1988]. 'Owen's progress', *PR* 97, 373–90.

———. [1990]. 'Knowledge and belief in *Republic* V–VII', in Everson [1990], 85–115.

———. [1992]. 'Inquiry in the *Meno*', in Kraut [1992a], chap. 6.

———. [1993]. *On Ideas*. Oxford.

Fitzgerald, W. [1853]. *Selections from the Nicomachean Ethics of Aristotle*. Dublin.

Flanagan, O. [1990]. 'Identity and strong and weak evaluation', in Flanagan and Rorty [1990], chap. 2.

Flanagan, O., and Rorty, A. O. [1990]. *Identity, Character, and Morality*. Cambridge, Mass.

Foster, L., and Swanson, J. W., eds. [1970]. *Experience and Theory*. Amherst.

Foster, M. B. [1936]. 'Some implications of a passage in Plato's *Republic*', *Phil* 11, 301–8.

———. [1937]. 'A mistake of Plato's in the *Republic*', *Mind* 46, 386–93.

———. [1938]. 'Rejoinder to Mr Mabbott', *Mind* 47, 226–32.

Frede, D. [1985]. 'Rumpelstilkin's pleasures', *Phr* 30, 151–80.

———. [1992]. 'Disintegration and restoration: Pleasure and pain in Plato's *Philebus*', in Kraut [1992a], chap. 14.

Frede, M. [1992]. 'Plato's arguments and the dialogue form', *OSAP* supp., 201–19.

Friedländer, P. [1964]. *Plato: The Dialogues*, vol. 2, E.T. Princeton.

Gallop, D. [1964]. 'The Socratic paradox in the *Protagoras*', *Phr* 9, 117–29.

———. [1965]. 'Image and reality in Plato's *Republic*', *AGP* 47, 114–31.

———. [1971]. 'Dreaming and waking in Plato', in Anton and Kustas [1971], 187–201.

———, tr. [1975]. *Plato: Phaedo*. Oxford.

Gauthier, D. P. [1982]. 'Three against justice', *Midwest Studies in Philosophy* 7, 11–29. Reprinted in Gauthier [1990], chap. 6.

———. [1986]. *Morals by Agreement*. Oxford.

———. [1990]. *Moral Dealing*. Ithaca.

Gauthier, R. A., and Jolif, J. Y. [1970]. *Aristote: l'Ethique à Nicomaque*. 2d ed., 4 vols., Louvain.

Geach, P. T. [1966]. 'Plato's *Euthyphro*', *Monist* 50, 369–82. Reprinted in Geach [1972], 31–44.

———. [1972]. *Logic Matters*. Oxford.

Gentzler, J. K. [1991a]. 'Knowledge and method in Plato's early and middle dialogues', PhD diss., Cornell University.

———. [1991b]. '*Sumphônein* in Plato's *Phaedo*', *Phr* 36, 265–76.

Giannantoni, G. [1957]. 'Il primo libro della "Repubblica" di Platone', *Rivista Critica di Storia della Filosofia* 12, 123–45.

———. [1983]. *Socraticorum Reliquiae*. 4 vols., Naples.

Gibbs, B. R. [1974]. 'Virtue and reason', *PASS* 48, 23–41.

Gifford, E. H., ed. [1901]. *Plato; Euthydemus*. Oxford.

Gill, C. J. [1985]. 'Plato and the education of character', *AGP* 67, 1–26.

Glidden, D. K. [1981]. 'The *Lysis* on loving one's own', *CQ* 31, 39–59.

Glucker, J. [1978]. *Antiochus and the Late Academy*. Göttingen.

Goldman, A. I. [1976]. 'Discrimination and perceptual knowledge', *JP* 73, 771–91. Reprinted in Dancy [1988], chap. 2.

———. [1986]. *Epistemology and Cognition*. Cambridge, Mass.

Gomme, A. W., Andrewes, A., and Dover, K. J. [1945–1981]. *A Historical Commentary on Thucydides*. 5 vols., Oxford.

Gomperz, T. [1905]. *Greek Thinkers*, vol. 2, E.T. London.

Gooch, P. W. [1974]. 'The relation between wisdom and virtue in *Phaedo* 69a–c', *JHP* 12, 153–59.

Görgenmanns, H. [1960]. *Beiträge zur Interpretation von Platons Nomoi*. Munich.

Gosling, J. C. B. [1960]. '*Republic* V: *ta polla kala*, etc.', *Phr* 5, 116–28.

———. [1973]. *Plato*. London.

———, tr. [1975]. *Plato: Philebus*. Oxford.

———. [1977]. 'Reply to White', *CJP* 7, 307–14.

———. [1978]. 'Plato's moral theory', *Philosophical Books* 19, 97–105.

Gosling, J. C. B., and Taylor, C. C. W. [1982]. *The Greeks on Pleasure*. Oxford.

Gould, C. S. [1987]. 'Socratic intellectualism and the problem of courage', *HPQ* 4, 265–79.

Graeser, A. [1975]. 'Zur Logik der Argumentationsstruktur in Platons Dialogen "Laches" und "Charmides"', *AGP* 57, 172–81.

———, ed. [1987]. *Mathematics and Metaphysics*. Berne.

Graham, D. W. [1992]. 'Socrates and Plato', *Phr* 37, 141–65.

Greenwood, L. H. G., ed. [1909]. *Aristotle: Nicomachean Ethics Book VI*. Cambridge.

Griswold, C. L. [1986]. *Self-Knowledge in Plato's Phaedrus*. New Haven.

———, ed. [1988]. *Platonic Writings, Platonic Readings*. London.

Grote, G. [1851]. *A History of Greece*. 2d ed., 10 vols., London.

———. [1888]. *Plato and the Other Companions of Socrates*. New ed., 4 vols., London.

Grube, G. M. A., tr. [1992]. *Plato: Republic*. 2d ed. (revised by C. D. C. Reeve), Indianapolis.

Guthrie, W. K. C. [1975]. *A History of Greek Philosophy*, vol. 4. Cambridge.

Hackforth, R. [1928]. 'Hedonism in Plato's *Protagoras*', *CQ* 22, 39–42.

———, tr. [1945]. *Plato's Examination of Pleasure*. Cambridge.

———, tr. [1952]. *Plato: Phaedrus*. Cambridge.

Hamilton, E., and Cairns, H., eds. [1961]. *Collected Dialogues of Plato*. Princeton.

Hampton, C. M. [1990]. *Pleasure, Knowledge, and Being*. Albany.

Hardie, W. F. R. [1936]. *A Study in Plato*. Oxford.

Harrison, E. L. [1962]. 'A red herring in Plato's *Republic*', *Eranos* 60, 122–26.

Hart, H. L. A. [1968]. *Punishment and Responsibility*. Oxford.

Hawtrey, R. S. W. [1981]. *Commentary on Plato's Euthydemus*. Philadelphia.

Heidel, W. A., ed. [1902]. *Plato: Euthyphro*. New York.

Henrich, D., et al., eds. [1960] *Die Gegerwart der Griechen in neueren Danken*. Tübingen.

Hirschberger, J. [1932]. 'Die Phronesis in der Philosophie Platons vor dem Staates', *Philologus* supp. 25.1.

Hobbes, T. [1968]. *Leviathan*, ed. C.B. Macpherson. Harmondsworth.

Holden, H. A., ed. [1886]. *Cicero: De Officiis*. 6th ed. Cambridge.

Hornblower, S. [1991]. *A Commentary on Thucydides*, vol. 1. Oxford.

Houston, A. C. [1986]. 'Plato's moral psychology', PhD diss., Cornell University.

Hume, D. [1888]. *A Treatise of Human Nature*, ed. L.A. Selby-Bigge. Oxford.

———. [1902]. *Inquiry concerning the Principles of Morals*, ed. L.A. Selby-Bigge. 2d ed. Oxford.

Irwin, T. H. [1977a]. *Plato's Moral Theory*. Oxford.

———. [1977b). 'Plato's Heracliteanism', *PQ* 27, 1–13.

———, tr. [1979]. *Plato: Gorgias*. Oxford.

———. [1982a]. 'Aristotle's concept of signification', in Schofield and Nussbaum [1982], chap. 12.

———. [1982b]. Review of Annas [1981], *Canadian Philosophical Reviews* 2, 49–54.

———. [1986]. 'Coercion and objectivity in Plato's dialectic', *RIP* 40, 49–74.

———. [1991]. 'Aristippus against happiness', *Monist* 74, 55–82.

———. [1992a]. 'Socratic puzzles', *OSAP* 10, 241–66.

———. [1992b]. 'Plato: The intellectual background', in Kraut [1992a], chap. 2.

Joseph, H. W. B. [1935]. *Essays in Ancient and Modern Philosophy*. Oxford.

———. [1948]. *Knowledge and the Good in Plato's Republic*. Oxford.

Jowett, B., and Campbell, L., eds. [1894], *The Republic of Plato*. 3 vols., Oxford.

Kahn, C. H. [1981a]. 'Did Plato write Socratic dialogues?' *CQ* 31, 305–20. Reprinted in Benson [1992], chap. 3.

———. [1981b]. 'Some philosophical uses of "to be" in Plato', *Phr* 26, 105–34.

———. [1983]. 'Drama and dialectic in Plato's *Gorgias*', *OSAP* 1, 75–121.

———. [1986]. 'Plato's methodology in the *Laches*', *RIP* 40, 7–21.

———. [1987]. 'Plato's theory of desire', *RM* 41, 77–103.

———. [1988]. 'On the relative date of the *Gorgias* and the *Protagoras*', *OSAP* 6, 69–102.

———. [1992]. 'Vlastos's Socrates', *Phr* 37, 231–58.

Kant, I. [1956]. *Grundlegung zur Metaphysik der Sitten*, tr. L. W. Beck. Indianapolis.

Karasmanis, V. [1988]. 'Plato's *Republic*: The Line and the Cave', *Ap* 21, 147–71.

Kerferd, G. B. [1947]. 'The doctrine of Thrasymachus in Plato's *Republic*', *Durham Univ. Jl*. 9, 19–27. Reprinted in Classen [1976], 545–63.

Kidd, I. G. [1988]. *Poseidonius: Vol. 2, Commentary*. Cambridge.

Kirwan, C. A. [1965]. 'Glaucon's challenge', *Phr* 10, 162–73.

———. [1974]. 'Plato and Relativity', *Phr* 19, 112–129.

Klosko, G. [1979]. 'Towards a consistent interpretation of the *Protagoras*', *AGP* 61, 125–42.

———. [1980]. 'On the analysis of *Protagoras* 351b–360e', *Phoenix* 34, 307–22.

———. [1981]. 'The technical conception of virtue', *JHP* 19, 95–102.

———. [1987]. 'Socrates on goods and happiness', *HPQ* 4, 251–64.

Kock, T. [1880]. *Comicorum Atticorum Fragmenta*, vol. 1. Leipzig.

Kosman, L. A. [1983]. 'Charmides' first definition', in Anton and Preus [1983], 203–16.

Krämer, H. J. [1990]. *Plato and the Foundations of Metaphysics*, E.T. Albany.

Kraut, R. [1973a]. 'Reason and justice in the *Republic*', in Lee, Mourelatos, and Rorty, [1973], chap. 11.

———. [1973b]. 'Egoism, love, and political office', *PR* 82, 330–44.

———. [1979]. 'Two conceptions of happiness', *PR* 88, 167–97.
———. [1983]. 'Comments on Gregory Vlastos, "The Socratic elenchus"', *OSAP* 1, 59–70.
———. [1984]. *Socrates and the State*. Princeton.
———, ed. [1992a]. *Cambridge Companion to Plato*. Cambridge.
———. [1992b]. 'Introduction to the study of Plato', in Kraut [1992a], chap. 1.
———. [1992c], 'The defence of justice in Plato's *Republic*', in Kraut [1992a], chap. 10.
———. [1992d]. 'Return to the Cave', *BACAP* 8, 43–61.
Kretzmann, N. [1971]. 'Plato on the correctness of names', *APQ* 8, 126–38.
Krohn, A. [1876]. *Der Platonische Staat*. Halle.
Kube, J. [1969]. *Technê und Aretê*. Berlin.
Lacey, A. R. [1971]. 'Our knowledge of Socrates', in Vlastos [1971b], chap. 2.
Lafrance, Y. [1969]. 'La problématique morale de l'opinion dans le *Gorgias* de Platon', *Revue Phil. de Louvain* 67, 5–29.
Larson, C. W. R. [1951]. 'The Platonic synonyms, *dikaiosunê* and *sôphrosunê*', *AJP* 72, 395–414.
Lear, J. [1992]. 'Inside and outside the *Republic*', *Phr* 27, 184–215.
Ledger, G. R. [1989]. *Re-counting Plato*. Oxford.
Lee, E. N., Mourelatos, A. P. D., and Rorty, R. M., eds. [1973]. *Exegesis and Argument*. Assen.
Lesher, J. H. [1987]. 'Socrates' disavowal of knowledge', *JHP* 25, 275–88.
Lesses, G. [1985]. 'Is Socrates an instrumentalist?' *PT* 13, 165–74.
———. [1987]. 'The divided soul in Plato's *Republic*', *HPQ* 4, 147–61.
Levin, D. N. [1971]. 'Some observations concerning Plato's *Lysis*', in Anton and Kustas [1971], 236–59.
Lewis, C. I. [1946]. *An Analysis of Knowledge and Valuation*. La Salle, Ill.
Lilla, S. R. C. [1971]. *Clement of Alexandria*. Oxford.
Locke, J. [1975]. *An Essay concerning Human Understanding*, ed. P. Nidditch, Oxford.
Long, A. A. [1988]. 'Socrates in Hellenistic philosophy', *CQ* 38, 150–71.
Long, A. A., and Sedley, D. N. [1987]. *The Hellenistic Philosophers*. 2 vols., Cambridge.
Luce, J. V. [1964]. 'The date of the *Cratylus*', *AJP* 90, 136–54.
Lycos, K. [1987]. *Plato on Justice and Power*. Albany.
Mabbott, J. D. [1937]. 'Is Plato's *Republic* utilitarian?' *Mind* 46, 468–74. Revised and reprinted in Vlastos [1971a], chap. 4.
Mackenzie, M. M. [1982]. 'A pyrrhic victory: *Gorgias* 474b–477a', *CQ* 32, 84–88.
———. [1986]. 'Putting the *Cratylus* in its place', *CQ* 36, 124–50.
———. [1988]. 'The virtues of Socratic ignorance', *CQ* 38, 331–50.
Mahoney, T. A. [1992]. 'Do Plato's philosopher-rulers sacrifice self-interest to justice?' *Phr* 37, 265–82.
Malcolm, J. [1981]. 'The Cave revisited', *CQ* 31, 60–68.
Markus, R. A. [1955]. 'The dialectic of eros in Plato's *Symposium*', *Downside Review* 73, 219–30. Reprinted in Vlastos [1971a], chap. 8.
McDonald, M. [1978]. *Terms for Happiness in Euripides*. Göttingen.
McDowell, J. H. [1980]. 'The role of *eudaimonia* in Aristotle's ethics', *Proc. African Classical Assoc.* 15, 1–15. Reprinted in Rorty [1980], chap. 19.
McKim, R. [1988]. 'Shame and truth in Plato's *Gorgias*', in Griswold [1988], chap. 2.
McKirahan, R. D. [1984]. 'Socrates and Protagoras on *sôphrosunê* and justice', *Ap* 18, 19–25.
McMurrin, S., ed. [1980]. *Tanner Lectures on Human Values*, vol. 1. Salt Lake City.

McPherran, M. L. [1985]. 'Socratic piety in the *Euthyphro*', *JHP* 23, 283–309. Reprinted in Benson [1992], chap. 13.
McTighe, K. [1984]. 'Socrates on desire for the good and the involuntariness of wrongdoing', *Phr* 29, 193–236. Reprinted in Benson [1992], chap. 15.
Mill, J. S. [1979]. *Utilitarianism*, ed. G. Sher. Indianapolis.
Mills, K. W. [1957]. '*Phaedo* 74bc, Part 1', *Phr* 2, 128–47.
———. [1958]. '*Phaedo* 74bc, Part 2', *Phr* 3, 40–58.
Mischel, T., ed. [1977]. *The Self*. Oxford.
Mohr, R. D. [1987]. 'A Platonic happiness', *HPQ* 4, 131–45.
Moline, J. [1978]. 'Plato on the complexity of the psyche', *AGP* 60, 1–26.
Moravcsik, J. M. E. [1971]. 'Reason and eros in the ascent-passage of the *Symposium*', in Anton and Kustas [1971], 285–302.
Moreau, J. [1939]. *La construction de l'idéalisme platonicien*. Paris.
Morris, C. R. [1933]. 'Plato's theory of the good man's motives', *PAS* 34, 129–42.
Morrison, D. R. [1987]. 'On Professor Vlastos' Socrates', *AP* 7, 9–22.
Morrow, G. R. [1960]. 'Aristotle's comments on Plato's *Laws*', in Düring and Owen [1960], 145–62.
Murphy, N. R. [1938]. 'The comparison of lives in Plato's *Philebus*', *CQ* 32, 116–24.
———. [1951]. *The Interpretation of Plato's Republic*. Oxford.
Nagel, T. [1980]. 'The limits of objectivity', in McMurrin [1980], 77–139.
Nakhnikian, G. [1973]. 'The first Socratic paradox', *JHP* 10, 1–17.
Nehamas, A. [1975a]. 'Plato on the imperfection of the sensible world', *APQ* 12, 105–17.
———. [1975b]. 'Confusing universals and particulars in Plato's early dialogues', *RM* 29, 287–306.
———. [1985]. 'Meno's paradox and Socrates as a teacher', *OSAP* 3, 1–30. Reprinted in Benson [1992], chap. 16.
———. [1986]. 'Socratic intellectualism', *BACAP* 2, 275–316.
———. [1992]. 'Voices of silence: On Gregory Vlastos' Socrates', *Arion* 2, 157–86.
Nettleship, R. L. [1901]. *Lectures on the Republic of Plato*. London.
Neu, J. [1971]. 'Plato's analogy of state and individual', *Phil* 46, 238–54.
Nicholson, P. P. [1974]. 'Unravelling Thrasymachus' argument in the *Republic*', *Phr* 19, 210–32.
Nozick, R. [1974]. *Anarchy, State, and Utopia*. New York.
Nussbaum, M. C. [1980]. 'Aristophanes and Socrates on learning practical wisdom', *YCS* 26, 43–97.
———. [1984]. 'Plato on commensurability and desire', *PASS* 58, 55–80. Reprinted in Nussbaum [1990], chap. 3.
———. [1986]. *The Fragility of Goodness*. Cambridge.
———. [1990]. *Love's Knowledge*. Oxford.
O'Brien, M. J. [1963]. 'The unity of the *Laches*', *YCS* 18, 131–47. Reprinted in Anton and Kustas [1971], 303–15.
———. [1967]. *The Socratic Paradoxes and the Greek Mind*. Chapel Hill.
O'Meara, D. J., ed. [1985]. *Platonic Investigations*. Washington.
Owen, G. E. L. [1953]. 'The place of the *Timaeus* in Plato's dialogues', *CQ* 3, 79–95. Reprinted in Owen [1986], chap. 4.
———. [1957]. 'A proof in the *Peri Ideôn*', *JHS* 77, 103–11. Reprinted in Owen [1986], chap. 9.
———. [1973]. 'Plato on the undepictable', in Lee, Mourelatos, and Rorty [1973], chap. 17. Reprinted in Owen [1986], chap. 7.

———. [1986]. *Logic, Science, and Dialectic*, ed. M.C. Nussbaum. Ithaca.
Parfit, D. [1984]. *Reasons and Persons*. Oxford.
Patzer, A., ed. [1987]. *Der historische Sokrates*. Darmstadt.
Penner, T. [1970]. 'False anticipatory pleasures', *Phr* 15, 166–78.
———. [1971]. 'Thought and desire in Plato', in Vlastos [1971a], chap. 6.
———. [1973a]. 'The unity of virtue', *PR* 82, 35–68. Reprinted in Benson [1992], chap. 10.
———. [1973b]. 'Socrates on virtue and motivation', in Lee, Mourelatos, and Rorty [1973], chap. 7.
———. [1987a]. 'Socrates on the impossibility of belief-relative sciences', *BACAP* 3, 263–325.
———. [1987b]. *The Ascent from Nominalism*. Dordrecht.
———. [1990]. 'Plato and Davidson: Parts of the soul and weakness of the will', *CJP* supp. 16, 35–74.
———. [1991]. 'Desire and power in Socrates', *Ap* 24, 147–201.
———. [1992a]. 'What Laches and Nicias miss', *AP* 12, 1–27.
———. [1992b]. 'Socrates in the early dialogues', in Kraut [1992a], chap. 4.
Polansky, R. M. [1985]. 'Professor Vlastos's analysis of Socratic elenchus', *OSAP* 3, 247–59.
Price, A. W. [1989]. *Love and Friendship in Plato and Aristotle*. Oxford.
Prichard, H. A. [1968]. *Moral Obligation*. Oxford.
Quincey, J. H. [1981]. 'Another purpose for Plato, *Republic* I', *Hermes* 109, 300–315.
Race, W. H. [1979]. 'Shame in Plato's *Gorgias*', *Classical Journal* 74, 197–202.
Raphael, D. D. [1969]. *British Moralists*. 2 vols., Oxford.
Raz, J. [1975]. *Practical Reason and Norms*. London.
Reeve, C. D. C. [1985]. 'Socrates meets Thrasymachus', *AGP* 67, 246–65.
———. [1988]. *Philosopher-Kings*. Princeton.
———. [1989]. *Socrates in the Apology*. Indianapolis.
Richardson, H. S. [1990], 'Measurement, pleasure, and practical science in Plato's *Protagoras*', *JHP* 28, 7–32.
Robin, L., tr. [1950]. *Platon: Oeuvres Complètes*. Paris.
Robinson, R. [1953]. *Plato's Earlier Dialectic*. 2d ed., Oxford.
———. [1956]. 'A criticism of Plato's *Cratylus*', *PR* 65, 324–41. Reprinted in Robinson [1969], chap. 6.
———. [1969]. *Essays in Greek Philosophy*. Oxford.
———. [1971]. 'Plato's separation of reason and desire', *Phr* 16, 38–48.
Roochnik, D. L. [1986]. 'Plato's use of the techne-analogy', *JHP* 24, 295–310. Reprinted in Benson [1992], chap. 11.
Rorty, A.O. ed. [1980]. *Essays on Aristotle's Ethics*. Berkeley.
Ross, W. D., ed. [1924]. *Aristotle: Metaphysics*. 2 vols., Oxford.
———. [1933]. 'The Socratic Problem', *Proc. Classical Assoc.* 30, 7–24. Reprinted in Patzer [1987], 225–39.
———. [1951]. *Plato's Theory of Ideas*. Oxford.
———, ed. [1955]. *Aristotelis Fragmenta Selecta*. Oxford.
Rowe, C. J. [1975]. 'A reply to John Cooper on the *Magna Moralia*', *AJP* 96, 160–72.
———, ed. [1986]. *Plato: Phaedrus*. Warminster.
Rudberg, G. [1953]. '*Protagoras*, *Gorgias*, *Menon*: eine platonische Uebergangszeit', *Symbolae Osloenses* 30, 30–41.
Rudebusch, G. [1989]. 'Plato, hedonism, and ethical Protagoreanism', in Anton and Preus [1989], 27–40.

———. [1992]. 'Callicles' hedonism', *AP* 12, 53–71.
Ryle, G. [1966]. *Plato's Progress*. Cambridge.
Sachs, D. [1963]. 'A fallacy in Plato's *Republic*', *PR* 72, 141–58. Reprinted in Vlastos [1971a], chap. 2.
Santas, G. [1969]. 'Socrates at work on virtue and knowledge in Plato's *Laches*', *RM* 22, 433–60. Reprinted in Vlastos [1971b], chap. 8.
———. [1972]. 'The Socratic fallacy', *JHP* 10, 127–41.
———. [1973]. 'Socrates at work on virtue and knowledge in Plato's *Charmides*', in Lee, Mourelatos, and Rorty [1973], chap. 6.
———. [1979]. *Socrates*. London.
———. [1980]. 'The Form of the Good in Plato's *Republic*', *Philosophical Inquiry* 2, 374–403. Reprinted in Anton and Preus [1983], 232–63.
———. [1985]. 'Two theories of the good in Plato's *Republic*', *AGP* 57, 223–45.
Saunders, T. J., tr. [1970]. *Plato: Laws*. Harmondsworth.
———, ed. [1987]. *Plato: Early Socratic Dialogues*. Harmondsworth.
Schaefer, H. J. [1981]. *Phronêsis bei Platon*. Bochum.
Schaerer, R. [1930]. *Epistêmê et Technê: études sur les notions de connaissance et d'art d'Homère à Platon*. Macon.
Schanz, M., ed. [1874–1879]. *Platonis Opera Omnia*. 13 vols., Leipzig.
Schleiermacher, F., tr. [1977]. *Platon: Werke*, revised by H. Hoffman. 8 vols., Darmstadt.
Schofield, M., and Nussbaum, M., eds. [1982]. *Language and Logos*. Cambridge.
Schopenhauer, A. [1966]. *The World as Will and Representation*, tr. E. F. J. Payne. 2 vols., New York.
Schulz, W. [1960]. 'Das problem der Aporie in den Tugenddialogen Platos', in Henrich, et al. [1960], 261–77.
Scott, D. [1987]. 'Platonic anamnesis revisited', *CQ* 37, 346–66.
Sharples, R. W., ed. [1985]. *Plato: Meno*. Warminster.
Sharvy, R. [1972]. '*Euthyphro* 9d–11b: Analysis and definition in Plato and others', *Nous* 6, 119–37.
Shorey, P. [1895a]. 'The idea of the good in Plato's *Republic*', in Shorey [1895b], 188–239; and Shorey [1980], 2:28–79.
———. [1895b]. *Studies in Classical Philology* 1. Chicago.
———. [1903]. *The Unity of Plato's Thought*. Chicago. Chap. 1 reprinted in Vlastos [1971a], chap. 1.
———, tr. [1930–1935]. *Plato: Republic*. 2 vols., London.
———. [1933]. *What Plato Said*. Chicago.
———. [1980]. *Selected Papers*, ed. L. Tarán. 2 vols., New York.
Sidgwick, H. [1907]. *The Methods of Ethics*, 7th ed. London.
Skemp, J. B., tr. [1952]. *Plato's Statesman*. London.
Smith, M. [1987]. 'The Humean theory of motivation', *Mind* 96, 36–61.
Snider, E. [1992]. 'The conclusion of the *Meno*', *AP* 12, 73–86.
Sprague, R. K., tr. [1965]. *Plato: Euthydemus*. Indianapolis.
———. [1976]. *Plato's Philosopher King*. Columbia, S.C.
———. [1977]. 'Plato's sophistry', *PASS* 51, 45–61.
Stählin, O., ed. [1906–1909]. *Clemenes Alexandrinus: Stromata*. 2 vols., Leipzig.
Stallbaum, G., ed. [1877]. *Platonis Opera Omnia*, revised by M. Wohlrab. 10 vols., Leipzig.
Stalley, R. F. [1983]. *Introduction to Plato's Laws*. Oxford.
Starr, W. C., and Taylor, R. C., eds. [1989]. *Moral Philosophy*. Milwaukee.
Stewart, J. A. [1892]. *Notes on the Nicomachean Ethics of Aristotle*. Oxford.

Stewart, M. A. [1977]. 'Plato's sophistry', *PASS* 51, 21–44.
Stokes, M. C. [1986]. *Plato's Socratic Conversations*. London.
Strang, C. [1963]. 'Plato and the Third Man', *PASS* 37, 147–64. Reprinted in Vlastos [1970], chap. 8.
———. [1986]. 'Plato's analogy of the Cave', *OSAP* 4, 19–34.
Striker, G. [1970]. *Peras und Apeiron*. Göttingen.
Sullivan, J. P. [1961]. 'The hedonism of Plato's *Protagoras*', *Phr* 6, 10–28.
Tarán, L. [1985]. 'Platonism and Socratic ignorance', in O'Meara [1985], chap. 4.
Taylor, A. E. [1928]. *A Commentary on Plato's Timaeus*. Oxford.
———, tr. [1934]. *Plato: Laws*. London. Reprinted in Hamilton and Cairns [1961].
———. [1937]. *Plato: The Man and His Work*. 4th ed. London.
Taylor, C. [1977]. 'What is human agency?' in Mischel [1977], 103–35; and Taylor, C. [1985], chap. 1.
———. [1985]. *Human Agency and Language*, vol. 1. Cambridge.
———. [1989]. *Sources of the Self*. Cambridge, Mass.
Taylor, C. C. W. [1967]. 'Pleasure, knowledge, and sensation in Democritus', *Phr* 12, 6–27.
———. [1969]. 'Forms as causes', *Mind* 78, 45–59.
———. [1979]. Review of Irwin [1977a], *Mind* 88, 597–99.
———. [1982]. 'The end of the *Euthyphro*', *Phr* 27, 109–18.
———, tr. [1991]. *Plato's Protagoras*. 2d ed. Oxford.
Thompson, E. S., ed. [1901]. *Plato: Meno*. London.
Tiles, J. E. [1984]. '*Technê* and moral expertise', *Phil* 59, 49–66.
Urmson, J. O., and Warnock, G. J., eds. [1979]. *Philosophical Papers*, 3d ed. Oxford.
Van Fraassen, B. C. [1980]. *The Scientific Image*. Oxford.
Versenyi, L. [1975]. 'Plato's *Lysis*, *Phr* 20, 185–98.
Vickers, B. [1985]. *In Defence of Rhetoric*. Oxford.
Vlastos, G., ed. [1956]. *Plato: Protagoras*. New York.
———. [1969a]. 'Socrates on acrasia', *Phoenix* 23, 71–88. Reprinted in Vlastos [1994], vol. 2.
———. [1969b]. 'Reasons and causes in the *Phaedo*', *PR* 78, 291–325. Reprinted in Vlastos [1981a], chap. 4.
———, ed. [1970]. *Plato I*. Garden City, N.Y.
———, ed. [1971a]. *Plato II*. Garden City, N.Y.
———, ed. [1971b]. *The Philosophy of Socrates*. Garden City, N.Y.
———. [1971c]. 'Justice and happiness in the *Republic*', in Vlastos [1971a], chap. 5.
———. [1972]. 'The unity of the virtues in the *Protagoras*', *RM* 25, 415–58. Reprinted in Vlastos [1981a], chap. 4.
———. [1973]. 'The individual as object of love in Plato', in Vlastos [1981a], chap. 1. (First published 1973.)
———. [1975]. 'Plato's testimony concerning Zeno of Elea', *JHS* 95, 136–62. Reprinted in Vlastos [1994], vol. 1.
———. [1977]. 'The theory of social justice in the *polis* in Plato's *Republic*', *Mnemosyne*, supp. 50, 1–40. Reprinted in Vlastos [1994], vol. 2.
———. [1981a]. *Platonic Studies*. 2d ed. Princeton. (1st ed., 1973.)
———. [1981b]. 'What did Socrates understand by his "What is F?" question?' in Vlastos [1981a], chap. 19.
———. [1981c]. 'Socrates on the "parts of virtue"', in Vlastos [1981a], chap. 20.
———. [1983a]. 'The Socratic elenchus', *OSAP* 1, 27–58. Reprinted in Vlastos [1993], chap. 1.
———. [1983b]. 'Afterthoughts'. *OSAP* 1, 71–74. Reprinted in Vlastos [1993], chap. 1.

———. [1985]. 'Socrates disavowal of knowledge' *PQ* 35, 1–31. Reprinted in Vlastos [1993], chap. 3.
———. [1990]. 'Is the Socratic fallacy Socratic?' *AP* 10, 1–16. Reprinted in Vlastos [1993], chap. 3.
———. [1991]. *Socrates: Ironist and Moral Philosopher*. Ithaca.
———. [1993]. *Socratic Studies*. Cambridge.
———. [1994]. *Studies in Greek Philosophy*. 2 vols., Princeton.
Von Arnim, H., ed. [1905]. *Stoicorum Veterum Fragmenta*. 4 vols., Leipzig.
Warner, M. [1979]. 'Love, self, and Plato's *Symposium*', *PQ* 29, 329–39.
Waterfield, R. A. H. [1980]. 'The place of the *Philebus* in Plato's dialogues', *Phr* 25, 270–305.
———, tr. [1982]. *Plato: Philebus*. Harmondsworth.
———, tr. [1987]. '*Euthydemus*', in Saunders [1987].
Waterlow, S. [1972]. 'The good of others in Plato's *Republic*', *PAS* 73, 19–36.
Weerts, E. [1931]. 'Platon und der Heraklitismus', *Philologus* supp. 23.1.
Weingartner, R. H. [1973]. *The Unity of the Platonic Dialogue*. Indianapolis.
Weiss, R. [1981]. '*Ho agathos* as *ho dunatos* in the *Hippias Minor*', *CQ* 31, 287–304. Reprinted in Benson [1992], chap. 14.
———. [1985]. 'Ignorance, involuntariness, and innocence: A reply to McTighe', *Phr* 30, 314–22.
———. [1986]. 'Euthyphro's failure', *JHP* 24, 437–52.
———. [1987]. 'The right exchange: *Phaedo* 69a6–c3', *AP* 7 57–66.
Westerink, L. G., ed. [1990]. *Prolégomènes à la philosophie de Platon*, tr. J. Trouillard. Paris.
White, F. C. [1977]. 'The "many" in *Republic* 475a–480a', *CJP* 7, 291–306.
———. [1978]. 'J. Gosling on *ta polla kala*', *Phr* 23, 127–32.
White, N. P. [1974]. 'Inquiry', *RM* 28, 289–310.
———. [1976]. *Plato on Knowledge and Reality*. Indianapolis.
———. [1979]. *A Companion to Plato's Republic*. Indianapolis.
———. [1984]. 'The classification of goods in Plato's *Republic*', *JHP* 22, 393–421.
———. [1985]. 'Rational prudence in Plato's *Gorgias*', in O'Meara [1985], chap. 6.
———. [1986]. 'The rulers' choice', *AGP* 68, 22–46.
———. [1987]. 'Forms and sensibles', *PT* 15, 197–214.
———. [1989a]. 'Perceptual and objective properties in Plato', *Ap* 22.4, 45–65.
———. [1989b]. 'Happiness and external contingencies in Plato's *Republic*', in Starr and Taylor [1989], 1–21.
———. [1992]. 'Plato's metaphysical epistemology', in Kraut [1992a], chap. 9.
Whiting, J. E. [1986]. 'Friends and future selves', *PR* 95, 547–80.
Whittaker, J., ed. [1990]. *Alcinoos: Didaskalikos*, tr. P. Louis. Paris.
Wiggins, D. [1978]. 'Weakness of will, commensurability, and the objects of deliberation and desire', *PAS* 79, 251–77. Reprinted in Rorty [1980], chap. 14; and Wiggins [1987], chap. 7.
———. [1987]. *Needs, Values, Truth*. Oxford.
Wilkes, K. V. [1979]. 'Conclusions in the *Meno*', *AGP* 61, 143–53.
Williams, B. A. O. [1959]. 'Pleasure and belief', *PASS* 33, 57–72.
———. [1965]. 'Ethical consistency', *PASS* 39, 103–24. Reprinted in Williams [1973b], chap. 11.
———. [1973a]. 'The analogy of city and soul in Plato's *Republic*' in Lee, Mourelatos, and Rorty [1973], chap. 10.
———. [1973b]. *Problems of the Self*. Cambridge.

Wilson, J. [1982]. '"The customary meanings of words were changed"—or were they?' *CQ* 32, 18–20.

Wilson, J. R. S. [1976a]. 'The argument of *Republic* IV', *PQ* 26, 111–24.

———. [1976b]. 'The contents of the Cave', *CJP* supp. 2, 117–27.

———. [1977]. 'Reason's rule and vulgar wrong-doing', *Dialogue* 16, 591–604.

Wolf, S. [1986]. 'Self-interest and interest in selves', *Ethics* 96, 704–20.

Wollheim, R. A., and Hopkins, J., eds. [1982]. *Philosophical Essays on Freud*. Cambridge.

Woodhead, W. D., tr. [1953], *Plato: Gorgias*, Edinburgh. Reprinted in Hamilton and Cairns [1961].

Woodruff, P. [1976]. 'Socrates on the parts of virtue', *CJP* supp. 2, 101–16.

———. [1986]. 'The sceptical side of Plato's method', *RIP* 40, 22–37.

———. [1988]. 'Aporetic Pyrrhonism', *OSAP* 6, 139–68.

———. [1990]. 'Plato's early theory of knowledge', in Everson [1990], chap. 4.

Woods, M. J. [1987]. 'Plato's division of the soul', *PBA* 73, 23–48.

Wright, J., tr. [1910]. *Plato: Lysis*. London. Reprinted in Hamilton and Cairns [1961].

Young, C. M. [1980]. 'Polemarchus' and Thrasymachus' definitions of justice', *Philosophical Inquiry* 2, 404–19.

Zeller, E. [1876]. *Plato and the Older Academy*. E.T. London.

———. [1885]. *Socrates and the Socratic Schools*. E.T. London.

Zeyl, D. J. [1980]. 'Socrates and hedonism', *Phr* 25, 250–69. Reprinted in Anton and Preus [1989], 5–25.

———. [1982]. 'Socratic virtue and happiness', *AGP* 54, 225–38.

Index Locorum

References are given to sections (e.g., '101') or to notes (e.g., '1n1').

Other Ancient Authors

Index Nominum

This index includes only names of modern scholars and philosophers. Other names are listed in the General Index.

General Index